MAY -- 2011

027.63 SERVING
Serving LGBTIQ library and arch ◁ **P9-CKC-869**
users :essays on outreach, service

WITHDRAWN

WITHDRAWN

Serving LGBTIQ Library and Archives Users

Essays on Outreach, Service, Collections and Access

Edited by ELLEN GREENBLATT

McFarland & Company, Inc., Publishers
Jefferson, North Carolina, and London

Alameda Free Library
1550 Oak Street

LIBRARY OF CONGRESS CATALOGUING-IN-PUBLICATION DATA

Serving LGBTIQ library and archives users : essays on outreach,
service, collections and access / edited by Ellen Greenblatt.
p.   cm.
Includes bibliographical references and index.

ISBN 978-0-7864-4894-4
softcover : 50# alkaline paper ∞

1. Libraries and sexual minorities — United States.
2. Libraries — Special collections — Sexual minorities.
3. Sexual minorities — Archives.   4. Sexual minorities —
Bibliography.   5. Sexual minorities — Electronic information
resources.   I. Greenblatt, Ellen, 1954–
Z711.92.S49S47   2011   027.6'3 — dc22   2010040472

British Library cataloguing data are available

© 2011 Ellen Greenblatt. All rights reserved

*No part of this book may be reproduced or transmitted in any form
or by any means, electronic or mechanical, including photocopying
or recording, or by any information storage and retrieval system,
without permission in writing from the publisher.*

Cover image © 2011 Shutterstock

Manufactured in the United States of America

*McFarland & Company, Inc., Publishers
Box 611, Jefferson, North Carolina 28640
www.mcfarlandpub.com*

In memory of
Yolanda Retter Vargas,
1947–2007,
herstorian, archivist, activist, librarian,
"gadfly on the body politic,"
and so much more

Contents

SECTION FIVE: BIBLIOGRAPHIC ACCESS

SECTION SIX: CENSORSHIP OF LGBTIQ RESOURCES

SECTION SEVEN: PROFESSIONAL CONCERNS — WORKPLACE ISSUES, LIBRARY EDUCATION, ORGANIZATIONS, AND NETWORKING

PROFILES

Acknowledgments

I've been planning this book for almost twenty years, and I can't believe it's finally a reality. I owe so much to the many people I've crossed paths with over the past two decades who have shared their stories and ideas with me. I cannot begin to thank you all enough for your help and encouragement.

The "book," which we lovingly referred to as "Spawn of *Gay and Lesbian Library Service*," went through several iterations on its journey to publication. I worked closely with Cal Gough, Anne L. Moore, John DeSantis, K.R. Roberto, and the late Yolanda Retter-Vargas on shaping the table of contents of the current volume. Thanks to you all for your support and suggestions.

I'd also like to thank Jim Van Buskirk for being my ever-reliable sounding board. Also Leslie Kahn for her pep talks. Plus Melodie Frances and Jeffrey Beall for their insights into cataloging issues and practices and Paul Weiss of the Library of Congress for help in tracing the history of subject headings.

Thanks to all the contributors to the book for their generosity in sharing their expertise. Working with you was an enriching experience, and I'm excited by the variety of perspectives you present and staggered by your knowledge about the subject matter.

I was fortunate to receive a sabbatical from the University of Colorado Denver, and I'd like to thank my colleagues at Auraria Library for covering for me during my absence, most notably Jeffrey Beall, Meg Brown-Sica, Mary Dodge, and Rosemary Evetts. Plus a hefty thanks to the folks in Interlibrary Loan for handling my many ILL requests so quickly and efficiently.

I'd also like to express my gratitude to the students in my online graduate classes on LGBTIQ issues and services at the San José State University School of Library and Information Science (SLIS). Your enthusiasm is a wonderful impetus for my continued research in this subject area, and your questions and insights have helped me focus on particular topics. Thanks as well to the SLIS administration for offering me the opportunity to teach the class, a truly rewarding and re-energizing experience.

Thanks to James LaRue for allowing us to reprint his fabulous letter in this book. Thanks also to the Canadian Teachers' Federation for giving us permission to use material from their publication *Challenging Silence, Challenging Censorship: Inclusive Resources, Strategies and Policy Directives for Addressing Bisexual, Gay, Lesbian, Trans-Identified and Two-Spirited Realities in School and Public Libraries*.

And last, but certainly not least, special thanks to Laura Reiman for her unfailing support and patience throughout this entire project.

Introduction

Ellen Greenblatt

A lot has happened in the twenty years since the collection of essays and resources titled *Gay and Lesbian Library Service* was published. In that book, our focus was limited, as the title suggests and the times dictated, to the gay and lesbian communities. However, in the 1990s, other groups based on more diverse sexual and gender identities began to emerge and become more vocal and politically active. These groups include bisexual, transgender, and intersex people. All these groups — lesbians, gay men, bisexuals, transgender, and intersex people — are bound together by common values, concerns, histories, and oppressions. Like gay men and lesbians, bisexual people form affectional and sexual relationships with members of the same sex and suffer from heterosexist prejudice because of these relationships. And like transgender and intersex people, lesbians, bisexuals, and gay men have been profoundly affected by social and legal repression stemming from sexism and genderism. All these groups share a history of pathologization, of existing outside "the norm." Throughout this book, I and the other contributors will use the acronym LGBTIQ (Lesbian, Gay, Bisexual, Transgender, Intersex, and Queer/Questioning) to represent these communities.[1]

In 1990, the Internet was unknown to most of us. Today it is so pervasive that few of us can imagine life without it. The Internet has had significant impact on LGBTIQ communities — most notably as a virtual lifeline helping questioning individuals explore their sexual orientation or gender identity and keeping those who live in geographic or personal isolation in touch with others. Long before Facebook and other social networking tools arrived on the scene, LGBTIQ people found the Internet to be an invaluable resource not only for networking and sharing resources, but also for mobilizing political and social activism.

The first section of this book speaks to these new considerations that have surfaced since the previous volume was published, containing essays discussing the impact of the Internet and introducing the communities that have been added under the LGBTIQ umbrella over the past two decades, addressing their needs and suggesting relevant resources. Rounding out this first section are some short profiles. The first, "It's Not Monopoly: Gender Role Explorations in Online Environments," demonstrates how virtual communities such as Second Life can help individuals get a "feel" for being another gender. The second profile, "Making a Difference," describes how one librarian partnered with a community member to enhance programming and collections at his library. The final profile features

OutHistory.org, an award-winning, collaborative, community-based website focusing on LGBTIQ history.[2]

Section Two examines the various types of libraries — public, school, and academic — and the particular LGBTIQ issues associated with these particular venues. An additional essay addresses services to a specific group of LGBTIQ users, young adults. Finishing off this section are profiles of the community-based Quatrefoil Library and its use of Web 2.0 technology and the "Out at the Library" exhibit of LGBTIQ images and materials from the James C. Hormel Gay and Lesbian Center at the San Francisco Public Library.

LGBTIQ archives are the focal point of Section Three, which begins with a historical overview. Following this essay is "It Was Only Supposed to Be Twenty Interviews: GLB-TIQ Oral History as Librarianship," which recounts the development of the Under the Rainbow Oral History project. The last essay in the section addresses the role of exhibits in LGBTIQ archives. Two profiles offering brief glimpses into two institutions — the Pacific Northwest Lesbian Archives in Seattle and the International Homo/Lesbian Information Center and Archives in the Netherlands — follow. And "Inside the Files of This Has No Name," a touching tale regarding the legacy of a donated collection completes this section.

Section Four offers essays on three aspects of collection development. The first is based on Cal Gough's award-winning[3] discussion of the major issues associated with gay and lesbian collection development, expanding it to include new communities and technologies. The second, "One for the Road," offers a personal reflection on LGBTIQ literature. And the last essay addresses collection assessment and user satisfaction of academic library collections. Supplementing these essays is a description of Rainbow Link, a grassroots collection development project, and a look at a major review resource, *The Gay and Lesbian Review/Worldwide*.

Section Five concerns access to resources, commencing with a discussion of how the Dewey classification system handles intersex concepts. As in the previous work, an examination of the Library of Congress subject headings will reveal how LGBTIQ concepts are treated. The final essay of this section delves into folksonomies and the recent Web 2.0 phenomenon of user-supplied tagging. Two profiles complement these essays — one detailing the creation of EBSCO's LGBT Life Thesaurus and another discussing Indigenous/Native LGBTIQ terminology.

Section Six covers attempts to restrict access to LGBTIQ resources, through challenges, censorship, and Internet filtering. As demonstrated by the essays in this section, LGBTIQ-related information and materials are disproportionately affected by these efforts. Appended to the end of the section is an example of a response to a book challenge.

And in the final section, seven, the first essay speaks to the workplace concerns of library workers. This is followed by an essay on integrating LGBTIQ representations into the library school curriculum focusing on the experience of the University of Tennessee Knoxville School of Information Sciences. The final essay, "When Collection Development Leads to Staff Development: The Transgender Resource Collection," as its title implies, shows that developing a library collection is a holistic experience, affecting staffing as well as services and collections.[4] A look at three professional groups, the American Library Association Gay, Lesbian, Bisexual, and Transgendered Round Table, the Society of American Archivists Lesbian and Gay Roundtable, and HQ76.3/New England (a regional group), concludes the book.

NOTES

1. Please see the Selective Glossary of LGBTIQ Terms immediately following for an explanation of the terms used throughout this book. Additionally, many of the contributors offer definitions of the terminology they employ in their essays and profiles. Further, some of the contributors may vary the order or number of letters included in the acronym due to already established names of projects, such as the Under the Rainbow oral history project which uses the acronym GLBTIQ, or the inclusiveness of communities, i.e., not all projects/activities referred to may include all of the communities under the LGBTIQ umbrella.

2. In 2010, OutHistory.org was awarded the inaugural Allan Bérubé Prize for outstanding work in public or community-based lesbian, gay, bisexual, transgender, and/or queer history by the Committee on Lesbian, Gay, Bisexual, and Transgender History, an affiliate society of the American Historical Association, and underwritten by the GLBT Historical Society in San Francisco. For more information, visit *http://clgbthistory.org/prizes.html.*

3. Blackwell bestowed its 1992 Scholarship Award which honors the author of the year's outstanding article or book on collection development or acquisitions to Cal Gough for "Key Issues in the Collecting of Gay/Lesbian Library Materials" in *Gay and Lesbian Library Service.* For more information, visit http://0-www.ala.org.sapl.sat.lib.tx.us/ala/mgrps/divs/alcts/awards/printmedia/blackwellssch.cfm.

4. The Transgender Resource Collection at the Oak Park Public Library in Illinois, which is featured in this essay, won the Public Library Association's 2010 Gordon M. Conable Award, which honors public librarians and libraries with a demonstrated commitment to the principles of intellectual freedom and the *Library Bill of Rights.* For more information, visit http://0-www.ala.org.sapl.sat.lib.tx.us/ala/mgrps/divs/pla/plaawards/gordonmconableaward/index.cfm.

Selective Glossary
of LGBTIQ Terms[1]

Ellen Greenblatt

Bisexuals are people who are affectionally, romantically, and/or sexually attracted to people of the same or opposite sex. They may or may not be non-monogamous or even sexually active.

Cisgender people is a relatively new term applied to non-transgender people, i.e., applied to people whose gender expression and identity are congruent with the sex they were assigned at birth.

Gay men are men who are affectionally, romantically, and/or sexually attracted to other men.

Gender is a cultural construct as opposed to sex, which is biologically defined. Used to classify attitudes, behaviors and other forms of expression, gender is applied in different ways by different cultures. In dominant Western society, the concept of gender is rigidly defined and limited to a male/female dichotomy. In other cultures, including many Native American cultures, gender is more fluid and broadly applied, covering a range of possibilities beyond the traditional Western binary system.

Gender expression is how people communicate their gender identity.

Gender identity is how people self-identify in regard to their gender. For example, they may self-identify as male, female, transgender, genderqueer, androgynous, etc. Individuals' gender identity may not be congruent with (i.e., correspond to) their appearance or the sex they were assigned at birth.

Gender variant people are those who choose not to or are unable to conform to societal gender norms.

Genderism manifests itself as the exclusion of people who do not conform to societal gender norms. It can also be defined as prejudice or bias against gender variant people.

Heterosexism is the belief in the inherent superiority of heterosexuality and its right to cultural dominance.[2]

Homophobia is prejudice against lesbian and gay people. It is sometimes also applied more broadly to LGBTIQ people.

Intersex people are people who are born with both or ambiguous male and female external genitalia, internal reproductive systems, gonads, or sex chromosomes. Previously they

were referred to as *hermaphrodites*, a term currently out of favor due to its pejorative con-
notations. A controversial new term for intersex conditions is *disorders of sex development*
(DSD).

Lesbians are women who are affectionally, romantically, and/or sexually attracted to other
women.

LGBTIQ people is the collective term used for lesbians, gay men, bisexuals, transgender,
intersex, and queer/questioning people in this book.

Queer: Originally derogatory when applied to LGBTIQ people, this word has been
reclaimed by some as an all-encompassing umbrella term. Others conceptualize it even
more broadly, using it to refer to any non-heterosexual-identified person or act. Still
others remain uncomfortable with its use due to its pejorative and oppressive connota-
tions/origins.

Questioning individuals are those who are engaged in self-discovery and exploration of
their sexual orientation and/or gender identity.

Sexual orientation is the inclination or capacity to develop intimate emotional and sexual
relationships with people of the same sex (lesbian or gay), the opposite sex (heterosexual),
or more than one sex (bisexual, pansexual).

Transgender people are people who literally "transgress" gender. An umbrella term applied
to people whose gender behavior, expression, or identity does not conform to the sex
they were assigned at birth, transgender is applied to a range of gender variant people.
There is some disagreement regarding the breadth of inclusion under this term. Sometimes
intersex people are included under the umbrella, while transsexuals opt out.

Transphobia is prejudice toward transgender people.

Transsexuals is a controversial term whose definitions vary. Some define the term in its
broadest sense to apply to people whose gender identity does not conform to their assigned
sex at birth. Others define the term more narrowly to include only those individuals who
are in the process of transitioning (physically and emotionally changing to align with
their gender identity) or have transitioned.

NOTES

1. This glossary first appeared in a slightly different form in the following article:
    Greenblatt, E. (2003). Lesbian, gay, bisexual, transgender library users: Overcoming the myths.
    Colorado Libraries, 29(4), 23–24.
    These definitions are based in part upon the following resources:
    Gender Education & Advocacy (2001). *Gender variance: A primer.* Retrieved from *http://www.
    gender.org/resources/dge/gea01004.pdf*
    Safe Schools Coalition (2005, June 27). *Glossary.* Retrieved from *http://www.safeschoolscoalition.
    org/glossary.pdf*
    An excellent resource that appeared just as this book was going to press is:
    Fenway Health. (2010, January). Glossary of gender and transgender terms. Retrieved from
    *http://www.fenwayhealth.org/site/DocServer/Handout_7-C_Glossary_of_Gender_and_Transgender_
    Terms__fi.pdf?docID=7081*
    Many of the contributors to this book also offer definitions of these terms (and several more) in
    their essays and profiles. Since these terms are fluid, their definitions may not always be in agreement
    with those offered above.
2. Lorde, A. (1983). There is no hierarchy of oppressions. *Interracial Books for Children Bulletin,
    14*(3), 9.

Library Resources and Services for Bisexuals

Jessica L. Howard

Library resources and services for bisexuals have traditionally been grouped together with those for gay and lesbian individuals. Like gays and lesbians, the bisexual community is often marginalized and underserved. In many ways, bisexual resources and services have benefited from being placed under the "gay and lesbian" umbrella, as these groups are starting to gain traction as acceptance increases and more libraries recognize the need for these resources and services. However, bisexuality is a distinct identity and as a result, bisexuals have their own distinct needs and concerns. They often face discrimination not just by the community at large, but also from within the gay and lesbian community. This dual marginalization (Oswalt, 2009) is at the heart of the need for libraries to acknowledge and validate bisexuals with affirming information resources and services.

Libraries should use many of the same collection development and service principles for bisexual-themed materials and services as have been established by the American Library Association (ALA) and used for those efforts directed at the gay and lesbian communities. However, it is necessary for libraries to make a concerted effort to provide distinct, bisexual-specific resources and services. Libraries can do this through collaboration with their local bisexual community or by turning to national bisexual organizations as a resource. They can also take advantage of bisexuality-focused review publications for identifying appropriate materials. In addition to including materials with bisexual themes in their collections, libraries can and should make these resources easy to find and use, and should highlight these materials within the library's physical and virtual spaces. This will be useful for bisexuals, their family and friends, and those who provide services to the bisexual community.

Bisexuality as a Unique Identity

The Bisexual Resource Center uses *bisexual* as "an umbrella term for people who recognize and honor their potential for sexual and emotional attraction to more than one gender" (2009). Similarly, the Healthy Teen Network (2006) defines a *bisexual* simply as "someone whose physical or romantic attraction for another person is not necessarily dependent upon sex or gender."

Just as there is diversity within the LGBTIQ community, the bisexual community is also quite diverse, including people of different genders, ages, cultural and socioeconomic backgrounds, and ways of expressing and defining their sexual identities. Bisexuals, as defined above, also include those — like pansexuals — who may not call themselves bisexual. The word *pansexual* acknowledges that gender is more diverse than the male-female binary, and refers to people who may be attracted to individuals of diverse genders.

As a group, bisexuals have a lot in common with the gay and lesbian community. As one of the so-called "sexual minorities," bisexuals face similar discrimination and societal challenges. In fact, some have suggested that biphobia and homophobia — because they are based on perceptions from the outside — provide the most significant overlap between bisexuals' needs and those of gays and lesbians (Ochs, 1996). Plus, bisexuals involved in same-sex relationships have similar information needs as gays and lesbians on topics including sexual health, relationships, and legal rights. This may be the reason why when we talk or think about bisexuality, it is usually under the umbrella of gay and lesbian issues.

Parents, Family, and Friends of Lesbian and Gays (PFLAG) notes in their *Bisexuality Resource Packet* that many organizations dedicated to supporting gay and lesbian individuals also include bisexuality in their mission statements, but "their programs and organizing do not specifically address this population." PFLAG also notes that bisexuals face a unique set of needs as a result, in part, of misunderstanding of bisexuality and resulting discrimination. Bisexuals often face criticism for what some view as indecision related to their sexual orientation, when in reality bisexuality is a firm sexual identity for many individuals.

Additionally, some might suggest that sexuality is based on a dichotomy between those who are heterosexual and those who are homosexual (Evans, 2003). When viewed within this framework, it may be erroneously assumed that bisexuals are "part gay" and "part straight," and therefore can have their needs met by resources designed for those audiences. However, this group is often invisible because, if someone doesn't overtly label themselves as bisexual, it is likely that others will not know that this is how they self-identify. People often view others' sexual orientation based on the type of relationship they are currently in, rather than their self-identified situation or expression (Burleson, 2005).

Additionally, bisexuals are unique in that they require information that provides insight on the struggles with identifying as bisexual, as well as resources that affirm their status as a bisexual. O'Brien (1998) describes the overwhelming response of her bisexual college students to a question about their needs as simply "unbiased and considerate treatment" (p. 33). Similarly, McLean (2001) points out that a lack of resources available for young bisexuals may cause them to feel that "bisexuality is not a valid identity, and therefore may [cause them to] suppress or deny their bisexuality" (p. 116). Affirming resources can cover topics of both same-sex as well as opposite-sex attraction, and the relationship between the two (Burleson, 2005). This is especially important because LGBTIQ individuals — particularly youth — seek out role models whose lives and situations reflect their own (Linville, 2005).

The general lack of societal acceptance of bisexuality highlights other ways in which bisexuals' information needs are unique. Research suggests, for example, that bisexuals receive less effective health services than gays, lesbians, and heterosexuals as a result of "invalidation of bisexual identity, lack of knowledge on bisexual issues, interpretations of bisexual attractions of behaviors as unhealthy, lack of skill in working with bisexual issues, and lack of proactive interventions" on the part of health care providers (Oswalt, 2009, p. 559). Therefore, even in cases where bisexuals' behaviors overlap with those of gays, lesbians, and heterosexuals, it is still necessary to explicitly acknowledge bisexuals via inclusive terminology and practice. This points to a need for affirming health information for bisexuals, as well as resources for individuals and organizations — like teachers, doctors, and librarians — that provide services for bisexuals. As Oswalt points out, validation of bisexuality is the first important step in providing effective service for bisexuals.

Lessons for Libraries

Because of their commonalities as marginalized sexual minorities, the ideas and principles applied to providing LGBTIQ or queer-themed library materials and services can be applied to those directed at bisexuals specifically. These principles, many of which have their foundation in the American Library Association's *Library Bill of Rights*, include provision of materials on diverse topics, resistance to censorship, promotion of ideas and free expression, and accessibility to all regardless of background, status, or views.

The ALA *Library Bill of Rights* (1996) states that libraries "should provide materials and information presenting all points of view on current and historical issues. Materials should not be proscribed or removed because of partisan or doctrinal disapproval" (para. 3). This re-affirms the role of all libraries in making affirming information on bisexuality and bisexual-themed materials available. Rather than being an indication that materials on bisexuality are not necessary, the invisibility of this community suggests that the maintenance of these collections is essential.

However, PFLAG notes that there is a lack of information about bisexuality in our libraries. Considering the relative lack of information and resources with bisexual themes, and knowing that resources for bisexuals are often erroneously assumed to be covered under the "gay and lesbian" umbrella, how can a library ensure that it is meeting bisexuals' information needs?

Collection Development and Access

First and foremost, a library should try to identify partners in the community who can assist in identifying valuable resources about bisexuality, or which incorporate bisexual themes. Once identified, these partners can be essential consultants on both how to reach out to the bisexual community, as well as what kinds of materials are of interest to that community. The *Library Bill of Rights* (1996) notes that libraries should work with "all persons and groups concerned with resisting abridgment of free expression and free access to ideas" (para. 5), and the case of providing materials related to bisexuality is a good opportunity to put this into practice. Who better to identify the needs of bisexual individuals than bisexuals themselves?

If possible, librarians should identify bisexual organizations within the community with which to collaborate. Understanding that strictly bisexual organizations may not exist, and that bisexuals can be difficult to identify in a community, other efforts may also be necessary in order to reach out to bisexuals. Groups dedicated to lesbian, gay, bisexual, and transgendered, intersex, and queer (LGBTIQ) rights might be good partners on this front. However, librarians should use caution in collaboration with organizations that claim to be LGBTIQ-focused because, bisexuals may be underrepresented, or not represented at all. For example, McLean (2008) found that there were antibisexual attitudes from within Australia's gay and lesbian community, and therefore bisexuals who are involved in this community tend not to be entirely forthcoming about their sexuality.

National bisexual organizations might also prove to be useful partners for librarians looking to reach out to bisexuals on a local level. Not only might these organizations be aware of locally-based bisexual organizations, but in the event that such groups don't exist, the national organizations might serve as a useful substitute for insight on appropriate resources and services. These organizations — which include the Bisexual Resource Center, BiNet USA, and the American Institute of Bisexuality — may prove especially useful in locating nonfiction resources, and may serve as important resources for use in pathfinders that incorporate bisexual content. The Bisexual Resource Center, for example, provides links to major bisexual organizations in the United States, Canada, and Europe, and also points to major bisexual media resources including magazines, book awards, and web sites. BiNet USA also links to bisexual organizations, highlighting bisexual, pansexual, and fluid groups in each U.S. state, and they also have a vast list of resources as well as a news and opinions section, email discussion groups, and Facebook groups. The American Institute of Bisexuality, the creator of the *Journal of Bisexuality* and *BiMagazine*, is also a hub for identifying bisexual-themed resources.

Also with regard to collection development of bisexual-themed materials, it is essential that librarians familiarize themselves with review resources specific to the bisexual community, as an alternative to the more general resources like *Choice, Booklist,* or *Library Journal.* Admittedly, these resources may be somewhat sparse because, despite the apparent boom in publications on lesbian, gay, and bisexual themes since the 1990s (Joyce, 2000), it is unclear how many of these are actually focused on bisexuality. If the appearance of bisexuals in films and other types of resources is any indication, there aren't many (Burleson, 2005). However, there are good examples of such publications, including *BiMagazine*. This resource, which is freely available online, incorporates bisexual book reviews and highlights bisexual-themed titles that are listed among the major queer book awards.

Additionally, there are some LGBTIQ-focused resources that highlight books and other materials that specifically contain bisexual content or themes. The Lambda Literary Awards, an important resource for identifying high quality LGBTIQ items, has an award category for items with bisexual themes, indicating that bisexuals hold a distinct place in the queer community. The resources that are selected in this category are important works which should be looked to for consideration for library collections (Lambda Literary Foundation, n.d.). The *Lambda Book Report* and the *Gay and Lesbian Review Worldwide* can also be good sources for identifying high quality resources with bisexual content, although it might take a bit of digging in order to separate the items with a bisexual focus, versus those that discuss bisexuality under the gay and lesbian umbrella.

Librarians should make every effort to make items with a bisexual theme easy to identify and use, while at the same time taking user privacy into account. Because many general resources directed primarily at gays and lesbians often include bisexual in the title, whether or not they include any bisexual-specific information, it can be hard to separate bisexual-specific resources from the batch. A keyword search for *bisexual* in a library catalog or databases, for example, will likely turn up some bisexual-specific items among many additional LGBTIQ items. Similarly, a search for *bisexual* that is limited to items that do not contain *gay* or *lesbian* as a keyword will likely eliminate useful bisexual-specific resources because bisexuality is rarely discussed without examining the relationship between this group and the gay and lesbian community. Librarians should keep this in mind and employ their own library-specific or advanced search strategies that will help the library patron sort through the materials in a way that works best with the library's specific catalog resources and systems.

Additionally, in the creation of pathfinders, librarians should not just point out LGB-TIQ resources as an all-encompassing group, but should point out bisexual (and transgender too, for that matter) materials. If labeling LGBTIQ books, either in the physical library, or via the online catalog, librarians should include specific ways of distinguishing bisexual items from others. This might include tagging items as *bisexual* in the library catalog, or adding physical, easily distinguishable, labels to the spine of books containing bisexual-specific information or themes. This will aid patrons in locating and using these items, and it will also send the message that the library recognizes bisexuality as distinct from gay and lesbian. However, as Linville's 2004 study points out, labeling should be done carefully so as to protect user privacy and ease patron discomfort, while making resources easier to locate.

Library Services

Providing reference services to bisexuals is quite comparable to providing them to gay and lesbian library patrons, or any other library users, for that matter. Reference inquiries should be handled in a welcoming, judgment-free manner, which maintains a high level of confidentiality for the patron. As Curry (2005) points out, even subtle actions of librarians can have an impact on whether library patrons feel welcomed and free to ask questions related to LGBTIQ issues. Additionally, it is important for librarians to be aware of their own perceptions when working with LGBTIQ patrons, avoiding the assumption that most people are heterosexual and, more specifically, the idea that one's sexual orientation can be assumed based on the gender of their partner.

Finally, it is important for libraries to incorporate bisexual resources and themes into library displays, events, and community outreach efforts, whether through bisexual-specific efforts, or as a part of larger LGBTIQ displays and events. By doing this, especially in conjunction with community organizations, librarians can ensure that they are supporting the section of the ALA *Library Bill of Rights* (1996), which states that libraries should make library spaces "available on an equitable basis, regardless of the beliefs or affiliations of individuals or groups requesting their use" (para. 7). This might also include incorporating bisexual-specific resources into work with gay-straight alliances and other LGBTIQ groups, whether or not the groups have an obvious bisexual focus.

Conclusion

The bisexual community has some commonalities with the lesbian and gay community as a result of similar social challenges related to discrimination against these groups and their identification as sexual minorities. As a result, libraries can employ similar philosophies and approaches to collection development and services in these areas, particularly with regard to supporting ALA's Library Bill of Rights. However, when bisexuality is placed under the umbrella of gay and lesbian concerns, the distinct challenges and needs of the bisexual community can sometimes be lost, forgotten, or ignored. Therefore it is essential that librarians ensure that their collections and services incorporate bisexual-specific items and activities in order to meet the needs of this "invisible" community.

REFERENCES

American Institute of Bisexuality. (n.d.). Inside BiMagazine: Books. Retrieved from http://www.bimagazine.org/books/index.html

American Library Association. (1996). *Library Bill of Rights*. Retrieved from http://www.ala.org/ala/aboutala/offices/oif/statementspols/statementsif/librarybillofrights.pdf

BiNet USA. (n.d.) BiNet USA home. Retrieved from http://www.binetusa.org/index.html

Bisexual Resource Center. (2009). Celebrating and affirming the diversity of identity and expression regardless of labels. Boston: Bisexual Resource Center. Retrieved from http://www.biresource.net/BRC_Brochure09.pdf

Bisexual Resource Center. (n.d.). Bisexual Resource Center. Retrieved from http://www.biresource.net/

Burleson, W. E. (Ed.). (2005). Bi America: Myths, truths, and struggles of an invisible community. New York: Harrington Park.

Curry, A. (2005, Fall). If I ask, will they answer? Evaluating public library reference service to gay and lesbian youth. *Reference & User Services Quarterly, 45*(1), 65–74.

Evans, T. (2003, March). Bisexuality: Negotiating lives between two cultures. *Journal of Bisexuality, 3*(2), 91–108.

Healthy Teen Network. (2006, September). Unique needs of lesbian, gay, bisexual, transgender, and queer (LGBTQ) youth. Retrieved from http://www.healthyteennetwork.org/vertical/Sites/%7BB4D0CC76-CF78-4784-BA7C-5D0436F6040C%7D/uploads/%7B48BB22A6-8A73-41A2-BD11-29FBBFCC6C15%7D.PDF

Joyce, S. (2000, September/October). Lesbian, gay, and bisexual library services: A review of the literature. *Public Libraries, 39*(5), 270–279.

Lambda Literary Foundation. (n.d.). Previous Lammy award winners. Retrieved from http://www.lambdaliterary.org/awards/previous_winners/paw_2004_2006.html

Linville, D. (2004, August). Beyond picket fences: What gay/queer/LGBTQ teens want from the library. *Voice of Youth Advocates, 27*(3), 183–186.

McLean, K. (2001). Living life in the double closet: Bisexual youth speak out. *Hecate, 27*(1), 110–118.

McLean, K. (2008). Inside, outside, nowhere: Bisexual men and women in the gay and lesbian community. *Journal of Bisexuality,* 8(1), 63–80.

O'Brien, K. M. (1998). The people in between: Understanding the needs of bisexual students. In R. L. Sanlo (Ed.), Working with lesbian, gay, bisexual, and transgender college students: A handbook for faculty and administration (pp. 31–35). Westport, CT: Greenwood.

Ochs, R. (1996). Biphobia: It goes more than two ways. In B. A. Firestein (Ed.), Bisexuality: The psychology and politics of an invisible minority (pp. 217–237). London: Sage.

Oswalt, S. B. (2009). Don't forget the "B": Considering bisexual students and their specific health needs. *Journal of American College Health*, 57(5), 557–560.

Parents, Families and Friends of Lesbians and Gays. (n.d.). Bisexuality 101: Bisexuality resource packet. Retrieved from http://www.pflag.org/fileadmin/user_upload/BisexualityResourcePacket.pdf

Intersex Resources in Libraries[1]

David Cameron Strachan and Jim Van Buskirk

"Is it a boy or a girl?" This seemingly straightforward query about a baby is not so simply answered when the child is born with ambiguous genitalia. Some experts estimate that as many as 1 in every 1,500 babies is born with genitals that cannot easily be classified as male or female. However, because experts disagree on exactly what qualifies as an intersex condition, they are not always accurately diagnosed, and government agencies do not collect statistics about intersex individuals. This, coupled with the stigma of having — or being — a baby that does not look "normal," has made dealing with intersex issues shameful and often traumatic. It is for this reason that it is imperative for libraries to provide objective sources of information — medical, social, and psychological — about intersex issues as they develop services to sexual and gender minorities.

Society assumes what men or women are and then reinforces gender and sex stereotypes and ideals. There is no legal definition of what a man or woman is; for every definition there is an exception. If one is intersex what is same or opposite sex? Some intersex people have gender identities other than the standard man equals male, woman equals female.

The following statement by renowned academic and intersex advocate Alice Domurat Dreger is intended to help you feel less frustrated if you are confused by this complicated topic.

> The challenging thing about talking about the history and politics of the term "intersex" is that the term is a moving target. That is to say, its meaning seems to change even as we talk about it ... let me define "intersex" the way it has usually been understood: a person is intersex when she or he is born with a body type that mixes or blends what are usually thought of as the standard male and standard female types. That mixing might occur at the level of "sex chromosomes," or gonads (ovaries, testes, or ovotestes) or external genitalia, or internal reproductive anatomy, or some combination of those [2007, para. 2].

Intersex, literally "between the sexes," is an umbrella term for variations in sexual anatomy, sex chromosomes and/or mixed sexual reproductive differences that have legal, social and medical implications. Intersex persons can be heterosexual, homosexual, bisexual, asexual or have another sexual orientation. They often face discrimination from the community at large as well as from within the gay and lesbian communities for not being readily identifiable as male or female.

Intersex people have lived in all cultures throughout history and there have been many terms used to describe them. As Dreger writes, *intersex* has been used in place of *hermaphrodite* steadily if irregularly in medical practice and literature since the mid-twentieth century

(2007, para. 7). Other common terms in English include *eunuch, hijras, people with disabilities,* and *mutation.* The phenomenon has been referred to as a difference, disorder, abnormality or a variation of sex development.

Like *intersex, transgender* is a relatively recent term applied differently to, and by, a variety of individuals, behaviors, and groups involving tendencies to diverge from the normative gender roles. While intersex relates to biological anatomy, transgender is socially constructed. Like intersex people, transgender people can have a variety of sexual orientations and gender identities.

People who identify as *genderqueer* or *intergender* may consider themselves as being both male and female, as being neither male nor female, or as falling completely outside the gender binary. Some genderqueer people see their identity as one of many possible genders other than male or female, while others see *genderqueer* as an umbrella term that encompasses all of those possible genders. Still others see *genderqueer* as a third gender to complement the traditional two, while others identify as genderless or agender. Genderqueer people are united by their rejection of the notion that there are only two genders. The term *genderqueer* can also be used as an adjective to refer to any people who transgress gender, regardless of their self-defined gender identity.

Intersex can be categorized into four basic divisions. "46XX" intersex individuals have female chromosomes and ovaries, but external genitals that appear male. Congenital Adrenal Hypoplasia is the most common cause of this condition. "46XY" intersex individuals have the chromosomes of a man, while the external genitals are either completely female or ambiguous. Internally, the testes may be normal, malformed or completely absent. Androgen Insensitivity Syndrome (AIS) occurs when the receptors to the male hormones (and androgen) do not function properly. "True Gonadal Intersex" individuals have both ovarian and testicular tissue and may have XX chromosomes, XY chromosomes or both. External genitals may be completely male or female or ambiguous. Conditions that fall under the category of "Complex or Undetermined Intersex" do not involve a discrepancy between internal and external genitalia, although there may be a problem with sex hormone levels, overall sexual development, or an altered number of sex chromosomes (Association for Women's Rights in Development, 2009).

Intersex children and adolescents born with ambiguous genitalia have been routinely surgically or hormonally "fixed" and "cured" of their variations/conditions, so they "fit visually" into the ordered "two sex-two gender" binary system. Some anatomical ambiguities become evident at puberty when children don't develop like others. It's estimated that one in two thousand persons have some birth ambiguity while one in one hundred fifty have other sex anatomical variations. It is estimated that between 0.1 percent and 0.2 percent of live births are ambiguous enough to become the subject of specialist medical attention, including surgery to disguise their sexual ambiguity. In "Queer Cut Bodies: Intersexuality and Homophobia in Medical Practice," M. Morgan Holmes argues vociferously about the connections between intersex issues and homophobia:

> Societally sanctioned homophobia is partly to blame for the invasive, violent and damaging treatment of intersexuality. When parents sign consent forms, allowing doctors to remove the erotogenic tissue of their children, they are willingly following a heterosexist requirement that humans live as either male or female. The cost is paid in terms of physical function and sensation, in terms of self-image and self-esteem and it is paid by the intersexed children [1995, para. 37].

Many discussions of sex and gender refer to the famous case of "John/Joan." On August 22, 1965, healthy twin boys, Bruce and Brian Reimer, were born in Canada. After his penis was accidentally destroyed during circumcision, Bruce was sexually reassigned and raised as a female named Brenda. John Money, the now-controversial pioneering psychologist in the field of sexual development and gender identity who oversaw the case, reported the reassignment was successful as evidence that gender identity is primarily learned. Academic sexologist Milton Diamond later reported that Reimer never identified as female, and that at the age of 14 he began living as male calling himself "David." Reimer later went public with his story to discourage similar medical practice, before committing suicide at the age of 38.

This cautionary tale points to the need for parents to be as well informed as possible when dealing with these complicated issues. Medical/scientific texts, personal accounts written by intersex people, and information from intersex advocacy organizations must all be made available to help parents understand that nothing irreversible should be done to children until they are old enough to understand and are ready and able to make their own decisions.

In August 2006 a new standard of care was published in *Pediatrics* (Lee, Houk, Ahmed, & Hughes). According to the Intersex Society of North America (ISNA), *The Consensus Statement on Management of Intersex Disorders* incorporates many of the concepts and changes long advocated by ISNA including progress in patient-centered care, more cautious approach to surgery, and replacing misleading language (2008).

To further complicate matters, in recent years the Intersex Society of North America, intersex activists, medical experts and parents have moved to eliminate the term *intersex* by introducing *disorders of sex development,* sometimes also referred to as *disorders of sex differentiation* (DSD). DSD has by no means been universally accepted and still another term is being put forth: *variations of sex development* (VSD). While it is posited that VSD is free of value judgment, feelings run high about the terms applied by outsiders to one's personal identity. Rather than make things more confusing and render this essay out-of-date even before it goes to press, we urge readers to stay abreast of ongoing developments by visiting the relevant websites listed in the resources section below as well as investigate new sites certain to appear.

Why is this important for librarians? As with all subject areas, patrons come to the library seeking to inform themselves. Users may personally identify as intersex or they may be doing research on behalf of a family member or friend. They might just be curious or working on an educational project. It is important to inform ourselves in order to develop collections, to provide reference and/or referral services, and to consider exhibits and/or public programs. Libraries need to acknowledge intersex people with affirming information resources and services, even if— or especially because — one cannot identify intersex individuals in the community served.

Using collection development and service principles established by the American Library Association, libraries are obligated to make a concerted effort to provide distinct, intersex-specific resources and services. One excellent way is by partnering with local and/or national intersex organizations and individuals.[2] Many of the issues raised by Jessica L. Howard in her excellent essay on serving the information needs of the "invisible" bisexual community are relevant to those of the intersex community.

Equally important as the materials in a library's collection are the points of access. Current LC subject headings include: *intersex people, intersex children, sex differences, sex differentiation, intersexuality, sex (biology), sex chromosome abnormalities,* and *hypogonadism.* Although *hermaphroditism* stopped being applied by Library of Congress in 2007, the term may not yet have been changed in all catalogs.

Terms for some but not all specific conditions may also be found, such as *Klinefelter's syndrome* and *Klinefelter's syndrome in children,* or *Turner Syndrome* or *Adrenal Hyperplasia, Congenital.* Keyword searching helps somewhat but it can remain challenging for patrons to find the information they seek. Because of the social stigma, some patrons may not be comfortable asking library staff for assistance. Developing and making available a bibliography or pathfinder may help patrons find the resources themselves.

Appearances of intersex characters in popular culture include the 2003 Japanese manga series *I.S.,* which features intersexed characters who deal with intersex-related issues and influence the lives of people around them. The anime and manga series *Nabari no Ou* by Yuhki Kamatani features an intersexed character known as Yoite. The multi-volume *Vorkosigan Saga* science-fiction series by Lois McMaster Bujold features the "herm" (Bujold's usage) character Captain Bel Thorne from the socially liberal Beta Colony, where genetically engineered hermaphrodites form a locally respected minority of the population.

At the time of this writing, there has been intense speculation about whether Caster Semenya, the South African middle-distance runner, is intersex and in doing so, publicizing a topic of which many people were previously unaware. It is essential to take to heart Thea Hillman's simple words.

> We're not actually all that different. We are women, men, and occasionally alternative genders such as transgender — just like non-intersex people. We are straight, gay, married, single — just like non-intersex people. We like to decide what happens to our bodies and like to be asked about our lives, rather than told [2003, p. 3].

Because intersex is a relatively new concept that librarians may not yet be aware of, we are including a lengthy list of useful and informative resources to help familiarize you with issues and concerns and to better help you serve the intersex community at your library.

Resources

In the resources listed below, works marked with [I] at the end of a listing indicate those written by an intersex-identified person.

Intersex Support Organizations

Organisation Intersex International (OII) <http://www.intersexualite.org>. The largest intersex organization in the world with a membership that "represents almost all known intersex variations," the OII maintains a multilingual website that offers a wealth of information, including an extensive library of documents in a variety of formats.

Intersex Society of North America (ISNA) <http://www.isna.org>. Although the ISNA, the first organization in North America to advocate for intersex rights, "closed its doors" in 2008, its website, although no longer maintained, still contains valuable information including a library of historically significant documents, bibliographies, and videos. The successor to this organization is the Accord Alliance (*see below*).

Accord Alliance <http://www.accordalliance.org>. A relatively new organization established in 2008, the Accord Alliance is the heir to the legacy of the ISNA. Its website contains several helpful resources, including educational materials, directories of support and advocacy groups, and a glossary of terms. This organization no longer uses the term *intersex,* preferring instead *disorders of sex development* (DSD).

Intersex Initiative <http://www.intersexinitiative.org/>. This Portland, Oregon-based organization, headed by intersex activist, Emi Koyama, offers articles and publications dealing with legal issues, intersex studies, activism and advocacy along with reports of intersex issues in the news.

Bodies Like Ours <http://www.bodieslikeours.org/forums>. Billing itself as "powered by the intersex community," this website provides forums on a variety of intersex issues, both general and specific. Designed as a large electronic support group, participants can "share and learn from others" on such wide-ranging topics as choosing a doctor, parenting issues, and current research. There are also forums for many specific intersex conditions.

Intersex Collective <http://www.intersexcollective.org>. Best known for its speakers bureau, featuring experts on the subject of intersex, this site also has a brief resources page listing other intersex organizations.

Advocates for Informed Choice <http://www.aiclegal.org>. Advocating for the civil rights of intersex children, this site offers an array of information to help parents make decisions about informed consent, school accommodations, medical privacy, and legal issues. Especially helpful are the section on "Know your rights!" and a bibliography of works addressing the legal and civil rights of intersex children.

Condition-Specific Support Organizations

Listed below are the sites for just a few intersex conditions. There are many more. For additional information about these and other conditions, visit the terminology portion of the OII site <http://www.intersexualite.org/intersex_medical_perspective.html> which offers explanations from a medical perspective. There is also a helpful glossary at the Accord Alliance web site <http://www.accordalliance.org/glossary.html>

Androgen Insensitivity Syndrome (AIS)

Androgen Insensitivity Syndrome Support Group <http://www.aissg.org>. According to the AISSG website: "AIS is a condition that affects the development of the reproductive and genital organs" (2009, para. 56) and "People with AIS have a functioning Y sex chromosome (and therefore no female internal organs), but an abnormality on the X sex chromosome that renders the body completely or partially incapable of recognizing [*sic*] the androgens [male sex hormones] produced" (para. 59). The UK-based AISSG site contains information regarding diagnosis, treatments, and an impressive historical bibliography on AIS concerns and treatments. Personal narratives of people with AIS appear on this site which also serves as a support and networking group. AISSG's site also presents abridged versions of the English language information in a variety of languages.

Congenital Adrenal Hyperplasia (CAH)

Congenital Adrenal Hyperplasia (CAH) Education and Support Network <http://www.congenitaladrenalhyperplasia.org/>. According to the Congenital Adrenal Hyperplasia

(CAH) Education and Support Network, "CAH is a genetic defect of the adrenal glands. A person with CAH will not be able to produce several vital hormones known as corticosteriods. CAH is treated with hormone replacement" (n.d., para. 1). The CAH Education and Support Network page includes frequently asked questions, a glossary, and lists of support groups, blogs, and family pages.

Hypospadias

Hypospadias and Epispadias Association (HEA) <http://www.heainfo.org/>. According to the Hypospadias and Epispadias Association: Hypospadias and epispadias are birth anomalies that affect formation of the penis during embryological development. When the urethra (the tube that serves as a conduit through the penis for the passage of urine and semen) fails to develop properly, the urethral opening is formed on the underside (hypospadias) or top side (epispadias) of the penis, instead of at the tip (2009, para. 4).

This organization's recently redesigned webpage is comprised of message boards and chat rooms, as well as links to resources, blogs, and personal stories.

Klinefelter Syndrome (KS)

The American Association for Klinefelter Syndrome Information and Support (AAKSIS) <http://www.aaksis.org/>.

Knowledge, Support, and Action (KS & A) <http://www.genetic.org/>. According to the Accord Alliance, "Klinefelter Syndrome (47,XXY or XXY syndrome) occurs when an individual has at least two X chromosomes and at least one Y chromosome. It typically results in small testes and reduced fertility" (2009, para. 2). Dr. Wolfram E. Nolten, the founding director of The American Association for Klinefelter Syndrome Information and Support (AAKSIS), expands upon the definition above on the AAKSIS website, stating: "Klinefelter Syndrome (KS) affects 1 in 500 male conceptions and is therefore the most common sex chromosome abnormality. It results in small testes, testosterone deficiency, infertility and often in swelling of glandular breast tissue (gynecomastia)" (n.d., para. 1).

The AAKSIS (pronounced "access") website offers direct support to people affected by KS as well as links to other regional support groups. It also provides educational information about KS and XXY.

Knowledge, Support, and Action's (KS & A) mission is slightly broader than AAKSIS, helping "individuals with one or more extra X and/or Y chromosomes and their families lead fuller and more productive lives"(2009, para. 1). The KS & A site includes online discussion groups and annotated reading lists, in addition to information directing individuals to local support groups.

Mayer Rokitansky Kuster Hauser Syndrome (MRKH)

MRKH Organization <http://www.mrkh.org/>. According to the MRKH Organization, MRKH is a "variation of female reproductive development ... [and] often involves missing vagina, cervix, uterus and fallopian tubes in genetic females. Uterine remnants are common with people who have MRKH" (2004, para. 6). The MRKH site includes support and networking information as well as links to medical information such as treatment options, photos of MRKH anatomy, and recommended doctors and therapists.

Turner Syndrome (TS)

Turner Syndrome Society of the United States (TSSUS) <http://www.turner-syn drome-us.org/>. According to the Turner Syndrome Society of the United States (TSSUS), "Turner syndrome (TS) is a chromosomal condition that describes girls and women with common features that are caused by complete or partial absence of the second sex chromosome" (2009, para. 1). The TSSUS site contains helpful information about this condition, including a guide for families and clinical practice guidelines, both downloadable.

About Kid's Health: How the Body Works: Sex Development: An Overview <http://www.aboutkidshealth.ca/HowTheBodyWorks/Sex-Development-An-Overview. aspx?articleID=7671&categoryID=XS>. While not a support organization, this website is included here because of its helpful explanations of various conditions related to sex development.

Online Articles and Reports

Arana, M. d. M. (2005). *A human rights investigation into the medical "normalization" of intersex people*. Retrieved from http://www.isna.org/files/SFHRC_Intersex_Report.pdf. This report, developed by the San Francisco Human Rights Commission (SFHRC) Intersex Task Force as the result of public hearings held by the commission, offers findings and recommendations, including testimony by intersex people, on medical intersex. The report was adopted by the Human Rights Commissioners in May 2005. (*See also the video of the hearings listed in the* Films and Videos *section of this resource guide*.)

Chase, C. (2005). *Intersex declared a human rights issue*. Retrieved from http://www. isna.org/node/841. Chase's response to the SFHRC Intersex Task Force report listed above in which she, the Executive Director of the ISNA at the time, states "In issuing this report, the San Francisco Human Rights Commission has essentially declared me a human being.... They have agreed that I — and children born like me — deserve the same basic human rights as others" (para. 2). [I]

Evans, W. (2004). *Those neither completely male or female speak out*. Retrieved from http://www.mermaidsuk.org.uk/bee001.html. Originally published in the *Sacramento Bee* on April 30, 2004, this article puts a personal face on the topic of intersex by highlighting the experiences of a variety of people.

Hinkle, C. E. (2006). *Intersex pride: Why the intergender community is so important to intersexuals*. Retrieved from http://intersexpride.blogspot.com/2006/03/why-intergender-community-is-so.html. Hinkle, founder of the Organisation Intersex International (OII), offers his views on the topic of intergender individuals whose identity does not conform with the traditional Western binary gender system. Speaking on the importance of the role of intergender activists in the intersex community, he states: "We clearly force society to deal with the fact that intersex bodies are not just mutilated but our identities are often mutilated too" (para. 6). [I]

Somers xxy, C., Reibel, T., and Whyatt, D. (2010). Intersex and androgyny and implications for provision of primary health care. Geraldton, Western Australia: Combined Universities Centre for Rural Health. Retrieved from http://www.cucrh.uwa.edu.au/fellowship/ files/Intersex%20and%20Androgyny%20Report%20Somers.pdf. Examines the knowledge and attitudes of primary care health providers (PCHPs) regarding intersex and androgyny. The researchers assessed the current status by conducting interviews with PCHPs in Western

Australia, concluding that, in order to better treat intersex or androgynous individuals, PCHPs must look beyond the traditional western binary system; gain a better understanding of the differences between androgynous and intersex conditions; improve their knowledge base so that they can improve their treatment of individuals with these conditions; and create an affirmative environment in order for individuals to feel comfortable in disclosing their intersex or androgynous status. [I]

Strachan, D. C. (2006). *Re: Variations of sex development instead of disorders of sex development.* Retrieved from http://adc.bmj.com/cgi/eletters/adc.2006.098319v1#2479. The co-author's contribution to the evolving discussion on appropriate terminology offered in response to the publication of the *Consensus Statement on Management of Intersex Disorders.* [I]

Strachan, D. C. (2006, June 15). Being different and fitting in. *San Francisco Bay Times,* Retrieved from http://www.sfbaytimes.com/index.php?sec=article&article_id=5096. Recounts the life journey of co-author David Cameron Strachan. [I]

Tamar-Mattis, A. (2006). *Exceptions to the rule: Curing the law's failure to protect intersex infants.* Retrieved from http://www.aiclegal.org/06_Tamar-Mattis_Final.pdf. Originally published in the *Berkeley Journal of Gender, Law & Justice,* this award-winning article discusses the role the law can play in changing the standards of care regarding intersex infants.

Books: Nonfiction

BIOGRAPHY

Bloom, A. (2002). *Normal: Transsexual CEOs, cross-dressing cops, and hermaphrodites with attitude.* New York: Random House. Novelist, psychotherapist and lesbian feminist Amy Bloom writes sensitively about male-to-female transsexuals, heterosexual male cross-dressers, and intersexed individuals — and challenges readers to question their concepts of gender.

Colapinto, J. (2000). *As nature made him: The boy who was raised as a girl.* New York: HarperCollins. A biography of David Reimer, the subject of the famous "John/Joan" case, which set the precedent for sex reassignment as standard treatment for thousands of intersex children. John Money used the "success" of this case to posit that a child's gender identity is fluid up to a certain age, until Milton Diamond and Keith Sigmundson disproved Money's claims.

Harper, C. (2007). *Intersex.* Oxford: Berg. Drawing heavily on the personal testimony of intersexed individuals, their loved ones, and medical carers, the impact of early sex assignment surgery on an individual's later life is examined within the context of ethical and clinical questions.

Holmes, R. (2002). *Scanty particulars: The scandalous life and astonishing secret of Queen Victoria's most eminent military doctor.* New York: Random House. James Miranda Barry, was raised as a boy, grew up to serve as a British Army physician, and became one of the leading and most controversial innovators of 19th-century medicine. (See also Patricia Duncker's novel, *The Doctor.*)

Preves, S. E. (2003). *Intersex and identity: The contested self.* New Brunswick, NJ: Rutgers University Press. Examines how intersexed individuals negotiate identity in a dual gendered culture. Based on interviews with adult intersexed individuals, Preves shows that medical intervention often causes more problems than it prevents.

Swan, R. (2004). *Assume nothing.* Auckland, NZ: Boy Tiger Press. Stunning black and white photographs accompanied by brief interviews explore 25 different embodiments of gender across cultures, nations, and generations. Text and captions in English; includes a foreword by Judith "Jack" Halberstam. (*See also the video of the same name below in the* Films and Videos *section.*)

HISTORY

Barbin, H. (1980). *Herculine Barbin: Being the recently discovered memoirs of a nineteenth-century French hermaphrodite.* New York: Pantheon. The diary of a French hermaphrodite who committed suicide after being forced to live as a man and separated from the woman he loved. Includes an introduction by Michel Foucault.

Dreger, A. D. (2000). *Hermaphrodites and the medical invention of sex.* Cambridge, MA: Harvard University Press. Focusing on events in France and Britain in the late nineteenth century, a moment of great tension for questions of sex roles, this book explores extraordinary encounters between hermaphrodites — people born with "ambiguous" sexual anatomy — and the medical and scientific professionals who grappled with them.

Fausto-Sterling, A. (2000). *Sexing the body: Gender politics and the construction of sexuality.* New York: Basic. Drawing on astonishing real-life cases and a probing analysis of centuries of scientific research, this title demonstrates how scientists have historically politicized the body.

Gilbert, R. (2002). *Early modern hermaphrodites: Sex and other stories.* New York: Palgrave. The author examines the ways in which inter-sexed individuals were viewed medically, erotically, legally, and literarily in Britain from the 16th to the 18th centuries.

Herdt, G. H. (Ed.). (1994). *Third sex, third gender: Beyond sexual dimorphism in culture and history.* New York: Zone. These eleven essays in history and anthropology offer a novel perspective by questioning the place of sexual dimorphism in culture and history. Of particular interest to scholars investigating intersexuality are the essays by Gilbert Herdt and Will Roscoe.

MEDICAL/SCIENTIFIC

Callahan, G. N. (2009). *Between XX and XY: Intersexuality and the myth of two sexes.* Chicago: Chicago Review Press. Every year in the United States, more than two thousand children are born with an intersex condition or disorder of sex development. Not even doctors or scientists are entirely clear whether maleness or femaleness is a result of external genitalia, chromosomes, environment, or some combination of these factors.

Cohen-Kettenis, P. T., & Pfäfflin, F. (2003). *Transgenderism and intersexuality in childhood and adolescence: Making choices.* Thousand Oaks, CA: SAGE. This book presents a cross-cultural overview of the research, clinical insights, and ethical dilemmas relevant to clinicians who treat intersex youth and their families.

Consortium on the Management of Disorders of Sex Development. (2006). *Clinical Guidelines for the Management of Disorders of Sex Development in Childhood.* Rohnert Park, CA: Intersex Society of North America. Retrieved from: http://www.dsdguidelines.org.

Consortium on the Management of Disorders of Sex Development. (2006). *Handbook for Parents.* Rohnert Park, Calif.: Intersex Society of North America. Retrieved from: http://www.dsdguidelines.org. These two handbooks were produced by a consortium consisting mainly of clinical specialists with experience helping patients with DSDs as well as family members (especially parents) of children with DSDs. Each handbook is available in a free, easily-downloadable PDF format.

Holder, T. J. (2006). *All points in between: Shifting on the scale of sex and gender.* New

York: iUniverse. This book explores sex and gender identities and argues that an understanding of both sex and gender as a spectrum, rather than binary categories, would help people to live healthier lives. [I]

Karkazis, K. A. (2008). *Fixing sex: Intersex, medical authority, and lived experience.* Durham, NC: Duke University Press. This book carefully exposes the contentious disagreements among theoreticians, clinicians, intersex adults, parents, and others involved in intersex issues.

Kessler, S. J. (1998). *Lessons from the intersexed.* New Brunswick, NJ: Rutgers University Press. Interviews with pediatric surgeons and endocrinologists as well as parents of intersexed children and adults who were treated for this condition in childhood lead Kessler to propose several new approaches for physicians in dealing with parents and children.

Parens, E. (Ed.). (2006). *Surgically shaping children: Technology, ethics, and the pursuit of normality.* Baltimore, MD: Johns Hopkins University Press. Written from the perspectives of affected children and their parents, health care providers, and leading scholars in philosophy, sociology, history, law, and medicine, this collection provides an integrated and comprehensive foundation from which to consider the complex and controversial issue of surgeries designed to make children born with physical differences look more normal.

Parker, J. N., & Parker, P. M. (2007). *Klinefelter syndrome: A bibliography and dictionary for physicians, patients, and genome researchers.* San Diego, CA: ICON Health. Designed for physicians, medical students preparing for board examinations, medical researchers, and patients who want to become familiar with research dedicated to Klinefelter syndrome, this book includes a complete medical dictionary, extensive lists of bibliographic citations, and information on how to use various Internet resources.

Parker, J. N., & Parker, P. M. (2007). *Turner syndrome: A bibliography and dictionary for physicians, patients, and genome researchers.* San Diego, CA: ICON Health. Similar to the book above on Klinefelter syndrome, this book helps both scholarly and casual researchers navigate the Internet in addition to providing a complete medical dictionary and extensive lists of bibliographic citations.

Roughgarden, J. (2004). *Evolution's rainbow: Diversity, gender, and sexuality in nature and people.* Berkeley: University of California Press. By examining the enormous gender and sexual diversity found in nature in animals and humans and the social barriers to acceptance of human diversity, Roughgarden explores how and why this range of bodies and behaviors evolved and exposes how biology, medicine, anthropology, and Christianity have obstructed the recognition and acceptance of this diversity.

Sytsma, S. E. (Ed.). (2005). *Ethics and intersex.* Dordrecht, Netherlands: Springer. This collection of twenty-one articles is designed to serve as a state-of-the-art reference book for intersexuals, their parents, health care professionals, ethics committee members, and anyone interested in problems associated with intersexuality.

Warne, G. L. (1989). *Your child with congenital adrenal hyperplasia.* Parkville, Victoria, Australia: Dept. of Endrinology and Diabetes, Royal Children's Hospital. This illustrated practical guide for parents is freely downloadable in English, French, Vietnamese and Chinese. Available at: http://www.rch.org.au/cah_book/index.cfm?doc_id=1375.

Warne, G. L. (1998). *Complete Androgen Insensitivity Syndrome.* Parkville, Victoria, Australia: Dept. of Endocrinology and Diabetes, Royal Children's Hospital. This twenty-eight page illustrated booklet is for women with Androgen Insensitivity Syndrome (AIS), parents of children with the condition, and health professionals involved in counseling and treating these patients. Free copies can be downloaded in German, French, and English at this URL: http://www.rch.org.au/chas/pubs/index.cfm?doc_id=6163.

MEMOIR

Connella, K. (2000). *Sugar and spice and puppy dog tails: Growing up intersexed: an intimate memoir*. Hollywood, CA: K. Connella. Actress/author Katherine Connella steps out of the shadows to frankly reveal her childhood and adolescence growing up intersexed. [I]

Dreger, A. D. (Ed.). (1999). *Intersex in the age of ethics*. Hagerstown, MD: University Pub. Group. This tightly focused collection, a reprint of a special issue of the *Journal of Clinical Ethics* edited by non-intersex academic Dreger, presents different points of view — personal, ethical, clinical, legal, anthropological, historical, sociological, and philosophical — all by intersex people. [I]

Hillman, T. (2008). *Intersex (for lack of a better word)*. San Francisco: Manic D Press. This poetic, political, and deeply personal book chronicles one person's search for self in a world obsessed with normal and in a series of compelling stories takes a no-holds-barred look at sex, gender, family, and community. [I]

Nestle, J., Howell, C., & Wilchins, R. A. (Eds.). (2002). *GenderQueer: Voices from beyond the sexual binary*. Los Angeles: Alyson. This groundbreaking anthology of thirty first-person testimonies deals with gender construction, exploration, and questioning, providing groundwork for cultural discussion, political action, and even greater possibilities of autonomous gender choices.

BOOKS: FICTION

Duncker, P. (1999). *The doctor: A novel*. New York: Ecco. This fictional account is based on the life of Dr. James Miranda Barry, a girl (or possibly a hermaphrodite), raised as a boy, who grew up to live as a man, serving as a British Army physician. (*See also Rachel Holmes' account*, Scanty Particulars *in the* Biography *section above.*)

Eugenides, J. (2002). *Middlesex*. New York: Farrar, Straus, Giroux. This Pulitzer Prize–winning novel explores the family history and life of a female-reared protagonist who has an intersex condition doctors call 5-alpha reductase deficiency.

Gentle, M. (2006). *Ilario: The lion's eye: A story of the first history*. New York: EOS/HarperCollins. Set in an alternate medieval world, the intersexed slave, Ilario flees existence as a King's toy when his/her mother tries to kill her/him. Ilario becomes dangerously pregnant following a brief encounter, is again enslaved, and travels one step ahead of his/her assassins. The story continues in book two, *Ilario: The Stone Golem* (2007).

Goyen, W. (1983). *Arcadio: A novel*. New York: C.N. Potter. Completed while he was dying, William Goyen's novel features Arcadio, a creature from beyond the normal walks of life. Half man, half woman, raised in a whorehouse and for years the veteran exhibitionist in an itinerant circus sideshow, he has escaped from the show and has been wandering in search of his lost family. Speaking intimately to the reader, he tells the bizarre and fantastic tale of his life.

Howe, J. W. (2004). *The hermaphrodite*. Lincoln: University of Nebraska Press. Written in the 1840s, but not published until 2004, this is the story of a hermaphrodite raised as a boy, who lives as a man, is loved by men and women alike, and can respond to neither. Howe (1819–1910), best remembered as the poet who wrote the words to *Battle Hymn of the Republic*, was also an activist for women's rights and known for her efforts to mobilize women for various peace efforts.

Odegard, T. (2006). *Friends well met & more*. Berkeley, CA: Beatitude. In this collection, poet Tom Odegard reflects on his friends, his loves, his multi-faceted self, and the fullness of a life well-lived. [I]

Films and Videos

As of this writing, some of these titles were only available in VHS versions. Some are also available online.

Clearway, A. (Producer & Director). (2006). *One in 2000* [DVD]. Available from http://fanlight.com/catalog/films/459_ots.php. At a time when five babies a day in the United States are having "gender reassignment" surgery, this provocative documentary argues that there is little evidence that such surgery is beneficial to the child. Interweaves the stories of several people born with ambiguous sexual anatomy, who have dealt with difficult family and social issues, and are today living "ordinary," productive lives.

Gale, P. & Soomekh, L. (Directors & Producers). (2000). *XXXY: A Short Documentary about Intersex Issues* [DVD]. Available from http://www.berkeleymedia.com/catalog/berkeleymedia/films/womens_studies_gender_studies/gay_lesbian_transgender_issues/xxxy. In this short (13 minute) documentary, Kristi Bruce and Howard Devore, both born intersex, talk eloquently and straightforwardly about their experience of a medical model based upon shame, secrecy, and forced "normalization." Physician Jorge Daaboul (Director of Pediatric Endocrinology at Oakland Children's Hospital in California) joins their call for an end to secrecy and mutilating genital surgery on intersex children. Viewable online with RealPlayer at http://www.film.com/movies/xxxy/14704261.

Intersex Society of North America. (2002). *First do no harm: Total patient care for intersex.* [VHS]. Available from http://www.fanlight.com/catalog/films/368_fdnh.php. This video outlines the problems with current practices and provides guidelines for a new standard of care that is more advanced both scientifically and ethically. Based on a panel discussion involving medical professionals, an adult with an intersex condition, and a parent, this video, while addressed primarily to medical and mental health professionals, is quite accessible to lay audiences as well.

Intersex Society of North America. (1997). *Hermaphrodites speak!* [DVD]. Available from http://www.isna.org/videos/purchase. A variety of people tell their stories (often for the first time) of growing up intersex and their joy at finally meeting other people who are intersex.

Keir, J. (Director). (2006). *Yellow for hermaphrodites: Mani's story* [DVD]. Available from http://www.isna.org/videos/purchase. This powerful documentary film explores the life of intersex activist Mani Bruce Mitchell (from *Hermaphrodites Speak!*) in her own words.

MacDonald, K. (Producer & Director). (2009). *Assume nothing.* [Documentary]. New Zealand. This pioneering film focuses on New Zealand photographer Rebecca Swan as she photographs the cultural diversity of the multi-gendered worldwide family. View the trailer on YouTube at: http://www.youtube.com/watch?v=4ISC6aJddYs. (*See also the book by the same name listed above in the* Biography *section.*)

San Francisco Human Rights Commission. (2004, May 27). *Intersex hearing.* [Video on demand recorded by SFGTV Cable Television]. Retrieved from http://sanfrancisco.granicus.com/MediaPlayer.php?publish_id=201. On May 27, 2004, the San Francisco Human Rights Commission was the first governmental entity in the United States to hold a public hearing, including testimony by intersex people, on medical intersex treatments that involved gender assignments. After the historic hearing, the San Francisco Human Rights Commission Intersex Task Force developed the *Intersex Report*, with findings and recommendations, and was adopted by the Human Rights Commissioners in May 2005. (*See also the report that was developed as a result of these hearings in the* Online Articles and Reports *section of this guide.*)

Ward, P. (Director). (2000). *Is it a boy or a girl?* [DVD]. Available from http://www.isna. org/videos/purchase. The question "Is it a boy or a girl" can be complicated when a third option is introduced; one out of every two thousand children in America is born intersexual. Sometimes biology malfunctions and children are born with mixed sexual characteristics, in what is called an intersexual birth. Intersexuals show us that gender is infinitely more complex than the shape of our genitals. Originally broadcast on the Discovery Channel on March 26, 2000.

NOTES

1. The coauthors would like to acknowledge the assistance and support of: Curtis Hinkle, founder of Organization Intersex International; Mani Bruce Mitchell, executive director of the Intersex Trust in Aotearoa New Zealand; Dr Margaret Sparrow, venereologist at the Wellington Sexual Health Service; and Anne Tamar-Mattis, founder of Advocates for Informed Choice.

2. For more on this topic, please see the profile "Making a Difference" in this section.

REFERENCES

Accord Alliance. (2009). Glossary of terms. Retrieved from http://www.accordalliance.org/component/glos sary/?task=list&glossid=1&letter=K

Androgen Insensitivity Syndrome Support Group. (2009, September 21). What is AIS? Retrieved from http://www.aissg.org/21_OVERVIEW.HTM#Introduction

Association for Women's Rights in Development. (2009, September 11). Are you intersexed? Retrieved from http://www.awid.org/eng/Issues-and-Analysis/Library/Are-you-intersexed

Congenital Adrenal Hyperplasia Education and Support Network. (n.d.). What is Congenital Adrenal Hyperplasia (CAH)? Retrieved from http://congenitaladrenalhyperplasia.org/

Dreger, A. D. (2007, November 17). Why "disorders of sex development"? (On language and life). Retrieved from http://www.alicedreger.com/dsd.html

Hillman, T. (2003, Spring). *Middlesex* and the limitations of myth. *ISNA News: Newsletter of the Intersex Society of North America*, 2–3. Retrieved from http://www.isna.org/files/hwa/spring2003.pdf

Holmes, M. M. (1995, March). *Queer cut bodies: Intersexuality & homophobia in medical practice*. Presented at the Queer Frontiers 1995 and Beyond Conference, University of Southern California. Retrieved from http://www.usc.edu/libraries/archives/queerfrontiers/queer/papers/holmes.long.html

Hypospadias and Epispadias Association. (2009). Understanding hypospadias & epispadias. Retrieved from http://www.heainfo.org/Brochure.html

Intersex Society of North America. (2008). A world free of shame, secrecy, and unwanted genital surgery. Retrieved from http://www.isna.org/

Knowledge, Support & Action. (2009). Welcome to KS&A. Retrieved from http://www.genetic.org/

Lee, P. A., Houk, C. P., Ahmed, S. F., & Hughes, I. A. (2006). Consensus statement on management of intersex disorders. *Pediatrics, 118*(2), e488–500. doi:10.1542/peds.2006–0738

MRKH Organization. (2004, July). Frequently asked questions. Retrieved from http://www.mrkh.org/files/home/Definitions.htm

Nolten, W. E. (n.d.). Nolten article. Retrieved from http://www.aaksis.org/WebPages.cfm?action=view Cat&BIZ_UNL_id=366

Turner Syndrome Society. (2009). Turner Syndrome-The basics. Retrieved from http://www.turnersyn drome.org/index.php?option=com_content&task=view&id=40&Itemid=63

Libraries and the
Transgender Community

Michael Waldman

Transgender people have been in the news a lot lately. The "pregnant man" did the rounds of the media and made it to Oprah and other major media outlets (Trebay, 2008). And even more recently, Chaz Bono went through a highly visible and public transition (Hall, 2009). *Transamerica* came out a few years ago and was considered a mainstream film (2005). While transgender people have been around for as long as there have been people, they have been at best ignored for most of that time and at worst, persecuted and killed (Feinberg, 1996). According to the National Center for Transgender Equality (2009) the percentage of transgender people in the general population is .025 to 1 percent, although it is hard to gather accurate statistics since most surveys do not track transgender people; however, these statistics indicate that there are probably transgender people in your community as well.[1]

Although there is not a lot of published research, it has been documented that transgender people attempt or commit suicide at higher rates than other populations. Dean et al. report that "both suicide attempts and completed suicides are common among transgendered persons" (2000, p. 129). The Washington Transgender Needs Assessment Survey (WTNAS) found that 35 percent of their sample of 252 participants "report experiencing suicidal ideation, and 64 percent of them attribute it to their gender issues. Of those with suicidal ideation, 47 percent report they have actually made attempts to kill themselves, 16 percent of the entire sample" (Xavier, 2000).

Finding out that there are others like yourself and that there are ways to deal with one's own gender dysphoria (feelings of disconnection between the gender you were assigned at birth and the one you feel you are) can be a way out of despair. But it can be hard to find information on transgender specific topics. One report on the experiences of transgender youth found for example that "less than half (46 percent) of transgender students reported that they could find information about LGBT people, history, or events in their school library and only a third (31 percent) were able to access this information using the school Internet" (Greytak, Kosciw, & Diaz, 2009, p. xiii).

Unfortunately, much violence is directed towards those who exhibit gender non-traditional behaviors (Erbentraut, 2009), and this ever-present threat of violence can make it difficult, if not impossible, to go searching for information. Every year we mark the Transgender Day of Remembrance when we remember the many who were killed because someone decided they did not like the way that person presented their gender.[2] It is hard to get an idea of the scope of the violence, as we do not have extensive statistics (see above) and because it might be difficult to differentiate violence against transgender people as opposed to violence against lesbian, gay or bisexual people. However based on data compiled by the Transgender Day of Remembrance, about one transgender person a month is killed in the United States (St. Pierre, 2009). In its latest report, the National Coalition of Anti-Violence Programs highlights an increase in murders, injuries, and bias violence from strangers and abusive treatment at the hands of law enforcement (2009, p. 8). Because transphobia is institutionalized to a great extent, many attackers are never brought to justice and when they are, they often are able to get lesser charges by claiming "transgender panic," a moment of temporary violent insanity brought on by the "transgender individual's deception about his or her biological sex" (Lee, 2008, p. 513).[3] Transgender youth suffer as well; they report being verbally and physically harassed (87 percent and 53 percent, respectively) and physically assaulted (26 percent) because of their gender expression (Greytak, Kosciw, & Diaz, 2009, p. xi).

Violence and discrimination certainly affect transgender people, but they also affect society as a whole, including cisgender people (i.e., nontransgender people, see definition below). When gender is policed to the extent that people are killed for transgressing gender rules, we all become a little more closed in, we lose a little freedom. Whether or not you understand transgender people, it is important for all of us to support the rights of everyone to access relevant information. In fact it is incumbent upon us as library professionals to do so per American Library Association's *Library Bill of Rights* and its statement on Freedom to Read. By providing hard to find information, libraries can have transformative effects on all of us.

Some Definitions

I think it is important to start with some central definitions so that we are all talking from a common understanding of basic terms. This is not presented as the ultimate list of terms or their definitions. In fact many of these are still somewhat in flux. However I believe these are the most common terms that information professionals may come across as they make their libraries trans-friendly.

It is also important to remember that although these are the most widespread terms, one can find variations of preferred terms among different groups by age, class, location and perhaps even finer distinctions. It is important to get to know your own particular community and the terms they prefer. That being said, even if a local transgender person does not identify with any of the terms below, I believe they will recognize them and be able to locate themselves in your library, and to see that the library is at least making an effort in reaching out to them.

I would like to first start with a brief differentiation of sex and gender. *Sex* tends to refer to biological facts, such as one's visible secondary sexual characteristics and chromosomes. It is important to note that there are not two sexes, people in fact have all sorts of sexual variations, some more visible than others. Some of these variations are referred to as *intersex*.[4] Intersex and transgender people have different gender experiences. Intersex individuals often have visible sexual differences, for example they may have ambiguous or non-traditional genitals. This is different from transgender or transsexual people who often are born with typical male or female anatomy but whose inner sense of gender is at odds with their physical gendered aspects. Because many intersex infants are assigned a gender by medical practitioners attending the birth, sometimes intersex people end up having a transgender experience, if the gender that was imposed on them is not the one they feel they are.[5]

Gender on the other hand refers to a social construct. One is not born a man or a woman, but becomes one through socialization. This becomes visible when looking at gender from a historical and cultural point of view — indeed what made a woman a woman has varied throughout history. For example, up until the recent past, women were not supposed to be firefighters but in fact that has nothing to do with female bodies — and we have women firefighters today. This was a cultural construct. Because for most people, their sex and gender match, it often seems as if they are one and the same, but in fact, the existence of gender non-conforming people shows that sex and gender are not always congruent. This is exacerbated, in Western cultures, by the construct that we live in a gender-binary system, where there are only two defined, clear-cut, fixed genders. Other cultures and times have believed differently, either accepting more than two genders, assigning genders according to a person's work, or letting people change genders "based on dreams and visions" (Stryker, 2008, p. 11). In our own time, Pakistan has just recently recognized a third "official" gender (Haider, 2009).

Transgender people feel that their gender identity does not match their assigned gender at birth (which is determined to a great extent by the baby's visible sexual characteristics). This term has gained acceptance in the 1990s, and acts as an

> umbrella term used to refer to all individuals who live outside of normative sex/gender relations — that is, individuals whose gendered self-presentation (evidenced through dress, mannerisms, and even physiology) does not correspond to the behaviors habitually associated with the members of their biological sex. A variety of different identities are included within the "transgender" label: cross-dressers, or individuals who wear the clothes associated with the "opposite" sex, often for erotic gratification; drag queens, or men who usually live and identify as gay men, but who perform as female impersonators in gay male bars and leisure spaces; and transsexuals, or individuals who take hormones and who may undergo surgery to align their biological sexes with their genders [Namaste, 2000, p. 1].

You may find that both *transgendered* and *transgender* are commonly used, and there is some debate as to which should be the correct term. The Gay and Lesbian Alliance Against Defamation (GLAAD) suggests in its Media Guide that *transgender* is the preferred term (2007, p. 6).

Trans is commonly used as a short hand to include, in their broadest sense, transgender, transsexual and genderqueer people (see below), and that is how I will be using it in this essay.

Transsexuals fall under the transgender umbrella but are in general understood to be individuals who feel the need to change their bodies via some form of medical intervention, be it hormones, surgery, or a combination of both.

Sometimes as a short hand, one can be referred to as *FTM*—female to male — someone assigned female at birth who identifies as male — also referred to as a *trans man;* or *MTF*— male to female — someone assigned male at birth who identifies as female — also referred to as *trans woman*. It is important to note here however that many transgender people do not feel like their transition is as simple as the acronyms seem to indicate, and many do not identify with such terms. These designations can be used regardless of transition status; i.e., some MTFs or FTMs are transsexuals, and some are not; some may decide to fully transition, some may decide never to.

Sexual orientation and *gender identity* are also two terms that are often confused. *Sexual orientation* relates to whom you are attracted. A man attracted to another man is a gay man, a woman attracted to another woman is a lesbian, while bisexuals are attracted to both. *Gender identity* on the other hand relates to a person's inner sense of gender. We do not know how gender identity develops and, for most people, their gender identity is congruent with whatever category they were assigned to at birth. However it is possible to form a sense of oneself that is unlike other members of the gender one has been assigned to, as shown by transgender people.

A slightly newer term, *genderqueer* usually refers to people who resist gender norms without "changing sex" necessarily, although some trans people, who feel they themselves belong in one particular gender still feel constricted by the narrow and unyielding nature of traditional Western binary concepts and so they may identify as genderqueer as well. This term is also often used by people who believe they are genderfluid, who feel like both genders, who will sometimes feel male, sometimes female, or who may not believe that there are only two genders. One of the problems faced by people who do not want to adhere to our currently strictly constructed binary gender system is that the English language only allows for two genders itself and people have to be gendered in *he* or *she* (*it* not being used for humans, unless in a very derogatory way). Leslie Feinberg has advocated the creation of new pronouns that would refer to a person (as opposed to *it*) but not denote a gender: *zelsie* for *he* or *she, and hir* for *his* or *her* (1998, p. 71). Additionally, many people opt to use *s/he* as a writing convention to circumvent these binary issues.

Cross-dressers usually refers to people who choose to wear the clothing generally associated with the opposite gender. Cross-dressing is a way that people express all of whom they are, both masculine and feminine. Use this term, rather than the word *transvestite*, which is outdated and offensive to many people.

Drag queen is a term historically used by men who dress in the clothing traditionally associated with women for the purposes of entertainment and/or personal fulfillment. There are also *drag kings*, women who dress in clothing traditionally associated with men. Unlike cross-dressing, drag is usually done for public performance and entertainment.

Gender variant or *gender non-conforming* refers to people who do not clearly follow society's rules for their gender. For example, a boy or man who wears makes-up may be considered gender non-conforming since in our society traditionally only women have worn make-up. There is not necessarily any correlation between gender non-conformity and being transgender or gay.

Gender expression refers to the physical, outward, manifestation of one's gender identity. This could be how one dresses, sits, relates to others, and/or which name one chooses for oneself. This usually only causes surprise and comment when one's gender expression matches one's gender identity and not one's assigned birth gender.

To transition refers to the process of moving from one gender to another, whatever that means for the individual who is *transitioning*. In strict terms it refers to the period of time when visible changes start to take place and one starts living in their chosen gender.

Sexual Reassignment Surgery, or SRS, refers to the surgical alteration that may happen as part of transition. Not all transgender people choose, want, or can afford to have surgery.

Cisgender/cissexual are fairly new terms that are starting to see wide use. "The idea behind the terms is to resist the way 'woman' or 'man' can mean 'nontransgendered woman' or 'nontransgendered man' by default, unless the person's transgender status is explicitly named" (Stryker, 2008, p. 22). This way the terms bring out the often implicit assumption that a person is nontransgender.

The following terms are considered offensive and should be avoided at all cost: *tranny, she-male, he-she, trannie, it*. These are used to dehumanize and sexualize transgender people.[6] The term *sex change operation* is also discouraged, as most trans people indeed feel that they are in fact realigning their bodies to the gender that they feel they have always been.

Now that we have a better idea of who we are talking about, I would like to talk about specific ways libraries can become welcoming places to the transgender community.

Libraries as Welcoming Places for Transgender People[7]

Relating to Transgender Users

While libraries try in general to be welcoming and safe places for their users, there are many things that librarians can do to make themselves and their institutions welcoming to transgender people. It is important to be proactive about implementing these, rather than reacting to specific incidents.

Foremost is having clearly written policies of non-discrimination and a zero-tolerance policy towards any harassment that may happen within the library. An unambiguous message from library administration that harassment will not be tolerated can go a long way to defuse any potential injurious encounters.

Although transgender people and topics have been more visible in the media of late, most people's knowledge of the topic is vague and imprecise, often reverting to stereotypes. Education of library staff, professional and paraprofessional, is therefore of paramount importance. It is preferable to have someone not affiliated with the library come and run workshops, even if you have an "out" trans person at work. That person should neither have the burden of educating all their co-workers nor be faced with the prospect of answering personal questions.

Meanwhile, I offer here some guidelines that may be helpful in dealing with users who have a non-traditional gender presentation. Two issues to keep in mind: you may be dealing with a transgender person and not know it and also, just like dealing with any member of the public, it is important to relate to the trans person with respect.

If you are unsure of someone's gender, the first thing to do is to ask yourself whether you really need to know that person's gender. While we usually take for granted the necessity of knowing a person's gender, in most cases, it is not a necessity. Will your answer to their question be different depending on the user's gender? I cannot think of a case when a circulation or reference question will be answered differently depending on the user's gender. If you are uncomfortable with someone's gender presentation, it is your problem, not theirs.

If you must know, the general rule is to refer to the person with the pronoun of the gender they are presenting in. If the presentation is unclear to you, it is best to ask, and then respect what the person says, even if you don't agree with it. Saying things like "but you look like a woman" or "what are you?" does not create a respectful and welcoming atmosphere. An alternative might be to use the gender-neutral pronouns presented above.

Asking about one's genitals, medical procedures or medical history is usually considered to be rude, and it is certainly rude to ask these questions to someone you perceive as gender non-conforming. How would *you* feel if someone asked you about your genitals?

Someone's gender status and history are private information that should not be shared. It is not information one should feel free to pass on, the individual's privacy and confidentiality should be respected at all times. In fact, there are situations in which you could actually create a potentially unsafe situation if an individual's gender status and history is not publicly known. By outing individuals, you could impact their job, relationships, housing and even their general physical safety. This is not to be taken lightly — transphobia and resulting violence are everyday realities — as "nearly 300 transgender people filed reports of violence against them" in 2008, and "on average, a transgender person is murdered once a month in the United States" (Transgender Legal Defense and Education Fund, 2009, para. 4).

Acting as an ally will go a very long way in making the library welcoming. If you know someone prefers a certain pronoun use it and correct those who don't. Speak up for the transgender patron who may be facing someone hostile.

The main point to remember here is that our users may and will define their gender identities in a variety of ways, from fluid to fixed identities, from feminine to masculine identities, some that will make sense to us, and some that we may not understand. The bottom line is that we are here to provide service to all our users and that is what we need to do.

Institutional Use of Language

While we have just seen how individuals within the library can make the place welcoming, the library as an institution does send clear messages in all its official literature. Pamphlets, websites, handouts, exhibits all contribute to create an image of the library. This can be used very powerfully to show that the library welcomes transgender users.

At the risk of stating the obvious, language conveys meaning even when the main idea is not explicitly stated. When one's literature speaks of "men" and "women" it is clear that it is favoring a binary view of gender. So while the following changes may seem minor, they actually do go a long way to indicate that the institution is making an effort to be trans-friendly. It might make the difference in whether a transgender person will approach a reference desk for example, and whether they will choose to return.

Some examples of gender inclusive language to be used on flyers, newsletters, event announcements, etc. might include "all genders welcome" or "for all genders" or "for people of any gender." In your forms or surveys, instead of using "Man" and "Woman" as the only categories, you might want to use "Man," "Woman" and "Transgender" for example, or leave it open so people can fill it with whatever they feel is more appropriate.

Consider an outreach plan. The world at large is not very welcoming to transgender people. Therefore, trans people often assume that they are not welcome or included — unless it is stated otherwise. If you want to include transgender people, state it explicitly. If you have an LGBT month for example, make sure that some of the books on display or events are inclusive of trans people. If there are local institutions that serve trans people, make sure you have some of their information on hand or include them in the community listings you may keep. Make connections with the local LGBT center and other local institutions serving trans people, for example.

Library Workers

It is important to remember as well that libraries may have transgender employees. Whether or not you are aware of this, some of your colleagues may be transgender and some may transition at your place of work. It is important to realize that while the Employment Non-Discrimination Act (ENDA) which would prohibit discrimination against employees on the basis of gender identity has not yet passed in the United States Congress as of fall 2009, many states have passed laws prohibiting discrimination on the basis of gender identity or expression.[8]

Library Cards

ID cards can be problematic for trans people who may not look like the picture or gender assigned in their ID. The ease of changing one's documents varies from state to state, and often depends on costly medical procedures that are rarely covered by insurance.[9] You could make your library more trans friendly by making the gender category optional on library card applications. Or, if that is not possible, train staff to deal with people who might pass as one gender but have either very gendered names or ID markers in a different gender.

Library Facilities

Restrooms often pose specific problems to transgender people. Indeed most library restrooms are sex-segregated and communal. A large number of transgender people have reported that they are routinely harassed and even assaulted when trying to use the restroom of their choice because they are perceived as not belonging to that restroom.[10] Are there any single-stall restrooms available in the library? Instead of labeling them "Men" or "Women," make them available to anyone. Can any other restroom be converted to an "all-gender restroom"? If you cannot find an available restroom, can a staff restroom be used if someone feels uncomfortable? If you are renovating or building a new library building, taking these issues into account will go a long way to make the library a safe place and a place in which transgender people feel comfortable.

Unfortunately, if there are no private restrooms available, you should be ready to be challenged by other users who may feel uncomfortable sharing a restroom with a transgender person. If someone feels uncomfortable using a particular restroom because of another individual's presence in the restroom, he or she may be encouraged to wait until that individual has left or to use another restroom in the facility. If someone has concerns about using public restrooms because of their gender identify or expression, the library should know how to deal with that, perhaps by making a private or staff restroom available.

Transgender Children and Youth and Parents of Transgender Children

Transgender children and youth and parents of transgender children face special challenges which we will examine in this section.[11] Although many trans people often describe knowing they were in the "wrong body" from a very young age, traditionally no one paid attention to those claims. We are seeing nowadays, however, that children are starting to be heard when they claim to be in the wrong body. This is, of course, controversial with others arguing that it might be a phase the child is going through, or that we cannot take seriously what a child is saying. Some parents have tried to be respectful of what the child says and let them explore whatever identity the child feels s/he is. This may cause problems however if the child is in school where gendered behavior tends to be fairly strictly enforced by peers if not also by teachers, as the child may want to dress in the gender they feel they are, not the one assigned at birth.

Youth face many of the same problems as children do: they may not be taken seriously, and peer pressure may be even stronger. According to a study by the Gay, Lesbian, Straight Education Network (GLSEN) entitled *Harsh Realities*, "90 percent of transgender students heard negative remarks about someone's gender expression sometimes, often, or frequently in school" and "a third of transgender students heard school staff make homophobic (32 percent) remarks, sexist (39 percent) remarks, and negative comments about someone's gender expression (39 percent) sometimes, often, or frequently in the past year" (Greytak, Kosciw, & Diaz, 2009, p. x). "Two-thirds of transgender students felt unsafe in school because of their sexual orientation (69 percent) and how they expressed their gender (65 percent)" (Greytak, Kosciw, & Diaz, 2009, p. xi).

In addition, young people face puberty. Most of the hormonal and surgical procedures that adult trans people go through happen because they have gone through the puberty of the gender they were assigned at birth, acquiring the sexual characteristics of the adults of their gender. Much anguish is also expressed by those who go through puberty and become visibly the gender they do not feel they are, some young people expressing the feeling that their body had betrayed them. It has been posited that much anguish could be saved by not going through the "wrong" puberty. While that may not be entirely possible, it is possible now to postpone puberty medically giving the young person time to sort out their feelings and decide whether or not transitioning is the right step for them. As mentioned earlier, transgender teens are at great risk of thinking about suicide and actually attempting to kill themselves.[12]

Parents are in a hard place as well. They may be distressed to find their child is gender non-conforming and at a loss about how to react and what to do about it. It is important to remember also that children and young people are not immune either to the culture at large and may withhold any information about their feelings about gender until they just cannot hide them anymore, surprising their parents. Parents may feel a range of emotions when told and unfortunately, there are few resources for them, and this is not an issue that comes up at PTA meetings.[13] Often parents may be blamed for not enforcing gender expression in their children. At the same time, some parents may not be able to deal with their children's gender non-conforming behavior and will reject them by throwing them out of the house.

Young people with no skills and no resources, these children often end up in the streets, homeless. Indeed some reports state that "Transgender youth are disproportionately represented in the homeless population" (Ray, 2006, p. 4). The situation is dire for those youth: many shelters are strictly segregated by sex and "homeless transgender youth are even ostracized by some agencies that serve their LGB peers" (p. 4). This makes transgender youth extremely vulnerable to exploitation and victimization.

In all of these situations, libraries can provide resources that would be helpful. Having a collection of books for children that show gender non-conforming children would be useful to children and to their parents.[14] Books that portray transgender families as "normal families" can also be helpful in easing the parents' anxieties.[15] For homeless transgender youth, the library can be a place where they can find information on local resources available to them, as youth, as homeless, and as transgender. It may also be a safe place where they can hang out and not be harassed, a safe haven.

Collections

One of the most important ways a library can serve its transgender population is by building and maintaining a collection of transgender materials.

For Research and Academic Purposes

While we are seeing the beginning of an accepted and more or less formalized area of studies called "Transgender Studies," most literature published in this area will not come in this "easy to recognize" category. What's more, most of this literature is interdisciplinary making it more difficult to collect comprehensively. Sometimes, the job of collecting in this area will fall to the selector of "gay and lesbian" materials, but it is important to note that not all trans material will be labeled that way. Publishers have often labeled this material as *gender studies, gay and lesbian studies* or *women's studies* for example, but one can also find books dealing with transgender topics in history, political science, anthropology, sociology, or literary theory, to name but a few.

The easiest way to make sure such material is collected is to have a designated selector for that area. While often it is assumed that the selector for gay and lesbian studies will collect in this area, it is best to formalize such understanding. In addition, because it is an interdisciplinary area, making sure that all selectors know that the library collects in this area and that they should either order the material themselves or pass it on to the main selector is very important. It is important also to highlight such material in the library's official literature, be it via handouts, on a subject guide web page, on a "suggested reading" bookmark, etc. This makes this material visible, but more importantly it shows the library is active in collecting in this area, and will create a welcoming atmosphere.[16]

It is important to keep tabs on this material as it may disappear. These books might go missing or be destroyed because some people disagree with the ideas presented or because someone might be too nervous to check them out. They may also just be misshelved for the same reasons. Especially in public libraries, if funds allow, it might be useful to have more than one copy of certain books and to have a clear collection development policy in case some of these books are challenged.

In general, it is not recommended to isolate this material in a separate area or provide access only through a librarian — the users most likely to need these resources might be too uncomfortable asking for the material and it will go unused.

For the Transgender User

While it is likely that transgender users will come to the library to find the same kinds of general information any other patron might want to find, there is specific information that might be of interest to transgender patrons.[17] For example, they may be interested in biographies and positive portrayals of other transgender people. Indeed in the general press, most portrayals of transgender people are exploitative and negative. Having resources that show the real lives of transgender people can be very informative to anyone interested in the topic, for themselves or others.[18]

Because of the complications in negotiating the legal issues associated with transitioning, many trans people are looking for information on changing names and genders in their documents. In addition, transgender people often face issues of housing and employment discrimination. The library can provide information on what the laws are, what to do in case of discrimination, and what the steps for a legal name change are, for example. Many national organizations offer resources and publications that are of interest to varying segments of the trans population. For example, the Sylvia Rivera Law Project has pamphlets in English and Spanish on how to get one's name legally changed.[19] There might also be local resources that provide such services. These should all be included in a trans subject guide and any handout that is created. The Gender Identity Project in New York City's Lesbian, Gay, Bisexual and Transgender Community Center offers a good example of making a variety of useful local information available to its users, with categories such as housing, legal, medical, and mental health.[20]

Another area where a library can be very helpful to trans people is when dealing with health information. Most trans people have many questions about available procedures, potential medical risks, and/or available options relating to their transition. In addition, having lists of local trans-friendly doctors for example would be helpful (or information on places where such information is available).

Making connections with local organizations that serve the transgender population would be very helpful. Have their literature in your library or library websites, among other community organizations and within any trans literature you might also make available. And make sure to let the organizations know that you are interested in serving transgender patrons and will welcome them. Ask them for input on collection development and service issues. Look into collaborating with them on projects/programming.

Even if the library does not have access to specialized medical or legal information, librarians can often point trans users to where they can find such information or they can facilitate getting that information via interlibrary loan or other inter-library agreements.

It is also recommended that access to such information be available on a publicly available web page or subject guide, maybe via suggested search terms, and/or canned cataloged searches, etc. so trans people can see that the library is friendly and welcoming but also does outreach to those users who might be at first uncomfortable talking directly to a librarian.

A Short List of Resources

I present here some resources that might be useful for starting a collection and subject page. Many of the organizations below also publish literature and studies that should find their place in one's collections. This is not meant to be a comprehensive list. Also, resources mentioned elsewhere have not been repeated here.

The Gay, Lesbian, Bisexual and Transgendered Round Table of the American Library Association (Silverrod, 2008) has a good starter list that might be useful in performing an initial assessment of your collection and building a basic library. Not all of the titles might fit your library's mission, but they will give you a good starting point. Steinberg (2005) and Taylor (2006) present additional insights in making the library trans friendly and offer collection suggestions.

Trans-academics.org <http://www.trans-academics.org/> is a site which contains not only an extensive listing of articles and books on transgender topics but is also a clearinghouse of information on grants, conferences and call for papers. As its name implies, it is geared primarily to the academic community.

The *International Journal of Transgenderism* (*IJT*), published by Routledge, is a peer-reviewed journal devoted to the study of all areas related to transgender studies, from medical to social research.

The World Professional Association for Transgender Health (WPATH), formerly known as the (Harry Benjamin International Gender Dysphoria Association (HBIGDA), is a professional organization devoted to the understanding and treatment of gender identity disorders. In addition to publishing *IJT*, it establishes the *Standards of Care for Gender Identity Disorders* (2001) which offer guidelines for practitioners in their care of transgender patients.

NYC's Lesbian, Gay, Bisexual and Transgender Community Center offers a Transgender Basics page that has much useful information, including the video *Transgender Basics* which presents transgender people talking about their own experiences (Nordentoft, 2009).

Another good general resource both for transgender people and for people who want to understand them is Matt Kaily's *Transgender and Transsexual Issues 101* blog where he examines a series of frequently asked questions. A listing of topics can be found at http://www.examiner.com/x-12237-Transgender — Transsexual-Issues-Examiner-topic 281395-Info-101-Project?selstate=topcat#breadcrumb

The National Center for Transgender Equality (NCTE) <http://transequality.org/>, the Transgender Law and Policy Institute <http://www.transgenderlaw.org/>, the Transgender Law Center <http://www.transgenderlawcenter.org/> and the Sylvia Rivera Law Project <http://srlp.org/> are good legal resources, providing information concerning name changes, fighting discrimination, transitioning in the workplace, etc.

FTMInternational (FTMI) <http://www.ftmi.org/> has a great deal of information primarily targeted to female to male transgender people as well as for parents of FTM sons. They also publish the *FTMI Newsletter*. IFGE, the International Foundation for Gender Education, <http://ifge.org/> presents information mostly on male to female population and also publishes *Transgender Tapestry*, one of the longest running transgender magazines.

Many transgender people have set up blogs to document their transition.[21] While personal in nature, they can give other transgender people hope and a connection. I offer here two that are more issues-focused. The Trans Group Blog <http://transgroupblog.blogspot.com/> is a place where a variety of well-known trans people and activists post their commentaries. The Transgender Workplace Diversity blog <http://transworkplace.blogspot.com/> looks at law and policy issues that affect transgender workers.

Again, many of the organizations will have publications on the basics of transgender issues, on how to transition, on issues one can expect to face, on coming out, etc. Take your time to explore them and see which resources would best suit your community.

Access to Transgender Materials

Catalog Access

Although its use is in decline, the library catalog is still often the main gateway to materials in the library. In particular, one of the strengths of the catalog is its subject classification which groups like materials together. However there are several challenges in accessing transgender material in this way since transgender subject headings leave much to be desired — although there has been some progress of late. Due to space considerations, I will not discuss the entire history surrounding "transgender" as a subject heading here.[22] Suffice it to say that the Library of Congress Subject Headings first authorized the use of *transgender* in 2007. At the same time, more and more libraries have been outsourcing their cataloging and reducing the number of cataloging staff. Thus, those cataloging the books do not know the community for which they are cataloging and what that community's specific needs and interests might be, leaving us with records that may be very generic in their subject treatment. A book on the police for example with a subject heading of "Criminal Justice, Administration of" in a criminal justice college would be correct but too vague when that whole collection is about criminal justice. In the same way, cataloging material under the often understood broader LBGTIQ umbrella will do a disservice to those looking specifically for transgender information.

On top of that, catalogers may not be aware of LGBTIQ terminology and many are probably not a part of that community and are assigning subject headings to topics they are not familiar with or understand. Because of this, materials are miscataloged or ambiguously identified. Material cataloged in this way often ends up obscuring the actual content of the book. Public service librarians who have knowledge of this area should be willing to speak up and offer guidance if something is cataloged inaccurately.

I wanted to offer one example of a "subject heading gone bad" to show how damaging this could be. One could assume that the book, *Transgender Equality: A Handbook for Activists and Policymakers* by Paisley Currah, Shannon Minter and Jamison Green (2000) has transgender content. If that wasn't enough, the authors are all noted writers on transgender topics. But it was cataloged in OCLC with the headings[23]:

> Homosexuality — Law and legislation — United States.
> Gay liberation movement — United States.
> Gay rights — United States.

If someone did a subject search for "Transgender people," they would not find this book. It is helpful that nowadays it would be found in a keyword search but not all books on transgender topics have the word transgender in their title. This is one way that such material can become invisible to the user, even if the library does have it. For this record, in April 2009, someone cataloged the electronic version of this document and created a new record with more appropriate subject headings. OCLC #45664323 now has the following subject headings:

> Transgender people — Civil rights — United States.
> Transgender people — Legal status, laws, etc.— United States.
> Transgender people — Government policy — United States.

Unfortunately if you already have the book in your collection chances are that it will not get re-cataloged, keeping it inaccessible.

Another problem with a controlled vocabulary system is that it implies a stability that simply does not exist in real life, especially in new communities, and communities that are in flux, and that embrace fluidity. What are the terms used by the community themselves? How long does it take for them to make it into established subject headings? Does your catalog allow tagging by patrons? They, and knowledgeable librarians, could add terms they relate to, so that others in their community can also find the information.

Conclusion

Transgender people challenge us to be aware of our own preconceptions about gender and how these affect everything from how we communicate to which restrooms we use.

Welcoming transgender people into our libraries builds on what libraries and librarians already do well, making people feel comfortable enough in our spaces to hang out, ask questions, and find information.

I hope this essay has given you some ideas on how to build gender awareness into our daily lives as librarians so that we may serve our users better.

Notes

1. There are several reasons that it is hard to gather accurate statistics about transgender people. Most surveys do not include transgender as one of their choices. Also, as frequent victims of harassment, discrimination and assault, transgender people may be reluctant to participate in surveys and/or not identify themselves as such. Additionally, it can be hard to find a random sample of transgender people large enough to draw statistical conclusions. See for example Jillian Weiss' interesting comments (2007) and Matt Kailey's insights (2009).

2. For more information, see the Transgender Day of Remembrance website: http://www.transgenderdor.org/

3. For a hopeful sign that perhaps change is coming, see Spellman (2009).

4. For more on this topic, see "Intersex Resources in Libraries," also in this section.

5. For an example of the trauma caused by this forced gender assignment, see Colapinto (2006).

6. See for example, Hill-Meyer (2008), for a good discussion of why these terms are offensive.

7. For an example of what one library has done, please see "When Collection Development Leads to Staff Development: The Transgender Resource Collection" in Section Seven.

8. See for example the Transgender Law and Policy Institute (2008).

9. To understand how this impacts people in a very real way, see for example, Melloy (2009). The National Center for Transgender Equality (NCTE) maintains a map with each state's requirements at http://transequality.org/Resources/DL/DL_policies.html. For a broader discussion on how access to documentation is problematic for transgender people see National Center for Transgender Equality (2009b).

10. For more on this topic, see, for example, the film "Toilet Training" and the accompanying toolkit available from the Sylvia Rivera Law Project. See also Let us Pee at http://letuspee.blogspot.com/

11. See for example Barbara Walters' *20/20* program on "Transgender children" (2007); Adriano (2007); and Rosin (2008).

12. See Bornstein (2006) and the accompanying blog, http://web.mac.com/katebornstein/iWeb/Hello_Cruel_World/Cruel%20Blog/Cruel%20Blog.html

13. For a couple helpful guides for parents, see Parents, Families and Friends of Lesbians and Gays Transgender Network (2007) and Children's National Medical Center, Outreach Program for Children with Gender-Variant Behaviors and Their Families (2009). Another useful resource is TransActive Education & Advocacy (2009).

14. For example, the ALA/GLBTRT/SRRT Rainbow Project updates and keeps a list of books for children and teens at http://rainbowlist.wordpress.com/; a list of books for trans teens can be found at http://www.hclib.org/pub/bookspace/myBooklists/ShowList.cfm?ListID=2252; Advocates for Youth publishes a brochure, *I think I might be transgender, now what do I do?*, in a fun, colorful way that might appeal to teens trying to figure things out; it also contains quotes and stories from other teens they may relate to.

15. See for example, Kaesar (1999) and Boenke (1999).

16. See for example, the "$200 Transgender Bookshelf" at http://www.oppl.org/media/trc_toolkit_shelf200.pdf

17. See for example Wilkinson & Gomez (2004).

18. See for example, Finn (2006), Green (2004), and Boylan (2003).

19. Sylvia Rivera Law Project.(n.d). How to legally change your name in New York City. Retrieved from http://srlp.org/resources/namechange; Sylvia Rivera Law Project. (n.d.). Cómo cambiar legalmente su nombre: Una guía para la gente Trans en la ciudad de Nueva York. Retrieved from http://srlp.org/node/280

20. Available at: http://www.gaycenter.org/gip
21. See for example Michael's blog "Be me for a day" at http://ftmichael.livejournal.com/
22. For a historical overview, please see "The Treatment of LGBTIQ Concepts in the Library of Congress Subject Headings" in Section Five of this book.
23. OCLC #45288973

REFERENCES

Adriano, J. (2007, April 27). Transgender children face unique challenges. *ABC News— 20/20*. Blog. Retrieved from http://abcnews.go.com/2020/story?id=3091754&page=1

Advocates for Youth. (n.d.). I think I might be transgender, now what do I do? A brochure by and for transgender youth. Retrieved from http://www.advocatesforyouth.org/storage/advfy/documents/transgender.pdf

Boenke, M. (Ed.). (1999). *Trans forming families: Real stories about transgendered loved ones*. Imperial Beach, CA: Walter Trook Pub.

Bornstein, K. (2006). *Hello, cruel world: 101 alternatives to suicide for teens, freaks, and other outlaws*. New York: Seven Stories Press.

Bornstein, K. (2008). Cruel blog. Retrieved from http://web.mac.com/katebornstein/iWeb/Hello_Cruel_World/Cruel%20Blog/Cruel%20Blog.html

Boylan, J. F. (2003). *She's not there: A life in two genders*. New York: Broadway Books.

Children's National Medical Center, Outreach Program for Children with Gender-Variant Behaviors and Their Families. (2009). If you are concerned about your child's gender behaviors: A guide for parents. Retrieved from https://www.childrensnational.org/files/PDF/DepartmentsAndPrograms/Neuroscience/Psychiatry/GenderVariantOutreachProgram/GVParentBrochure.pdf

Colapinto, J. (2006). *As nature made him: The boy who was raised as a girl*. New York: HarperCollins Publishers.

Currah , P, Minter, S, & Green, J. (2000). *Transgender equality: A handbook for activists and policymakers*. Washington, D.C.: National Gay and Lesbian Task Force.

Dean, L., Meyer, I. H., Robinson, K., Sell, R. L., Sember, R., Silenzio, V. M. B., et al. (2000). Lesbian, gay, bisexual, and transgender health: Findings and concerns. *Journal of the Gay and Lesbian Medical Association, 4*(3), 102–151.

Erbentraut, J. (2009, Sept. 29). Violence against the transgendered only getting worse. *The Edge, Boston*. Retrieved from http://www.edgeboston.com/index.php?ch=news&sc=&sc2=news&sc3=&id=96920

Feinberg, L. (1996). *Transgender warriors: Making history from Joan of Arc to RuPaul*. Boston: Beacon Press.

Feinberg, L. (1998). Trans liberation: Beyond pink or blue. Boston: Beacon Press.

Finn, R. (2006, November 10). Battling for one's true sexual identity. *The New York Times*. Retrieved from http://www.nytimes.com/2006/11/10/nyregion/10lives.html?_r=1&adxnnl=1&oref=slogin&adxnnlx=1163174945-tEPB38d+BVfPbKkK5fYhAw

Gay and Lesbian Alliance Against Defamation (2007). *GLAAD media reference guide*. (7th ed). Retrieved from http://www.glaad.org/Document.Doc?id=25

Green, J. (2004). *Becoming a visible man*. Nashville, TN: Vanderbilt University Press.

Greytak, E.A., Kosciw, J.G., & Diaz, E.M. (2009). *Harsh realities: The experiences of transgender youth in our nation's schools*. New York: Gay, Lesbian and Straight Education.

Haider, Z. (2009, December 23). Pakistan's transvestites to get distinct gender. *Reuters India*. Retrieved from http://in.reuters.com/article/lifestyleMolt/idINTRE5BM2BX20091223?pageNumber=2&virtualBrandChannel=0&sp=true

Hall, K. (2009, October 28). Chaz Bono: My outsides are finally matching my insides, I shave (Video). *The Huffington Post*. Blog. Retrieved from http://www.huffingtonpost.com/2009/10/28/chaz-bono-my-outsides-are_n_337647.html

Harry Benjamin International Gender Dysphoria Association (2001). *Standards of care for gender identity disorders*, (6th version). Retrieved from http://www.wpath.org/documents2/socv6.pdf

Hill-Meyer, T. (2008, September 9). Is "tranny" offensive? *The Bilerico Project*. Blog. Retrieved from http://www.bilerico.com/2008/09/is_tranny_offensive.php

Johnson, M. (2007, Spring). *Gay, lesbian, bisexual, and transgender subject access: history and current practice*. Retrieved from: http://www.lib.washington.edu/msd/norestriction/b58062361.pdf

Kaeser, G. (1999). *Love makes a family: Portraits of lesbian, gay, bisexual, and transgender parents and their families*. Amherst, Mass: University of Massachusetts Press.

Kailey, M. (2009, August 27). Are there more trans women than trans men? Part one. *Transgender & Transsexual Issues 101.* Blog. Retrieved from http://www.examiner.com/x-12237-Transgender — Transsexual-Issues-Examiner-y2009m8d27-Transgender — Transsexual-Issues-101-Are-there-more-trans-women-than-trans-men-Part-one

Lee, C. (2008). The gay panic defense. *UC Davis Law Review, 42*(2), 471–566.

Lesbian, Gay, Bisexual & Transgender Community Center, Gender Identity Project. (n.d.) *Trans basics.* Retrieved from http://www.gaycenter.org/gip/transbasics

Let us pee. (2009). Retrieved from http://letuspee.blogspot.com/

Mateik, T. (2003). *Toilet training.* DVD, New York, NY: The Sylvia Rivera Law Project.

Melloy, K. (2009, August 17). Trans battlefield: Drivers' licenses. *The Edge, Boston.* Retrieved from http://www.edgeboston.com/index.php?ch=news&sc=&sc2=&sc3=&id=95133

Namaste, V. K. (2000). *Invisible lives: The erasure of transsexual and transgendered people.* Chicago ; London: University of Chicago Press.

National Center for Transgender Equality. (2007). Driver's license policies by state. Retrieved from http://transequality.org/Resources/DL/DL_policies.html

National Center for Transgender Equality. (2009a). *Teaching transgender.* Washington, D.C.: Retrieved from http://transequality.org/Resources/NCTE_Teaching_Transgender.pdf

National Center for Transgender Equality. (2009b, February). *Transgender equality and the federal government.* Retrieved from http://transequality.org/Resources/NCTE_Federal_Government_web.pdf

National Coalition of Anti-Violence Programs. (2009). *Hate violence against lesbian, gay, bisexual and transgender people in the Unites States.* Retrieved from http://www.transgenderlegal.org/media/uploads/doc_163.pdf

Nordentoft, R. J. (2009). *Transgender basics.* Available at http://www.gaycenter.org/gip/transbasics/video

Parents, Families and Friends of Lesbians and Gays Transgender Network. (2007). Our trans children. Retrieved from http://www.pflag.org/fileadmin/user_upload/Publications/OTC_5thedition.pdf

Ray, N. (2006). *Lesbian, gay, bisexual and transgender youth: An epidemic of homelessness.* New York: National Gay and Lesbian Task Force Policy Institute and the National Coalition for the Homeless. Retrieved from http://www.thetaskforce.org/downloads/HomelessYouth.pdf

Rosin, H. (2008, November). A boy's life. *The Atlantic.* Retrieved from http://www.theatlantic.com/doc/200811/transgender-children

St. Pierre, E. (2009). Statistics and other info. *Transgender Day of Remembrance.* Retrieved from http://www.transgenderdor.org/?page_id=192

Silverrod, N. (2008). *TRANScending identities: A bibliography of resources on transgender and intersex topics.* Gay, Lesbian, Bisexual and Transgendered Round Table of the American Library Association. Retrieved from http://its.usc.edu/-trimmer/glbtrt/TRANScendingIdentitiesMarch2008.pdf

Spellman, J. (2009, April 23). Transgender murder, hate crime conviction a first, CNN.com, Retrieved from http://www.cnn.com/2009/CRIME/04/22/transgender.slaying.trial/index.html

Steinberg, R. (2005). *Addressing the "T" in GLBT: Issues in transgender collections management.* Retrieved from http:// www.slais.ubc.ca/PEOPLE/students/student-projects/R_Steinberg/520issuespaper.pdf

Stryker, S. (2008). *Transgender history.* Berkeley, CA: Seal Press.

Sylvia Rivera Law Project. (2003). Toilet training toolkit. Retrieved from http://srlp.org/films/toolkit

T., C. (2009). Books for trans teens. *Hennepin County Library bookspace.* Retrieved from http://www.hclib.org/pub/bookspace/myBooklists/ShowList.cfm?ListID=2252

Taylor, J. K. (2006, January-February.). The library collection and transgender individuals. *Versed.* Retrieved from http://www.ala.org/ala/aboutala/offices/diversity/versed/versedbackissues/january2006abc/transgendercollection.cfm

TransActive Education & Advocacy. (2009). TransActive — Serving Trans Youth and Their Families. Retrieved from http://transactiveonline.org/

Transgender children. (2007, April 28). *ABC News — 20/20.* Retrieved from http://abcnews.go.com/Video/playerIndex?id=3084254

Transgender Law and Policy Institute. (2008, December 15). Non-discrimination laws that include gender identity and expression. Retrieved from http://www.transgenderlaw.org/ndlaws/index.htm

Transgender Legal Defense and Education Fund. (2009.) The Lateisha Green murder: Violence against transgender people resource kit. Retrieved from http://www.transgenderlegal.org/headline_show.php?id=122

Trebay, G. (2008, June 22). He's pregnant. You're speechless. *The New York Times.* Retrieved from http://www.nytimes.com/2008/06/22/fashion/22pregnant.html

Tucker, D. (2006). *Transamerica* [Film]. New York: The Weinstein Company.

Weiss, J. T. (2007, July 9). National statistics on transgender unemployment. *Transgender Workplace Diversity*. Blog. Retrieved from http://transworkplace.blogspot.com/2007/07/national-statistics-on-transgender.html

Wilkinson, W., & Gomez, P. (2004, May). Assessing the needs of female-to-male transgendered people of color and their partners. Retrieved from http://www.hawaii.edu/hivandaids/Assessing_the_Needs_of_FTM_TG_People_of_Color_and_their_Partners.pdf

Xavier, J.M. (2000). *The Washington transgender needs assessment survey*. Retrieved from http://www.glaa.org/archive/2000/tgneedsassessment1112.shtml

The Internet and
LGBTIQ Communities

Ellen Greenblatt

"Sometimes I think the Internet is simultaneously the best and worst thing that has happened to the GLBT movement."

— Wayne Besen

When *Gay and Lesbian Library Service* was published in 1990, few of us used — or even knew about — the Internet. In the intervening two decades, it has become ubiquitous, transforming our daily lives. Internet connectivity facilitates quicker and more expansive communication, improves the capacity for gathering and disseminating information, and frees community building from the constraints of geography.

In the mid–1990s, an Associated Press article noted that "It's the unspoken secret of the online world that gay men and lesbians are among the most avid, loyal, and plentiful commercial users of the Internet," going on to cite that a third of all chat rooms on America Online (AOL), the largest online content provider at the time, were gay-related (Weise, 1996, p. 6B; Haeberli, 1996). By 1996, the Gay and Lesbian Forum, which traces its roots back to 1989, was the "most popular space on AOL," garnering almost 1.8 million hits a month (Weise, 1996, p. 6B).

Studies confirm that LGBTIQ people use the Internet more than their straight counterparts. For example, a recent survey by Harris Interactive and Witeck-Combs Communications shows that more than half (55 percent) of lesbian and gay respondents reported reading blogs as compared to only 38 percent of straight people (2009, p. 1).[1] The same survey also examined social networking use, with gays and lesbians again coming in with consistently higher percentages.[2] An earlier survey conducted by Harris Interactive showed that 32 percent of lesbians and gays used the Internet between 24 and 168 [*sic*] hours a week, as compared to 18 percent of straight people (2007, para. 4). The report goes on to say:

> We have consistently benchmarked strong online usage by the gay community. Gays and lesbians have shown their need to build and maintain an early and major presence on the web.... Social networks also appear to be second nature for the gay and lesbian consumer [para. 5].

These studies indicate that LGBTIQ individuals' Internet use is above average and a significant part of their everyday life.

While entire books could be (and have been) written about the Internet and its impact on and importance to LGBTIQ users, this essay will focus on topics that are particularly relevant in the context of libraries: coming out, identity formation, support, and activism. It will also address some negative aspects related to Internet use, such as cyberbullying and filtering. Throughout, it will offer examples and suggestions of how libraries can use the Internet to better serve their LGBTIQ users.

Coming Out, Forming Identities,[3] and Forging Support

Because of the stigma often attached to LGBTIQ identities,[4] individuals exploring their sexual orientation, gender identity, and/or intersex conditions have turned to the Internet for the relative anonymity, privacy, and safety it affords. Whether socially or geographically isolated, these marginalized individuals have found the Internet to be a lifeline to which they turn in their quest for identity and support. While earlier generations of sexual and gender minorities visited library shelves in search of relevant information, the Internet is today the primary destination for such searches (Adams & Peirce, 2006; Beiriger & Jackson, 2007; Bond, Hefner, & Drogos, 2008; Hamer, 2003).

Although the situation has improved somewhat in recent years, many LGBTIQ young people are still unable to find support from families and peers. Many face hostility (or worse) at school on a regular basis. According to the most recent Gay, Lesbian and Straight Education Network (GLSEN) National School Climate Survey, 60 percent of students responding felt unsafe due to their sexual orientation (Kosciw, Diaz, & Greytak, 2008) while 65 percent felt unsafe due to their gender expression (Greytak, Kosciw, & Diaz, 2009). And roughly nine out of ten respondents had been harassed due to being LGBTIQ (Kosciw, Diaz, & Greytak, 2008).

Because of these "harsh realities," many young people turn to the Internet to find the support and validation that are missing in their daily lives. For them, the Internet is a safe haven in which to explore their burgeoning identities, a sanctuary where they can freely express themselves, and a refuge where they can interact with others like themselves. And while these virtual worlds allow them to explore and "try on" their emerging identities, they are not always immune to the intrusions of harassment and cyberbullying.[5]

An important consideration that we must keep in mind regarding young people's reliance on the Internet is that while today's teens may be technologically savvy, their critical thinking and evaluation skills often lag far behind. There is a wide variety of information about sexuality and gender expression/identity available on the Internet, ranging from the well-informed to the outrageously misinformed. And although it may be considered controversial for libraries and schools to point teens to appropriate sexuality and gender sites (and perhaps not even possible in certain circumstances, given filtering issues), libraries and schools can still help teach teens how to make informed decisions in regard to determining whether the sites they consult offer reliable advice and factual information.

The Internet has been instrumental in forging support and advocacy groups, not only for young people, but for people of all ages. This is especially evident in the evolution of newer movements, such as the transgender and intersex movements, which have benefited from their work in these areas arising simultaneously with the development of the Internet. Prior to the 1990s, transgender and intersex individuals often faced isolated, closeted existences, with only the medical establishment to rely upon for information. The Internet has provided a venue in which such individuals can turn to those who have shared similar experiences, thereby reaching "beyond the clinic" (Preves, 2003, p. 95).

"D," one of the participants in a study on information seeking in the transgender community conducted by Adams and Peirce (2006), speaks to the primacy of the Internet in her community:

> I feel confident saying that the development of the Internet is the single-most important tool fueling the development of the transgender community, and in fostering empowerment within it. When we realize that we're *not* alone, that there *is* hope for a fulfilling life, that others have already walked this path and have shared their experiences — that's an incredibly powerful thing [p. 5].

The literature is full of accounts of people who turn to the Internet to seek the support of lesbian, gay, bisexual, transgender, intersex, and/or queer communities (Correll, 1995; Haag & Chang, 1998; Hegland & Nelson, 2002). Through Internet support groups, LGBTIQ individuals overcome their sense of isolation, meet others with similar issues and concerns, and begin to build virtual communities. Other groups, besides those who are LGBTIQ themselves, also seek support on the Internet. For example, parents of LGBTIQ children or young adults often turn to online support groups to help them cope with situations such as the recent coming out of one of their children, a child's variant gender expression, or the birth of an intersex child.

Activisim

The community building that arises from these support groups often leads to the formation of advocacy groups. As Sharon Preves observes in relation to the intersex community: "The use of the Internet as a primary means of contact, education, and support has afforded the development of a geographically diverse advocacy movement" (2005, p. 257). By connecting with others who share the same identity and concerns, LGBTIQ people become empowered, moving beyond their former isolated, stigmatized status and working towards gaining visibility, broader social acceptance, and civil rights.

LGBTIQ people have a long history of involvement in activism, and the Internet is no exception. For example, in 1993, America Online prohibited discussions of transgender issues. After what one activist termed "electronic civil disobedience," AOL changed its terms of service and eventually hosted a transgender forum (Shapiro, 2003, p. 174). Nancy Nangeroni (1997) credits the mobilization of the Brandon Teena demonstration in 1995, what she terms the "first broad-based demonstration on behalf of a transgender victim of violence," as starting with an email she and Riki Anne Wilchins sent to the community (para. 6). In 1997, when America Online outed sailor Timothy McVeigh to Navy investigators, McVeigh leveraged the power of the Internet to fight against his discharge, becoming what *The Advocate* dubbed "the most famous beneficiary of gay connections in cyberspace to date" (Friess, 1999, p. 35).

Web 2.0 has increased the speed, capacity, and effectiveness of Internet activism exponentially. The immediacy and interactivity of such social networking sites as Facebook, Twitter, blogs, and the like have "given multiple people/groups ... the ability to form ... literally overnight and to motivate and lead [them] toward a common goal" (Garcia, 2009, p. 38). For example, the website Join the Impact, which was formed on November 7, 2008, just days after the California electorate's passage of Proposition 8 (which banned same-sex marriage), was instrumental in helping organize protests in 300 cities worldwide on November 15 (Join the Impact, 2008). In the space of little over a week, Join the Impact's "viral activism" bounced around the Internet driven by other social networking sites, receiving wide coverage from sources as diverse as CNN and LGBTIQ blogger Perez Hilton, and itself receiving more than a million visitors to its site in just four days (Basgil, 2009; Villemez, 2008).

According to Dann Dykas of Human & Equal Right Organizers (HERO), "The Internet, along with social networking utilities such as Facebook, MySpace, and Twitter, has revolutionized the process of the revolution. With its vastness and accessibility, Web-roots organization ... simply blows away any antiquated localized movements" (Garcia, 2009, p. 38).

One attempt at focusing LGBTIQ power on the Internet is the proposed new .gay[6] (dotgay) top level domain (TLD). The proposal will be brought before the Internet Corporation for Assigned Names and Numbers (ICANN) in 2010, and, if approved, will go live in 2011 or 2012 ("Activists push for top level domain dedicated to the gay community," 2009). Dotgay is intended to be an Internet domain composed of LGBTIQ people, organizations, and businesses. It will pump 51 percent of its profits back into the community by offering grants to organizations involved in LGBTIQ causes (Dot Gay Alliance, 2009). Joe Dolce, founder and executive director of the Dot Gay Alliance, states:

> The LGBT community has always supported itself and its causes — no one was there to help us. We've made amazing progress in the 40 years since Stonewall. Now in the digital era a .GAY top-level domain is a logical evolution in our history of self sustenance" [Melloy, 2009].

While many support the new top level domain, some are wary, viewing it as a form of ghettoization. Others see this as making it easier to filter or block LGBTIQ sites. Still others fear it will remove the anonymity for those tentatively exploring sexual and gender identity information on the Internet.

I'll close this section with some recent examples of the power of Internet activism within library-related contexts. The first case in point concerns the controversy at West Bend (Wisconsin) Community Memorial Library (WBCML) over the fate of several dozen LGBTIQ young adult books. Conservative blogger Ginny Maziarka and her husband Jim petitioned the library in March 2009 to relocate what she characterized as "Youth-Targeted Pornographic Books" from the young adult to the adult area of the library (2009, para. 3). An opposing blog soon appeared, West Bend Parents for Free Speech, with its own petition to the library "to enforce (and if necessary, adopt) policies that protect the collection from attempts at censorship" (Hanrahan, 2009, para. 1).[7] Other blogs devoted to the West Bend controversy quickly followed (Lawson, 2009).[8] The battle of the bloggers generated quite a bit of media attention, as other cyberspace entities picked up on and passed along information, eventually drawing the attention of major news outlets such as CNN, ABC News, and Fox News.[9] In July of 2009, the Pew Research Center's Project for Excellence in Journalism reported that the West Bend controversy was the third largest story in the blogosphere (2009).[10] Coverage of the incident went viral, with references showing up all over the Internet including YouTube and Facebook.[11] Eventually the West Bend library board unanimously voted to keep the LGBTIQ books in the library's young adult section (Whelan, 2009). Because of the continuous and extensive coverage, this is perhaps one of the most detailed examples to date documenting both sides of a book challenge.[12]

Another instance involves a leading educational press, Scholastic, who in the fall of

2009, decided to exclude Lauren Myracle's *Luv Ya Bunches* from being sold at its book fairs because one of the elementary school age protagonists had lesbian parents, a portrayal which the company deemed "offensive and inappropriate for children" (Jones, 2009, para. 6). Change.org, which bills itself as "the central platform informing and empowering movements for social change around the most important issues of our time" (2009, para. 2), hosted a petition to get Scholastic to reverse its decision and within 48 hours had collected over 4000 signatures. Scholastic contacted all of the petitioners and informed them that "Scholastic editors recognize Milla's two moms as a positive and realistic aspect of the story" and that they would carry the book in their middle school fairs (K. Good, email communication, October 30, 2009).[13]

Before the Internet, the West Bend Library incident would likely have received little attention outside the local community, except perhaps with those groups who monitor such situations. Similarly, the Scholastic episode would not have received such an immediate and widespread response. With the advent of the Internet, we now live in a glocalized goldfish bowl.

Problems/Concerns

While the Internet plays an important positive role in the support and information seeking of LGBTIQ communities, it also has its negative aspects — in particular, cyberbullying and filtering.

Cyberbullying

The Internet makes it easier to bully and intimidate young people online, in the form of "cyberbullying," which is defined as "Willful and repeated harm inflicted through the use of computers, cell phones, and other electronic devices" (Hinduja & Patchin, 2008, p. 5).

The anonymity of the Internet serves not only as protection for those seeking information and community, but also to cloak those who seek to antagonize or humiliate others. No longer confined to school hallways, bullies can now torment others from anywhere. The statistics are staggering. Hinduja and Patchin state that about 15–35 percent of students claim to be victims, while 10–20 percent admit to being perpetrators (2009). Another survey (i-SAFE, 2009) places the number of students bullied online at 42 percent, with one in four of these students facing repeat bullying. Involvement in cyberbullying seems to climax during junior high/middle school (Hinduja & Patchin, 2009).

LGBTQ students (or those who are perceived to be LGBTQ) are cyberbullied at even higher rates. GLSEN's most recent school climate survey stated that 55.4 percent of the students surveyed were subjected to cyberbullying incidents in the prior school year, with 17.6 percent being subjected "often" or "frequently" (Kosciw, Diaz, & Greytak, 2008, p. 54).

As with traditional bullying, cyberbullying can undermine the self-esteem of those being targeted. Often they withdraw either socially by keeping to themselves or physically by dropping out of school (Cassels, 2002). Cyberbullying can have even more drastic effects on its victims: for example, one survey found that four percent of students had suicidal thoughts as a result of their experience (Cassidy, Jackson, & Brown, 2009). Another study places the proportion even higher for non-heterosexual students at eleven percent (Dillavou, 2009).

Cyberbullies often experience what Warren Blumenfeld refers to as the "disinhibition effect," where people's inhibitions are decreased because of their perceived anonymity or indirect involvement with the target during the cyberbullying act (Dillavou, 2009, para. 5). This enables cyberbullies to partake in behavior in which they may not participate were the encounter face-to-face rather than online.

If cyberbullying originates from the school grounds, school administrations have the authority to deal with the situation. However, when it originates elsewhere, school administrators are often hamstrung in addressing the situation. First Amendment issues can arise in these latter situations, where courts have found that punishing cyberbullies violates freedom of speech (Kim, 2009; Willard, 2009).

In helping to counter cyberbullying, schools and other community institutions (such as libraries) can offer net etiquette, sensitivity, and assertiveness training to young people as well as create anonymous mechanisms for students to report incidents of cyberbullying. Striving to build a culture that is more inclusive, welcoming, and responsive will go a long way in counteracting cyberbulling (Cassidy, Jackson, & Brown, 2009).

Filtering

A full-blown discussion of filtering appears elsewhere in this book,[14] so this topic will receive only a brief mention here. Filtering access to the Internet has a disproportionate effect on young people seeking LGBTIQ information and communities. Because of the anonymity and confidentiality the Internet offers, many see it as their sole avenue of information and support. Blocking LGBTIQ teens from making informed choices based on their queries and/or connecting with supportive communities can lead to dire consequences including unsafe sexual practices, despair, and suicide.[15]

The restrictions mandated by the Children's Internet Protection Act and the ramifications of losing federal E-rate funding for non-compliance leave libraries with few options to avoid Internet filtering. However, libraries can mitigate the effects somewhat by evaluating filtering software and choosing the least restrictive products as well as instituting clearly defined and comprehensive Internet use policies.

Conclusion

The Internet has transformed not only how communities communicate, connect, and mobilize, but also how libraries and archives work with these same communities. Throughout this book, you'll find creative ways that librarians, archivists, and others have used the Internet to reach out and serve LGBTIQ users and their communities, including guided tours of archival facilities offered through videos on YouTube[16]; collaborative projects that blend grassroots activism with scholarly endeavor on wikis[17]; oral histories of LGBTIQ individuals from the U.S. heartland hosted on a university's institutional repository site[18]; and small community-based libraries that have radically expanded their visibility and outreach through Web 2.0.[19]

Notes

1. This is a marked increase from 2006, with 32 percent lesbians and gays reporting reading blogs as compared to only 26 percent of straight people (Light, 2009).

2. For example, 55 percent are members of Facebook (as compared to 46 percent of straight people); 43 percent are members of MySpace (as compared to 30 percent of straight people); 23 percent are members of LinkedIn (as compared to 13 percent of straight people); and 20 percent use Twitter (as compared with 12 percent of straight people).

3. For a fuller discussion of this topic, please see the essay in Section Six on "LGBTIQ Teens—Plugged In and Unfiltered: How Internet Filtering Impairs Construction of Online Communities, Identity Formation, and Access to Health Information."

4. Not all intersex people view *intersex* as an identity. For example, activist Emi Koyama, states, "What makes intersex people similar is their experiences of medicalization, not biology. Intersex is not an identity" (Still, 2008, p. xv).

5. For more on this topic, see the section on Cyberbullying.

6. Although the suffix is "gay," the intent is to be inclusive of all the groups under the LGBTIQ umbrella. As Joe Dolce explains: "'gay' is an internationally recognized word, while the L.G.B.T. acronym differs across different languages." Plus "gay is a nice three-letter word, which fits Internet naming convention" (Lee, 2009, para. 17).

7. Both these petitions can be found on their respective blogs: Maziarka's on her blog, WISSUP = Wisconsin Speaks Up at http://wissup.blogspot.com/2009/03/petition-for-child-safe-family-friendly.html and Hanrahan's on West Bend Parents for Free Speech at http://westbendparentsforfreespeech.webs.com/petition.htm

8. These include: Sleepless in West Bend <http://sleeplessinwestbend.blogspot.com/> and WIS-SUP-Uncensored <http://wissup-uncensored.blogspot.com/>

9. A listing of "News Sources, Blogs & Organizations" can be found on the West Bend Community Memorial Library website at: http://www.west-bendlibrary.org/alahandout.pdf

10. In fact, the West Bend Parents for Free Speech blog encourages people on its home page to "Go Viral!"

11. Several videos of the West Bend Library Board June 2 meeting appear on YouTube. Also there is an "I Support Intellectual Freedom and the West Bend (WI) Public Library" page on Facebook at http://www.facebook.com/group.php?gid=64270851441

12. More information on this specific incident can be found in the essay on "Censorship of Children's and Young Adult Books in Schools and Public Libraries" in Section Six.

13. Many claim that this is a hollow victory, because since the book is about elementary school age girls, there is some doubt that it would be of interest to middle school students.

14. See Section Six for the essay on "LGBTIQ Teens — Plugged In and Unfiltered: How Internet Filtering Impairs Construction of Online Communities, Identity Formation, and Access to Health Information."

15. As recently as 2009, Tennessee schools were blocking access to affirmative LGBTQ sites, while allowing access to anti-gay sites dealing with such topics as reparative therapy and ex-gay matters (Staino, 2009). After the intervention of the American Civil Liberties Union, which termed the practice "illegal viewpoint discrimination," the situation was rectified (American Civil Liberties Union, 2009, para. 2).

16. The GLBT Historical Society in San Francisco provides a nine-part guided tour of its facilities on YouTube <http://www.youtube.com/watch?v=nMnqFFCwtC4>. Other archival facilities and libraries also offer virtual tours on their websites or YouTube, including the Lesbian Herstory Archives at http://www.lesbianherstoryarchives.org/tourintro.html; the Leather Archives and Museum at http://www.youtube.com/watch?v=HQwbuzBpaYM; and Quatrefoil Library at http://www.youtube.com/watch?v=aXJX-iUdFbd4.

17. These include OutHistory.org which is profiled in this section and also the IRN (International Resource Network) <http://www.irnweb.org/>, a global, multilingual digital library which strives to increase access to scholarly resources in the areas of sexuality and gender, provide opportunities for networking and collaboration, and aid in curriculum development.

18. See "'It Was Only Supposed to Be Twenty Interviews': GLBTIQ Oral History as Librarianship — The Under the Rainbow Collection" in Section Three.

19. See "Quatrefoil Library: The Next Generation" in Section Two.

References

Activists push for top level domain dedicated to the gay community. (2009, August 24). *PinkNews.co.uk.* Newspaper, Retrieved from http://www.pinknews.co.uk/news/articles/2005–13780.html

Adams, S. S., & Peirce, K. (2006). *Is there a transgender canon? Information seeking and use in the transgender community.* Presented at the Annual Conference of the Canadian Association of Information Science, Toronto. Retrieved from http://www.cais-acsi.ca/proceedings/2006/adams_2006.pdf

American Civil Liberties Union. (2009, August 13). Franks v. Metropolitan Board of Public Education — case profile. Retrieved from http://www.aclu.org/lgbt-rights_hiv-aids/franks-v-metropolitan-board-public-education-case-profile

Basgil, T. (2009, March). New visions in organizing the Internet's importance in LGBT activism. *Out in Jersey, 14*(2), 15.

Beiriger, A., & Jackson, R. (2007). An assessment of the information needs of transgender communities in Portland, Oregon. *Public Library Quarterly, 26*(1), 45–60. doi: 10.1300/J118v26n01_03

Besen, W. (2007, December 6). A weekend without e-mail. *Outlook Weekly,* 8.

Blumenfeld, W. (2005). *Cyberbulling: A new variation on an old theme.* Presented at Abuse I: The Darker Side of Human-Computer Interaction. Retrieved from http://www.agentabuse.org/blumenfeld.pdf

Bond, B. J., Hefner, V., & Drogos, K. L. (2008). Information-seeking practices during the sexual development of lesbian, gay, and bisexual individuals: The influence and effects of coming out in a mediated environment. *Sexuality & Culture, 13*(1), 32–50. doi: 10.1007/s12119–008–9041-y

Cassels, P. (2002, December 19). LGBT youth singled out with cyber bullying. *Bay Windows — New England's largest GLBT newspaper.* Retrieved from http://www.baywindows.com/index.php?ch=news&sc=glbt&sc2=news&sc3=&id=69750

Cassidy, W., Jackson, M., & Brown, K. N. (2009). Sticks and stones can break my bones, but how can pixels hurt me? Students' experiences with cyber-bullying. *School Psychology International, 30*(4), 383–402. doi: 10.1177/0143034309106948

Change.org. (2009). About us. Retrieved from http://www.change.org/info/about

Correll, S. (1995). The ethnography of an electronic bar: The Lesbian Cafe. *Journal of Contemporary Ethnography, 24*(3), 270–298. doi: 10.1177/089124195024003002

Dillavou, L. (2009, January 21). Blumenfeld's cyberbullying study confronts growing problem. Retrieved from http://www.hs.iastate.edu/news/inside/view/181/

Dot Gay Alliance. (2009). Dot Gay. Retrieved from http://www.dotgay.org/

Friess, S. (1999, March 2). Cyber activism. *Advocate,* (780), 34–39.

Garcia, L. (2009, February 5). The instant connector. *Echo Magazine, 20*(10), 36, 38–39. Retrieved from http://www.echomag.com/echopdfs/Echo_506.pdf

Greytak, E. A., Kosciw, J. G., & Diaz, E.M. (2009). *Harsh realities: The experiences of transgender youth in our nation's schools.* Retrieved from http://www.glsen.org/binary-data/GLSEN_ATTACHMENTS/file/000/001/1375–1.pdf

Haag, A. M., & Chang, F. K. (1998). The impact of electronic networking on the lesbian and gay community. *Journal of Gay & Lesbian Social Services, 7*(3), 83–94. doi: 10.1300/J041v07n03_07

Haeberli, E. (1996, July 9). Balancing act. *The Advocate,* (711), 36–37.

Hamer, J. S. (2003). Coming-out: Gay males' information seeking. *School Libraries Worldwide, 9*(2), 73–89.

Hanrahan, M. (2009). Petition. *West Bend Parents for Free Speech.* Retrieved from http://westbendparentsforfreespeech.webs.com/petition.htm

Harris Interactive. (2007, January 2). Gays, lesbians and bisexuals lead in usage of online social networks. Retrieved from http://www.harrisinteractive.com/news/allnewsbydate.asp?NewsID=1136

Harris Interactive & Witeck-Combs Communications. (2009, June 9). Gay and lesbian adults more likely to read blogs and use social networking tools. Retrieved from http://www.harrisinteractive.com/news/pubs/Harris_Interactive_Witeck_Combs_News_2009_06_09.pdf

Hegland, J. E., & Nelson, N. J. (2002). Cross-dressers in cyber-space: Exploring the Internet as a tool for expressing gendered identity. *International Journal of Sexuality and Gender Studies, 7*(2/3), 139–161.

Hinduja, S., & Patchin, J. W. (2008). *Bullying beyond the schoolyard: Preventing and responding to cyberbullying.* Corwin.

Hinduja, S., & Patchin, J. W. (2009, September). Cyberbullying: Fast Facts and School Strategies. *School Climate Matters, 3*(3), 4–6.

Human Rights Campaign. (2009). Cyber bullying and the GLBT community. Retrieved from http://www.hrc.org/issues/9682.htm

i-SAFE. (2009). Cyber bullying: Statistics and tips. Retrieved from http://www.isafe.org/channels/sub.php?ch=op&sub_id=media_cyber_bullying

Join The Impact. (2008, December 31). About us. Retrieved from http://jointheimpact.com/about-us/

Jones, M. (2009, October 26). Tell Scholastic to stop censoring gay friendly books. Change.org. Retrieved from http://gayrights.change.org/actions/view/tell_scholastic_to_stop_censoring_gay_friendly_books

Kim, V. (2009, December 14). Judge backs student's first amendment rights: Cruel remarks online are not unconstitutional. *The Boston Globe*. Retrieved from http://www.boston.com/news/nation/articles/2009/12/14/judge_rules_students_cruel_remarks_online_are_not_unconstitutional/

Kosciw, J. G., Diaz, E. M., & Greytak, E. A. (2008). The 2007 national school climate survey: The experiences of lesbian, gay, bisexual and transgender youth in our nation's schools. New York: Gay, Lesbian and Straight Education Network. Retrieved from http://www.glsen.org/binary-data/GLSEN_ATTACHMENTS/file/000/001/1290–1.pdf

Lawson, R. (2009, June 16). Small-town Wisconsin has its own blog wars, thank you very much. Gawker. Retrieved from http://gawker.com/5292791/small+town-wisconsin-has-its-own-blog-wars-thank-you-very-much

Lee, J. (2009, October 23). Competing groups press for a ".gay" Internet suffix. *New York Times City Room Blog*. Retrieved from http://cityroom.blogs.nytimes.com/2009/10/23/competing-groups-press-for-a-gay-internet-suffix/?hp

Light, L. (2009, July 17). Gay and lesbian adults more likely to embrace 21st century tech. *Over the wire: A researcher's perspective on current events*. Blog. Retrieved from http://overthewire.typepad.com/my_weblog/2009/07/gay-and-lesbian-adults-more-likely-to-embrace-21st-century-tech.html

Maziarka, G. (2009, March 26). Petition for a child-safe, family-friendly library. *WISSUP = Wisconsin Speaks Up*. Blog. Retrieved from http://wissup.blogspot.com/2009/03/petition-for-child-safe-family-friendly.html

Melloy, K. (2009, October 23). Coming online: "Dot-Gay?" *EDGE Boston*. Retrieved from http://www.edgeboston.com/index.php?ch=news&sc=&sc2=news&sc3=&id=98104

Nangeroni, N. R. (1997). The virtual movement. Retrieved from http://www.gendertalk.com/articles/oped/virtual.shtml

Nangeroni, N. R. (2009, September 24). Missing trans history: The Brandon Teena demo. *Nancy's blog on GenderTalk*. Retrieved from http://www.gendertalk.com/?q=node/338

Pew Research Center Project for Excellence in Journalism. (2009, July 30). Bloggers seize on Obama's slipping poll numbers. Retrieved from http://pewresearch.org/pubs/1299/new-media-conservatives-applaud-lower-obama-ratings

Preves, S. E. (2003). *Intersex and identity: The contested self*. New Brunswick, NJ: Rutgers University Press.

Preves, S. E. (2005). Out of the O.R. and into the streets: Exploring the impact of intersex media activism. *Cardozo Journal of Law & Gender, 12*, 247–288.

Shapiro, E. (2003). "Trans"cending barriers: Transgender organizing on the Internet. *Journal of Gay & Lesbian Social Services, 16*(3/4), 165–179. doi: 10.1300/J041v16n03_11

Staino, R. (2009, August 17). TN school district dumps filters that block LGBT sites. *School Library Journal*. Retrieved from http://www.schoollibraryjournal.com/article/CA6676896.html?rssid=190

Still, B. (2008). *Online intersex communities: Virtual neighborhoods of support and activism*. Amherst, N.Y.: Cambria.

Villemez, J. (2008, November 21). Making a difference, online and off. *Philadelphia Gay News*, 32.

Weise, E. (1996, June 21). Gay, lesbian net surfers dream market for on-line world. *Moscow-Pullman Daily News*, 6B. Retrieved from http://news.google.com/newspapers?nid=2026&dat=19960620&id=1cUjAAAAIBAJ&sjid=GtEFAAAAIBAJ&pg=6016,1892853

Whelan, D. L. (2009). WI's West Bend Library Board says "no" to relocating YA books. *School Library Journal*. Retrieved from http://www.schoollibraryjournal.com/article/CA6663173.html

Willard, N. (2009, December 16). There is no constitutional right to be a cyberbully: Analysis of J.C. v Beverly Hills Unified School District. Center for Safe and Responsible Internet Use. Retrieved from http://www.cyberbully.org/documents/JCcyberbullyingcase.pdf

Witeck-Combs Communications & Harris Interactive. (2000, April 27). New Witeck-Combs / Harris Interactive Internet survey confirms gays and lesbians are among heaviest Internet users. witeck-combs communications. Retrieved from http://www.witeckcombs.com/news/releases/20020427_internet.pdf

It's Not Monopoly: Gender Role Explorations in Online Environments

K. Fisher

No exploration of the powerful effect of new technologies would be complete without at least a passing reference to the work of Marshall McLuhan, who's most famously known for the quote, "the medium is the message." Those who think that the newest technologies can only be understood by the young or those technically savvy enough to understand computers would do well to consider the following quotes from an interview with McLuhan done in 1969. The time was well before the advent of personal computers that sat on our desks, let alone anything even imagined like the Internet.

Consider these three observations by McLuhan on the effects of media:

- All media—*in and of themselves and regardless of the messages they communicate*—exert a compelling influence on man [*sic*] and society.
- Technological innovations are extensions of human abilities and senses that alter this [natural] sensory balance—an alteration that, in turn, inexorably reshapes the society that created the technology.
- All technology has the property of the Midas touch; whenever a society develops an extension of itself, all other functions of that society tend to be transmuted to accommodate that new form; once any new technology penetrates a society, it saturates every institution of that society. New technology is thus a *revolutionizing* agent [italics mine] (*Playboy* interview, 1969, para. 4).

Forty years later I find McLuhan's observations made in 1969 to be remarkably prescient, revealing a profound and deep understanding of the effect of the medium itself beyond the content. Even further than that, I have experienced precisely what McLuhan predicts in my exploration of being transgendered in the online virtual world called Second Life. This is just one personal account, albeit I hope an informed one, of what it's like to use this new technology to experience what it's like to be another gender. Please note that I have deliberately used the phrase "be another gender" and not "pretending to be another gender."

Second Life is a virtual reality software program accessible on the World Wide Web (Second Life official site, 2009). The virtual world of Second Life is an online 3-D environment created by users known as Residents. At any given time 38,000 people, on average, are logged into Second Life and occasionally as many as 80,000 are "in-world" (Second Life, 2009, para. 5). Each of these users has created an "avatar" to interact in the environment of Second Life and with other users. The variety of avatars is not limited to human forms but most users do seem to choose an avatar that is human. The ability to shape the image of an avatar is almost without limits. One can shape each and every part of the body, change hair color, height, weight, and yes, even gender.

A vibrant economy has developed in Second Life to allow people to have more control over the appearance of their avatar. This economy deals in virtual dollars (called Lindens after the virtual names of the creators) but do in fact represent real dollars being exchanged. Over $35 million are exchanged each month in Second Life (Second Life — The Marketplace, 2009). In a recent journal article on the business potential of Second Life gleaned from 29 in-depth interviews, the authors found that users do not consider Second Life as a "mere computer game" but *as an extension of their real lives* [italics mine] (Kaplan & Haenlein, 2009).

Though anecdotal, I do know people in real life that met in Second Life and have fallen in love, married, been divorced, and carried on real romantic affairs both in Second Life and in the real world. What kind of a "game" could possibly attract so many people to expend so much time, effort, and money unless it was exerting some powerful attraction to significant numbers of people? The electronic environment takes the whole idea of "playing a game" to another level.

I have a personal interest in all of this, and my experience of Second Life confirms McLuhan's point of view. I am a transgendered male. For over 50 years I have been contending, pretending, denying, and in many other ways dealing with my own inner feeling of being differently gendered than what my biological gender would indicate. I have been, at turns, ashamed and embarrassed as well as inspired and exhilarated. It's been a roller coaster ride of acceptance and denial with sharp turns into and out of marriages, traditional male gender roles, and secret behaviors. It was after one of these sharp turns into a traditional husband role and then out of it after a divorce that I discovered Second Life and its power to allow me to reconnect with my lifelong urge to be female and experience the other gender.

It started as an innocent library school assignment to go into Second Life and create an avatar to interact in the school's new virtual environment. And so I did. I created an avatar and went exploring. And what I found stunned me. With a simple click of a button I could change my avatar's gender. When I did click that gender button I felt a palpable jolt go through me. As I gazed at my avatar on my computer screen I experienced what McLuhan suggests. My avatar felt like an extension of my own nervous system. *She* felt like *me*. This feeling persisted and grew.

For the next several weeks I engaged in an intensive interactive process to get the look of my avatar just right. I met people in Second Life who helped me. I spent money buying upgraded skin and hair. I went shopping for clothes. Each night for weeks I would turn on my computer when I walked in the house and spend hours in this virtual world as my feminine self. I also began to realize what many in Second Life said was their experience as well — that SL — the shorthand way of writing Second Life — actually meant Sleep Less. I dragged myself away from the screen bleary-eyed each night and sometimes got up early to log on in the morning. I realize I am describing perhaps an almost addictive relationship to Second Life but when you aren't living your real life in real life then a virtual world where you can actually feel authentic exerts a very powerful attraction. And my experience with this electronic medium has reshaped my reality just as McLuhan suggests.

As I worked with my avatar each night I found myself going back to my transgendered way of life in the real world, a life I had been living in one way or another since the age of six, and it felt good. It felt good to be authentic. And now this new way of being in the world has become my reality. I don't participate in Second Life like I did when I first encountered it because two years later I'm living the life in the real world that I discovered, or perhaps more accurately, re-discovered in Second Life. I'm transitioning to be female now. I am on hormones. I live a substantially female life now in the outer world. And for me it was all set off in a very real way by my participation as the gender of my choice in Second Life.

I am not alone. I have no proof other than anecdotal evidence, but the fact is there are many people in Second Life choosing avatars of the other gender and posing as authentic persons of the other gender. There is a Transgender Resource Center in Second Life, a kind of support group and place where people can go to get help and find resources for being transgendered. But the rest of Second Life is full of people who are living secret lives of the other gender. Some are predators, no doubt, engaging in covert forms of sexual fantasies for their own benefit. Some are simply ashamed or afraid of "coming out" and are just used to keeping their true selves a secret. But many others are enjoying, often for the first time, their authentic selves in a sincere way. I know. I've met many of them online and the only difference between most of them and me is my willingness to live my life in the real world as I do in Second Life. I can afford to. I live in a liberal part of the country and work for an institution that is supportive of equal rights for all persons. I'm not married and have no children. The social cost I have to pay, though not insignificant, pales in comparison to what other transgendered folks have to pay in other areas of the country and the world in the form of discrimination, ridicule, and social stigmatizing.

At the very least, for those with the means for computers and Internet access, Second Life and other virtual reality programs offer a way for transgendered people to experience authenticity, community, and support for a way of life that is still viewed by the heterosexual majority as strange, weird, or neurotic. Transgendered people have the right to determine and define their unique experience of life on their own terms. Online virtual communities are helping transgendered people like me find a place in the world where our experience is not simply defined by a heterosexist point of view of someone else but by *our* authentic feelings and experiences of *our* authentic selves.

If McLuhan is right, and I think he is, using these virtual extensions of the human nervous system are reshaping not just the individuals who participate in them but the societies in which they live. In short, the revolution is here and it can't be stopped. The heterosexist monopoly game is over.

REFERENCES

Kaplan, A., & Haenlein, M. (2009). Consumer use and business potential of virtual worlds: The case of "Second Life." *International Journal on Media Management, 11*(3), 93–101. doi: 10.1080/142412709030 47008

Playboy interview: Marshall McLuhan. (1969, March). Retrieved from http://www.playboy.com/articles/marshall-mcluhan-playboy-interview/index.html

Second Life. (2009, December 5). In *Wikipedia, The Free Encyclopedia.* Retrieved from http://en.wikipedia.org/w/index.php?title=Second_Life&oldid=329959927

Second Life official site: Virtual worlds, avatars, free 3D chat, online meetings. (2009). Retrieved from http://secondlife.com/

Second Life — The Marketplace. (2009). Retrieved from http://secondlife.com/whatis/marketplace.php

Making a Difference

Jim Van Buskirk

When I first met David Cameron Strachan, I was a bit intimidated by his 6-foot-10-inch frame towering over me. Being 6' 3" myself, I was not used to having to look up at others. I needn't have worried; this gentle giant was friendly, knowledgeable and determined as he presented his agenda about promoting intersex issues. While David's build, balding head, deep voice and beard register as male, he explained that instead of the typical male XY sex chromosomes or the female XX set, David has XXY ones. Born with male genitalia (and undescended gonads), David began growing breasts during puberty and didn't sprout chest hair until testosterone treatment kicked in, after he was diagnosed, at the age of 29, with Klinefelter Syndrome. Since then David has used his personal experience and his expertise to educate others about intersex issues.

Early in 2001, David proposed a library program on intersex topics to be sponsored by the James C. Hormel Gay & Lesbian Center of the San Francisco Public Library. I interrupted him immediately to confess I didn't know the first thing about intersex. He explained that I might be more familiar with the older term *hermaphrodite*. That helped a little until David brought in VHS copies of several documentaries to preview. He was very strategic as he assisted my education, encouraged me to consider materials to develop the library's collections, and help shape a public program. The documentaries, including *Hermaphrodites Speak!; XXXY: A Short Documentary about Intersex Issues; Is It A Boy or a Girl?;* and *Intersexuality: Redefining Sex,* brought home some of the basic issues of intersex.

As pleased as I was to have my horizons broadened, I was dismayed that I had no real understanding of this important and prevalent condition. I was eager to learn more and to educate my community. Fortunately, I had an excellent teacher.

Once David had provided me with a rudimentary education, we began to develop the program. Of course, we wanted to do everything in those ninety minutes: screen a film, have a panel discussion, and answer questions. We decided on one of the films, and David recommended several potential panelists, including himself. When the panelists arrived, I was shocked that they all presented as normal. Out of this context, I would never have suspected any deviation/variation in their sexual conditions. Thea Hillman, Howard Devore, Taylor Holder and David spoke eloquently and candidly about their painful journeys to accept the bodies that in some ways had betrayed them. Because David obtained the co-sponsorship of the Intersex Society of North America (ISNA), the local intersex community turned up for the program which was well attended and very successful.

From there, David helped me augment the collection of the San Francisco Public Library so that it contained relevant and up-to-date materials on various aspects of the intersex experience. We made sure to include a balance of historical, medical, and personal experience. In 2002, Jeffrey Eugenides' novel *Middlesex* was chosen for the Oprah book club and became a bestseller, recounting the unusual story of Cal Stephanides, a 41-year-old hermaphrodite who had been raised as Calliope. The novel's depiction of the very rare condition, 5-alpha-reductase deficiency syndrome, may have done more to bring intersex issues to the awareness of the general public than any other work. However, as Thea Hillman notes,

> *Middlesex* was written by a non-intersex man who never interviewed an intersex person before writing his book. He's an author who used intersex as a metaphor, but he is in no way an advocate for intersex people, nor has his work sparked any activism (except activism targeted at him) [quoted in Roth, 2008, para. 22].

In 2004, David gave me a VHS copy of *Yellow for Hermaphrodites: Mani's Story*, the documentary that follows the life story of New Zealand intersex activist Mani Bruce Mitchell. When David told me that Mani would soon be visiting San Francisco, we planned another successful program, featuring the film and Mani being interviewed onstage by local sexologist Carol Queen. The library's 240-seat Koret auditorium was filled and the post-program reception honoring Mani was abuzz with networking intersex activists.

I was lucky to have been found by David, who expediently used my position and my eagerness to learn to the advantage of his important agenda. The intersection of libraries, librarians and passionate library users *can* make a difference.

REFERENCES

Roth, M. (2008, December 11). Thea Hillman: The inner sanctum of intersex. *Jewcy.com*. Blog. Retrieved from http://www.jewcy.com/post/thea_hillman_heart_and_sex

OutHistory.org: Fostering Community-Created LGBTQ Histories

Lauren J. Gutterman

OutHistory.org is the first freely accessible, collaboratively written website on lesbian, gay, bisexual, transgender and queer (LGBTQ) U.S. history. OutHistory.org uses the Internet to compile community created histories of LGBTQ life in the U.S. and to make the insights of LGBTQ history broadly accessible. Using MediaWiki software, the site allows anyone to create articles, add discussion threads or upload images, audio and video files. OutHistory.org thus enables those within, as well as outside of the academic world to record the history of the LGBTQ community by posting collections, memorabilia, personal memories, and historical narratives. Historically, authorities have cast LGBTQ people's lives and experiences as stories of pathology or perversion. OutHistory.org provides a unique venue for LGBTQ people to tell their own stories and share them with a vast audience.

Independent scholar and pioneering gay historian Jonathan Ned Katz conceived of and founded OutHistory.org, which is hosted by the Center for Lesbian and Gay Studies (CLAGS) at the City University of New York Graduate Center and supported by grants from the Arcus Foundation and individual donations. Katz, author of *Gay American History: Lesbians and Gay Men in the U.S.A.,* first published in 1976, was one of the first scholars to begin publishing on gay history, to argue that homosexuality had a history and that it warranted telling. Katz's first books, *Gay American History* and *Gay/Lesbian Almanac: A New Documentary,* are collections of historical documents describing men and women who engaged in homosexual sex, women who lived together as married couples, men and women who lived their lives as the opposite sex, and materials on the oppression and resistance tactics of homosexuals. In some ways, OutHistory.org is a continuation of the project Katz began with *Gay American History.* The site aims to encourage people to consider how understandings of sexuality are historically specific, to bring materials about LGBTQ history to light, and to empower people beyond the academic world to create history for themselves.

OutHistory.org features both collaboratively written, continually evolving articles — like those on Wikipedia — and completed, unchanging entries created by named authors which can be found on the Exhibits page of OutHistory.org <http://www.outhistory.org/wiki/Exhibits>. The site currently highlights several completed exhibits including one written and researched by anthropologist C. Todd White about homophile organizations and gay-themed pulp fiction from the 1950s or "pre-gay" era. Pauline Park, co-chair and co-founder of the New York Association for Gender Rights Advocacy, created an exhibit on the campaign for a transgender rights law in New York City between 2000 and 2002. Lesbian Herstory Archives co-founder Joan Nestle has also contributed a series of "blogs" or musings on lesbian history.

In 2008 OutHistory.org awarded two fellowships to journalist Joey Plaster and Ph.D. candidate Tristan Cabello for their proposed online exhibits. Plaster's exhibit "The Polk Street History Project" features oral history interviews with residents of this San Francisco neighborhood, which has been home to some of the most underrepresented members of the queer community since the 1950s: seniors, immigrants, transgender women and homeless youth. Tristan Cabello's "Queer Bronzeville: The History of African American Gays and Lesbians on Chicago's South Side" uses music, images and video clips to cover nearly 100 years of this community's history from the turn of the century through the HIV/AIDS crisis.

Artists and collectors can use OutHistory.org too. Photographers Ron Schlittler and Suzanne Poli have created exhibits featuring their images of openly gay and lesbian politicians, and New York City Pride Parades from the 1970s and 1980s, respectively. Collectors Sharon Weinman and Marshall Weeks have uploaded early twentieth-century postcards featuring cartoon drawings and photographs of masculine women and feminine men. These images can serve as useful tools in helping people visualize LGBTQ communities and cultures that existed long before the gay liberation movement of the 1970s.

OutHistory.org's content is searchable by keyword, timeline and time era making it a valuable resource for teachers and students of LGBTQ history alike. Teachers can use the text and audio-visual resources on OutHistory.org to create lectures and classes on LGBTQ history, and their students can use it to do research and to publish their own historical writing. OutHistory.org also lists links to other online LGBTQ history resources across the country for those doing more advanced research projects. Some professors have incorporated OutHistory.org into their curricula by requiring students to create new LGBTQ history exhibits on the website. OutHistory.org's exhibit on queer youth activism was created by Sharon Ullman's undergraduate students at Bryn Mawr and Haverford Colleges and the exhibit on lesbians in the twentieth century was created by Esther Newton and her graduate students at the University of Michigan.

OutHistory.org also makes out-of-print material on LGBTQ history and hard-to-find primary documents accessible. The website features nine pages of a recently released New York City Police Department report from the morning of the Stonewall riots, June 28, 1969. A searchable 1981 edition of Barbara Grier's bibliography *The Lesbian in Literature* and digitized copies of the New York City Gay Liberation Front's *Come Out!* magazine from the early 1970s can also be found on OutHistory.org. Leading gay historian John D'Emilio's series of articles on Chicago's LGBTQ past, originally published in the *Windy City Times*, are available on OutHistory.org as are numerous primary documents on gender-crossing women, LGBTQ Native Americans and sodomy in colonial America taken from Katz's out-of-print books.

While most histories of LGBTQ life focus on cities like New York, Los Angeles and San Francisco, OutHistory.org has made an effort to draw attention to the histories of LGBTQ life outside of major metropolitan centers. June 28, 2009, marked the fortieth anniversary of the Stonewall riots, the event that has come to symbolize the beginning of today's mass LGBTQ rights movement. In honor of this important milestone OutHistory.org announced a "Since Stonewall Local Histories Contest" inviting students, archivists, activists, academics, and others to create exhibits on OutHistory.org about the last forty years of LGBTQ life in their local town, village, county, city or state. The resulting "Since Stonewall" exhibits describe the history of LGBTQ communities in places such as Champaign-Urbana, Illinois; Gainsville, Florida; Richmond, Virginia; Watauga County, North Carolina; and Tippecanoe County, Indiana, to name a few.

OutHistory.org is just in its beginning stages, but has already demonstrated its tremendous potential. Since its official debut in October 2008, OutHistory.org's content has grown immensely. The media interest in LGBTQ history spurred by the fortieth anniversary of Stonewall also helped draw attention to the wonderful resources OutHistory.org has to offer; articles about OutHistory.org were published in the Associated Press and in online versions of the *New York Times* and *The Village Voice*. OutHistory.org is fast becoming an important site to turn to in order to learn about new research, to post research queries, to find out-of-print texts, or to find information about LGBTQ archives and websites. It is also becoming a site that students visit, in order to research a project where the school library is of little help. On OutHistory.org the work of LGBTQ history is very much alive and in the present.

References

Katz, J. (1976). *Gay American history: Lesbians and gay men in the U.S.A.: A documentary*. New York: Crowell.

Katz, J. (1983). *Gay/lesbian almanac: A new documentary in which is contained, in chronological order, evidence of those persons now called lesbians and gay men, and of the changing forms of an the responses ... in the early American colonies, 1607 to 1740, and in the modern United States, 1880 to 1950*. New York: Harper & Row.

LGBTIQ Issues in Public Libraries

Catherine Ritchie and *Dale McNeill*

Introduction

From any viewpoint, the public library is indeed a miraculous institution. Where else can one find, or begin the attempt to find, any and all knowledge about everything created, loved, hated, and/or destroyed by mankind throughout all historical millennia? Not to mention free and open to all. Public libraries truly embody a world of knowledge within the world that is every library's own community, be its locale a vast metropolitan area or a rural township.

By their very nature, public libraries assume a monumental task on a daily basis: to serve all their constituent citizens with accuracy and integrity. With today's increasingly multicultural environment, combined with a questionable economy and its concomitant shrinking revenues, this task becomes both more urgent and more challenging to tackle. But the fact remains that all patrons of a public library deserve the best professional commitment possible, regardless of any controversy, real or imagined, attached to a given group of persons.

Earlier studies have shown that LGBTIQ persons, along with their friends and loved ones, have traditionally relied on the public library for presumably non-judgmental enlightenment and entertainment. While other institutions' acceptance of this particular group may have proven unenthusiastic or lacking altogether, the library, by its very "public" nature, has been viewed as a potential refuge from discrimination and as a repository of knowledge, impartially rendered (Ritchie, 2001).

While the past decades may have brought more general acceptance of LGBTIQ concerns and voices, the challenges faced by public libraries in addressing them remain demanding, though far from insurmountable. This essay addresses a few of the issues still viable in the quest to serve this particular group with fairness and completeness, all the while maintaining that delicate balance between the needs of the LGBTIQ population and a library's other equally worthy demographic groups.

In any given economy, funding in general and for specific projects or groups is an ongoing preoccupation. When dealing specifically with ideas for the LGBTIQ population, one might ask: from whence can special funds be derived above and beyond sources already utilized for a library's budget as a whole? Should there indeed be separate "funds" demarcated for individual demographic groups? What broad ramifications should be considered vis-à-vis such money-seeking?

In dealing one-on-one with the LGBTIQ patrons visiting every public library, regardless of its size and community composition, other questions arise. What sort of staff training should be implemented specifically for this group? How can LGBTIQ sensitivity coaching be best integrated into employee orientation as a whole? What special considerations regarding LGBTIQ persons should be discussed with library staff?

While staff training is a must, a library's actual building and the items found therein lend themselves to additional considerations pertinent to the LGBTIQ demographic. Are LGBTIQ patrons *finding* their desired materials easily? Is it more user-friendly for LGBTIQ-related items to be shelved separately, or blended with other collections? If there is to be no demarcation among collections, is any particular "labeling" called for instead? How should such major decisions be reached? Is the cause of customer convenience truly being addressed?

Once LGBTIQ items are on the shelves, in whatever fashion, how best can in-house displays be utilized as a further aid to access and to draw attention to topics of special interest to those patrons, and to the many others in their lives? Should LGBTIQ materials be spotlighted via separate exhibits observing special occasions, or as an integral part of a library's year-round "exhibit plan" as a whole? How can annotated bibliographies/booklists supplement — or perhaps serve as the main vehicle for — the act of calling attention to a library's uniquely LGBTIQ holdings?

And as a means of outreach to this segment of a community, how best can LGBTIQ-themed programming be created? As with the shelving and display questions, is "separate but equal" the most feasible approach, or can thoughtful integration with a library's other programming efforts be a facility's best option?

In this new era of greater general acceptance of LGBTIQ rights and concerns, the public library still embraces a formidable mandate: fairness to all the groups it serves, no matter how potentially controversial said groups' visibility may seem. For patrons to see themselves reflected in the world of knowledge within a library's four walls is perhaps that institution's greatest challenge — combining visibility with equity, laced with physical and intellectual convenience, and leavened with staff approachability and acceptance. A truly *public* library must strive for nothing less.

Collection Development

In theory, building a public library collection for LGBTIQ patrons should be no more challenging than amassing materials for African-American, Jewish, or Asian-American customers, but reality may say otherwise. When some elements of society would deny a given group the very right to exist at all, and take public or private actions to illustrate that point, collection development for said persons could be subconsciously, unintentionally, relegated to a lower priority in terms of budgets and time constraints.

Yet it is that inherent controversy surrounding LGBTIQ patrons that makes it all the more imperative that attention must be paid. Numerous studies have shown that for LGBTIQ users, along with their heterosexual friends and loved ones, the public library has consistently been viewed as a potential refuge from discrimination, as a repository of knowledge, impartially rendered, and a source of both personal validation and current information relevant to their lives. Our very "public" institutions represent a kinder, gentler world to the LGBTIQ community, and so our collection development mandate, guaranteeing full inclusion, is clear.

Fortunately, thanks to greater LGBTIQ visibility within the publishing industry, worthwhile materials for this group are no longer solely the domain of small presses with finite print runs (though, to be sure, many excellent titles emanate from such sources). No matter the means of obtaining such materials, however, our professional training still dictates that balance and quality must be primary considerations.

With materials budgets shrinking rapidly, it would be understandable to an extent to let our patron requests do our selecting for us, i.e., wait for LGBTIQ *customers* to alert us to titles worth purchasing, just as we would welcome suggestions for the latest vegan cookbook, or genealogical study of Barack Obama's family. However, once again, we face challenges: many LGBTIQ library users may be reluctant to ask directly that particular titles be purchased, since by such an act, they may, in effect, "out" themselves. Invisibility may be a factor in their lives to an extent, but we must break the cycle by acting as their requestors in a public library variation of *in loco parentis*. We must become their eyes and ears.

Review sources for LGBTIQ-related materials are plentiful, as is illustrated elsewhere in this essay. But another, somewhat more indirect, option for seeking out materials for purchase may actually serve a dual purpose: spreading the word that the public library is listening.

If there is an active LGBTIQ community of any size in your city (and chances are likely that is indeed the case), use the Internet or any personal contacts you may have to seek it out, and then introduce it to the library as a positive source of information. Ask prominent LGBTIQ individuals for book and audio-visual recommendations, or encourage them to submit ideas to the library via e-mail.

The public library may need to form further partnerships to facilitate its collection development efforts. The existence in your area of either an LGBTIQ center, or semi-regular publication geared to that population would also be boons; the people in charge will likely be glad to publicize your library's outreach efforts and will encourage members/readers to contact you with suggestions.

In evaluating LGBTIQ-related titles for possible purchase, be aware that one size does not fit all. Do not assume that a non-fiction book pertaining to gays and lesbians will automatically appeal to your bisexual and transgender patrons as well. Even within the wide-ranging LGBTIQ community itself, bisexual and transgender persons may at times feel alienated or ignored. Be aware that the well-used, multi-letter acronyms encompass multiple shades and categories.

Do be aware of small presses, some of which may focus almost exclusively on LGBTIQ materials. Examples include Alyson Books; Cleis Press; and Bella Books, among others. Your materials vendors might not carry their product, which may necessitate direct orders and some greater expense, but such publishing houses can be a bountiful source of material directly relevant to this population.

As for periodicals: since the long-time "core" magazine *The Advocate* is now available only online or as an insert within the serial *Out* <http://www.out.com>, collection development librarians will need to turn their attention to other titles, bearing in mind those focusing on lesbian issues and concerns as well. Examples of the latter include *Curve* and *LN: Lesbian News*. For general LGBTIQ audiences, *Out* might also be considered, along with *GayParent* for interested families. Patrons could also be directed to online titles, such as *10,000 Couples* <http://www.10thousandcouples.com>; *Ambiente* <http://ambiente.us> and *Bi Magazine* <http://www.bimagazine.org>.

Collection Development Tools

Thanks to the Internet, along with society's overall increased acceptance of LGBTIQ issues and individuals, librarians seeking collection development guidance in this area have a far wider array of options than was possible even a decade ago.

All of the major selection journals now review LGBTIQ-themed fiction and non-fiction for both adults and teenagers, and periodically devote significant portions of an entire issue to LGBTIQ-related titles and publishing trends. *Library Journal* also occasionally offers LGBTIQ-relevant general articles.

Lambda Book Report and *The Gay & Lesbian Review* are useful online journals devoted solely to discussion of current LGBTIQ materials. *Lambda Book Report,* published exclusively online at <http://www.lambdaliterary.org>, features author interviews and sponsors annual book awards in multiple categories and age groups. Lists of Lambda Literary Award ("Lammies") nominees and winners are also available via this website, making it a unique starting point for LGBTIQ collection development.

First published in 1994, *The Gay & Lesbian Review* <http://www.glreview.com> devotes each issue to a central theme, including essays and a large number of book and other reviews. The year following its debut, *Library Journal* dubbed the *Review* "the journal of record" for the intellectual discussion of LGBTIQ topics.[1]

The American Library Association's Gay/Lesbian/Bisexual/Transgendered Round Table (GLBTRT) publishes a quarterly newsletter including an extensive book review section. Perhaps most significantly, the Round Table also sponsors the annual Stonewall Book Awards, presented to each year's outstanding titles in fiction and non-fiction, and now expanding to include young adult literature as well. Lists of previous winners are available at http://www.ala.org/ala/mgrps/rts/glbtr/stonewall/honored/index.cfm.

For school and public librarians seeking suitable titles for the LGBTIQ young people they serve, the Rainbow Project, also sponsored by ALA's GLBT Round Table and the Social Responsibilities Round Table, offers a website with recommended titles for different age groups, in both fiction and nonfiction. The site <http://rainbowlist.wordpress.com> also offers links to other sources and titles.

In 2010, a new Stonewall Youth Award, also sponsored by the GLBTRT, will be presented for the first time to an LGBTIQ-themed book written for a pre K–12 audience.

Public and college library websites may also offer suggestions of relevant LGBTIQ titles, both popular and scholarly, in the form of "research guides" or perhaps annotated booklists. Many public libraries now post samplings of their relevant LGBTIQ-related titles on their websites, right next door to the latest romance and "true crime" additions to their collections.

A basic Google search will uncover many of these libraries, but selectors may begin with the New York Public Library <http://www.nypl.org/>; San Francisco Public Library, in particular its Harvey Milk Branch <http://sfpl.lib.ca.us>; Hennepin County (MN) Public Library <http://www.hclib.org/>; and sites for somewhat smaller venues, including San Antonio (TX) <http://www.mysapl.org>, and Waterboro (ME) Public Library, the latter of which also offers links to other LGBTIQ booklists throughout the nation <http://www.waterborolibrary.org/>. These sites, and the valuable information contained within, can be of immeasurable use to collection developers.

Another non-library-related website devoted to LGBTIQ readers advisory is Rainbow

Sauce <http://www.rainbowsauce.com/>. In addition, many nationwide LGBTIQ libraries and archives maintain useful sites, including Chicago's Gerber-Hart Library <http://www.gerberhart.org>, Quatrefoil in St. Paul, Minnesota <http://www.quatrefoillibrary.org>,[2] and the Tretter Collection at the University of Minnesota <http://special.lib.umn.edu/rare/tretter.phtml>.

Building a relevant and entertaining collection for LGBTIQ patrons is no longer doomed to frustration verging on futility. Just as the average person's worldview has reportedly broadened to accept the importance of LGBTIQ issues and needs, so has the publishing world responded in kind. Spending some time in cyberspace will yield many riches for these patrons, and will enrich a public library's entire collection.

Funding

In any public library, at all decision-making levels from the board and director to the branch librarian, funding for services to defined segments of the community must be considered. If the LGBTIQ community and individuals interested in LGBTIQ materials are to be well served over the years, funding may be the single most important decision to be made. Funding affects collections, programming, hiring staff, and every facet of the public library.

To the extent possible, the library should make funding for LGBTIQ services routine. In many libraries, this will mean intentionally including the needed materials, services, and staffing as part of the routine request of funds from the funding authority. Since public libraries in most of the United States and in many other countries are local services, decisions about the best way to make these requests will need to be made locally — and may need to change from year to year to take available funding, local government support and other important factors into consideration. The ultimate goal might be that LGBTIQ materials, services, staff, and training are considered such a routine part of library service that funding in these areas will increase and decrease in proportion to the overall library budget, rather than being thought of as an outreach service.

In addition to routine funding, the public library may choose also to seek additional sources to enrich collections or programs. Examples could include funds for books with bookplates, a named series of programs, and an archivist to conserve local history materials. Libraries can consider local government, family foundations, area businesses, state associations, national programs such as the federal Institute of Libraries and Museums, and LGBTIQ organizations. Often, partnering with another cultural organization will add to the effectiveness of such requests. Remember that staff time equals money in the form of in-kind contributions to your funding agency. Grants and other special funds should have more value than the time spent in procuring them.

With some funding authorities, there will be greater or lesser advantages to making specific requests for LGBTIQ services and materials. Consider the method of making the request that makes the most sense locally. With a smaller funding agency, it's worth considering the relative merits of discussing LGBTIQ services at the beginning of the budget cycle or after materials have been purchased.

Each library should have policies that relate to funding. It is important to follow these policies or to seek explicit approval if an exception needs to be made. For example, if a particular library has a policy of not accepting donations that require the funder be named in promotional materials, it is important to be clear about this with outside funders or to work with library administration to seek an exception or a change in policy when a particularly attractive opportunity arises. Be aware that funding always has political ramifications so make sure to involve library/local government administration in decisions to seek outside funding or to designate funds for LGBTIQ services or programs.

Shelving

Once you have made the decision to purchase LGBTIQ materials (or more such materials or to develop a specialized collection), consider the collection as a whole and other community-oriented collections. How are books (and other materials) in non–English languages shelved? What about materials by Native American authors? Or collections developed for African-American communities? It isn't necessary to make the same decision for all collections, yet it is important to think about the most effective way to connect books with readers and readers with books.

There are advantages to having all collections shelved in one order, using whatever classification system the library prefers. Such an arrangement generally makes it easier for readers to find specific books. In the case of LGBTIQ readers (and family, friends, and others), it may be less stressful to browse the entire library, rather than to be in a particular LGBTIQ section. When one classification scheme is used, it's also easier to decide where to shelve particular books. (For example, if there is an LGBTIQ section, would it include non–LGBTIQ materials from a well-known lesbian writer?)

This decision does not have to be the same in every location of a multi-branch public library. One way to think about the relative advantage of separate LGBTIQ sections is simply by the number of times that customers ask for such materials. If customers ask several times a week for materials that could be shelved together, such as LGBTIQ fiction, a separate section might be needed. This would mean both that LGBTIQ materials are in high demand and that many community members are comfortable asking specifically for these materials. There is value to engaging these customers in conversation, if a separate section is being considered, regarding their opinion of the merits of such a plan.

When different decisions are made in different locations, it is important to have a plan to denote these materials in the catalog. How will the location be named? At least one public library allows each branch to have one such community-based collection, each using the generic location "special collection." While simple, this plan can also lead to confusion, as the "special collections" at each location are quite different. The purpose should always be to make both browsing and locating specific items as effective as possible for customers.

While there is not a great deal of research, there is some evidence that at least genre collections are more effective when shelved separately (Baker & Wallace, 2002). One way to think about this is to ask whether "every book its reader" is more likely to be true *in this community at this time* if the LGBTIQ collection is shelved together or if it is shelved with other materials. This question is not only about fiction, but also about film, history, biography, and many other subjects.

More thoughtful decisions about the collection can be made if shelving, subject cataloging, and classification are thought of as a whole. When items are shelved together, they will need to be labeled in some way to identify them. Some libraries also provide various labels to assist with readers' advisory or for browsing customers, when collections are not shelved together. This labeling could be the words "special collection" or "LGBTIQ" or a symbol (a rainbow or a pink triangle, for example). The ALA statement on "Labels and Rating Systems" says "Viewpoint-neutral directional aids facilitate access by making it easier for users to locate materials. The materials are housed on open shelves and are equally accessible to all users, who may choose to consult or ignore the directional aids at their own discretion" (American Library Association, 2009, para. 4). The same statement reminds librarians that it is important for labels not to be "used to forbid access or to suggest moral or doctrinal endorsement" (para. 5).

To determine the most effective viewpoint-neutral label, if one is to be used, might involve creating a focus group with customers or with staff. It would generally involve determining what usage is common locally. If symbols are used, it is important to consider whether the symbol is viewpoint-neutral and whether it is clearly understandable to customers of various ages. Pragmatically, it's also worth considering whether the desired label is commercially available or easy to produce in the library or by the library's vendors. Although shelving arrangements are usually managed by public services, they are an integral part of the classification and cataloging processes as well, so be sure to include library administration and cataloging staff in any discussions.

Staff Training

Training for public library staff can be as informal as a conversation in the workroom or as formal as a symposium. When training touches on diversity, LGBTIQ issues should always be included, even if not the main focus. For example, when discussing the needs of homebound users, consider that among the diverse groups being served may be a bisexual man. Since public libraries exist for the use of the entire public, staff training is vital to ensure employees serve library users in a culturally competent fashion.[3]

Because some staff members aren't familiar with LGBTIQ themes in fiction, it's worthwhile to include at least a few books in any readers' advisory training. Library workers should also carefully consider usage of LGBTIQ materials in collection maintenance, as the materials may receive more in-library usage than circulation. In fact, customers may use and re-shelve materials. They may not feel comfortable checking out these materials due to the stigma often associated with being LGBTIQ. Library staff should be encouraged to discuss and learn about the use of cultural materials, such as materials by and about LGBTIQ individuals. Users of this material and related programs may consider themselves part of the LGBTIQ community, may want to learn about family or friends, or may simply be curious. Readers and program attendees may be of any race, age, national origin, religion, sexual orientation, gender identity, and so forth. Use of collections may be for extremely personal reasons, school assignments, scholarship, or for some other reason. That is, about the only thing these customers have in common is the use of the same materials and programs. This is true for many, if not all, library collections — it is not unique to LGBTIQ collections.

Staff training should place emphasis on treating all customers with respect and empathy. Respect and empathy relate to interactions with library workers, collections, physical design of library buildings, and library policies and procedures. Is there any way for your library to provide a unisex or family restroom if one isn't already being provided? Transgender and intersex patrons may not feel comfortable using gender-specific restrooms. Is there even a need for large restrooms in the building? If buildings are designed with respect and empathy to all people, it is much easier for staff to continue that same treatment.

Does your library require customers to check "male or female" on account applications? Generally, there is no particular reason to do so. Again, when policies and procedures are thought through to be respectful and empathetic, staff can more easily follow that lead. When this information isn't required, no staff member needs to make an exception when asked — or even be asked to make such an exception.

Group discussions with local LGBTIQ groups, customers, outside speakers, and staff can be a way to facilitate learning how the library can be intentionally empathetic. It's useful to remember that one solution may work for several community groups. That is, providing single-person restrooms may be just as useful for mothers with toddlers, a person who isn't feeling well, the person who just wants to be next in line, or the person who doesn't want to have to explain gender identity right now.

Training relating to LGBTIQ library service can be planned by human resources, legal services, public service librarians, library administration and others. Specific sessions of a formal symposium or event could focus on the LGBTIQ community, but perhaps the most effective means of training is to include LGBTIQ concerns — along with those of the entire community being served — into all kinds of library training.

Displays

Without a doubt, and with a nod to the perennial competition of bookstores, displays are a foolproof method of attracting attention to specific aspects of a library's holdings. Whether permanently mounted to address a topic of continuous interest to patrons, or quickly assembled in order to stay abreast of a particular current event or significant trend, exhibits of books and other relevant material offer excellent "topics at a glance" opportunities for all involved.

Displays as simple as the end of a half-filled row in a shelving unit or as elaborate as a full table with printing-press-produced signage can be enlightening, entertaining, and *inclusive,* as they remind the public of *all* your facility has to offer.

Along with all the other population groups a public library serves, a library's LGBTIQ patrons deserve to see themselves reflected in a facility's displays, as do African Americans, Asian Americans, Latinos, and aficionados of gardening, mystery novels, or true crime accounts. To exclude any single population from representation is prejudicial and a violation of the *Library Bill of Rights.*

As the American Library Association has stated in its "Interpretation" of the *Library Bill of Rights* pertaining to LGBTIQ users: "Librarians have a professional obligation to ensure that all library users have free and equal access to the entire range of library services, materials, and programs" (ALA, 2008, para. 9).

Ideally, a public library should have a written policy governing display assembly calling for the inclusion of materials in as many subject areas as feasible, and representing all demographic groups. If your library's guidelines are less well-defined, simply alerting a manager to the need for fairness and breadth in what is exhibited will hopefully suffice.

Every public library serves LGBTIQ patrons, plus their family and friends, no matter how understated their presence may be. Neglecting this population in display planning is inherently unfair and contradicts a public library's very mission of serving a community with thoroughness and approachability. For example, an "LGBTIQ Awareness Month" display each June, along the lines of Black History and Hispanic Heritage Months, would demonstrate the library's awareness of, and respect for, all points of view and traditions.

Such an exhibit could include fiction by LGBTIQ authors; biographies of LGBTIQ-identified people of note; titles on LGBTIQ history; financial guides aimed towards that population, and much more. No sense of catering to an "agenda" of any kind should be implied — is such an assumption ever made in February, when we celebrate Black History Month?

What *is* illustrated, rather, is that the public library serves *all* the people in its community. At a point in our history when a May 2009 Gallup Poll tells us that 58 percent of Americans now claim to be personally acquainted with an LGBTIQ person (Morales, 2009), such visible inclusion should be expected as a matter of course — not looked upon as something inherently controversial, or inspiring fear and trepidation. Displays can and should be an "issue" worthy of thoughtful consideration in public libraries, but one whose time has come and should now be looked upon as an opportunity, rather than a burden of political correctness.

While annually devoting an entire table or floor surface to an LGBTIQ-related exhibit would be the ideal, there are other ways of raising public awareness about such materials all year round. In cooperation with other colleagues and departments, add LGBTIQ-authored books to displays on seemingly non-related topics: mysteries (or any other literary genre); performing arts biographies; film/theatre history; business; politics; childrearing; travel; and so forth. If having LGBTIQ-related titles "stand alone" is ultimately not feasible on a regular basis, integrating such materials into already-established, or even year-round, exhibits nevertheless sends a positive message, one of inclusion and fairness.

If your library assembles "quick and dirty" displays in commemoration of newly deceased famous folks, or topics suddenly "hot" and newsworthy, try to include LGBTIQ-related items as feasible. If a well-known figure was known to be LGBTIQ in his/her lifetime, the decision to memorialize that person should be arrived at no differently than if s/he had been an evident heterosexual, married with children. Once again, fairness first and foremost.

If you are comfortable offering free handouts promoting LGBTIQ-related events in your community, exhibits offer an apt opportunity for just that. Also such notices could (and probably should) be posted on your library's community bulletin board. Once again, your facility's written policy regarding distribution/display of such items should allow for a broad range of subject matter and potential audience, with all items presented tastefully and suitable for multiple ages.

Finally, as a supplement to your displays, or as a welcome library service in and of itself, offering printed booklists with recommended LGBTIQ-related titles is a guaranteed (and arguably subtler) way of making patrons aware of such materials 365 days a year. Once again, these (ideally annotated) lists can be as simple or elaborate as your computer publishing software program allows: perhaps with titles in categories by age group, featuring both fiction and non-fiction. Booklists (and bookmarks: an even "quicker" undertaking) are invaluable tools via which a patron demographic can *see* itself included in the world within the world that is your library. (Posting such lists on your facility's website will also send the public the undeniable message that the library embraces all facets of its community.) The benefits reaped via a minimum of staff time are truly incalculable.

Programming

Public programming is time-consuming, stressful, exhausting and potentially frustrating — but when done successfully, it is also an indisputably excellent means of bringing a library's community together in a positive way. As with displays and exhibits, it is important that, as much as possible, *all* aspects of the patron population are offered events of particular relevance to them and the special people in their lives.

In formulating programming of interest to the LGBTIQ community, it is vital above all to secure solid support and guarantees of "backup" from your library's administration, as your top managers will then be willing and able to offer a public face in case problems arise.

If your library plans programs "by committee" in any way, joining such a group yourself or at least making your own ideas known to the members could also provide you with welcome allies in a common cause. And if, by happy circumstance, your library staff includes personnel primarily devoted to "multicultural" activities, those folks should be able to offer invaluable guidance and encouragement.

Making personal connections within your city's LGBTIQ community is also highly desirable, both as a means of formulating programming ideas and for publicity and word of mouth as your event begins to take shape. A direct partnership between your library and a local interest group vis-à-vis securing a speaker, for example, can be fruitful for all concerned, though it is important that all involved parties agree early on regarding the aim and intentions of said potential event — especially since a public library almost always has regulations regarding program suitability (all of which should be delineated in the facility's official "meeting room" policy).

If, for whatever reasons, "stand-alone" LGBTIQ-related programming is not immediately feasible for your library, do not despair. With permission as necessary, you can perhaps "piggy-back" your ideas onto other more established event series in your venue, be they weekly, monthly, or seasonal. In other words, seek to include an LGBTIQ speaker as part of a concert and lecture series; as a featured author at book festivals; as a film series guest lecturer; on panel discussions of current events; or as an exhibitor in an art show. These participants obviously need not focus on exclusively LGBTIQ topics, of course; the speaker's background or curriculum vitae may in fact be the only clue to his/her connection to the event. Even so, such inclusion should be a matter of course, especially if the person is an expert on the given topic.

Use these same public opportunities to advertise local LGBTIQ events via handouts, flyers, or announcements made before or after the event. As with inanimate displays, it is important to let your potential audiences know that your library welcomes ideas and creativity from the *entire* community, albeit always subject to the institution's own official policies and procedures governing all public events. With policy in hand, no programming concept should be automatically included simply on the basis of subject matter, but neither should it be excluded.

Finally, as with all public programming, be sure to allow ample time for adequate publicity, including media targeted towards the LGBTIQ community as feasible. Make sure all press releases, posters and flyers are thoroughly reviewed and approved before distribution. With at least one or two layers of administrative "backup" behind any given undertaking — as would be necessary and desirable for *any* program — your efforts should be able to withstand whatever slings and arrows may come your way from the less "inclusive" patrons among you. And bear in mind the mantra: programming for the PUBLIC library is programming for ALL.

Conclusion

Public libraries have always represented a "first stop" source of information for the LGBTIQ population — both for those newly questioning their identities and for those already comfortable with themselves, but seeking to learn more about their history and coping with the normal struggles of everyday life. These libraries thus bear a mighty burden and an extraordinary privilege, as they indirectly play a role in shaping lives and influencing futures.

This simultaneous burden and privilege is admittedly more challenging in today's daunting economic climate, but despite whatever lingering controversy the LGBTIQ presence in a given community may inspire, these patrons nevertheless deserve no more and no less than public libraries' best efforts, as they mingle and thrive along with their fellow African-American, Asian-American and Latino citizens. Public libraries must strive to the best of their abilities, to work towards serving all their various constituencies, while celebrating the diversity and richness surrounding them.

NOTES

1. For more information on *The Gay and Lesbian Review Worldwide,* please see "'The Journal of Record': *The Gay and Lesbian Review Worldwide*" in Section Four.
2. For more information on Quatrefoil, please see "Quatrefoil Library: The Next Generation," also in this section.
3. For more information related to the subject of staff development in public libraries, see also the essay "When Collection Development Leads to Staff Development: The Transgender Resource Collection" in Section Seven.

REFERENCES

American Library Association. (2008, July 2). Access to library resources and services regardless of sex, gender identity, or sexual orientation: An interpretation of the library bill of rights. Retrieved from http://www.ala.org/ala/aboutala/offices/oif/statementspols/statementsif/interpretations/accesslibrary.cfm
American Library Association. (2009, July 15). Labeling and rating systems: An interpretation of the library bill of rights. Retrieved from http://www.ala.org/ala/aboutala/offices/oif/statementspols/statementsif/interpretations/labelingrating.cfm
Baker, S. L., & Wallace, K. L. (2002). *The responsive public library: How to develop and market a winning collection* (2nd ed.). Englewood, CO: Libraries Unlimited.
Morales, L. (2009, May 29). Knowing someone gay/lesbian affects views of gay issues. Retrieved from http://www.gallup.com/poll/118931/Knowing-Someone-Gay-Lesbian-Affects-Views-Gay-Issues.aspx
Ritchie, C. J. (2001, Spring). Collection development of gay/lesbian/bisexual-related adult non-fiction in medium-sized Illinois public libraries. *Illinois Libraries, 83*(2), 39–70.

School Libraries Can Make a Difference

Arla A. Jones

School libraries have changed significantly since 1990, when *Gay and Lesbian Library Service* (Gough & Greenblatt, 1990), the first book on this topic, was published. The most drastic and obvious change is that there are fewer books on the shelves, and many more computers on the tables. Where LGBTQ students are concerned, the increased availability of technology in the library has made it easier for students to safely and anonymously learn about themselves, and the issues that are of interest to them. There are more positive images of openly LGBTQ people in the media than ever, and — in some schools — more literature featuring LGBTQ topics on the library's shelves. School libraries, often located at the heart of a school, are in a position to provide a safe and accepting environment for a school's LGBTQ students, who — like all students — deserve an equal opportunity to thrive both personally and academically.

Current Status of LGBTQ Students

We are living in a society that is much more accepting of diverse sexual orientations and gender identities than ever before. Those who support equal rights for LGBTQ people generally agree that a positive cultural shift is taking place. One indicator of that shift is that according to a Gallup Poll taken in June of 2008, our country is now evenly divided on the "morality" of homosexuality — 48 percent consider homosexual relations morally acceptable, and 48 percent say that they are morally wrong (Saad, 2008). The 2000 Census provided a unique glimpse into our country by counting unmarried same-sex couples. Even in Kansas, there are unmarried same-sex couples who were willing to identify themselves in the census. In fact, there is at least one gay or lesbian couple living in every county of the state (unmarried, since Kansas passed an amendment banning same sex marriage in 2005) (Romero, Rosky, Badgett, & Gates, 2008).

Students Define Themselves

There are myriad words that today's young people use to describe their sexual orientation or gender identity/expression. While some choose words that are designed to be more

70

inclusive, such as *pansexual, asexual, bi-gender, gender-queer, bi-curious, gay-curious, questioning*, among other words, most young people embrace the more traditional terms of *gay, lesbian, bisexual* or *transgender*. Research shows that adolescents are coming out at a younger age than in previous decades (Diaz & Kosciw, 2009; Russell, Clarke, & Clary, 2009). Many of those young people are choosing to label their sexual orientation as bisexual, to temper the reaction that some may have to their coming out, at least in the early stages, before they have established a loving relationship that may or may not involve sexual contact.

It is up to adults to educate themselves on new ways of thinking and talking about sexual orientation and gender identity. The role of the school librarian is to ensure that resources are available to meet the needs of *all* students.

Bullying and Homophobia

A number of surveys over the last twenty years indicate that students are feeling more freedom to come out while they are still in school, but that their classmates may not be nearly as open-minded as the LGBTQ students are, themselves. Students of color, transgender students and middle school students are the demographic groups which are the most likely to experience bullying and homophobia at school.

GLSEN, the Gay, Lesbian and Straight Education Network (2009b), provides a number of publications on its website which can all be downloaded. One, entitled *Shared Differences: The Experiences of Lesbian, Gay, Bisexual and Transgender Students of Color in Our Nation's Schools* (Diaz & Kosciw, 2009), reports that secondary students of color experience higher levels of harassment based on sexual orientation or gender identity and are more likely to feel unsafe at school than their White classmates. Also online, the National Education Association's *Report on the Status of Gay, Lesbian, Bisexual and Transgender People in Education: Stepping Out of the Closet, Into the Light* (Kim, Sheridan, & Holcomb, 2009), finds as well that students of color experience increased levels of harassment and violence based on their actual or perceived sexual orientation or gender expression.

An article in the *Journal of Youth Adolescence* (Kosciw, Greytak, & Diaz, 2009) also examines in detail the empirical research being done in the area of hostile school climates for LGBTQ youth. The authors analyzed GLSEN's biennial National Climate Survey. Of the 5,420 students surveyed, about two-thirds were White, more than half identified as female and slightly more than half identified as gay or lesbian. Almost all were in enrolled in public schools. The survey reveals that gay and bisexual males may be more likely to experience victimization than their lesbian or bisexual female classmates. Youth in the South and the Midwest were significantly more likely to hear homophobic language in school and to experience harassment related to sexual orientation than youth in the Northeast or West. LGBTQ youth in rural communities were the most unsafe, while those in urban or suburban communities experienced fewer incidences of harassment. Although many schools have anti-bullying policies, they do not always clarify that teasing based on sexual orientation and gender identity/expression is not acceptable.

Middle School Trauma

Another recent publication of interest on GLSEN's website is a research brief, the first of its kind to look exclusively at the climate of U.S. middle schools. *The Experiences of Les-*

bian, Gay, Bisexual and Transgender Middle School Students: Findings from the 2007 National Climate Survey (Gay, Lesbian, and Straight Education Network, 2009a) analyzes the results of GLSEN's 2007 National Climate Survey of 5,420 LGBT secondary students (ages 13 to 21) including all 50 states and the District of Columbia. The complete report can be downloaded from the GLSEN website, but the major findings are as follows:

- 82 percent of LGBTQ middle school students reported hearing homophobic comments from their classmates and school staff.
- 39 percent of LGBTQ middle school students have been assaulted (e.g., punched, kicked or injured with a weapon) in school because of their sexual orientation (compared to 20 percent of high school students) and 24 percent because of their gender expression (compared to 13 percent of high school students).
- Harassment of LGBTQ students resulted in a negative impact on the middle school students' academic performance, in terms of absenteeism and a lower G.P.A., than harassment of their heterosexual classmates.
- Only 4 percent of middle school students and 43 percent of high school students reported that their school had an extra-curricular club or support group for LGBTQ students.

The report also states that having LGBTQ resources (this includes materials in school libraries!) contributes to a more positive environment for LGBT students in their school.

Transgender Students at School

As of 2009, only eleven states and the District of Columbia have laws that specifically protect students from bullying and harassment on the basis of sexual orientation, while only seven states and the District of Columbia protect students based on their gender identity or expression. Another important aspect of school-based harassment can be found in GLSEN's 67-page report entitled "*The Harsh Realities of Transgender Youth*" (Greytak, Kosciw, & Martinez, 2009) which details the struggles that transgender students experience on a daily basis at school. The "harsh realities" are that transgender students face even higher levels of harassment and violence than lesbian, gay, and bisexual students. Increased victimization creates a domino effect of more missed school, lower grades, and feelings of isolation, which can increase the student's potential for experiencing mental health issues. In addition, transgender students have difficulty accessing traditionally gender-segregated areas, such as restrooms and locker rooms, which puts them at risk for both verbal and physical abuse. They can be in grave danger because they must choose which restroom or locker room to use — is it ok, or mandatory, to use the boy's restroom if you are wearing a dress? How do you decide which room is better to use, especially if you are openly transgender at school, or within your community? The verbal threats in class are one thing, but using an unsupervised restroom or locker room creates great stress for the transgender student. It's no surprise that many transgender students frequently cut class and school altogether because there are just too many complications to deal with.

Alternative Education

The Safe Schools Coalition has a wealth of information that is tailored to schools and those who are working to counter bullying and homophobia. Their website contains hundreds of bookmarks for LGBTQ organizations all around the country and in Canada.

Virginia Uribe's Project Ten concept was developed in the Los Angeles Public Schools during the 1980's. There are seven elements to the program, including one that helps librarians develop library collections for LGBTQ students. Project Ten is also a school-based support program that deals not only with general support and education of students, but also deals with issues of substance abuse, dropout and suicide prevention, creating a safe space for students in school. At the high school level there are trained facilitators who work with students on these issues.

Since 1985, the Harvey Milk High School in New York City has been serving at-risk LGBTQ students who were unable to complete their high school education in their neighborhood school due to their experience of extreme bullying. Starting in 2010, LGBTQ students will have access to the GLBTQ Online High School at http://www.glbtqonlinehigh school.com/. The virtual school should prove to be an extremely important option for all LGBTQ students, especially those who live in rural areas of the country where statistics indicate that conventional schools are more dangerous for LGBTQ students.

The Importance of Friends and Family

While some students come out as LGBTQ to loving and accepting friends and family, other students experience rejection, bullying or even violence. For LGBTQ youth who have — or fear having — a negative experience, coming out can be depressing, and may also put them at increased risk for suicidal behaviors due to feelings of self-loathing, and/or internalized homophobia.

The Family Acceptance Project at San Francisco State University at http://familypro ject.sfsu.edu/ has conducted the first ever study to assess the relationship between health problems in LGBTQ youth and their home environments. When parents or guardians respond negatively to their child's coming out, young gays or lesbians are more likely to attempt suicide, experience severe depression, or use drugs than students whose families accept the news that their child is gay. The Acceptance Project is finding that parents who try — even minimally — to accept their child's sexual orientation can dramatically improve a child's health outlook.

The incidence of suicide (and attempted suicide) among people of all ages who are struggling with accepting their own same-sex attractions or gender identity is a critical issue. One non-profit organization that can help is the Trevor Project, whose mission is to promote acceptance for LGBTQ youth and to aid in crisis and suicide prevention. The Trevor Project's website <http://www.thetrevorproject.org/home2.aspx> provides statistics from 2007 which state that LGBTQ youth who come from a rejecting family are up to nine times more likely to attempt suicide than their heterosexual peers. The Trevor Project receives 20,000 calls per year on their hotline for suicidal youth.

One example of an organization that is taking positive steps to counter the hateful speech that some LGBTQ students experience in their daily lives is a series of public service announcements produced by The Advertising Council. The campaign, called "Think Before You Speak" at http://www.thinkb4youspeak.com/, features the actress Hilary Duff and comedian Wanda Sykes in scenarios designed to address anti-gay language among teens. The Ad Council also hopes to reach adults, including school staff and parents, since their support of the ads' message can contribute to the success of schools' efforts to effect climate change.

Finding Support

One of the best ways to help students is to let them know that there are supportive adults working in their school or living within their community. Is there a PFLAG (Parents, Families and Friends of Lesbians and Gays) chapter nearby? PFLAG is a national organization with local chapters that works to promote the health and well-being of LGBTQ people, with a focus on supporting their families and friends. The PFLAG website at http://www.pflag.org/ has a wealth of free, easily downloadable booklets in English and Spanish that deal with a broad range of LGBTQ topics. Most PFLAG chapters meet monthly, so one suggestion for helping find support for students in your school would be to request that your local chapter meet in the library. Inviting supportive parents and school staff to attend a PFLAG meeting is one way to identify allies.

Extra-Curricular Clubs

Kevin Jennings, the founder of GLSEN, originated the idea of the GSA (Gay-Straight Alliance), which is an extracurricular club for secondary schools. Today, GLSEN has registered over 3,000 GSA's in cities and towns of all sizes. One way to support LGBTQ students is to start a Gay-Straight Alliance club in your school. It's best to find some students who are willing to request that your school start such a club. If you don't know any LGBTQ students, then perhaps you can find some students who have LGBTQ parents or family members, or simply have an interest in becoming allies for LGBTQ students and working to develop social awareness in their school. GLSEN's website has a downloadable document entitled *Dealing with Legal Matters Surrounding Sexual Orientation and Gender Identity* (National School Boards Association, et al., 2004) which explains in detail the legal reasons that GSA's should be allowed to form in public schools. The Federal Equal Access Act (20 U.S.C. §§ 4071–4074 2004) says that if a school permits non-curricular clubs to meet, like the Drama Club or Chess Club, a school has to treat a GSA the same way as any other club. In some communities, students have opted to call their group a "diversity" club or "social awareness" club to allow LGBTQ students and their allies to meet "under the radar." There are other ways to make your school a safe place for all students by working within the framework of community acceptance. If you are unsure about forming a GSA in your school, consider forming your own GLSEN chapter, thus providing you and other like-minded people with a framework to organize within your community.

Turning Off the Internal Censor[1]

Looking back, it's ironic that one of the most famous censorship cases of the 20th century involved two high schools in suburban Kansas and the teen lesbian romance, *Annie on My Mind* by Nancy Garden. Things appear to have improved in Olathe, Kansas, since the *Annie* trial in 1995. An online search of the library catalogs for Olathe public high schools revealed that in addition to *Annie on My Mind*, a few other fiction and nonfiction titles with the subject headings of gay and/or lesbian are in their collections.

There is no question that censorship cases like the *Annie on My Mind* trial have had a chilling effect on collection development in school libraries. Every school librarian struggles to justify purchasing materials that might draw criticism from parents or community members. It is definitely easier to play it safe and not buy anything that might be considered controversial in any way. However, if you do decide to purchase some LGBTQ books, make certain that you have a clear and well-defined collection development policy and procedures for dealing with a challenge. The idea that students will be "turned gay" by reading books with gay themes is not logical. The American Library Association's (ALA) *Library Bill of Rights* specifically mentions the necessity of including LGBTQ materials in every library collection, including school libraries. ALA has an Office for Intellectual Freedom and there are sample collection development policies and procedures that you can consult on their web page <http://www.ala.org/ala/aboutala/offices/oif/index.cfm>. If a book does get challenged, do not hesitate to contact the staff in the ALA Office for Intellectual Freedom. They have a lot of experience with all types of censorship cases and will help you react in a calm and logical manner.

Collection Development

Buying a copy of *Annie on My Mind* is a start, but today's publishing world has so much more to offer. An excellent overview of the development of the LGBTQ fiction genre is *The Heart Has Its Reasons: Young Adult Literature with Gay/Lesbian/Queer Content, 1969–2004*. Co-written by Christine Jenkins and Michael Cart, it is an outstanding history and analysis of teens and homosexuality in literature.

The American Library Association's divisions of YALSA (Young Adult Library Services Association) at http://www.ala.org/ala/mgrps/divs/yalsa/yalsa.cfm and ALSC (Association for Library Service to Children) at http://www.ala.org/ala/mgrps/divs/alsc/index.cfm publish many book lists each year. In fact, one of YALSA's newer book awards was named for openly gay high school librarian, Mike Printz. Mike was a librarian in Topeka, Kansas, and a lifelong advocate for young adult fiction that could be enjoyed by all types of readers. In 2000, YALSA inaugurated the Printz award, given to cutting edge books that deal with topics that were considered too mature for the Newbery Medal. Today, most ALA-endorsed lists include titles with LGBTQ content.

Most significantly, the Rainbow Project, a joint committee supported by the American Library Association Roundtables of SRRT (Social Responsibilities Round Table) and GLB-TRT (Gay Lesbian Bisexual and Transgendered Round Table), was started in 2007. The Rainbow Project <http://rainbowlist.wordpress.com/> compiles an annual bibliography, the Rainbow List, of quality fiction and nonfiction books with LGBTQ content for youth of all ages. This committee is seeking to increase the number — and improve the quality — of LGBTQ materials for young people ages birth to age eighteen.[2]

If you feel that your school district simply cannot purchase materials from the Rainbow List, you may be able to refer students, teachers and parents to your local public library. Many public librarians will be happy to request LGBTQ titles though interlibrary loan, even if they are unwilling or unable to purchase them for their own collections. Check the websites of public libraries in larger cities in your state for resource lists to share with your colleagues and principal. Sharing these bibliographies and reader's guides for LGBTQ materials with your colleagues and administration might help persuade them that your library will not be the first to purchase them in your area. It is most important that you communicate with your colleagues, administration and even the parents at your school about issues of censorship and developing an open atmosphere of intellectual freedom. A wonderful example of what someone can accomplish is that of Pat Scales, a librarian in Greenville, South Carolina (home to ultra-conservative Bob Jones University). Pat took the bull by the horns and taught her junior high students and their parents about banned books. By doing so, she was able to instill in them respect for intellectual freedom. Her book, *Teaching Banned books: 12 Guides for Young Readers,* is an excellent example of how we as librarians can minimize controversy by encouraging an open discussion of hot button issues as a part of the curriculum.

Don't hesitate to include your library's LGBTQ books when you do book talks with classes. Robert Trachtenberg's anthology of stories entitled, *When I Knew* (2005), is a great book to share with students who want to know about others who are just like them, or who want to know the answer to the question — "when I knew" I was LGBTQ.

In the *VOYA* article "Beyond Picket Fences — What Gay-Queer-LGBTQ Teens Want from the Library," New York Public librarian Darla Linville (2004) surveyed self-identified LGBTQ teens in the New York City area to see what they wanted. A little more than half of the teens said they had gone to the library to find answers about being gay, or questions about someone they know who is gay. Their most common interest was to read stories of real people, including information about transgender persons, and they wanted to read both fiction and non-fiction. Eighty-two percent of the youth surveyed were library users, but many felt that the library purposely hid LGBTQ materials. Eighty percent said they wanted to read books with gay characters and wanted their own branch library to have at least one LGBTQ book that didn't have to be requested through inter library loan. They also wanted to know that it was safe to ask for help finding information, and they wanted to know that gay people lived in every neighborhood, not just "over there."

While it's important to determine the needs of our lesbian and gay students, we must also make a concerted effort to provide resources to our bisexual and transgender students. Sometimes there are reviews for books or other resources with some bisexual or transgender content. This book's essays on bisexual and transgender issues cite a number of good resources. The Rainbow List and other YALSA book lists have recognized a few young adult books with bisexual and transgender content, but this is definitely a subject that is covered minimally.

Health Information

It is ironic that young people could access health information via the Internet but, because of federal funding restrictions, all public school libraries must have filtered internet access.[3] If you are not able to prevent any health-related websites from being filtered out, you should refer your students to the public library where they might have access to an unfiltered computer. It's only natural for young people to be curious about sexuality, and there are good, safe places where they can find helpful answers to their questions. One website, Go Ask Alice <http://www.goaskalice.columbia.edu>, administered by Columbia University's Health Services, has a sexuality page and offers users the opportunity to ask any question, anonymously.

Even though a very high percentage of North American private homes and many cell phones have 24/7 access to all types of databases and resources, the younger generation grew up after the AIDS Crisis. The high school class of 2012 was in born in 1991, which means that they don't necessarily understand the gravitas that HIV/AIDS brings to mind for those who lived through the AIDS crisis. Many youth assume that AIDS is a tolerable condition that can simply be controlled with pills, or that it is only a problem in the developing world. Even though the rate of teen pregnancy continues to rise, and young people mature at younger and younger ages, teachers are still restricted in many locales from discussing anything but abstinence.

There is a need for safer-sex information to be distributed widely and in multiple languages. If your school curriculum offers sex education, or your library has any materials, including videos, it is vitally important to check their publication dates. Like other health resources, HIV/AIDS information can become outdated and therefore, unsafe. Your county health department, or a number of organizations accessible via the internet, can provide timely information.

It is so important to help students find accurate information when they do research for their school assignments and for their own personal information needs. Students must also be taught how to evaluate websites and the information found on them.

Nurturing Change

Even though some students may be afraid to attend a GSA meeting, they may find solace in hearing about the club's meetings through their school's daily announcements over the intercom. Putting a rainbow sticker on your office or library door will indicate to the school community that the library is a safe place for LGBTQ students. The rainbow flag has become a universal symbol of gay pride, so even if your school is not a very accepting place, offering a rainbow sticker to other teachers who are accepting to put up in their classrooms can serve as a small symbol of safety to LGBTQ students. If you are successful in getting a GSA started in your school, find ways for the group to participate in the school as fully as they are willing to extend themselves. Try reaching out to other clubs to do joint activities, even marching in the school's annual Homecoming Parade. The GSA can put up a display of books and posters in the school and/or the library for a pride recognition day, week or month. If your school is not in session during the month of June when most pride celebrations are going on, then choose a time that works for your group. One idea would be to create a pride celebration honoring the anniversary of Harvey Milk's election to public office, or to commemorate his receiving the Presidential Medal of Freedom from President Obama. This would be an opportunity for students to learn more about the history of the LGBTQ struggle for equal rights. Participating in the National Day of Silence and Transgender Day of Remembrance can be very powerful and positive ways to recognize those who are silenced by bullying and violence. GLSEN's website at http://www.glsen.org/cgi-bin/iowa/all/home/index.html provides all of the resources you need for these days of recognition, including a comprehensive checklist of tasks to help make your activities successful.

One day of awareness that is somewhat popular, but should be given careful consideration before celebrating it in a school setting, is National Coming Out Day, which is actually celebrated internationally on October 11th. As teacher-librarians, we must always be cognizant of the dangers associated with a young person's coming out. There is no easy answer as to when a young person should come out. Some young people live in families where support for their LGBTQ status is clear and stable, but many may not. The risks of coming out depend on whether a student's parents will react negatively — or even violently — when their child discloses that they are LGBTQ. Students may get kicked out of their home. LGBTQ youth have a very difficult time living in homeless shelters or in foster or group home situations. The Safe Schools Coalition at http://www.safeschoolscoalition. org, identifies numerous programs across the country that help students who become homeless after disclosing their status to their parents or guardians. Chris Beam's memoir, *Transparent: Love, Family and Living the T with Transgender Teenagers* (2007) describes the experiences of transgender young people living in the Los Angeles area. Perhaps instead of celebrating National Coming Out Day, your school could recognize October as being LGBT History Month, an opportunity to bring attention to famous events and heroes without focusing on the concept of coming out.

One activity that causes angst for all high school students is the annual prom. Look for other groups in your school, or within the community, who might be willing to help organize an LGBTQ prom. PFLAG (Parents, Friends and Families of Lesbians and Gays) is a logical choice, since they are a group of mostly parents and grandparents, whose own children and grandchildren probably did not have the opportunity to participate in their own proms when they were high school students.

If you are teaching in a supportive school, consider screening both LGBTQ documentary and feature films, which is a fun activity as well as being educational. Many films are rated PG or PG-13, and are quite appropriate for discussion. If your school allows teachers to offer independent study courses to students, you might consider teaching an LGBTQ literature or history course using books, films or a combination of both. A syllabus for an independent study course on queer history and culture that is currently being offered at Lawrence (Kansas) High School can be provided by emailing Arla Jones at arlajones@gmail. com.

Another idea that can be very helpful to LGBTQ students is to find a way for them to spend their lunch time in the library. Start a book discussion group that allows students to eat their lunches while chatting about the books they have been reading. If you find that you have enough money in your budget to purchase multiple copies of a single title for the traditional book club format, that's great, but an inexpensive way to organize a book discussion group is to have the participants choose a book that they would like to read (preferably one with LGBTQ content), and then share their book with the whole group. Lunch time can be the loneliest time for any student, but LGBTQ students often skip lunch altogether because the lunch room can be a perfect setting for them to experience bullying and harassment.

Libraries Are the Answer

The role of the librarian has expanded over the years to include activities that never seemed possible before. We should not underestimate the important role that the library can play in any LGBTQ student's life. One example comes from 1998–1999 American Library Association President, Ann Symons (and former school media specialist in Juneau, Alaska), who felt that she had failed as a school librarian when she read the introduction to

Young, Gay and Proud. The author was one of her former students, Don Romesburg, who wrote in the book's introduction that he didn't find anything in his school library to define his sexuality while he was growing up. Symons' immediate response to Don's statement was to start building an LGBTQ collection in her school. When she became the ALA President, she made services to LGBTQ youth a central platform during her term as president.

Another public declaration of how important library services to LGBTQ youth can be came about ten years later, in 2007, when Alison Bechdel accepted the Stonewall Book Award's Israel Fishman Non-Fiction Award for her illustrated memoir, *Fun Home: A Family Tragicomic.* In her acceptance speech, Alison reminisced about the first time she went into the library and looked up the word *homosexual* and thought to herself, "that's me!" LGBTQ students are in our schools. It is up to us to ensure that they feel welcome in our libraries as well!

NOTES

1. For more on self-censorship, see "Censorship of Children's and Young Adult Books in Schools and Public Libraries" in Section Six.
2. The Gay and Lesbian Roundtable (GLBTRT) of the American Library Association has been recognizing exemplary adult fiction and non-fiction since 1971, and starting in 2010, the GLBTRT's Stonewall Book Awards will recognize titles that are appropriate for children and young adults.
3. For more information about filtering, see "LGBTIQ Teens — Plugged In and Unfiltered: How Internet Filtering Impairs Construction of Online Communities, Identity Formation, and Access to Health Information" in Section Six.

REFERENCES

American Library Association. (2009). Access to library resources and services regardless of sex, gender identity, gender expression, or sexual orientation: An interpretation of the library bill of rights. Retrieved from http://www.ala.org/ala/aboutala/offices/oif/statementspols/statementsif/interpretations/accesslibrary.cfm

American Library Association Gay, Lesbian, Bisexual, and Transgendered Round Table & Social Responsibilities Round Table. (2009). The rainbow project. Retrieved from http://rainbowlist.wordpress.com/

American Psychological Association Task Force on Appropriate Therapeutic Response to Sexual Orientation. (2009). *Appropriate therapeutic response to sexual orientation.* Retrieved from http://www.apa.org/pi/lgbc/publications/therapeutic-response.pdf

Beam, C. (2007). *Transparent: Love, family and living the T with transgender teenagers.* New York: Harcourt.

Bechdel, A. (2006). *Fun home: A family tragicomic.* Boston: Houghton Mifflin.

Cart, M., & Jenkins, C.A. (2006). *The heart has its reasons: Young adult literature with gay/lesbian/queer content, 1969–2004.* Lanham, MD: Scarecrow.

Curwood, J. S, Schliesman, M., & Horning, K. T. (2009). Fight for your right: Censorship, selection, and LGBTQ literature. *English Journal, 98*(4), 37–43.

Denizet-Lewis, B. (2009, September 23). Coming out in middle school. *New York Times Magazine.* Retrieved from http://www.nytimes.com/2009/09/27/magazine/27out-t.html

Diamond, L. M. (1998). Development of sexual orientation among adolescent and young adult women. *Developmental Psychology, 34*(5), 1085–1095. doi: 10.1037/0012-1649.34.5.1085.

Diaz, E.M., & Kosciw, J.G. (2009). *Shared differences: The experiences of lesbian, gay, bisexual and transgender students of color in our nation's schools.* Retrieved from http://www.glsen.org/binary-data/GLSEN_ATTACHMENTS/file/000/001/1332-1.pdf

Family Acceptance Project, Marian Wright Edelman Institute, San Francisco State University. (2009). Family Acceptance Project. Retrieved from http://familyproject.sfsu.edu/

Gay, Lesbian, and Straight Education Network (2009a). The experiences of lesbian, gay, bisexual and transgender middle school students (GLSEN Research Brief). Retrieved from http://www.glsen.org/binary-data/GLSEN_ATTACHMENTS/file/000/001/1475-1.pdf

Gay, Lesbian, and Straight Education Network . (2009b). Gay, Lesbian and Straight Education Network. Retrieved from http://www.glsen.org/cgi-bin/iowa/all/home/index.html

Gay, Lesbian, and Straight Education Network & Ad Council. (2009). Think before you speak. Don't say "That's So Gay." Retrieved from http://www.thinkb4youspeak.com/

GLBTQ Online High School. (2009). Retrieved from http://www.glbtqonlinehighschool.com/

Gough, C., & Greenblatt, E. (Eds.). (1990). *Gay and lesbian library service.* Jefferson, NC: McFarland.

Greytak, E. A., Kosciw, J. G., and Diaz, E.M. (2009). *Harsh realities: The experiences of transgender youth in our nation's schools.* Retrieved from http://www.glsen.org/binary-data/GLSEN_ATTACHMENTS/file/000/001/1375-1.pdf

Health Services at Columbia. (n.d). Go Ask Alice! Columbia University's health Q&A internet service. Retrieved from http://www.goaskalice.columbia.edu/

Jenkins, C.A. (2003, June). Annie on her mind: Edwards award-winner Nancy Garden's groundbreaking novel continues to make a compelling case for sexual tolerance. *School Library Journal, 49*(6), 48–52.

Kim, R., Sheridan, D., & Holcomb, S. (2009). *A report on the status of gay, lesbian, bisexual and transgender people in education: Stepping out of the closet, into the light.* Retrieved from http://www.nea.org/assets/docs/glbtstatus09.pdf

Kosciw, J., Greytak, E.A., Diaz, E.M. (2009). Who, what, where, when, and why: Demographic and ecological factors contributing to hostile school climate for lesbian, gay, bisexual, and transgender youth. *Journal of Youth and Adolescence, 38*(7), 976–988. doi: 10.1007/s10964-009-9412-1.

Linville, D. (2004, August). Beyond picket fences: What gay/queer/LGBTQ teens want from the library. *Voice of Youth Advocates, 27*(3), 183–186.

Martin, H.J., & Murdoch, J.R. (2007). *Serving lesbian, gay, bisexual, transgender, and questioning teens: A how-to-do-it manual for librarians.* New York: Neal-Schuman.

National School Boards Association, et al. (2004). Dealing with legal matters surrounding students' sexual orientation and gender identity. Retrieved from http://www.glsen.org/cgi-bin/iowa/all/news/record/1742.html

Pascoe, C.J. (2007). *Dude you're a fag: Masculinity and sexuality in high school.* Los Angeles: University of California Press.

Perrotti, J., & Westheimer, K. (2001). *When the drama club is not enough: Lessons from the Safe Schools Program for Gay and Lesbian Students.* Boston, MA: Beacon.

Romero, A.P., Rosky, C.J., Badgett, M.V.L., & Gates, G.J. (2008, January). Census snapshot: Kansas. Los Angeles: Williams Institute. Retrieved from: http://www.law.ucla.edu/Williamsinstitute/publications/KansasCensusSnapshot.pdf

Romesburg, D. (Ed.). (1995). *Young, gay and proud!* Los Angeles, CA: AlyCat.

Russell, S. T., Clarke, T. J., & Clary, J. (2009). Are teens "post-gay"? Contemporary adolescents' sexual identity labels. *Journal of Youth and Adolescence, 38*(7), 884–890. doi: 10.1007/s10964-008-9388-2.

Saad, L. (2008, June 18). Americans evenly divided on morality of homosexuality. Retrieved from http://www.gallup.com/poll/108115/americans-evenly-divided-morality-homosexuality.aspx

Savin-Williams, R. C., & Diamond, L .M. (2000, December). Sexual identity trajectories among sexual-minority youth: Gender comparisons. *Archives of Sexual Behavior, 29*(6), 607–627. doi: 10.1023/A:1002058505138.

Scales, P. (2001). *Teaching banned books: 12 guides for young readers.* Chicago: American Library Association.

Scales, P. (2007, December). Freedom for all? Focus on the first amendment. *School Library Journal, 53*(12), 54–57.

Trachtenberg, R. (Ed.). (2005). *When I knew.* New York: Regan.

Walling, D.R. (Ed.). (1996). *Open lives: Safe schools.* Bloomington, IN: Phi Delta Kappa Educational Foundation.

Whalen, D.L. (2006, January). Out and ignored: Why are so many school libraries reluctant to embrace gay teens? *School Library Journal, 52*(1), 46–51.

Whalen, D.L. (2009, February). A dirty little secret: Self-censorship is rampant and lethal (effects of self censorship among librarians). *School Library Journal, 55*(2), 26–31.

LGBTIQ Users and Collections in Academic Libraries

K. L. Clarke

College and university climates have improved for LGBTIQ students over time. To support LGBTIQ students, many campuses have worked to become more inclusive by offering the following options to their communities:

- Safe spaces: Designated and clearly identified campus zones that are non-judgmental places for LGBTIQ-identified people
- LGBTIQ undergraduate and graduate programs
- Campus departments that plan and offer LGBTIQ programming for the campus community
- LGBTIQ student associations, as well as gay/straight alliances
- LGBTIQ Greek organizations: Delta Lambda Phi <http://www.dlp.org/> is the only national LGBTIQ social fraternity, although several city and state LGBTIQ fraternities and sororities exist[1]
- Inclusive language in non-discrimination clauses on college and university websites and publications

As observed by the National Gay and Lesbian Task Force's 2003 report, the *Campus Climate for Gay, Lesbian, Bisexual and Transgender People: A National Perspective,* there is still much work to be done to ensure that LGBTIQ students (and by extension, staff, faculty and community members) attend educational institutions that are more open to all. Several questions in the report asked about college and university campuses regarding curriculum, classes, and the amount of visible resources pertinent to LGBTIQ issues and concerns. Forty-three percent of the respondents disagreed or strongly disagreed with the statement that the university adequately reflected the contributions of LGBTIQ people.

While it isn't the sole response to this persistent issue, strong, current LGBTIQ collections in academic libraries are one way colleges and universities can employ to improve the campus climate. College and university libraries help support the curriculum; the reason academic libraries exist is to support the teaching, learning and research of the institution. A strong academic library, with rich collections, supportive and helpful staff, and useful services, can help make a more inclusive campus for LGBTIQ students.

This essay outlines the work that is undertaken in academic libraries. Sections include researching LGBTIQ topics, the role of the LGBTIQ Studies subject liaison, and building an academic collection in LGBTIQ studies.

Researching LGBTIQ Topics

How do researchers locate information on LGBTIQ issues and concerns? They use search engines such as Google, article indexes, and library catalogs, and get recommendations from friends about the most helpful resources. Some users prefer to interact with a librarian to get research assistance; others do not need or want to have searching help. Often, there is reluctance on the part of students to disclose their topics if they are working on something they perceive as sensitive or stigmatic. LGBTIQ topics are an example of this. To ensure that help is available at the point of need, any system, either print or electronic, that allows the researcher to search and locate information without a librarian to mediate will help empower these students. One way to surmount this obstacle is to provide highly visible access to print or electronic lists of resources to students so that they are able to obtain guidance without asking for it.

Many LGBTIQ librarians have created printed and electronic pathfinders that offer access to key works and reputable and authoritative online information. Several academic libraries now use LibGuides, a Web 2.0 platform created by the company Springshare, which allow librarians to easily incorporate listings of titles that are augmented by embedded video, chat software, and RSS feeds (see examples of LGBTIQ LibGuides at Yale University at http://guides.socialsciencelibraries.yale.edu/content.php?pid=75228 and at the University of Wisconsin at http://researchguides.library.wisc.edu/content.php?pid=33052). An example of a more extensive, more traditional bibliography of books and media titles is the gay and lisbian Bibliography offered online by the University of Chicago at http://www.lib.uchicago.edu/e/su/gaylesb/glguide.html.

Although keyword or natural language searching is a useful way to discover information, and is a method that novice users are more likely to meet with success, subject searching is still a beneficial method of retrieving comprehensive results in article databases. The Library of Congress Subject Headings are continually evolving in terms of using contemporary and varied inclusive language regarding sexual and gender minorities,[2] but often users won't know how extensive this specialized vocabulary is, and consequently, may not receive the most extensive results. Further, in order to be most thorough while searching, researchers, of necessity, must use a bevy of terms, those currently in use and those used in the past: *homosexuals, homosexuality, lesbians, gays, gay men, gay males, same sex, sexual deviance*, etc., because the search terms describing this population vary between search tools.

The rise of the Internet in the 1990s has made searching for LGBTIQ topics less complex, in some ways. The new researcher can find more of what they want precisely because of the lack of subject indexing. Using one's own natural language will find results using Internet search engines (although the problem then becomes sorting through the overwhelming results retrieved).

Where Should LGBTIQ Materials Be Housed on Campus?

Because of the stigma[3] that may be associated with researching LGBTIQ subjects, some students try to rely solely on Internet sources in order to avoid having to visit the library and interact with library staff. At the same time, students often will be required by their professors to use books and journals that are only available in print in the library collection, and not online. Add in the difficulty of searching library catalogs, and the near-impossibility of browsing LGBTIQ books in a campus library (which are likely to be in several different call number areas due to the interdisciplinary nature of the field), it is easy to understand that some users might be frustrated and abandon using the library and its resources altogether.

In an effort to offer more access to these resources, some campuses make LGBTIQ materials available in more places than the academic library. In addition to the main library collections, collections may also be available at other locations on campus: the LGBTIQ cultural center/student organization or the programs office (for examples, see Duke University, New York University, Tufts University and the University of Wisconsin at Madison). The materials may not be solely scholarly; they may lean toward more leisure reading, a selection of periodicals, a select list of reference titles, and DVDs. For these alternative spaces, it's more important to have a safe and welcoming place for students to browse and use materials rather than having a comprehensive academic library collection. To assist with discoverability of items, some collections are searchable in an online catalog (see the University of California at Riverside at http://out.ucr.edu/programs/books.htm and Tuft's use of Web 2.0 using the LibraryThing platform at http://www.librarything.com/catalog/TuftsLGBT). The collections are often developed and maintained by donations, such as the University of Kentucky's collection at the LGBT Resource Center. Materials should be available wherever students are likely to encounter them. Students who require more scholarly materials are typically referred to the LGBTIQ librarian.

Academic Liaisons

The role of an academic librarian has changed dramatically over the past twenty years. No longer the subject bibliographer of old, tethered to a library office, buying books for the collection; academic librarians are now encouraged to leave their quiet towers to work with their communities of users: in academic departments, at the student union, on campus committees — wherever they happen to be. Being out and about on campus affords the LGBTIQ Studies Librarian opportunities she may have missed otherwise by staying close to the library.

An LGBTIQ Studies Librarian can keep faculty updated about recent library innovations by attending faculty department meetings in-person, or develop a wiki or blog to keep faculty abreast of newly purchased electronic journals. She can interview faculty to find out more about their teaching and research interests, and use this information to help build the library collection. She can also arrange to offer a walk-in reference service at the LGBTIQ student center, located at the campus student union, perhaps, a natural crossroads for students, to assist them with finding materials, in the flow of their daily student lives. She can ensure that fliers advertising LGBTIQ resources be kept in stock at the LGBTIQ Programming Office. Additionally, being a presence at LGBTIQ-related campus events, such as a guest lecture, a movie screening, or campus beautification event, can go a long way to start building relationships with users who may never actually visit a physical library.

An LGBTIQ Studies Librarian can also instruct students on how to use the library to find LGBTIQ information for their coursework. She can offer classroom sessions tailored to a particular course or hold individual research appointments for students working on intensive research. The librarian can demonstrate how to use the online library catalog to find books, access articles using an LGBTIQ specific database such as LGBT Life with Full Text (if it is available), as well as other subject-specific databases that index LGBTIQ journals, such as Academic Search Premier, Alternative Press Index, PsycInfo, and Sociological Abstracts, among others, using LGBTIQ search examples. She can suggest search strategies to maximize the number of relevant results. As mentioned above, electronic guides are useful to offer as well because they "provide instruction to LGBT students in a way that respects their need for independence and privacy" (McDowell, 2000). Because LGBTIQ information can be hard to locate, it's very helpful to have a librarian on staff to provide assistance in this subject area.

An LGBTIQ Studies Librarian can also, when in non-library situations, clearly identify herself as such, to help establish herself as an ally. Further, while it's not necessary to be out to do the work, it can often be a bonus to do so.[4] Coming out in service to students in order to deliberately identify one's self as queer can be quite beneficial, both for the LGBTIQ librarian and the student. When a student meets a librarian for a research appointment, if the librarian feels that is appropriate to disclose her sexual orientation during the course of the meeting time (if the situation merits it and it is safe to do so) that openness can help work to disrupt Audre Lorde's notion of the "mythical norm"—in this case, a not-straight librarian (1984, p. 116). "Openly gay instructors (or librarians) send a powerful message to their gay and straight students that college is a place where differences are respected, valued and celebrated rather than simply tolerated" (Russ, Simonds, & Hunt, 2002). For a college student struggling with defining her sexual identity, knowing and working with an out LGBTIQ librarian can be a powerful affirmation; the librarian can serve as a role-model and unofficial mentor to students questioning their sexual orientation.

LGBTIQ Collections in the Academic Library

U.S. colleges and universities are creating new programs or extending existing programs in the area of LGBTIQ Studies, and academic libraries need to keep with up the continuing and increasing demand of appropriate library resources for the new undergraduates, graduates, faculty and scholar-researchers in this field. According to John Younger's website, University LGBT/Queer Programs: Lesbian, Gay, Bisexual, Transgender, Transsexual, Queer Studies in the USA and Canada, which has been tracking LGBTIQ programs since 1997, currently in the United States:

- Six colleges or universities offer majors in LGBTIQ studies
- More than 30 offer LGBTIQ minors
- 11 offer certificates.

While only one graduate program offers a Ph.D. in LGBTIQ Studies (the California School of Professional Psychology, a division of Alliant International University) as of this writing, several others offer doctoral degrees in Gender Studies, Lesbian and Gay Studies, and Sexuality Studies. Most of these programs, both undergraduate and graduate, were established in the first decade of this century. As campus climates improve for LGBTIQ-identified persons and their allies, as more students graduate from LGBTIQ programs, and as libraries continue to normalize the discipline within the university by developing inclusive collections, the number of LGBTIQ programs is sure to rise.

Selecting LGBTIQ Materials

Choosing which LGBTIQ materials to select in order to build an inclusive academic library is based primarily on two factors: The appropriateness of a particular resource for the curriculum as well as the information needs of the user. Materials appropriate for a LGBTIQ collection for an academic audience must fit a range and a variety of purposes: the formats must include print and electronic journals and books and non-print media, including films, music and online article indexes and databases; the subjects must include works on the perennially hot topics used for speech assignments and research projects such as same-sex marriage, gay adoption, HIV/AIDS, and homophobia, the classic texts of the field, and work that supports the course content in the program. Resources also must be acquired that speak to non-academic and personal interests, such as coming out, health, intimate relationships, parenting, religion, and safer-sex practices. Additionally, materials must be purchased that reflect the research interests of scholars, faculty, and graduate students both within the discipline of LGBTIQ Studies and beyond.

The collection will certainly serve people who identify as LGBTIQ, but also those from allied disciplines, and those who are interested in learning about a group of people different from themselves. Librarians, in their selection of these materials, must develop a core collection of both current standard titles, and anticipate future topics of interest.

Although more research needs to be conducted on the information needs of a diverse LGBTIQ campus community (as there is no monolithic queer experience) there are still conclusions to be made from the studies that have been completed thus far on certain groups of sexual minorities that can inform and direct the selection decisions of librarians in charge of growing these collections at colleges and universities. Here is a summary of research findings regarding the information needs of LGBTIQ-identified information seekers:

- Regarding gays and lesbians, "Creelman and Harris, 1990; Joyce and Schrader, 1997; and Whitt, 1993 conclude[d] that the library was either the first or the second most important source of information to people during their coming out [process] and continued to be a vital ongoing information source to them (McDowell, 2000).
- Underneath the overarching issue of coming out, researchers found that the gay men (teens to college age) surveyed had three sub-issues: self-labeling, consequences for self-identifying as gay, and understanding their gay identity (Hamer, 2003).
- For transgendered persons early in the coming out process, their information needs included finding out more about transgender identity, and the experiences of other transgender individuals; learning about transsexualism and cross-dressing; and finding support networks; later in the process, their information needs included: workplace discrimination, hate crimes, and transgender activism (Taylor, 2002).

Adding LGBTIQ Materials Into the Academic Library Collection

Finding reviewing sources for LGBTIQ titles, in any format, for academic libraries, can be a time-consuming undertaking because it requires the use of several types of resources in order to be comprehensive: core book bibliographies, reviewing sources, approval plans, award-winning titles, and electronic mailing lists, among other methods. While some newer and bestselling titles will be featured in mainstream publications, selection doesn't have to be limited to this handful of titles. Indeed, it is necessary to be a bit more creative when seeking out LGBTIQ titles to add to the collection. Many of these resources are free and available on the Internet.

Core Books Bibliographies

Titles that appear on core books bibliographies are those that are deemed the most essential to the discipline. Core lists are especially useful if one is trying to create an LGBTIQ collection from scratch, if one is new to collecting in this area, or if one has a limited materials budget.

- Gay and Lesbian Studies: A Guide to the Collections of The New York Public Library <http://www.nypl.org/research/chss/grd/resguides/gay/index.html>. The librarians at the rich NYPL research collections have assembled a lengthy bibliography comprised of thirteen sections, from reference titles, biographies and memoirs, health, legal and social issues, history, religion and philosophy, and Internet sites. Lightly annotated. Undated.
- Guide to Gay and Lesbian Resources: A Classified Bibliography Based upon the Collections of the University of Chicago Library <http://www.lib.uchicago.edu/e/su/gaylesb/glguide.html>. This is the second bibliography created by University of Chicago librarians F. Conaway, S. Hierl, and S. Sutter and includes more than 4500 books and periodicals divided into 22 sections. Annotations are comprised of Library of Congress Subject Headings. Includes an index and local call numbers. Dated October 2002.
- The Men's Bibliography: A Comprehensive Bibliography of Writing on Men, Masculinities, Gender, and Sexualities <http://mensbiblio.xyonline.net/index.html>. The nineteenth edition of M. Flood's (Researcher at Victorian Australia Health Promotion Foundation) bibliography includes more than 22,000 books and articles, organized in more than 30 sections. Browseable and searchable. See especially these sections: Gay men, homophobia, and masculinity; Sexuality; Violence and responses to violence. No annotations. Last updated in 2008.
- TransBiblio: Transgender bibliography: A Bibliography of Print, Audio-visual, and Online Resources Pertaining to Transgendered Persons and Transgender Issues <http://www.library.illinois.edu/edx/womensstudies/transbiblio.html>. C. Ingold (Women and Gender Studies Librarian at the University of Illinois at Urbana-Champaign Library) created an extensive bibliography of 24 subjects, including audiovisual materials, intersexuality, and Internet sites. Extensively annotated. Local call numbers. Last updated in 2006.
- WSSLinks: Lesbian Studies <http://www.people.carleton.edu/~htompkin/ACRL/WSS Links.html>. H. Tompkins (Librarian at Carleton College) lists and annotates Internet sites about lesbianism. Last updated in 2008.

Reviewing sources

Lambda Book Report at http://www.lambdaliterary.org/lambda_book_report/lbr.html is a great source for reviews for LGBTIQ books, and bills itself as "the country's most established review of contemporary LGBT literature" (from site). In operation since 1987, the now quarterly *Book Report* is moving to an all-online format, and is indexed in the following databases: Academic Search Premier, Book Review Index, Contemporary Women's Issues,

Expanded Academic Index, GenderWatch, and LGBT Life. While it's possible to find reviews of books, periodicals or media, or at the least, lists, of new LGBTIQ materials in more mainstream periodicals such as *Publisher's Weekly*, it's a good practice to routinely scan other sources, too — online versions of national newspapers, such as the *New York Times, Los Angeles Times, Washington Post* and *Chicago Tribune*, feature reviews from the mid–1980s to the present. The reviews tend to be longer and more descriptive than in *Booklist, Choice, Kirkus Reviews*, and *Library Journal*. Additionally, don't overlook book review indexes, such as *Book Review Digest, Book Review Plus Online*, and *Women's Review of Books*. Lastly, *Alternative Press Index, Feminist Periodicals: A Quarterly of Women's Studies Resources*, and *Studies on Women and Gender Abstracts* also cover reviews. Popular magazines, such as the *Advocate* and *Curve*, cover reviews, as well.

For more scholarly items, a search for academic LGBTIQ journal titles that include book reviews in Ulrich's Periodicals Directory turned up eight relevant titles:[5]

- *Gay and Lesbian Issues and Psychology Review*. Established: 2005. Published by: Australian Psychological Society. Frequency: 3 times per year. Indexed in: GenderWatch and LGBT Life.
- *Gay & Lesbian Review Worldwide*. Established: 1994. Published by: Harvard Gay and Lesbian Review Inc. Frequency: Bimonthly. Indexed in: Academic Search Premier and GenderWatch.
- *GLQ: A Journal of Lesbian and Gay Studies*. Established: 1993. Published by: Duke University Press. Frequency: Quarterly. Indexed in: Academic Search Premier, Expanded Academic Index, and LGBT Life.
- *Journal of Bisexuality*. Established: 2000. Published by: Routledge. Frequency: Quarterly. Indexed in: Academic Search Premier and LGBT Life.
- *Journal of Gay and Lesbian Mental Health*. Established: 1988. Published by: Routledge. Frequency: Quarterly. Indexed in: Academic Search Premier, GenderWatch, and LGBT Life.
- *Journal of Homosexuality*. Established: 1974. Published by: Routledge. Frequency: Eight times per year. Indexed in: Academic Search Premier, Book Review Digest Plus, Expanded Academic Index, GenderWatch, and LGBT Life.
- *Journal of Lesbian Studies*. Established: 1997. Published by: Routledge. Frequency: Quarterly. Indexed in: Academic Search Premier, Feminist Periodicals, GenderWatch, and LGBT Life.
- *Law & Sexuality*. Established: 1991. Published by: Tulane University School of Law. Frequency: Annual. Indexed in: Academic OneFile and LGBT Life.

Additionally, academic journals often offer a "Books Received" list — listings of books that the journal has received, but hasn't reviewed.

Approval Plans

Approval plans have streamlined the selection-to-access pipeline tremendously. Librarians can search for books, as well as have their library profile developed by the approval plan vendor, in order to have appropriate books shipped and book slips emailed automatically to the librarian. Once the titles are selected and purchased, they arrive at the library, already marked and cataloged, and ready to be checked out. While many publishers that offer LGBTIQ books are included in approval plans,[6] many are not.[7] It is necessary for the

LGBTIQ librarian to seek out titles from small, alternative, or independent presses, since they may not be included in book vendors' plans, in an effort to be comprehensive, and to build a more diverse and less homogenous collection. Arrange to get on the publishers' mailing lists in order to find out about newly published titles for those presses that seem relevant.[8]

Award-Winning Titles

The Lambda Literary Awards, the American Library Association's Stonewall Awards, and the Publishing Triangle Awards are awarded annually and the finalists and winners are available on each award's site. These awards have a long history, making it easy to identify titles that may not been added to an LGBTIQ collection in the past.

- ALA's Stonewall Award (Established: 1971) <http://www.ala.org/ala/mgrps/rts/glbtrt/stonewall/stonewallbook.cfm>.
- Lambda Literary Awards (Established: 1989) <http://www.lambdaliterary.org/awards>.
- Publishing Triangle Awards (Established: 1989) <http://www.publishingtriangle.org/>.

Electronic Mailing Lists

Subscribing to electronic mailing lists, such as the Gay, Lesbian, Bisexual and Transgender Network or Trans-Academics, enables the librarian to interact with others about working in the discipline, as well as receiving messages about upcoming and newly available books, journals and websites.

- GAY-LIBN, Gay/Lesbian/Bisexual Librarians Network <http://www-lib.usc.edu/~trimmer/gay-libn.html>. Established in 1993, Gay-Libn is a "forum for gay, lesbian, and bisexual library workers and friends. As such, issues discussed may include outreach programs, social programs, finding out what other groups, individuals, and libraries are doing, and general library issues." From http://www.lib.umd.edu/MCK/LGBTForum.html.
- Gay, Lesbian, Bisexual, and Transgendered Round Table <http://www.ala.org/ala/mgrps/rts/glbtrt/socialnetworking/index.cfm>. Established in 2000, "the GLBTRT electronic mailing list is a forum for open communication among GLBTRT members and others" (from site).
- Qstudy-L <https://mailman.rice.edu/mailman/listinfo/qstudy-l>. "Qstudy-L is a forum for academic discussions pertaining to queer theory, an umbrella term encompassing lesbian, gay, bisexual, and transsexual/transgender studies. QSTUDY-L is also intended to promote networking and information sharing between teachers, researchers, librarians, and students. It also serves as a repository for syllabi, bibliographies, and other items of interest relating to Queer Studies." Archives primarily from 2000-present (from site).
- Trans-Academics <https://www.jiscmail.ac.uk/cgi-bin/webadmin?A0=trans-academic>. "Trans-Academics members are transgendered / transsexual academics, or other academics in any field involved in the study of transsexual and transgender people, culture, medicine, law and social welfare." Archives span 1998-present (from site).
- WMST-L <https://listserv.umd.edu/archives/wmst-l.html>. Established in 1998, "WMST-L is ... for teachers, researchers, librarians, and/or program administrators [, and focuses on] current research, teaching strategies, useful texts and films, online

resources, innovative courses, building Women's Studies majors, minors, and graduate programs, and other academic issues. [The list] welcomes announcements about relevant conferences, calls for papers, job opportunities, publications, and the like" (from site).

Bookstores: Online and Independent

Mainstream online bookstores, such as Amazon.com and Powells.com organize materials using a more commonsense categorization scheme than what one typically finds at an academic library, making them easier to navigate. When available, titles are linked to editorial and reader reviews, as well as reader comments, which allows for easier selection. Independent bookstores specializing in LGBTIQ materials, including True Colors (Minneapolis, formerly named Amazon) http://www.truecolorsbookstore.com/; Calamus (Boston) <http://www.calamusbooks.com/>; A Different Light (San Francisco) <http://www.adlbooks.com/>; and Giovanni's Room (Philadelphia) <http://www.giovannisroom.com/> are all excellent options. For a list of LGBTIQ bookstores, see Lori Lake's List of GLBT Bookstores< http://www.lorillake.com/bookstores.html>

Media

Aside from Amazon.com, the following vendors offer videos suitable for an LGBTIQ collection:

- Frameline <http://www.frameline.org>. This non-profit distributor of LGBTIQ films offers a catalog comprised of more than 200 titles. Established in 1977.
- Wolfe Video< http://www.wolfevideo.com/>. "Wolfe is the oldest and largest exclusive distributor of gay and lesbian films." Catalog includes more than 150 titles. Established in 1986 (from site).
- Women Make Movies <http://www.wmm.com>. Non-profit feminist distributor whose 500+ title catalog includes films on gender, sexual orientation, and sexuality. Established in 1972.

To find more video catalogs (and video reviewing sources), visit the Association of College and Research Libraries' Women's Studies Section site: Women's Studies Resources for Film and Video at http://libr.org/wss/committees/film-video.html. Although the focus is on videos related to women's studies, the list also includes LGBTIQ-friendly vendors.

And Some Additional Ideas

- Patron recommendations: Encourage faculty, staff and students to share their interests in new and interesting topics. Make it easy for them to offer their suggestions by having a contact email available from LGBTIQ library pages.
- Blogs and wikis and social networking: Use blogs, wikis and social networking to find out what's going on in the LGBTIQ world. Librarians can discover new authors, titles, and themes, read reviews, and keep abreast of current events.
- The GLBT Bookshelf <http://bookworld.editme.com/Home>. This wiki's focus is on fiction, a genre that academic libraries do not often purchase enough of for LGBTIQ users. The site includes a bookstore, publishers' lists, snippets of books, and reviews.

- Gay, Lesbian, Bisexual, Transgender Roundtable Blog <http://blogs.ala.org/glbtrt.php>. Keep up with LGBTIQ news from the American Library Association committee.
- Facebook: Gay Librarians <http://www.facebook.com/group.php?gid=2364945898>. Network with nearly 200 librarians and library students.

Challenges of LGBTIQ collection-building

As one considers the selection work of an LGBTIQ librarian, inevitably some difficult questions will arise:

- Because of the interdisciplinary nature of LGBTIQ Studies, is it solely the responsibility of the LGBTIQ selector to make purchasing decisions?
- What's the best way to manage potential purchase overlaps with other subject librarians in other disciplines: sociology, politics, psychology, and women's studies?
- How can LGBTIQ librarians do more (purchase materials) with less funding?

The answer to the question, "Who owns LGBTIQ Studies?" is a bit murky, due to the interdisciplinary nature of the field (and for practical purposes here, interdisciplinary is defined "as work that is carried out utilizing insights and techniques from one or more disciplinary sources" [Wilson & Edelman, 1996]). LGBTIQ librarians primarily select items that can be cataloged in the HQ71-HQ77.95 range, according to the Library of Congress classification system. Outside of this range (and if the budget allows), the LGBTIQ librarian can purchase materials depending on the research activities of the students and faculty of the LGBTIQ department.

Budgets, or the lack thereof, are a challenge that LGBTIQ librarians can expect to encounter in their work. Typically, the funding for LGBTIQ collections, which include print and electronic books, journals, magazines and newspapers; audio-visual media; and article indexes and databases, is rather small compared to other disciplines because the allocation is usually based on the number of students enrolled in the department — which is tiny, compared to say, English Literature, or Psychology, or other historically large academic departments. What complicates matters, and what makes allocating budgets so problematic when the amount of the budget is based solely on the number of enrolled students, is that this system does not account for the interdisciplinary aspect of the subject. Sure, students and faculty in designated LGBTIQ departments use the materials purchased with these funds, but also students, staff and faculty in allied studies, such as Women's Studies and Gender studies, as well as those in Education, History, Medicine, Psychology, and Sociology also use the LGBTIQ collection. It's hard to capture this information to use it for lobbying for a larger piece of the budget. Allocating budgets for LGBTIQ collections using this method will always be an underestimation of the population who ultimately use it. Alternative methods such as bibliometrics (Wilson & Edelman, 1996), circulation data (Kao, Chang, & Lin, 2003) and the costs of the books purchased (Williams and Schmidt, 2008) are a few options where the number of enrolled students is not a variable that needs to be considered.

Collaborative collection development can be the solution to many of the questions posed above. Library work is collegial in nature; and selecting and purchasing materials is no different. In some cases, one librarian may be designated to select and purchase all the LGBTIQ materials, and have a dedicated budget for those materials, but there may not be a librarian so named in every educational institution; instead, there is rather an understanding among several librarians to consciously buy materials in LGBTIQ Studies to ensure that there are no gaps in coverage. Whether a sole librarian works with the LGBTIQ budget or in conjunction with related subject librarians and their budgets, collaborative collection development can work if all librarians involved possess the broad understanding that everyone can have a hand in selecting and purchasing relevant materials. For larger, more expensive purchases, selectors can join together to buy materials, or, if the LGBTIQ librarian's budget is running low, he or she can ask a colleague to purchase the title instead. The keys to successful collaborative collection development hinges on good communication, a descriptive collection development policy, and routine checking to monitor the collection.

Further, since the LGBTIQ materials selected and purchased for an academic library are intended to support the teaching and learning of students, faculty and staff at a college or university, there are large swaths of materials that are unlikely to be part of the circulating collection, since the content is not part of the curriculum, such as sex manuals and self-help books. Partnering with public libraries to ensure that users can get access to those materials that are outside of the collection development scope is a good practice.

In order to stretch collection dollars further, college and universities have increasingly over time teamed up to purchase and share electronic materials in consortia (examples of library consortia include OHIOLink, from Ohio; VIVA, from Virginia, and TexShare, from Texas). Building academic collections using this method enables groups of libraries to band together in order to get the resources they need for the best price — and at a greater discount than they would have been able to command without consortial membership. Consortial purchasing has made very pricey full-text aggregator databases and electronic book packages more affordable for the member librarians to buy. For the LGBTIQ librarian, consortial purchasing is quite beneficial: while her small budget would not cover the cost of an expensive set of electronic journals, her library organization's membership in the consortia that made the big deal to obtain the titles for all member libraries will enable her community of users to access them in her library.

Existing research tells us how essential libraries are to the coming out process of LGBTIQ people; we also know that those who identify as LGBTIQ think that it's important to have a library on campus that reflects their concerns and interests, both academic and personal. Yet, the literature is curiously silent on many vital issues:

- Twice- or thrice-blessed LGBTIQ-identified library users: How are LGBTIQs of color, differently-abled, or other "non-traditional" patrons served?
- What are the core journals in LGBTIQ studies? By what measure should this be determined?
- Is censorship of LGBTIQ materials a problem in college and university libraries?
- How do LGBTIQ users employ electronic resources in their work?
- What are the key databases that graduate students use in their dissertations in the field of LGBTIQ Studies?

In order for college and university libraries to continue on the path towards true inclusion for the whole community, solid LGBTIQ collections must be a priority. Answering these initial research questions can help start this vital conversation.

Notes

1. Please see the List of LGBT and LGBT-friendly fraternities and sororities at http://en.wikipedia. org/wiki/List_of_LGBT_and_LGBT-friendly_fraternities_and_sororities/.

2. For information on this topic, please see the essay on "The Treatment of LGBTIQ Concepts in the Library of Congress Subject Headings" in Section Five.

3. Please see Curry's 2005 article which describes some of the reference interactions between a proxy patron and several librarians who seemed uncomfortable and/or unhelpful with the topic she asked for: reference assistance about gay/straight alliances at schools.

4. For more information on this topic, please see the essay on "LGBTIQ Librarians and Workplace Issues" in Section Seven.

5. This author located periodical titles in Ulrich's Periodicals Directory by searching for Homosexuality as a subject, then focusing the results to those titles currently active, refereed, academic or scholarly in nature, and including book reviews. Indexes were listed only if they were one of the following: a general index, such as Academic Search Premier or Expanded Academic Index, and an LGBTIQ or related subject-specific index, such as Contemporary Women's Issues, Feminist Periodicals, GenderWatch or LGBT Life.

6. On the Lambda Literary site <http://lambdaliterary.org/resources/find_a_publisher.html>, the publishers list is compiled from user submitted suggestions, out of 61 presses that cover LGBTIQ content, 49 are included in the YBP Library Services approval plan. Examples are: Alyson, Firebrand Books, New Victoria, Spinsters Ink, and Wildcat Press.

7. This author searched for lesbian interest and gay male interest small presses in YBP Library Services' Gobi search, using titles from the 2009–2010 International Directory of Little Magazines & Small Presses. For lesbian-interest small presses, 34 of 38 are not included in YBP; for gay male-interest small presses, 60 of 62 are not included. Inquire whether the small presses of interest can be added to an existing approval plan: it's often possible to do so.

8. See a list of LGBTIQ publishers at Lori L. Lakes' GLBT Publishing Links page: http://www.loril-lake.com/glbt_pub.html

References

Curry, A. (2005). If I ask, will they answer? Evaluating public library reference service to gay and lesbian youth. *Reference and User Services Quarterly, 45*(1), 65–75.

Creelman, J. A. E., & Harris, R. M. (1990). Coming out: The information needs of lesbians. *Collection Building, 10*(3/4), 37–41. doi: 10.1108/eb023281.

Hamer, J. S. (2003). Coming-out: Gay males' information seeking. *School Libraries Worldwide, 9*(2), 73–89.

Joyce, S. L., & Schrader, A. M. (1997). Hidden perceptions: Edmonton gay males and the Edmonton Public Library. *Canadian Journal of Information and Library Science, 22*, 19–37.

Kao, S. C., Chang, H. C., & Lin, C. H. (2003, January). Decision support for the academic library acquisition budget allocation via circulation database mining. *Information Processing & Management, 39*(1), 133–148.

Kinner, L. & Crosetto, A. (2009). Balancing act for the future: How the academic library engages in collection development at the local and consortial levels. *Journal of Library Administration, 49*(4), 419–437.

Lorde, A. (1984). Age, race, class, and sex: Women redefining difference. In *Sister outsider: Essays and speeches* (pp. 114–123). Berkeley: Crossing.

McDowell, S. (2000). Library instruction for lesbian, gay, bisexual, and transgendered college students. In Jacobson, T. E., & Williams, H. C. (Eds.), *Teaching the new library to today's users: Reaching international, minority, senior citizens, gay/lesbian, first generation, at-risk, graduate and returning students, and distance learners* (pp. 71–86). New York: Neal-Schuman.

Rankin, S. R. (2003). Campus climate for gay, lesbian, and transgender people: A national perspective. New York: Policy Institute of the National Gay and Lesbian Task Force. Retrieved from http://www.thetaskforce.org/downloads/reports/reports/CampusClimate.pdf

Russ, T. S., Simonds, S. J., & Hunt, S. K. (2002, July). Coming out in the classroom ... An occupational hazard? The influence of sexual orientation on teacher credibility and perceived student learning. *Communication Education, 51*(3), 311–324.

Taylor, J. K. (2002). Targeting the information needs of transgender individuals. *Current Studies in Librarianship, 26*(1/2), 85–109.

Whitt, Alisa. (1993). The information needs of lesbians. *Library Information Science Research, 15*, 275–288.

Williams, V. K., & Schmidt, J. (2008, January). Determining the average cost of a book for allocation formulas. *Library Resources & Technical Services, 52*(1), 60–70.

Wilson, M. C., & Edelman, H. (1996, May). Collection development in an interdisciplinary context. *Journal of Academic Librarianship, 22*, 195–200.

Younger, J. G. (2009, November 15). University LGBT/Queer programs: Lesbian, gay, bisexual, transgender, transsexual queer studies in the USA and Canada plus sibling societies & study-abroad programs. Retrieved from http://people.ku.edu/~jyounger/lgbtqprogs.html

Queering Libraries and Classrooms: Strategies to Build Inclusive Collections and Services[1] for Sexual Minority and Gender Variant Youth

Alvin M. Schrader and *Kristopher Wells*

Books and other library resources should be provided for the interest, information, and enlightenment of all people of the community the library serves.
  –American Library Association, *Library Bill of Rights* (1996)

It is the responsibility of libraries to guarantee and facilitate access to all expressions of knowledge and intellectual activity, including those, which some elements of society may consider to be unconventional, unpopular or unacceptable.
  –Canadian Library Association, *Statement on Intellectual Freedom* (1985)

Not all minorities are visible. In increasingly multicultural and pluralistic societies such as the United States and Canada, the legal and ethical right of sexual minority and gender variant youth to be visible, have their voices heard, and to be able to access safe, caring, and inclusive learning environments is challenged every day (Egale Canada, 2009; Gay, Lesbian, and Straight Education Network, 2009). Name-calling, homophobic bullying, intimidation, explicit and implicit censorship, and other forms of aggression directed against sexual minority, gender variant, and questioning youth work in insidious ways and are deeply entrenched systemic concerns in our schools, libraries, and communities.

As service professionals we should ask: Do librarians and teachers believe that all young people deserve the dignity, respect, and safety in the library and in the classroom that will help them realize their full potential to become engaged, productive citizens in adulthood? Do educational and library communities recognize and support the core values of their own professions such as the importance of embracing diversity, inclusivity, understanding, acceptance, mutual respect, and the right to a safe and affirming learning environment? Contemporary research tells us that students cannot learn if they live in perpetual fear of harassment, bullying, and alienation. Ultimately, they cannot develop healthy and happy personal identities and relationships if they feel vulnerable and unsafe in their schools, libraries, families, and communities.

With this awareness, we ask, what is the responsibility of school and public librarians to assume a key role in examining diversity and inclusivity issues that affect today's youth? In particular, what is the responsibility of librarians and educators to improve the institutional social climate and everyday educational experiences of sexual minority, gender variant, and questioning youth and for children from same-gender parented families? How can we find common ground, so that the unbearable pain of rejection, silence, isolation, and alienation experienced on a daily basis by these youth will be eradicated? This question is especially poignant for sexual minority, gender variant, and questioning youth and families in rural communities who frequently do not have access to traditional sources of community-based support, outreach, and information. Will librarians be there for *every* child who walks into the library?

This essay weaves together research and policy perspectives for social justice advocacy and inclusive practice, which are grounded in the core values and ethical principles common to both K–12 teaching and to school and public librarianship. We articulate the need for an ethos of social responsibility guided by key democratic principles such as intellectual freedom in schools and libraries; non-discrimination; equality; and safe, caring, and inclusive learning environments. This ethos is manifested in several guiding principles, which include the promotion of inclusive and respectful learning communities for all young people and their families; respect for their inherent dignity and rights; acceptance and endorsement of the infinitely wide range of diversity in students' characteristics and needs; acknowledgment of adolescence as a critical period in healthy identity formation; support for equal opportunities for the learning achievement of all to the best of their abilities; and stewardship for a democratic culture of peace, non-violence, and social justice. Moreover, these values and principles are interwoven so tightly that any one of them — inclusivity, dignity, diversity, equity, social responsibility, and stewardship — endures only if all of them endure. In essence, each principle signifies the presence of the others, and the absence of one breaks the bonds of integrity and trust in our key civic institutions.

Recent research indicates that teachers and school officials are largely unaware of resources available in their communities to support sexual minority, gender variant, and questioning students; are unfamiliar with relevant policies and legislation; and do not know how or feel confident enough to support these students (Kittelberg, 2006). To address these critical absences, this essay identifies key strategies for school and public librarians, educators, parents, and students in developing a critical literacy and knowledge base of sexual minority and gender variant issues and concerns. These strategies are intended to create schools and libraries as welcoming spaces for all students, regardless of their actual or perceived differences. In pluralist democracies, we firmly believe that equal access to all civil institutions by all citizens is non-negotiable. The heteronormative status quo is no longer an option as our silence signals consent in the very act of discrimination and intolerance.

We believe, as do the other authors in this book, that school and public librarians are an often underrepresented and underserved segment of the educational community. When supported they can become critical catalysts in the building of inclusive learning communities. When empowered, librarians can and *do* change lives.

Core Values and Ethical Responsibilities for Social Justice

New understandings and representations of sexual minority and gender variant persons and their communities have emerged over the last fifty years as one of the most challenging arenas of cultural dissonance and controversy in North America. Fortunately, critical developments in culture, politics, science, ethics, and law have served as key catalysts to liberate our learning institutions from shallow rhetoric, stereotypical beliefs, and discriminatory practices.

Clearly, access to multiple voices and differing perspectives through school curricula, books, and other materials in classrooms and libraries is in the public interest. It is equally clear that the silencing of sexual minority voices through persistently tolerated bullying and name-calling is not in the public interest — a position that has found voice in courts throughout North America. For example, as a result of recent cases heard before the Supreme Court of Canada, discriminatory practices have been pushed back in schools and school libraries (see Chamberlain v. Surrey School District No. 36, 2002) and in the federal customs agency (see Little Sisters Book and Art Emporium v. Canada [Minister of Justice], 2000). Importantly, in the Chamberlain case the Supreme Court sent a clear message to educators, parents, and communities when it stated:

> Learning about tolerance is therefore learning that other people's entitlement to respect from us does not depend on whether their views accord with our own. Children cannot learn this unless they are exposed to views that differ from those they are taught at home.... Tolerance is always age appropriate [para. 66, 69].

Such declarations are indicative of the broad legislative and ethical framework within which all educational personnel are required to act professionally — to move beyond tolerance and the "putting up with difference." For public librarians, this legislative and ethical framework is less explicit, mandated under various state and provincial legislation, and embraced within a less regulated professional environment than the public school system. Nevertheless, the larger constitutional frameworks of the United States *Bill of Rights* and the *Canadian Charter of Rights and Freedoms* and human rights legislation apply to the professional conduct of all public librarians and speak to the value of diversity and difference as a significant asset in our society that should be nurtured and supported.

Concomitantly, there is also an international context, which stipulates that the provision of school and public library services must occur without prejudice and discrimination. The international framework starts with the *Universal Declaration of Human Rights* (1948) promulgated by the United Nations and is affirmed in its *Convention on the Rights of the Child* (1989) along with other international covenants and agreements. Grounded in these ethical imperatives, the International Federation of Library Associations and Institutions (IFLA) and UNESCO have crafted policy frameworks more specific to librarianship (IFLA, 2009), which include:

- *IFLA/UNESCO Public Library Manifesto* (1994);
- *Statement on Libraries and Intellectual Freedom* (1999);
- *IFLA/UNESCO School Library Manifesto* (2000), endorsed by the International Association of School Librarianship in 2002 (See Clyde, 2003);
- *IFLA/UNESCO School Library Guidelines* (2002);
- *Glasgow Declaration on Libraries, Information Services and Intellectual Freedom* (2002), which explicitly prohibits discrimination on the basis of "sexual preference";
- *IFLA Internet Manifesto* (2002), which also explicitly mentions sexual orientation; and
- *IFLA Position on Internet Governance* (2005).

Even when sexual orientation and gender identity are not specifically identified, all of these international documents enjoin librarians to provide inclusive services to "all people" and to avoid discriminatory censorship practices. Correspondingly, international and national association documents on codes of ethics echo these principles of inclusivity and respect.

This is similarly true of the policy framework developed by the American Library Association (ALA) for supporting inclusivity and diversity in library collections and services, as reflected in the *Code of Ethics* (1938/2008), the *Library Bill of Rights* (1948/1996) and its many "statements of interpretation" as well as other Association declarations (American Library Association, 2009), including:

- *Labels and Rating Systems* (1951/2009);
- *Challenged Materials* (1971/2009);
- *Free Access to Libraries for Minors* (1972/2008);
- *Evaluating Library Collections* (1973/2008);
- *Expurgation of Library Materials* (1973/2008);
- *Restricted Access to Library Materials* (1973/2009);
- *Diversity in Collection Development* (1982/2008);
- *Library-Initiated Programs as a Resource* (1982/2000);
- *Access to Resources and Services in the School Library Media Program* (1986/2008);
- *Access for Children and Young Adults to Nonprint Materials* (1989/2004);
- *The Universal Right to Free Expression* (1991);
- *Exhibit Spaces and Bulletin Boards* (1991/2004);
- *Meeting Rooms* (1991);
- *Access to Library Resources and Services Regardless of Sex, Gender Identity, Gender Expression, or Sexual Orientation* (1993/2008);
- *Access to Digital Information, Services, and Networks* (1996/2009);
- *Libraries: An American Value* (1999);
- *Privacy* (2002);
- *Core Values of Librarianship* (2004);
- *Minors and Internet Interactivity* (2009); and
- *Resolution on Threats to Library Materials Related to Sex, Gender Identity, or Sexual Orientation* (2005), which was adopted to counter legislative proposals in the United States that would restrict or prohibit access to materials related to sexual orientation within publicly-funded libraries.

In addition, the American Library Association is home to the Gay, Lesbian, Bisexual, and Transgendered Round Table (GLBTRT), originally founded in 1970 as the Task Force on Gay Liberation and considered to be the first such professional organization in the world. Its many advocacy activities include annual book awards, programs at ALA annual conferences, a quarterly newsletter, a clearinghouse of resources, and a website of policies and information of special interest to sexual minority and gender variant persons (American Library Association. Gay, Lesbian, Bisexual, and Transgendered Round Table, 2002).[2]

Also of special note is the Standing Committee on Lesbian and Gay Issues established in 1985 by the American Association of Law Libraries (AALL). The Standing Committee's activities include: educational programs at AALL annual conferences on topics such as hate crimes, sexual minority legal library collection development, the military, international human rights, transgender law, and queer kids' legal needs (American Association of Law Libraries. Standing Committee on Lesbian and Gay Issues, 2008). They also include publications such as the 2006 annotated bibliography *Sexual Orientation and the Law: A Research Bibliography* (with updates posted online at http://www.lgbtbib.org); anti-discrimination resolution proposals; and encouragement of the inclusion of sexual orientation in the Association's anti-discrimination policy. For example, in 1987, AALL adopted a specific *Sexual Orientation Resolution* <http://www.aallnet.org/sis/social_responsibilities.asp>.

Fundamental principles of equality and equity are also reflected in the policy framework of the Canadian Library Association (CLA), which emphasizes the importance of inclusivity and diversity in library collections and services, which is most notably affirmed in its *Statement on Intellectual Freedom* (1974/1985) as well as in the Association's other "position statements" (Canadian Library Association, 2008), including:

- *Code of Ethics* (1976);
- *Young Adult Services in Public Libraries* (1987);
- *Information and Telecommunication Access Principles* (1994);
- *Internet Access* (1997/2000);
- *Effective School Library Programs in Canada* (2000);
- *Diversity and Inclusion* (2008); and
- *Students' Bill of Information Rights / Charte des droits de l'élève à l'ère de l'information*, endorsed by the Canadian Association for School Libraries (1995), which states that: We believe that all students should have the right to:
  - access a wide range of print, non-print and electronic learning resources at an appropriate level;
  - explore materials expressing a variety of opinions and perspectives; and
  - freely choose reading, viewing and listening materials for recreational and study purposes.

The real test of the strength of these principles, and the bond of trust between students and professionals, lies in how effectively marginalized groups are served by librarians and teachers. Or put another way, this policy framework is only as good as the librarians who put it into practice and actively reach out to support sexual minority, gender variant, and questioning youth and their families.

Research on the Experiences of Sexual Minority and Gender Variant Youth

Contemporary research and personal testimonies paint a disturbing picture of hostile school climates, denial, and indifference among those entrusted with the emotional well-being and physical safety of young people in the United States and Canada (Egale Canada, 2009; GLSEN, 2009; Grace & Wells, 2005, 2007, & 2009; Kosciw, Diaz, Colic, & Goldin, 2005; Kosciw, Diaz, & Greytak, 2008; Wells, 2006 & 2008a). In a 2007 survey exploring the experiences of sexual minority and gender variant students in the United States, the report found that nearly 86 percent of sexual minority and gender variant students surveyed were verbally harassed at school within the previous year, 44 percent were physically harassed, and 22 percent were physically assaulted (Kosciw, Diaz, & Greytak, 2008). Almost 61 percent felt unsafe at school and one out of three students skipped a class or a day of school due to concerns for their safety. Youth in rural and impoverished areas faced especially hostile school environments, greater victimization, higher rates of bullying, and increased harassment.

Middle school students encounter even harsher school climates, with 91 percent reporting verbal harassment in school in the previous year because of their sexual orientation or gender expression, 59 percent experiencing physical harassment, and 39 percent being physically assaulted (GLSEN, 2009). Half of the students surveyed reported missing at least one day of school in the previous month because they felt unsafe.

Similar patterns characterize the Canadian educational system. Indeed, the first national study of sexual minority and gender variant students in Canada revealed that more than two-thirds of responding students in grades 8 through 12 said they felt unsafe in their schools, and more than one-third skipped classes because of safety concerns (Egale Canada, 2009). Over half had been verbally harassed, a rate twice as high as for heterosexual students. Almost half reported malicious rumors had been spread about them on the Internet or through text messages, and 25 percent had been victims of physical threats because of their sexuality.

Study after study demonstrates that sexual minority and gender variant youth are more likely than their heterosexual peers to feel alienated, attempt suicide, drop out of school, abuse alcohol and other drugs, engage in prostitution, run away from home, become teen parents, or be rejected by their parents and forced out of the family home (California Safe Schools Coalition, 4-H Center for Youth Development, & University of California, Davis, 2004; Saewyc, Poon, Wang, Homma, Smith, & The McCreary Centre Society, 2007; Suicide Prevention Resource Center, 2008).

The evidence is overwhelming. The time is past when society can ignore the pressing health needs, safety concerns, and social alienation of sexual minority, gender variant, and questioning youth and still believe that these young people will grow up unaffected, invisible, and passive in the face of discrimination, abuse, and violence. For many of these youth, invisibility and silence are no longer an option they are willing to endure. These youth want to live proud, open, visible, and confident lives based upon who they are, rather than upon who their schools and communities tell them they should be. How can librarians assist these youth in finding the support to develop pride in their identity and a sense of connectedness to their school and larger community?

Challenging Neutrality, Silence, and Censorship

Aware of both pervasive institutional silence and the broad national and international policy frameworks already in place, school and public librarians should revisit their collections and assess the services being provided for and about the sexual minority and gender variant communities they serve. Relevant resources for young people are significantly underrepresented in school and public library collections, and these absences are even more acute in conservative and rural communities. Reference services, access and search terminologies, library collection holdings, and Internet access all serve as sources of systemic concern in both rural and urban school and public libraries. When these concerns are coupled with the gradual disappearance of qualified teacher librarians from schools, it becomes increasingly difficult to develop inclusive resources and to effect positive social and institutional change (Canadian Coalition for School Libraries, 2004; Canadian Library Association, 2000; Haycock, 2003; National Coalition, 2002).

Among the most troubling concerns is the quality of school and public library reference services provided to sexual minority and gender variant students. In a "mystery shopper" type of unobtrusive reference research, a female proxy appearing to be a teenager asked for information in twenty public libraries in the greater Vancouver, British Columbia, area about several needs including principally how to start a gay-straight student alliance (Curry, 2005). "Definite censure" was communicated by public librarians in three out of the twenty interactions, and the proxy student indicated she would not return to them or to another nine locations. The study identified several critical areas for improvement: library and information studies curricula; professional self-assessment by practicing librarians of their attitudes towards sexual minority and gender variant youth; awareness of sexual minority and gender variant youth concerns and their information needs; and familiarity with local resource centers and other information sources for support and referral. These areas of concern echo conclusions drawn by Carmichael and Shontz a decade earlier: formal education and professional values were not ideologically cohesive on women's issues and on sexual minorities or on the relationship between social responsibilities and professionalism (Carmichael & Shontz, 1996).

Given that attitudes towards library collections and services to sexual minority and gender variant persons and families range from cold indifference to outright antagonism, it should come as little surprise to learn that sexual minority and gender variant publications are significantly underrepresented in both school and public library collections in Canada and the United States, and that subject access to them is problematic and deeply ideological.[3]

At the same time, one of the earlier Gay, Lesbian, and Straight Education Network (GLSEN) national school climate surveys indicated that nearly 50 percent of high school students had no access to gay-related resources in their school libraries (Kosciw, 2004). At the same time, many young people attest to library visits to find answers about their identity, such as Jewelle Gomez, who recounts her early teen ventures in these eloquent reminiscences in a recent documentary film about sexual minority and gender variant youth experiences of public libraries in San Francisco: "I thought I'd find myself in the library, I thought I'd find myself in the word" (Barnes, 2004; Linville, 2004).

Other important factors that should not be discounted when it comes to selection and censorship involve a librarian's fear of controversy, criticism, and censure. In a national survey of censorship pressures on Canadian public libraries during 1985–1987, 5 percent of the more than 500 titles challenged were because the items "promoted homosexuality" (Schrader, 1995 & 1997). A number of survey respondents also noted restrictive selection approaches with respect to lesbian and gay materials that amounted to self-censorship. Numerous incidents have been reported in the media since then, including several high profile legal cases, and in three recent annual surveys sponsored by the Canadian Library Association 2006–2008, which document objections to titles on grounds of homosexuality at the rate of 8 percent per year over the three survey years and reaching 20 percent in 2007. The only title challenged in all three years was *And Tango Makes Three* (Bowman, 2009). This echoes patterns in the United States, where *Tango* was the most challenged title during the same three year period, and over the decade of the 1990s almost 8 percent of all titles reported to ALA's Office for Intellectual Freedom were about sexual minority themes (American Library Association, 2005).[4] Earlier research investigating how school librarians in the United States make selection decisions supports the existence of widespread self-censorship. Callison (1990) reviewed more than 170 research studies about school library collections, concluding that written collection policies should be adopted because they might prove to be "the difference between an unwillingness to 'take a risk' and the willingness to 'innovate with a progressive collection' in support of the information needs faced by today's young people" (p. 8).

Sadly, almost twenty years later, this recommendation does not seem to have had much impact in either Canada or in the United States. Notably, researchers such as Hopkins (1991), Coley (2002), and Roberts (1996) all point to continuing self-censorship practices by school librarians in both the United States and Canada of potentially controversial materials. Indeed, four sexual minority titles included in Coley's checklist study of self-censorship in public high schools in Texas ranked near the bottom of title ownership frequencies, between 1 percent and 16 percent of schools compared to 41 percent of schools for general titles (Coley, 2002, See Table 1). Roberts (1996) also found a great deal of "soft censorship, or pre-censorship" (p. 83) of materials in Saskatchewan public school libraries. There is no reason to think that sexual minority publications in other educational jurisdictions — either in the United States or in Canada — have escaped these practices.

In addition to censorship, new opportunities for homophobic and transphobic bullying have emerged with advances in Internet technologies, for example, instant messaging and chat lines (Wells, 2008b&c). A 2006 survey of children between the ages 8 and 12 revealed that nearly 20 percent had been bullied online (Weeks, 2006). School officials and legislators in the United States, in particular, have become increasingly alarmed about reports of cyber predators. They have often responded in knee-jerk fashion, banning e-mail and social networking sites such as the highly popular Facebook and MySpace. Rather than teaching responsible use of the Internet, moral panic has triggered draconian state legislation and a rush to adopt technological band-aid solutions through the installation of filtering systems that in reality are so extensive they block students, teachers, and school librarians alike from essential websites and services. The cumulative effect is a strongly negative impact on young people's ability to find relevant information, particularly information on health issues impacting sexual minority and gender variant youth (Rideout, Richardson, & Resnick, 2002; Schrader, 2000 & 2002).[5]

The chilling effect on inclusivity and diversity of these pressures and propensities to censor school and public library collections, to self-censor, to obfuscate subject access, and to block reputable sexual minority content on the Internet should not be misjudged or condoned. At the same time, we should neither undervalue nor ignore the power of literature to influence attitudes towards sexual minority and gender variant youth, even if it is just helping to make them visible (Lane, 2002). Whether sexual minority-inclusive literature and information is avoided or merely veiled, the result is the same: the stories of sexual minority and gender variant young people are taken away, rendered inaccessible, and invisible. Young people themselves are censored. And the losers are not only sexual minority, gender variant, and questioning youth, and the larger educational community, but also the body politic, which misses out on the opportunity to learn from diversity, rather than continuing to fear it.

An Ethical Guide for Developing Inclusive Policies and Practices

Ethical and professional responsibility requires more than neutrality. Individual practitioners and organizations in both education and librarianship need to reflect critically on service gaps and harmful practices that alienate sexual minority, gender variant, and questioning youth from their fundamental right to enjoy access to information, resources, and assistance reflecting the diversity of their lived experiences.

In librarianship this social responsibility must occur on several fronts in order to create

ALAMEDA FREE LIBRARY

safe, caring, and inclusive learning environments for sexual minority, gender variant, and questioning youth in their school and public libraries. We recommend that all librarians work together to:

- acquire current and age-appropriate materials;
- ensure relevant subject indexing access;
- evaluate filtering products and monitor Internet practices; and
- implement positive, respectful reference and interloan services to aid in retrieving information and materials.

Equally important is a need to revisit the traditional claims to librarian "neutrality" with respect to ideology, which ignores the postmodernist view that neutrality itself represents a definite point of view that reinforces the status quo (Carmichael, 1998). Silence is never neutral nor is the omission of sexual or gender minority content in the library. These absences send a loud and clear message to sexual minority, gender variant, and questioning youth about their value in our society.

In education, social responsibility points in several key directions that are pivotal to the creation of safe, caring, and inclusive learning environments for sexual minority, gender variant, and questioning students in public schools. As a result, libraries and schools ought to work collectively to:

- develop a more inclusive library and classroom curriculum;
- enhance policy development such as book censorship and challenges;
- promote intergenerational mentoring; and
- improve counseling and outreach services.

For both school and public librarians, this social responsibility begins with critical self-reflection that invites librarians and teachers to examine their feelings, attitudes, prejudices, and biases toward sexual minority and gender variant persons in general, and sexual minority and gender variant youth in particular who are vulnerable as youth and doubly vulnerable as minority youth. It is the complex combination of diverse knowledge, compassionate attitudes, and a caring orientation to professional service that can provide a lifeline of support for sexual minority, gender variant, and questioning youth. Never doubt the power that one trusted adult can play in the lives of youth.

Next to the family, school and public libraries can serve as important refuges of safety from an otherwise hostile and uninviting world. Only when physical, symbolic, and institutional violence have disappeared from the schoolyard, the classroom, the hallways, and the libraries, will the true acceptance of sexual minority and gender variant persons become within our grasp. Visionary leadership in both teaching and librarianship requires nothing more — nor less — than the simple will to reach out and make a difference in a young person's life. Will you be that person?

If librarians are to move beyond the multiple mantras of service to all, equitable access to materials, value-free impartiality, and libraries as the great social equalizers, it will be essential to reexamine staff attitudes and library policies, particularly with respect to services for sexual minority, gender variant, and questioning youth. As Carmichael (1998) has observed:

> American librarians generally seem torn between the mandates of social responsibility and impartiality, and confused or indifferent about the role they should play in addressing homosexual materials, clients and colleagues. Until research conventions and library school curricula are

modified to accommodate gay concerns, it is likely that the growth in gay research will occur in spite of rather than because of the library profession [Abstract].

However, the potential is still there. Among the assets and strengths of Canadian public libraries that are identified in a policy review by Newman (2004) is the "understanding of diversity" and "commitment to inclusion and culture" (p. 3). We also echo the words of Tadei (2002) in her policy and resource guide for Saskatchewan educators when she states:

> Teacher-librarians can make a difference to a student who is dealing with gay and lesbian issues. By having resources available to your students in your public school library, you may save a life, physically or psychologically. Your students who are living with gay or lesbian parents will see that you accept their family members for who they are. Your students who are struggling with their sexual identity will be able to read books that help them to understand the meaning of sexual orientation. Your students who are gay or lesbian will be able to read novels depicting gay and lesbian characters in a positive light. And you, as a teacher-librarian, will have "Broken the Silence" for gay and lesbian students in your school [p. 3].

Our call is therefore also for stronger and more sustained programs of formal education for both librarians and teachers, together with research and evidentiary practice as the foundations for effective policy development in schools and libraries alike. In the twenty-first century the time has come to help practitioners and their institutions come out of the closet.

Strategies for Building Inclusive Collections and Services

Building inclusive collections for sexual minority, gender variant, and questioning youth and their families involves considerations of both policy and process. Sometimes this may seem like a chicken-and-egg situation; for example, the primary recommendation for developing a robust and meaningful library collection is to know your communities of student users — but if there is nothing in the collection to attract certain student communities to the library, how can this be done? Take the time to build slowly, seek resources, find kindred spirits, form networks, strategize thoughtfully, and know that you are not alone. Above all, and in all that you do, *seize the teachable moment to educate your school, staff, and community!*

The following strategies are drawn from the work of Gough & Greenblatt (1998), Jenkins (1990), Kravitz (2002), Resichman (2001), and Whelan (2006), and are elaborated in our book (Schrader & Wells, 2007).

Board Policies and Legislation

Policy is protection. Most public libraries have well-established policies and procedures in these regards, but many school libraries do not. Ensure your school district has clear written policies in place that reflect the spirit and intention of international, federal, and state policy guidelines, laws, and legislation to support inclusive library collections, which specifically include sexual minorities and gender variant people and their issues.

Community Development

Librarians should initiate community development approaches to build inclusive, responsive, and collaborative collections and services by seeking out and listening to local sexual minority and transgender communities and by developing relationships with gay-straight student alliances (GSAs) and other local youth support and/or community groups.

Professional Networking

Librarians should build and maintain working relationships with teachers, counselors, school administrators and other local librarians regardless of the type of institution they are employed in. They should frequently review their sexual minority and gender variant resource collections and consult with each other on a regular basis.

Selection Criteria

Guidelines for selecting library materials should be clearly identified and procedures should be established for obtaining input to aid the school librarian in selection decisions. These guidelines should include opportunities and procedures for input from teachers, students, parents, and other community members.

Challenges and Reconsideration of Materials

Policies and procedures for responding to objections, complaints, and challenges (informal as well as formal) should be clearly defined with an escalating series of steps including formal appeal.

Collection Development

Sexual minority and gender variant collection development efforts must be proactive (Downey, 2005). School and public librarians should keep abreast of bibliographies, "best" books lists, book award lists, catalogues of LGBTIQ publishers, and multiple sources of book reviews.

Collection Access

Materials are irrelevant if students cannot find them. Both fiction and non-fiction should be catalogued under an imaginative diversity of user-friendly subject headings. Produce relevant bibliographies and make sure these materials are visible, accessible, and available without going through the normal checkout process.

Web Access

Ensure that filtering software does not exclude sexual minority and gender variant sites and information. If possible, we suggest abolishing filtering altogether. Instead, develop acceptable use policies with comprehensive student training and parental awareness information.

Library Access

Promote the library as a "safe space" through signage and other communications and ensure that inclusive language is used in all library communications and on websites. Turn the library into an essential element in the culture of an inclusive, safe, and caring learning environment for every student and staff member.

Promotion and Marketing

Maintain a sexual minority presence on the library website, including bibliographies, new titles alerts, and links to relevant websites including those of other libraries. Include sexual minority and gender variant titles in displays, book talks, programs, and other presentations and communications. Produce brochures, resource listings, and exhibits or displays that affirm diversity and difference as a source of community strength.

Community Advocacy

School and public librarians should engage in well-planned public education programs to inform their constituencies about the library's mission to serve inclusive populations and oppose social exclusion. In particular, develop a support network of like-minded teachers, counselors, parents, local police services, social workers, local librarians, and other community leaders.

Professional Development

Challenge your personal biases and continue to expand your knowledge of sexual minority and gender variant issues and information by attending conferences and symposia and by staying current with the latest research on LGBTIQ issues, especially as they pertain to library collections, access, and service.

Library Service Charter or Guarantee

Ensure your library has a broadly constituted and mandated service guarantee policy. The adoption of this strategy underlines the authentic service role of library staff and provides for accountability (Block, 1993).

Transforming School and Library Cultures

Cultural transformation within schools and communities needs to be accompanied by yet another important project in the arsenal of social justice. Freedom from sexual oppression and harassment must also be linked to confronting misogyny, resisting sexism, and dismantling patriarchy. We believe there can be no hierarchy of oppression. If we fight against one form of injustice we must strive to fight against them all. Ignorance is based in fear that leads to violence (Grace, 2001). And just as there is no hierarchy of oppression, there can be no hierarchy of equality and equality rights.

Our goal is the development of a personal and professional ethical responsibility for school and public librarians to create an environment where diversity is embraced as our greatest strength, rather than feared as our worst enemy. When ethical values prevail over prejudice, we will finally begin to witness respect for our young people in all of their psycho-cultural and sexual developments, and hopefully we will see an end to the legacy of homophobic name-calling and bullying in our schools. When this happens, when under-standing trumps ignorance, when truth speaks to power, we will finally begin to trust our librarians and teachers with the just treatment of sexual minority, gender variant, and questioning youth.

Our focus is on the well-being and future citizenship of young people who self-identify as sexual or gender variant minorities, are questioning their sexual or gendered identities, or come from same-gender parented families. Our concern is to suggest a framework for developing and maintaining safe, caring, and inclusive learning environments so that librarians and teachers can and will help to raise healthy young people who will be supported to realize their full potential to become engaged and productive citizens. We ought to ask ourselves: Do we as public service professionals believe that all young people deserve basic dignity and respect in our libraries and schools?

We hope the information, policy background, and practical strategies in this essay help to convince librarians and teachers that they can — and must — play a critical role in fostering diversity and inclusivity. We also hope that school and public librarians will:

- question their religious, moral, and personal views and recognize that their focus as professionals should be on serving the educational interests and needs of sexual minority, gender variant, and questioning youth;
- recognize their professional and ethical obligations to work to enhance the self-esteem and self-identity of all youth and families they serve;
- understand the ethical imperative that libraries and classrooms must be safe places for all youth regardless of their difference;
- help sexual minority, gender variant, and questioning youth, and youth from same-gender parented families, find themselves "in the word" and see themselves in the library; and
- develop the power to help turn pain into opportunity, tolerance into celebration, and validation into resiliency.

The rhetoric that librarians and teachers make a difference, that libraries and classrooms change lives, must become the reality. Otherwise,

What message do we give to children, teenagers, families, friends, and indeed our communities, if we leave the life experiences of sexual minority and gender variant youth out of our classrooms, schools, and libraries?

APPENDIX I: SEXUAL MINORITY AND GENDER VARIANT STUDENTS' CHARTER OF RIGHTS AND FREEDOMS[6]

All sexual minority and gender variant students have the inalienable right to:

- Attend schools free of verbal, physical, and symbolic violence and harassment; where education, not survival, is the priority.
- Attend schools where safety, respect, and dignity for all is a standard set by the Ministry or Department of Education and enforced by every school district, board, administrator, teacher, and librarian.
- Gain access through libraries and the Internet to accurate and unbiased information about themselves, which is free from negative judgment and delivered by trained adults who not only inform, but affirm them.

- See a variety of positive role models in their classrooms, curriculum, and libraries.
- Be included in all support programs that exist to help children and youth build the resiliency necessary to positively address the challenges of growing up in a complex, global world.
- Be represented by national and state or provincial/territorial legislatures that advocate for their individual, human, and civil rights, rather than reinforce or legislate hatred and prejudice.
- Enjoy a heritage free of crippling self-hatred and unchallenged discrimination.

APPENDIX 2: LIBRARY SERVICE AND COLLECTION STRATEGIES FOR SUPPORTING SEXUAL MINORITY AND GENDER VARIANT COMMUNITIES

Board Policies and Legislation

- "Policy is protection"— develop and approve policies on inclusive education, curriculum-based library support, intellectual freedom, and challenges to school and library materials, within the context of board philosophy, mandate and mission, legislative frameworks, esp. the *Bill of Rights* in the United States or in Canada the *Canadian Charter* and *Canadian Human Rights Act,* and national library association policy statements highlighting social responsibility

Community Development

- Utilize community development approaches to build inclusive, responsive, and collaborative libraries and collections
- Seek out and listen to local sexual minority and transgender communities
- Develop and maintain relationships with gay-straight student alliances (GSAs) and other local sexual minority support groups such as PFLAG (Parents, Families and Friends of Lesbians and Gays)

Professional Networking

- Develop relationships and a support network with other librarians, teachers, counselors, parents, police, social workers and other community leaders and groups
- Stay current through local publications of community organizations, news and issues, reviews of books, movies, etc.

Selection Criteria

- Establish inclusive selection guidelines and practices that go beyond the traditional selection canon
- Identify LGBTIQ-related areas for collection development such as travel, consumer information, same-sex marriage, parenting, adoption, homelessness, violence, religion, and ethnic minorities

- Include alternate formats such as graphic novels and zines
- Develop procedures for obtaining input from teachers, students, parents, and other community members

Challenges and Reconsideration of Materials

- Frame policies and procedures in accordance with the ALA *Library Bill of Rights* or the CLA *Statement on Intellectual Freedom*

Collection Development

- Consult bibliographies, "best" books lists, award lists, multiple sources of book reviews, the catalogues of independent publishers, and the alternative press
- Seek recommendations from local youth, community groups, parents, teachers, bookstores, and websites

Collection Access

- Adopt a user-centered approach to classification and cataloguing and ensure fiction and non-fiction are catalogued under an imaginative diversity of user-friendly subject headings
- Ensure that materials are visible, accessible, and promoted through book lists, bibliographies, etc.
- Make materials available through an honor system or alternative checkout process

Web Access

- Ensure Internet filtering software does not exclude sexual minority sites and information, which otherwise violates non-discrimination laws and library policies — better yet, avoid filtering for teens and adults and develop acceptable use policies with user training and parental awareness information
- Ensure easy web access to owned materials and maintain links to other websites and resources
- Endorse and distribute the ALA or CLA policy documents on Internet access
- Consult the *Directory of Internet Access Policies* adopted by Canadian public, school, and post-secondary libraries

Library Access

- Promote the library as a "safe space" through signage, etc. (see promotion & marketing)
- Use inclusive language in all library communications and on websites

Promotion and Marketing

- Post "safe space" signs and symbols
- Maintain a visible sexual minority presence on the library website, including bibliogra-

phies, new title alerts and links to relevant websites including those of other libraries and LGBTIQ organizations
- Include sexual minority and gender variant titles in displays, book talks, presentations, and public and internal communications
- Produce brochures, resource listings, and exhibits or displays (such as LGBTIQ History Month or National Coming Out Day)
- Support and promote awareness of local events and national issues of interest, e.g., pride week celebrations, same-sex marriage, gay-straight student alliances, same-sex parenting, adoption, bullying awareness, violence prevention, critical literacy, homelessness, mother's and father's days, *No Name-Calling Week, International Day against Homophobia*, etc.
- Promote *Banned Books Week* in the United States or in Canada *Freedom to Read Week* as well as local initiatives to build awareness and an appreciation for inclusivity and diversity
- Ensure the school or public board and senior administration are regularly and fully aware of all LGBTIQ initiatives and activities undertaken by library staff

Community Advocacy

- Develop a support network of like-minded teachers, parents, police, social workers, public health officials, and other community leaders and librarians
- Establish working relationships with key local media and engage in well-planned public education programs to inform constituencies about the library's mission to serve inclusive populations and oppose social exclusion

Professional Development

- Expand your knowledge of sexual minority and gender variant issues and information resources by attending conferences, staying current with research, and fostering cultural awareness training for other staff, volunteers, and trustees

Library Service Charter

- Develop a board-approved, user-centered guarantee of superior inclusive collections and services in school and public libraries

Seize the teachable moment to educate your school, staff, and community!

NOTES

1. This essay is an abridged version from our book *Challenging silence, challenging censorship: Inclusive resources, strategies and policy directives for addressing BGLTT realities in school and public libraries* published by the Canadian Teachers' Federation (2007) and reproduced with permission.

2. For more information about the GLBT Round Table, please see the organizational profile in Section Seven of this book.

3. For more information about terminology and subject access, see the essay on "The Treatment of LGBTIQ Concepts in the Library of Congress Subject Headings" in Section Five.

4. See the essay on "Censorship of Children's and Young Adult Books in Schools and Public Libraries" in Section Six for further examples.

5. For more information, see "LGBTIQ Teens — Plugged In and Unfiltered: How Internet Filtering

Impairs Construction of Online Communities, Identity Formation, and Access to Health Information" in Section Six. See also the essay on "The Internet and LGBTIQ Communities" in Section One for additional discussion regarding cyberbullying.

6. Adapted from the work of Dr. Virginia Uribe, Project 10, Los Angeles: http://www.project10. org/Laws%20And%20Policies/billofrights.html

REFERENCES

American Association of Law Libraries (AALL). *Standing committee on lesbian and gay issues*. (2008). Retrieved from http://www.aallnet.org/sis/srsis/lgbt/index.html

American Library Association (ALA). (1996). *Library bill of rights*. Retrieved from http://www.ala.org/ala/ aboutala/offices/oif/statementspols/statementsif/librarybillrights.cfm

American Library Association. (2005). *The 100 most frequently challenged books of 1990–2000*. Retrieved from http://www.ala.org/ala/oif/bannedbooksweek/bbwlinks/100mostfrequently.htm

American Library Association. (2009). *Interpretations of the library bill of rights*. Retrieved from http://www. ala.org/ala/aboutala/offices/oif/statementspols/statementsif/interpretations/default.cfm

American Library Association. Gay, Lesbian, Bisexual, and Transgendered Round Table. (2002). *What is the GLBTRT?* Retrieved from http://www.ala.org/ala/mgrps/rts/glbtrt/index.cfm

Barnes, L. (2004). *Reaching out: Library services for lesbian, gay, bisexual, transgender, and questioning youth.* Documentary film directed by Lynne Barnes. San Francisco, CA: Friends of the San Francisco Public Library.

Block, Peter. (1993). *Stewardship: Choosing service over self-interest.* San Francisco, CA: Berrett-Koehler.

Bowman, D. (2009). *CLA challenged materials survey: Some results and trends.* Presentation at the Annual Conference, Canadian Library Association, Montreal, Quebec. Retrieved from http://www.cla.ca/con ference/2009/sessions/A5_Challenge_Materials_Survey_presentation.ppt

California Safe Schools Coalition, 4-H Center for Youth Development, & University of California, Davis. (2004). *Consequences of harassment based on actual or perceived sexual orientation and gender non-conformity and steps for making schools safer.* San Francisco, CA: California Safe Schools Coalition.

Callison, D. (1990). A review of the research related to school library media collections: Part I. *School Library Media Quarterly, 19*(1), 27–34.

Canadian Coalition for School Libraries. (2004). *Research.* Retrieved from http://www.peopleforeducation. com/librarycoalition

Canadian Library Association (CLA). (1974/1985). *Statement on intellectual freedom.* Retrieved from http://www.cla.ca/AM/Template.cfm?Section=Position_Statements&Template=/CM/ContentDis play.cfm&ContentID=3047

Canadian Library Association (CLA). (2000). *Statement on effective school library programs in Canada.* Retrieved from http://www.cla.ca/AM/Template.cfm?Section=Position_Statements&Template=/ CM/ContentDisplay.cfm&ContentID=3038

Canadian Library Association (CLA). (2008). *Position statements.* Retrieved from http://www.cla.ca/AM/ Template.cfm?Section=Position_Statements

Carmichael, J. V., Jr. (1998). *Homosexuality and United States libraries: Land of the free, but not home to the gay.* Paper presented at the World Library and Information Congress, International Federation of Library Associations and Institutions, Amsterdam. Retrieved from http://www.ifla.org/IV/ifla64/002– 138e.htm

Chamberlain v. Surrey School District No. 36. 2002. SCC 86 [2002] 4 S.C.R. 710. Retrieved from http:// csc.lexum.umontreal.ca/en/2002/2002scc86/2002scc86.html

Coley, K. P. (2002). Moving toward a method to test for self-censorship by school library media specialists. *School Library Media Research, 5.* Retrieved from http://www.ala.org/ala/mgrps/divs/aasl/aaslpubs andjournals/slmrb/slmrcontents/volume52002/coley.cfm

Curry, A. (2005). If I ask, will they answer? Evaluating public library reference service to gay and lesbian youth. *Reference and User Services Quarterly, 45*(1), 65–75.

Downey, J. (2005). Public library collection development issues regarding the information needs of GLBT patrons. *Progressive Librarian, 25,* 86–95.

Egale Canada. (2009). *Youth speak up about homophobia and transphobia: The first national climate survey on homophobia in Canadian schools.* Retrieved from http://www.egale.ca/index.asp?lang=&menu=1& item=1401

Gay, Lesbian, and Straight Education Network (2009). The experiences of lesbian, gay, bisexual and transgender middle school students (GLSEN research brief). Retrieved from http://www.glsen.org/binary-data/GLSEN_ATTACHMENTS/file/000/001/1475-1.pdf

Gough, C., & Greenblatt, E. (1998). Gay and lesbian library materials: A book selector's toolkit. In A. K. Stephens (Ed.), *Public library collection development for the information age* (pp. 151–170). New York: Haworth.

Grace, A. P. (2001). Being, becoming, and belonging as a queer citizen educator: The places of queer auto-biography, queer culture as community, and fugitive knowledge. *Proceedings of the 20th annual conference of the Canadian Association for the Study of Adult Education* (pp. 100–106), Laval University, Quebec City, PQ.

Grace, A. P., & Wells, K. (2005). The Marc Hall prom predicament: Queer individual rights v. institutional church rights in Canadian public education. *Canadian Journal of Education, 28*(3), 237–270.

Grace, A. P., & Wells, K. (2007). Using Freirean pedagogy of just ire to inform critical social learning in arts-informed community education for sexual minorities. *Adult Education Quarterly, 57*(2), 95–114.

Grace, A. P., & Wells, K. (2009). Gay and bisexual male youth as educator activists and cultural workers: The critical praxis of three Canadian high-school students. *International Journal Of Inclusive Education, 3*(1), 23–44.

Haycock, K. (2003). *The crisis in Canada's school libraries: The case for reform and re-investment.* Toronto: Association of Canadian Publishers. Retrieved from http://www.peopleforeducation.com/librarycoalition/Report03.pdf

Hopkins, D. M. (1991). *Factors influencing the outcomes of challenges to materials in secondary school libraries: Report of a national study.* Washington, DC: U.S. Department of Education, Office of Educational Research and Improvement, Library Programs.

International Federation of Library Associations and Institutions (IFLA). (2009). *Policies and Procedures.* Retrieved from http://www.ifla.org/V/cdoc/policies.htm#Statements

Jenkins, C. (1990). Gay and lesbian issues for school libraries and librarians. In C. Gough and E. Greenblatt (Eds.), *Gay and Lesbian Library Service* (pp. 11–24). Jefferson, NC: McFarland.

Kittelberg, L. (2006). Study to gauge queer support in schools. *Xtra! West*, August 30. Retrieved from http://www.xtra.ca/public/viewstory.aspx?AFF_TYPE=1&STORY_ID=2043&PUB_TEMPLATE_ID=2

Kosciw, J. G., Diaz, E. M., Colic, D. M., & Goldin. R. (2005). *No name-calling week project: Year one evaluation; No sticks. No stones. No dissing.* New York: GLSEN. Retrieved from http://www.nonamecallingweek.org/binary-data/NoNameCalling_ATTACHMENTS/file/25-1.pdf

Kosciw, J. G., Diaz, E. M., & Greytak, E. A. (2008.) *2007 national school climate survey: The experiences of lesbian, gay, bisexual and transgender youth in our nation's schools.* New York: GLSEN. Retrieved from http://www.glsen.org/cgi-bin/iowa/all/library/record/2340.html?state=research&type=research

Kravitz, N. (2002). *Censorship and the school library media center.* Westport, CT: Libraries Unlimited.

Lane, D. (2002). The emergence of gay literature for young people. *Young Adult Library Services, 1*(1), 18–21.

Linville, D. (2004). Beyond picket fences: What gay/queer/LGBTQ teens want from the library. *Voice of youth advocates, 27*(3), 183–186.

Little Sisters Book and Art Emporium v. Canada (Minister of Justice). 2000. SCC 69, [2000] 2 S.C.R. 1120. http://csc.lexum.umontreal.ca/en/2000/2000scc69/2000scc69.html. See also "Court Case History/Documents" at http://www.littlesisters.ca/docscc/index_court.html, and the 2002 feature documentary film *Little sisters vs big brother*, written and directed by Aerlyn Weissman. Vancouver, B.C.: Moving Images.

McCreary Centre Society. (1999). *Being out: Lesbian, gay, bisexual, and transgender youth in BC: An adolescent health survey.* Burnaby, BC: Author.

National coalition calls for more teacher-librarians, increased acquisition budgets. (2002). Retrieved from http://www.peopleforeducation.com/librarycoalition/may28_02.html

Newman, W. (2004). *Public libraries in the priorities of Canada: Acting on the assets and opportunities.* Prepared for the Provincial and Territorial Library Directors Council. Retrieved from http://www.lac-bac.gc.ca/6/7/s7-3000-e.html

Reichman, H. (2001). *Censorship and selection: Issues and answers for schools* (3rd Edition.). Chicago: American Library Association.

Rideout, V., Richardson, C., & Resnick, P. (2002). *See no evil: How Internet filters affect the search for online health information.* Kaiser Family Foundation. Retrieved from http://www.kff.org/entmedia/20021210a-index.cfm

Roberts, E. A. (1996). *A survey of censorship practices in public school libraries in Saskatchewan.* Master's thesis, Department of Curriculum and Instruction, University of Saskatchewan, Saskatoon, SK.

Saewyc, E., Poon, C., Wang, N., Homma, Y., Smith, A., & The McCreary Centre Society. (2007). *Not yet equal: The health of lesbian, gay, & bisexual youth in BC*. Vancouver, BC: McCreary Centre Society.

Schrader, A. M. (1995). *Fear of words: Censorship and the public libraries of Canada*. Ottawa, ON: Canadian Library Association.

Schrader, A. M. (1997). Community pressures to censor gay and lesbian materials in the public libraries of Canada. In Norman G. Kester (Ed.), *Liberating minds: The stories and professional lives of gay, lesbian, and bisexual librarians and their advocates* (pp. 149–160). Jefferson, NC: McFarland.

Schrader, A.M. (2000). *Internet filters: Library access issues in a cyberspace world*. Address at the annual conference of the International Federation of Library Associations and Institutions. Retrieved from http://archive.ifla.org/faife/papers/others/schrader.htm

Schrader, A.M. (2002). *Technology and the politics of choice: Information literacy, critical thinking, and intellectual freedom*. Keynote address to the Alberta Teachers' Association Learning Resources Council and ATA Computer Council. Retrieved from http://aslc.teachers.ab.ca/SiteCollectionDocuments/ASLC. teachers.ab.ca/Publications/Technology and the Politics of Choice.pdf

Schrader, A.M., & Wells, K. (2007). *Challenging silence, challenging censorship: Inclusive resources, strategies and policy directives for addressing BGLTT realities in school and public libraries*. Ottawa, ON: Canadian Teachers' Federation.

Suicide Prevention Resource Center. (2008). *Suicide risk and prevention for lesbian, gay, bisexual, and transgender youth*. Newton, MA: Education Development Center.

Tadei, K. (2002). *It's okay to have this book in your public school library!* Research Report Project #74. Saskatoon, SK: Dr. Stirling McDowell Foundation for Research into Teaching. Retrieved from http:// www.mcdowellfoundation.ca/main_mcdowell/projects/research_rep/74_ok_to_have_book.pdf#xml= http://www.mcdowellfoundation.ca/cgi-bin/texis.exe/main_mcdowell/webinator/mcdsearch/xml. txt?query=tadei&db=mcddbl&id=4421ec212b

Weeks, C. (2006). One in five kids bullied on Internet. *Edmonton Journal*, May 8: A6.

Wells, K. (2004). Safe in my heart: Found poetry as narrative inquiry. In J. McNinch and M. Cronin (Eds.), *I could not speak my heart: Education and social justice for gay and lesbian youth* (pp. 7–18). Regina, SK: Canadian Plains Research Centre, University of Regina.

Wells, K. (2006). *The gay-straight student alliance handbook: A comprehensive resource for Canadian K–12 teachers, administrators, and school counsellors*. Ottawa, ON: Canadian Teachers' Federation.

Wells, K. (2008a, Winter). Generation queer: Sexual minority youth and Canadian schools. *Education Canada, 48(1), 18–23*.

Wells, K. (2008b). *Homophobic bullying* [Fact Sheet]. Government of Alberta. Edmonton, AB.

Wells, K. (2008c). *Homophobic bullying* [Web Resources]. Office for the Prevention of Family Violence and Bullying, Government of Alberta. Retrieved from http://www.bullyfreealberta.ca & http://www. b-free.ca

Whelan, D. L. (2006). Out and ignored. *School Library Journal*. Retrieved from http://www.schoolli braryjournal.com/index.asp?layout=articlePrint&articleid=CA6296527

Quatrefoil Library:
The Next Generation

Karen P. Hogan

Quatrefoil Library is a member-based, volunteer-run LGBTQ library, serving the Minneapolis-St. Paul area since 1986. While we are very much a "bricks and mortar" library — i.e., a physical building with print books, print magazines, and DVDs — we have also increased our presence in cyberspace, and have an active virtual community.

Our first venture into the online realm began in 1996, when Metronet, a Minnesota multitype library network, included a webpage about Quatrefoil on its "special libraries" page. It was a listing in a directory, but it got the word out that there was this unique library in the Twin Cities area.

In 2001, our Internet service provider SCC.net, donated the labor and server space to host our first web page at http://www.quatrefoillibrary.org. There was basic information about our hours and location and collections plus some links to other local organizations and community resources. Though it was primitive by today's standards, it represented a huge leap in our publicity and outreach. As a volunteer-run organization we managed to staff the desk about 24 hours a week. With a website, we were "open" 24 hours a day. We did not have to pay to be put in a directory. People could search the Internet for "Quatrefoil, gay library" or even "porn" and learn about our existence.

And let us not forget, that even today, there still remains some shame and stigma regarding homosexuality. People who may be fearful of being "outed" because they are a member — or even because they visited Quatrefoil — could now check us out in the privacy of their own homes. People could research resources that the public library does not own. Just because someone has an information need, does not always mean they feel safe enough to ask in person. I hope this is one barrier to access that has been removed.

In 2007, with the help of Quatrefoil volunteer Brian Mangin and his company Start Spark, the library launched a newly designed website. This professionally designed site had a big purple "Q" logo, rotating photographs of volunteers, a calendar of events, and more information about the history of the library. This new design did not just look pretty; volunteer Kris Anderson added the functionality of our book catalog to the web site. This feature opened up our collection to the world, and led to even more web traffic and visitors.

Over the years we have migrated static lists of our DVDs, erotic videos, and archive collections to our online catalog. While we now have all our collections indexed in the catalog, it is still a basic title-author-subject database. We have seen the advances in "Next Generation" catalogs: book covers, reviews, and table of contents, web links and would like to do that as well.

But before we could figure out how to do it on our own, Tim Spalding, a web developer in Maine, started LibraryThing.com. This new website was launched in August 2005, and I put Quatrefoil's holdings there in September 2005. "Website" is inadequate to describe what LibraryThing.com is. It is a place for book lovers to catalog their books, but also to share their collections. It was one of the first "social networking" sites I had participated in. I was not the target demographic of sites like Friendster or MySpace, but book people do love to talk about books. The site attracted not just book lovers, but librarians, authors, publishers and booksellers as well.

So now we had a catalog with the Quatrefoil Library logo, with book covers, links to purchase from a bookstore, borrow from a library, or swap with other users. LibraryThingers could use "tags" to describe the books the way they thought they ought to be organized. Oh sure, us librarian types could still use Library of Congress Subject Headings, but they would also be supplemented with more accurate descriptors. (I don't know if "lesbian vampire porn" has made the Weekly Headings list yet.)

This represented a shift away from "everything needs to be on OUR website" to using better tools someone else has developed. LibraryThing developers are a very creative bunch and have come up with features we never would have dreamed of. UnSuggester anyone? If you like this book, you'll HATE this one. There are statistics and data mashed up in unusual ways. The "Vous et nul autre" ("You and No Other") lists books that you and only one other user have in common. When you have such a unique collection like Quatrefoil does, it really helps us stand out. By the time I figure out one new widget, another one is rolled of the beta forge.

Yet there is a downside to this. We lose some control — since LibraryThing only catalogs books, our users don't see half of our collection: DVDs, magazines, newsletters, games, and music. But others around the world are able to make use of our collections, in ways we could not have anticipated before.

This year, we had a researcher contact us, after seeing that we owned a particular edition of the book *Quatrefoil* by James Barr. He was writing a book on pre–Stonewall gay novels, and wanted to know if we had a copy of the original book jacket. He could see the image fine on the LibraryThing.com site, but we were able to scan a higher quality image of an out-of-print edition for the author. That is a connection which, while it may have been possible in the pre–Internet, pre-social networking days, would certainly have been much harder.

Since my day job is at a college campus, I was exposed to Facebook way before it took over the world. Facebook started as a way for students to network. The one requirement for joining was you needed to be a student with an ".edu" email address. In 2006, Facebook opened to the world so anyone could join. One feature of Facebook was the ability to create "Groups" — formal, informal, and "random." When I saw other local groups creating Facebook groups, I created a group for Quatrefoil Library.

It was a great way to promote events, initiate discussions, create polls, and talk about books. Since it was linked to my personal account, people needed to "friend" me first before they could join the Quatrefoil Library group. Right after I created the Group, Facebook developed the Fan Page. The Fan Page allows the organization to create targeted advertising, offers different levels of admin. access, and permits other people to create content for the site. For the time being, we run the dual sites, since there are hundreds more on the Groups site than the Fan page.

Facebook has allowed us to reach many people who may not be members of the library or have even visited the library. They know about Quatrefoil because they have "friended" me, or are a friend of a friend, or someone commented on a status update, or got tagged in a photo. When we need emergency substitutes for a desk shift, we get a faster response from a Facebook post than an email. When we needed to get the word out quickly about a Board member's death, the Facebook status appeared before the online newspaper obituary. While the jury may still be out regarding the etiquette of Facebook being the first notification about a death, it allowed friends and supporters to publicly mourn and plan the memorial.

Facebook was the entry into another social networking phenomenon, Twitter. When the "link to Twitter from your Facebook page" feature emerged, I did not have to worry about maintaining yet another site. I just had to create a Twitter account for Quatrefoil, and whatever I post on the Quatrefoil Fan page is auto-magically posted to the Twitter feed ... the first 140 characters that is. LibraryThing has also rolled out an "LT for Facebook application," where recent title cover images are added to the Facebook page.

Rounding out the sacred social networking trinity is YouTube. Our sole video on YouTube <http://www.youtube.com/watch?v=aXJXiUdFbd4> is one that was created by our local cable access channel. Kurt Pawlak interviewed me as I gave a tour of the library. It was a great way for people who are outside the area to become familiar with the library. Brochures, photographs, and web sites are wonderful, but lack the perspective that a video can bring. One gets a better sense of the size of the library, and how packed full of books and materials it is.

Just as I was about to wrap up this piece, we had yet another online tool launch this week. Various non-profit foundations partnered with Razoo.com and Network For Good. Social networking + philanthropy = GiveMN.org "Give To The Max Day." While Quatrefoil has been exploring online giving via a Paypal link on our homepage, along comes a powerhouse that did it better, easier and FREE. GiveMN.org created a single site for processing credit card transactions. Did I mention it is FREE? Any Minnesota non-profit registered with the state was automatically enrolled, and given a web site template. GiveMN.org contributes the credit card processing fees as part of its business model. We customized our site, with our logo, mission statement, and story, and how-we-use your dollars statement. November 17, 2009 was the big rollout day, with foundations matching donations to $500,000. In 24 hours over $14 million was raised for 3,000 Minnesota non-profits.

The timing was quite fortuitous for Quatrefoil since we had just launched our Annual Giving campaign. We receive no government money to run the library. For the past several years, we have sent out printed fundraising appeal letters through the mail. We did that plus added a social network component. Our funding comes from donations and membership fees. We were able to use many social networking tools to spread the word about the "Give To The Max" campaign and our Annual Campaign. We used our email mailing list on Yahoo.com and messaged our Facebook and MySpace friends. We tweeted on Twitter. There was radio and television coverage all day as well.

In the end, one 24-hour social networking/fundraising blitz brought in over $4,000.00. Whether this was "year-end-giving-six-weeks-early" or new money raised, it is certainly a testament to the power of online social networks on special libraries like ours.

By the time this essay goes to print, there may well be several other hacks, mash-ups and online tools. That is the way of the online world: constant change, constant tweaks, and rapid development. For every tool that I have mentioned, I do an "oh yeah, I forgot about Constant Contact and email marketing, oh and Slideshare! And Google groups! And Blogger! And Vimeo! And online research databases and RefWorks, iPhone apps..." Some tools are new, some just unknown to me, some just an "I wonder if we can do this..." gleam in a programmer's eye.

Though the techno wizardry may change, the mission of Quatrefoil Library remains the same: creating community connections, providing and preserving LGBTQ materials in a safe space to combat homophobia and to promote understanding. Whether that means curling up with a good queer book at the library or blogging about the latest Twitter trending topic, the library lives on.

Quatrefoil: The Next Generation

Library home page: http://www.qlibrary.org
Email contact: info@qlibrary.org
LibraryThing: http://www.librarything.com/catalog/Quatrefoil_library
Quatrefoil Library group: http://www.facebook.com/#!/group.php?gid=18817789576& ref=ts
Quatrefoil Library Fan Page: http://www.facebook.com/#!/pages/Saint-Paul-MN/Qua trefoil-Library/5691874707?ref=ts
Razoo: http://givemn.razoo.com/story/Quatrefoil-Library
Twitter: http://twitter.com/Q_Library
YouTube: http://www.youtube.com/watch?v=aXJXiUdFbd4.

San Francisco Public Library's "Out at the Library: Celebrating the James C. Hormel Gay & Lesbian Center"

Jim Van Buskirk

The James C. Hormel Gay & Lesbian Center, which opened to the public in April 1996 on the third floor of the main San Francisco Public Library (SFPL), serves as the gateway to collections documenting lesbian, gay, bisexual and transgendered history and culture, with a special emphasis on the San Francisco Bay Area. In addition to book, periodical and archival collections, the Center sponsors changing exhibitions and public programs.

"Out at the Library: Celebrating the James C. Hormel Gay & Lesbian Center" is an example of a library using its collections to mount an exhibit, publish an accompanying catalog, offer an online presence, develop related public programming, and create a panel version which traveled across the country.

My early idea was to display selected images from the various portfolios of photographs that the Center had purchased over the years. Many of these images by Ann P. Meredith, Dan Nicoletta, Lynda Koolish, Chloe Atkins, Robert Giard, and Rick Gerharter, had never been displayed at the library. The Exhibitions and Public Programming staff suggested expanding the scope by exhibiting even more artifacts from the Center's rich collections.

The Hormel Endowment Committee, the Center's fundraising and oversight board operating under the auspices of the Friends of the SFPL, rose to the occasion and quickly established a Leadership Committee, co-chaired by Charles Q. Forester and Jan Zivic, which diligently solicited the funds to support the exhibition. As funding goals were met, various components of the project were put into place. Recognizing the importance of a permanent record documenting the exhibit, an accompanying catalog was planned from the inception; it would be SFPL's first publication in its 125-year history. The Leadership Committee was especially committed to raising funds to travel a version of the exhibition across the country.

The project director was Catherine King, SFPL's Head of Exhibitions and Public Programming, who did a masterful job coordinating and overseeing the myriad components of the complicated project. She brought on guest curator Barbara Levine, who in turn assembled a team including exhibition designer Stephen Jaycox, catalogue editor and designer Stephanie Snyder, and researcher Léonie Guyer, to work with Library staff including Everett Erlandson, Ann Carroll, Joan Jasper, Tim Wilson, and many others.

Having curated nearly ten years' worth of exhibitions from the Hormel's ever-growing collections, it was inspirational to work with the outside team's fresh perspective and unmitigated enthusiasm for the material. As non-librarians, they were eager to demystify for the public what archival collections were, how they came to the library, how they are processed, and how elements of the various collections begin to "talk" to one another over time.

They immediately considered how to present the archival material in an engaging way, including developing an eye-catching pallet (bright pink, purple, green, and brown) to reflect the vibrancy of the collected materials. Thematic "pods" were conceived including "Public & Private," "The Personal into the Political," "Gay Games," "Barbara Grier," "Harry Hay," "Pulp Paperbacks," and "Periodicals." Highlights of the exhibition included:

Leather boots belonging to Dr. Mary Edwards Walker (1832–1919), the first female surgeon in the U.S. Army, a humanitarian, and an early advocate for women's rights, including dress reform. The curators were immediately captivated by the boots, feeling they would appeal to diverse audiences — men, women, straight, gay, questioning, young, and old. Their mystery — who had these very tiny, very old boots belonged to? — became the signature iconic image throughout the branding of the exhibition.

A volume of *Der Eigene*, considered the world's first gay periodical, which became the voice of a small movement that advocated Classical Greek pederasty — highly ritualized sexual relationships between men and boys — as a cure for what some saw as the alarming effeminacy of German culture.

Pulp paperback covers included titles such as *Warped Desire, Odd Girl Out,* and *The Gay Year*. Related materials included pseudonyms used by LGBT authors and activists, and correspondence between Barbara Grier, founder of Naiad Press, and Patricia Highsmith, who in 1952 wrote *The Price of Salt*, under the pseudonym Claire Morgan.

An appointment book and a hand-edited draft of a speech by gay rights activist Harvey Milk (1930–1978), the first openly gay man elected to the San Francisco Board of Supervisors, was also featured. The grief caused by the assassinations of Milk and Mayor George Moscone unified the LGBT community as it continued to emerge as a political force.

In addition there were materials from various archival collections, including the personal papers of Harry Hay (1912–2002), the dynamic, visionary man considered by many to be the father of the modern gay rights movement. Using the Olympic Games as a model and in keeping with other events such as the Special Olympics, physician Tom Waddell had conceived of the "Gay Olympic Games" to promote sports and positive self-image within what was then a largely bar- and club-centered community.

As the exhibition was in the process of being developed, the library accessioned a remarkable collection of material documenting the Cockettes, the psychedelic drag queen troupe founded in the late 1960s, which performed outrageous parodies of show tunes gaining an underground cult following. The donor, former Cockette Kreemah Ritz, was thrilled to learn that some of this material would be included in the exhibition.

There were multiple sets of texts — for the original exhibition, the catalog, the online presence, the traveling exhibition, and the marketing — each with its own space requirements and timeline. Keeping track of the various edited versions was no mean feat. In addition, King engaged the services of Cara Storm, Principal of Marketing by Storm to assist with promotion. An online presence, developed by SFPL staff members Joan Lefkowitz and Adam Markosian, remains online at http://sfpl.org/news/onlineexhibits/out/.

The original exhibition ran from June 18 through October 16, 2005, in three separate venues: the Main Library's Jewett Gallery on the lower level, the Hormel Center on the third floor and the Eureka Valley/Harvey Milk Memorial Branch Library. King arranged that *Nazi Persecution of Homosexuals 1933–1945*, a traveling panel exhibit by curator Ted Phillips, deputy director of exhibitions at the United States Holocaust Memorial Museum, would be on view concurrently in the SFPL's Skylight Gallery on the sixth floor.

A full color, 144-page catalog featured a foreword by James C. Hormel, the philanthropist and activist whose initial generous donation spearheaded the fundraising campaign; "Tracking Past and Present," a moving essay by seminal lesbian poet and writer Judy Grahn; a roundtable conversation on the founding of the Center; and my own reminiscences on having served as its manager, "Reflections: Stewarding the Collections."

There was a wide variety of related public programs, which took place at both the main library and the Eureka Valley/Harvey Milk Memorial Branch. These included an Opening Day Celebration, "Nazi Persecution of Homosexuals: Curating Invisible History," "Lesbian Publishers: A Historical Perspective and a Current View," "Lesbian Pulp Fiction: The Sexually Intrepid World of Lesbian Paperback Novels 1950—1965," "Home Team: The Growth of the Gay Games and GLBT Sports," and a screening of *Not in Our Town Northern California: When Hate Happens Here*, featuring the Library's *Reversing Vandalism* exhibition. During "Hidden Secrets & Lost Treasures," Bay Area authors read from unpublished works and little known literary and historical writings from the Hormel Center Archives. *2005 Queer Youth Speak: In and Out at the Library* was a short video featuring the voices of queer youth in response to the "Out at the Library" exhibition.

While the ambitious project did not break attendance records, the anecdotal response was gratifying. Most viewers took time to read each document and the wall text, contemplate each object, and share comments in a guest book.

Between Spring 2006 and Spring 2009, the exhibition had traveled to carefully selected venues throughout the country. The itinerary was intended to represent a balance of academic libraries, public libraries, large and small, as well as a community center. Venues included: Lesbian, Gay, Bisexual & Transgender Community Center, New York, NY; Provincetown Public Library, Provincetown, MA; Atlanta-Fulton Central Library Branch, Atlanta, GA; Swarthmore College Library, Swarthmore, PA; Oak Lawn Library, Dallas, TX; Minneapolis Central Library, Minneapolis, MN; College of William and Mary, Williamsburg, VA; Missoula Public Library, Missoula, MT; St. Louis Public Library, St. Louis, MO; Portland State University, Portland, OR; and University of Pennsylvania, Philadelphia, PA. The reported response to these regional presentations was inspiring. Communities developed their own opening celebrations, programming, and in several cases were inspired to begin collecting their own local LGBT history.

While the scope of this project and the resources to realize it may be beyond the range of most institutions, it nevertheless provides an excellent example of ways to use collections creatively to educate library constituents about LGBT history and culture.

How Queer "Pack Rats" and Activist Archivists Saved our History: An Overview of Lesbian, Gay, Bisexual, Transgender, and Queer (LGBTQ) Archives, 1970–2008

Aimee Brown

The term archives refers to both the place where archival material is stored as well as the collections themselves. The place can be online, in a closet at a LGBTQ[1] community center, or in a traditional brick and mortar building such as the Lesbian Herstory Archives in Brooklyn, New York. The collections can be photographs posted on a queer-straight alliance Facebook page, the box under a bed containing old lesbian T-shirts, or in a community-based institution like the Lambda Archives of San Diego.

For the purposes of this essay, LGBTQ archives are defined as archives that are intentionally LGBTQ, specifically archives that preserve queer[2] history primarily to provide access for sexual and gender minorities and to ensure cultural visibility. Community-based archives tend to be activist by nature and an active part of local communities by sponsoring events and providing a safe gathering space. Doing a comprehensive study of the history of these archives worldwide or even in North America is beyond the scope of this essay. Profiles of a few archives in particular will be included as examples as there is not room to go into detail about many LGBTQ archives. This essay discusses the history of LGBTQ archives during the twentieth century and into the current decade in North America and Europe, primarily focusing on those founded from 1970 to 2008 after the Stonewall Riots. These riots were a series of violent protests sparked by a police raid of the gay bar the Stonewall Inn in New York City in 1969. Although there have been LGBTQ individuals and organizations working on securing civil rights, ending discrimination, and building culture throughout the twentieth century, the Stonewall Riots are considered a major milestone in the history of the contemporary LGBTQ liberation movements.

At least seventeen of the LGBTQ archives founded during the 1970s and 1980s in North America and Europe still exist independent of mainstream archives.[3] Without further research, it is hard to say how many LGBTQ archives started up during and since the 1970s as many merged with others, became part of mainstream archives, or closed. There are currently several institutionally supported collections that actively collect and advertise their LGBTQ holdings.[4] This is primarily the result of the work of community LGBTQ archives staff and "out" LGBTQ historians who have over the past forty years demonstrated how valuable these materials are to professional academics and students. Another result of their work is that some non–LGBTQ archivists and historians began to view LGBTQ history as a valuable part of social history. For example, some realized that you can't accurately document feminist history without including lesbians. LGBTQ and allied archivists employed by mainstream archives also helped to make LGBTQ history more visible by encouraging the collecting, processing, and accurate cataloging of related collections in their institutions. Some also volunteered at community archives. The most important accomplishment of LGBTQ archives has been making LGBTQ history and culture visible and more accessible to LGBTQ people.

Before Stonewall (1900–1968)

It is likely that there have always been LGBTQ individuals and groups who have collected materials documenting their history and shared them with others. The collections of individuals such as Jim Kepner, "a self-described 'pack rat' credited with assembling the nation's largest single collection of gay and lesbian materials" (Russell, 1988) which later became the nucleus of some LGBTQ archives. Kepner, who had been collecting material since 1942, founded the Western Gay Archives in 1971 in Los Angeles. It was later known as the Natalie Barney/Edward Carpenter Library of the International Gay & Lesbian Archives and then merged with ONE, Inc.'s library and archives in 1995 to form the ONE National Gay & Lesbian Archives (Society of American Archivists, Lesbian and Gay Archives Roundtable, 2007). Kepner was also instrumental in starting ONE, Inc.'s, library in the 1950s (Potvin, 1998). ONE, Inc., was the publisher of *ONE Magazine* which was the first pro-homosexual magazine in the United States. Another example of this is the Lambda Archives of San Diego, founded in 1987 by Jess Jessop, which grew out of the personal collections of Jessop and Doug Moore (Lambda Archives of San Diego, n.d.).

The only two documented LGBTQ archives that were formed before 1940 are the Institute for Sexual Science (Institut für Sexualwissenschaft) founded in 1919 in Berlin by Magnus Hirschfeld and the library of the Dutch Scientific Humanitarian Committee (Nederlandsch Wetenschappelijk Humanitair Komitee) founded by Jacob Schorer in The Hague in 1912. The Institute for Sexual Science grew out of the Scientific Humanitarian Committee (Wissenschaftlichhumanitares Komitee) which Hirschfeld founded in 1897. Both collections were destroyed by the Nazis.[5]

In the 1940s, three archives were founded in the United States at academic institutions which acquired large collections that were later used to study homosexuality and lesbian culture. These included a collection on women writers at Smith College (1942) which later became the Sophia Smith Collection, the Women's Archives at Radcliffe College (1943) later known as the Schlesinger Library on the History of Women in America, and the Institute for Sex Research, Inc. (1947) that is now known as the Kinsey Institute for Research in Sex, Gender, and Reproduction at Indiana University Bloomington.

Many traditional and academic archives already contained material on the history of queer people, but the staff was either unaware of it, didn't value it in terms of documenting

LGBTQ culture, or actively tried to hide it. Material that was identified as related to queer lives tended to be documents created by people who viewed them as criminals or degenerates. LGBTQ material in mainstream repositories was often hidden by inaccurate subject headings or "coded" language such as using the words friend, roommate or travel companion. These subject headings were misleading at best, and were often overlooked by researchers as relevant to their research. Sometimes archivists would not provide any subject headings that would indicate LGBTQ activity, for instance, leaving out any mention of same sex behavior at a girls' school or women's college (D. Hamer, personal communication, November 5, 2009).

Much of the archival material created by LGBTQ people was intentionally destroyed or not considered valuable enough to save. Papers that were saved in mainstream archives were generally those of elite white men. In order for paper documents to survive an individual's lifetime, it generally required that they had the space, stability, financial resources and clout to collect, save, and convince others that their materials were worth saving after their death. Countless collections were destroyed by relatives of LGBTQ people. Even more tragic are the collections destroyed by LGBTQ individuals themselves out of a fear of discrimination or the reaction of their families and friends. Some simply didn't consider their own lives a valuable part of history and were not encouraged to do so by mainstream society. There were also many collections that were destroyed by flooding in the basements of tenement buildings, that grew mold in shacks in the woods, or that an individual could not afford to move or lost as a result of being made homeless.

The 1970s

The 1970s were a particularly active and visible phase of what were then known as the gay liberation and women's liberation movements in the United States. The LGBTQ archives founded during this time were formed out of the private collections of individuals and the records of LGBTQ organizations, publications, and businesses. For example, the previously mentioned Western Gay Archives was founded in 1971 by Jim Kepner. Two years later, in 1973, four more community-based archives were established: the Canadian Lesbian and Gay Archives in Toronto, the Lesbian Herstory Archives in New York City, the Stonewall Library and Archives in Fort Lauderdale (Society of American Archivists, Lesbian and Gay Archives Roundtable, 2007), and Spinnboden Lesbenarchiv und Bibliothek in Berlin — all of which are still going strong today (International Information Centre and Archives for the Women's Movement, n.d.).

It was clear that these archives were formed by activists in the context of the gay and women's liberation movements in their approach to organizing and running the archives. For example, many archives were run as collectives and some of the lesbian feminist archives were for women only. Many of them viewed the gay and women's liberation movements as part of a greater struggle for social justice for all people. They were a vibrant part of creating LGBTQ community, hosting events such as book clubs, film nights, and lectures. These were not quiet tombs run by archivists who expected researchers to have academic qualifications to use the materials. James Fraser wrote in an article on the Canadian Gay Archives in 1977, "The Archives itself is a part of the movement whose story it attempts to preserve" (p. 159).

There are countless stories of young people going to libraries looking for information on being LGBTQ and only finding a few books portraying them as mentally ill, criminals, suicidal, or homicidal. Some of the founders of LGBTQ archives that started in the 1970s were reacting to the experience of growing up without an awareness that an LGBTQ culture existed. They also considered the destruction of their history by the mainstream or patriarchal society to be a part of their oppression. Some of the main reasons LGBTQ activists started archives were to come out of the closet as a culture, a desire to know their history, to combat the active destruction of their history, to own and control their own history, to provide material for the creation of publications both celebrating and telling the truth about their lives, and to provide safe places to read and study LGBTQ materials. Ed Jackson, of the Canadian Gay Liberation Movement Archives in Toronto (now known as the Canadian Lesbian and Gay Archives), said at a Gay Academic Union conference at Columbia University in 1975:

> Typically such repositories of historical records have been seen as neutral, passive receptacles ... In the case of a gay archives or library, this simply is not true. Given the nature of social attitudes toward homosexuality, such a centre of information is and will remain a threat to a society organized like ours [Bebout, 1979].

During the 1970s, mainstream archives generally did not want visibly LGBTQ materials.

Collecting material to document an invisible culture from donors who, if "outed," risked losing jobs, housing, and custody of children was a challenge. In addition, after an individual's death, homophobic families were often the legal owners of the material unless a will leaving the material to a partner or friend existed. Even then, families would sometimes try to destroy or hide any evidence of their relative's sexual orientation or identity. As LGBTQ archives grew, there were occasionally homophobic families who attempted to take back materials from them. Some families whose LGBTQ relatives had papers at mainstream archives asked that they be covered up or at least not be identified as LGBTQ.

While not having documentation of the legal transfer of ownership and copyright for collections has been a problem at times for mainstream archives, this problem is especially endemic for LGBTQ archives for the reasons described above. Valuable collections are still being left on the doorstep of archives and being salvaged from the trash. Discrimination against LGBTQ people has greatly affected their ability to preserve their history. Archivists are generally able to provide access to materials as the owner of the physical property if not of the copyright without such donation documentation. The burden of obtaining permission to publish from the copyright holder falls on the researcher. This becomes a more thorny issue regarding providing online access to archives as posting documents on the Internet is considered a form of publishing. Federal orphan works legislation, intended to enable the use of copyrighted works without permission when the copyright owner cannot be found, may make this easier in the future.

Activists found starting and maintaining community archives to be taxing. The challenges included: adequate funding, space for storage and providing access, staff to process materials, and long term preservation of materials, particularly those in audiovisual formats. Most institutional archives struggle with similar issues, but tend to have more resources through their parent institutions and broader community and alumni support. Some LGBTQ archives were housed in LGBTQ community centers, at Metropolitan Community Churches,[6] and in the offices of LGBTQ publishers, businesses, and activist organizations. Several collections spent years in individuals' homes or in storage which contributed to access and preservation problems. Funding sources, if they had any, varied, but included membership fees, individual donations, and community fundraising events. Working within an all volunteer organization can be both challenging and liberating. Many of the volunteers were not trained archivists or librarians although most of the community-based archives that started in the 1970s had at least one volunteer with professional training and experience. Some of the volunteers involved in these early community-based archives later got professional training if they didn't start out with it. The stability and continuity of funding, staff, and housing were also a struggle for some archives. These issues caused several archives to eventually place their holdings at mainstream institutions.

Profile: The Canadian Lesbian and Gay Archives (CLGA), Toronto

CLGA was founded in 1973 as the Canadian Gay Liberation Movement Archives in Toronto by members of the collective that published the gay newspaper *The Body Politic*. Part of the newspaper's files became the basis for the archives. The volunteers collected materials locally and solicited them from LGBTQ organizations across Canada. The introduction to their 1975 flyer states:

> A conspiracy of silence has robbed gay people of their history. A sense of continuity, which derives from the knowledge of a heritage, is essential for the building of self-confidence in a community. It is a necessary tool in the struggle for social change [Bebout, 1979].

In 1975, a six person collective was formed to give the archives an organizational structure independent of the newspaper although they still shared resources and space. Not only did it take the staff of the archives three years to get their own desk, they also survived a police raid on the office they shared with The Body Politic Collective in 1977 ("Police raid archives," 1978). In 1978, the volunteers included two professional archivists, one professional librarian, and one library technician (H. Averill, personal communication, October 8, 2009). In addition, the archives was a member of the Toronto Area Archivists Group (Fraser, 1977/1978). In the late 1970s, the Provincial Archives of Ontario offered to take the collection, but was turned down by CLGA (H. Averill, personal communication, October 8, 2009). The reasons included concerns about cataloging accuracy, denial of access to people not considered to be conducting "serious" research, and placement of restrictions on materials (Bebout, 1979). The archives was incorporated in 1980 and run as a collective until 1992 (H. Averill, personal communication, October 8, 2009).

The vision and hard work of the volunteers led to many impressive accomplishments including: becoming the first LGBTQ organization in Canada to receive charitable status (1981); having the largest collection of LGBTQ periodicals in the world; compiling and publishing the first bibliography specifically on gay men and AIDS (1982) (A. Miller, personal communication, October 1, 2009); and publishing a manual on archives administration management with limited space and financial resources (1983). The book, *Organizing an Archives: The Canadian Gay Archives Experience* by James A. Fraser and Harold A. Averill, went through three printings and was sold to many small archives (most of them "straight") across North America despite being held up by Customs staff on one occasion as potentially obscene material (H. Averill, personal communication, October 23, 2009). CLGA has been an active and vital part of the community including being a cofounder of the Gay Community Dance Committee, organizing conferences, and supporting other LGBTQ organizations and political movements (H. Averill, personal communication, October 8, 2009).

CLGA is now the second largest LGBTQ archives in the world[7] and on September 26, 2009, celebrated the grand opening of its new home which contains a gallery and meeting rooms along with space for research and storing collections (Canadian Lesbian & Gay Archives, 2009). The CLGA website, launched in 1997, includes the full-text of back issues of their newsletter, *The Lesbian and Gay Archivist*, recordings of speeches given at the grand opening celebration of their new facility, and images that can be downloaded onto mobile phones and MP3 players. They also have a blog and post on Facebook and Twitter.

The 1980s

Several more LGBTQ archives were founded in the 1980s including: the Gerber/Hart Library (1981); June L. Mazer Lesbian Archives (1981); Lambda Archives of San Diego (1987); and the Archives Gaies du Quebec (1985) (Society of American Archivists, Lesbian and Gay Archives Roundtable, 2007). In 1987, two groundbreaking publications on LGBTQ archival collections appeared: the *Directory of the International Association of Lesbian and Gay Archives and Libraries* compiled by Alan V. Miller, and Elizabeth Knowlton's article "Documenting the Gay Rights Movement" published in *Provenance: The Journal of the Society of Georgia Archivists*.

Knowlton's article exposed the ignorance of many mainstream archivists of the existence of LGBTQ archives in their local communities and of LGBTQ material in their own collections. She wrote,

> Unfortunately, most archivists cannot separate their attitude toward homosexuality from their care and protection of gay records. Although none of the traditional archivists surveyed admitted to destroying gay papers..., there are many ways for documents to "disappear" without actually shredding them. Archivists return papers to the family, never get around to processing them, catalog them vaguely and incompletely.... If an archivist does not want homosexual records in his institution, he will never see the ones he has [Knowlton, 1987, p. 25].

Knowlton encouraged archivists at mainstream institutions to take an active role in preserving the history of the gay rights movement including offering advice on funding and preservation to community-based archives.

The *Directory of the International Association of Lesbian and Gay Archives and Libraries*, also based on a survey, made LGBTQ archives more visible especially to each other and the larger LGBTQ community. It included responses from thirty-four archives and a list of eighty-eight organizations that were sent surveys.

Feminist Archives

As part of the second wave of the feminist movement, a new generation of women's libraries and archives were founded worldwide. Many of them proudly collected material on lesbians as part of the history of the women's movement such as the Feminist Library in London, founded in 1975. Several of the feminist archives were focused on lesbian feminism and lesbian history. From 1973 to 1985, at least 18 archives[8] were founded with the word "lesbian" in the title. Several of these libraries and archives were for women only and some remain so, such as STICHWORT, Archiv der Frauen und Lesbenbewegung (STICHWORT, Archives of the Women's and Lesbian's Movements) in Vienna, Austria, whose website states "women only, transgenders [*sic*] welcome" <http://www.stichwort.or.at/english/frames-

e/index-e.htm>. These archives were crucial to preserving lesbian history. Some lesbians either didn't want to work with gay men or felt that lesbian history would not be a priority at male-dominated LGBTQ archives.

Profile: Spinnboden Lesbenarchiv und Bibliothek, Berlin

Spinnboden Lesbenarchiv und Bibliothek was founded in 1973 in the context of the resurgence of the gay and women's liberation movements. The collection started with the files of the women's section of the lesbian and gay liberation group Homosexual Action Westberlin (HAW) which documented their own activities and work with other West German lesbian groups. The lesbians who founded it wanted to make sure that no more of their history was lost. In 1983, it was registered as a charitable association and was named Spinnboden — Archiv zur Entdeckung und Bewahrung von Frauenliebe (Archive for the Discovery and Preservation of Women's Love). The first part of the name "Spinnboden" is a reference to the medieval workplaces where spinsters, independent women who supported themselves by spinning yarn or weaving, shared their thoughts and passed on knowledge. Spinnboden has received government funding since 1993, but remains an independent organization. Spinnboden's collection is international in scope and, except for the Lesbian Herstory Archives, has the world's largest collection of materials by and about lesbians. Spinnboden has been an active part of the lesbian community stemming from their position that it is not enough to keep the documentation of lesbian culture, but that they also need to engage with that culture. To that end Spinnboden, like many community-based archives, is also a meeting place and hosts films, lectures, and support groups. In addition, their staff does outreach and education which they feel is essential to the liberation of lesbians in a society where heterosexual culture is considered the norm. Spinnboden is involved in i.d.a (Dachverband deutschsprachiger Frauen/Lesbenarchive, bibliotheken und dokumentation-sstellen, informieren, dokumentieren, archivieren) the umbrella organization of German-language lesbian/women's libraries, archives and documentation centers and is affiliated with local public libraries (Spinnboden Lesbenarchiv und Bibliothek Berlin, n.d.).

AIDS Epidemic and Archives

During the 1980s, the AIDS Epidemic created a new urgency to document the lives of gay men who were dying and to preserve their papers. David Mixner, gay activist and political strategist, commented on why he saved so many of his papers in an interview published in *The Advocate*:

> I've saved my huge collection because I saw so many of the papers of my nearly 300 friends who died from AIDS being destroyed by their families after their deaths. I saw our community's history vanishing right in front of me, and I was devastated that so many of their stories were being lost. Most of their papers were burned by their families in shame [Allen, 2005].

The University of California San Francisco (UCSF) AIDS History Project, the most well known of the AIDS archives, started in 1987. Although it is housed and owned by UCSF, it is a collaboration between AIDS activists, archivists, and historians and focuses on documenting AIDS activist groups and community based organizations (University of California San Francisco Library and Center for Knowledge Management, 2009). The

Happy Foundation Archives founded in 1988 by Gene Elder in San Antonio, Texas, collected the papers of many gay men who died from complications of HIV/AIDS. Sarah Fisch, who interviewed Elder for the *San Antonio Current* in 2008, asked him if working with the collection made him sad. Elder replied "Attending to the Archives helps me feel less sad. It's a way of honoring them, of course" (Fisch, 2008). Existing LGBTQ archives also collected material documenting the AIDS Epidemic and the lives of people living with HIV/AIDS.

Profile: Gay, Lesbian, Bisexual, Transgender Historical Society, San Francisco

The GLBT Historical Society was founded in 1985 as the San Francisco Bay Area Gay and Lesbian Historical Society (SFBAGL) by historians, librarians, and activists who were members of the San Francisco Lesbian and Gay History Project. The SFBAGL grew out of the San Francisco Gay and Lesbian Periodical Archives which was created from a number of private collections in 1982 by founders Willie Walker and Greg Pennington (Bryer, 2005). Willie Walker was an archivist and a nurse who worked at San Francisco General Hospital on the so-called AIDS ward. Marjorie Bryer wrote about Walker in a brief history of the Society, "Like others who witnessed the AIDS Epidemic firsthand, Walker was convinced that if no one collected and preserved these records, before long, vital information about the collective past of San Francisco's queer community ... would be lost forever" (2005). At first, the Society's materials were kept in private homes and storage units and were accessible only by appointment. The volunteer staff included professionally trained archivists and librarians. According to the *Directory of the International Association of Lesbian and Gay Archives and Libraries* published in 1987, their annual budget was $1000 or less and was funded by membership fees and donations and their collecting policy was to "accept any historically significant gay/lesbian related material which would otherwise be lost or destroyed" (Miller, 1987). From this humble beginning, the Society grew to be one of the largest queer archives in the world. One of the most impressive things about the Society, along with its valuable collections, has been its work providing access to the public in multiple ways to its materials and the history they document. The Society's public history work includes lectures, conferences, exhibits, and tours of the archives on YouTube. Since 2008, the Society has had a satellite exhibit space in the Castro neighborhood which, with its heavy tourist traffic, draws more visitors than the one at their downtown location (Bajko, 2008). In addition to having a full-time professional archivist and an archives that is open to the public, the Society has some manuscript collections on deposit at the San Francisco Public Library to allow greater researcher access and participates in the Online Archive of California (OAC) which provides access to finding aids to and digital facsimiles of primary resource collections held by institutions in California at http://www.oac.cdlib.org/.

The 1990s

The 1990s brought even more LGBTQ history projects and archives into existence and witnessed the continued growth of some that had survived for 20 or more years. The Lesbian Herstory Archives bought their own building in 1990 which officially opened in June 1993. More mainstream archives started to be willing to identify LGBTQ holdings, but it was still not a priority for most and others were still actively opposed to doing so. The reasons for this included concerns about the homophobic reactions of donors of collections, financial supporters, and the administration. Some archivists simply did not understand how to better identify LGBTQ subject content or consider it important to learn.

A major milestone of the 1990s was the publication of the *Lavender Legacies* guide by the Society of American Archivists, Lesbian and Gay Archives Roundtable in 1998. It was the first formal guide to LGBTQ primary source material held by both mainstream and LGBTQ archives in North America (Society of American Archivists, Lesbian and Gay Archives Roundtable, 2007). The reasons listed for compiling the *Lavender Legacies* guide in its introduction are similar to those that activists who started LGBTQ archives expressed for founding them. They include "the need to identify responsive archives during a time of many deaths of early community activists," "our desire to participate in the effort to ensure preservation and access to the materials that document our contributions to society," and to "facilitate the continued study of the history and culture of a marginalized people traditionally ignored and sometimes deliberately hidden from researchers by mainstream institutions" (Society of American Archivists, Lesbian and Gay Archives Roundtable, 2007). In addition to providing a source of information on repositories collecting LGBTQ material for donors and researchers, the guide encouraged mainstream archives to identify their holdings in this area and make information about them available to the public.

The 2000s

By 2000, more mainstream archives were openly collecting and accurately cataloging LGBTQ materials, and collaborations between mainstream and LGBTQ archives and history projects began to be more common. These included local history projects that collected material, conducted oral histories, and did public history projects, but donated and encouraged others to donate their materials to mainstream archives. An early and especially notable example founded in 1980 is The History Project (THP) which is an all volunteer organization focused on preserving and making accessible the history of Boston's LGBT community. In addition to conducting research and collecting materials, THP brings Boston's LGBTQ history to the public in a variety of ways including exhibits and publications such as *Improper Bostonians: Lesbian and Gay History from the Puritans to Playland* published in 1998. They also assist Northeastern University in identifying collections that may be transferred to their Archives and Special Collections at http://www.historyproject.org/.

A significant development for LGBTQ history and archives was the first international conference on GLBT Archives, Libraries, Museums, and Special Collections (GLBT ALMS) held in 2006. It was hosted by the Quatrefoil Library, a GLBT lending library in St. Paul, Minnesota, and the Jean-Nickolaus Tretter Collection in Gay, Lesbian, Bisexual and Transgender Studies at the University of Minnesota. The keynote speakers included long time LGBTQ liberation activists Barbara Gittings and Frank Kameny. It was followed by a second one in 2008 at the Graduate Center of the City University of New York and more are planned for the future. The next one will be in Los Angeles in 2011.

Many LGBTQ archives have tried to collect materials from the broad spectrum of the LGBTQ community, although they often focused on specific geographical areas. Some have intentionally focused on specific groups within the community, such as lesbian specific archives and the Black Gay Archive in Philadelphia.[9] In 1996, Fritz Klein and Regina Reinhardt, preeminent leaders of the bisexual movement, founded the Bisexual Archives. More recently the Black Gay and Lesbian Archive (BGLA) was founded in 2000,[10] the rukus! Black LGBT Archive Project in 2005,[11] and the Houston Transgender Archives in 2008.[12]

Regarding women's history, although archivists at some women's colleges were at their worst hostile to lesbian students and historians and kept the history of lesbians hidden though inaccurate cataloging, if identified at all, several did preserve incredibly rich collections on lesbians. Things have changed so much in forty years that the three largest women's history collections in the United States, the Schlesinger Library at Harvard University, the Sophia Smith Collection at Smith College, and the Sallie Bingham Center for Women's History and Culture at Duke University have competed (in a sisterly manner) to have the honor of adding the papers of famous "out" lesbians to their collections. They have also become major collectors of the records of lesbian organizations and the papers of individuals such as lesbian feminists Alix Dobkin (Schlesinger Library), Noel Phyllis Birkby (Sophia Smith Collection), and Julia Penelope (Sallie Bingham Center). In addition, the list of sponsors of the 2008 GLBT Archives, Libraries, Museums, and Special Collections conference included the Sophia Smith Collection and the Sallie Bingham Center as well as the Lesbian Herstory Archives at http://web.gc.cuny.edu/clags/glbtalms/.

Since 2000, the collections of several LGBTQ archives were transferred to mainstream archives due to a lack of funding, staffing, or loss of archival facilities. The inability to provide adequate storage for the long term preservation of the collections was also an issue. For example, the National Transgender Library & Archive, one of the largest collections of transgender research materials in the world, was donated to the Labadie Collection at the University of Michigan in 2000.

Several well-know activists involved in the gay liberation and lesbian feminist movements of the twentieth century have donated their papers to mainstream archives since 2000. For example, Barbara Gittings' papers[13] were donated to the New York Public Library in 2007 and Frank Kameny's[14] to the Library of Congress and the Smithsonian's National Museum of American History in 2006. In situations where collections were purchased, the need for money may have been an important factor. There are many long time LGBTQ activists who are now living in poverty and without adequate medical care or those who have died in similar situations over the past twenty years. Other concerns that may have led to some individual's decisions to place material in mainstream archives may have been a desire to support the archives of women's colleges and/or their alma mater; for their papers to be at an institution that they felt had the stability and resources to catalog, preserve, and provide access to their papers long term; or for their papers to be in the company of those of some of their friends. Deborah Edel, co-founder of the Lesbian Herstory Archives, commented at the session on "Community-Based Archives: What Now?" at the 2008 GLBT ALMS conference that some of these donors could request that a community-based archives such as the Lesbian Herstory Archives also get copies of their papers as a condition of donating papers to mainstream archives (2008). Traditionally archivists did not want duplicates of their original materials being held by other institutions,[15] but some may be willing to consider this arrangement. The presence of more archival material on the Internet may change the way this issue is handled.

Despite changes at some mainstream archives, LGBTQ archives continue to be founded by queer people for similar reasons as in the 1970s. These reasons include combating the active destruction of their history, owning and controlling their own history, and providing safe places to read and study LGBTQ materials. There are also many donors who still prefer to give their papers to LGBTQ archives and community members who feel more comfortable doing research there. For example, pioneer lesbian activists Phyllis Lyon and Del Martin both sold and donated their papers to the Gay, Lesbian, Bisexual Transgender Historical Society in San Francisco in 1993. Some LGBTQ people continue to be concerned that although institutions that were once hostile to them now want their papers, the situation could change or be reversed again in the future. Several LGBTQ archives such as the ONE National Gay & Lesbian Archives and the Lesbian Herstory Archives continue to thrive and grow even though some mainstream archives would now be happy to have their collections.

Profile: ŠKUC-LL Lezbična Knjižnica (ŠKUC-LL Lesbian Library & Archive) Ljubljana, Slovenia

The ŠKUC-LL Lesbian Library & Archive was founded in Ljubljana, Slovenia in 2001. ŠKUC-LL, founded in 1987, was the first lesbian organization in the former socialist Eastern European countries and grew out of the lesbian section of the feminist organization Lilith. The LL stands for "Lesbian Lilith" (T. Greif, personal communication, September 28, 2009) and ŠKUC is the Students' Cultural Centre "which is one of the leading organizations for the promotion of nonprofit artistic activity in Slovenia, formed in 1972" ("Škuc LL lesbian section," n.d.). ŠKUC-LL is still rooted in leftist, feminist theory and activism and is involved with other civil rights movements. Before 2001, ŠKUC-LL collected books and archival materials, but they were stored in locations that were not accessible to the public. Natasa Velikonja, current coordinator of the library and archives, sociologist, and the first "out" lesbian poet in Slovenia, gathered materials for the archives and was an important founder (T. Greif, personal communication, November 16, 2009). One of the other founders is a professional librarian and other volunteers include an archivist and women with advanced degrees in the social sciences. Once the archives was founded, they received many more donations of materials and are now the most comprehensive collection on LGBTQ culture and sexuality in the Balkan States. Although the collection is mainly lesbian, they also have other LGBTQ materials. Magnus, the first Slovenian gay men's group which was founded in 1984, donated most of their archives. The University of Ljubljana rejected ŠKUC-LL Lezbična Knjižnica's invitation to work collaboratively although many of their students in the social sciences do research there (T. Greif, personal communication, September 28, 2009). The reasons for founding and continuing to build the library and archives include preserving lesbian history and making sure it will be well cared for and made accessible. According to Tatjana Greif, Coordinator of Lesbian Section ŠKUC-LL, the women's groups that currently exist in Slovenia do not recognize lesbian issues as women's issues and "we have to keep our heritage independently, otherwise we can easily get lost in the dominant, mainstream culture, which has a tendency to assimilate and normalize minorities" (T. Greif, personal communication, September 28, 2009).

LGBTQ Archives Online

Some LGBTQ archives and history projects use their resources and volunteers to create online archives and exhibits instead of focusing on sustaining a brick and mortar archive. A recent example, the Thai Rainbow Archive Project: A Digitized Collection of Thai Gay, Lesbian and Transgender Publications is a collaboration between Thai organizations, the Australian National University, and the National Library of Australia. The project plans to preserve and make accessible LGBTQ materials that have not been collected by any Thai institutional archive. This project received a grant from the British Library's Endangered

Archives Programme in 2008 to digitize Thai LGBTQ magazines and make them available on the project's website at http://thairainbowarchive.anu.edu.au.

LGBTQ archives are using a variety of Web 2.0 technologies such as Facebook, Twitter, and YouTube to provide more access to their collections and information about them. These are great tools for outreach and community building and can encompass a wider audience than the local community and usual researchers. A wonderful example is the tour of the Gay, Lesbian, Bisexual, Transgender Historical Society on YouTube. This nine part series includes information on how the archives works, examples from the collections, and a tour for a student group.

OutHistory.org, produced by the Center for Lesbian and Gay Studies at the City University of New York Graduate Center and directed by pioneering LGBTQ historian Jonathan Ned Katz, is a website that functions as an online museum, encyclopedia, archives, and a place to collaboratively document LGBTQ and heterosexual history. Some of the slogans listed on the website sum up what the goals of many of the archives founded in the 1970s were such as "OutHistory.org: History from the Community Up" and "Out History.org: The Story of LGBTQ people by LGBTQ people" at http://www.outhistory.org/wiki/About.[16] Another example of Web 2.0 technologies being used to create collaborative online LGBTQ history sites is the Gay History Wiki which documents the history of gay men in Philadelphia, Pennsylvania, and the organizations, bars, culture and social networks they created from 1960 through the present at http://gayhistory.wikispaces.com/Welcome+to+Gay+Networks+in+Philadelphia. According to Chris Bartlett, founder of the wiki, it also "aims to collect the life stories of at least 4,600 gay Philadelphia men who since 1981 have died following complications to their battles with AIDS/HIV" (Wink, 2009).

Conclusion

Community-based archives have more competition for LGBTQ materials now that some mainstream archives also consider them valuable. However, there is still an abundance of material to collect. LGBTQ community-based archives continue to do what they do best — collecting and providing access to material on LGBTQ people who have pushed the boundaries of how those identities are defined and expressed and those who are often underrepresented in mainstream archives such as transgender people, people of color, women, the working class and poor, and people who are not famous. Another success of LGBTQ archives is providing open, free, and welcoming access to their collections to the LGBTQ community and others, from homeless LGTBQ teenagers to "straight" academics. They continue to be places where LGBTQ people and history are the number one priority for the staff, funders, and administration. As supportive of LGBTQ history as several mainstream archives are, the work of community-based archives directly sustains and is part of current movements toward LGBTQ liberation and community building. Mainstream archives can maintain the preservation of this history by making accessible and identifying collections that contain documents relevant to the study of LGBTQ culture, political movements and individuals whether or not the individual or organization who created the materials identified as LGBTQ.

The history of LGBTQ archives is an activist history. Most mainstream archives would not have started openly collecting and valuing that history unless LGBTQ activists, librarians, archivists and historians made sure that archival materials were preserved, accessible, published and used in public history projects. The work of these pioneers raised the expectations of access in mainstream archives to these materials as well as made them more widely available. The collections at community and mainstream archives made it possible for historians to produce the growing number of books and articles on LGBTQ history published during the past forty years. Young people can now find information on LGBTQ culture in most libraries that is not degrading. In addition, queer "pack rats" now have options. There are LGBTQ and mainstream archives that will welcome their papers and accurately catalog them as well as online history sites where they can deposit their "papers" and participate in documenting LGBTQ history.

NOTES

1. The "Q" in the acronym LGBTQ stands for both queer and questioning individuals.
2. For the purposes of this essay, "queer" is meant to be synonymous with LGBTQ.
3. Western Gay Archives, Los Angeles, CA, 1971 (later known as the the Natalie Barney/Edward Carpenter Library of the International Gay & Lesbian Archives which in 1995 merged with ONE, Inc., to become the ONE National Gay & Lesbian Archives); Canadian Lesbian and Gay Archives, Toronto, Ontario, 1973; Lesbian Herstory Archives, New York, NY, 1973; Spinnboden Lesbenarchiv und Bibliothek, Berlin, Germany, 1973; Stonewall Library and Archives, Ft. Lauderdale, FL, 1973; Sexual Minorities Archives / New Alexandria Lesbian Library, Florence, MA (founded in Chicago, IL, as the New Alexandria Lesbian Library), 1974; International Homo/Lesbian Information Center and Archives (IHLIA), Amsterdam, Netherlands, 1978; Ohio Lesbian Archives, Cincinnati, OH, 1978; Up the Stairs Community Center Archives & Resource Library, Fort Wayne, IN, 1978; Gerber/Hart Library, Chicago, IL, 1981; June L. Mazer Lesbian Archives, West Hollywood, CA, 1981; Lesbisch Archief Nijmegen, Nijmegen, The Netherlands, 1981; Archives Gaies du Quebec, Montreal, Quebec, 1983; STICHWORT — Archives of the Women's and Lesbian Movements, Berlin, Germany, 1983; Lesbian Archive and Information Centre, Glasgow, Scotland (founded in London), 1984; Lambda Archives of San Diego, San Diego, CA, 1987; and the HAPPY Foundation's LGBT History Archives, San Antonio, TX, 1988.
4. Examples are the Human Sexuality Collection at Cornell University Library's Division of Rare & Manuscript Collections founded in 1988 and the Jean-Nickolaus Tretter Collection in GLBT Studies in the Special Collections and Rare Books Department of the University of Minnesota Libraries founded when Tretter donated his personal collection in 2001. For more examples, see the Lavender Legacies Guide by the Society of American Archivists, Lesbian and Gay Archives Roundtable http://www.archivists.org/saa groups/lagar/index.html.
5. For more information on the Dutch Scientific Humanitarian Committee, see the profile on the Internationaal Homo/Lesbisch Informatiecentrum en Archief (IHLIA) in this section.
6. The Metropolitan Community Church (MCC) or the Universal Fellowship of Metropolitan Community Churches (UFMCC) is a LGBTQ-centered Protestant Christian denomination.
7. ONE National Gay & Lesbian Archives is the world's largest research library on Gay, Lesbian, Bisexual, and Transgendered heritage, at http://www.onearchives.org/.
8. Lesbian Herstory Archives, New York, NY, 1973; Spinnboden Lesbenarchiv und Bibliothek, Berlin, Germany, 1973; Sexual Minorities Archives / New Alexandria Lesbian Library, Florence, MA (founded in Chicago, IL as the New Alexandria Lesbian Library), 1974; Ohio Lesbian Archives, Cincinnati, OH, 1978; June L. Mazer Lesbian Archives, West Hollywood, CA, 1981; Stichting Lesbisch Archief Leeuwarden, Leeuwarden, the Netherlands, 1982; Victorian Women's Liberation and Lesbian Feminist Archive, Melbourne, Victoria, Australia, 1982; Archives Recherches et Cultures Lesbiennes (ACRL), Paris, France, 1983; San Francisco Lesbian Archives, San Francisco, CA, 1983; STICHWORT — Archiv der Frauen- und Lesbenbewegung, Berlin, Germany, 1983; the archives of the Colectiva Lesbica Feminista Ayuquelen, Santiago, Chile, 1984; Lesbian Archive and Information Centre (LAIC), London, England, 1984.The following archives were listed in the *Newsletter of the Canadian Gay Archives*, No. 4, September 1981 http://www.clga.ca/About/LGArchivist/v4.htm, but did not indicate the year they were founded: Atlanta Lesbian-Feminist Alliance, Southeastern Lesbian Archives; Florida Collection of Lesbian Herstory; Kentucky Lesbian Herstory Archives; Lesbian Community Center Library; Tennessee Lesbian Archives.
9. This was listed in the *Directory of the International Association of Lesbian and Gay Archives and Libraries* published in 1987 as one of the archives contacted which failed to respond.

10. The Schomburg Center for Research in Black Culture became the official repository for the Black Gay and Lesbian Archive (BGLA) in 2004.

11. http://www.rukus.co.uk/content/view/12/27/.

12. http://tgctr.org/archive.shtml.

13. Formal title: Barbara Gittings and Kay Tobin Lahusen Gay History Papers.

14. Formal title: Frank Kameny Papers.

15. This was partly due to the responsibility of an archive, as custodian of the materials entrusted to them by the donor, to try to control the dissemination of copies and use of the collection. In addition, processing and caring for archival material can be so costly that archives usually prefer to use their resources to care for original material that is not available elsewhere. The absence of copies at other archives also makes the material more valuable.

16. For more information, please see the profile on OutHistory.org in Section One.

References

Allen, D. (2005, November 22). Mixner goes to Yale — at least on paper. *Advocate*, (951), 44.

Bajko, M. S. (2005, September 22). Keepers of gay past focus eyes on future. *Bay Area Reporter Online*, Retrieved from http://www.ebar.com/news/article.php?article=175&sec=news

Bajko, M. S. (2008, July 3). Historical society to open Castro site. *Bay Area Reporter Online*, Retrieved from http://bayareareporter.net/news/article.php?sec=news&article=3132

Bebout, R. (1979, August). Stashing the evidence. *The Body Politic, 55*, pp. 21–22, 26.

Bryer, M. (2005). A brief history of the GLBT Historical Society. In Gay, Lesbian, Bisexual and Transgender Historical Society & Primary Source Microfilm (Eds.), *Gay and lesbian community, support, and spirit: Selected newsletters and periodicals from the holdings of the Gay, Lesbian, Bisexual, Transgender History Society. Series 9, Parts 1 through 3*. Woodbridge, CT: Primary Source Microfilm.

Canadian Lesbian & Gay Archives. (2004, June 16). What we've published. Retrieved from http://www.clga.ca/About/publish/pubint.htm

Canadian Lesbian & Gay Archives. (2009). New home for archival gold. Retrieved from http://clga.ca/aboutus/new_home.shtml

Edel, D., Wandel, R., & McElhinney, G. (2008, May 10). Community-based archives: What now? [Podcast]. Panel presented at the GLBT Archives, Libraries Museums, and Special Collections Conference, New York. Retrieved from http://library.gc.cuny.edu/GLBTALMS2008recordings/Community-Based%20Archives.mp3

Fisch, S. (2008, November 26). The archivist. *San Antonio Current*. Retrieved from http://sacurrent.com/printStory.asp?id=69586

Fraser, J. A. (1977/1978). Canadian gay archives. *Archivaria, 5*, 158–159.

International Information Centre and Archives for the Women's Movement. (n.d). Spinnboden Lesbenarchiv und Bibliothek. Mapping the World Database. Retrieved from http://www.iiav.nl/scripts/wwwopac.exe?%250=00255&DATABASE=mapdetail&DEBUG=0&GEZOCHTOP=Spinnboden+Lesbenarchiv+und+Bibliothek&INGANG=&OPAC_URL=&OPNIEUWZOEKEN=&SRT1=A1&TAAL=eng&isutf8=1&os=x

Knowlton, E. (1987). Documenting the gay rights movement. *Provenance, 5*(1), 17–30.

Lambda Archives of San Diego. (n.d). About the archives. Retrieved from http://www.lambdaarchives.us/about.htm

Miller, A. V. (1987). *Directory of the international association of lesbian and gay archives and libraries*. Toronto, Ont., Canada: The Association.

Police raid archives. (1978, May). *Gay Archivist: Newsletter of the Canadian Gay Archives*, 2. Retrieved from http://clga.ca/aboutus/LGArchivist/v2.htm

Potvin, E. (1998, January 25). A brief history of ONE Institute & Archives 1942–1994. Unpublished manuscript.

Russell, R. (1988, October 20). Collective crisis: Loss of storage space leaves future uncertain for gay activist's unique archives. *Los Angeles Times*. Retrieved from http://articles.latimes.com/1988-10-30/news/we-667_1_gay-organization

Škuc LL lesbian section. (n.d). Retrieved from http://www.ljudmila.org/lesbo/english.htm#1

Society of American Archivists, Lesbian and Gay Archives Roundtable. (2007, November 30). Lavender legacies: Lesbian and Gay Archives Roundtable guide to sources in North America. Retrieved from http://www.archivists.org/saagroups/lagar/guide/index.html

Spinnboden Lesbenarchiv und Bibliothek Berlin. (2008). Geschichte des Spinnboden. Retrieved from http://www.spinnboden.de/wir/geschichte.html

University of California San Francisco Library and Center for Knowledge Management. (2009). About the AIDS History Project. Retrieved from http://www.library.ucsf.edu/collections/archives/manu scripts/aids/about

Wink, C. (2009, October 26). TNT: Chris Bartlett of the Gay History Wiki Project. *Technically Philly.* Retrieved from http://technicallyphilly.com/2009/10/26/tnt-chris-bartlett-of-the-gay-history-wiki-project.

"It Was Only Supposed To Be Twenty Interviews": GLBTIQ Oral History as Librarianship — The Under the Rainbow Collection

Tami Albin

"And finding information was really difficult, because if it had anything about sex in the title or in the book itself, the librarians usually kept it behind the counter. And I think they still do that sometimes. But it was really hard. So one of my strategies around that was I went to work at the public library so that I could get access to this material, so that I would know what was out there so I could — so I could answer people's questions, answer my own questions" (McKinney, 2008).

When I go to a conference and mention that I live in Kansas or work at the University of Kansas (KU), I have come to expect a barrage of recycled jokes about the *Wizard of Oz* generally followed with a "look of pity." The type of conference does not seem to matter, whether it's libraries, oral history or gay, lesbian, bisexual or transgender issues. When people tell these jokes, it seems I am supposed to respond as if I've never heard them before and actually laugh at jokes that mock my home. Usually after *they* have stopped laughing at *their* Oz jokes, their voices drop into a hushed whisper. Even if they've never set foot in Kansas, they usually remark, "It's so flat, like a pancake," or, "It must be so hard to be gay in Kansas." When this first started to happen, I used to take the time to explain the multifaceted topography of Kansas, or I would delve into what I knew about the documented gay, lesbian, bisexual, transgender, intersex or queer (GLBTIQ) history of Kansas, rattle off the names of newsletters or newspapers such as *Land of Awes, Liberty Press,* or *Shades of Gray* the acclaimed documentary on gays and lesbians living in Kansas. People eventually understand the topography once I explained it, but they rarely understand why anybody who identifies as GLBTIQ would live in Kansas. These comments, sometimes from complete strangers, combined with conversations with colleagues and friends led me to the question: Why do GLBTIQ people live in Kansas? Which then, in turn, led me to many other questions: Is it financial? Is it family? Do people who identify as GLBTIQ lead fulfilling lives in Kansas or would they rather be living in a different location? Is it really such a "bad" place to live? As far as I knew, nobody had attempted to do an oral history of GLBTIQ people in Kansas.[1] Was this an opportunity to help fill in a gap about GLBTIQ life and history in Kansas? Would anybody let me interview them? Would anybody be interested? Would anybody care? And would filling in such a gap count as librarianship?

I should point out a few things before continuing. I love my job as the undergraduate instruction and outreach librarian for KU Libraries. I am the subject librarian for our Women, Gender and Sexuality Studies program and also work with undergraduates (specifically first-year students). My area of expertise includes information and technology fluency, and while I have important skill sets and knowledge, I have not had much experience with oral history projects. I knew how to work the equipment, and I had an elementary understanding of the interview process. Additionally, when I decided to design *Under the Rainbow: Oral Histories of GLBTIQ People in Kansas*, I needed to make a connection between oral history and librarianship so that I could get funding and support from the libraries' administration.[2] Plus, it was essential that any research that came out of this project would count towards tenure.

Fortunately, I see oral history and librarianship as two areas that are intrinsically connected. My personal philosophy as an instruction librarian involves a commitment to understanding issues of diversity and access to information. On one hand, I am dedicated to teaching students from various experiences how to access and comprehend information; on the other hand, I am dedicated to making visible and accessible the experiences of GLBTIQ people in Kansas, a population that seldom sees itself included in history.

In 1968, Martha Jane Zachert, a librarian, published "The Implications of Oral History for Librarians." This article makes an excellent argument as to why librarians should be involved in oral history.[3] She states, "oral history, for a library, is a way of *creating* primary source materials in contrast to its time-honored responsibilities of acquiring them. For the librarian, then, building an oral archive becomes a unique opportunity for creative intellectual contribution" (p. 102). The creation of oral histories about GLBTIQ people in Kansas contributes unique, one-of-a-kind documentation for the Libraries' collections. This also assists with filling in the gaps about GLBTIQ history in Kansas, of which, little has been documented historically (Fogerty, 1983).

Also, by making these stories available through our open access institutional repository, KU ScholarWorks, we are not just sharing with KU, but rather, we are also reaching out on a global scale. Oral history is a methodology that is, by its nature, interdisciplinary. "Human beings do not belong to any one field of scholarly inquiry" (Portelli, 1991, p. xi). Thus, even though these interviews are about a specific group of people, at a certain time and location, they can be used more than once. Oral histories can be drawn upon in a variety of ways for research or as a teaching tool, by various disciplines including, but not limited to, Sociology, Women, Gender and Sexuality Studies, History, Political Science, American Studies, Linguistics, Communication Studies, Anthropology and Religious Studies.

An open access collection allows the searcher/reader an opportunity to access and connect with the narrator's experience; this enables the searcher/reader to recognize that they are not alone and who knows, maybe even save a life.[4] As John T. Sears (1997) remarks in the introduction to *Lonely Hunters: An Oral History of Lesbian and Gay Southern Life, 1948–1968*, "[w]e come to know our place within the world through the stories we hear and retell. Our images of lesbians and gay men are shaped by stories learned from school, family and community" (p. 1). He also points out "[d]ocumenting, writing and reading narratives of *our* communities provide lesbian and gay men with a collection of sacred communal stories

that for too long have been lost or devalued in the larger cannon of heterosexist history —
presented to us as fact"[5] (p. 1). When we, as GLBTIQ people in Kansas document and share
our experiences, we challenge what has or, in many instances, has not been documented in
books about GLBTIQ history and experiences, making things not so "straightforward."
Under the Rainbow seeks to create access and share experiences between the narrator and
the searcher/reader regardless of location. Experiences specific to Kansas and other parts of
the world are highlighted in this study.

Oral history in its most basic form "is a recorded interview of an individual or group
of individuals by an historian, researcher, or another interested individual doing the interview" (Butler, 2008, p. 34). "[I]t is largely a learning situation, in which the narrator has
information we lack" (Portelli, 1991, pp. viii–ix). According to the work of Ellen D. Swain
(2006) the "origins of oral history in the United States are rooted firmly in archives and
libraries" with the "Columbia University Oral History Research Office, founded in 1948 ...
[being] one of the first and most notable programs" (p. 344).[6] It is also important to acknowledge that prior to the creation of oral history programs in academic institutions the Federal
Writers Project during the 1930s involved interviewing over "10,000 life stories of men and
women from a variety of occupations and ethnic groups" including former slaves (Library
of Congress, n.d.; Library of Congress, 1980; Erdmans, 2007, p. 10; Portelli, 1991, p. viii).
Historically, these programs, spread throughout the United States, sought to capture specific
oral histories based on gender, class, and race. Paul Thompson (2006) suggests "by introducing new evidence from the underside, by shifting the focus of new areas of inquiry, by
challenging some of the assumptions accepted judgments of historians, by bringing recognition to substantial groups of people who had been ignored, and cumulative process of
transformation is set in motion" (p. 29).

One area where transformation relies "heavily on oral history methods" is the study of
gay, lesbian, and queer history; a field of research that is approximately twenty-five years
old and influenced by the works of feminist ethnographers (Boyd, 2008, p. 177). "Feminist
researchers try to empower (rather than exploit) historical narrators by trusting their voices,
positioning narrators as historical experts, and interpreting narrators' voices alongside the
narrators' interpretation of their own memories" (Boyd, 2008, p. 177). Many researchers
including Elizabeth Lapovsky Kennedy and Madeline D. Davis (*Boots of Leather, Slippers
of Gold*, 1993), and Allan Bérubé (*Coming Out Under Fire*, 2000) saw the need to create
"an archive of oral history tapes that they would 'give back to the community' in the form
of public presentations" (Boyd, 2008, p. 181). Nan A. Boyd (2003), the author of *Wide
Open Town*, also comments that she "was an archivist seeking to save certain histories from
the historical dustbin" (p. 187). The ground work laid by these and many other oral historians
doing GLBTIQ research created a space from which I could design and implement a GLB-
TIQ oral history project in Kansas. I, too, would be able to work with narrators "on a
ground of equality to bring together ... [our] ... different types of knowledge and achieve
a new synthesis from which both will be changed" (Portelli, 1991, p. xii).

As mentioned earlier, KU librarians in tenure-track lines are required to do research
and publish in scholarly journals or books. I am involved in a lot of instruction-related
activities that I could have easily converted into research, but for some reason none of it
was really grabbing my attention, engaging me or causing me to say, "Hey, this could really
help out students." My mind kept on wandering back to all of the comments and jokes
people had made over the years about being "gay-in-as-flat-as-a-pancake-Kansas." I realized
that interviewing GLBTIQ people in Kansas about their experiences in Kansas could be a

research project, one that just might create awareness for those both inside and outside of the state. This project could, as described by Alessandro Portelli in Linda Shopes' (2006) article, "'amplify narrators' voices so that their experiences and views extend outward to others who otherwise would not hear what they have to say" (p. 155).

Oral history projects can be expensive but worth the cost. They can be large projects or small depending on funding, assistance, and support from administration. I will not lie or gloss over facts and say that a well-thought out oral history project can be done cheaply, that isn't fair to your narrators or you. I was able to start my project with a new faculty research grant of approximately $8,000.00 and since then received an additional $17,000.00 in internal funding — in total approximately $25,000.00.

Before I could even consider writing the application for funding I had to think through what I wanted to achieve by doing this oral history project. I read books and articles on how to do oral histories, why one should do oral histories, what the end results can be from doing oral history. I labored over the Oral History Association's *Evaluation Guidelines* (Oral History Association, 2000); I talked to oral historians on campus, to GLBTIQ people in the Lawrence community and on campus. I fussed over where the interviews would be housed, questioned if I would be able to keep the promises I made to narrators and spent a lot of time floating out in the ether asking myself all sorts of questions. To some this may sound like a waste of time but "[t]he concept of research design almost by definition encompasses most aspects of an oral history project, since it guides work on a project from its inception to its completion" (Larson, 2006, p. 105).

After sorting through my thoughts and conversations with people, I began working on my funding request. One of the requirements for applying for funding at KU is completing the Human Subjects Tutorial and Human Subjects Application.[7] This process included outlining my project, estimating how many people would be interviewed, sharing potential interview questions, suggesting ways that I would contact potential narrators and explaining how these interviews would be carried out. Along with the application I also had to create an Informed Consent Form, which walks the potential narrator through the oral history process, stating what I will and will not do, such as, there will be no payment for the interview, that their interview in the future can be transferred into other digital formats, and lastly, if the narrators want to be removed from the project at any point in time, they have the right to remove themselves. I designed the form to also give narrators options such as using their real name or a pseudonym and making their interviews available online via a text document (in this case a PDF), streaming audio and/or video. I didn't know if people I interviewed would want to use their real names because of safety or privacy concerns, and I felt that this was an extremely important option to give narrators.[8]

Other options that I felt were important included sealing oral histories until a certain date (e.g., after the narrator has passed away), and lastly, if people did not want their interviews online they could donate their transcript to the Kansas Collection in the Spencer Research Library (one of the seven libraries on campus), the home of University Archives, Special Collections and the Kansas Collection. In addition to the required Informed Consent Form, I also created a Deed of Gift Form. While not a requirement for the University, it was a requirement for me. I wanted it to be very clear to the narrators that by signing the Deed of Gift Form they would be signing copyright over to me as the steward of the collection.[9] These are two of the most important documents one will need for an oral history project and will be discussed in further detail later.

The proposal for the new faculty grant forced me (in a good way) to think through each step of the process and plan with great detail how I was going to initiate, implement and complete this project. The application asked several questions regarding the significance of the project and funding requirements which I've addressed earlier. It also asked for what I saw as the final outcomes of the project, which are:

- Providing the first fully digitized open access oral history collection of GLBTIQ people in Kansas through KU ScholarWorks
- Exploring the advancement of the role of cultural repositories in online teaching, learning, and research
- Helping to fill in the gap in knowledge about GLBTIQ people in Middle America (as most research is performed on either coast)
- Writing at least one scholarly article about working on this GLBTIQ oral history project

(Since my initial plan was to interview twenty people in the Lawrence/Douglas County area, I did not factor in travel cost for interviews in different locations across Kansas.)

When I found out in September of 2007 that my project had been fully funded, I was ecstatic and terrified at the same time. I was about to reach beyond my comfort zone as a chatty instruction librarian and enter the realm of oral historian, where I had to learn how to listen more deeply (and be quieter than ever before). Every year librarians at KU are fortunate enough to be allotted professional development funds. I used my professional fund to attend the Oral History Association's conference in October of 2007. Since it was in Oakland and in such close proximity to San Francisco and Berkeley, I used my grant money to cover the cost of a hotel to stay a few extra days. I was able to do site visits to the GLBT Historical Society in San Francisco and the Regional Oral History Office at Berkeley. While at the conference and at both of these locations, I was able to ask questions about preservation, ethics, storage, file formats, ways to approach potential narrators, how to work with narrators with editing their transcript and the biggest question of all: how does one create an oral history center? Everybody I spoke with was unbelievably generous and shared so much information with me. I gained insight that I could not have gotten over the phone, or by email or even by Facebook. A few months later in May of 2008, I went to New York and did more site visits to several LGBTIQ archives, including the National Archive of Lesbian, Gay, Bisexual & Transgender History at The LGBT Community Center, the Black Gay & Lesbian Archive, housed in the Schomburg Center for Research in Black Culture and the Lesbian Herstory Archives in Brooklyn. I also visited the Oral History Office at Columbia University, where I asked questions related specifically to creating an oral history center.

In November 2007, I began drafting letters of introduction and tracking down the names of potential narrators in the Lawrence/Douglas County area. In addition to the letters, I also began creating packets of information for GLBTIQ organizations across Kansas. The packets were very similar to the letter I sent, but included more business cards and posters. Through all of this I was trying to work in a forward-thinking manner. If I was able to get twenty interviews in Lawrence, then maybe if I got a larger grant I could do a few more interviews with people from outside of the Lawrence/Douglas County area.

I honestly had no idea how many people would talk to me, and then, of course, I wondered, what if after all of this, nobody would talk to me? I wouldn't have a project and what would that say about Kansas? My three main resources for accessing names of prospective narrators included newspaper articles from the local newspaper, the *Lawrence Journal World*, stories in the *Liberty Press*, Kansas' only and longest running GLBT newspaper, and by word of mouth.[10] I then looked up addresses using the White Pages website. So I sent off many letters and packets of information. I also got a couple of friends to send out information via two electronic discussion lists on the Sunday of Thanksgiving. As soon as word went out over the electronic discussion lists, I had people from across Kansas contacting me, interested in the project, wanting to know more and interested in sharing their stories. After fifteen minutes I had received emails from five people outside of the Douglas County area, after an hour I had a few more people, by the end of the week I had made contact with over forty people. The numbers kept growing and growing. I realized while sitting in front of my computer, one day early in December that my project had morphed into something much larger than I was expecting and little did I know how large it would continue to grow.

After initial contact, I continued to correspond with narrators via email and mail.[11] Prioritizing and scheduling interviews can be a bit of a juggling trick. Initially most interviews happened on weekends or evenings, and it was on a first-come-first-serve basis. As more people contacted me, I prioritized according to the logistics of location and schedules. Prior to doing interviews, I would send narrators pre-interview questionnaires. The questionnaire enabled me to know a bit about the narrator beforehand. Questions included where they were born, places they lived, what was their gender identity and/or sexual orientation, topics that they would like to cover and areas that they would not discuss. Of course, in the interview people can refuse to answer any question I ask. I designed my schedule so I would only do one interview a day and devote my time and energy on that individual. I did not want to put the narrator in a position where they would only be allotted a certain amount of time to share their stories. That would have been rude and extremely insensitive to their stories and their time.

Interviewing people can be a little nerve-wracking if you've never done before, and it is very different than doing a reference interview. It is beneficial for both you and the narrator if you have practiced asking questions and understand how your equipment works. I practiced a few times with a friend using the different features on my digital recorder, an Olympus D-40. Initially, I was using my personal MiniDV recorder, a very inexpensive Sony with an internal microphone. I discovered after videotaping practice interviews with my cats (not the most engaging test subjects) that the internal microphone was picking up the "clicking" sound of the MiniDV tape recording in the cassette compartment. The constant "clicking" sound was extremely distracting and could not be removed from the audio of the tape. Fortunately, KU Libraries has a small research fund for ongoing projects. I was able to write a small grant for a new video camera, a Canon HV20 with a Directional Stereo Mic. The addition of an external mic allowed for better audio capture than what I would get with the internal mic. The new High Definition (HD) MiniDV camera introduced a new complication that I hadn't anticipated—file size. A standard 60 minute recording usually took up 3 gigabytes (GB) on a hard drive, whereas an HD recording took up to 10 GB. I ended up also purchasing a 1 terabyte (1000 GB) external hard drive to store the majority of the video.

I began interviewing narrators in January 2008 and tried to weave interviews around my other job responsibilities. If I had a week where I didn't have any instruction classes, I would book the entire week to do interviews. Within a few months I had completed over twenty interviews, but people continued to contact me wanting to share their stories. I spoke to my immediate supervisor, the Assistant Dean for User Services, and the Dean of the Libraries, to see if there was a way for me to continue interviews. With some negotiating, some of my responsibilities were temporarily shifted to another librarian for 2009, and once again, thanks to the KU Libraries Research Fund and a campus wide yearly General Research Fund, I could apply for grants to cover the cost of transcription, hotel, food and travel as I navigated up, down and across Kansas. Over two years I was able to secure two General Research grants, each for approximately $4,700.00 and roughly five smaller Library Research grants, which totaled approximately $7,000.00. To date, I have interviewed over fifty-two people from across Kansas and have at least one hundred and ten potential additional narrators.

I never knew what to expect with doing an interview, but planning ahead allowed me to be flexible with whatever type of situation was presented. Some interviews happened at my house, while others happened in narrators' places of employment, or in their home. Sometimes, beforehand, I would be invited over for breakfast or a tour of a farm and be given the opportunity to feed baby goats. In other instances, in mid-interview, a narrator's partner might walk in the room and ask us if we would like some popcorn or something to eat. The biggest challenge of all would be when a narrator would talk about the loss of a loved one — a partner, parent, sibling, or friend. Those moments were so moving and powerful. At times I was at a loss for words, and in some instances had no idea what to say next or if I should say anything. Each narrator volunteered to share their experience; by doing so they have created a very powerful collection of oral histories about the lives of GLBTIQ people in Kansas.[12]

Even before I would set up my equipment, I would sit down with the narrator and explain both the Informed Consent Form and the Deed of Gift Form. I would outline their options and also suggest that, if at any point they wanted to modify the Informed Consent Form after the interview, they could contact me and we would negotiate changes, such as using only their first name or only providing the print transcript and audio online but not the video. I was extremely concerned about the safety of the people participating in this project and recognized that it was my responsibly to respect their wishes. While setting up the equipment, I would explain that I needed a recording of the interview in order to create the transcript. Narrators also had the option to be video recorded as well. Some did not want to be videotaped at all. And for those who agreed, I would stop videotaping right away if I sensed their hesitancy or discomfort. I wanted my narrators to be as comfortable as possible, and I most certainly did not want to impose on them in any way.

One area that I found extremely daunting was getting the interviews transcribed. I had initially earmarked funds to have a graduate student transcribe my interviews for me. This did not work out. In fact, it failed miserably. I would suggest to anybody that, unless you have a transcription service on your campus, outsource to a transcription service and allocate the majority of funding for transcription. Trust me, transcribing interviews is extremely challenging. Fortunately, I was able to change my budget lines around so I could outsource my interviews to a professional transcriptionist. She is extremely efficient and accurate with a very fast turnaround.

As the transcripts are returned to me, I send them back to the narrators for a final read through. Along with the transcript I include a letter asking the narrator to make sure the interview meets their approval and request that they return the transcript within six to eight weeks after receipt in the stamped, self-addressed envelope which I had also provided. Narrators have the option to add additional information and to cross out anything they would like removed from the interview which includes any audio or video versions as well as the transcript itself. The one thing that I ask narrators not to do is formalize the conversation.[13]

This is sometimes difficult for narrators who have a background in English, writing or copy-editing. Most of the time narrators review and return their transcripts within the allotted time frame. If they don't, I contact them and give them a gentle nudge or offer them more time.

As narrators returned their transcripts to me, I started to create a rough index. As an instruction librarian who had minimal indexing experience, I found this to be quite challenging. I needed to think about how people, not librarians, might use this collection and decided to create a taxonomy that could be used across the entire collection. KU Scholar-Works has the capability to keyword search the full text, but I didn't think keyword searching was sufficient enough. People using the transcripts need to be able to locate terms and concepts quickly, and sometimes keyword searching takes more time than necessary. Creating indexes involved listening to narrators for what they identified as important through their stories. These significant moments combined commonalities across all of the oral histories, such as coming out, and allowed me to identify key terms that covered specific and common experiences. In addition to indexing the oral histories, I also created a collection index for all of the oral histories. Oral histories often use the *Chicago Manual of Style*, 15th ed., which I used as a guideline for formatting the indexes. If narrators had corrected mistakes or added supplemental information, a footnote was used to denote the changes/additions. When narrators occasionally asked me to remove small portions of their interviews, I inserted the notation "[section removed by narrator]" into the text of the transcript.

Because these can be very personal narratives, I was surprised to find that, when I talk to narrators about this project and they find out that there is an option to have their stories online, they jump at the chance. As narrators have mentioned, they don't want their story to be left sitting on a shelf in an archive. They want people to have access to it when they want. While deleting changes in the audio and video versions of the interviews will take more time, eventually they too will be available online. Because it is often easier to edit a transcript, supplemental information by the narrator can be added during the review process and noted. Video and audio are seen as being more authentic than the transcript and should therefore not be modified to a great extent, just edited to remove sections the narrator wants removed. The final stage involves preparing the transcript for inclusion in the digital repository. Besides the text of the interview, each transcript contains additional information including a title page featuring the names of the participants, titles of the interview, and grant and copyright statements. A subsequent information page includes biographical information about the narrators, abstracts of the content of the interviews, metadata regarding technology and formats used, and acknowledgements of those assisting with the transcription, editing, and time-stamping of the final version. Once the transcript and all of its components are complete, it is turned into a PDF and uploaded into KU ScholarWorks. All of the interviews will be housed in the *Under the Rainbow Collection* and will be accessible via http://kuscholarworks.ku.edu/dspace/handle/1808/5330.

So now when I'm at an out-of-state conference and people share their assumptions about landscape and/or GLBTIQ life in Kansas, I can respond with a discussion about *Under the Rainbow* and the stories people have shared. There are common themes throughout the interviews: coming out or not coming out to friends, family and relatives, relationships, experiences in school, and so on. These transcripts are so rich with experiences and can be used for books, journal articles, dissertations, and many other types of projects by researchers, students, and those just looking for information. I think this is one of the most important ways we as librarians can participate in collection development. As Thompson points out "[r]eality is complex and many-sided; and it is a primary merit of oral history that to a much greater extent than most sources it allows the original multiplicity of stand-point to be recreated" (2006, p. 28). By creating this collection people can see, hear, read and connect on multiple levels with those presently living in Kansas. So does assisting in the creation of oral histories about the lives of GLBTIQ Kansans and making it accessible via open access count as librarianship? I would definitely say yes.

NOTES

1. For this project I am asking people to self-identify as gay, lesbian, bisexual, transgender, intersex or queer.

2. Eventually this project will expand to include GLBITQ people who have lived in Kansas and relocated out of state.

3. Even though the article is dated, I still think she has a valid argument.

4. Please see the Trevor Project at http://thetrevorproject.org/helpline.aspx for more information.

5. Examples of some books and chapters that have used GLBTIQ oral histories include Bérubé, A. (1990). *Coming out under fire: The history of gay men and women in World War Two*; Boyd, N. A. *Wide open town: A history of queer San Francisco to 1965*; Chauncey, G. (1994). *Gay New York: Gender, urban culture, and the makings of the gay male world, 1890–1940*; D'Emilio, J. (1983). *Sexual politics, sexual communities*; Dews, C. L., & Law, C. L. (Eds.). (2001). *Out in the South*; Estes, S. (2007). *Ask & tell: Gay and lesbian veterans speak out*; Fellows, W. (1996). *Farm boys: Lives of gay men from the rural Midwest*; Hall Carpenter Archives, Gay Men's Oral History Group. (1989). *Walking after midnight: Gay men's life stories*; Hill, D.B. (2008). A method for the margins: A trans feminist oral history. In W. Meezan & J. Martin (Eds.), *Handbook of research with lesbian, gay, bisexual, and transgender populations*; Howard, J. (1999). *Men like that: A southern queer history*; Johnson, P. (2008) *Sweet tea: Black gay men of the south*; Kennedy, E. L., & Davis., M. D. (1993). *Boots of leather, slippers of gold: The history of a lesbian community*; Lemke, J. (1991). *Gay voices from East Germany*; Lucas, I. (1998). *Outrage! An oral history*; Marcus, E. (1993). *Making history: The struggle for gay and lesbian equal rights, 1945–1990*; Newton, E. (1995). *Cherry Grove, Fire Island: Sixty years in America's first gay and lesbian town*; Power, L. (1995). *No bath but plenty of bubbles: An oral history of the Gay Liberation Front, 1970–73*; Sears, J. T. (1997). *Lonely hunters: An oral history of lesbian and gay southern life, 1948–1968*; Sears, J. T. (2001). *Rebels, rubyfruit, and rhinestones: Queering space in the Stonewall South*; and Wat, E. C. (2002). *The making of a gay Asian community: An oral history of pre–AIDS Los Angeles*.

6. The Columbia Oral History Office is a part of Columbia University Libraries. http://www.columbia.edu/cu/lweb/indiv/oral/.

7. The Human Subjects Committee of Lawrence (HSCL) is our Internal Review Board (IRB).

8. I interviewed many people in the mental health field who did not want their clients to be able to identify them and find out personal information.

9. Of course, if donors decided that they do not want their transcript online they must work directly with archivists at SRL and sign the SRL's Deed of Gift Form.

10. In August 2007 the city of Lawrence passed a Domestic Partnership Registry. The couples who register as domestic partners have their names published once a week in the local newspaper, the *Lawrence Journal World*.

11. If people wanted to meet me to talk about the project prior to an interview, we would schedule a time to meet and discuss the project. This allowed people to find out a little about me and ask questions about the project.

12. Grammar note: You will notice that when I refer to the "narrator" I do not use singular terms such as "s/he," rather I use the term "they." Some of the people I have talked to and interviewed do not necessarily conform or agree with binary language such as female/male or she/he, therefore I think it is inappropriate to use in this essay.

13. Martin Meeker at Berkeley's Regional Oral History Office was extremely helpful with providing examples of letters.

References

Bérubé, A. (2000). *Coming out under fire: The history of gay men and women in World War Two.* New York: Free.

Boyd, N. A. (2003). *Wide open town: A history of queer San Francisco to 1965.* Berkeley: University of California Press.

Boyd, N. A. (2008). Who is the subject? Queer theory meets oral history. *Journal of the History of Sexuality, 17*(2), 177–189. doi: 10.1353/sex.0.0009

Butler, R. P. (2008). Oral history as educational technology research. *TechTrends, 52*(4), 34–41. doi: 10.1007/s11528-008-0175-4

Erdmans, M. P. (2007). The personal is political, but is it academic? *Journal of American Ethnic History, 26*(4), 7–23.

Fogerty, J. E. (1983). Filling the gap: Oral history in the archives. *American Archivist, 46*(2), 148–157.

Kennedy, E. L., & Davis, M. D. (1993). *Boots of leather, slippers of gold: The history of a lesbian community.* New York: Routledge.

Larson, M. (2006). Research design and strategies. In T. L. Charlton, L. E. Myers, & R. Sharpless (Eds.), *Handbook of Oral History* (pp. 105–134). Lanham, MD: AltaMira.

Library of Congress. (1980). *Federal Writers' Project: Interview Excerpts.* Retrieved from Voices from the Thirties: Life Histories from the Federal Writers' Project: http://rs6.loc.gov/wpaintro/exinterv.html

Library of Congress, (n.d.). *WPA life histories about the Federal Writers' Project.* Retrieved from http://rs6.loc.gov/wpaintro/wpafwp.html

McKinney, B. (2008, February 23). Interview with Bruce McKinney. Interviewer: Tami Albin. Under the Rainbow: Oral Histories of GLBTIQ People in Kansas. University of Kansas, Lawrence.

Oral History Association. (2000, September). *Oral history evaluation guidelines.* Retrieved from Oral History Association: http://www.oralhistory.org/do-oral-history/oral-history-evaluation-guidelines/

Portelli, A. (1991). *The death of Luigi Trastulli and other stories: Form and meaning in oral history.* Albany: State University of New York Press.

Sears, J. T. (1997). *Lonely hunters: An oral history of lesbian and gay southern life, 1948–1968.* Boulder, CO: Westview.

Shopes, L. (2006). Legal and ethical issues in oral history. In T. L. Charlton, L. E. Myers, & R. Sharpless (Eds.), *Handbook of Oral History* (pp. 135–169). Lanham, MD: AltaMira.

Swain, E. D. (2006). Oral history in the archives: Its documentary role in the twenty-first century. In R. Perks, & A. Thomson (Eds.), *The Oral History Reader, 2nd Ed.* (pp. 343–361). New York: Routledge.

Thompson, P. (2006). The voice of the past: Oral history. In R. Perks, & A. Thomson (Eds.), *Oral History Reader* (pp. 25–31). New York: Routledge.

University of Chicago Press Staff. (2003). *Chicago manual of style* (15th ed.). Chicago: University of Chicago Press.

Zachert, M. J. (1968). The implications of oral history for librarians. *College and Research Libraries, 29*, 101–103.

Now on Exhibit: Bringing Out Materials from LGBTIQ Archives

Jennifer K. Snapp-Cook

Over the last twenty to thirty years, the Lesbian, Bisexual, Transgender, Intersex, and Queer (LGBTIQ) community has placed a growing emphasis on reclaiming their queer history by establishing and maintaining LGBTIQ archives and libraries around the world. While a good deal has been written about the importance of LGBTIQ archives in both the Library and Information Science (LIS) and LGBTIQ literature, less time has been devoted to examining the impact of LGBTIQ exhibitions, especially those which draw their materials from LGBTIQ archive collections. By highlighting some of the outstanding LGBTIQ archive exhibitions that have taken place throughout the U.S. recently and exploring their effect on the community, I will attempt to show that LGBTIQ exhibitions play an integral role in the archiving process.

A Brief History of LGBTIQ Archives

Around the turn of the twenty-first century, the number of LGBTIQ archives and libraries in the U.S. and Canada hovered at just over 80 (Clark, 2002), with another estimate at 110 institutions worldwide (Lukenbill, 2002, p. 97). However, a more recent list of LGBTIQ archives and libraries that appears on a webpage of the Gay/Lesbian International News Network (GLINN) contains over 100 resources in the U.S. alone (GLINN Gay Lesbian Queer Libraries and Archives in the United States, 2009). This recent and rapid increase in the number of organizations offering LGBTIQ collections serves as evidence of the relative newness of the concept.

The ONE National Gay and Lesbian Archives in Los Angeles is among one of the best known LGBTIQ archives and indeed, one of the oldest at nearly 60 years old ("Nation's Oldest," 2003). Other longstanding LGBTIQ archives, such as the Lesbian Herstory Archives in Brooklyn, just recently celebrated its thirty-fifth year, while the Gerber-Hart Library and Archives in Chicago was founded in 1981.

Many LGBTIQ archives have their roots in the post–Stonewall years of the '70s as the gay liberation movement was reaching full speed and the need for recognizing the "unique characteristics of gay and lesbian culture and social life" (Lukenbill, 2002, p. 93) became a significant goal for LGBTIQ community organizers. By the early '80s however, institutions with LGBTIQ archives were still few and far between. As Jess Jessop, founder of the Lambda Archives of San Diego noted in a 1989 interview, "Mostly they are poverty stricken ... programs in some state of disarray" (Fitzsimmons, p. D-2). Jessop also expressed what many others in the gay community were feeling at the time, saying "archives [are] all the more important now because so many of us are dying of AIDS" (p. D-2). This sentiment was echoed by UC Berkeley historian Martin Meeker who noted, in reference to the 1985 founding of the GLBT Historical Society Archives in San Francisco, as the AIDS crisis began to devastate the gay community, "there was this pressing need to preserve materials" (Marech, 2005). Perhaps in direct response to this notion, many of the LGBTIQ archives that exist today were started during this decade.

Throughout the '90s and into the twenty-first century, community groups and universities in the United States continued to establish smaller but notable LGBTIQ archives and libraries. Local and regional LGBT archives, such as the Gay and Lesbian Archives of the Pacific Northwest, as well as archives serving specific groups within the LGBTIQ community, such as the LGBT Religious Archives Network (LGBT-RAN) and the Black Gay and Lesbian Archive Project, also began to crop up. While these newer archives work to actively collect current LGBTIQ materials in an effort to preserve them, Lukenbill (2002) also notes that in many cases historical materials are sought out and collected as well.

Perhaps the biggest breakthrough to come to the LGBTIQ archival world in quite some time was the organization of the first conference for GLBT Archives, Libraries, Museums, and Special Collections (ALMS) in 2006. Jean Tretter, who founded the Tretter Collection in LGBT Studies archive at the University of Minnesota, organized and hosted the first GLBT ALMS conference in an effort to address the urgent need for "more cohesion ... in the world's gay archives" (Allen, 2005, p. 43).

Bringing together LGBTIQ archivists from around the globe, the conference featured three days of programming devoted entirely to preserving LGBTIQ history. Among the keynote speakers was Barbara Gittings, the well-known gay-rights activist and library advocate. Presentations ranged from "Archiving and Exhibiting Oral Histories" to "Community/Government Partnerships" to "Private to Public: Transitioning GLBT Collections" (LGBTIQ ALMS 2006). The GLBT ALMS conferences (a second one was held in 2008) have significantly raised the awareness of LGBTIQ archivists to the unique issues, as well as the commonalities, that each faces at their respective institutions and certainly addresses Tretter's initial concerns over finding some cohesion amongst them all.

From Photo Albums to Riotous Shoes: The Collections

In general, LGBTIQ archives seek to collect "any medium pertaining to gay and lesbian ... history and culture" (Lukenbill, 2002, p. 98) due to the fact that throughout history these materials have largely been "hidden and ignored" (Marston, 1990, p. 66). Among the most common materials collected by LGBTIQ archives are manuscripts. These are typically personal papers of LGBTIQ individuals, including correspondence and diaries or journals, or the professional records of LGBTIQ businesses and organizations.

Increasingly, LGBTIQ archives are also collecting a wide array of objects and ephemera as well. The GLBT Historical Society Archives in San Francisco holds a particularly colorful collection of artifacts ranging from the sewing machine used to create the first rainbow flag to the shoe worn (and eventually lost) by mayoral candidate Frank Jordon as he was chased by groups of queer protestors who were angry with his actions as former police chief. Items in some of the larger LGBTIQ collections include photographs, scrapbooks, clothing and costumes, artwork, buttons, activist materials, periodicals, posters, fliers, signs, and even architectural pieces from famous LGBTIQ landmarks.

There are a variety of ways in which materials end up in a LGBTIQ archive. Oftentimes individuals or organizations will officially donate their papers or items to a collection, but in other cases there may be reluctance for the "makers of gay history ... to part with their materials" (Allen, 2005). It becomes an important aspect of a LGBTIQ archivist's job to have some sense of what's out there, particularly with respect to individuals who are known to have desirable materials (Allen, 2005). Some LGBTIQ archivists may even have the opportunity to purchase materials from dealers, as suggested by the 2006 GLBT ALMS presentation, "Role of Dealers in Building LGBT Collections" (GLBT ALMS, 2006).

There are also many instances where materials just appear. Rich Wandel, archivist at the National Archive of LGBT History in New York, says that it's not uncommon for materials to be left on their doorstep (Out at the Center, 2008). Terrence Kissack, former executive director of the GLBT Historical Society Archives, also notes that individuals will often find materials that may have been sitting somewhere for decades but "because they know of us, they'll pause before they get rid of it" (Allen, 2005).

Regardless of how the materials are acquired, all of them become incredibly important objects for preservation as each piece speaks to a unique perspective within the LGBTIQ community. LGBTIQ scholars, researchers and those curious enough to seek out materials in LGBTIQ archive collections are well aware of the value of these items, but what about the general public or even those in the LGBTIQ community who may not know that these resources exist? This is where I believe exhibitions can play a vital and necessary role in raising awareness of LGBTIQ history, and LGBTIQ archives hold a unique responsibility to be leaders in this area.

Outing LGBTIQ Archives

By definition, archives are typically thought of as repositories for documents and manuscripts of historical interest; places reserved strictly for scholarly research, especially those collections which reside in an academic environment like a university library. While there are many LGBTIQ archives that still adhere to this standard way of thinking, there are more and more that do not. In a 2007 video tour of the GLBT Historical Society Archives, Gerard Koskovich comments that with their collection, "we crept into being a museum around the edges, in terms of keeping physical culture as well as documentary materials." This is one of the key elements of what Koskovich refers to as the concept of "queer[ing] the archive." Taking the next step and exhibiting these materials (once again akin to a museum), and making them accessible to a wider audience, is another way in which LGBTIQ archives can set themselves apart.

So, why are so many of these fabulous collections being kept locked away, accessible only to a handful of users during the archive's precious few open hours? The most obvious challenge that LGBTIQ archives face in getting their materials out is the same one that plagues these archives in their general day-to-day operations — a lack of resources like funding, personnel, time and most notable to this scenario, an exhibition space. There are, of course, several shining exceptions. Those institutions that have managed to overcome some of these obstacles and present to the world the treasures that lie in their collections. I present here just a few examples as inspiration.

Stonewall Library and Archives

In 2006, the Stonewall Library and Archives in Fort Lauderdale, Florida mounted an exhibition entitled, "Pride: Party or Protest?" The exhibit featured T-shirts, buttons, bumper stickers, and posters from South Florida Pride festivals dating back to the 1970s, as well as early Pride memorabilia from New York and Washington, D.C., from the archive's collection. According to co-curator Ken Clark, the exhibit was meant to stir conversation within the LGBTIQ community over whether South Florida's Pride events had become less politicized and more of a party over the years (Lapadula, 2006). Opinions on the subject among LGBTIQ activists and other members of the community were decidedly split.

But organizers of the exhibit were wise in that they timed its run to coincide with one of the two Pride events that South Florida hosts each year, the Stonewall Street Festival, which is known as a sort of block party that doesn't even allow political speakers (Lapadula, 2006). In this respect, Stonewall Library was able to use historical pieces from their collection, pieces that hold an inherent attraction to the target audience, to raise awareness of and create a dialogue about the different facets of South Florida's Pride events, including its more political origins. Without being exhibited, Stonewall Library's collection runs the risk of not being accessible to this segment of the community.

This fact was made all the more clear when over a year later, the Stonewall Library and Archives faced opposition from public officials (the mayor had deemed the archive's materials "pornographic") as they were set to move to a new location within a city park. Their original location was inside the local Gay and Lesbian Community Center which was only open to adults 18 years and older. According to the Library's Board Director, the archives are "locked and open to researchers by appointment only" (Baier, 2007). If not for exhibitions such as "Pride: Party or Protest?" issues like what Pride events mean to the LGBTIQ community may never have been addressed.

The Kinsey Institute

The Kinsey Institute in Bloomington, Indiana, is home to another celebrated archive of LGBTIQ materials. No stranger to exhibitions, the Kinsey Institute regularly lends its materials to exhibitions throughout the world and is fortunate enough to operate its own gallery space as well. Last year, the Institute's Gallery staged the exhibition, "Pre–Revolutionary Queer: Gay Art and Culture before Stonewall" featuring materials from the archive that documented "the existence of a vibrant but largely underground gay culture prior to the start of the modern gay rights movement in the late 1960s" (The Kinsey Institute, 2009).

While the Kinsey Institute attracts researchers from around the globe in the broad areas of human sexuality, gender, and reproduction, they should also be credited (at least partly) for attracting LGBTIQ visitors to Bloomington with their outstanding LGBTIQ exhibitions. In fact, in 2008, Bloomington was named the #1 Small Town Gay Destination by *Out Traveler Magazine* and even has a website specifically aimed at LGBTIQ visitors at http://www.visitgaybloomington.com. This just goes to show that by exhibiting their materials, LGBTIQ archives have the potential to reach out beyond their local communities to a new audience: the queer tourist. Generating tourism may even help to raise the level of clout an archive has with other community businesses and organizations, queer or mainstream.

Lesbian, Gay, Bisexual, and Transgender Historical Society Archive

Perhaps one of the best examples of a LGBTIQ exhibit that reached out beyond its typical LGBTIQ audience is the LGBT Historical Society Archive's "Passionate Struggle: Dynamics of San Francisco's LGBTIQ History." This exhibit is currently on display at a storefront gallery in the Castro, perhaps the most famous gay neighborhood in the U.S., and features a wide variety of materials from the archive's collection which serve to illustrate four key themes in LGBTIQ history, "People," "Places," "Politics," and "Pleasure."

Prior to "Passionate Struggle," the GLBT Historical Society archive had been described as "our community's Smithsonian" (McMillan, 2007) by executive director Paul Boneberg, and was a fairly well-known resource within the LGBTIQ community and certainly among LGBTIQ studies scholars. Although the exhibit was set to officially open in December 2008, the Society opened it in previews a month earlier, to coincide with the opening of Gus Van Sant's biopic *Milk*, about slain San Francisco Supervisor Harvey Milk, some of whose artifacts are part of the Society's collection and are included in the exhibit.

The timing and the placement of the exhibit were all very calculated moves on the part of the Society, which was quick to acknowledge this fact. "We wanted the people who saw the film to see the exhibit" Boneberg said (Bajko, 2008). And when a major article about the exhibit and the film ran in the *Los Angeles Times*, Boneberg was enthusiastic about the possibilities of people traveling from outside of San Francisco to see the exhibit saying, "by having ... that kind of attention we draw people to the Castro" (Bajko, 2008). He went on to say, "To what degree it brings attention to [the historical society], I don't know. But I think a lot of people who come to San Francisco come to look for a deeper understanding of that history, and we're the ones who can help" (Gordon, 2008).

Although thousands of people did attend the exhibit during its previews, as *Milk* screened just a few steps away at the Castro Theater, Boneberg noted that not all of the exhibit attendees are filmgoers. In addition to tourists, "both gay and straight," some of the visitors are people who are just passing by. And co-curator of the exhibit Don Romesburg has also mentioned speaking with visitors including, "straight couples, families, long-time Castro residents, queer youth groups, tourists, and politicians." This, he noted, was a sure testament to "how relatable our community's history can be to so many people" ("GLBT Historical Society Celebrates Castro Exhibit Opening," 2008). Boneberg seconds, "It is a good sign that there is broad appeal for the exhibit and not just from LGBTIQ people or people who live in the neighborhood" (Bajko, 2008).

The No-Space Case: Advantages and Challenges

While these few examples serve to highlight some of the best case scenarios for LGBTIQ archive exhibitions and the power they have to transform their audiences, there are still many LGBTIQ archives that are keeping their materials to themselves. Earlier I alluded to some of the potential obstacles that LGBTIQ archives may face with respect to exhibiting their collections and most notable among them was a lack of exhibition space. One obvious solution to this quandary is for LGBTIQ archives to establish a web presence and to mount exhibitions online. Several LGBTIQ archives are already doing this with great success (Stonewall Library and Archives has an excellent web site and online access to their exhibits), yet others are still struggling in this department (The ONE National Gay and Lesbian Archive's web site is surprisingly and disappointingly sparse). Maintaining access to LGBTIQ archives online is a rich subject and worthy of its own analysis which is beyond the scope of this paper, but it does offer possibilities for some organizations.

In terms of finding a physical exhibition space however, while there are a handful of LGBTIQ archives and museums in the U.S. in addition to the ones profiled here that have a dedicated exhibition space (others include The Leslie/Lohman Gallery and the Tom of Finland Foundation), many LGBTIQ archives are part of special collections at public or academic libraries. In cases such as these, LGBTIQ archives may want to consider partnering with other institutions and lending their materials for exhibition purposes.

There are a couple of major advantages to working cooperatively with other organizations to mount an exhibition, especially if they offer a venue to host it. Libraries, museums, galleries and LGBTIQ community centers are just a few possible sites that may be receptive to collaboration. Not only would this solve the space dilemma but as Gough (1990) states, if an exhibit is properly planned and shared amongst a variety of institutions, then it "could maximize the number of people who see it while minimizing the amount of work and expense of assembling it" (p. 128). Furthermore, collaboration offers a unique opportunity for LGBTIQ archivists to work with colleagues from other LGBTIQ or mainstream institutions and will undoubtedly raise the visibility of each of the participating organizations.

Of course as is often the case when dealing with the exhibiting of LGBTIQ materials to the public, there are a few concerns that LGBTIQ archivists may want to make note of when considering a partnership. First and foremost is the potential for censorship and opposition to an exhibition of LGBTIQ materials, whether expressed by members of the community, political officials, or even staff associated with one of the organizations, especially mainstream organizations.

LGBTIQ exhibits at libraries are particularly vulnerable to these contentious situations as a library is generally perceived of as a neutral site where no one point of view should take precedence over another. Some mainstream library users, clouded by the heterosexist attitudes that seem to permeate U.S. culture, will see a LGBTIQ exhibit and be inclined to feel that suddenly the library is "endorsing" a pro-gay point of view (Gough, 1990, p. 132).

There is certainly no shortage of news stories to support this notion either. In 2001, the mayor in Anchorage, Alaska pulled a gay pride exhibit from a local public library because he believed the display violated the library's policy against exhibiting materials that could "trigger 'substantial disruptions or material interference with primary library business' or takes an advocacy position" ("Anchorage Mayor Faces Legal Action for Pulling Gay-pride Display," 2001). The exhibit featured gay pride posters and a banner that urged, "Celebrate Diversity."

Perhaps an even more insidious form of censorship may come from within the organizations themselves. In 1994, the New York Public Library (NYPL) hosted an exhibition entitled, "Becoming Visible," featuring materials donated and loaned by the Lesbian Herstory Archives, among other LGBTIQ archives and organizations. At the time, the exhibit was largely regarded by the mainstream as groundbreaking and the first major exhibit on the topic of LGBTIQ history in the United States.

As much as the exhibit was lauded by queer audiences, Lesbian Herstory archivist Polly Thistlethwaite (1995) criticized NYPL for resisting public acknowledgment of contributions from various LGBTIQ individuals and organizations that played major roles in creating the exhibition. Thistlethwaite argued that in doing so, "the exhibit was falsely framed to appear as though it was berthed [*sic*] from the stacks, goodwill, and native savvy of the New York Public Library." She warns that LGBTIQ archives must use caution when collaborating or merging with mainstream institutions as their motives are often aimed at assimilation rather than community building.

Conclusion

There could be no doubt in the minds of LGBTIQ studies scholars that LGBTIQ archives are of supreme importance to the LGBTIQ community, as they are acutely familiar with the richness of the collections housed in these institutions. But how about the rest of the world? As the examples in this essay have shown, LGBTIQ exhibitions culled from LGBTIQ archives have the power to reach across social boundaries and illustrate in vivid detail the many facets of LGBTIQ history and culture that are so often ignored or shunned by the mainstream. While there are definitely some challenges that may arise in mounting an exhibition from a LGBTIQ archive's collection, it is most certainly worth the effort. And just as the LGBTIQ community has struggled to overcome the many heterosexist obstacles placed in their path over the years, LGBTIQ archivists must endure in their quest to preserve these wonderful stories and share them with all.

References

Allen, D. (2005, November 22). Where our history lives. *Advocate*, 43–44.
Anchorage mayor faces legal action for pulling gay-pride display. (2001, June 11). *American Libraries*. Retrieved from http://www.ala.org/ala/alonline/index.cfm
Baier, E. (2007, October 18). Ribbon-cutting at Fort Lauderdale library celebrates controversial move of gay archives. *Knight Ridder Tribune Business News*.
Bajko, M.S. (2008, December 4). Gay history museum opens in Castro. *The Bay Area Reporter*. Retrieved from http://www.ebar.com/
Clark, D. (2002). Free access without judgment. *The Illinois Library Association Reporter, 20*(5), 1, 4–6.
Fitzsimmons, B. (1989, May 21). Local archives may make life easier for lesbians, gays. *The San Diego Union*.
Gay Bloomington. (2009). Retrieved from http://www.visitgaybloomington.com/
GLBT ALMS 2006. (2005). *University of Minnesota Libraries*. Retrieved from http://www.lib.umn.edu/events/GLBTalms/topics.phtml
GLBT Historical Society. (2009). Retrieved from http://www.GLBThistory.org/
GLBT Historical Society celebrates Castro exhibit opening. (2008, December 15). *Gay News Bits*. Retrieved from http://gaynewsbits.com/
GLBThistory. (2007, February 16). Archive tour: 1. A queer archive [Video file]. Video posted to http://www.youtube.com/watch?v=nMnqFFCwtC4
GLINN, Gay Lesbian Queer libraries and archives in the United States. (2009). Retrieved from http://www.glinn.com/news/lar1.htm
Gordon, L. (2008, November 30). On film and in exhibits, a full picture of Harvey Milk. *Los Angeles Times*. Retrieved from http://articles.latimes.com/
Gough, C. (1990). Library exhibits of gay and lesbian materials. In C. Gough & E. Greenblatt (Eds.), *Gay and lesbian library service* (pp. 125–140). Jefferson, NC: McFarland.

Kinsey Institute. (2009). Retrieved from http://www.kinseyinstitute.org/

Lapadula, P. (2006, June 17). The great Pride debate: Party or protest? Stonewall Library exhibit traces history of Pride events in South Florida. *South Florida Blade.* Retrieved from https://www.florida blade.com/

Lukenbill, B. (2002). Modern gay and lesbian libraries and archives in North America: A study in community identity and affirmation. *Library Management, 23*(1), 93–100.

Marech, R. (2005, January 29). Treasure trove of gay and lesbian artifacts: "Queer Smithsonian" in S.F. celebrates its 20th anniversary. *San Francisco Chronicle.* Retrieved from http://www.sfgate.com/

Marston, B. (1990). Lesbian and gay materials in Cornell's collection on human sexuality. In C. Gough & E. Greenblatt (Eds.), *Gay and lesbian library service* (pp. 65–72). Jefferson, NC: McFarland.

McMillan, D. (2007, September 13). LGBTIQ Historical Society to honor queer military leaders at gala. *San Francisco Bay Times.* Retrieved from http://www.sfbaytimes.com/

Nation's oldest. (2003, April-July). *Lambda Book Report, 11,* 41.

Out at the Center. (2008, December 8). The center story: An exhibition from the National LGBT Archives [Video file]. Video posted to http://www.gaycenter.org/centerblog/2008-12-08-the-center-story-an-exhibition-from-national-lgbt-archives/

Stonewall Library & Archives. (2009). Retrieved from http://www.stonewall-library.org/

Thistlethwaite, P. (1995). The lesbian and gay past: An interpretive battleground. *Gay Community News, 20*(4), 10.

From a Vision to a Reality:
The Birth of the Pacific Northwest
Lesbian Archives

Lisa A. Cohen

Here I sit in our neighborhood café, my unofficial office for the Pacific Northwest Lesbian Archives (PNLA). I am drinking a large cup of decaf coffee and thinking about how many people I have met here over the years to hatch my plan of opening a repository for lesbian primary source materials in the Pacific Northwest. There were many — from prospective board members, volunteers and co-directors, to web designers and networking partners. This café has seen and heard countless ideas, laughter, tears and heartfelt conversation about the importance of starting PNLA and creating a place for our life's work, our love for one another and our accomplishments. New parents and parents-to-be clamber over each other and their children, trying to claim space on the two comfy overstuffed blue couches while my meeting date and I conspire and gesture wildly at a table by the window, our talk leads to fundraisers we will throw for the Archives that coming season.

In 1996, I attended a workshop at the Michigan Womyn's Music Festival called "How to Start Your Own Lesbian Archives" presented by women from the Ohio Lesbian Archives and June Mazer Lesbian Archives. I returned from that sacred place in the Michigan woods a new woman. I knew my life's purpose. Later, I applied for grad school and moved an hour and a half north to Bellingham, Washington to be trained in the craft of archives work. Two years later I returned to Seattle to start the Archives. The process took about 10 years from me sitting in that circle on the summer-scorched August grass in a field in western Michigan until the June day I saw that blessed IRS stamp declaring that PNLA was a 501c3 organization in 2006. It took *a lot* of patience and luck.

As a woman of child-bearing age but yet to fulfill my desire to have an actual child, PNLA became my baby.

Conception (or, Boy, Do I Have Control Issues!)

I had quite a creative vision. The plan was that the PNLA would own and inhabit a two or three story building centrally located in the heart of Seattle. The space would be part archival facility, part community center and venue. The stacks would be climate and humidity controlled. There would be a beautiful well lit research room, spacious processing area, a small conservation lab and space for a rotating exhibit. There would be a multi-purpose classroom for lectures and programs, a venue for community events, comfy couches and a spacious volunteer area. There would be a café attached to the building which would generate revenue for the Archives and a place where we could meet with potential financial and archival donors in a less formal setting. There would finally be a space for lesbians to connect the important aspects of their lives together; celebrating current, past and future work and life. Our focus was not only on collecting and providing access to herstorical materials, but also welcoming women who had donated archival collections to come give talks about their lives and why the materials were significant to them. We would create an archives education curriculum to be utilized by LGBTQ community groups and presented and facilitated by PNLA volunteers. The skill and craft of Archives would be passed down from one generation of lesbians to the next in the tradition of the Lesbian Herstory Archives — making the scholarly skills of processing an archival collection accessible to everyday lesbians who want to preserve their herstory and are interested in giving back to the community.

We're Pregnant!

I ran around like a frantic parent trying to gather as much info as I could. Instead of reading books on childbirth, I connected with the women who had come before me to gain insight and wisdom. I called and emailed the founders of the June Mazer Archives in West Hollywood. I completed an internship at the Lesbian Herstory Archives. I attended conferences and presented information about PNLA and watched the reactions. I appealed to community leaders in Seattle. I made random phone calls and asked people if they had herstorical stuff or if they knew who did. I made presentations to small groups of lesbians and asked them to spread the word. Little by little I began to see that another plan beyond my control percolated softly in the background.

I assembled a board of directors. Our main focus was reviewing and revising our vision and mission statements. In 2009 we came up with:

PNLA's vision: A community in which lesbians are embraced, honored and respected for their past, present and future contributions and accomplishments.

PNLA's mission: PNLA gathers, preserves and shares primary source materials of lesbians to enhance public and scholarly understanding of our diverse, regional *herstory*; bringing our *herstory* out of obscurity to promote learning, visibility and community strength.

PNLA defines the Northwest as Oregon, Washington, Idaho, Alaska and southwestern British Columbia.

It Was a Long and Complicated Labor and Delivery

In the 2000s, Seattle began losing its LGBTQ stronghold organizations due to improper management and lack of community support. The Lesbian Resource Center (LRC) was the longest running organization of its kind and was always an essential stop when lesbians moved to town or visited Seattle. It was a referral service as well as a drop in center with a dynamic meeting space. It folded in 2003 after many moves and many changes of leadership.

Locating the surviving records could best be described as a wild goose chase. If I hadn't talked to just the right person at just the right time, the records, which had been languishing in a storage unit, would have been pitched and Seattle would have lost a significant part of lesbian herstory.

In 2008, Verbena Health, the only lesbian, queer women's and transgender health organization in Seattle closed due to a sad case of mismanagement. Verbena was the result of several incarnations of Lesbian health organizations. The records in this collection reflected the need for an all encompassing center for health which would provide for the growing needs of the community. Verbena and its predecessor organizations started with a focus on lesbians with cancer and eventually grew to a focus on general health and wellness, also providing a much needed social space, sponsoring softball teams and putting on community celebrations. Verbena pioneered the LGBTQ health care field by providing health care services to the transgender community.

Both the LRC and Verbena collections are comprised of meeting minutes, correspondence, budget and financial records, newsletters and printed materials, project files, programs and events, photographs and ephemera. Our smaller collections donated by individuals are made up of journals from 1973 to 2003, correspondence from the 1980s and 1990s, political and social action files from the 1970s-2000s, scrapbooks, ephemera and sound recordings. There are some really great trophies from a Lesbian Resource Center sponsored softball team during the 1980s and colorful handmade bras and bustiers made by cancer survivors during a Verbena social event.

The Baby Was Beautiful and It Needed Help

PNLA spent four years in my basement. It was time to find a safe, clean, accessible home for our growing Archives. I sing praises to the universe that volunteers were able to come to my home every week for almost two years and pre-process collections, and that we had a water-proof basement in Seattle! Luckily no collections suffered any kind of damage.

The Baby Learned to Walk, and in Doing So, Hit a Lot of Walls

I spent a lot of vital life energy pushing forward, trying to drum up the interest of people who were willing to invest time and money into finding a physical autonomous space for the Archives. I heard "NO" a lot. I again turned toward my sister archivettes and they told me to take it slow, one thing at a time; focus and just do the next indicated action. I was a maniac. I felt stressed out and defeated. It was hard to carry on. Was this the end of my dream? I longed for the Archives to be strictly a community-based Archives, owned and operated by lesbians who would tell our own stories and preserve what we saw fit.

During many long philosophical phone discussions with the Head of Special Collections at the Washington State Historical Society (WSHS) about user accessibility and preservation, I'd walk my dog in our favorite forest, ruminating over what the lesbian community would think, and how it would all go down. The vision of the Archives as a free standing building with a lot of maintenance and money required to sustain it slowly faded away and in its place, shimmering like an oasis, was WSHS with climate controlled shelving and a gorgeous 1880s reading room. That library smell coated the wood paneled interior and marble entrance hall. There were employees to answer research questions, retrieve and copy materials and answer the phone. This decision was not made lightly. Over several years, I saw the demonstrated commitment of WSHS to the lesbian community in Washington, as the director courted other community collections relating to lesbians and gay men, Washington's Human Rights Commission and AIDS/HIV.

Her First Day at School

Like a proud parent, I ushered those boxes out of my basement and into the world. PNLA and WSHS worked out an agreement. We came to a mutual decision that because of the flexibility and environment provided, the collection was much better off at the museum than it was sitting in a basement. The records became property of WSHS, and PNLA as an entity has shifted to become more of a clearing house of sorts, bringing materials to WSHS for processing, storage, care and access but our mission has not changed. PNLA focuses on outreach to donors and promoting visibility and processing collections. Appropriate provisions were made in the deed of gift document should WSHS wish to purge the PNLA collection, though this would be highly unethical and unprofessional. The lesbian community seemed genuinely delighted and excited to know we have a space for our herstory to reside.

The most important piece from that original vision of having our own space was teaching the skill and craft of archives work to lesbians of all generations; that past-present-future connection actually came true. In our agreement, WSHS agreed to let PNLA volunteers process collections and make decisions about preservation, conservation and restrictions. Volunteers spend about five hours per week organizing the collection and making it available. WSHS staff separated and cataloged the three-dimensional items from the collection and they will be cross-referenced in finding aids. When we moved in, we brought about $500 worth of archival supplies with us. I love that the State of Washington covers the cost of future supplies needed to process collections, provides space for lesbian herstory, and encourages diversity in their archival collections. That the Lesbian Resource Center records share space with pioneer diaries is itself a marvel. It is a great match, literally moving from obscurity in a basement to visibility in a museum. Collections are preserved and accessible. Finding aids are available online as collections are processed, enabling research from a distance and is in line with our vision and mission.

Today at the café, many of the seats at the tables are cluttered with people like myself, wholeheartedly engaged in typing on laptops, occasionally stopping for sips of coffee or looking up to admire the evergreen trees out the window. I'm thinking about how grateful I am that I got to work out my parenting skills on PNLA because one day soon I'll be one of the parents clambering around trying to find a good book on the café's worn bookshelf to read to our little one, the product of much patience and lots of luck, kind of like what happened with the Pacific Northwest Lesbian Archives!

If you are interested in contacting the Pacific Northwest Lesbian Archives or you just want to find out more about us, visit www.pnwlesbianarchives.org.

IHLIA — Making Information on LGBTIQ Issues in the Past and the Present Accessible and Visible

Jack van der Wel

Located in the Netherlands, IHLIA (Internationaal Homo/Lesbisch Informatiecentrum en Archief or International Gay and Lesbian Information Centre and Archives) is Europe's largest and leading lesbian and gay research library and archive, providing resources and services to all persons wishing to use the library and archival materials for their research or information needs. While its name only refers to lesbians and gay men, IHLIA interprets its mission broadly by collecting, cataloguing, and indexing all print materials in any way relevant to LGBTIQ life. IHLIA not only plays a key role in preserving our heritage, but also offers a unique public reference service. It is one of the best sources for gay and lesbian studies research in the world.

IHLIA has two branches: IHLIA-Homodok in Amsterdam and IHLIA-Anna Blaman Huis in Leeuwarden (located in the northern part of the Netherlands in the Province of Friesland). IHLIA-Homodok is housed on the sixth floor of the Amsterdam Public Library,[1] and IHLIA-Anna Blaman Huis is housed in its own building at the edge of the city centre. Each of these branches has a different primary purpose. While the Amsterdam information centre serves as a research library and does not circulate its materials, the Leeuwarden location also serves as a lending library.

The roots of IHLIA can be traced back to three separate entities. The first of these, Homodok, was founded in 1978 as a response to gay and lesbian studies initiatives in the Netherlands. At that time gay and lesbian students and lecturers from the Universities of Amsterdam and Utrecht demanded opportunities for research and education on homosexuality which until then were nearly absent from the universities' curriculum. The two other entities, the Lesbian Archives Amsterdam and the Lesbian Archives Leeuwarden, were both founded in 1982 as grassroots efforts aimed at collecting and preserving resources related to the lesbian subcultures in each of those cities. In 1987, the Lesbian Archives Leeuwarden transformed itself into the Anna Blaman Huis, an LGBTQ library and information centre named after a renowned Dutch lesbian novelist. Homodok, the Lesbian Archives Amsterdam, and the Anna Blaman Huis merged into IHLIA in 1999.

Collection

The large multilingual and geographically diverse collections of gay and lesbian periodicals, the most comprehensive collection of its kind in Europe, and so called "grey literature" (i.e., annual reports, student papers, conference proceedings and other hard-to-find non-book documents) form the heart of IHLIA's holdings, together with the extensive library of thousands of books, ranging from dissertations to pulp fiction. In 1996, the COC (Cultuur en Ontspannings-Centrum, or Centre for Culture and Leisure, the Dutch national LGBTQ association, which incidentally, is the oldest such organization in the world, founded in 1946) decided to move its modern library collection, consisting of several thousand volumes of reference books and purple prose, to IHLIA. Together with the Van Leeuwen Bibliotheek, the historical library collection of the COC which IHLIA acquired earlier in 1988, these collections greatly enhanced Homodok's positition as a gay and lesbian research institution. Since 2000, we have provided online catalogue access to both these library collections via the Internet.

IHLIA has also succeeded in reconstructing most of the gay library of Jacob Anton Schorer, who in 1912 founded the Nederlandsch Wetenschappelijk Humanitair Komitee (NWHK, i.e., Dutch Scientific Humanitarian Committee) based on Magnus Hirschfeld's German Wissenschaftlich-humanitares Komitee (WhK, or Scientific Humanitarian Committee) founded previously in 1898. Similar to Hirschfeld in Germany, Schorer was a pioneer in the campaign for legal and social equality for gay men and women. First and foremost, Schorer's campaign was an educational one. With this aim in mind he built an impressive library of 1800 books and many periodicals. He collected as many scientific works on (homo)sexuality as possible, as well as literary works dealing with homosexuality. As soon as the Germans invaded the Netherlands in May 1940, Schorer decided to dissolve the NWHK and destroy the records and all correspondence. Shortly thereafter the Germans confiscated his library. The library has gone missing since that time, and there has been no clue as to what happened to it. With the help of the salvaged catalogue and its supplements, IHLIA has reconstructed most (1400 books) of this unique historical library with support from the Dutch government.

Database and Thesaurus

IHLIA has its own cataloging and indexing system. Its bibliographic database was created in 1982 and is accessible online at http://www.ihlia.nl/, available in both in Dutch (under the tab "Catalogi") and English (under the tab "Catalogs"). The database currently includes almost 125,000 records indexed with the help of the *Homosaurus*, a specially-designed thesaurus of about 3000 LGBTQ index terms. Using the *Homosaurus*, the database provides easy and highly detailed access to both IHLIA's own holdings and the holdings of other institutions. It is an invaluable tool in helping users to retrieve the wealth of available resources on LGBTQ existence.

In May 1997, Homodok and Anna Blaman Huis, produced a bilingual (Dutch/English & English/Dutch) version of the *Homosaurus* which they dubbed the *Queer Thesaurus*.[2] The major objective of the *Queer Thesaurus* is to provide all lesbian, gay, bisexual and transgender archives, libraries and documentation centres around the world, as well as those persons or organizations wishing to set up such an archive, library or documentation centre, with a ready-to-use international thesaurus of LGBTQ index terms.

Archives and Exhibits

IHLIA is a depository of the records of LGBTQ organizations and groups. It stores the records of several Dutch gay and lesbian organizations and activists' groups as well as personal archives of gay men and lesbians.

IHLIA organizes small exhibitions on the 6th floor of the Amsterdam Public Library. Some examples include:

- Oog voor Vrouwen (Eye4Women), a photographic exhibition by Marian Bakker that spans 20 years of lesbian life in the Netherlands http://www.eye4women.nl/
- Monument van Trots (Monument of Pride), an exhibition in honor of the 20th anniversary of the Homomonument http://www.monumentvantrots.nl/index.html; English: http://www.monumentvantrots.nl/eng/index.html
- Wie Kan Ik Nog Vertrouwen? Homoseksueel in Nazi Duitsland en Bezet Nederland (Who Can I Still Trust? Homosexual in Nazi Germany and the Occupied Netherlands), a look at gay and lesbian life during World War II http://www.vertrouwen.nu/
- Wij Gaan Ons Echt Verbinden: Exposities over het "Homohuwelijk" (We Are Really Going to Be Joined Together: Exhibitions about "Same-Sex Marriage"), a photographic exhibition on the history of same-sex marriage in the Netherlands, the first country in the world to legalize marriages for gay and lesbian couples http://www.wijgaanonsecht verbinden.nl/

Holdings

- Books: 23,000 titles
- Grey Literature: 10,000 titles
- Video's/DVD's: 7,500 titles
- Periodicals: 4,500 titles
- Posters: 5,400 titles
- Database: 126,000 titles
- Archives: 230–240 linear meters
- Clippings: 50 linear meters

Contact Information

IHLIA-Homodok

Visiting address
  Oosterdokskade 143
  Amsterdam
  6th floor
Hours:
  Monday–Friday: 12:00 P.M.–5:00 P.M.
  Saturday and Sunday: 1:00 P.M.–5:00 P.M.

Postal address
  Oosterdoksstraat 110
  1011 DK Amsterdam
  The Netherlands
  Telephone: +31.20.5230837
  Email: info@ihlia.nl
  Homepage: http://www.ihlia.nl/

IHLIA-Anna Blaman Huis

Visiting address
  Noordvliet 11
  Leeuwarden
Hours:
  Monday–Thursday 9:00 A.M.–5:00 P.M.

Postal address
  PO Box 4062
  8901 EB Leeuwarden
  The Netherlands
  Telephone: +31.58.2121829
  Email: abh@ihlia.nl
  Homepage: http://www.ihlia.nl/

NOTES

1. IHLIA-Homodok is not a part of the Amsterdam Public Library; rather it is an independent foundation with its own board. We get space for free in return for providing information and reference services and organizing exhibitions and activities. We pay our own staff and therefore receive government support.

2. Staalduinen, K.v., & Brandhorst, H. (1997). *A queer thesaurus: An international thesaurus of gay and lesbian index terms.* Amsterdam: Homodok and Anna Blaman Huis.

Inside the Files of *This Has No Name*

tatiana de la tierra

I remember being young and feeling so alone, imagining that there was a Latina Lesbian nation somewhere, yet not knowing where it was or how to get there. This yearning for community is what impelled me to be at the core of publishing the Latina lesbian magazines *esto no tiene nombre* (this has no name) and *conmoción* (commotion and "with motion") in the 1990s.[1] For fifteen years I schlepped the boxes that held the archives of the zines across the country, from Miami, Florida to El Paso, Texas, then on to Buffalo, New York, and finally, to Long Beach, California. After years of ruminating, I invited the archives manager of UCLA's Chicano Studies Research Center Library and Archive into my garage. Among the dusty mementos of my life were ten linear feet of Latina lesbian herstory. I picked out the plastic file boxes and watched Mike Stone load them into the back of his Subaru, bidding them farewell as he headed off down 7th Street and onto highway 405 North, 31 miles away.

It's in the loving that I was able to let them go. Inside the boxes are the behind-the-scenes documents of a five-year publishing affair. We edited 12 issues from 1991 until 1996 — a total of 341 entries in 332 pages between *esto* and *conmoción*. While it wasn't easy to find writers and artists who openly self-identified as Latina lesbians back then, we got 136 contributors from all across the country (and a few from Mexico, Latin America and the Caribbean) into print. We published poetry, essays, short stories, letters and news in Spanish, English or Spanglish. We even had a cheesy sexy counselor, Erotiza Memaz (a play on words, meaning "eroticize me more"). Our graphics were no joke; we published striking photographs, evocative and representative artwork, and sported some cool layouts.

That was a magical moment in Miami, when four of us — two Puerto Ricans, one Cuban, and one Colombian — decided to make a publication from scratch, without a recipe. Inside the boxes I handed over just the other day is the intrigue of discovery as Vanessa Cruz, Patricia Pereira-Pujol, Margarita Castilla and myself explored fonts and layouts along with the fine print of editing. There are the original contributions, letters to the editor, and the layout drafts. There also is the initial spark of joy crushed by deception, as the Latina lesbian group Las Salamandras de Ambiente we belonged to and which *esto* was originally affiliated with presented us with a petition demanding we cease publication because of a disagreement about overtly sexual language. Inside the boxes is our vision, which expanded out of Miami and across the country as a result of being locally rejected.

We believed that what we were doing mattered, that it made a difference to us as well as to others. Inside the boxes is our seriousness, along with the Articles of Incorporation of Esto No Tiene Nombre, Inc., and our raucous laughter at having to send the Florida Department of State a document saying that the English translation of our corporation is "This Has No Name, Inc." There are grant proposals that we wrote, along with reward letters. The funding was proof that we had support and that others believed in our mission as stated in our first proposal to the Astraea Lesbian Foundation for Justice in 1992: to "open minds, provoke discussion, create controversy, break isolation, celebrate the diversity of our communities, provide space where there is none and nurture a passion for our roots."

In the files are our economics — the handwritten income and expense ledger, statements from our bank account, and receipts for office supplies, postage, printing and phone calls. These, along with correspondence with distributors, the handwritten subscription roster, calls for submission and subscription flyers, were our reality checks. While a sense of adventure and collective vision got us started, it was evident as we grew that we could only keep going as long as we had funds, contributors, and subscribers.

We kept going, and as we did, the magazines got into the hands of lesbians and organizations farther and farther away from us. In the files are newsletters, magazines, flyers and tidbits from Latina lesbian organizations in Los Angeles, New York City, San Antonio, San Francisco, Mexico City, Buenos Aires and elsewhere, hard evidence of the Latina lesbian nation I had yearned for. I remember the days when I walked into libraries and bookstores looking for anything by or about Latina lesbians and leaving frustrated. There, in the boxes of *esto no tiene nombre* and *conmoción*, are my dreams of unearthing a South American Sappho and my delight in connecting the dots of our existence around the globe.

Maybe I am romanticizing those days, something easy to do, since publishing is the thing that twirls my curls. In the files are all those nights we stayed up typesetting, designing, editing and proofreading until we were seeing double. There is our exhaustion, our addiction to detail. There we are, having editorial committee meetings in our homes and in South Beach restaurants, gossiping about Las Salamandras, egging each other on. There we are having sex, as Vanessa and Patri were lovers, and so were Margarita and I. And there are our bitter fights, our disagreements, our inability to work with others who tried to join us, and our breakup. There is Margarita, demanding that we cease publication and there I am, resisting. Inside the boxes is the death of *esto no tiene nombre* and the subsequent and immediate birth of *conmoción*. As stated in the editorial box (1995), the new publication was "an international Latina lesbian vision that uses the published word to empower and terrorize, to destroy and create (p. 4)."

Conmoción was an expanded version of *esto no tiene nombre* and it was produced by everyone previously involved with *esto*, with the exception of Vanessa. I became the official editor and Amy Concepción, who was Margarita's ex lover, joined as the associate editor; we also established an editorial advisory board. Inside the boxes now at the UCLA Chicano Studies Research Center are documents related to the Latina lesbian writer's *telaraña* (network) newsletter that I edited. There is my stubbornness and dedication to the Cause. There is everything that we accomplished without emails or the Internet.

But there is something else, bigger than all of the above, inside those boxes. Margarita Castilla. She was a working class stone butch from Cuba who came to Miami in 1980 during the Mariel exodus. Margarita was tall and handsome in her prime. She smoked Marlboros and sipped espresso at all hours, wore guayaberas and walked Little Havana's 8th Street with a hot pink "Clit Power" button clipped to her clothes. I never saw anyone mess with her. Inside the archives of *esto no tiene nombre* and *conmoción* is Margarita's courage to be herself at all times.

Margarita kept the records for the finances and subscriptions and more often than not, she kept the peace between the four of us. She was a saleswoman; she sold insurance policies, funeral arrangements, knockoff garments and Avon, and she peddled *esto no tiene nombre* to anyone who would give her the chance. In her contributor statement she describes herself as "Cuban, anti-communist, Christian and not feminist, a lover of women, sexuality and communication." Her right-wing views of the world often clashed with the rest of ours; we were forced to consciously agree to disagree in order to work together. Within the drafts of our publications is our remarkable ability to come together for a project we each fully believed in despite our political differences.

Out of all my lovers, Margarita was the one that lasted the longest and riled me up the most. She pissed me off and she turned me on. At one point she left me for a woman she met as a result of my appearing on a show on Telemundo Television to promote the magazines. At another point she was my secret lover as I was in a primary relationship with someone else. There was no getting away from her; the karma was too strong.

Margarita was diagnosed with colon cancer that metastasized to the liver; she died on March 21, 2009. I flew to Miami to say goodbye and to help her leave the planet. The cancer and the chemotherapy transformed and aged her; she was tiny and frail at the end. Yet there she was in hospice, days away from dying, commanding the night nurse to get the supervisor so she could have her way. She gave me the instructions for her funeral, which included that she be buried in her guayabera and that mariachis play as the procession walked with the coffin to the burial plot.

After she died, Margarita's brother took all her possessions that he couldn't make a profit on and dumped them in the trash. This included her books, photographs, journals, personal correspondence, and a folder that had my name on it. In there were all my love letters and miscellaneous mementos of our long and crazy relationship. She had asked him to give it to me, and I reminded him. But in the end, he could care less about our lesbian love story.

Inside the files of *This Has No Name* is everlasting Latina lesbian lust, the same lust that Margarita's brother, and many others, deem garbage. There is our fuel, the sexual essence that defines us as lesbians. There is our Caribbean heat. There is our love and the stories of our lives in Spanish, English, and Spanglish. There is our sisterhood. There are our lesbian footprints and our loud voices. There we are.

NOTES

1. For an in-depth account of the making of *esto no tiene nombre* and *conmoción*, see:
de la tierra, t. (2002). Activist Latina Lesbian Publishing: *esto no tiene nombre* and *conmoción*. *Aztlán: A Journal of Chicano Studies*, *27*(1), 139–178.

REFERENCES

Editorial box. (1995) *Conmoción* 1. p. 4.
Telemundo Television. (1992). Cuando su hijo es gay. *Contacto*. Miami, Florida.

Barriers to Selecting Materials about Sexual and Gender Diversity[1]

Cal Gough and Ellen Greenblatt

Since the mid–1980s, materials intended for non-scholarly readers, listeners, and viewers about the experiences, creations, aspirations, and struggles of sexual and gender minorities have not been in short supply. Despite this fact, adequate inventories of these materials have not found their way into the collections of all libraries (Alexander & Miselis, 2007; Boon & Howard, 2004; Bryant, 1995; Downey, 2005; Greenblatt, 2003; Howard, 2005; Joyce, 2000; Loverich & Degnan, 1999; Moss, 2008; Murden, 1993; Oberg & Klein, 2003; Ritchie, 2001; Rothbauer, 2004; Rothbauer & McKechnie, 1999; Whelan, 2007).

The obstacles that can lead to a library selector's (or group of selectors') lack of attention to stocking materials of particular interest to sexual and gender minorities take a variety of forms. Most of these barriers, however, are rooted in unexamined or mistaken beliefs or attitudes.

"My library doesn't cater to specialized needs."

Although most library collections intentionally focus on either scholarly or non-scholarly materials, most library collections contain some of both. That's because most librarians feel obliged to address the information and/or recreational reading/viewing/listening needs of a relatively wide variety of identifiable blocs of users, including specific ethnic and age groups.

Selectors for public library collections in particular are expected to address the *different* information needs and recreational reading preferences of *multiple* groups of users. To cite only the most obvious example, few large-city U.S. public libraries are still collecting materials exclusively written or performed in English.

Whatever the regrettable defects in the number, range, or depth of materials intentionally assembled for other groups of users, the extent of those deficiencies often pales in comparison to the number, range, and depth of materials purchased to address the interests and concerns unique to individuals belonging to sexual or gender minority groups.

"Only heterosexuals live in the area my library serves."
"Lesbians, gay men, etc. don't seem to use my library."

Although the urban-based mass media tend to focus on the organized activities of LGBTIQ individuals and groups who live in large cities, LGBTIQ-identifying individuals live in virtually every community.[2] They certainly live in every village, town, and city large enough to support one or more libraries, and they attend (and/or are employed by) virtually every educational institution with one or more libraries.

The fact that in most areas heterosexuals outnumber the total number of individuals with sexual or gender minority self-identities doesn't mean these latter groups of library users don't exist, nor does that fact exempt library selectors from a responsibility to address the unique information needs and priorities and leisure reading/listening/viewing interests of all groups of library users.

In any case, the sexual identities of the individuals who patronize a particular library are difficult if not impossible to determine. For every gay male, lesbian, bisexual, transgender, or intersex person a library employee thinks he or she recognizes as such, there are others whose sexual or gender identification an employee will not recognize. Library selectors are as likely to buy into stereotypes as anyone else, but sexual/affectional orientation is not as readily apparent as a person's race, native language, vocabulary level, etc.

Nor can you rely on verbalized requests as a barometer of the information needs or habits of your library's LGBTIQ constituencies. Expecting these individuals to approach a librarian for help in locating (or purchasing) LGBTIQ materials is unrealistic for a number of reasons. For one thing, some of the information needs of gay people —*especially younger ones*— are personal and/or deeply felt (Curry, 2005; Linville, 2004; A. Martin & Hetrick, 1988; H. Martin, 2006; Mehra & Braquet, 2006). LGBTIQ library users who are unsure or anxious about their sexual or gender identities look to libraries — especially public libraries — to help cope with or sort out their uncertainty and anxiety, and partly because of the complete or near-complete anonymity surrounding the use of library materials, and because of the anonymity afforded by library-based computers with Internet access.

A few LGBTIQ patrons may approach a library employee with a question or a purchase request, but the majority will not — as, indeed, most heterosexual patrons looking for materials do not, regardless of the subject matter, as many people are simply not inclined to discuss their information needs or reading/listening/viewing preferences with strangers.

Furthermore, even when users do involve library staff in their searches for LGBTIQ-related materials, these interactions are not necessarily satisfactory (Curry, 2005; H. Martin, 2006; Mehra & Braquet, 2006). Librarians should also remember that most users' disappointments and frustrations with library collections go unreported, despite our occasional formal and informal efforts to solicit user comments, recommendations, and personal interactions with library staff.

Infrequent direct communication between library users and selectors means, among other things, that librarians must take an inclusive approach to selection rather than basing selection decisions on patron feedback. Selectors should see themselves as advocates for all their users' information needs, not merely responders to formal acquisition requests.

In addition to the certainty that LGBTIQ people use your library whether or not you are aware of that fact, most of these library users have acquaintances, a circle of friends, and families — including, in some cases, their own children as well as parents, grandparents, siblings, etc. Some of those individuals will be patronizing your library seeking information about sexual or gender identities because the sexual or gender identity of their family member, friend, or acquaintance is unfamiliar, puzzling, or makes them uneasy.[3]

There are also professional people — teachers, clergy members, doctors, social workers, therapists, attorneys, law enforcement personnel, etc.—who at some point may be visiting the nearest library for information on the subject of gender or sexual nonconformity.

And there are still other library users — most of them heterosexual — who need, want, or would benefit from accurate information about sexual or gender minorities: the uninformed, the curious, the sympathetic, the voyeuristic, even the homophobic. People from these groups, seeking information about a subject that is either controversial or personally unsettling, will at some point head for the nearest library to find what they hope will be "objective" information, preferring to do that in the atmosphere of anonymity that using a library usually offers. If that library is the one where you're working, does your collection contain the information these people are seeking?

In short, most individuals in our society are related to, or know personally, or work with, or come into professional contact with, or are periodically exposed to mass media treatments of sexual or gender minorities. Taken together with LGBTIQ people themselves, this is a relatively large constituency for justifying the collecting of LGBTIQ materials in non-specialized libraries, regardless of the library's location, size, or budget.

"It's too difficult to identify worthwhile LGBTIQ materials."

Reviews of LGBTIQ materials show up frequently in standard print and online reviewing sources. Also, Internet search engines and the reviews from mainstream reviewing sources as well those generated by users available on sites like Amazon.com make it easy to find information that can help with selection decisions.

Given the availability of favorably-reviewed materials produced for sexual or gender minorities, there's no need for selectors to change or lower their standards or ignore standard selection criteria (currency, accuracy, price, etc.) when considering potential purchase of materials about these groups. But selectors should likewise not subject such materials to a higher or different standard, or limit their purchases to an arbitrarily narrow scope of subjects or genres.

Selectors should remember that each of the constituencies under the LGBTIQ umbrella deserves access to materials across all genres, including not only the full range of non-scholarly treatments of nonfiction topics, but also novels, biographies and memoirs, poetry, and plays. And, as LGBTIQ teenagers especially tend to seek out fiction featuring LGBTIQ characters, fiction purchases for this age group shouldn't be neglected (Linville, 2004). Selectors should also remember to select materials created for different age groups and reading levels — and in every format purchased for other types of materials and target audiences: relevant feature film and documentary videos as well as books, a sampling of sound recordings — audiobooks as well as music — and pertinent online databases.

An important caveat here: gender and sexuality cannot be sufficiently addressed by purchasing two batches of materials — one batch for straight library users, another batch for "non-straight" users. Each gender or sexual minority deserves its own materials.

It's also worth pointing out that the objection to purchasing "trendy" materials is seldom mentioned with respect to materials purchased by and for heterosexual users. In fact, most public libraries go to quite a bit of trouble — and expend many dollars — to select bestselling and/or otherwise "trendy" items and/or materials of questionable value that are of primary interest to heterosexual library patrons. Librarians who stock bestselling LGB-TIQ-related titles will find that they circulate often. In-house use of these materials is likely to be even more impressive (Greenblatt, 2003).

"I don't feel qualified to order these materials."

Libraries would be in deep trouble if librarians or library users believed that only children could make sensible decisions about which children's materials should be purchased for libraries, or required a credentialed scientist to order the library's science books. The same reasoning applies to the qualifications for selecting LGBTIQ materials. You don't need to be a member of a sexual or gender minority yourself to select materials for these library users.

True, a selector's belonging to a sexual or gender minority himself or herself might have a bearing on the extent of that selector's background knowledge, enthusiasm, or diligence, but the selector's self-identity is not otherwise relevant to systematically pursuing user-friendly collection improvements.

Certainly in no case should the selection of these materials be neglected merely because no otherwise-qualified selector publicly self-identifies as a member of a sexual or gender minority, or because no one, regardless of their presumed sexual orientation, has volunteered to take on selection responsibilities in this area.

"Can't people just use the Internet or interlibrary loan?"

The existence of Internet resources does not automatically relieve librarians of their responsibility for stocking their libraries with printed and audiovisual materials for other subject areas, patron interests, and target audiences. Why should an exception be made with respect to LGBTIQ-related materials?

Besides, Internet access is not universal (even in U.S. libraries), and many public- and school library-based Internet terminals deliberately filter out LGBTIQ content. Furthermore, the extent, stability, and reliability of LGBTIQ resources on the Internet vary widely. The Internet is no substitute for a thoughtfully-stocked library collection.

The abundance of LGBTIQ-related resources available on the Internet should prompt library staff to create and distribute — and/or post on library websites — lists of relevant Internet sites for their LGBTIQ patrons. However, the abundance of Internet-based tools for *identifying* quality LGBTIQ-related materials does make purchasing these materials more convenient.

Relying on interlibrary loan to obtain LGBTIQ materials instead of buying them for your library is also unrealistic, because even some research libraries under-collect these materials. Furthermore, the inconvenience of a patron's being forced to wait for an interlibrary loan to arrive — not to mention the inconvenience of needing to return interlibrary loan items after relatively short loan periods — should not fall disproportionately upon the group of library users wanting access to information about gender or sexual diversity. Certainly, no LGBTIQ library user should be forced to resort to interlibrary loan to obtain *non-obscure* information, such a bestselling gay novel, or a parenting manual designed specifically for gay or lesbian parents. Submitting interlibrary loans for non-scholarly treatments of gender or sexual diversity information should be a rare experience, not a routine one, for any single group of library users.

"Buying LGBTIQ materials would be promoting gender or sexual nonconformity."

Purchasing LGBTIQ-related materials is evidence that the library acknowledges the diversity of its constituencies and affirms diversity in its collections. Using library funds to purchase diverse materials does not constitute the exalting of one group of users over other groups. Creating an affirming environment for all library users is not the same as endorsing a particular group's social or political agenda (Hedgepeth, 2004). Besides, librarians are professionally obligated "to resist efforts that systematically exclude materials dealing with any subject matter, including gender or sexual orientation" (American Library Association, 2009).

"I'm personally uncomfortable with exposing myself to what some of these materials describe."
"That stuff doesn't belong in my library."
"I don't approve of people who don't conform to conventional behaviors or reading/listening/viewing interests."

Librarians are used to coping with — or at least to reading about others coping with — periodic attempts by library users to remove from a library items they object to finding there. But some librarians practice a form of "prior censorship" themselves through selection decisions that deny access to library information of interest to some library patrons (Braun, 2008; Coy, 2008; Jones, 1983; Tsang, 1990; West, 1983; Whelan, 2009).[4]

The ethical issues and vagaries of exclusive vs. inclusive selection practices are hardly confined to the selection or non-selection of gender- or sexuality-related materials. And although many library school students receive training about the ethical ramifications of library work, most librarians have been thoroughly socialized in a heterosexist culture long before they arrive in graduate school. One or two discussions about the dangers of selection bias, a classroom assignment on that topic, or even an entire course in LGBTIQ collection development will not always penetrate the results of many years of social conditioning.

Nevertheless, the professional's job is to strive to minimize the effects of his/her personal feelings and biases when selecting library materials, and to focus instead on addressing the indisputable and probable information needs of all the library's user groups.

At a minimum, one would hope that a librarian who is philosophically opposed to censorship of library materials by other individuals or by organized groups would ponder very carefully his/her own reluctance or refusal to purchase LGBTIQ library materials, and to do so as systematically and responsibly as s/he selects for other groups of library users.

Unfortunately, even if ordering LGBTIQ materials is not a problematic moral issue for you personally, it might be for someone else on the library staff. You may work with heterosexist colleagues, supervisors, managers, administrators, or funding agency representatives. Your community may include an individual willing to attack your library to garner support during a local election campaign. And there's no denying that providing gay-oriented materials for your gay and lesbian library users may offend more than a few (heterosexual) patrons who regard the library as "their" library and not everyone's.

What's often forgotten, however, when a librarian decides *not* to order LGBTIQ items in the hopes of avoiding a possible confrontation with an offended (heterosexual) patron is the fact that *the absence of these materials* in a library is a failure to serve—and offensive to—LGBTIQ library users. The choice facing every librarian responsible for selecting library materials is not whether s/he can avoid offending people, but *which people the librarian chooses to risk offending.* And while it's usually politically safer to ignore the information needs of even large user groups as long as it isn't the perceived largest group, "usually safe" doesn't mean "professional," much less "ethical."

"Usually safe" also isn't the same thing as "always safe." It's interesting to speculate on how a librarian or library administrator would respond if "enough" members of various sexual and gender minorities became as vocal in their demands for a fair return on their library tax or tuition dollars as heterocentric users can often be in expressing their outraged sensibilities at noticing some non-heteronormal book, magazine, or film on the shelves of "their" library. If logic and professional ethics can't motivate a selector to select materials of interest to sexual and gender minority members, perhaps organized (and/or highly publicized) clamoring would result in a more even playing field among the multitude of equally-deserving but very different library constituencies.

In any case, should you yourself be relatively unencumbered by a heterocentric bias, some library patron, a colleague, an administrator, or someone else outside the library selection and de-selection process may try to get you (or your supervisor) to collude with him/her in interfering with, postponing, or even blocking your selecting LGBTIQ materials, or in surreptitiously removing certain LGBTIQ-related items your library already owns. Can you, the selector, resist these pressures, regardless of how subtle or blatant they are?

It also may be worth realizing that sometimes when a person disparages any subject or user group that s/he does not belong to, that person's expressions of discomfort, disapproval, or indignation about what's suitable and not suitable for the shelves of a library should be left to that person to cope with, not taken on as a problem you must address to that unhappy user's satisfaction. In other words, life is full of disappointments, and when it comes to access to library collections there's no reason why LGBTIQ library users should always be the disappointed group. Coping with people who object to the presence of certain materials in "their" library seems a lesser evil than knowing you are systematically depriving some library users of materials they would undoubtedly find interesting, entertaining, or helpful.

On the other hand, selectors should acknowledge that it's part of a selector's job—an occupational hazard, really—to defend library selection principles whenever called on to do so. Managing our personal anxiety at being questioned about our purchasing decisions will probably better serve librarians and library users in the long run better than will pursuing a strategy we hope will totally protect us from other people's negative reactions to our selection decisions. And, while we're on this subject, it's interesting that some librarians seem more threatened by the possibility of complaints or observations about what someone may discover is in our library's collection than they feel guilty about what's *not* there, but probably should be.

In any case, if the American Library Association's freedom-to-read and diversity-in-collections policies have not been incorporated into your library's collection development policy already, they should be, as they are very useful in handling complaints from patrons and politicians. You can find these policies in the annual *ALA Handbook of Organization,* available in print and at ALA's website. Of particular relevance is ALA's "Access to Library Resources and Services Regardless of Sex, Gender Identity, Gender Expression, or Sexual Orientation" (American Library Association, 2009).

"My library can't afford these materials."

Probably the most often-used reason for not routinely purchasing LGBTIQ materials is the inadequate amount of money most libraries have available for buying new or retrospective materials of any kind. But even a severely limited budget doesn't mean you can't afford to select any such materials; it does mean that you must work harder to be sure you're choosing the best and/or the most useful or the most popular materials available.

Also, don't overlook the potential of donated materials. If you can find a way to communicate your library's willingness to stock donated materials of interest to sexual and gender minorities, your users' donations, especially if promptly and officially acknowledged, can help fill some gaps in library collections that can't be filled through purchases.[5]

Whatever the merits or defects of these varied explanations for ignoring or refusing to purchase LGBTIQ-themed books, periodicals, databases, videos, and sound recordings, the *consequences* for the library's users are the same: the collections of very few libraries reflect the fact that not all library users are heterosexuals.

In addition to the practical difficulties for LGBTIQ people that result from this dearth of library materials of particular interest to them, the psychological consequences for individual users are profound:

> When those who have the power to name and to socially construct reality choose not to see you or hear you ... [you feel] as if you looked into a mirror and saw nothing.... Invisibility is not just a matter of being told to keep your private life private; it's the attempt to fragment you, to prevent you from integrating love and work and feelings and ideas, with the empowerment that that can bring [Rich, 1986, p. 199].[6]

Some people expect library collections to contain materials of interest to them, and a library is therefore a natural place for them to patronize. Other people, repeatedly finding that their particular interests are not adequately reflected in library collections, abandon libraries and seek information of particular interest to them elsewhere.

As professional librarians, we have commitments to numerous constituencies. We are encumbered by various constraints on our desire to better serve all these user groups. Lesbians, gay men, bisexuals, intersex, and transgender persons are not the only groups of users a librarian needs to be mindful of, but meeting these groups' unique information needs, like those of other groups, deserves our best professional efforts.

NOTES

1. An earlier version of this essay appeared in *Gay and Lesbian Library Service* edited by Cal Gough and Ellen Greenblatt (McFarland, 1990).

2. Estimates of the prevalence of gay people in the population vary. Although there is no official count, librarians who examine service area federal census data to help guide their selection decisions will find the same-sex household occupancy data somewhat helpful. Another useful demographic resource is ePodunk's Gay Index, a fairly good indicator of gay and lesbian relationships in various communities. Slightly over 1300 communities are indexed, so not all communities are included. For more information, see: http://www.epodunk.com/. For an example of how census information has been used to evaluate libraries' holdings of lesbian fiction, please see Pecoskie & McKenzie (2004).

3. The information needs of parents who suspect or learn their child is not heterosexual are particularly worthy of the librarian's attention. See Ben-Ari (1995).

4. For more information on self-censorship, see "Censorship of Children's and Young Adult Books in Schools and Public Libraries" in Section Six.

5. For an example of what one person can do, see the profile "Shoulders to Stand On," also in this section of the book.

6. Rich made this remark with respect to Western culture's relentless eradication and distortion of female reality; it is equally true of the routine erasing of the histories and the routine denial of the sensibilities, activities, aspirations, and contributions of lesbians, gay men, bisexuals, transgender and intersex persons.

REFERENCES

Alexander, L. B., & Miselis, S. D. (2007). Barriers to GLBTQ collection development and strategies for overcoming them. *Young Adult Library Services, 5*(3), 43–49.

American Library Association. (2009). Access to library resources and services regardless of sex, gender identity, gender expression, or sexual orientation. Retrieved from http://www.ala.org/ala/aboutala/offices/oif/statementspols/statementsif/interpretations/accesslibrary.cfm

Ben-Ari, A. (1995). The discovery that an offspring is gay: Parents', gay men's, and lesbians' perspectives. *Journal of Homosexuality, 30*(1), 89–112. doi: 10.1300/J082v30n01_05

Boon, M. H., & Howard, V. (2004). Recent lesbian/gay/bisexual/transgender fiction for teens: Are Canadian public libraries providing adequate collections? *Collection Building, 23*(3), 133–138. doi: 10.1108/01604950410544674

Braun, L. W. (2008, July 19). What are we scared of? *YALSA Blog.* Retrieved from http://yalsa.ala.org/blog/2008/07/19/what-are-we-scared-of/

Bryant, E. (1995). Pride & prejudice. *Library Journal, 120*(1), 37–39.

Coy, John. (2008, October 9). Protecting students from "those people." *AS IF! Authors Support Intellectual Freedom:* Blog, retrieved from http://asifnews.blogspot.com/2008/10/protecting-students-from-those-people.html

Curry, A. (2005). If I ask, will they answer? Evaluating public library reference service to gay and lesbian youth. *Reference and User Services Quarterly, 45*(1), 65–75.

Downey, J. (2005). Public library collection development issues regarding the information needs of GLBT patrons. *Progressive Librarian,* (25), 86–95.

Greenblatt, E. (2003). Lesbian, gay, bisexual, transgender library users: Overcoming the myths. *Colorado Libraries, 29*(4), 21–25.

Hedgepeth, E. (2000). What does it really mean to "affirm" versus "promote"? Retrieved from http://www.safeschoolscoalition.org/affirmation-vs-promotion.pdf

Howard, V. (2005). Out of the closet ... but not on the shelves? An analysis of Canadian public libraries' holdings of gay-themed picture books. *Progressive Librarian,* (25), 62–75.

Jones, F. (1983). Internal censorship. In *Defusing censorship: The librarian's guide to handling censorship conflicts* (pp. 115–127). Phoenix, AZ: Oryx.

Joyce, S. L. (2000, September/October). Lesbian, gay, and bisexual library service: A review of the literature. *Public Libraries, 39*(5), 270–279.

Linville, D. (2004). Beyond picket fences: What gay/queer/LGBTQ teens want from the library. *Voice of Youth Advocates, 27*(3), 183–186.

Loverich, P., & Degnan, D. (1999, June 15). Out on the shelves? Not really. *Library Journal, 124*(11), 55.

Martin, A., & Hetrick, E. S. (1988). The stigmatization of the gay and lesbian adolescent. *Journal of Homosexuality, 15*(1), 163–183. doi: 10.1300/J082v15n01_12

Martin, H. J. (2006, Summer). A library outing: Serving queer and questioning teens. *Young Adult Library Services, 4*(4), 38–39.

Mehra, B., & Braquet, D. (2006). A "queer" manifesto of interventions for libraries to "come out" of the closet! A study of "queer" youth experiences during the coming out process. *LIBRES: Library and Information Science Research Electronic Journal, 16*(1). Retrieved from http://libres.curtin.edu.au/libres16n1/MehraBraquet.pdf

Moss, E. (2008). An inductive evaluation of a public library GLBT collection. *Collection Building, 27*(4), 149–156. doi: 10.1108/01604950810913715

Murden, S. (1993). Gay and lesbian materials: Are Virginia's public libraries meeting the challenge?" *Virginia Librarian, 39*(4), 5–8.

Oberg, L. R., & Klein, G. M. (2003). Gay-themed books in Oregon public and academic libraries: A brief historical overview. *OLA Quarterly, 9*(2), 8–12.

Pecoskie, J. L., & McKenzie, P. J. (2004). Canadian census data as a tool for evaluating public library holdings of award-winning lesbian fiction. *The Canadian Journal of Information and Library Science / La Revue canadienne des sciences de l'information et de bibliothéconomie, 28*(2), 3–23.

Rich, A. (1986). Invisibility in academe. In *Blood, Bread, and Poetry: Selected Prose, 1979–1985* (pp. 198–201). New York: Norton.

Ritchie, C. J. (2001). Collection development of gay/lesbian/bisexual-related adult non-fiction in medium-sized Illinois public libraries. *Illinois Libraries, 83*(2), 39–70.

Rothbauer, P. (2004). "People aren't afraid anymore, but it's hard to find books": Reading practices that inform the personal and social identities of self-identified lesbian and queer young women. *The Canadian Journal of Information and Library Science / La Revue canadienne des sciences de l'information et de bibliothéconomie, 28*(3), 53–74.

Rothbauer, P. M., & McKechnie, L. E. F. (1999). Gay and lesbian fiction for young adults: a survey of holdings in Canadian public libraries. *Collection Building, 18*(1), 32–39. doi: 10.1108/01604959910 256526

Tsang, D. C. (1990). Censorship of lesbian and gay materials by library workers. In C. Gough & E. Greenblatt (Eds.), *Gay and lesbian library service* (pp. 166–170). Jefferson, NC: McFarland.

West, C. (1983). The secret garden of censorship: Ourselves. *Library Journal, 108*(15), pp. 1651–1653.

Whelan, D. L. (2007). Gay titles missing in most AR libraries. *School Library Journal, 53*(1), 18.

Whelan, D. L. (2009). A dirty little secret: Self-censorship is rampant and lethal (effects of self censorship among librarians). *School Library Journal, 55*(2), 26–31.

One for the Road: Personal Reflections on LGBTIQ Literature

James V. Carmichael, Jr.

At the 2009 Book Awards luncheon meeting of the American Library Association's Gay, Lesbian, Bisexual and Transgender Round Table (GLBTRT), which roughly coincided with the fortieth anniversary of the Stonewall riots, I received indirect absolution for my relatively late development as an openly gay man from historian and two-time ALA GLB-TRT Book Award winner John D'Emilio (1984, 2003), who pointed out how very few in the LGBTIQ community were aware of the so-called Stonewall Riots of June 28, 1969, since coverage of the event was limited to a minor news item in *The New York Times* ("4 policemen hurt in 'Village' raid," 1969, June 29). I surely wasn't tuned in, because ten days earlier, I had been married in Decatur, Georgia, and was already at work in a defense plant that manufactured C-130s to carry troops and munitions to Viet Nam. In my weekend psychedelic haze, I barely registered the fact that Judy Garland died on June 22, although note it I did; not until years later when I came out did I discover that I was not her only gay fan (ditto a secret passion for Margaret Mitchell's novel *Gone with the Wind*). I find the gall of Rufus Wainwright in recreating Garland's legendary April 23, 1961, Carnegie Hall concert on June 14, 2006, somewhat hubristic.

Gay liberation certainly did not seem as important to me as the other aspects of the social revolution then going on, but then, up until about the time of the Kent State shootings on May 4, 1970, the success of the social revolution seemed possible — no more bigotry, bureaucracy, international bullying, or banking. My revolution ended in a whimper, however: shortly after the Atlanta Pop Festival at Byron, Georgia, on July 4, 1970, I started working in the trust department of an Atlanta bank. Jimi Hendrix and Janis Joplin died that fall of variations on the overdose.

Not until I was professionally credentialed as a librarian at a small college in Georgia did I discover a book entitled *The Gay Academic* on the library shelves, containing Barbara Gittings' (1979) seminal essay, "Combating the Lies in Libraries" on the subject of the misinformation about homosexuality in libraries. Gittings referred in her title to the psychological literature by reputable psychiatrists that described homosexuality as a disease. She was one of the activists who crashed the 1971 American Psychiatric Association (APA) convention in the successful effort to have homosexuality reclassified as a natural orientation or preference. (The most complete account of these events is Drescher and Malino, 2007.)

Gittings' essay seemed to be addressed to me, personally. I was so excited that I called the book's editor, Louie Crew, and over Sunday afternoon tea with him and his partner Ernest at Fort Valley State College, an hour away, Louie encouraged me to call Barbara. The next night, Barbara and I talked for over an hour like old chums — we hooted and we hollered. While I've extolled Barbara and her importance in my life for years, I have never reflected on how her essay resonated with my personal experience of gay literature. So belatedly, I send this love note in memory of Barbara, and join in the chorus of those who have stated how prescient and pertinent her writings and presence were, particularly for LGBTIQ librarians.

The LGBTIQ community is now so inured to the fact of having a literature written by and for them that it is difficult to imagine a time when that was not the case, yet in 1998, when I checked the OCLC records for titles that appeared under any of the admittedly inadequate subject headings for gay literature published up to and including 1969, I found only 161 unique fiction and non-fiction print titles, with an additional 77 serials, many but not all of which were nude male soft-core pornography (Carmichael, 2002, esp. p. 80). This finding is not as grim as it sounds if one stops to reflect that the fictions of Mary Renault, for example, were not included in this total, and moreover, the Library of Congress was not in the habit of assigning subject headings to fiction.

Outside of the big cities, the subject of homosexuality was breached *sub rosa* if discussed at all. There may have been individual acceptance or derision, but as my senior year high-school English teacher admonished me, it was not a "socially acceptable" topic for fiction, on the grounds that it wasn't polite to "frighten the horses." It is not surprising that a lot of what today would be called gay literature was not then understood as such, nor was all of it produced by gay writers: Oscar Wilde's *The Picture of Dorian Gray* (1890), for example; Sherwood Anderson's short story "Hands," in his collection *Winesburg, Ohio* (1919) ; and Thomas Mann's *Death in Venice* (1928). These works were studied in honors English classes in the prep school I attended, albeit with only oblique references to the fact that the subject matter was gay.

Just as today one hears the straight "tolerant" individual who will coexist with LBGTIQ people as long as they don't "flaunt" or discuss their sexual or romantic preferences, gay people of the pre–Stonewall era were accepted as long as they used their talents to non-gay ends like age-old gay religious who sublimated their sexuality in prayer and good works; florists arranging flowers for the wedding; hairdressers doing mother's hair; coaches of the women's basketball and softball teams; directors of straight love stories (Dorothy Arzner, George Cukor); gay actors and lesbian actresses performing straight roles (Alla Nazimova, Agnes Moorehead, Claudette Colbert, Billy Haines, Rock Hudson) — hence the emphasis on gay special artistic "talents" and "creativity," a claim one doubts would be heard if the creative activity had as its object gay subject matter. Besides that, however, the lives of most gay people in most backwaters seemed to be about furtive sex and the desperate attempt to pass or fit in. To a degree, these were still the facts of gay life when I grew up, with the added conflation of "gay" with "Commie" and "[name of minority]-lover," leftovers of the McCarthy era perpetuated by the FBI's director (Johnson, 2004 discusses the relationship between anticommunism, racial liberality, and homosexuality).

Of course, to this mix, one should add the puritan obsession with sex still characteristic of the socio-political climate of the United States today: Walt Whitman's poetry was shocking to nineteenth-century readers, but his ambisexuality made the exact nature of his social offense harder to pin down. The open discussion of homosexuality was confined to the police court and the psychiatric couch. The psychiatrists wanted to "cure" us, which made C. A. Tripp's (1975) sympathetic treatment in *The Homosexual Matrix* so refreshing. My parents had a library for reference and "serious" literature where they gathered for drinks in the late afternoon, and another book shelf for popular fiction in what was basically a den, and although Hall's *The Well of Loneliness* (1929) was on the fiction shelves — why, I can't imagine, since Mother had a horror of lesbians after being pursued by one on a business trip with my father — I was much more interested in what Rod and Betty were doing on the rocks in Grace Metalious's *Peyton Place* (1956), and public discourse about sex had an outlying barrier at about the point where Eustace Chesser's *Love Without Fear* (1941, originally published as a sex manual) expressed the then somewhat daring opinion that sexual expression of love outside of marriage could be healthy and beautiful. Chesser was vindicated in a landmark censorship trial, and the book became something more philosophical, even a cause célèbre, to a later generation of readers.

Tennessee Williams' *One Arm* (1954), on the other hand, also on my parents' library shelf, contained, among other stories, the lurid tale of a male predator in a movie house balcony, "Hard Candy." Besides these glimpses of gay life, the ambiguity of art books that my parents collected profligately, the occasional peek at *Physique Pictorial* in a short-lived Marietta, Georgia, newsstand, and my father's admonitions to curb my emotive behavior, these manifestations constituted what little I knew about being gay, and my education was completed only when a sexually aggressive Cuban classmate advanced on me in seventh grade at military school in the only private spot available, my closet.

Meanwhile, the Supreme Court, under Chief Justice Earl Warren, changed the terms of debate of what was considered "obscene." By the time *Our Lady of the Flowers* by Jean Genet was published, relatively peacefully, in 1963, the major battles over literary censorship were almost over, and those over gay censorship *per se* had occurred over beefcake (Green, 1990). Sears' breathtaking history (2006) contains the most vivid description of how gay "pornographers" like Hal Call fought the police, the courts, and the U.S. Postal Service.

During my sophomore year in prep school, a new teacher came to campus. His library in his apartment suggested that he was gay. He was the first person to whom I ever admitted my sexual proclivities, and we still talk about once a month by phone. On his shelves, I discovered and read in 1961 James Barr's *Quatrefoil* (1950), Gore Vidal's *The City and the Pillar* (1954, unrevised), and Jean Cocteau's *Le Livre Blanc* (1930). By 1965, when I returned from a year in France with a contraband copy of an Olympia Press edition of William Burroughs's *The Soft Machine* (1961) hidden in my luggage, I had fallen in love with a straight Englishman, and on my way back up North to finish my senior year, I picked up a paperback copy of John Rechy's *City of Night* (1964) at the Pennsylvania train station. The book still haunts me, and its hellish vision of Los Angeles "youngmen," hustlers, and Miss Divine in an endless nocturnal miasma of tricks, drugs, booze, hilarity and despair, all overseen by a huge neon sign spelling out the word "F*A*S*C*I*N*A*T*I*O*N," defined my reaction and my vision of gay night life for years to come, and dulled my senses to the allure of other gay novels extolling the gay world both before and after Stonewall, such as Gordon Merrick's *The Lord Won't Mind* (1970), Andrew Holleran's *Dancer from the Dance* (1978), and Andrew Hollinghurst's *The Swimming Pool Library* (1988). For this reader, at least, *City of Night* was the fictional equivalent of Allen Ginsberg's *Howl* (1956), and callow youth that I was, I had no humor whatsoever and even less sense of camp about my sexual condition, although there was a lot of gay humor in the era: Paul Lynde on television; the movie *Flesh Gordon* (1974); and best of all, the porn classic series of that era, Richard Armory's *Fruit of the Loon*

(1968). Not until relatively recently did I discover a group of novels by Joseph Hansen, who wrote in the 1960s under the pseudonym James Colton, describing the gay life of Nathan Reed in California in the 1940s, which seem to me to be honest, and certainly are among the best gay fiction (Hansen, J., 1993, 1995, 2001). Legal liberality is not a precondition for good writing or bearable living conditions.

My entry into librarianship reaffirmed my gay identity, thanks to my "discovery" of Barbara Gittings and the Gay Task Force, lesbian and gay colleagues across campus at Georgia College, the presence of Laud Humphries' (1970) *Tearoom Trade* and *The Journal of Homosexuality* on the library shelves, the latter first published in 1974, and my first ALA Conference in San Francisco in 1981. Not only did I see the Gay Day Parade with the Sisters of Indulgence and the Dykes on Bikes putting in memorable appearances, but I stayed with a friend, poet Steve Abbott (1942–1992), who had been president of our senior class at Emory, was married about the same time I was, and who started a gay liberation movement of a sort when he followed a beautiful young man to San Francisco.

It's probably fair to say that the gay poets whose work I like the most are among those I've known personally, like my old friend Steve Abbot (Abbott, A.), GLBTRT member Steven Riel (1992, 2003), or North Carolina's Jeffrey Beam (2008). Maybe it's the troubadour in my soul, or the fact that I used to read my own ghastly productions from an Atlanta coffeehouse stage in my sexually conflicted early twenties. I am mystified by the appeal of the poetry of Frank O'Hara, Robert Duncan, and Dennis Cooper, the poets Steve Abbott seemed to admire. On the other hand, I will always be grateful to him for reading aloud with me in tandem the long progressively drunker tirade, "The Prophet" by Alice Notley (1981). I laughed until I cried.

In my experience, some of the best gay literature, or representations of gay people or gay sensibility, occur outside of what is now called LGBTIQ literature, and in fact, includes titles in which the word "gay" or its equivalents never occur. These writers show instead of tell: I am thinking in particular of Truman Capote's *Other Voices, Other Rooms* (1955), Cecil Beaton's *My Royal Past* (1939), and Patrick Denis's *Auntie Mame (1955)*, *Around the World with Auntie Mame* (1958), and *Little Me* (1961), the first an exposition of southern gothic, the rest all primers in camp. My favorite contemporary example is James Wilcox, whose gay novel, *Plain and Normal* (1998) is pleasant enough, yet is hardly a match for the hysterical and limpid takes on southern culture he gives in *Heavenly Days* (2003) and *Hunk City* (2007). One needs a gay guide, on the other hand, or a very wise straight reader, to fathom the gay subtext of Joseph Conrad's short story "The Secret Sharer" (Conrad, 1912), anything by Pierre Loti, or Herman Melville's *Redburn* (1849) — (Hardwick, 2000, June 15).

Indirection confers the power of denial, or not, upon the story teller, and there are still writers who prefer something more than the labeling that "gay," "lesbian," or "bisexual" provide, whether or not class snobbery, self-protection, or privacy is the ostensible reason for it. The classic example is Gore Vidal, one of my favorite social commentators, who eschews the label "gay" for its attendant cultural baggage and claims in his memoir *Palimpsest* (1995, p. 132) that the reason his relationship with Howard Austen (d. 2003) endured for so many years was that they never had sex. His recounting of his "gay" re-writing of the biblical clunker *Ben-Hur* in 1958 (pp. 303–307) and the subsequent subterfuge necessary to keep leading man Charlton Heston from catching on is one of the most exquisite tales in Hollywood lore. Other gay writers have canvases difficult to classify: James Purdy's *Eustace Chisholm and the Works* (1967) depicts a sadistic gay love affair ending with a disembowelment as grisly as any devised by a Tudor tribunal, but like Tennessee Williams, some of his most convincing characters are women, in particular the heroine of the title novella *63, Dream Palace and Other Stories* (1981). The clearest indication that the lesbian, gay, and bisexual movements will endure is the presence of a multiplicity of voices and viewpoints, other than purely political ones, *pace* Bruce Bawer (1993), Andrew Sullivan (1996), et al., which of course is not to deny the presence of official gay party lines outside of politics, among cultural conservatives as well as among radicals. I am speaking of course of public commentators who seem contrarian by design, although Sullivan's work is admittedly more complex and diffuse than others in the genre.

I don't think about my sexuality as a matter of sex primarily, since my libido has never been particularly strong, but very much a matter of gender. I distinguish between the two by saying that my sex (male) is what I am, my sexuality is who I choose, my gender is what I do, and how I do it. This formulation is eidetic and not original with me, but I have no idea as to its source. The United States media panders to prurience of the Clinton/Lewinsky variety, but *gender* difficulties are responsible for much of the evil resulting from sexuality — bullying, macho and feminine expectations, "difference" measured against the most tenuous scale of normality. It is easy to spot these evils on older iterations of the Minnesota Multiphasic Personality Inventory (Newmyer, 1976); not so easy to see how they infiltrate everything we do. Interestingly men were penalized for femininity, but few officials seemed to care whether females were masculine or not — they were, as the saying goes, "doubly invisible." Johnson (2004) found that only men lost federal positions as a result of the homosexual purge in the federal government, because lesbians seemed to pose no "security threat."

Within the LGBTIQ communities, the standoff between various shades of gender manifestations — femme and butch, queen and trade — have entered a new phase of elaboration with the transgender movement, and how those individuals self-identify. Basically non-sexual manifestations of gender had some articulation in the 1960s and 1970s (the uniform of a Castro Street clone, the ostracization for non-allergenic reasons of males who wear cologne in certain bars, walking "butch"). The societal expectations on which these manifestations are based are toxic to any inclusion project, whatever aphrodisiac effects they may produce in the excluders.

My search for the limits of the glass ceiling in southern libraries in my doctoral work led me quite naturally to ask if gay men shared with women any professional barriers. Could one remain a reference librarian if one preferred to do so, or was that professional suicide in the case where one was offered the position of Head of Public Services? I broke a cardinal rule of survey research on the male librarian survey I conducted in the early 1990s, and asked respondents to identify their sexual orientation, but it did not affect my response rate (73 percent) as my academic mentor feared (Carmichael, 1992). I found that while the proportion of gay men in the profession was only slightly larger than in the population as a whole, 83 percent of straight and gay librarians alike admitted to the "effeminate, probably gay" male stereotype they had encountered from time to time. Christine L. Williams, who had conducted research similar to mine in sociology among men in feminine professions (1995), called the phenomenon of men who felt pressured to assume administrative work in feminized professions "the glass escalator." In terms of "tokenism," i.e., the presence of a token number of males in a "feminized" profession in which women formed a majority of the workforce (e.g., nursing, librarianship, school teaching, or social work), men were rewarded for being in the minority, but were afraid of being perceived as gay; whereas female "tokens" in "male" professions, held down as they were in scut work or menial jobs, nevertheless felt empowered by their work.

Gender, not sex, permits empathy between the sexes, just as it can undermine understanding in apposite circumstances. Thus, Dorothy Parker's barbs become camp *bon mots* for gay men, not because her sexual objects are male but because gay men can identify with the wit and dogged resilience with which Parker dismisses the put-down, the lover's rejection, or societal expectations, e.g., "*You cannot persuade her with gun or a lariat / To come across for the proletariat*" (Whitman, A., 1967, June 8). I like to think how lucky I was that gender, that social force that wanted to push me towards "male" activities rather than more reflective pursuits like reading, failed to prevent me from discovering Emily Dickinson's poetry and letters when I was thirteen or fourteen. I don't share the opinion that Dickinson was a lesbian, although her dining room table certainly provided the setting for some of the most salacious Victorian sexual melodrama one can imagine (Longworth, ed. 1983). Her poetic life was almost totally interior; unless one makes the case that her gargantuan cake recipes and domestic chores provided her with at least a part of her inspiration or imagery (Mudge, Brose, & Dupre, J.M., 1976). At any rate, her personal life can hardly alter the fact that, with the possible exception of Walt Whitman, hers is the most startling voice in all of nineteenth-century American literature, and it presages most of literary modernism. In spite of the fact that the academic industry and the ubiquitous one-woman show has at times made of her life something more fey and twee than profound, she represents for me a very high poetic standard against which one aspect of literary achievement can be measured: not instructive, except incidentally; entertaining, only subliminally; stream-of-consciousness, only as a spider's filament is so, vitally and essentially, not accidentally.

During a particularly vicious ice-storm in Greensboro, I began trekking through Bloomsbury with Virginia Woolf (1975–1980), who, more than she was a lesbian, was, I believe, affectionately asexual. Within a year, I had read the letters, the diaries, the essays, the fiction, and while I relished it all, I felt that what Sally Fitzgerald had said about Flannery O'Connor — that her fiction was really a gloss on the letters — was perhaps true of Woolf as well (Fitzgerald, 1979). It was her manner of living, observing, and imagining, her "habit of being," and what I like to think of as Woolf's invention of the twentieth century approach to her subject matter — an exasperated roll of the eyes and an eruption of smoke from a Gauloise as she contemplated the latest bêtise from Dame Sybil Colfax — and her unspeakable vulnerability for all of that, defined her. Although perhaps best known for her series of lectures, *A Room of One's Own* (1929) because of Eileen Atkins' brilliant portrayal of Woolf in a BBC/PBS production, my personal favorite example of Woolf's bravado is *Three Guineas* (1938), her finest and most sustained feminist critique of, among other things, the non-equivalency of "women's education," the useless pageantry of war, and the male vanity behind that pageantry. On the other hand, I confess that I like Gertrude Stein's *Autobiography of Alice B. Toklas* (1933), but very little else in her oeuvre, since it is hard for a layperson to like a literary exemplar of obscure effect. I suspect, too, that Stein may have lacked some of Woolf's generosity of spirit, and needed more control of the people around her, just as Alice needed control of Stein (Malcolm, 2007).

AIDS changed what it meant to be gay for myself and my contemporaries. My lesbian friends became so weary of caring for and burying gay men that there almost came a parting of the ways between us, out of sheer exhaustion. I did not read Paul Monette's celebrated volumes of memoirs, but I lived with the illness and death of a large and important part of my community, including poet Steve Abbott, mentioned above. AIDS meant that we could no longer be merely "numbers" (John Rechy's 1967 title of a further look at the gay skin trade); we had names; our names appeared on quilts; we became friends instead of tricks;

we became citizens with demands instead of hidden statistics. Many writers documented what happened to the gay community because of AIDS, none more poignantly or poetically than Tony Kushner (1995). My own remembrance of those dark years before the miracle cocktails became available is symbolized in Susan Sontag's *AIDS and Its Metaphors* (1989) and *Illness as Metaphor* (1978) that had originally appeared as a series of essays in *The New York Review of Books*. Sontag explains, for me at least, how fear of the foreign "other" and terror of plague are related. Without saying so in so many words, she also described the heartlessness of the Reagan administration and the unprecedented phenomenon of parents rejecting and disowning their own fatally ill sons (for they were usually sons at the beginning), supposedly on moral grounds. AIDS also cleared the way for the many straight-gay alliances that followed and the recognition by at least a portion of the American public that the gay community consisted of their sons, daughters, neighbors, bosses, neighbors, and in some cases, husbands and wives. Holleran's (2006) Gittings Award-winner, *Grief,* is a finely-crafted AIDS-themed meditation on death and survival.

Many of the important gains made in LGBTIQ literature have occurred since the discovery of the HIV virus. There is now at least one comprehensive world history of homosexuality (Crompton, 2003). Moreover, D'Emilio's seminal 1983 history of the pre–Stonewall Mattachine Society (1998) has now been complemented by Gallo's (2006) superb history of the Daughters of Bilitis. Wayne Dyne's (1987) bibliography of scholarly literature about homosexuality and the GLBTRT's Gay Bibliographies created by Barbara Gittings have now been fleshed out by histories of all aspects of gay and lesbian publishing (Strietmatter, 1995, 2009; Meeker, 2006; Bronski, 2002; Forrest, 2005; Cart & Jenkins, 2006, plus a plethora of histories of individual beefcake/pornography studios and artists). Biographies and autobiographies of LGBTIQ individuals, both famous and relatively unknown, are almost too numerous to name, although one has to mention Katherine Cummings' diary (Cummings, 1992) as representative of the numerous transgendered voices available in print and elsewhere in the years since Christine Jorgensen's (1967) story first appeared, especially as Cummings' book won the 1992 Australian Human Rights Award for Non-Fiction, and, fortuitously, she is a retired librarian. Certainly the greatest boon for the LGBTIQ community is having reliable, well researched biographies of important historical figures who were born somewhere other than the heterosexual end of the sexual continuum, and who contributed significantly to society. Two that have appeared recently treat Jeannette Howard Foster (Passet, 2008), librarian at the Kinsey Institute and author of *Sex Variant Women: A Historical and Quantitative Survey* (1956), the first bibliography of lesbian literature; and Edward Carpenter (Rowbotham, 2008), English demi-aristocrat who defended homosexuality and the "Uranian" lifestyle well before and long after the Oscar Wilde legal debacle of 1895. There are now gay histories of every city, not only George Chauncey's (1994) exhaustive panorama of the gay Big Apple, but also a grass-roots history of gay Chicago (Baim, 2009), and more evocative intellectual gay histories of New York City and the Village from within the artistic and intellectual communities (Field, 2005; Lerman, 2007; and especially McCourt, 2004).

Mainly, however, there are the works I love because they appear out of nowhere and delight me, not because they were recommended by *Lambda Book Report* but because they surprise me: Terry Castle's biographical encomium on the "great love" between lesbians and gay men (1996), and her personal essays, especially those in the *London Review of Books*; plus any novel by Sarah Waters (2006, tells the story of a mysterious death in chronological pastiche; 2009, revisits the themes of Henry James' *The Turn of the Screw* from the male point of view in postwar austerity England); Colm Tóibín (2006, a fictional portrait of Henry James that is perhaps definitive), the late Timothy Findley (1984, a feminist re-telling of the story of the Ark from the point of view of Mrs. Noah) ; or Michael Cunningham,(1998, beautifully evokes Virginia Woolf, AIDS, and the messiness of modern relationships in three parallel streams of stories). All four authors deserve to be ranked among the profound novelists of our era, and not only for "gay" content.

The growth of LGBTIQ literature since 1969 has borne reassuring witness to the fact that the public is indeed getting used to us. Even more profound, however, not least because it was unplanned by the gay community, has been the coming of age in LGBTIQ literature since AIDS, and perhaps, to a different degree, since Matthew Shepard's death. The federal government at last has begun collecting and publishing LGBT hate crime statistics based on a broader population than urban centers; can U. S. Census re-classification be far behind, at last? The sodomy laws are gone, although Mr. Backlash is not. Fun (gaiety, if you will) has been replaced to some degree with vigilance, and rightly so. The Fishman and Gittings book awards have been fully endowed, recession notwithstanding, and GLBTRT is currently raising funds for a separate award for Young Adult literature. GLBTRT book award gatherings these days are very swank at $65/head, even though the hugs almost make it worth the price.

REFERENCES

Abbott, A. Steve Abbott.Com: A daughter's memoir. Steve Abbott, 1943–1992. Retrieved from http://www.steveabbott.org

Anderson, S. (1919). *Winesburg, Ohio: A group of tales of Ohio small town life.* New York: Modern Library.

Armory, R. (1968). *Fruit of the loon: A novel in seven turgid books and a few frantic interludes.* San Diego, CA: Greenleaf Classics.

Baim, T., (Ed.). (2008). *Out and proud in Chicago: An overview of the city's gay community.* Chicago: Surrey.

Barr, J. (1950). *Quatrefoil.* New York: Greenberg.

Bawer, B. (1993). *A place at the table: The gay individual in American society.* New York: Poseidon.

Beam, Jeffrey. (2008). *The beautiful tendons: Uncollected queer poems, 1969–2007.* Brooklyn, NY: White Crane.

Beaton, C. (1939). *My royal past.* London: n.p.

Bronski, M. (2002). *Pulp friction: Uncovering the golden age of male pulps.* New York: St. Martin's.

Burroughs, W. (1961). *Ten episodes from The soft machine.* Paris: Olympia.

Capote, T. (1955). *Other voices, other rooms.* New York: Random House.

Carmichael, J. V. (1992). The male librarian and the feminine image: a survey of stereotype, status, and gender perceptions. *Library and Information Science Research, 14*(4), 411–447.

Carmichael, J. V. (2002). Effects of the gay publishing boom on classes of titles retrieved under the subject headings "Homosexuality," "Gay Men," and "Gays" in the OCLC WorldCat database. *Journal of Homosexuality, 42*(3), 65–88.

Cart, M., & Jenkins, C. A. (2006). *The heart has its reasons: Young adult literature with gay/lesbian queer content, 1969–2004.* Lanham, MD: Scarecrow.

Castle, T. (1998). *Noel Coward & Radclyffe Hall: Kindred spirits.* New York: Columbia University Press.

Chauncey, G. (1994). *Gay New York: Gender, urban culture, and the making of the gay male world, 1890–1940.* New York: Basic.

Chesser, E. (1941). *Love without fear.* London: n.p.

Cocteau, J. (1930). *Le Livre blanc, précédé d'un frontispice et accompagné par 17 dessins de Jean Cocteau.* Paris: ditions Signac.

Conrad, J. (1912). *'Twixt land and sea: Tales.* London: J. M. Dent & Sons.

Crompton, L. (2003). *Homosexuality and civilization.* Cambridge MA: Belknap Press of Harvard University Press.

Cummings, K. (1992). *Katherine's diary: The story of a transsexual.* Brisbane: Heinemann.

Cunningham, M. (1998). *The Hours.* New York: Farrar, Straus, Giroux.

D'Emilio, J. (1998). *Sexual politics, sexual communities: The making of a homosexual minority in the United States, 1940–1970* (2nd ed.). Chicago: University of Chicago Press.

D'Emilio, J. (2003). *Lost prophet: The life and times of Bayard Rustin.* New York: Free.

Dennis, P. (1955). *Auntie Mame: An irreverent escapade in biography.* New York: Vanguard.

Dennis, P. (1958). *Around the world with Auntie Mame.* New York: Harcourt Brace.

Dennis, P. (1961). *Little me: The intimate portrait of that great star of stage, screen, and television, Belle Poitrine.* New York: Dutton.

Drescher, J., & Malino, J. P. (2007). *American psychiatry and homosexuality: An oral history.* New York: Harrington Park.

Dynes, W. R. (1987). *Homosexuality: A research guide.* New York: Garland.

Field, E. (2005). *The man who would marry Susan Sontag, and other intimate literary portraits of the Bohemian era.* Madison: University of Wisconsin Press.

Findley, T. (1984). *Not wanted on the voyage.* Markham, Ontario: Penguin.

Fitzgerald, S. (Ed.). (1979). *The habit of being: The letters of Flannery O'Connor.* New York: Farrar, Straus, Giroux.

Forrest, K. (2005). *Lesbian pulp fiction: The sexually intrepid world of lesbian paperback novels, 1950–1965.* San Francisco: Cleis.

Foster, J. (1956). *Sex variant women in literature: A historical and quantitative survey.* New York: Vantage.

4 policemen hurt in "Village" raid. (1969, 29 June). *The New York Times,* A33.

Gallo, M. M. (2006). *Different daughters: A history of the Daughters of Bilitis and the rise of the lesbian rights movement.* New York: Graf & Graf.

Genet, J. (1963). *Our lady of the flowers.* New York: Grove.

Ginsberg, Allen. (1956). *Howl and other poems.* San Francisco: City Lights Pocket Bookshop.

Gittings, B. (1978). Combating the lies in libraries. In L. Crew (Ed.), *The Gay Academic* (pp. 108–117). Palm Springs, CA: ETC.

Green, J. (1990). *The encyclopedia of censorship.* New York: Facts on File.

Hall, R. (1929). *The well of loneliness.* New York: Covici Friede.

Hansen, J. (1993). *Living upstairs.* New York: Plume.

Hansen, J. (1995). *Jack of hearts.* New York: Dutton.

Hansen, J. (2001). *The cutbank path.* New York: Xlibris.

Hardwick, E. (2000, June 15). Melville in love. *New York Review of Books, 47*(10). Retrieved from http://www.nybooks.com/articles/57.

Holleran, A. (1978). *Dancer from the dance: A novel.* New York: Morrow.

Holleran, A. (2006). *Grief.* New York: Hyperion.

Hollinghurst, A. (1988). *The swimming pool library.* New York: Random House.

Humphries, Laud. (1970). *Tearoom trade: Impersonal sex in public places.* Chicago: Aldine.

Johnson, D. K. (2004). *The lavender scare: The cold war persecutions of lesbians and gay men in the federal government.* Chicago: University of Chicago Press.

Jorgensen, C. (1967). *Christine Jorgensen: A personal autobiography.* New York: Paul S. Eriksson.

Kushner, T. (1995). *Angels in America: A gay fantasia on national themes.* New York: Theatre Communications Group.

Lerman, L. (2007). *The grand surprise: The journals of Leo Lerman.* New York: Knopf.

Longworth, P. (Ed.). (1983). *Austin and Mabel: The Amherst love affair and love letters of Austin Dickinson and Mabel Loomis Todd.* New York: Farrar, Strauss, Giroux.

McCourt, J. (2004). *Queer street: The rise and fall of an American culture, 1947–1985.* New York: W. W. Norton.

Malcolm, J. (2007). *Two lives: Gertrude and Alice.* New Haven, CT: Yale University Press.

Mann, T. (1928). *Death in Venice.* London: Secker.

Meeker, M. (2006). *Contacts desired: Gay and lesbian communications and community, 1940s-1970s.* Chicago: University of Chicago Press.

Melville, H. (1849). *Redburn: His first voyage, being the sailor-boy confessions and reminiscences of the son-of-a-gentleman, in the merchant service.* London: Bentley.

Merrick, G. (1970). *The Lord won't mind: A novel.* New York: Avon.

Metalious, G. (1956). *Peyton Place.* New York: Messner.

Mudge, J.M., Brose, N.H., & Dupre, J.M. (1976). *Emily Dickinson: Profile of the poet as cook: With selected recipes.* Amherst, MA: n.p.

Newmyer, J. (1976). The image problem of the librarian: Femininity and social control. *The Journal of Library History, 11(1):* 44–67.

Notley, A. (1981). *How spring comes.* West Branch, IA: Toothpaste.

Passet, J. (2008.) *Sex-variant woman: The life of Jeanette Howard Foster.* New York: DaCapo.

Purdy, J. (1967). *Eustace Chisholm and the works.* New York: Farrar, Straus, and Giroux.

Purdy, J. (1981). *63, dream palace and other stories.* New York: Penguin.

Rechy, J. (1964). *City of Night.* New York: Grove.

Rechy, J. (1967). *Numbers.* New York: Grove.

Riel, S. (1992). *How to dream.* Amherst, MA: Writers & Artists Press.

Riel, S. (2003). *The spirit can crest.* Amherst, MA: Writers & Artists Press.

Rowbotham, S. (2008). *Edward Carpenter: A life of liberty and love.* New York: Verso.

Sears, J. T. (2006). *Behind the mask of the Mattachine: The Hal Call chronicles and the early movement for homosexual emancipation.* New York: Harrington Park.

Sontag, S. (1978). *Illness as metaphor.* New York: Farrar, Straus, and Giroux.

Sontag, S. (1989). *AIDS and its metaphors.* New York: Farrar, Straus, and Giroux.

Stein, G. (1933). *The autobiography of Alice B. Toklas: Illustrated.* New York: Harcourt Brace.

Streitmatter, R. (1995). *Unspeakable: The rise of the gay press in America.* New York: Faber and Faber.

Streitmatter, R. (2009). *From "perverts" to "Fab Five": The media's changing depiction of gay men and lesbians.* New York: Routledge.

Sullivan, A. (1996). *Virtually normal: An argument about homosexuality.* New York: Vintage.

Tóibín, C. (2004). *The master: A novel.* Toronto: M&S.

Tripp, C. A. (1975). *The homosexual matrix.* New York: McGraw-Hill.

Vidal, G. (1950). *The city and the pillar.* New York: Dutton.

Vidal, G. (1995). *Palimpsest: A memoir.* New York: Random House.

Waters, S. (2006). *The night watch.* New York: Riverhead.

Waters, S. (2009). *The little stranger.* New York: Riverhead.

Whitman, A. (1967, 8 June). Dorothy Parker, 73, Literary Wit, Dies. *The New York Times.* Retrieved from http://www.proquest. umi.com

Wilcox, J. (1998). *Plain and normal.* Boston: Little, Brown.

Wilcox, J. (2003). *Heavenly Days.* New York: Viking.

Wilcox, J. (2007). *Hunk City.* New York: Viking.

Wilde, O. (1890). *The picture of Dorian Gray.* London: Ward, Lock & Co.

Williams, C. L. (1995). *Still a man's world: men who do women's work.* Los Angeles: University of California Press.

Williams, T. (1954). *One arm, and other stories.* New York: New Directions.

Woolf, V. (1929). *A room of one's own.* London: Hogarth.

Woolf, V. (1938). *Three guineas.* New York: Harcourt Brace.

Woolf, V. (1975–1980). *The letters of Virginia Woolf.* New York: Harcourt Brace.

Meeting the Needs of LGBTIQ Library Users and Their Librarians: A Study of User Satisfaction and LGBTIQ Collection Development in Academic Libraries[1]

Melissa Adler

Without question, LGBTIQ Studies (also sometimes referred to as Queer Studies or Gender and Sexuality Studies) has been a rapidly growing field in academia over the past twenty years. Depending on the size and scope of library collections, budgets, academic curricula, and the attitudes and knowledge held by librarians, people seeking information on LGBTIQ issues may find that their campus libraries are a rich resource for research or personal use, or they may become so disenfranchised that they seek information through other sources, such as the Internet or bookstores. Sadly, there are very few tools to assist librarians in their efforts to grow their libraries' LGBTIQ collections. A tremendous gap in the professional and scholarly literature persists with regard to research that focuses on the needs of LGBTIQ library users in academic settings, or on academic library collections of LGBTIQ-related materials. This essay is part of a larger project that assessed how academic librarians make decisions regarding selection and acquisition of LGBTIQ resources. The study aimed to ascertain what librarians need to assist them in their development of LGBTIQ collections.

Together, the University of Wisconsin (UW)–Madison Women's Studies librarian, a librarian at UW-Stevens Point, and I deployed two web-based surveys to constituents in Wisconsin: one was sent via LGBTIQ listservs and targeted people who seek information on LGBTIQ-related topics, and the other was sent to librarians at all Wisconsin public and private academic libraries. Twenty-six faculty, 26 students (undergraduate and graduate), and 13 academic staff completed the user survey, and 33 librarians responded to the librarian survey. A few of the librarians were from the same schools, but overall, we got a nice representation of institution types and sizes.

The user survey was intended to assess users' satisfaction with their campus libraries; the kinds of materials and topics they seek; whether they seek information for personal or academic reasons; and where, other than libraries, they find resources. The survey of librarians aimed at understanding their decision-making processes for acquiring LGBTIQ-themed resources. The questions asked whether the libraries have a collection development policy for LGBTIQ materials; what sources librarians used to make selection decisions; whether or not LGBTIQ-themed instruction sessions had been taught at their libraries; whether there is a librarian who is responsible for selecting LGBTIQ-themed materials; and for what purposes the libraries collect such materials. The results of the surveys reveal that, while we have come a long way since the 1990 edition of *Gay and Lesbian Library Service*, many of the challenges revealed by Suzy Taraba still remain. Sentiments about the availability of LGBTIQ-themed resources in college and university libraries reflect a wide range of experiences and attitudes ranging from utter disappointment and frustration to great appreciation and satisfaction.

What's Changed in Two Decades?

To place the importance of libraries within the academy, it's worth noting some of the key developments with regard to LGBTIQ Studies over the past twenty years. *Gay and Lesbian Library Service* was published in 1990, just as gay and lesbian courses and programs were beginning to emerge. The first Gay and Lesbian Studies department in higher education was launched at the City College of San Francisco in 1988, and the Center for Lesbian and Gay Studies (CLAGS) at the City University of New York was founded in 1991 as the "first university-based research center in the United States dedicated to the study of historical, cultural, and political issues of vital concern to lesbian, gay, bisexual, and transgender individuals and communities" (CLAGS, n.d.). *GLQ: A Journal of Lesbian and Gay Studies* was first published in 1993, and Transgender Studies was launched around 1992 following the presentation and publication of Sandy Stone's "The Empire Strikes Back: A Posttranssexual Manifesto."

Today most colleges and universities at least offer courses on some facet of LGBTIQ Studies. Many offer certificates and some offer major or minor degrees in the field, while others provide opportunities for interdisciplinary degrees, for which LGBTIQ Studies may be a concentration. Nearly every school in the United States, depending on the size and type of institution, has some kind of LGBTIQ student group, resource center, or other type of organization to support the college or university LGBTIQ community.

Despite such advances, it is very difficult for librarians to find resources on developing LGBTIQ collections. Turning to the professional and scholarly literature published since 2000, one finds a fair amount of articles and books on LGBTIQ collections in school and public libraries, particularly with regard to young adult and teen collections. However, while some research does incorporate a consideration of collection development within the wider context of library services for LGBTIQ users or diverse collections in academic libraries, no books or articles specifically address LGBTIQ collection development in college and university libraries (Mehra & Braquet, 2007; Jacobson & Williams, 2000; Switzer, 2008; Young, 2008). One study out of Canada comprehensively addresses LGBTIQ users' satisfaction with and perceptions of academic libraries (Lupien, 2007).

A handful of collection development policies is available via the Internet, and certainly these provide excellent models to guide librarians in developing their own policies or in selecting materials. Special and university collection policies available online include those drafted by the ONE Institute, the Leather Archives and Museum, Michigan State University, New York University, University of California Santa Barbara, University of Illinois-Urbana/Champaign, and the Canadian Lesbian and Gay Archives.

We asked Wisconsin librarians if their libraries had collection development policies for LGBTIQ materials, and although two of the librarians said that they did, the policies did not include the components that a comprehensive policy should have, such as a statement of purpose, and explication of the scope of the collection, the types of materials held, and the criteria upon which choices for selection are based. The present study's intended contribution is to ascertain the needs of users of LGBTIQ collections and to serve as a starting point to guide librarians in developing LGBTIQ collections.

The University of Wisconsin System

The University of Wisconsin system is comprised of 13 four-year universities, two of which are doctoral degree granting institutions, and 13 two-year colleges. The state of Wisconsin is also home to 20 private colleges. The UW System prides itself on its mission and success in drawing upon and bringing together faculty, staff, students, and curricula across the state, and across types of institutions. Collaborative efforts, such as the Inclusivity Initiative whose mission is to "promote the success of all UWS [UW System] students, staff, and faculty and support the development and dissemination of new knowledge concerning LGBTIQ people and issues," enable and enhance the capacity to act and promote equity in access to education and resources (UW-System Inclusivity Initiative, 2007). The Women's Studies Consortium, permanently established in 1989, is another system-wide program. It promotes Women's Studies programs and resources, advocates for anti-discriminatory policies, and has held an annual conference for 34 years. The first year that the conference was held jointly with the Wisconsin LGBTQ Conference was 2009.

The UW System also shares a catalog and the resources owned by all of the system libraries. Universal borrowing allows faculty, staff, and students from any of the UW System schools to borrow library materials from any of the system libraries with relative ease. The Council of University of Wisconsin Libraries (CUWL, 2007b) was "established to provide a forum and structure for library and information planning within the University of Wisconsin System." The System-Wide Collections and Resource Sharing Initiatives Coordinating Committee of CUWL oversees system-wide development and sharing of collections system-wide to become "One System, One Library" (CUWL, 2007a).

Findings

Essentially, we found that LGBTIQ library users are a lot like other library users: most are generally satisfied with their campus libraries; they are cognizant of budget constraints; they are aware of and use universal borrowing (although it isn't always fast enough for their needs); and they do not always know about all of the resources their libraries have to offer. Six major themes arose out of the survey results with regard to the unique challenges and opportunities presented by LGBTIQ collections and their users. Each of these themes provides insight into the needs of users and measures that librarians can take to meet those needs. The first three areas — the interdisciplinarity of LGBTIQ Studies and the vast research interests of users, the gaps in and currency of collections, and accessibility — offer indications of what should be collected and what is missing from collections. The remaining themes — collaboration and communication, personal interests of users, and the potential for proactive librarians to make a difference — focus more on how librarians can approach building LGB-TIQ collections.

Interdisciplinarity

Interdisciplinarity has long presented a challenge for the management of Women's Studies collections, and it clearly raises issues for LGBTIQ collections. Suzy Taraba wrote in 1990, "Where gay and lesbian studies ends and another discipline begins may remain forever problematic" (p. 26). While this is still and may indeed forever remain true, the rise of LGBTIQ programs in college and university curricula has changed ways of thinking about the problem. As Taraba (1990) observed:

the discipline-oriented thinking in most colleges and universities (and, consequently, in most academic libraries) can mask the need for academic librarians to collect materials to support gay and lesbian studies. Gay and lesbian studies departments, programs, majors or even minors are virtually unknown. Few colleges and universities currently offer courses dealing specifically with aspects of gay and lesbian studies, although this number is increasing" [p. 25–26].

Twenty years later there are numerous LGBTIQ departments or programs within Women's and Gender Studies departments. Still, some questions may prove to be irresolvable: Who is responsible for selecting these materials and how should they be organized? Should materials be shelved in the HQs with other materials specifically dealing with sexuality, or should they be shelved by related disciplines; e.g., should a book on the "Don't ask/Don't tell" rule be shelved with works on the military or with books on gays? Do libraries need LGBTIQ subject specialists, and should they select materials for every discipline that might touch upon this area? Indeed, the users that we surveyed do have very diverse research streams. Table 1 illustrates the variety of topics on which people seek information.

Table 1. For which topics do you seek information in your campus libraries?

Gender or sexuality studies	Number of respondents (of 67 total)	Percentage	Discipline/area of study	Number of respondents (of 67 total)	Percentage
Gender/Sexuality	58	91%	Identity	43	66%
Homosexuality	53	83%	Discrimination	42	65%
Lesbians	42	66%	Sex	38	58%
Queer theory	42	66%	History	36	55%
Bisexuality	30	47%	Same-sex marriage/ Domestic partners	35	54%
Transgender	41	64%	Coming out	33	51%
Gay men	39	61%	Education	30	46%
Feminism	35	55%	Literature	29	45%
Masculinity	31	48%	Law	27	42%
Women	27	42%	Psychology	25	38%
Heterosexuality	25	39%	Families	25	38%
Intersex conditions	25	39%	Race	24	37%

Gender or sexuality studies	Number of respondents (of 67 total)	Percentage	Discipline/area of study	Number of respondents (of 67 total)	Percentage
Femininity	20	31%	AIDS	22	34%
Men	19	30%	Media	21	32%
			Health	21	32%
			Harassment/Security	21	32%
			Access to healthcare	19	29%
			Arts	19	29%
			Youth	18	28%
			Social Services	16	25%
			Religion	16	25%
			Geographical areas	13	20%
			Occupations	8	12%
			Sports, recreation	3	5%

In addition to the choices supplied by the survey questions, respondents added pansexuality, asexuality, demisexuality, the intersections of identity (i.e., disability), and LGBTIQ social movements, aging, immigration, popular culture, language, military, alcohol and drug abuse, pornography, and LGBTIQ youth homelessness.

The responses to the survey distributed to librarians varied, depending on the size and type of library for which they worked. Thirteen stated that there is a librarian who is responsible for LGBTIQ collections. Of course, at smaller schools it is common to have only one librarian assigned to the task of selecting materials for the entire library. One librarian's comment illustrates the point: "The staff member assigned to the campus LGBT task force has a special responsibility to collect, but obviously the material falls into many disciplines and therefore can be selected by any selector."

Gaps and Currency

Eighty-eight percent of the users responding to the survey said that they have used their campus library to research an LGBTQ-related topic for academic work. Among these users, 54 percent are moderately to very satisfied with their campus library's collection overall, 20 percent are moderately to very dissatisfied, and the remaining 36 percent are neutral. A large share of the respondents had serious complaints about their libraries' collections. When asked what kinds of materials they were unable to obtain, they had a lot to say:

"Oh, there are huge holes in the collection. I get a lot of stuff via interlibrary loan or just buy it."

"DVD selection on LGBT history is atrocious. I've had better luck finding documentaries through the Wisconsin public library system than even the UW interlibrary loan."

"Transgender-related topics, LGBTQ topics in general."

"LGBTQ-related journals, whether through our physical library or via e-journals"

"My campus library has virtually NO useful academic books on LGBTQ issues so I have to borrow all my books from other UW system libraries."

"Older journals, manuscript collections"

"We lack videos, current research, and journals on LGBT issues. It's pathetic."

"I tend to rely more on my own personal collection because it is usually more complete than what the library has available."

Regarding the last remark, it must be noted that, while this may be possible for faculty with salaries and department funding, for any user who has a tight budget (as most college students do) this is simply an impossibility. This statement brings to mind issues of class and privilege in the academy and questions of access for all LGBTIQ library users.

Similarly, the acquisition of LGBTIQ-themed materials can often be cost-prohibitive, both in terms of money and the time and efforts of librarians. Many books of interest are published by small presses and don't usually get reviewed in mainstream publications. Important films may make the LGBTIQ film festival circuit but might not be widely marketed or easily acquired. Such films on DVD are frequently very expensive, with prices reaching three to five hundred dollars. The price range of independently produced videos is reflected by the fact that six of the fifteen videos on the ALA Video Round Table's 2009 list of "Notable Videos for Adults" cost between $170.00 and $395.00.

Accessibility/Availability of Materials, Universal Borrowing

UW-System libraries strive to be "One System, one library," and one way that they work toward that goal is through a resource sharing system called Universal Borrowing. The system works like most other library consortia do; within the system, faculty and students can borrow books, videos, microforms, and other types of materials from other UW-System libraries. The benefits to the smaller campuses are that they have access to an abundance of materials, and can obtain them in two to four days. There are limits to this system, though, as members of the larger campus communities may find that access to their own campus resources are limited by the fact that their desired resource has been loaned to a person at another campus. Also, librarians are advised not to duplicate holdings if possible, so if another campus holds a title, the librarian should strongly consider not purchasing that item. This can be highly problematic, as one user observes: "In my experience, not only are the collections limited, but those recent publications that the library has are in high demand, so there's a lot of recall activity." "My campus is very small so I don't EXPECT them to have a lot of LGBTQ resources. I've been very pleased, however, with the entire UW System and have had a great deal of success borrowing books from other libraries."

Interlibrary loan functions in ways that are similar to Universal Borrowing. While providing access to collections worldwide via resource sharing options such as WorldCat, it generally takes longer to obtain the requested materials, and there is frequently a shorter loan period, as observed by a respondent: "The problem is that if the resource is only available via interlibrary loan, I may have little time to work with the materials before they must be returned." Additionally, lending libraries sometimes place restrictions on the types of items circulated, e.g., libraries will often refuse requests for videos.

The UW System does not share all of the article databases, although articles from these may also be requested via ILL or Universal Borrowing. The article request process is rather cumbersome, though, and does present a barrier to access. The lack of access does present a problem for people who attend or work at smaller colleges and universities, as a user's description illustrates: "The UW System's e-journal selection is minimal in terms of older publications, like magazines and journals pre–2000. I can typically access ½ of what I am seeking."

Exactly half of the respondents said they made purchase requests, and most of them thought that the library did purchase the requested items. One very satisfied user exclaimed, "The library at my university has ordered every single item (books, videos and DVDs) I've ever requested — and over the past 14 years, I've ordered a lot!"

DVDs seem to present the greatest challenge for librarians and source of frustration for library users. Only 38 percent of users said that they check out videos from their academic library. In response to a question asking why users do not go to the library for videos, they cited the following reasons:

"Location"

"Lack of selection"

"The paucity of videos makes it close to impossible."

"I have experienced long delays in obtaining them for a course and found little that I was looking for."

"To the best of my knowledge, they don't have them."

"The thought never occurred to me to do it."

"Have seen most of collection."

As discussed earlier, DVDs present particular problems as they can often be very costly and are not generally reviewed or advertised in mainstream library publications. The cost and scarcity of videos can lead libraries to create and enforce policies that ensure that the videos do not circulate to patrons at any other libraries through interlibrary loan.

Collaboration and Communication

The most common resources consulted for making decisions regarding selection of LGBTIQ materials (along with reviews in library publications) are faculty. Students are also key sources of information regarding purchases (See Table 2). This suggests that a strong working relationship between librarians and faculty and students, and openly inviting recommendations for purchase are key to developing collections that will meet the needs of users.

Table 2. What sources do you or someone else at your library use for information on LGBTQ materials to make decisions regarding acquisition of LGBTQ materials? Please choose all that apply.

Recommendations or requests from faculty or staff	29	94%
Reviews in library publications	29	94%
Recommendations or requests from students	23	74%
Reviews in LGBTQ, feminist, or other publications	14	45%
Online reference tools	14	45%
Blogs, listservs, etc.	14	45%
Vendor profiles or standing orders	9	29%
ALA GLBT Round Table Web site/newsletter	7	23%
Other	0	0%

Taraba (1990) points out that "the library also has a responsibility to serve the information needs of campus gay and lesbian organizations" (p. 28). In some cases student organizations consult librarians and make requests. One two-year college library director is the faculty/staff adviser for the campus Gay Straight Alliance. The group meets in the library and is the major source of material requests, particularly films and videos. While not every LGBTIQ student organization can have a librarian as an advisor, librarians can certainly take this example as a model and directly seek out groups to find out what they need and desire.

Instruction sessions are another way for librarians to reach out to the greater college or university community. We asked both instructors and librarians if they had requested or taught library instruction sessions on LGBTIQ resources. Three faculty members said that they had LGBTIQ-themed library instruction sessions taught by librarians for their classes, and seven librarians said that instructors had requested LGBTIQ-focused instruction sessions. Librarians could certainly invite students and faculty to instruction sessions to raise awareness of their collections and promote services. Such sessions, as well as meetings with library liaisons and faculty, might launch a dialogue about community needs.

Personal Interests of Users

According to users, they seek out LGBTIQ-themed information resources primarily for personal reasons. Unfortunately, this is a very broad term, and because among LGBTIQ scholars and students, professional interests often coincide with or relate to personal interests, it is difficult to determine how meaningful this result is, and the question demands follow-up. Nevertheless, it does raise a few crucial points to be aware of when selecting materials.

Table 3. For what purposes do you seek information in your campus library?

Personal	88%
Research	50%
Coursework	42%
Entertainment	29%

Taraba (1990) noted that it is imperative that academic libraries offer materials for personal use because young adults often explore their gender and sexual identities and many come out during their college years. Larger campuses house LGBTIQ centers, and as these centers are typically intended to provide social and educational support to students and organizations, they tend to have collections of books, magazines, and videos that are primarily for personal or non-academic use.

Half of the librarians said that there is an LGBTIQ center on campus, but upon further investigation, we found that a few of these were actually student organizations, such as Gay/Straight Alliances. Perhaps that was a flaw in the question, or it may be an indication that some librarians aren't clear about the LGBTIQ offerings on their campuses. As with the responses to most questions, the results revealed a range of experiences. Most of the respondents who elaborated on the working relationships between the LGBTIQ center and the library expressed that the centers are mostly independent and do not collaborate or consider each others' holdings when selecting materials. One librarian stated that the LGBTIQ Center doesn't affect how they collect "because their mission is different, more popular focus, and we do not collaborate with them; we support each other." Two did say that they work with LGBTIQ centers on a limited basis, either referring students to the center or considering the center's collections when making purchases. But an LGBTIQ center director stated, "As an LGBTIQ Director I do not even know the name of the person who deals with the LGBTIQ collections. We should work together."

The LGBT Campus Center at UW-Madison is a unique case among campus centers. Housed in the student union, it has a very strong collection, and its holdings have actually been added to the general library catalog. This means that all UW System campuses can search and borrow from the Center's collection.

Local public library holdings may be worth considering when purchasing LGBTIQ items. In some communities, public libraries have excellent collections of LGBTIQ resources for personal use. But in small towns or conservative areas, the public libraries may lack quality materials, and it may fall upon the academic library to provide access to local and college and university communities. Three librarians said they do consider public library holdings when selecting LGBTIQ materials. One user stated, "Sometimes I am appalled that I can often find a more current selection of LGBT books at my public library, and a local LGBT Community Center, than the university library."

Such observations suggest that librarians should take care to assess the needs of their users, as well as the resources that are available in the wider community. In developing collections, academic librarians need to determine how much they should collect to meet the personal needs of their users.

Librarians Make a Difference

More than anything, this study revealed that librarians who strive to offer a strong LGBTIQ collection and services can have a tremendous impact on library users' experiences. By assessing their users' needs, turning to alternative sources for reviews and publications, educating users on resource sharing and other library services, and working closely with students and faculty, librarians can greatly add to users' success in their research endeavors. To close this essay, I'll leave you with an inspiring comment from a very satisfied library user:

> I feel very fortunate to have such a responsive and knowledgeable library system and staff. In addition to the likelihood that the library will seek to purchase requests, there are people working in the library system who proactively find out what's out there and keep up to date with the various LGBTQ-related fields. It is very reassuring to know that people are more on top of things than I am so that I can get the resources I need for my research and teaching.

These words speak volumes of the power that librarians hold to influence, affect, and assist their users and the research they produce.

NOTES

1. Phyllis Holman Weisbard, the women's studies librarian at the University of Wisconsin-Madison, and Nerissa Nelson, the interim women's studies director and librarian at UW-Stevens Point, were kind enough to let me join them in their research. I am truly grateful to them for allowing me to work on such an important project.

REFERENCES

American Library Association Video Round Table (2009). Notable list of videos for adults. Retrieved from http://www.ala.org/ala/mgrps/rts/vrt/initiatives/notablevideos/notables2009.cfm

Canadian Lesbian and Gay Archives. (1998). Our mandate: What we collect and why. Retrieved from http://www.clga.ca/About/mandate.htm

Center for Lesbian and Gay Studies. (n.d.). Home page. Retrieved from http://web.gc.cuny.edu/Clags/

Colmenar, G. (2004). UCSB Libraries: Gay, lesbian, bisexual, and transgender collection development policy. Retrieved from http://www.library.ucsb.edu/services/policies/collections/glbtpolicy.html

Council of Wisconsin Libraries (CUWL). (2007a). Collections & Resource Sharing Coordinating Committee. Retrieved from http://uwlib.uwsa.edu/committees/collections/index.htm

Council of Wisconsin Libraries (CUWL). (2007b). Home page. Retrieved from http://uwlib.uwsa.edu/

Jacobson, T. E., & Williams, H. C. (2000). *Teaching the new library to today's users: Reaching international, minority, senior citizens, gay/lesbian, first-generation, at-risk, graduate and returning students, and distance learners.* New York: Neal-Schuman.

Leather Archives and Museum. (2005). Collection policy. Retrieved from http://www.leatherarchives.org/about/collect.htm

Lupien, P. (2007). GLBT/Sexual Diversity Studies students and academic libraries: A study of user perceptions and satisfaction. *Canadian Journal of Information & Library Science, 31*(2), 131–147.

Mehra, B., & Braquet, D. (2007). Library and information science professionals as community action researchers in an academic setting: Top ten directions to further institutional change for people of diverse sexual orientations and gender identities. *Library Trends, 56*(2), 542–565.

ONE National Gay & Lesbian Archives. (n.d.). Collection policy statement. Retrieved from *http://www.onearchives.org/collections_policy*

Phillips, J. (2007). New York University Bobst Library: Lesbian, bisexual, gay, and queer studies collection development policy. Retrieved from http://library.nyu.edu/collections/policies/lbgq.html

Stone, A.R. (1996). The empire strikes back: A posttranssexual manifesto. In K. Straub and J. Epstein (Eds.), *Body guards: The cultural politics of sexual ambiguity* (pp. 280–304). New York: Routledge.

Switzer, A.T. (2008). Redefining diversity: Creating an inclusive academic library through diversity initiatives. *College and Undergraduate Libraries, 15*(3), 280–300. doi: 10.1080/10691310802258182

Taraba, S. (1990). Collecting gay and lesbian materials in an academic library. In C. Gough and E. Greenblatt (Eds.), *Gay and lesbian library service* (pp. 25–37). Jefferson, N.C.: McFarland.

Tracy, A.E. (2000). Collection development policy statement: Lesbian, gay, bisexual, and transgender. Retrieved from http://guides.lib.msu.edu/page.phtml?page_id=1776

University Library, University of Illinois Urbana-Champaign. (n.d.). Lesbian, gay, bisexual, and transgender Collection. Retrieved from http://www.library.illinois.edu/administration/collections/about/statements/lgbt.html

UW-System Inclusivity Initiative for LGBTQ People. (2007). Vision/mission/goals. Retrieved from http://lgbtq.uwsa.edu/vision.htm

Young, C. L. (2006). Collection development and diversity on CIC academic library web sites. *The Journal of Academic Librarianship, 32*(4), 370–376. doi: 10.1016/j.acalib.2006.03.004

Shoulders to Stand On

Peter Bernier

Rainbow Link's mandate is to help connect LGBT people in Canada to each other and the global LGBT community and to help them to take part in and make their contribution to the LGBT community as well. Initially I am collecting LGBT materials, mostly books so far, and offering them to LGBT groups and university and college libraries outside of the major urban areas of Canada.

It started with a plea for donations from one of my universities. Being poor meant that donating money was not really an option. However the 519, the local community centre, had an area where people left items they no longer needed and this often included books. In 2005, I contacted the Technical Services Librarian at the Cape Breton University Library and started picking up books I thought they might be interested in and sending her a list to choose from. Librarians are understandably ambivalent about book donations. It is hard to balance the benefits and appreciation with the extra work dealing with unwanted items, especially if the donor is likely to notice the absence of some treasured donation. This way they only receive books they choose, and I do not waste money shipping unwanted books. Perhaps libraries should do more to encourage this sort of donating rather than accepting nothing or everything. They could also post wish lists. The library also gives me a list of general topics they are currently interested in so I sometimes pick up titles on those topics if I see any.

As the 519 is in the heart of the Toronto LGBT community many of the books left there are LGBT oriented. I thought back to my youth and how little was available that I could relate to as a young gay man so I offered the library as many LGBT books as I could to improve their collection of such material. The books I offered them were often nonfiction that was clearly LGBT by title or topic, but I also offered books that were not so obviously LGBT, such as biographies of LGBT persons, books written by LGBT people, books with LGBT characters, etc. The books on LGBT topics will show up when anyone does a search with those parameters but the other things would add a subtle LGBT flavour to the whole collection for those straight students who were not specifically looking for LGBT material. So far I have sent the university library more than 1200 books of their choice, mostly LGBT in some way or other.

As I started sending books to the library, I also started to accumulate leftovers because as they added to their collection, I acquired duplicates and books they already had. What to do with them? The university has a Sexual Diversity Centre so I sent the leftovers to them. This was fine for awhile but now there were triplicates. This was when I came up with the idea to expand the number of places to send books.

The Sexual Diversity Centre suggested the Youth Project in Halifax and a gay straight alliance (GSA) in Cape Breton. I contacted them and added them to my list. I had to change my system for offering the books as I started to accumulate more books and places to send them. Now I send out the same list to all and set up an allocation system to decide who gets what when more than one group requests the same book. As shipping books is expensive and some groups will ask for everything if there is no cost for them, I have instituted a small fee of $1 per book to cover the shipping costs and to encourage judicious selection of desired books by the group, but the books are free. This system made it easier to deal with more groups, and with more sources I started to have too many books around. I started to investigate other places that might be interested in LGBT books.

I first looked at other places in the Atlantic Provinces in *Wayves*, the area's LGBT paper. I found some other possibilities and contacted them. Several were very interested in my offer. In the province of Prince Edward Island the local chapter of Parents, Families, and Friends of Lesbians and Gays (PFLAG) actually got together with a couple of other LGBT organizations to found an LGBT library in Charlottetown. Other places welcomed the opportunity to cheaply add to their collections. As well I came across two other GSAs in Cape Breton. I am now looking for university and college libraries and LGBT organizations across Canada to add to my groups. I plan to apply for charitable status which I hope will make it easier to acquire more, especially current books and other material, as well as donations to help cover costs and perhaps purchase harder to find material.

Although I do not intend to discriminate regarding age, I feel that it is most important to bring LGBT culture to youth, and thus my main priority is groups that serve younger people such as GSAs. University and college libraries primarily serve young students but in addition to serving young LGBT people, their collections are also available to straight students, and the addition of specifically LGBT material and the overall addition of LGBT flavoured material will subtly introduce many of them to LGBT concepts.

One of the groups I send to has said that with one box of books from me they probably have more LGBT books than the local library. This can make a big impact on the local LGBT people who access the group's collection. These people have a better concept of what LGBT people do and can be, thus improving their self image and visions of their future. They will find "shoulders to stand on" to reach further than their LGBT predecessors.

When the 519 was temporarily unavailable as a source of books due to renovations, I looked around for other sources. The Toronto Library has two Book Ends shops where they sell withdrawn and donated books, and these became a good source as books are usually $1 each there. They also have occasional sales. The local used book stores usually have an area of cheap books that sometimes have LGBT material. Then there are the book sales at the University of Toronto; several of the colleges there have sales in the fall and there are good bargains, especially at the end of the sale when they sell a boxful for $5 to $10. Of course if you have a bigger budget you can pay more for books or even buy to fulfill a wish list.

I am fortunate to have the Canadian Lesbian and Gay Archives here in Toronto and their new home is only a block away. I have an agreement with them that they give me all the books donated to them that they do not need for their collection in exchange for first choice of the other books I acquire. This is fantastic for both of us as they constantly receive books and have had a hard time dealing with the surplus, and I can send them to LGBT groups across Canada. I have given the Archives about 120 books in the last three months.

I feel it is important to get books to people across Canada but I feel it is more important to make sure that the Archives have at least one copy for researchers and posterity.

The next priority for giving books to is university and college libraries as it means the books are available to both LGBT and straight students but also because these libraries are more likely to take better care of the books and they are likely to be available there for a long time. As the books cease to be up-to-date they become useful for historical research of the fast-changing lives of LGBT people. The community LGBT groups are important, and I want to get stuff out to them. I tend to give the groups that cater to youth rather than adults a bit higher priority as youth cannot as easily obtain the material. I do try to spread the largesse around as well as I can though.

I acquire a wide range of LGBT material; so far most of it is used and thus dates from the '70s to '90s, with some from earlier and increasingly more from this century. Occasionally I find items more than 100 years old, items published this month and interesting material from outside North America. The value of the items as indicated on the Internet also varies considerably from a low of $1 to hundreds of dollars for a rare item. With charitable status I hope to have publishers donate some books or at least sell me their remainders cheaply. Most of the books are soft cover although about one third are hard covers. The books I acquire range from non-fiction to fiction, from literature to light mysteries, science fiction to erotica, etc. Fortunately the different groups have different preferences. The university and college libraries generally prefer non-fiction, and since many did not buy a lot of LGBT material in the latter part of the previous century, they like to fill in their collection with older books. The local LGBT groups like some non-fiction but are more interested in the fiction. The more youth-oriented groups like a variety but do like to have material aimed at the young adult market. This is not easy to find as it did not sell well originally since youth often cannot afford it new nor have the credit cards to buy it over the Internet, and parents rarely buy LGBT material for their kids. Books aimed at children are even harder to come by, as well as trans and bisexual material.

Although I am aiming to be a national organization, you could work on a smaller level and just gather and send LGBT material to your university, college or high school library, or to a local LGBT group or one "back home." Some groups and libraries have "wish lists" that you could specifically try to fulfill. Of course you could also ask your LGBT archives what sort of material they would like to have. They are always on the lookout for LGBT material of all kinds, not just books. It is important to save our history.

I hope I have given you an idea of what I am doing and have encouraged you to use your imagination to see how you can help other LGBT people where you live now or "back home."

"The Journal of Record": *The Gay & Lesbian Review/Worldwide*

Martha E. Stone

After *Library Journal*'s Eric Bryant examined issues 1 to 4 of the first volume of what was at that time a quarterly magazine titled the *Harvard Gay & Lesbian Review*, he wrote in his review that it was the "journal of record for the examination of broader questions such as the origins of homosexuality, theory vs. practice of sexual politics, and the future of gay literature in an age of assimilation.... Miraculously, the mix is as consistently readable and jargon free as it is provocative and informative. Essential for all but small public libraries" (Bryant, 1995). A vote of confidence by such a trusted name in librarianship was of immeasurable importance.

Early issues of the magazine included an interview with Edward Albee; articles by major names in American gay and lesbian arts and letters, such as Sarah Schulman and Edmund White; and scholarly essays by academicians such as Bernadette Brooten and Camille Paglia. Poetry, book reviews, and theatre and film reviews have appeared since the beginning. Representative Barney Frank (D.-Mass.) has been a contributor since the magazine's earliest days, as have such instantly-recognizable and wildly different writers as Gore Vidal, Patricia Nell Warren, Samuel Delaney and Lillian Faderman. Topics featured frequently over the years, as articles or book reviews, have included the gay, lesbian, and bisexual figures of the Harlem Renaissance; the lesbian writers and artists associated with the Parisian salons of Gertrude Stein and Natalie Barney; Bloomsbury writers and artists; and such notable artistic and literary icons as Andy Warhol, Oscar Wilde and Marcel Proust. Once-forgotten names have been brought back to light, thanks to reviews of biographies of early twentieth century gay American writers Charles Flandreau and Myron Brinig. Intersex and transgender, as well as the science of sexuality, have been the topics of articles and essay-length reviews by psychiatrist and historian of medicine Vernon Rosario.

The magazine's history is related in the current *Wikipedia* entry ("The Gay & Lesbian Review Worldwide," 2009). The original goal was to provide a vehicle for publishing gay-related talks given at Harvard University. One such talk was that of novelist Andrew Holleran, who agreed to the publication of his 1992 address, "My Harvard: Self-portrait of the Novelist as a Young Man," a recollection of his undergraduate years — but only if the 8,000-word entry were published in its entirety. This called for a new vehicle, and the idea for a supplementary publication was born. The *Harvard Gay & Lesbian Review* (HGLR) began its life as a one-time-only "gift" for subscribers to the quarterly newsletter of Harvard University's gay and lesbian organization, the Harvard Gay and Lesbian Caucus (HGLC), at that time edited by Richard Schneider, Jr. Schneider, who holds a doctorate in sociology from Harvard, put together a 32-page magazine, with no ads and a few black-and-white illustrations. It contained both full-length and brief book and theatre reviews; a handful of poems; three feature articles; and an interview. Though much expanded (and in color) today, this still stands as the magazine's format, whose slogan since the first issue has been "just good writing" and whose mission, to quote the magazine's web site <http://www.glreview.com> is to "provide a forum for enlightened discussion of issues and ideas of importance to lesbians and gay men; to advance gay and lesbian culture by providing a quality vehicle for its best writers and thinkers; and to educate a broader public on gay and lesbian topics" ("About the Gay & Lesbian Review Worldwide," 2008).

In 1997, Temple University Press approached Richard Schneider, proposing a hardcover compilation, *The Best of the Harvard Gay and Lesbian Review*. Published in late 1997, as part of Temple's American Subjects series, and edited by Robert Dawidoff, it included articles by such notables as Karla Jay, Holly Hughes, Cheryl Clarke, Edmund White (who also wrote the Foreword), Felice Picano, and Andrew Holleran, covering a wide-ranging variety of topics including the science of homosexuality, politics, literary criticism and cultural assimilation. *Library Journal's* Jeffery Ingram, in his November 15, 1999, review, stated that the collection "reads like the liveliest café society debate." The book's cover art was by Charles Hefling, a frequent contributor of caricatures, whose style is reminiscent of the *New York Review of Books'* illustrator David Levine.

The greatest praise, though, came in 1998 when the newspaper of record — the *New York Times* — ran a feature article by Robin Pogrebin. In it, author Gabriel Rotello was quoted as saying, "Anybody who's anybody in the gay world tends to read that publication [and its] influence far exceeds its circulation." The article also quoted Larry Kramer, "It's our intellectual journal, for better or worse.... If you want to deal with scholarly intelligent arguments, there's really no place else we can publish" (p. B9).

With the January-February 2001 issue, the magazine changed its name to the *Gay & Lesbian Review Worldwide* (referred to as GLR) — with no loss of readership — and began to publish on a bimonthly basis. Noted writer and poet David Bergman became the poetry editor. Featured in that 52-page issue were a new poem by Marilyn Hacker and several articles about the 2000 presidential election.

By spring of 2001, GLR's web site <http://www.glreview.com> was going through the first of its iterations. Once housed on the Harvard Gay & Lesbian Caucus's web site <http://www.hglc.org/review.htm> (archived at http://web.archive.org/), GLR's web site offers several free articles and reviews per issue. A complete index of the magazine's contents, dating back to its first issue, is available as a PDF file at http://www.glreview.com/pdfs/GLR-Index-1994-2007.pdf and is enhanced with *see* references to subject headings gleaned from the Harvard University's online catalog at http://hollisweb.harvard.edu. The web site is constantly growing and adding content.

Features have been gradually added to the magazine: a bulletin board listing upcoming conferences and calls for submissions; a "BTW" (by the way) column of sound-bytes and news notes; international perspective essays about contemporary gay and lesbian life in countries ranging from Uganda to Italy to Costa Rica; profiles of living artists; and a highly selective "In Memoriam" column in each January-February issue. The entire spectrum of sexual orientations and gender identities is covered in brief biographies of individuals who have made noteworthy contributions to any form of human endeavor but who may not have been memorialized outside of their local communities. Essay-length obituaries of major names of importance to members of the LGBTIQ community are also featured year-round.

Over the past 15 years, about 1176 books have been reviewed. This number includes both essay length and brief reviews, and of these, almost 300 (25 percent) were fiction. Books written by LGBTIQ authors with no evident LGBTIQ content are usually not considered for review; conversely, books by heterosexual authors with LGBTIQ themes will gladly be considered. Genre fiction and young adult books are reviewed only on occasion and self-published books must have something special about them to be considered for review. The sizable number of scholarly books reviewed mirrors the number of books received from university publishers. Small, independent presses such as Beacon, Copper Canyon, Greywolf, and the Canadian publishers Arsenal Pulp Press and Insomniac Press are reliable sources of books, and of the mainstream presses, Knopf, Norton, and Morrow are representative. The demise of such presses as Haworth (and its imprints Alice Street, Southern Tier, and Harrington Park); Masquerade; Firebrand; and Carroll & Graf has decreased the number of independent press options available for authors, while the premature loss of so many gay and lesbian writers to AIDS, cancer, and other causes has been felt dramatically.

The closing of many independent gay and lesbian bookstores, the inclusion of large LGBTIQ sections in major chain bookstores, and the rise of online bookstores and online publishing, are all changing the world for readers of LGBTIQ books. Such journals as the *Lesbian Review of Books* and the *James White Review: A Gay Men's Literary Quarterly*, stopped publishing. The book review sections in monthly magazines *Out* and *The Advocate* have shrunk dramatically. The quarterly *Lambda Book Report* moved from print to all-digital. Duke University's *GLQ: A Journal of Lesbian and Gay Studies*, which has been published from 1993, appeals, with its "queer studies" focus, almost exclusively to an academic audience.

It should be noted that the GLR has been indexed from the beginning by the print publications Alternative Press Index and American Humanities Index, and is currently indexed, comprehensively or partially, by the following: Academic OneFile (full text from 2000); Academic Search Biography Resource Center (full text from 2000); Contemporary Women's Issues (full text from 2002–2007); Expanded Academic ASAP (full text from 2001); Factiva (full text from 1999); General Reference Center Gold (full text from 2000); LGBT Life with Full Text (depending on the supplier: full text from 1994–1999 via EBSCO); LexisNexis Academic (selected full-text only, from 2002); and Gay, Lesbian, Bisexual and Transgender Life & Issues Collection (full text from 2001). Genderwatch indexes the magazine back to 1994.

Whatever the future holds, it is sure to include a much larger web presence. As the twenty-first century progresses, there is hope that the younger generation, many of whom are coming out and feeling comfortable with their sexual orientation even before their teen years, will find that reading a magazine containing a variety of well-written articles and reviews, carefully selected and edited with great care, will serendipitously lead to new discoveries about LGBTIQ life and culture, its history and its future.

REFERENCES

About the Gay & Lesbian Review Worldwide. (2008). Retrieved from http://www.glreview.com/about.php

Bryant, E. (1995, July 1). Reviews: Magazines. *Library Journal, 120*(12), 142.

The Gay & Lesbian Review Worldwide. (2009, April 9). In *Wikipedia, The Free Encyclopedia.* Retrieved from http://en.wikipedia.org/w/index.php?title=The_Gay_%26_Lesbian_Review_Worldwide& oldid=282730533

Ingram, J. (1997, November 15). The best of the *Harvard Gay and Lesbian Review. Library Journal, 122*(10), 68.

Pogrebin, R. (1998, April 18). Think tank: For the thinking student, a hotbed of gay and lesbian ideas. *New York Times,* B9.

Interfiling Intersex: How Dewey Classifies Intersex in Theory and in Practice

Ben Christensen

The primary purpose of classification is to bring similar things together. This proves to be more difficult than at first it seems when we take into account changing definitions of what "similar" things are, across time, cultures and subcultures. Despite its ubiquitous use, particularly among public libraries in the United States, the Dewey Decimal Classification system (DDC) has been widely criticized for its inability to change with the times and to accurately reflect minority interests (Johnson, 2007; Olson, 1998). In the past half-century, as women, people of color, and other underprivileged and oppressed groups have worked to gain a stronger voice in public discourse, librarians and classificationists have worked to reshape DDC to more accurately represent these voices. Change for the most part has been slow, hindered primarily by two obstacles: the difficulty of keeping up with ever-changing terminology and knowledge structures as minorities redefine themselves; and the reticence to make drastic changes to a classification system already in use in library collections around the world. All in all, adapting DDC to changing times has proven as easy as changing the temperature of an ocean.

An interesting example of the complexities involved in changing DDC to reflect minority interests and current structures of knowledge is that of intersex. In the first place, *intersex* is a relatively new term, having replaced the medically inaccurate term *hermaphrodite* as part of a movement in the 1990s to recognize people with atypical reproductive or sexual anatomy as just that—atypical, but not deformed, broken, or in need of repair (Intersex Society of North America, 2008). Given the relative youth of the terminology and shifting cultural perceptions of intersex, looking at how DDC responds to these changes allows us a glimpse at the process in motion. Secondly, the status of intersex people as a minority-within-a-minority-within-a-minority makes it a uniquely demonstrative case study of where DDC succeeds and fails at balancing the needs of the few with those of the many. In public discourse, intersex is often buried in the LGBTIQ acronym, tacked on as a sort of extension of transgender which is itself often treated (incorrectly) as a sub-topic of homosexuality.

In the following pages I hope to shed light on how intersex is represented in DDC, both in theory and in practice. I will examine the progress as well as the missteps DDC has made, and make suggestions for future improvements.

Intersex in the Schedules

At the time of this writing, there is only one reference to intersex in the DDC Relative Index:

> **Intersexuality**
> **medicine 616.694**

This reference leads to **616.694 Hermaphroditism**, placed in the hierarchy at

> **600 Technology**
> **610 Medicine & Health**
> **616 Diseases**
> **616.6 Diseases of urogenital system**
> **616.69 Sexual disorders.**

That is to say, intersexuality or hermaphroditism is represented solely as a disease or disorder to be treated medically. This was an accurate representation of the generally-accepted view of what we now refer to as intersex for much of the twentieth century. The reference to "intersexuality" in the Relative Index is an acknowledgment of changing terminology, a sign of transition. This would be appropriate through the early 1990s, when the intersex movement was gaining momentum but not yet firmly established. The fact that DDC still reflects this quickly-fading status quo in 2009 is an example of the lag often seen between evolving cultural definitions and the corresponding evolution of library classification. When it comes to library subject access accurately representing minorities according to the most current terminology and conceptual framework, unfortunately the Library of Congress's anticipation of the American Psychiatric Association's depathologization of homosexuality (Greenblatt, 1990) is the exception, not the rule.

Nonetheless, the Dewey editorial team should be applauded for recognizing this discrepancy and working to rectify it. In June of 2007, Dewey editor-in-chief Joan Mitchell posted a discussion paper on transgendered people on the Dewey blog, proposing that transgendered people be provided for in DDC separate from groups of people by sexual orientation (Mitchell, 2007). This proposed change would remove transgendered people (represented in DDC22 only as "transsexuals" in a scope note) from **T1–0866 Persons by sexual orientation** to a newly created position, **T1–0867 Transgendered people**, with the following scope note: "Class here transsexuals [*formerly*–0866], cross-dressers, intersexed people, transgenderists" (*Transgendered people*, 2007). Before implementing the change, the editorial team sought feedback from the classification community at large, many of whom objected to the inclusion of intersexed people under transgendered people. For example, one blog commenter noted, "The classification of 'Intersexed' under transgender is a mistake, and should be separately classified as a unique classification" (Donna, 2007). The proposal was revised to establish that transgender and intersex are not overlapping concepts by changing the new position on Table 1 to –0867 **Transgender and intersex people**. In January 2008, Mitchell explained on the Dewey blog that the concept of intersex people was then considered to be in "standing room," a temporary place to acknowledge its existence until literary warrant justified its own class number. "When the literature devoted exclusively to intersexuality / intersex people reaches our threshold for the creation of a new class ... we will provide a specific number under T1–0867 for intersex people and under 306.768 for intersexuality / intersex people" (Mitchell, 2008a). Mitchell's comment illustrates a tension in the process of revising DDC, between maintaining a "universal language" that encompasses all areas of knowledge as currently understood, and working within the necessary (and far more practical) confines of the knowledge contained within the literature DDC classifies. If we assume that in January 2008 there was indeed not enough literature devoted exclusively to intersex to warrant the creation of a new class, then in a way the creation of "standing room" for the anticipated class can be considered a case of DDC being slightly ahead of the curve.

At any rate, it appears that literary warrant was found before the proposed changes were released as PDF draft revisions in August 2008; the revision to Table 1 includes, under **–0867 Transgender and intersex people**, a subclass devoted to Intersex people,–08675. This places intersex people in the Table 1 hierarchy at

> **–08 Groups of people**
> **–086 People by miscellaneous social attributes**
> **–0867 Transgender and intersex people.**

The decision to place transgender and intersex under miscellaneous social attributes rather than under **–081 People by gender or sex** was a conscious one on the part of the Dewey editorial team. While acknowledging that transgender and intersex are attributes of gender and sex, respectively, the editorial team argued that this approach

> ensures that transgendered people are given preference over other groups in T1–081–T1–086 by the class-with-the-last instruction under T1–081–T1–088. It also locates transgendered people closer to T1–0866 People by sexual orientation, a group with whom transgendered people are often allied in struggles against discrimination [*Transgendered people*, 2007].

Additionally, a note, "for transgendered people, see T1–0867," would be added at T1–081, "to acknowledge the notational displacement of the group in the structural hierarchy" (*Transgendered people*, 2007). The structural hierarchy referred to here is defined in the introduction to DDC, which explains the difference between structural hierarchy and notational hierarchy. Usually the two coincide, but in cases where they don't, "A see reference leads the classifier to subdivisions of a subject located outside the notational hierarchy" (Dewey, Mitchell, et al., 2003). In other words, the proposed see reference at T1–081 would tell the classifier that transgender and intersex are structurally subtopics of gender and sex, even if notationally they are not. Though they proposed this approach, this is one of the questions the editorial team put out for discussion: whether it would be more appropriate to class transgendered and intersex people in the notational hierarchy under **T1–081 People by gender or sex**.

Parallel to the addition of transgender and intersex to Table 1 is an addition to the schedule at **306 Cultures and institutions**. Again, the decision was made not to place them under **305.3 People by gender or sex**, but rather near their LGB allies against discrimination, and again a see reference under 305.3 would indicate the structural relationship. In this case, the adjacent placement puts intersex at an interesting place in the notational hierarchy:

> **306.7 Sexual relations**
> **306.76 Sexual orientation, transgenderism, intersexuality**
> **306.768 Transgenderism and intersexuality**
> **306.7685 Intersexuality.**

And so a decision made for justifiable, practical reasons results in an unintentional ideological statement: that intersex is a subtopic of sexual relations. Some of the other classes

located at 306.7x are **306.732 Celibacy, 306.74 Prostitution, 306.772 Masturbation,**
and **306.775 Sadism**. All of these topics are practices defined by sexual relations. Even
sexual orientation is defined at least in part by the type of sexual relations one has or desires,
though relatively few LGB individuals consider sex to be the single defining characteristic
of their lesbian, gay, or bisexual identity. In the case of transgendered and intersex people,
sexual relations are completely independent of their transgendered or intersex identity.
Whereas the notational placement of transgender and intersex in Table 1 merely moves them
away from the most logical position, their placement in 306 actually places them in an
illogical position.

Beyond the illogic of this placement, it's unfortunate that it contributes to an all too
common misconception — that lesbians, gay men, bisexuals, transgendered people, transsexuals, intersex people, and all others who fall under some variation of the LGBTIQ
umbrella form a single, homogeneous minority group whose needs and concerns are all the
same. Certainly there is some overlap in experience; many intersex people whose gender
was incorrectly chosen by their parents at birth grow up feeling very similar to transgendered
people, and those who undergo surgical correction of their sexual organs may identify with
transsexuals. And certainly there are intersex people who are also gay, lesbian, or bisexual.
But the intersex experience is not the gay experience. A classification that places works about
intersex people next to works about transgender people and works about gay people only
reinforces the belief — held not only outside the LGBT community but also by many
within — that intersex is, for all intents and purposes, just another sexual orientation.

I don't intend to villainize the Dewey editorial team here. As I said earlier, the editorial
team decided where to place transgender and intersex neither out of ignorance nor out of
malicious intent. Rather, they acknowledged that their job is not to create a theoretically
perfect classification system that exists in a vacuum but to build on one that exists in the
context of literary warrant and current cultural constructions. All classifications are artificial
constructs that reflect social constructs of knowledge (Olson, 1998), so perhaps the most
honest approach is to acknowledge this and work with it. The social reality we have constructed in twenty-first-century America is one composed of a straight majority and a queer
minority. Another social construct might perceive the same reality as simply a plurality of
unrelated groups of people. But the social construct we live in is built on a history of
assumptions of heterosexuality, gender identity based on one's biological sex, and biological
sex that is either male or female without exception. Given this context, it's no surprise that
minorities of sexual orientation, gender identity, and biological sex have banded together
in the recent past. Just as the village of tiny Whos living on Horton's clover, many small
voices together can make a much louder voice, more likely to be heard. This allegiance is
particularly beneficial to transgendered and intersex people, who have entered the fight
against discrimination relatively recently, and so can benefit from the association with a
more established, more visible movement. The flip side of the coin is that by doing so, we've
conflated the very aspects that make each group unique — orientation, gender, and sex.

Can we blame DDC for reflecting this reality that the LGBTIQ movement has created?
Should classification systems construct a "purer" classification of people than the classifications those people themselves construct? In order to answer this question, we need to consider
the fact that if DDC were to class transgender and intersex people separately from minorities
of sexual orientation, the benefit of grouping these less visible minorities with their more
visible allies would be lost — at least on library shelves. And, of course, there's still literary
warrant to consider. It's very common for books to discuss lesbians, gays, bisexuals, trans-

gendered people, transsexuals, and intersex people together (you're reading one such book right now). Given this literary warrant, it's convenient to have a class such as 306.76 that groups sexual orientation, transgender, and intersex together. And given such a class, the logical location for each of those elements that comprise it is as subclasses thereof. And from a practical point of view, the reason books that span the LGBTIQ spectrum are written is because readers interested in Ls, Gs, and Bs tend to be the same readers who want to read about Ts, Is, and Qs. For browsing, then, the best decision is to place these subjects adjacent to each other.

As willing as I am to defend Dewey's implicit conflation of orientation, gender, and sex, I am not so quick to forgive its classification of transgender and intersex as aspects of sexual relations. Yes, the see reference at 305.3 classifies the topics appropriately in the structural hierarchy, but this does not eliminate the implications of the placement in the notational hierarchy. Perhaps the problem, only made obvious by the inclusion of transgender and intersex, is that sexual orientation doesn't belong here at all. The placement under **306 Culture and institutions** and **306.7 Sexual relations** implies that sexual orientation is a culture or institution defined by its sexual relations. It could be argued that this is an accurate reflection of the pre–AIDS gay culture championed by many activists during the 1970s, a culture that rejected heterosexual norms such as marriage and family in favor of free sex without commitment. In the past three decades, however, the lesbians and gay men who have come to the forefront of the gay rights movement are those who seek long-term relationships and families, who are defined by sexual relations no more than heterosexual people are. Yet still there are homosexual people who have no interest in subjecting themselves to the heteronormative institution of marriage. There are those who are happy to define their committed relationships on their own terms, and those who reject committed relationships. There are all kinds of homosexual people who participate or don't participate in all kinds of cultures and institutions. In short, homosexuality is not a culture or institution. Like gender, religion, and race, sexual orientation defines a social group. And social groups are classed in 305.

Sexual orientation was in fact once classed as a social group. In DDC 22, schedule 305 includes the following:

> [.906 6] Persons by sexual orientation
> Relocated to 306.76.

Previous to this relocation, then, persons by sexual orientation were found under **305.906 Persons with special social status**, under **305.9 Occupational and miscellaneous groups**. The problem with this placement, of course, was the marginalizing effect of classifying sexual minorities as "miscellaneous" or "special." An oft-criticized weakness of DDC is its tendency to give ample coverage to privileged classes in the zeroes through eights, and cram unprivileged classes into the nines, as is the case with Christianity in 200–289 and all other religions in the 290s. And so in order to address this, sexual orientation was given its own place in 306, but in the process was removed from other social groups. The problem of finding a place for sexual orientation in 305 is that the schedule is rather full:

> 305.2 Age groups
>   .3 Men and women [changed in the 8/08 draft to "People by gender or sex"; note that this topic spans 305.3–305.4, with Men at 305.31 and Women at 305.4]

.4   Women
.5   Social classes [changed in the 8/08 draft to "People by social and
      economic levels"]
.6   Religious groups
.7   Language groups
.8   Ethnic and national groups
.9   Occupational and miscellaneous groups [changed in the 8/08 draft
      to "People by occupation and miscellaneous social statuses; people
      with disabilities and illnesses, gifted people"]

We've already ruled out 305.9 for its emphasis on otherness, and 305.2 and 305.5–305.8 clearly don't fit. This leaves **305.3–305.4 People by gender or sex**. Can sexual orientation be considered a gender or sex?

Certainly the concept of homosexuality as a third gender exists (and has for a while; this was in fact one of the earliest senses of the term *intersex*; see Johnson, 2007), but it's hardly accepted widely enough to justify a classification as such. However, if we look at current discourse surrounding sexual orientation, there is justification for considering orientation a closely related topic to gender and sex. Easily the most visible public forum where orientation is discussed is the ongoing debate over same-sex marriage. Again, this discourse reinforces the classification of people by sexual orientation as a social group, not an institution. The debate is not over whether to allow people to participate in the institution of homosexuality; this is a battle the religious right lost long ago. The debate is over whether to allow homosexual couples to participate in the institution of marriage. The actual *sexual relations* hardly enter the discourse at all. On the opposing side the discourse tends to center around children: whether same-sex couples provide the family situation children need, and whether children should be exposed to homosexuality in schools. On the side of same-sex marriage proponents, the question largely boils down to one of sexual discrimination: Is it just to restrict a couple's right to marry based solely on their genders? Should a man be allowed the right to marry a woman while a woman is not given that same right? This argument is humorously articulated by a video released by the Courage Campaign Issues Committee in October 2008 (at the peak of the debate over California's Proposition 8, a ballot initiative amending the constitution to define marriage as between a man and a woman), in which a man and woman go to a California court to obtain a marriage license, only to be accosted by a team of "Gender Auditors" who look under her dress and inside his pants to verify that they have "state-approved equipment" (Courage Campaign, 2008). As this example demonstrates, sexual orientation as it currently exists in public discourse is linked to questions of gender and sex.

The appropriate place for sexual orientation, then, would be under **305.3–4 People by gender or sex**, perhaps amended to "People by gender, sex, or sexual orientation." This placement would not only put sexual orientation at a more logical place in the schedule, but, more germane to the present discussion, it would allow transgender and intersex to have their cake and eat it too: the two could be placed in the notational hierarchy under gender and sex as is logically appropriate while remaining adjacent to their political allies of sexual orientation. Another way of looking at this proposal is that transgender and intersex are being moved to the class most appropriate for them, and sexual orientation is "tagging along" as a closely related concept; this perspective nicely subverts the minority-within-a-minority status of transgender and intersex.

There are certainly problems with this proposal. First and foremost is the problem that comes with moving any existing class in Dewey — the corresponding titles in thousands of libraries need to be recataloged and the corresponding items, relabeled and reshelved. Secondly, there's little room for growth in 305.3–4. The only logical placement of sexual orientation, transgender, and intersex without moving other existing classes would be at 305.39 or 305.49, either of which returns the sexual minorities to the dreaded ninth position of otherness. Just as ideological sacrifices had to be made when placing transgender and intersex under 306.76, either ideological or practical sacrifices would be made by any placement. Benefits must be weighed against these sacrifices, a decision made, and the consequences lived with — not only by those who make the decision, but by librarians and patrons of every library that uses DDC. Perhaps these limitations are evidence that any classification system that has been in use for over a century is going to be inherently biased against minorities who weren't even named at the time of its creation. Altering theoretical systems is difficult enough; altering the realities born of them can be next to impossible.

Intersex in Application

In order to properly weigh the advantages of changing the classification of intersex against the disadvantages, we need to step away from the theoretical and look at the practical. It's one thing to say that the placement of intersex in DDC schedules and tables is theoretically incorrect, but if this incorrectness has no impact on real people in the real world, then the question is purely academic. So that we might get a better idea of how works about intersex are classed at present, I will look at two examples: *Bodies in Doubt: An American History of Intersex* by Elizabeth Reis and *Unseen Genders: Beyond the Binaries* by Felicity Haynes and Tarquam McKenna. For each example I will look at the DDC numbers applied to it by libraries found through OCLC's WorldCat, its context among other books in those libraries' online catalogs, and the implications thereof.

According to the publisher's description, *Bodies in Doubt: An American History of Intersex* "traces the changing definitions, perceptions, and medical management of intersex (atypical sex development) in America from the colonial period to the present day" (Reis, 2009). Its author, Elizabeth Reis, is an associate professor of women's and gender studies and history. This book appears to be primarily a history, though there are also strong elements of social sciences and medicine. Immediately, a problem inherent in mapping works about gender and sexuality to DDC is highlighted: these works tend to be multidisciplinary in nature, and unitary classification systems such as DDC simply do not work well with multidisciplinary works (Hurt, 1997). The cataloger is forced to choose whether to emphasize the historical aspect by placing this book in the 900s, the social science aspect in the 300s, or the medical aspect in the 610s. Catalogers at libraries using DDC to classify this book seem to have gone one of two routes. The first is to place *Bodies in Doubt* at 616.694, where it is found in the Multnomah County Library system in Oregon. As I stated earlier, 616.694 is currently the only class referred to under Intersexuality in the Relative Index. The book does examine the "medical management of intersex," but the publisher's description also says that a major argument of the book is "that medical practice cannot be understood outside of the broader cultural context in which it is embedded" (Reis, 2009). This seems to indicate that medicine is not the primary focus of the book, so placement at 616 seems inappropriate. The book's immediate neighbors at Multnomah County are also about intersex, or at least discuss intersex among other related topics: to the left is *Fixing Sex: Intersex, Medical Authority, and Lived Experience*, and to the right is *Gender Identity: The Ultimate Teen Guide*. If nothing else, at least books about intersex are grouped together. However, just three books down from *Bodies in Doubt* is *Office Orthopedics for Primary Care: Diagnosis and Treatment*, and just six books before it is *The Andropause Mystery: Unraveling Truths About the Male Menopause*. One would be hard-pressed to argue that the average shelf browser interested in intersex would also likely be interested in orthopedics and male menopause, as opposed to other issues related to gender and sexual identity. This choice of classification, so long as it is consistently made, achieves the purpose of grouping like items together within the narrow topic of intersex, but it fails at grouping like topics together. Nor is this the intuitive place to find the topic.

Other libraries, such as King County Library in Washington, classify *Bodies in Doubt* at 362.196694. Neither DDC 22 nor the 2008 draft list this number in the Relative Index under Intersexuality, but the classification is justified within the schedules. Obviously, this number emphasizes the social sciences aspect of the book by placing it in the 300s. As we move down the hierarchy, though, we see that the medical aspect is also accounted for:

> **360 Social problems & services; associations**
> **362 Social welfare problems & services**
> **362.1 Physical illness**
> **362.19 Services to patients with specific conditions.**

This latter class includes the scope note "Class here living with a physical condition" and the instruction to class specific conditions in .196–.198 by adding to .19 the numbers following 61 in 616–618. Hence **616.694 Hermaphroditism** gives us 632.196694, indicating services to patients with hermaphroditism or living with hermaphroditism. Like the placement at 616, this placement emphasizes the medical aspect of intersex, though it shifts the focus from the medical practice to the patient. And, lest we miss the elephant in the room, intersex is treated as a physical illness or social problem. This is hardly a flattering classification to the people represented by it and, judging by the publisher's description, not an accurate representation of this particular book's stance. Certainly *Bodies in Doubt* examines attitudes such as that implied by this classification, but in order to do so it must by necessity not partake in those attitudes. One doesn't even have to be familiar with the complexities of DDC in order to interpret what this classification says about intersex: On the King County Library shelves, *Bodies in Doubt*'s neighbor to the left is *Empty Womb, Aching Heart: Hope and Help for Those Struggling with Infertility*, and to the right is *Live Strong: Inspirational Stories from Cancer Survivors—From Diagnosis to Treatment and Beyond*. Intersex, then, is akin to infertility and cancer.

Although the Decimal Classification Editorial Policy Committee approved the Dewey editorial team's proposed changes to Table 1 and 305–306 in November 2008, with plans to implement the changes by mid–2009 (Mitchell, 2008b), as of November 2009 these changes have not yet been officially released. Mitchell (personal communication, November 20, 2009) expects the changes to be implemented sometime in 2010. Let us suppose for a moment, though, that catalogers at Multnomah County Library or King County Library were to apply these changes and place *Bodies in Doubt* and other books about intersex at 306.7685. At Multnomah County, their neighbors on one side would be books such as *The Testosterone Files: My Hormonal and Social Transformation from Female to Male* and *The Transgender Child*; on the other side would be *The Gender Frontier* and *The Man in the Red*

Velvet Dress: Inside the World of Cross Dressing. These latter two are due to Dewey's classifi-cation of transvestism and cross dressing under **306.77 Sexual and related practices**, and the former because of the current use of 306.768 for transsexuality, which has the same practical effect as the proposed **306.768 Transgenderism and intersexuality** will, in that works on transgender as well as transsexuality are placed here. The books on either side of the theoretical 306.7685 at King County are also on these same topics. As discussed earlier, these immediate neighbors are not altogether inappropriate; intersex people share many things in common with transgendered people, transsexuals, and transvestites. One doesn't have to zoom out much more, though, to see where this position on the shelves is not quite logically sound: also in 306.77 are books such as *Thanks for Coming: One Young Woman's Quest for an Orgasm* and *Pop-Porn: Pornography in American Culture*. Here we jump from transgender and intersex to orgasm and pornography. Perhaps the strongest link between these topics is that they are all taboo in traditional American society. The purpose of clas-sification, however, is not to separate the "naughty" books from the rest. To the left of our theoretical section devoted to intersex at 306.7685 are several shelves worth of books about lesbianism, homosexuality, and bisexuality, at either library. As I concluded earlier, the col-location of intersex, transgender, and sexual orientation is somewhat of a logical concession, but one with cultural and literary warrant. Beyond those books about sexual orientation, though, we find *Child Prostitution in Thailand: Listening to Rahab* and *The Happy Hooker: My Own Story.* Again, what we have here is essentially a grouping of taboo subjects. Intersex, transgender, and sexual orientation are hardly related to prostitution. This placement hear-kens back to the perception of homosexuality as identified by an illicit sexual act rather than by the shared features of a minority social group, with intersex and transgender grandfathered in by virtue of their political association with homosexuality.

An interesting counterexample is *Unseen Genders: Beyond the Binaries*, a book about how "Transsexuals, homosexuals, lesbians, cross dressers, and transgender and intersex per-sons share an invisibility in their performativities in, through, and across male or female stereotypes" (Haynes & McKenna, 2001). When this book appears in Dewey-based catalogs, such as at the San Francisco Public Library (SFPL), it tends to be classed at 305.3 Men and women (in the revised draft, 305.3 People by gender or sex). Browsing through several libraries' catalogs at 305.3, one finds not only books about traditional male and female gender identity, but also books such as *Who's Who & Resource Guide to the Transgender Com-munity, Changing Ones: Third and Fourth Genders in Native North America*, and *Evolution's Rainbow: Diversity, Gender, and Sexuality in Nature and People.* These books seem to be placed here for a variety of reasons: because they fall under the scope note "Class here inter-disciplinary works on sex role, the sexes, gender identity"; because in the current schedule there is no better place to put works on transgender or intersex, at least from a non-medical perspective; and because, like *Unseen Genders*, these books cover a variety of topics that are best summed up under the umbrella of gender and sex. The advantage of this placement is that it puts works about minority sexual and gender identities next to works about traditional gender and sex. The disadvantage is that this places works about gender, sex, and sexual orientation in a broader sense several shelves away from more specific works about these topics, placed at 306.76. In SFPL's catalog, there are nearly 5000 titles between *Unseen Genders* and the first title at 306.76, covering several completely unrelated topics such as religious groups, racial and ethnic groups, and, again, prostitution. The proposed see ref-erence at 305.3, "for transgender and intersex people, see 306.768," may connect these classes for the classifier, but this does nothing to help the casual browser. This patron may well come across either 305.3 or 306.768, not both, and believe she's found all there is to find on her topic of interest. If works on intersex, transgender, and sexual orientation were classed somewhere in 305.3–305.4, on the other hand, this wouldn't be such a problem.

Conclusion

The Dewey editorial team has made a lot of progress toward classifying intersex in the Dewey Decimal System in such a way that accurately reflects current cultural understanding and appropriate sensitivity, but in order to fully reach these goals a mass overhaul is needed, not just of the classification of intersex, but also of other minorities of sex, gender, and orientation. The placement of intersex and transgender with sexual orientation is problematic, but the advantage of reflecting cultural and literary warrant outweighs the disadvantage of potential confusion. The placement of these three concepts in the notational hierarchy under cultures and institutions defined by sexual relations, however, is both theoretically and practically unsound. The most logical placement, and the one that would best serve library patrons, would be under **305.3 People by gender or sex**. I therefore propose that the heading for 305.3 be changed to "People by gender, sex, or sexual orientation," and that classes be created within 305.3–305.4 to house the concepts currently classed under 306.76 by DDC 22 or the revised draft released in August 2008. I suggest that further research be done to identify the best positions within this range, weighing the advantages and disadvantages of each possibility, as well as to estimate the workload such a change would create for libraries currently using DDC.

In response to my suggested changes, Mitchell acknowledged that the heading at 306.7 is problematic, and suggested that the editorial team might consider changing the heading to "Sexual relations, sexual orientation, transgenderism, intersexuality" (personal communication, November 23, 2009). Such a change, together with the adjustments made to the structural hierarchy by see references, would address the theoretical problems associated with the currently proposed placement of transgender and intersex at T1–0867 and 306.768. Nonetheless, the practical problems remain. Library users see only the notational hierarchy as represented on library shelves, not the structural hierarchy in the schedules themselves. Until the type of massive overhaul of DDC I've suggested becomes practical — an overhaul that would likely need to address many problems besides just those related to sex and gender — I recommend that libraries using DDC find other ways to practically address the discrepancies between DDC's structural hierarchy and its notational hierarchy. Signs placed on shelves at 305.3 and 306.768 referring users to related works at the other location, for example, might help close the physical gap between these classes. A logical next step in addressing these problems would be further research into such solutions that may already be in use, and how well they work. Practical problems, after all, call for practical solutions.

References

Courage Campaign. (2008). *Gender auditors: no on Prop 8* [Web video]. Retrieved from http://www.you tube.com/watch?v=UiYmjDzSg3o

Dewey, M., Mitchell, J., et al. (Ed.). (2003). Dewey decimal classification and relative index. Dublin, OH: OCLC.

Donna. (2007, August 15). [Blog comment]. On J. Mitchell, *Transgendered people*. Retrieved from http://ddc.typepad.com/025431/2007/06/transgendered_p.html?cid=79631711#comment-6a00d8341d500f53ef00e54edf9c868834

Greenblatt, E. (1990). Homosexuality: The evolution of a concept in the Library of Congress Subject Headings. In C. Gough & E. Greenblatt (Eds.), *Gay and lesbian library service* (pp. 75–101). Jefferson, NC: McFarland.

Haynes, F., & McKenna, T. (2001). *Unseen genders: Beyond the binaries.* New York: Peter Lang.

Hurt, C.D. (1997). Classification and subject analysis: Looking to the future at a distance. In J. R. Shearer & A. R. Thomas (Eds.), *Cataloging and classification: Trends, transformations, teaching, and training* (pp. 97–112). New York: Haworth.

Intersex Society of North America. (2008). *What is Intersex?* Retrieved from http://www.isna.org/faq/what_is_intersex

Johnson, M. (2007). *Gay, lesbian, bisexual, and transgender subject access: History and current practice.* Retrieved from http://www.lib.washington.edu/msd/norestriction/b58062361.pdf

Mitchell, J. (2007). *Transgendered people.* Retrieved from http://ddc.typepad.com/025431/2007/06/transgendered_p.html

Mitchell, J. (2008a). *Transgendered and intersex people.* Retrieved from http://ddc.typepad.com/025431/2008/01/transgendered-a.html

Mitchell, J. (2008b). *EPC meeting 130.* Retrieved from http://ddc.typepad.com/025431/2008/11/epc-meeting-130.html

Olson, H.A. (1998). Mapping beyond Dewey's boundaries: Constructing classificatory space for marginalized knowledge domains. *Library Trends, 47*(2), 233–254.

Reis, E. (2009). *Bodies in doubt: An American history of intersex.* Baltimore, MD: Johns Hopkins University Press.

Relative index [Draft revision]. (2008). Retrieved from http://www.oclc.org/dewey/discussion/papers/T1_08-09 305-306 idx.pdf

Table 1. Standard subdivisions [Draft revision]. (2008). Retrieved from http://www.oclc.org/dewey/discussion/papers/1_08-1_09.pdf

305 Groups of people — 306 Culture and institutions. [Draft revision]. (2008). Retrieved from http://www.oclc.org/dewey/discussion/papers/305-306.pdf

Transgendered people: A discussion paper. (2007). Retrieved from http://www.oclc.org/dewey/discussion/papers/transgendered_people.pdf

The Treatment of LGBTIQ
Concepts in the Library
of Congress Subject Headings[1]

Ellen Greenblatt

In the current technically sophisticated environment where keyword searching reigns supreme, some may question the continued importance of controlled vocabularies such as the Library of Congress Subject Headings (LCSH). However, while keyword and full text searching are quick and convenient, they do have their drawbacks.[2] With the variations in terminology pertaining to LGBTIQ people and concepts over the years, a controlled vocabulary is an essential component in successful information discovery. Controlled vocabularies help make searching more efficient and precise. A well-constructed controlled vocabulary has a syndetic structure which brings together synonyms that keyword searching would miss, for example *lesbians, dykes,* and *gay womyn.* It also links historical and obsolete usages to current terminology — e.g., the terms *lesbigay* and the more inclusive *lesbigaytr* (to a lesser extent), while extremely popular in the 1990s, have virtually disappeared in the last decade.[3] Further, controlled vocabularies help navigate the "alphabet soup" — LGBTIQ, GLBT, LGBTST-GNC, LGBTIQAA — used to encompass the various iterations of queer communities.[4]

As you can see, syndetic structure, the linking of related concepts and terms through cross-references which provide three main types of relationships — equivalence, associative, and hierarchical[5] — trumps the flat, hit-or-miss nature of keyword searching. These linkages enable users to navigate between concepts or terms during information discovery.

Web 2.0 innovations, such as the use of folksonomies through tagging, while offering user-generated terminology which may be more relevant and current, can exacerbate this problem even more, by offering a plethora of unlinked terms for a single concept — once again inhibiting efficient, exhaustive, and accurate discovery of LGBTIQ materials.[6]

This essay will examine how well LCSH works as a controlled vocabulary in its treatment of LGBTIQ concepts.

LCSH: An Overview

The Library of Congress first made its subject headings available to other libraries in 1898, and over the past century, LCSH has evolved into one of the most ubiquitous subject heading schemes employed in libraries today. It has become a "worldwide standard" (Library of Congress, 2009), employed not only in countries where English is a primary language, such as Australia and South Africa, but also in translation in non–English-speaking countries, such as Brazil, the Czech Republic, and Greece (Heiner-Freiling, 2000). Used not only in library catalogs, LCSH also forms the basis of several thesauri, such as those produced by EBSCO, most notably in regard to the topic of this essay, its LGBT Life database.

Library of Congress headings are established based on the principle of literary warrant. For the first ninety plus years of its existence, the literary warrant for LCSH headings was limited to the terminology appearing in materials in the Library of Congress collections. That is to say, subject headings in LCSH solely reflected the holdings of the Library of Congress, and as such may not have addressed all topics. However, the implementation of the Subject Authority Cooperative Program (SACO) in 1992 broadened the subject base (and thus the literary warrant) as other libraries began to submit headings to LCSH (Wiggins, 1998).

Despite its pervasiveness in libraries, LCSH has had its share of critics, mostly in regard to user warrant, which, as its name suggests, is based upon the terminology employed by users. One of the most vociferous critics is Sanford Berman who for the past 40 years has advocated for more relevant and less biased subject headings. Berman characterizes LCSH's failure to employ common usage, current, and unprejudiced terminology as "bibliocide by cataloging" stating that these practices effectively render books and other media inaccessible to library users (Augustyn, 1993). Furthermore, says Berman, "[C]atalog users should (ideally) be able to reach desired subjects on their first try and should not be offended, prejudiced, confused, misled, or repelled by the very terminology used to denote specific topics" (Berman, 1981, p. 110).

Universalization vs. Minoritization

LCSH traces its roots back to Charles A. Cutter's *Rules for a Dictionary Catalog* which stresses the importance of uniform terminology in enabling the collocation function of the catalog. Cutter states that "in choosing between synonymous headings, prefer the one that is most familiar to the class of people who consult the library" (1889, p. 50), thus advocating for what Hope A. Olson terms "a universal language of subject representation" (1996, para. 7).

Criticisms such as Berman's are based on the fact that such a universal language is of necessity based on mainstream concepts and perceptions and does not incorporate marginalized groups — i.e., to paraphrase Olson, universality precludes diversity (para. 17).

Extrapolating upon his readings of queer theorist, Eve Kosofsky Sedgwick, Grant Campbell (2000) discusses the tension between these two approaches. Universalization emphasizes integration within the larger community, while minoritization emphasizes the visibility of the marginalized community. Christensen (2008) explains the difference between these two viewpoints as a "question of marked or unmarked representation," in which the minoritizing view calls attention to difference, while the universalizing view emphasizes the unified whole (p. 236).

As this essay examines the treatment of concepts pertaining to groups under the LGB-TIQ umbrella, it will of necessity assume a minoritizing approach to the topic taking the stance that marginalized identities should not be invisible and that controlled vocabularies, such as LCSH, should enable users to easily find the information they seek using culturally sensitive and relevant terminology.

Historical Overview of LGBTIQ Concepts and LCSH

This section will examine the terminology associated with LGBTIQ subjects, offering etymological and historical information about each term and its incorporation into LCSH.[7]

Homosexuality, Homosexuals

The term *homosexual*, connoting same-sex orientation, was coined by the Austro-Hungarian writer Károly Mária Kertbeny[8] from the Greek *homo-* meaning "same" and the Latin *sexualis* meaning "sexuality." The word, *Homosexualisten* (German for *homosexuals*), first appeared in a letter Kertbeny wrote to Karl Heinrich Ulrichs in 1868 and appeared in two pamphlets he published the following year. (Endres, 2006; Feray & Herzer, 1990). He also coined the words *Homosexualität* and *Homosexualismus,* the German equivalents of our term *homosexuality* (Feray & Herzer, 1990). Though other terms such as *invert, urning, catamite, androgenic, Platonist, similisexual, contrasexual, homogenic, intersexual, morphadite, pathic, sodomist,* and their equivalents in other languages were also used around this time, *homosexual* appears to have won out because of its flexibility (Sell, 1997). Based upon Greek and Latin roots, it had an international appeal due to its adaptability in different languages and its potential for deriving opposable terminology, i.e. such terms as *heterosexual* and *bisexual.* The terms *homosexual* and *homosexuality* appeared for the first time in medical journals in the United States in the 1890s, and, by the 1920s, the terms began to appear in mainstream publications (Alyson Publications, 1989).

Homosexuality (sh85061780)[9] was not, however, to become an authorized subject heading in LCSH until a couple decades later. Early subject headings reflected a pathologized approach to the terminology chosen to represent this concept. Until 1946, the concept of *homosexuality* was subsumed under the heading *Sexual perversion.* The term *homosexuality* did not even appear until 1945 and then only as a cross-reference to the heading *Sexual perversion.* It was not until 1946 that *Homosexuality* first appeared as an authorized heading. However, a "see also from" reference to *Sexual perversion* continued to appear as late as 1972 (M. K. D. Pietris, Chief, Office for Subject Cataloging Policy, personal communication, November 28, 1989). Terms denoting classes of persons, i.e., *Homosexuals* and *Homosexuals, Male,* did not appear until as recently as 1976 (M. K. D. Pietris, Chief, Office for Subject Cataloging Policy, personal communication, November 28, 1989).

Lesbianism, Lesbians

The terms *lesbian* and *lesbianism,* the female equivalents of *homosexual* and *homosexuality* respectively, are traditionally credited with being derived from Lesbos, the Greek island which was home to the poet Sappho and her students. While the word, *lesbian* appears in older English and French texts as long as four centuries ago (Chen, 2004), Emma Donoghue (1993) points out that the word *lesbian* was used in its current sense in English as far back as 1732 as an adjective (as a reference to "Lesbian Loves" in William King's *The Toast*) and 1736 as a noun (as "Tribades or Lesbians" in a later edition of the same work), almost 140 years before the *Oxford English Dictionary* (*OED*) establishes its origins (2000). However, *Lesbians* (sh85076160) did not appear as an authorized heading in LCSH until as recently as 1976, while *Lesbianism* (sh85076157) appeared as an authorized heading in 1954 (M. K. D. Pietris, Chief, Office for Subject Cataloging Policy. personal communication, November 28, 1989).

Gay

The term *gay* evolved into its current meaning as a synonym for *homosexual* over the past three centuries. It is derived from the Old French word *gai*, which means "full of mirth" (Herbst, 2001). In addition to this original meaning of *happy*, in the seventeenth century the word was used to describe what today would be called a playboy, e.g. *gay Lothario, gay blade*, etc. Somewhere around the nineteenth century, the term was applied to fallen women and both male and female prostitutes (Cohen, 2004). Eventually the term took on its present meaning referring to homosexual men, perhaps because of their promiscuity and marginality. Its first manifestation in print in the United States is in Noel Ersine's *Dictionary of Underworld Slang* (1933) where it appears as *gaycat*, referring to a homosexual boy (Dynes, 2008). Two years later in 1935, *gay* itself appeared in Ersine's book *Underworld and Prison Slang*. (Herbst, 2001). Its first documented mainstream usage in film was in 1938's *Bringing Up Baby*, in which Cary Grant appears dressed in a frilly dressing gown claiming he "just went gay all of a sudden"[10] (Russo, 1987). Though the term *gay* was used extensively in the gay and lesbian community beginning around the 1920s, it was not until after the Stonewall Rebellion in 1969 and the activism of the 1970s that the term entered into mainstream usage. Since then *gay* has become the term of choice over *homosexual*, which is seen as a clinical, sexually objectifying, and limiting term. *Gay* expands the meaning of the term, taking it outside of the bedroom and "affirm[ing" the] 'truly joyous lifestyle'" of the gay and lesbian community (Cordova, 1974, p. 22).

Nevertheless, although the term *gay* has been the term of choice of the gay and lesbian community for decades and has become ensconced in popular usage during the last forty years, it was not sanctioned by the Library of Congress until as recently as 1987 (other than its uses as an adjective in *Gay liberation movement* [sh85053580] and *Gay bars* [sh85053577]). While the heading *Gay liberation movement* first appeared in 1972, it was the only appearance of the vernacular synonym for *homosexual* until the appearance of the heading *Gay bars* in 1974 (M. K. D. Pietris, Chief, Office for Subject Cataloging Policy, personal communication, November 28, 1989). The first appearance of *gay* as a cross-reference occurred in 1976: *Gays, Male see Homosexuals, Male* (M. K. D. Pietris, Chief, Office for Subject Cataloging Policy, personal communication, November 28, 1989). In 1987, after years of petitioning from Sanford Berman and other library activists, the Library of Congress effected a major change in LCSH, exchanging the term *Gays* (sh85061795) for the previously authorized term *Homosexuals* (Library of Congress Acquisitions and Bibliographic Access Directorate, 1987). It took the Library of Congress almost twenty years to change this subject heading to reflect vernacular usage. Even the conservative *New York Times*, whose previous editorial policy had been to use the word *gay* only if it was part of an organization's name or if it occurred in a direct quote, authorized the use of *gay* before the Library of Congress.[11]

Bisexuality, Bisexuals

The meaning of the term bisexuality has evolved over the past two centuries. When it first appeared in the dictionary in 1824, it was synonymous with the term *hermphroditism*[12] in that it referred to a person or organism possessing both male and female anatomical traits (Fairyington, 2005; Harper, 2001; OED, 2000).[13] A few decades later, *bisexuality* transitioned from these biological foundations to become what early sexologists Richard Krafft-Ebing and Havelock Ellis referred to as *psychosexual hermaphroditism*, pertaining to people who were perceived to psychologically display both masculine and feminine traits (Beemyn, 2006; Storr, 2002). As the fledgling discipline of psychoanalysis emerged in the early twentieth century, the concept of *bisexuality* began take on its current meaning as a sexual orientation. Sigmund Freud is generally credited as being the first (and certainly the most influential) in this regard (Beemyn, 2004; Fairyington, 2005; Zaretsky, 1997).

However, despite its use in the early decades of the twentieth century, *Bisexuality* (sh85014412) was not established as an authorized heading in LCSH until 1959, while *Bisexuals* (sh93003390) as a class of persons first appeared in 1993.

Transvestism, Transsexualism, and Transgender

In the interests of space, I will examine only these three concepts of the many relating to *trans*[14] issues. Historically, the term *transvestism*[15] came first, coined by noted German sexologist Magnus Hirschfeld in 1910 in his book *Die Transvestiten* (Hill, 2005). The term, which he defines as "the strong drive to live in the clothing of that sex that does not belong to the relative build of the body" derives from the Latin *trans* meaning "over or opposite" and *vestis* meaning "clothing" (1991, p. 124). Hirschfeld applied this term to a broader spectrum of people than we would today, conflating this concept with homosexuality and transsexuality (Hill, 2005; Hines, 2004; Meyerowitz, 2002). In its contemporary sense, the concept is not associated with sexual orientation or cross-gender identity, but instead refers to "practices ... based largely around bodily appearance" (Hines, 2004, p. 235). Gilbert (2000) elaborates, applying the concept to "a person who has an apparent gender identification with one sex, and who has ... been birth-designated as belonging to [that] one sex, but who wears the clothing of the opposite sex because it is the clothing of the opposite sex" (para. 10).

For many, the terms *transvestitism* and *transvestites* are seen as defamatory due to their association with fetishism, deviance, and perversion. Starting in the 1970s, these terms began to be gradually replaced by *cross-dressing* and *cross-dressers* respectively, terms which are preferred today as they are perceived to be more neutral (Herbst, 2001; Kelly, 2008; Lovaas, 2004; Stryker, 2008).

According to Stryker (2008), *transsexual* was established to differentiate "between those 'transvestites' who sought medical interventions to change their physical bodies (that is, their 'sex') and those who merely wanted to change their gendered clothing (the 'vestiments' in the root of 'transvestite')" (p. 18). Although Hirschfeld is also credited with coining the term, *Transexulismus* (*transsexualism/transsexuality*) in his paper "Die intersexuelle Konstitution" (The Intersexual Constitution) in 1923 (Hill, 2005), it was not used in its current sense until the mid–twentieth century, when David O. Cauldwell published a paper called "Psychopathia transexualis" in the journal *Sexology* in 1949. It was further popularized by Harry Benjamin in the 1950s, following in the wake of publicity surrounding Christine

Jorgensen's historic "sex change" (Bullough, 1987; Ekins & King, 2001; King, 1995; Meyerowitz, 2002; Stryker, 2008). The term *transsexualism,* which first appeared in the medical literature in the late 1940s, was in vogue in the 1950s and 1960s, but during the past four decades *transsexuality* has been the preferred term (Herbst, 2001; Meyerowitz, 2002).

Transgender traces its roots back to 1969 when Virginia Prince coined the word *transgenderal* (in opposition to *transsexual*) to describe herself as someone changing her gender rather than her sex (Ekins & King, 2005). Over the next decade, the term morphed into *transgenderist,* first appearing in print in her 1978 article "The 'Transcendents' or 'Trans' People" (Prince, 2005, p. 42).[16] Leslie Feinberg is credited with being the first to use *transgender* in print in its current sense, i.e., as an umbrella term encompassing the broad spectrum of gender-variance, in the 1992 pamphlet *Transgender Liberation: A Movement Whose Time Has Come*[17] (Stryker, 2005; Valentine, 2007).

LCSH's treatment of headings concerning *trans* concepts has been problematic. *Transvestism* (sh85137104) and *Transvestites* (sh89002495) are still authorized headings, each containing cross-references regarding cross-dressing and cross-dressers (with and without hyphens) respectively. *Transvestism* first appeared in LCSH in 1948 (Paul Weiss, Library of Congress, Acquisitions and Bibliographic Access Directorate, Policy and Standards Division, personal communication, February 23, 2009). And *Transvestites* was created in 1989, despite prior long term community preference for the terms *cross-dressing* and *cross-dressers.* *Transvestism* continues to be pathologized in LCSH with its inclusion under the BT (broader term) *Psychosexual disorders* (sh85108504). And until recently, *Two-Spirit people* (sh95004103) was an NT (narrower term) subsumed under *Transvestites,* no doubt based on the scope note in the record which reads: "Here are entered works on North American Indians, especially men, who assume the dress, role, and status of the opposite sex" (Library of Congress Acquisitions and Bibliographic Access Directorate, 2009b). De Vries (2008) states this concept is much broader, being applied to "[Native American/First Nations] people who embody characteristics of multiple genders, sexes, or sexualities" (p. 63).[18]

Transsexualism (sh94005829) was added to LCSH in 1994, despite the term going out of vogue in the 1960s in favor of the currently preferred term, *transsexuality,* which does appear as a cross-reference in the subject authority record. But aside from the currency of the choice of heading, the biggest problem concerning *trans* headings in LCSH is that until 2007, it conflated the concepts of *transsexuality* and *transgender.* Before the change, terms such as *Transgenderism, Transgender orientation, Transgendered people, Transgenders* served as cross-references to the authorized headings *Transsexualism* and *Transsexuals* (sh85137086). In 2007, LCSH authorized the headings *Transgenderism* (sh2007003716) and *Transgender people* (sh2007003708), providing the following scope note to the former: "Here are entered works on the various manifestations of cross-gender orientation, such as transvestism, transsexualism, male or female impersonation, intersexuality, etc., treated collectively." However, the only NT listed in the subject authority record for *Transgenderism* is *Transsexualism* and not any of the other concepts mentioned in the scope note, while the subject authority record for *Transgender people,* on the other hand, includes NTs for *Transsexuals, Transvestites, Female Impersonators* (sh85064634), and *Male Impersonators* (sh85064636),[19] among others.

Hermaphroditism, Intersexuality, and DSDs

There is much debate both within the intersex community and beyond regarding appropriate terminology. As Elizabeth Reis explains:

> How to name a diverse set of conditions involving aspects of external genitalia, sex chromosomes, internal reproductive anatomy, and gender identity raises political as well as medical questions. The choice of nomenclature influences not only how doctors interpret medical situations but, equally as important, how parents view their affected children, how intersex people understand themselves, and how others not directly involved in medical settings — such as gender and legal scholars, historians, and media commentators — conceive of and theorize about gender, sex, and the body [2007, p. 536].

For several centuries the terms in common usage were *hermaphroditism* and *hermaphrodites,* words that derive their origin from the Greek mythological figure, Hermaphroditus, son of the gods Hermes and Aphrodite (Callahan, 2009; Eckert, 2003; Reis, 2005). As the myth relates, when the youth Hermaphroditus bathes in a pool belonging to the water nymph Salmacis, she is struck by his attractiveness and jumps in the pool to be with him. She asks the gods to unite them, that they may never be parted. The gods grant her request, joining them together forever "so when they were mated together in a close embrace, they were not two, but a two-fold form, so that they could not be called male or female, and seemed neither or either" (Ovid, 2000, Book IV: 346–388, para. 3).

Intersexuality was first applied to biological sex categories ranging from male to female and in between by Richard Goldschmidt in 1917 in an article entitled "Intersexuality and the Endocrine Aspect of Sex" in *Endocrinology,* a new journal appearing that year (Dreger & Herndon, 2009). Prior to this the term was used to describe *homosexuality, bisexuality,* and *transsexuality.*[20] The term *intersexed* began to appear in medical literature in the mid-twentieth century to refer to what had previously been termed *hermaphroditic* (Dreger, 1998). In the 1990s, activists reclaimed the medical term *intersex* in much the same way that LGBT activists reclaimed *queer.* And so *intersex* became an identity, not just a medical condition.[21]

In 2005, the medical community put forward new nomenclature —*disorders of sex development (DSDs)*— at a conference hosted in Chicago by the Lawson Wilkins Pediatric Endocrine Society and the European Society for Paediatric Endocrinology (Reis, 2007). Not everyone was happy with this new development.[22] Some felt that this new terminology was foisted on the intersex community by the medical community without consultation (Hinkle, n.d.). Many found the term *disorders* to be a negative term which pathologizes intersex conditions[23] (Diamond, 2009; Hinkle, n.d.). Alternatives have been proposed, including *differences in sex development* (Diamond, 2009) and *divergences in sex development* (Reis, 2007), which maintain the acronym *DSD,* as well as *variations in sex development* (Cameron, 2006). Proponents state that *DSD* puts the focus on the medical condition, not the person, so that people with *DSD* will be "human beings with a diagnosis" (Vilain et al., 2007, p. 66).

This concept has been present in LCSH early on, if not right from the beginning of the establishment of the subject authority file. According to Paul Weiss, of the Acquisitions and Bibliographic Access Directorate at the Library of Congress, "[Hermaphroditism] appears to have been established some time in the early part of the 20th century. It is listed in the oldest edition of LCSH that we have available, which was published during the period 1910–1914" (Personal communication, January 29, 2009). Apparently there was never any heading for the class of people known as *hermaphrodites*. In 2007, the Library of Congress changed the authorized heading from *Hermaphroditism* to *Intersexuality* (Library of Congress Acquisitions and Bibliographic Access Directorate, 2007a). Later that same year, the heading *Intersex people* was also added (Library of Congress Acquisitions and Bibliographic Access Directorate, 2007b). The subject authority record for *Intersexuality* (sh85060401) contains cross-references from the earlier heading *Hermaphroditism* along with *Intersex conditions* and *Bisexuality (Biology)*. There are no references to *DSDs*, *disorders [or divergences or differences] in sex development*, or *variations in sex development*.

In cases such as this, where the terminology is fluid and not agreed upon by all stakeholders, it is understandable that the Library of Congress may hesitate to establish new headings. However, it would be useful to cross-reference these terms to existing headings helping users to find the information which they seek using terminology with which they are familiar.

Queer

Depending on one's generation, queer can be a politically or emotionally charged term. It is definitely a contested term—fluid and varied in its many applications. Its original meaning of odd or abnormal can be traced back to the seventeenth century (Herbst, 2001). In the past century, *queer* was a derogatory term applied to non-heterosexuals. By the 1990s, however, *queer* was reclaimed by lesbian, gay, bisexual, and transgender activists as a radical act — most notably by the group Queer Nation.

While most would agree that queer is a term that encompasses both sexuality and gender and that it draws its meaning from its opposition to heteronormativity, it is difficult to find an agreed upon definition. In fact, as Annamaria Jagose explains, "[Queer's] definitional indeterminacy, its elasticity, is one of its constituent characteristics.... For part of queer's semantic clout, part of its political efficacy depends on its resistance to definition, and the way in which it refuses to stake its claim" (1996, p. 1). In other words, "Once a definition of queer congeals, it ceases to be queer at all" (Bobotis, 2002, para. 6).

Because of the controversy and vagueness surrounding this term, it is not surprising that LCSH has not embraced it. The term *queer* does not appear in LCSH except for the heading *Queer theory* (sh2006001835) which was added in 2006. But, as K.R. Roberto (2009) wryly asks, "if there are no queers, what does queer theory study?" (p. 3). Other subject headings containing the word *theory* are linked to the topics about which they theorize — e.g., *Lesbian feminist theory* (sh00002434) falls under the BT *Lesbian feminism* (sh93000705); likewise *Feminist theory* (sh90002282) falls under the BT term *Feminism* (sh85047741). *Queer theory* has no UFs and only one RT, *Gender identity* (sh91003756). Why is there no parallel reference to *Sexual orientation* (sh91005179)? *Queer theory* is adrift in LCSH, unanchored and disconnected (except for one lone RT) from other relevant subject headings.

As the above overview suggests, when it comes to establishing headings for LGBTIQ concepts, the Library of Congress has been slow to respond to changes in usage. In my earlier work, "Homosexuality: The Evolution of a Concept in the Library of Congress Subject Headings," I suggested two changes to then-current headings and proposed seven new headings. While most of these headings were eventually added or amended (although not necessarily in the form I suggested), it took 20 years for all of them to be addressed. As this situation has been fully discussed elsewhere (Christensen, 2008), I will not repeat it here, other than to add that the last of these, *Lesbian separatism,* was not established as a heading until April 22, 2009 (Library of Congress Acquisitions and Bibliographic Access Directorate, 2009a).

Key Problem Areas

Continued Use of Gays as an Umbrella Heading

One of the issues I raised in my earlier work concerned LCSH's policy of using the term *gays* as a collective term for *gay men* and *lesbians* which I suggested be changed. Twenty years later, this situation remains unaltered. This practice is confusing. Do users understand the fine distinction between *gays* and *gay men*? To add to the confusion, in 2006, LCSH added an explanatory record (sh2006002250) that directed users from terms beginning with "*Gay male*" to the preferred term "*Gay*" (Library of Congress Acquisitions and Bibliographic Access Directorate, 2006).

In the citations included in the Library of Congress subject authority record for *Gays,* (sh85061795), the catalogers offer a statement from the publisher of the local gay and lesbian newspaper, the now defunct *Washington Blade,* whom they consulted for guidance on this issue:

> Phone call to Don Michaels, publisher, The Washington Blade, 5/20/88 (editorial policy of the Blade is to use the terms "gay" and "gays" to include both men and women, both for editorial and stylistic convenience and because the term is not considered pejorative to the majority of lesbians, some of whom prefer to be called "gay" rather than "lesbian." Criticism of this policy surfaces occasionally but it is generally acceptable to the majority of gay people.)

In a 2005 article, William Safire asks then current *Washington Blade* editor Chris Crain "Why is *gay* no longer encompassing enough?" (para. 5) and Crain answers:

> Historically, *gay* represented both homosexual men and women and technically still does ... but a number of gay women felt that *gay* was too male-associated and pressed to have lesbians separately identified so they weren't lost in the gay-male image [para. 5].

The National Lesbian and Gay Journalists Association, which provides a stylebook offering guidelines on LGBTIQ usage on its website, gives advice which clearly runs counter to the earlier *Washington Blade* statement cited in the subject authority record above:

> *Gay*: An adjective that has largely replaced "homosexual" in referring to men who are sexually and affectionally attracted to other men. Avoid using as a singular noun. For women, "lesbian" is generally used, but when possible ask the subject which term she prefers. *To include both, use gay men and lesbians.* In headlines where space is an issue, "gays" is acceptable to describe both [italics added for emphasis] [2008, para. 20].

Safire (2005) also quotes lesbian magazine editor Diane Anderson-Minshall's explanation of the preference of *lesbians and gays* over *gays*:

> When, in the queer world, you say "the gay community," the majority of the time that conjures up San Francisco's largely male Castro District, or West Hollywood or "Queer Eye for the Straight Guy," so interjecting the word *lesbian* into the mix is a necessary reminder that we — gay women — are not simply a subset of that larger male world but rather our own distinct community of individuals.

Another citation in the subject authority record for *gays* leaves some room for questioning the appropriateness of using the term as a collective noun:

> Random House 2 (Usage: Gay as an adjective meaning "homosexual" goes back at least to the early 1900's. After World War II, as social attitudes toward sexuality began to change, "gay" was applied openly to homosexuals themselves, first as an adjective and later as a noun. *Today the noun often designates only a male homosexual: gays and lesbians.* The word has ceased to be slang and is not used disparagingly) [Italics added for emphasis].

Since both of the citations included in this particular subject authority record reveal an awareness that there is controversy concerning the use of *gays* as an umbrella-term for *gay men and lesbians*, the Library of Congress may fairly be criticized for not exploring this issue further. In formulating this heading, the catalogers at the Library of Congress should have examined lesbian publications for insight into their editorial usage concerning preference of the dual usage of gay and lesbian or the omnibus term *gays* much as William Safire did in his investigation of the usage of the term.

This is another example of the minoritization vs. universalization issue discussed above. By using *gays* as an umbrella term to encompass both *gay men* and *lesbians,* LCSH is contributing to the longstanding issue of lesbian invisibility. As Adrienne Rich states in her classic essay, "Compulsory Heterosexuality and Lesbian Existence," "to equate lesbian existence with male homosexuality because each is stigmatized is to erase female reality once again" (p. 26).

Sex vs. Gender

Many of the problems relating to LGBTIQ terminology in LCSH stem from its conflation of the concepts of *sex* and *gender*, i.e., viewing them as synonymous terms. However, social theorists distinguish these concepts, explaining that sex is biologically founded, while gender is a social construct. Sex relates to one's genitalia, hormones, and chromosomes, while gender is determined by social and cultural indicators. Sexual categories include male, female, intersex, etc., while gender categories refer to man, woman, and other forms of gender identity and expression. To put it bluntly: "Sex is between your legs, while gender is between your ears."

Feminist and queer theory and the emergence of the transgender and intersex movements in the 1990s influenced the evolution of the distinction between these two concepts. For example, transgender scholar, Susan Stryker (2008), explains:

> [G]ender is historical (it changes through time) ... it varies from place to place and culture to culture, and ... it is contingent (it depends on a lot of different and seemingly unrelated things coming together). This takes us to one of the central issues of transgender politics — that the sex of the body does not bear any *necessary* or *deterministic* relationship to the social category in which that body lives [p. 11].

However, since LCSH does not make these distinctions, users face confusing terminology in their attempts at information discovery on these topics.

An examination of LC subject headings demonstrates this confusion. For example, the heading for *Sex* (sh 85120549) includes the following cross-references (UFs): *Gender (Sex)* and *Sex (Gender)*. These are rather ambiguous (tautological in fact!) and it is clear from these references that LCSH does not distinguish the two concepts.

Alternatively, *Gender identity* (sh91003756) includes the UFs *Sex identity (Gender iden-*

tity) and *Sexual identity (Gender identity).* And while this time it is *gender* that is authorized over *sex,* the ambiguous references again demonstrate LCSH's predilection for conflating the two concepts. This subject authority record also includes links to the narrower terms (NTs) *Intersex people — Identity* and *Transgender people — Identity* and to the broader term (BT) *Sex (Psychology).* While *Transgender people — Identity* clearly makes sense as an NT in this context because it is a gender-related concept, and perhaps *Intersex people — Identity* could be related by conceptualizing it in the broadest possible sense, the other term, *Sex (Psychology),* which is sexually-based, is not an appropriate linkage.

In 2004, LCSH established the term *Sexual minorities* (sh2004003385) to serve as the collective term for LGBTQ people with the UF *Gender minorities.* The following explanation of the authorized term from the Library of Congress Cataloging and Support Office reinforces how once again they equate *sex* and *gender* by confusing *sexual orientation* with *gender identity*:

> The exisiting heading Sexual minorities is a term that refers collectively to all sexual groups who are not in the majority. Any group that is not the majority is by definition a minority group. So the term Sexual minorities encompasses not only transgender people, but also gay men, lesbians, tranvestites, bisexuals, intersex people, etc. [Paul Weiss, Email communication to Nancy Silverrod shared on the Lezbrian email list, June 13, 2007].

These terms are not equivalent. In fact, resources specifically point out that "'Sexual minority' should not be used as a synonym for, or as inclusive of, 'gender minority'" (Fenway Health, 2010, p. 8). When members of the American Library Association Gay, Lesbian, Bisexual and Transgendered Round Table questioned the appropriateness of the term, the Library of Congress responded that:

> Since the vast majority of the population are not transsexual or transgender, those who are transsexual or trangender are by definition minorities, regardless of whether they happen to be homosexual or heterosexual. Sexual minorities is an appropriate broader term for the headings Transsexuals and Transgender people [Paul Weiss, Email communication to Nancy Silverrod shared on the Gay/Lesbian/Bisexual Librarians Network email list, June 15, 2007].

While the answer addresses the issue of minority status, it does not address the issue of *sexuality* vs. *gender identity,* demonstrating the Library of Congress's lack of understanding in this area. As such, transgender and gender variant people again disappear from the catalog.

Resolving These Issues

Sandy Berman has long circulated petitions to propose and change Library of Congress Subject Headings.[24] With the advent of Web 2.0 applications, such petitions have reached a broader audience in a shorter time frame, enabling such grassroots efforts as the Radical Reference "Library of Congress Subject Heading Suggestion Blog-a-Thon," which invited readers to

> [S]uggest subject headings and/or cross-references which will then be compiled and sent to the Library of Congress. You can either choose one previously suggested by Sandy Berman (pdf or spreadsheet) or propose your own. This is a chance to positively impact the catalog of the de facto national library of the United States, which also impacts cataloging all over the world! [Freedman, 2008, para. 3–4].

Individuals can also propose new subject headings or request changes to existing headings, directly to the Library of Congress, one heading at a time. The Library of Congress

Subject Cooperative Program (SACO) home page provides links to guidelines and forms at http://www.loc.gov/catdir/pcc/saco/saco.html

Additionally, institutions can become members of the SACO program, and after training, submit proposals for LCSH. One such LGBTIQ institution is the Leather Archives & Museum (LA&M), which, as a *bona fide* member of SACO, has submitted dozens of headings concerning leather-related topics over the past decade, most of which have been accepted by the Library of Congress ("LA&M creates new Library of Congress leather subject headings," 2000).

Another method to submit or edit headings is for groups of individuals or libraries who contribute records regarding a particular subject area or region to form a "funnel." One of the existing funnel groups is the African American Subject Funnel Project, whose web page states:

> The funnel project is concentrating on the creation of new subject headings and the changing or updating of old subject headings relating to the African American experience. Through this project participants of the funnel will focus on providing and improving access to African American resources. To date, a variety of headings have been proposed such as: African Americans — Reparations and African American social reformers. Subject changes have also been proposed and accepted which include changing the heading Afro-American to African American [Library of Congress Subject Cooperative Program, 2009a, para. 2].

Establishing a funnel to create and amend LGBTIQ subject headings would be a good way to work with the Library of Congress in addressing the issues brought up in this essay.[25]

Ben Christensen states that having a controlled vocabulary such as LCSH which "reflect[s] current terminology and ideologies is not an end result but an ongoing process that requires constant vigilance on the part of catalogers, other librarians and scholars, and library users" (2008, p. 237). Language is fluid and there is not always a consensus, even within LGBTIQ communities, on appropriate terminology. The Library of Congress has demonstrated its openness to feedback[26] and its willingness to collaborate through the programs outlined above. Working together we can optimize the discovery process for library users, ensuring that they find the information they seek in an efficient and inoffensive manner.

NOTES

1. Portions of this essay appeared in a different form in Greenblatt, E. (1990). Homosexuality: The evolution of a concept in the Library of Congress Subject Headings. In C. Gough & E. Greenblatt (Eds.), *Gay and lesbian library service* (pp. 75–101). Jefferson, NC: McFarland.

2. For more on this topic, see Beall (2008).

3. These terms are composed of the first two-three letters of "lesbian, bisexual, gay" (with the addition of "transgender" for the latter term).

4. These abbreviations stand for "Lesbian, Gay, Bisexual, Transgender, Intersex, and Queer/Questioning," "Gay, Lesbian, Bisexual, and Transgender," and "Lesbian, Gay, Bisexual, Two Spirit, Trans and Gender Non Conforming," and "Lesbian, Gay, Bisexual, Transgender, Intersex, Queer, Questioning, Asexual, and Allies," respectively.

5. Equivalence relationships are designated by the following abbreviations: USE or UF [Used for]"); associative relationships are designated by RT [Related term] or SA [See also]; and hierarchical relationships are designated by BT [Broader term] or NT [Narrower term]. These conventions will be used throughout this essay when discussing syndetic structure.

6. For more information about this topic, please see the essay on "Queer as Folksonomies," also in this section. Another pertinent resource is Adler, M. (2009).

7. As these concepts have a rich and complex history, a essay could easily be devoted to each term.

However, due to limited space, these overviews will of necessity be overly simplistic, designed to give readers a general impression rather than a full understanding. For more detailed information, please refer to the works cited. Additionally, please see the appropriate essays in Section One of this book for further information regarding bisexual, intersex, and transgender concepts.

8. Since he wrote in German, his name is often germanicized to Karl Maria Benkert.

9. I am including the LC subject authority file control numbers (cited in parenthesis after the heading) for each of the subject headings discussed. Also, for the sake of clarity, when discussing particular subject headings, I will capitalize these to distinguish them from discussion of the terms themselves — i.e. *Lesbianism* (the subject heading) vs. *lesbianism* (the concept).

10. See the video clip "Bringing Up Baby: 'Gay All of a Sudden'" on YouTube: http://www.youtube.com/watch?v=_A8U6aUPW48.

11. Armstrong (1989) mentions "the reluctance of the *New York Times* to use the word 'gay,' the word gays vastly prefer, instead of 'homosexual,' until two years ago [1987]." This date slightly precedes LC's shift in usage, for in sh8561795, LC cites, among other sources, the usage of the *New York Times* to justify its selection of "gays" as an authorized heading: NY Times, 5/26/87: sec. 4, p. 6 ("Gay man named to AIDS panel"); NY Times, 5/26/87: sec. 1, p. 31 ("Insurers and gay groups angered by ... ").

12. See the section on "Hermaphroditism, Intersexuality, and DSDs" for more information on this term.

13. MacDowall (2009) dates the initial use of the term "bisexuality" to 1859 when it appeared in Robert Bentley Todd's *Cyclopaedia of Anatomy and Physiology.*

14. I use *trans* as a truncated stem to refer generically to all three concepts: *transgender, transsexuality* (or *transsexualism* as LCSH terms it), *transvestism,* and the related classes of people: *transgender people, transsexuals,* and *transvestites.*

15. The German word Hirschfeld coined was *Transvestitismus.*

16. Feinberg (1996) states that Prince told hir that "I coined the noun *transgenderist* in 1987 or '88" (p. x).

17. For a fascinating discussion of *transgender* as an umbrella term see Davidson (2007).

18. For more information about this concept, please see "LGBTIQ History Starts Here: Indigenous/Native Terminology" also in this section.

19. These last two headings are also problematic as female and male impersonators are not necessarily the same as drag queens or drag kings, but space limitations prohibit further discussion here. A brief mention of this appears in "The LGBT Life Thesaurus Creation Experience" also in this section.

20. See, for example, Hirschfeld (1923).

21. Not all intersex people view *intersex* as an identity. For example, activist Emi Koyama, states "What makes intersex people similar is their experiences of medicalization, not biology. Intersex is not an identity" (Still, 2008, p. xv).

22. According to Reis (2007), of the 50 participants invited to the conference, only two were intersex themselves with no parents of intersex children included.

23. Intersex activist Sophia Seidlberg pronounces the acronym "DSD" as "dissed."

24. In fact, Berman included a petition in the foreword he wrote for *Gay and Lesbian Library Service.*

25. I first proposed such a project at the Gay, Lesbian, Bisexual, and Transgender Archives, Libraries, Museums, and Special Collections conference in 2006.

26. See, for example, "LGBTIQ History Starts Here: Indigenous/Native Terminology," also in this section, which mentions the Library of Congress response to Karen Vigneault's request to remove the linkage between *Two-spirit people* and *Transvestites.*

REFERENCES

Adler, M. (2009). Transcending library catalogs: A comparative study of controlled terms in Library of Congress Subject Headings and user-generated tags in LibraryThing for transgender books. *Journal of Web Librarianship, 3*(4): 309–331.

Alyson Publications. (1989). Homosexual. In *The Alyson Almanac* (p. 94). Boston: Alyson.

Armstrong, D. (1989, June 6). Gays make media inroads: But some criticize slow rate change and lack of sensitive coverage. *San Francisco Examiner.*

Augustyn, F. J. (1993, February 22). Cataloging the 1990s: Sanford Berman's challenge to LC. *Library of Congress Information Bulletin, 52*(4), Retrieved from http://www.loc.gov/loc/lcib/93/9304/berman.html

Beall, J. (2008). The weaknesses of full-text searching. *The Journal of Academic Librarianship, 34*(5), 434–444. doi: 10.1016/j.acalib.2008.06.007

Beemyn, B. (2004). Bisexuality, bisexuals, and bisexual movements. In M. Stein (Ed.), *Encyclopedia of lesbian, gay, bisexual and transgendered history in America* (Vol. 1, pp. 141–145). Detroit: Charles Scribner's Sons.

Beemyn, B. G. (2006). Bisexuality. In *glbtq: An encyclopedia of gay, lesbian, bisexual, transgender, and queer culture*. Retrieved from http://www.glbtq.com/social-sciences/bisex.html

Berman, S. (1981). Gay access. In *The joy of cataloging: Essays, letters, reviews, and other explosions* (pp. 110–112). Phoenix, AZ: Oryx.

Bobotis, A. (2002, Autumn-Winter). Queering knowledge in Flann O'Brien's The third policeman. *Irish University Review: A Journal of Irish Studies, 32*(2), 242–259.

Boswell, H. (1991–1992, Winter). The transgender alternative. *Chrysalis, 1*(2). Retrieved from http://www.ifge.org/Article58.phtml

Bullough, V. L. (1987). A nineteenth-century transsexual. *Archives of Sexual Behavior, 16*(1), 81–84. doi: 10.1007/BF01541843

Callahan, G. N. (2009). *Between XX and XY: Intersexuality and the myth of two sexes.* Chicago: Chicago Review Press.

Cameron, D. (2006, August 2). Re: Variations of Sex Development Instead of Disorders of Sex Development — ADC — eLetters for Hughes, et al., 0 (2006) 200609831. Retrieved from http://adc.bmj.com/cgi/eletters/adc.2006.098319v1#2479

Campbell, G. (2000). Queer theory and the creation of contextual subject access tools for gay and lesbian communities. *Knowledge Organization, 27*(3), 122–131.

Chan, L. M. (2005). *Library of Congress Subject Headings: Principles and application.* (4th ed.). Westport, CT: Libraries Unlimited.

Chen, M. (2004). Lesbian. In J. Eadie (Ed.), *Sexuality: The essential glossary* (pp. 114–116). London: Arnold.

Christensen, B. (2008). Minoritization vs. universalization: Lesbianism and male homosexuality in LCSH and LCC. *Knowledge Organization, 35*(4), 229–238.

Cohen, T. (2004). Gay. In J. Eadie (Ed.), *Sexuality: The essential glossary* (pp. 77–78). London: Arnold.

Cordova, J. (1974). What's in a name? *Lesbian Tide, 3*(10), 21–22.

Davidson, M. (2007). Seeking refuge under the umbrella: Inclusion, exclusion, and organizing within the category "transgender." *Sexuality Research and Social Policy: Journal of NSRC, 4*(4), 60–80. doi: 10.1525/srsp.2007.4.4.60

Davidson, R. J. (2009). DSD debates: Social movement organizations' framing disputes surrounding the term "disorders of sex development." *Liminalis,* 60–80. Retrieved from http://www.liminalis.de/2009_03/Artikel_Essay/Liminalis-2009-Davidson.pdf

de Vries, K. M. (2008). Berdache (Two-spirit). In J. O'Brien (Ed.), *Encyclopedia of gender and society* (pp. 62–65). Los Angeles: Sage.

Diamond, M. (2003). What's in a name? Some terms used in the discussion of sex and gender. *Transgender Tapestry,* (102), 18–21.

Diamond, M. (2009). Human intersexuality: Difference or disorder? *Archives of Sexual Behavior, 38*(2), 172. doi: 10.1007/s10508-008-9438-6

Donoghue, E. (1993). *Passions between women: British lesbian culture, 1668–1801.* London: Scarlet.

Dreger, A. D. (1998). *Hermaphrodites and the medical invention of sex.* Cambridge, MA: Harvard University Press.

Dreger, A. D., & Herndon, A. M. (2009). Progress and politics in the intersex rights movement: Feminist theory in action. *GLQ: A Journal of Lesbian and Gay Studies, 15*(2), 199–224.

Dynes, W. R. (2008). Gay. In *Homolexis glossary.* Retrieved from http://www.williamapercy.com/homolexis/index.php?title=Main_Page#G

Ekins, R., & King, D. (2001, April-June). Pioneers of transgendering: The popular sexology of David O. Cauldwell. *International Journal of Transgenderism, 5*(2). Retrieved from http://www.iiav.nl/ezines/web/IJT/97-03/numbers/symposion/cauldwell_01.htm

Ekins, R., & King, D. (2005). Virginia Prince: Transgender pioneer. *International Journal of Transgenderism, 8*(4), 5–15. doi: 10.1300/J485v08n04_02

Endres, N. (2006). Kertbeny, Károly Mária. In *glbtq: An encyclopedia of gay, lesbian, bisexual, transgender, and queer culture.* Retrieved from http://www.glbtq.com/social-sciences/kertbeny_km.html

Evans, D. (2004). Homosexuality. In J. Eadie (Ed.), *Sexuality: The Essential Glossary* (pp. 94–95). London: Arnold.

Fairyington, S. (2005, July-August). Bisexuality and the case against dualism. *Gay & Lesbian Review, 12*(4), 32–34.

Feder, E. K. (2009). Imperatives of normality: From "intersex" to "disorders of sex development." *GLQ: A Journal of Lesbian and Gay Studies, 15*(2), 225–247. doi: 10.1215/10642684-2008-135

Feder, E. K., & Karkazis, K. (2008). What's in a name? The controversy over "disorders of sex development." *Hastings Center Report, 38*(5), 33–36. doi: 10.1353/hcr.0.0062

Feinberg, L. (1992). *Transgender liberation: A movement whose time has come.* New York: World View Forum.

Feinberg, L. (1996). *Transgender warriors: Making history from Joan of Arc to Dennis Rodman.* Beacon.

Fenway Health. (2010, January). Glossary of gender and transgender terms. Retrieved from http://www.fenwayhealth.org/site/DocServer/Handout_7-C_Glossary_of_Gender_and_Transgender_Terms_fi.pdf?docID=7081

Feray, J., & Herzer, M. (1990). Homosexual studies and politics in the 19th century: Karl Maria Kertbeny. *Journal of Homosexuality, 19*(1), 23–48. doi: 10.1300/J082v19n01_02

Freedman, Jenna. (2008, April 22). Library of Congress subject heading suggestion blog-a-thon. *Radical Reference.* [Blog] Retrieved from http://www.radicalreference.info/lcsh/2008/blog-a-thon

Gilbert, M. M. A. (2000). The transgendered philosopher. *International Journal of Transgenderism, 4*(3). Retrieved from http://www.iiav.nl/ezines/web/IJT/97-03/numbers/symposion/gilbert.htm

Goldschmidt, R. (1917, October). Intersexuality and the endocrine aspect of sex. *Endocrinology, 1*(4), 433–456. doi: 10.1210/endo-1-4-433

Greenblatt, E. (1990). Homosexuality: The evolution of a concept in the Library of Congress Subject Headings. In C. Gough & E. Greenblatt (Eds.), *Gay and lesbian library service* (pp. 75–101). Jefferson, N.C.: McFarland.

Haeberle, E. J. (2003). Homosexuality: Healthy or sick? In *Sexual dysfunctions and their treatment.* Berlin: Magnus Hirschfeld Archive for Sexology. Retrieved from http://www2.hu-berlin.de/sexology/ECE5/homosexuality.html

Harper, D. (2001, November). Bisexuality. *Online etymology dictionary.* Retrieved from http://www.etymonline.com/index.php?term=bisexuality

Heiner-Freiling, M. (2000). Survey on subject heading languages used in national libraries and bibliographies. In A. T. Stone (Ed.), *The LCSH century: One hundred years with the Library of Congress Subject Headings system* (pp. 189–198). New York: Haworth Information.

Herbst, P. H. (2001a). *Wimmin, wimps & wallflowers: An encyclopaedic dictionary of gender and sexual orientation bias in the United States.* Yarmouth, ME: Intercultural.

Hill, D. B. (2005). Sexuality and gender in Hirschfeld's Die Transvestiten: A case of the "elusive evidence of the ordinary." *Journal of the History of Sexuality, 14*(3), 316–332.

Hines, S. (2004). Transvestite. In J. Eadie (Ed.), *Sexuality: The essential glossary* (pp. 234–235). London: Arnold.

Hinkle, C. E. (n.d.). Why is OII not using the term DSD or "disorders of sex development"? Retrieved from http://www.intersexualite.org/Response_to_Intersex_Initiative.html

Hirschfeld, M. (1910). *Die Transvestiten: Eine Untersuchung über den erotischen Verkleidungstrieb.* Berlin: Pulvermacher.

Hirschfeld, M. (1923). Die intersexuelle Konstitution. *Jahrbuch für sexuelle Zwischenstufen, 23*, 3–27.

Hirschfeld, M. (1991). *Transvestites: The erotic drive to cross-dress.* Buffalo, NY: Prometheus.

Jagose, A. (1996). *Queer theory: An introduction.* Melbourne: Melbourne University Press.

King, D. (1995). Gender blending: Medical perspectives and technology. In R. Ekins & D. King (Eds.), *Blending genders: Social aspects of cross-dressing and sex changing* (pp. 79–98). Routledge.

Koyama, E. (2008, June 29). Intersex Initiative: DSD controversy FAQ. Retrieved from http://www.intersexinitiative.org/articles/dsdfaq.html

"LA&M creates new Library of Congress leather subject headings." (2000, Summer). *Leather Archives & Museum Newsletter,* (12), 1, 8.

Library of Congress. (2009, August 11). *Thesauri & controlled vocabularies.* Retrieved from http://www.loc.gov/library/libarch-thesauri.html

Library of Congress Acquisitions and Bibliographic Access Directorate. (1987). Library of Congress Subject Headings weekly list 37.

Library of Congress Acquisitions and Bibliographic Access Directorate. (2006a, April 19). Library of Congress Subject Headings weekly list 16. Retrieved from http://www.loc.gov/catdir/cpso/wls06/awls0616.html

Library of Congress Acquisitions and Bibliographic Access Directorate. (2006b, April 26). Library of Congress Subject Headings weekly list 17. Retrieved from http://www.loc.gov/catdir/cpso/wls06/awls0617.html

Library of Congress Acquisitions and Bibliographic Access Directorate. (2007a, October 24). Library of

Congress Subject Headings weekly list 47. Retrieved from http://www.loc.gov/catdir/cpso/wls07/awls0743.html

Library of Congress Acquisitions and Bibliographic Access Directorate. (2007b, November 21). Library of Congress Subject Headings weekly list 47. Retrieved from http://www.loc.gov/catdir/cpso/wls07/awls0747.html

Library of Congress Acquisitions and Bibliographic Access Directorate. (2009a, April 22). Library of Congress Subject Headings weekly list 16. Retrieved from http://www.loc.gov/cgi-bin/gourl?URL=%2Fcatdir%2Fcpso%2Fwls09%2Fawls0916.html

Library of Congress Acquisitions and Bibliographic Access Directorate. (2009b, October 21). Library of Congress Subject Headings weekly list 42. Retrieved from http://www.loc.gov/catdir/cpso/wls09/awls0942.html

Library of Congress Program for Cooperative Cataloging. (2009, April 17). *About the SACO Program.* Retrieved from http://www.loc.gov/catdir/pcc/saco/sacopara.html

Library of Congress Subject Cooperative Program. (2009a, November 23). African American Subject Funnel Project. Retrieved from http://www.loc.gov/catdir/pcc/saco/aframerfun.html

Library of Congress Subject Cooperative Program. (2009b, November 23). SACO funnel FAQ. Retrieved from http://www.loc.gov/catdir/pcc/saco/funnelfaq.html

Library of Congress Subject Cooperative Program. (2009c, November 23). PCC SACO funnel projects. Retrieved from http://www.loc.gov/catdir/pcc/saco/funnelsaco.html

Library of Congress Subject Cooperative Program. (2009d, December 10). Subject Cooperative Program (SACO), Library of Congress. Retrieved from http://www.loc.gov/catdir/pcc/saco/

Lovaas, K. (2004). Cross-dressing. In J. Eadie (Ed.), *Sexuality: The essential glossary* (pp. 43–44). London: Arnold.

MacDowall, L. (2009). Historicising contemporary bisexuality. *Journal of Bisexuality, 9*(1), 3–15. doi: 10.1080/15299710802659989

Meyerowitz, J. (2002). *How sex changed: A history of transsexuality in the United States.* Cambridge, MA: Harvard University Press.

National Lesbian and Gay Journalists Association. (2008). Stylebook supplement on LGBT terminology. Retrieved from http://www.nlgja.org/resources/stylebook_english.html

Olson, H. A. (1996). *Between control and chaos: An ethical perspective on authority control.* Presented at Authority Control in the 21st Century, OCLC, Dublin, Ohio. Retrieved from http://www.worldcat.org/arcviewer/1/OCC/2003/06/20/0000003520/viewer/file97.html#1

Olson, H. A. (2000). Difference, culture and change: The untapped potential of LCSH. *Cataloging & classification quarterly, 29*(1), 53–71. doi: 10.1300/J104v29n01_04

Ovid. (2000). Book IV, 346–388: Salmacis and Hermaphroditus merge. In A. S. Kline (Tran.), *Metamorphoses.* University of Virginia E-Text Center. Retrieved from http://etext.virginia.edu/latin/ovid/trans/Metamorph4.htm#478205198

Oxford University Press. (2000). *OED online.* Oxford, England: Oxford University Press.

Prince, V. (2005). The "transcendents" or "trans" people. *International Journal of Transgenderism, 8*(4), 39–46. [Reprint of original article appearing in *Transvestia, 16*(95), 1978] doi: 10.1300/J485v08n04_07

Reis, E. (2005). Impossible hermaphrodites: Intersex in America, 1620–1960. *Journal of American History, 92*(2), 411–441.

Reis, E. (2007). Divergence or disorder? The politics of naming intersex. *Perspectives in Biology and Medicine, 50*(4), 535–543. doi: 10.1353/pbm.2007.0054

Rich, A. (1996). Compulsory heterosexuality and lesbian existence. In M. Eagleton (Ed.), *Feminist literary theory* (pp. 24–29). Oxford, England; Cambridge, MA: Wiley-Blackwell.

Roberto, K. R. (2009). Bodies in the library catalog: Subject analysis for non-normative sexualities and bodies. Unpublished manuscript.

Russo, V. (1987). *The celluloid closet: Homosexuality in the movies* (Revised ed.). New York: Harper & Row.

Safire, W. (2005, November 6). Homolexicology. *New York Times.* Retrieved from http://www.nytimes.com/2005/11/06/magazine/06safire.html

Sell, R. L. (1997). Defining and measuring sexual orientation: A review. *Archives of Sexual Behavior, 26*(6), 643–658. doi: 10.1023/A:1024528427013

Siedlberg, S. (n.d.). Disorder sex, sex disorder, dissed? Retrieved from http://www.intersexualite.org/English_OII/IAIA/Sophie/Dissed.html

Still, B. (2008). *Online intersex communities: Virtual neighborhoods of support and activism.* Amherst, NY: Cambria.

Storr, M. (Ed.). (2002). *Bisexuality: A critical reader.* London: Routledge.

Stryker, S. (2005). Transgender. In *glbtq: An encyclopedia of gay, lesbian, bisexual, transgender, and queer culture*. Retrieved from http://www.glbtq.com/social-sciences/transgender.html

Stryker, S. (2008). *Transgender history*. Berkeley, CA: Seal.

Valentine, D. (2007). *Imagining transgender: An ethnography of a category*. Durham, NC: Duke University Press.

Vilain, E., Achermann, J. C., Eugster, E. A., Harley, V. R., Morel, Y., Wilson, J. D., & Hiort, O. (2007). We used to call them hermaphrodites. *Genetics in Medicine, 9*(2), 65–66. doi: 10.1097/GIM. 0b013e31802cffcf

Wiggins, B. (1998). The Program for Cooperative Cataloging. Retrieved from http://research.calacademy. org/research/informatics/taf/proceedings/wiggins.html

Zaretsky, E. (1997). Bisexuality, capitalism and the ambivalent legacy of psychoanalysis. *New Left Review*, (223), 69–89.

Queer as Folksonomies

Analisa Ornelas

Introduction

For the past few years, the Internet and information science community has been engaged in a lively and largely online debate regarding the benefits and flaws of social book-marking and tagging, popularly defined as folksonomies. Jessica Dye (2006) assesses the situation as such, "Whether they succeed in overthrowing the controlled vocabulary hierarchy and setting up a free-for-all folksonomy in its place remains to be seen, but experts agree — now that 'every man' has power over the language of classification, searching will never be the same" (p. 38).

In the 1990 groundbreaking publication, *Gay and Lesbian Library Service*, Ellen Greenblatt challenged the Library of Congress regarding the subject headings for lesbian and gay books and materials. She declared, "Until LC departs from its ethnocentric, heterosexist, WASPish, and middle class approach ... subject headings will never provide adequate access to the rich cultural diversity of information concerning groups outside mainstream American culture" (p. 96). Twenty years later, the amount of "rich cultural diversity of information" has mushroomed to unknowable proportions on the Internet — a resource not beholden to a specific taxonomy. With this knowledge, LGBTIQ tags used on Delicious, Flickr and LibraryThing were surveyed for the current essay.

What Are Folksonomies?

In "Tag — You're It," Mary Ellen Bates succinctly describes folksonomies as "taxonomies built by just plain folks" (2006, p. 64). In *Library 2.0 and Beyond*, Ellyssa Kroski writes that folksonomies are "created from the aggregate of user-created tags within a website and therefore provides an inclusive categorization scheme reflective of the collective intelligence" (2007, p. 94).

Another feature associated with folksonomies is the tag cloud. Tag clouds are graphic representations of the nature of the metadata that tagging has created. For example, Flickr maintains a tag cloud of the most used tags. As of October 4, 2009, "wedding" and "party" were the tags used most often on Flickr and therefore appear in the largest point size.

Folksonomies: Friend or Foe?

The issue of folksonomies has been debated with vigor, with the lion's share occurring in online articles, lengthy blog entries and the trading of blog comments. Social tagging has a strong and vocal contingent of supporters. In a blog posting entitled, "The hive mind: Folksonomies and user-based tagging," Ellyssa Kroksi (2005) declares that with folksonomies users have the power to tag according to their own cataloging and that "Metadata is now in the realm of the Everyman" (para. 1). Echoing Kroksi's sentiments, David Weinberger, a Berkman Center for Internet and Society fellow at Harvard Law School, praises the flexibility (to access information how the user desires) and sociability (accessing information that other users have discovered) of tagging.

One of the most vocal supporters of folksonomies, Clay Shirky boldly suggests in "Ontology is overrated: categories, links and tags," that social tagging and the arising folksonomies, not traditional, hierarchical classifications serve best to organize the large body of resources available on the Internet. He also contends "much of the appeal of [traditional] categorization comes from this sort of voodoo, where people doing the categorizing believe, even if only unconsciously that naming the world changes it. Unfortunately, most of the world is not actually amenable to voodoo categorization" (Shirky, 2006, para. 62).

The concept of folksonomies has its skeptics. Entitling his blog posting, "Clay Shirky's viewpoints are overrated," Peter Merholz (2005) criticizes Shirky's ideas, "Has he ever talked to a cataloguer? This statement suggests not. He sets up cataloguers as some faceless elite trying to enforce their will on the world" (para. 18). Based largely on the absence of authority control, in a posting on Educause Connect, Stuart Yeates (2006), of Oxford University, asks, "Where's the fight-back from formal classificationists?" He describes tagging as, "the assigning of arbitrary tags to content by amateurs (typically content creators, editors or readers) and folksonomies are systems built from the ground up using these tags" (para. 2).

Also participating in this discourse are those whose beliefs lie somewhere in between. Hammond, Hannay, Lund and Scott surmise that "Despite all the current hype about tags ... tags are just one kind of metadata and are not a replacement for formal classification systems ... Rather, they are a supplemental means to organize information and order search results" (2005, para. 24). One of the more measured voices in the folksonomy/taxonomy debate, Laura Gordon-Murnae (2006) concludes, "Think of it this way: Combine the Library of Congress Subject Headings or the Dewey Decimal System with tagging and you could create both a hierarchical structure and a flat taxonomy search engines could use to give you a really rich user experience. Now how cool would that be?" (p. 38). Vera Fessler (2007) echoes this in her discussion of the future of technical services. She puts forth the idea that "users themselves are entering into the indexing arena via 'tagging'— an area (a 'folksonomy') where user-provided tags, i.e., subject assignments, might also be an enhancement to library-created catalogs and databases" (p. 142).

Folksonomies in Libraries

In the context of libraries, the question of tagging and folksonomies is included in discussions of Library 2.0— the incorporation of technologies such as blogs, wikis and podcasts into library services. In her 2006 article, "The use of folksonomies in public library catalogues," Louise Spiteri noted that "there has been little examination of folksonomies within Library and Information Science (LIS)" (p. 84). Since then, the conversation has surfaced quite a bit in the LIS community. The American Society for Information Science and Technology devoted a special section of their *Bulletin* to the subject of tagging and folksonomies.

Peter J. Rolla (2009) highlights findings of the Library of Congress Working Group on the Future of Bibliographic Control who concluded that "allowing user-supplied data in online catalogs will make the catalogs more relevant to users ... [and] will improve access to the materials in library collections" (p. 175). Indeed, the current sentiment expressed in library journals brims with optimism and regards user-created metadata as an opportunity to create more efficient systems for information retrieval. In fact, Tim Spalding of LibraryThing was named a 2008 Mover & Shaker by *Library Journal*. Karen Schneider (2008) wrote the following in support of Spalding, "Tim has ported the fun of reading to the web and in doing so honors the best of our profession and suggests a path for its future" (p. 20).

Library 2.0 guru Meredith Farkas (2007), while skeptical of the overall value of folksonomies, does believe that "It isn't always easy to know what a book is about by looking at records in most library catalogs. Tagging the catalog is one way library users could offer feedback on the 'aboutness' of materials" (p. 140).

Research on LGBTIQ Tagging

Why do the folksonomies applied to LGBTIQ content matter? The answer lies in Ellen Greenblatt's (1990) comment about the treatment of the "concept of homosexuality" directed to the Library of Congress, "The Library of Congress must realize that the power to name generates the power to control" (p. 96). With this in mind, tagging and folksonomies seem tailor-made for usage by the LGBTIQ community. As described in *Library Technology Reports,* "they don't privilege one hierarchy or worldview over another" (Anonymous, p. 49). Therefore, studying how social tagging treats LGBTIQ issues and resources appears a prudent exercise.

In order to examine how LGBTIQ terms are being used in creating folksonomies, the author conducted an informal survey by selecting words of significance to the LGBTIQ community to use as search terms. The tag-terms used were: lesbian, gay, transgender, queer, bisexual, lgbt/glbt, homosexual, intersex, and transsexual. The author searched the tags of popular web sites that utilize social software: Delicious, Flickr, and LibraryThing. After each query, the author examined the URLs, photos, blogs, and books indexed with these terms to assess the tag-term's relevance.

Delicious

Owned by Yahoo!, Delicious is a social bookmarking web site where users can save URLs that are tagged for retrieval and discovery by other users. For the most part, the first ten URLs retrieved on Delicious for the LGBTIQ terms searched were appropriately tagged. Of URLs retrieved for *lesbian,* all were from the LGBTIQ community such as the magazines *Curve* and *The Advocate* and the "Dykes to Watch Out For" web site. The retrieved URLs tagged with *gay* consisted of two pornography web sites and suitably tagged URLs such as the Human Rights Campaign web site, Queerty, and an article entitled "The Science of

Gaydar" in *New York* magazine. A search on *transgender* yielded all relevant URLs from the top ten. The URLs ranged from a story on NPR, "Two Families Grapple with Sons' Gender Preferences," to the web site for The Transgender Law and Policy Institute to a transgender comic entitled "Venus Envy." For *queer,* the URLs tagged were relevant and included glbtq.com, queertheory.com and 365gay.com. The URLs tagged with *bisexual* were relevant and included three web sites specifically for the bisexual community and remaining URLs were targeted to the LGBTIQ community in general. Almost twice as many URLs were tagged with *lgbt* as with *glbt* and each search retrieved a different set of appropriate URLs.

The term *homosexual* retrieved a pornography web site, a blog with a disparaging video entitled, "one never knows when a homosexual is about," the web site for National Association of Research and Therapy of Homosexuality, the Prime Minister of England's official statement about the treatment of Alan Turing, and a web site, religioustolerance.org. Of the 148 URLs tagged with *intersex,* the first ten were germane and included the web sites of the Intersex Society of North America and that of an intersex activist, Emi Koyama. The search on *transsexual* also yielded relevant URLs from the first ten retrieved excepting two. Four URLs linked to porn web sites. The appropriately tagged URLs included the "Venus Envy" comic strip, and an article on the BBC web site titled "Transsexual gene link identified."

Flickr

On Flickr photographs are uploaded and tagged by the contributors. When searching on the tag *lesbian,* the first ten retrieved photographs seemed to originate from inside the LGBTIQ community. They ranged from a photograph of the cover of Elana Dykewomon's most recent book to a mocked-up image of Michelle Obama at the 2009 NYC Pride celebration.

The photographs recalled with *gay* as a tag were an assortment of photographs documenting the Tampa International Gay and Lesbian Film Festival, a self-portrait of a man in celebration of National Coming Out Day, and those that after investigation appeared to be posted by someone in the LGBTIQ community. The search executed on *transgender* retrieved mostly self-portraits. Many of the photographs were uploaded by the user MiraDee and were tagged with *tgirl, tranny,* and *crossdresser.* Her profile states that MiraDee also belongs to the Flickr group "TransSisters."

For the term *queer,* the first ten could be deemed appropriately tagged by a member of the LGBTIQ community. Most of the first ten photographs for the tag *bisexual* were from an Albuquerque Pride celebration with one photograph of the androgynous German band Cinema Bizarre. Searching for photos that were tagged *lgbt* resulted in five photograph mashups with a decidedly queer-bent from bobster855, a self-described "caucasian queer" (n.d. para.1).

In addition, there were photographs posted by the Metro DC GLBT Community Center. The *glbt* tag retrieved photographs again from an Albuquerque Pride celebration. Of the first ten photographs tagged *intersex,* most were from "real life" and "Second Life" posted by Luminis Kanto whose Flickr profile reads "I was born intersexed in RL, and find genderexpression in SL to be endlessly fascinating" (n.d. para. 1). All of the first ten photographs retrieved with a tag of *homosexual* were photographs from the Chicago rally held in conjunction with the National Equality March on October 11, 2009.

LibraryThing

LibraryThing is a web site that allows users to create a catalog of sorts for their personal book collection by tagging the books with keywords that can be used for retrieval and aggregation. In the LibraryThing database, the first twenty books most often tagged *lesbian* were appropriately done so and included *Oranges Are Not the Only Fruit, Rubyfruit Jungle* and *Tipping the Velvet.* The term *gay* was applied 29,478 times and the titles most often tagged included *Giovanni's Room, Me Talk Pretty One Day* and books by Armistead Maupin. In searching for those books tagged with *transgender*, 5,739 titles were retrieved. The titles highlighted as being most often tagged with this term included the teen novel, *Luna,* as well as well-known authors in the arena such as Leslie Feinberg and Kate Bornstein. *Queer* was applied 12,638 times and the first twenty results included books by authors well regarded in the LGBTIQ community such as Sarah Waters, Alison Bechdel, and Jeffrey Eugenides. LibraryThing taggers used the tag *bisexual* 1,008 times and included books such as *Vice Versa, Invisible Life* and *Dual Attraction: Understanding Bisexuality.*

Previously merged, the acronyms *lgbt* and *glbt* are separate tags that yield different results in the LibraryThing database. The tag *glbt* was applied 14,256 times and the tag *lgbt* was used 8,485 times. The works of Alison Bechdel and Jeanette Winterson were in both lists of those most often tagged with either of these two terms. Of the 181 titles tagged with *intersex,* the first twenty included the novels *Middlesex* and *The Left Hand of Darkness* and non-fiction titles concerning the study of gender as expected. Titles in the LibraryThing catalog were tagged with *homosexuality* (and its aliases) 9,129 times and the twenty most often tagged included *Celluloid Closet, The Amazing Adventures of Kavalier and Clay,* and *Christianity, Social Tolerance and Homosexuality. Transsexual* occurred as a tag for 606 titles. The twenty titles most tagged appeared apt and included fiction, such as *Trans-Sister Radio,* and non-fiction titles, such as *She's Not There: A Life in Two Genders.*

I Tag, Therefore I Am

"The tagging movement says, in effect, we're not going to wait for the experts to deliver a taxonomy from on high. We're just going to build one ourselves. It will be messy inelegant and inefficient, but it will be Good Enough [*sic*]. And, most important, it will be *ours* [*sic*], reflecting our needs and our ways of thinking" (Weinberger, 2005, p. [1]). In examining the research results of LGBTIQ tagging, this has shown to be quite true. With gusto, the LGBTIQ community has been providing access and meaning to the resources on the Internet — both personal and otherwise. On Flickr, the LGBTIQ presence is well documented.

For example, in the tag cloud for a user named gretchl2000, one finds a powerful example of a lesbian naming herself and her community. The words *lesbian, dyke, butch, boifriend, lgbt,* and *femme* leap from the cloud defining, labeling and controlling the meaning of her photographs.

In studying the recall for *transgender* and *transsexual,* one can surmise again that those from the LGBTIQ community have performed the tagging. The Gay, Lesbian & Straight Education Network (GLSEN) defines transgender as those "who transgress social gender norms; often used as an umbrella term to include transsexual, genderqueer, gender non-conforming or cross-dressers" (GLSEN, 2004, p. 7). The statistical differences between the retrievals for each term exhibit this concept. For example on Delicious, the number of web sites tagged with *transgender* was 6,589 and for *transsexual* 1,299 were retrieved. Clearly, with a difference of five times, *transgender* is being used as an umbrella term. The tagging on Flickr echoes this result retrieving nine times the number for *transgender* than *transsexual*.

The tagging studied also reflects the contemporary usage of words such as *homosexual* by the LGBTIQ community. Greenblatt (2005) explains, "The term 'homosexual' has long been thought too clinical by gays and lesbians themselves, although it continues to appear in publications by non-gay and lesbian writers" (p. 87). Certainly, the web sites Delicious retrieved with the tag *homosexual* mirror that preference. As well, Shirky (in his argument against controlled vocabularies and in support of free tagging) imagines a cataloguer's response to folksonomies not collapsing the terms *gay/queer/homosexual*, "Oh, the people talking about 'queer politics' and the people talking about 'the homosexual agenda,' they're really talking about the same thing.' Oh no they're not" (n.d., para. 69). Indeed. Most of the uses of the tag *homosexual* resonated with either the pejorative, like the blog that allowed comments such as "kill all fags," or the ignorance of an outsider, such as the well-meaning preacher's blog who welcomed "homosexuals" at his church. Another clue to who is using *homosexual* as a tag can be found in the co-occuring tags. As an example, on Delicious the URL for Exodus International, the infamous Christian organization whose "*ministry*" is to convert gays, was tagged with *homosexual, homosexuality, christian, ministry,* and *religion*. It can be surmised that the LGBTIQ community did not apply these tags. Those LGBTIQ web sites that included the word *homosexual* and therefore tagged accordingly, brimmed with tongue-in-cheek irony in their usage.

In addition to Shirky, other folksonomists have been tackling the issues particular to the LGBTIQ community. In 2005, an interesting conversation on LibraryThing ensued about the treatment of *lgbt* and *glbt* tags on their blog. The original posting announced, "this is a *perfect* example of seeming synonyms having a very different nuance as tags" (LibraryThing, 18 December 2005, para. 2). The comments to the blog included musing that lesbians use LGBT and all others GLBT, to those who admitted to using the two terms interchangeably and a healthy discussion about whether it truly mattered to keep them separate. For a time, LibraryThing decided to merge the *lgbt* and *glbt* tags and titles tagged with either were retrieved. Eventually, at least at the time of the author's search in 2009, the tags again had been separated.

In another example from LibraryThing, Abby Blachly (2006), LibraryThing Librarian, commented on the limitations of LCSH:

> Take Armistead Maupin's Tales of the City, for example. The top tags include queer and gay fiction, whereas the subject headings are City and town life Fiction, Humorous stories and San Francisco (Calif.) Fiction. Someone looking for Tales of the City is unlikely to start their search under City and town life Fiction (San Francisco, however, might prove a good access point, which is also highlighted in the tags) [para. 3].

Uncannily, this post could have been written by Sanford Berman. In fact, a blogger has questioned, "Could Berman be the original freetagger?" (Wright, 2005, para. 7).

The survey of LGBTIQ folksonomies also illuminates the way in which the LGBTIQ items are tagged — without hierarchy and including multiplicity of communities. For example, the LibraryThing tag cloud that represents those tags used in conjunction with *transgender* include the terms *gay, trans, lesbian, gender,* and *glbt*. The tag cloud for *queer* indicates that often those books tagged *queer* were also tagged with *lesbian, gay, feminism,* and *trans.* From the research, it appears as if those tagging LGBTIQ resources, with an understanding of the fluidity of identity specific to this community, apply multiple tags to provide multiple points of access.

Exploring the use of LGBTIQ terms as tags exposes the familiar specters of prejudice, bias, and hate. True, most of the resources tagged with one of the LGBTIQ terms were appropriate — yet enough were done with a derogatory subtext to make one pause. Liz Lawley (2005) comments on this in a posting to *Many 2 Many,* a social software blog, "Unfortunately, too many of the paeans to tagging that I've read have completely ignored some of the key social and cultural issues associated with public and collaborative labeling of content, opting instead for a level of technology-driven optimism that I see as overly naïve" (para. 3). Indeed. On Flickr if you search on the text rather than the creator-created and controlled tags, you will retrieve different results for the LGBTIQ search terms. Many of the results link to pornography web sites. These results seem to confirm the notion that queer people are perverse and morally suspect.

Questioning the absence of authority control in social classification, Melanie Feinberg (2006) states:

> instead of being without bias, [the hive mind] as described by Kroski (2005), let all biases thrive simultaneously ... resources indexed with "feminism" in del.icio.us [*sic*] include an article on how feminized education short changes boys and one how "feminism has destroyed the real men." As a feminist, this is not what I expect, or want [*sic*], to see when I use this term, but I can't limit my search to exclude those semantics that I don't care about or don't agree with [p. 6].

Feinberg's reaction to her search on *feminism* is understandable, but even systems with authority in place, such as the Library of Congress Subject Headings (LCSH), leave room for prejudice and bias.

LibraryThing in Libraries

Whether under duress or with exuberance, overall the library community has embraced utilizing user-generated metadata such as tagging for catalog enhancement. As of September 2009, 1,512 libraries are incorporating LibraryThing metadata into their catalogs. In an article about its implementation at the Libraries of the Claremont Colleges, the authors reported that they received enthusiastic responses from users about their improved research experience (Westcott, Chappell, & Lebel, 2009). Studying bibliographic records in two libraries enhanced by LibraryThing for Libraries (LTFL) demonstrates the possible impact on LGBTIQ access and academics.

For example, using LibraryThing tags as a discovery tool in the catalog of the Libraries of the Claremont Colleges could produce illuminating results for a young scholar interested in LGBTIQ literature. Most academics are aware of Oscar Wilde's sexual orientation and would not be surprised to find the tag *gay* listed under *LibraryThing Tags* in the bibliographic record for *De Profundis.* However, if a user clicks on the tag *gay* to find other items in the catalog tagged as such, *Leaves of Grass* is one of the titles retrieved. For some young scholars, it could be a quite a discovery to find a Walt Whitman book in the list. This discovery — a link between the American poet of the people Whitman and the British aesthete and dandy Wilde could lead to fascinating LGBTIQ scholarship.

If a user looked at the bibliographic record for *Genêt: A Biography of Janet Flanner* in the Seattle Public Library catalog without LibraryThing tags, Flanner's part in the vibrant Left Bank lesbian culture in the years between the wars would not be revealed. The subject headings assigned to this book are: Women authors, American — 20th century — Biography, Americans — France — Paris — History — 20th century, Paris (France) — Intellectual life — 20th century. When looking at this bibliographic record with LibraryThing tags, a patron would see *lesbian* included in the list of tags associated with this title. The LibraryThing metadata unveils a more complete description of what content might be found in the biography.

The case can be made that the subject headings can certainly do justice to Flanner — the heading Lesbian — Biography could easily be applied to the bibliographic record. In fact, the Library of Congress bibliographic record for another biographical work about Flanner, *Janet, My Mother, and Me: A Memoir of Growing up with Janet Flanner and Natalia Danesi Murray*, does include the LCSH Lesbians — United States — Biography. That being stated, even the most devoted catalogers, burdened by their current cataloging responsibilities, would find it difficult to retroactively catalog titles that when originally cataloged suffered from the woefully inadequate, or worse absent, LGBTIQ subject headings. In the case of *Genêt*, a critical facet of the work's "aboutness" — the life of a lesbian writer — was utterly missed or dismissed. User-created metadata such as tagging can address this void in description and access.

These LTFL-enhanced bibliographic records not only illustrate the enhanced access that tags deliver, but also their ability to free LGBTIQ content from the margins. Whether folksonomies have an inherent nature that is either friendly or particularly supportive of LGBTIQ indexing, one cannot state with certainty. Yet, one can surmise that folksonomies allow LGBTIQ communities to name themselves and apply meaning to significant resources by providing access using their own language.

Conclusion

Technology will continue to propel libraries, librarians and society's ideas about information retrieval into uncharted territories. Librarians and information professionals must involve themselves in the discussions of information science technology, even in their most nascent stages. Folksonomy, as others have voiced, does have its weaknesses and provides latitude for a tyranny of the "hive mind," but it also provides the flexibility for users to employ their own language — perhaps a more authentic language. For example, the Library of Congress created *sexual minorities* as a subject heading to approximate the inclusive nature of LGBTIQ. Unfortunately, this clinical terminology "does not truly address the gender-based concerns of transgender and gender-variant people" (Greenblatt, 2005, p. 85). Not surprisingly, *sexual minorities* did not appear as a related tag in any of the searches conducted in the test web sites.

In her article "How Libraries Can Employ Metadata," Sheila Intner makes the case that in order to serve patrons better, libraries "must strike new balances between uniformity and flexibility. While uniformity fosters wide interchangeability — something we have prized highly, and rightfully so — it strictly limits individuality" (2003, p. 84). I believe that integrating tagging capabilities into library catalogs would provide the best of both worlds — the individuality and flexibility inherent in folksonomies and the uniformity of controlled vocabularies. For instance, a student researching LGBTIQ issues could tag books and other materials in a library catalog with *lgbtq, glbt, queer, lgbtstgnc,*[1] etc., which would facilitate access to these resources more so than the non-intuitive LCSH *sexual minorities.*

In the early conversations about tagging and library catalogs, skeptics concluded that "Folksonomists are confusing cataloging structure with personal opinions" (Peterson, 2006, para. 19). Now these same skeptics concede that there is value added when including user-created metadata to catalogs. Two years later, Peterson (2008) writes "In sum, library subject cataloging is based on established rules and principles. It is restrictive rather than inclusive because choices are made by an information specialist who assigns a limited number of relevant subject headings ... In contrast to subject cataloging, folksonomy is a reflection of personal preference" (p. 1). Although to the mainstream library community this may appear to be promising, those considering the ramifications of catalogs and user-created metadata to the LGBTIQ community might find the word choice of "preference" eerily familiar. Our community has memory of being told we were not "born that way" that we merely had a "preference" (possibly a wrong one) — not an inherent orientation.

In "Burning Down the Shelf: Standardized Classification, Folksonomies, and Ontological Politics," Andrew Lau (2008) acknowledges the difference between "opinion" and "identity" when he writes:

> Shirky presents the example of the political connotations of categorizing information relating to same-sex attraction as "queer" as opposed to other similar terms such as "gay" or "homosexual." Each conveys an experience and a history and has been used in a variety in [*sic*] contexts (i.e., "queer" is often used in more politicized, sexual identity-affirmative contexts, while "homosexual" is often used in more neutral or in de- politicized contexts and/or used pejoratively) [p. 6].

When considering the LGBTIQ community, the profound worth of user-created metadata cannot be trivialized as mere opinion or preference.

In studying LGBTIQ tagging, the research has revealed that perhaps LGBTIQ people are natural taggers. A community that embraced the declaration of feminist and gender theorist Monique Wittig that "Lesbian are not woman" [*sic*] (1992, p. 32) has a long history teasing out the complexities inherent in the relationship between words and the entities they purport to represent. Without question, as people who have had to supersede semantics to survive and thrive, queer folks tag with an eye to inclusiveness and sensitivity to the power that words hold.

NOTES

1. The acronym "lgbtstgnc" stands for lesbian, gay, bisexual, two spirit, transgender, and gender-nonconforming people.

REFERENCES

Anonymous. (2005). Current issues and developments related to metadata. *Library Technology Reports*, *41*(6), 45–57.

Bates, M.E. (2006). Tag — you're it [Electronic version]. *Online, 30*(1), 64.

Blachy, A. (2006, May 14). Tagging meets subject headings. Message posted to http://www.librarything.com/thingology/2006/05/tagging-meets-subject-headings.php

Bobster855 (n.d.) About bobster855 / Bob Bobster. Retrieved from http://www.flickr.com/people/32912172@N00/

Dye, J. (2006). Folksonomy: A game of high-tech (and high-stakes) tag: Should a robot dictate the terms of your search? In an age when whole lives are lived online — via blogs, picture albums, dating, shopping lists — digital content users are not only creating their content, they're building their own infrastructure for making it easier to find [Electronic version]. *EContent, 29*(3), 38–43.

Farkas, M. (2007). *Social software in libraries.* Medford, NJ: Information Today.

Feinberg, M. (2006, November 4). *An examination of authority in social classification schemes.* Paper presented at the 17th SIG/CR Classification Research Workshop, Austin, TX. Retrieved from http://dlist.sir.ari zona.edu/1783/

Fessler, V. (2007). The future of technical services (It's not the technical services it was) [Electronic version]. *Library Administration and Management, 21*(3), 139–144.

Gay, Lesbian & Straight Education Network (2004). GLSEN jump-start #8: Where's the "T" in GSA? Making your student club trans inclusive. Retrieved from http://www.glsen.org/binary-data/GLSEN_ ATTACHMENTS/file/414-1.pdf

Gordon-Murnae, L. (2006). Social bookmarking, folksonomies, and Web 2.0 tools: How do we find information that can help us do our jobs, pursue our interests and hobbies, or answer any other needs we may have? How do we keep track of information that we have already found, vetted, and deemed useful? [Electronic version]. *Searcher, 14*(6), p. 26–38.

Greenblatt, E. (1990). Homosexuality: The evolution of a concept in the Library of Congress Subject Headings. In C. Gough & E. Greenblatt (Eds.), *Gay and lesbian library service* (pp. 75–101). Jefferson, NC: McFarland.

Greenblatt, E. (2005). Exploring LGBTQ Online Resources [Electronic version]. *Journal of Library Administration, 43*(3/4), 85–101.

Hammond, T., Hannay, T., Lund, B. & Scott, J. (2005). Social bookmarking tools (I): A general review. *D-Lib Magazine, (11)*4. Retrieved from http://www.dlib.org//dlib/april05/hammond/04hammond. html

Intner, S.S. (2003). How libraries can employ metadata. *Cataloging & Classification Quarterly, 35*(3/4), 71–86.

Kroski, E. (2005, December 7). The hive mind: Folksonomies and user-based tagging. Message posted to http://infotangle.blogsome.com/2005/12/07/the-hive-mind-folksonomies-and-user-based-tag ging/

Kroski, E. (2007). Folksonomies and user-based tagging. *Library 2.0 and beyond: Innovative technologies and tomorrow's user.* Westport, CT: Libraries Unlimited, p. 91–103.

Lau, A. J. (2008). Burning down the shelf: Standardized classification, folksonomies, and ontological politics. *InterActions: UCLA Journal of Education and Information Studies, 4*(1). Retrieved from http://escholarship.org/uc/item/74p477pz

Lawley, L. (2005, January 20). Social consequences of social tagging. Message posted to http://many. corante.com/archives/2005/01/20/social_consequences_of_social_tagging.php

Libraries of the Claremont Colleges. (n.d.) Leaves of grass. Retrieved from http://blais.claremont.edu/ record=b3090830~S0

Libraries of the Claremont Colleges. (n.d.) De profundis. Retrieved from http://blais.claremont.edu/ record=b2417365~S0

Library Journal (2008, March 15) Metadata man: Tim Spalding, LibraryThing, LLC [Electronic version]. *Library Journal, 133*(5), 20.

Luminis Kanto. (n.d.). About Luminis Kanto. Retrieved from http://www.flickr.com/people/ 12609729@N07/

Merholz, P. (2005, August 17). Clay Shirky's viewpoints are overrated. *peterm.com: Links, thoughts, and essays from Peter Merholz.* Retrieved from http://www.peterme.com/archives/000558.html

Peterson, E. (2006, November). Beneath the metadata: Some philosophical problems with folksonomy. *D-Lib Magazine 12*(11). doi:10.1045/november2006-peterson

Peterson, E. (2008, April). Parallel systems: The coexistence of subject cataloging and folksonomy [Electronic version]. *Library Philosophy and Practice*, 1–5.

Rolla, P. J. (2009). User tags versus subject headings: Can user-supplied data improve subject access to library collections? [Electronic version]. *Library Resources & Technical Services, 53*(3), 174–184.

Seattle Public Library. (n.d.) Genêt: A biography of Janet Flanner. Retrieved from http://catalog.spl.org/ ?index=ISBNEX&term=0899194427

Shirky, C. (2006). Ontology is overrated: Categories, links, and tags. Retrieved from http://shirky.com/writ ings/ontology_overrated.html

Spalding, T. (2005, December 18). Tags again: GLBT vs. LGBT. Message posted to http://www.library thing.com/blog/2005/12/tags-again-glbt-vs-lgbt.php

Weinberger, D. (2005, May 13). Tagging and why it matters. Retrieved from http://cyber.law.harvard.edu/home/uploads/507/07-WhyTaggingMatters.pdf

Westcott, J., Chappell, A. & Lebel, C. (2009). LibraryThing for libraries at Claremont [Electronic version]. *Library Hi Tech, 27*(1), 78–81.

Wittig, M. (1992). The straight mind. In *The Straight Mind* (pp. 21–32). Boston: Beacon.

Wright, A. (2005, January 24). Sandy Berman, freetagging old school. Message posted to http://www.alexwright.org/blog/archives/000945.html

Yeates, S. (2006). Where's the fight-back from formal classificationists? Retrieved from *http://connect.educause.edu/blog/StuartYeates/wheresthefightbackfr/2359?time=1190593731*

The LGBT Life Thesaurus Creation Experience

Linda Rudell-Betts

I was recruited in June 2002 by Denny Auld on behalf of EBSCO Publishing to assemble a team that would compile an information retrieval thesaurus for a new bibliographic database. EBSCO saw an opportunity to build a database for the LGBTIQ studies community that would not place any restrictions on content. Other databases targeted for LGBTIQ studies had declined to include content that may have been offensive to certain database constituents. The board of the new EBSCO database was comprised of members of the LGBTIQ community who stipulated that the database and its information retrieval thesaurus be built from within the community to reflect the community and the inclusive nature of the new database.

My expertise on the project was that of an information retrieval lexicographer and project manager. By the time I was brought on to the LGBT Life thesaurus project, I had compiled several indexing vocabularies and had worked within the Internet software industry. And I was a woman-born-woman married for many years to a man-born-man. I have friends and relatives who are LGBTIQ people, but I would not be considered part of the community other than being what I later learned was an ally.

The initial task was to find subject experts who would also be able to create indexing terms for the thesaurus, identify and establish relationships between terms, and navigate the Library of Congress Subject Headings (LCSH). LCSH formed the basis of EBSCO Publishing thesauri and its terms would be updated and gently modified to meet the needs of the LGBT Life database. It should be noted that the database was first published as GLBT Life and in term examples, GLBT will be used instead of LGBT. EBSCO Publishing changed the name to LGBT Life in 2007.

It was critical to have members of the LGBTIQ community as our subject experts to insure a community-generated and community-responsive product. I needed to find a lesbian and a gay man who each had the library and information science background to contribute to the thesaurus. Any knowledge that either contributor might have regarding the bisexual and transgender communities would be a fabulous bonus. The database board provided some candidate contacts and I also had my own resources.

After many telephone calls and email messages, Ellen Greenblatt and Russ Castonguay were signed up as subject experts. Both had worked for many years as professional librarians with expertise in subject cataloging and special collections. To have librarians create the thesaurus meant that the resource would be created by people who had training similar to the indexers and searchers who would be using it everyday. Librarians specialize in information seeking, retrieval and storage, all elements supported by the thesaurus.

Ellen was assigned the areas specific to lesbians, transgender and intersex people. Russ was assigned subject areas pertinent to gay men and bisexual people. I focused on subject hierarchy structures, merging of subject areas and project management. We pooled bibliographies and subject guides to get an initial scope. I created a tutorial for Ellen and Russ on building robust indexing vocabulary and guided them in learning the thesaurus construction software we used to build the thesaurus, MultiTes version 8.0. Both were very adept at MultiTes because of their significant library and information science expertise, and easily grasped the why's and how's of thesaurus compilation.

A brief note about thesaurus terminology: Most standard information retrieval thesauri are built in hierarchies, from general to specific. In this way, they are similar to biological taxonomies or navigational taxonomies seen in e-commerce sites. Information retrieval thesauri usually include related terms that are closely associated with the main descriptor as well as scope notes that explain how to apply the descriptor or other usage information.

There are some similarities between LCSH and a hierarchical thesaurus, but the subject heading conventions (sub-headings, geographic subdivisions, etc.) make LCSH an entity unto itself. By contrast, standard thesaurus inheritance structure is much stricter than what LCSH requires and thesaurus terms are most frequently used in a post-coordinate fashion. All that said, LCSH displays may offer a familiar parallel to many readers. BT means "broader term," or a more general expression of an object, concept or action. NT means "narrower term," or a more specific expression of the object, concept or action. NT1 is the first level, followed by NT2 which is more specific. SN is the abbreviation for scope note which may give the descriptor's coverage or usage guidelines.[1]

As mentioned above, the foundation vocabulary was LCSH, fully licensed by EBSCO Publishing as the basis of their database indexing language. Other LGBTIQ indexing vocabularies were consulted throughout the construction of the LGBT Life thesaurus. We also harvested concepts and terms from LGBTIQ articles retrieved from existing EBSCO databases. As we developed the thesaurus, we found some well-known LC subject headings that were outdated and derogatory. Placement in LC hierarchies were also called into question such as the historic instance of *sexual deviation* being the related term (or see also) for *homosexuality* and *lesbianism* (Knowlton, 2005, p. 133). Obviously, in a LGBTIQ thesaurus such a linkage would be unsustainable.

A profound specification that might not exist for other thesauri was that portions of the LGBTIQ indexing vocabulary and the database itself would likely be incorporated into other EBSCO databases. Since some percentage of indexing terms were sexually explicit, the terms had to be flagged so they would not appear in the general database retrieval. The terms would also have to be modified so that indexers, both human and machine, would not misapply terms: a database devoted to athletics wouldn't be a good place to have *Water sports (Sexual behavior)* show up, nor would a civil engineering database be a good fit for *Dental dams (Sexual hygiene)*. The team generated the list and submitted it to the LGBT Life board and EBSCO for consideration. The EBSCO programmers were able to flag the terms so they would appear only in the LGBT Life database.

Along the creation path, we discovered other alerts for sexually "hot" language: when we sent email messages amongst our team, explicit terms would spawn a graphic of one or two chili peppers in the Eudora email program being used. Sometimes the messages were shuttled into spam files as pornographic. In my own household, I would have occasional discussions with my spouse about racy unsolicited email messages or webpages with descriptions of decidedly explicit sex acts and how this was all really research for validating literary and user warrant, two vital measures in determining term inclusion.

We found that the principles regarding thesaurus construction applied no matter the subject material, that there were hierarchies in most elements of LGBTIQ living that we were striving to represent. In addition to covering all aspects of LGBTIQ living, the project was charged with being as inclusive as possible. We chose to apply pattern headings to many terms about people such as types of jobs or families in order to specifically identify any member of the LGBTIQ community.

> GLBT journalists
>   BT1: Journalists
>   NT1: Bisexual journalists
>   NT1: Gay journalists
>   NT2: Gay male journalists
>   NT2: Lesbian journalists
>   NT1: Transgender journalists

and

> GLBT physicians
>   BT1: Physicians
>   NT1: Bisexual physicians
>   NT1: Gay physicians
>   NT2: Gay male physicians
>   NT2: Lesbian physicians
>   NT1: Transgender physicians

We also strove to remove judgment from our descriptors and where they were placed within hierarchies. Including a concept such as *ephebophilia* that may be unacceptable to some (being that consummation is against United States law), we assured that articles about sexual attraction to adolescent boys would be accurately indexed. The descriptors are available to provide access to the articles regardless of the content.

> Ephebophilia
>   SN: Sexual attraction to adolescent boys.
>   BT: Sexual practices
>   RT: Androphilia
>   RT: Intergenerational relations
>   RT: Korophilia
>   RT: Pedophilia
>   RT: Variant sexuality

As a development team, we had long-running email messages, color coding our responses to one another to keep threads comprehensible. We also had telephone conference calls when that mode was deemed most efficient. These discussions often were regarding teasing apart concepts that LCSH grouped together.[2] In the example below, *Female impersonators* is the preferred LCSH heading and *Drag queens* is a lead in term or UF. Drag queens are related to female impersonators, but just as RuPaul is distantly related to Milton Berle, the two worlds are quite distinct.

Drag queens
    BT: Transgender people
    RT: Crossdressers
    RT: Drag (Clothing & dress)
    RT: Drag balls
    RT: Drag kings
    RT: Female impersonators

Just as frequently, we worked to resolve perceptions each of us brought to term development. We had an memorable discussion regarding domestic partnerships: were such partnerships limited to LGBT couples? Or could unmarried, cohabitating heterosexual couples also be considered domestic partners? This is the thesaurus entry we settled upon:

Domestic partners
    UF: Cohabitation
    UF: Living together
    BT: Couples
    RT: Common law marriage
    RT: Domestic partner benefits
    RT: Free love
    RT: GLBT couples
    RT: Life partners
    RT: Unmarried couples

The experience I had creating the LGBT Thesaurus for the EBSCO database remains a career milestone. Although I had considered myself to be knowledgable about human sexuality and subcultures, I regularly found myself discarding newly exposed assumptions about gender and treatment of sexual minorities in the broader world. The team as a whole was also challenged by younger LGBTIQ advisors who came of age in a social environment that viewed queer living largely without stigma. Some of the descriptors suggested by younger LGBTIQ advisors were startling and may have simply highlighted the pan-human generational divide.

The final draft of the thesaurus was submitted to EBSCO in May 2003. It is hoped that the thesaurus continues to provide a solid backbone for scholarly search in the LGBTIQ studies field.

NOTES

1. For more information on information retrieval thesauri, please see the current ANSI/NISO standard for additional information at ANSI/NISO Z39.19 — Guidelines for the Construction, Format, and Management of Monolingual Controlled Vocabularies at *http://www.niso.org*.

2. See also the essay on LCSH in this same section.

REFERENCES

Knowlton, S. A. (2005). Three decades since Prejudices and antipathies: A study of changes in the Library of Congress Subject Headings. *Cataloging & Classification Quarterly*, *40*(2), 123–145. doi: *10.1300/J104v40n02_08*

LGBTIQ History Starts Here: Indigenous/Native Terminology

Karen Vigneault

Lesbian, gay, bisexual, intersexed (hermaphrodite), transgendered, queer and 2 spirit/ two spirit.[1] So many colonized labels for what used to be simply being what the creator made you to be. If we look at the original terms for what is now labeled as LGBTIQ in this country we would have a word used in a Native language for whatever tribe was in that state or county. Where has all this terminology come from and what are the terms librarians and those classifying these cultures should be made aware of?

While much has been written about the history of the LGBTIQ community, most of the printed history timeline starts from a non-native perspective. If one looks at the true history of the LGBTIQ culture and community it would and should begin with the aboriginal people of Turtle Island or what is now called America.

One must remember that in historical times in Indigenous/Native cultures there was no such concept as gender; you were born either male, female or intersex. You were born to be as you were created to be. If the creator made you a woman and you chose to live your life as a man or vice versa then it was done. It was known in tribal ways that the creator makes no mistakes.

Another point to remember is that many terms used by non-natives were mostly used to describe men. As with most patrilenial societies, women's lives were not focused on or recorded as widely as men's.

> According to ethnographers' accounts, among the tribes there were women warriors, women leaders, women shamans, women husbands, but whether any of these were lesbians is seldom mentioned. On the few occasions lesbianism is referred to, it is with regard to a specific individual who is noted because she is a lesbian [Allen, 1992, p. 245].

With the arrival of the colonizers much of the historical terminology and traditional ways of life were destroyed and only religiously biased views were recorded. Which in turn meant that surviving terminology would be recorded in non-tribal languages. Historically, the earliest writings were taken from journals and letters written by non-natives. These writings were merely observations taken from people whose perceptions were based on their own Eurocentric cultural milieu — not within the cultural context of the peoples being viewed. The English, French, and Spanish words they used to describe these peoples and their practices were woefully inadequate at best, but mostly demeaning and deplorable.

The first term applied to LGBTIQ Natives is the term *berdache*. From the 1600s until the 1990s, this term was used extensively by writers and anthropologists despite it being an offensive term to many LGBTIQ Natives. Used to predominantly describe LGBTIQ males, *berdache* first appeared in Jesuit documents in the 1660s. The documents contained mentions of men who wore women's clothing, performed "women's work," lived as women, and/or had sexual relations with other men. Based on the Persian word *bardaj*, the term morphed into *bardaje* in Spanish and *bardache* in French. Anglicized as *berdache*, the term was defined as "a young man who is shamefully abused" (Stryker, 2006, para. 3). Others have defined it as "kept boy" or "male prostitute" (Thomas & Jacobs, 1999). Anthropologists and ethnologists later appropriated the term, applying it "to Native American/First Nations people who were gender variant, sexually variant, and/or anatomically (sex) variant" (de Vries, 2008, p. 63).

Many of the old words used by tribal nations have been either forgotten, are rarely used, or again were mostly used in describing men. Will Roscoe (1992) claims that the concept is widespread, documented in "over 130 North American tribes, in every region of the continent, [and] among every type of Native culture" (p. 5). Many LGBTIQ Native Americans are trying to reclaim these traditional terms. Here are just a few examples of the many terms that exist: *winkte* (Lakota), *egwakwe* (Ojibwa), *alyha* (Mohave), *lhamana* (Zuni) and nádleehí (Navajo). Will Roscoe's book *Changing ones: Third and fourth genders in Native North America* contains an extensive glossary of terms (1998, p. 213–222).

For many urban Indians well-known terms such as gay and lesbian were frequently used to self identify. This is self-evident with the creation of the first lesbian and gay Native group, GAI (Gay American Indians), founded in San Francisco, California by Randy Burns (Paiute) and Barbara Cameron (Lakota) (Williams, 1992).

In the 1990s things began to change on Turtle Island when the term *two-spirit* was proposed to replace *berdache* at the third annual Native American/First Nations gay and lesbian conference in Winnipeg, Manitoba, Canada.

> It was specifically chosen to distinguish and distance Native American/First Nations peoples from non–Native peoples. Two-spirit serves as a self-identifying term in place of Western concepts and identities such as gay, lesbian, bisexual, transgender, intersex, queer, cross-dresser, and so on [de Vries, 2008, p. 64].

Based on the Objibwa terms, *niizh manidoowag*, the term was coined both in English and Ojibwa (a First Nations language spoken in the Manitoba region) at the conference. It has "no traditional cultural significance" or "linguistic equivalent" (de Vries, 2008, p. 64).

What does all this mean to librarians, especially those who catalog and classify books? Because information regarding 2 spirit / LGBTIQ people can be either historical, contemporary (or both) in nature, deciding where to classify this information may be an intimidating task. In researching how the Library of Congress Subject Headings (LCSH) classified LGBTIQ Indigenous peoples, I found that they used the term *Berdaches* until 2006 when the heading was changed to *Two-spirit people*, sixteen years after the term was coined. *Two-spirit people* were also listed under the broader term of *Transvestites*. I am assuming it was placed under this term due to the fact most of the writings were describing men dressing as women and just an assumption on their part or something that didn't get changed when *Berdache* was superseded by *Two-spirit people*. I contacted the Library of Congress to advise them that relating those two terms was inappropriate, and they responded that they would no longer group *Two-spirit people* under the broader term *Transvestite*.

When patrons are searching for information on LGBITQ / 2 spirit Native Americans they may not know what terms to use. Also, librarians may not be aware of the various terminologies used in locating books or materials on this subject. One must first decide if they are looking for historical documents or contemporary books by or about contemporary LGBTIQ Natives. Terminology may vary depending on whether the book is written by an LGBTIQ Native vs. a non-native person. Some of the examples of words a librarian might experience a patron using are:

- the antiquated term *berdache*
- two-spirit or 2 spirit
- popular indigenous terms such as the Navajo term *nádleehí,* Zuni term *lhamana,* or the Lakota term *winkte*

I would also like to note that the term *two-spirit* is a relatively new term, despite it being created almost twenty years ago. I say new because not all Indians that are LGBTIQ have heard the term until recently, especially amongst West Coast Indians. Accordingly, not all LGBTIQ Natives/indigenous peoples define themselves as 2 spirit. Some LGBTIQ Natives/indigenous people prefer the traditional gay terms as well as others who do not believe they are 2 spirits.

Libraries and the Library of Congress have many issues to face regarding the LGBTIQ/2 spirit/Native/Aboriginal communities. As time moves forward and new words are added to our dictionaries and into our cultures, libraries and classification schemes must also change. Both those creating the classifications and those implementing them must be in sync.

NOTES

1. I will use *2-spirit* and *two-spirit* interchangeably throughout this piece.

REFERENCES

Allen, P. G. (1992). *The sacred hoop: Recovering the feminine in American Indian traditions.* Boston: Beacon.

de Vries, K. M. (2008). Berdache (Two-spirit). In J. O'Brien (Ed.), *Encyclopedia of gender and society* (pp. 62–65). Los Angeles: Sage.

Roscoe, W. (1992). *The Zuni man-woman.* Albuquerque: University of New Mexico Press.

Roscoe, W. (1998). *Changing ones: Third and fourth genders in Native North America* (1st ed.). New York: St. Martin's.

Stryker, S. (2006). Berdache. In *glbtq: An Encyclopedia of Gay, Lesbian, Bisexual, Transgender, and Queer Culture.* Retrieved from http://www.glbtq.com/social-sciences/berdache.html

Thomas, W., & Jacobs, S. (1999). "—And we are still here": from berdache to two-spirit people. *American Indian Culture and Research Journal, 23*(2), 91–107.

Williams, W. L. (1992). *The spirit and the flesh: Sexual diversity in American Indian culture.* Boston: Beacon.

Censorship of Children's and Young Adult Books in Schools and Public Libraries

Laura Reiman and *Ellen Greenblatt*

Introduction

Censorship has been around since before the invention of the printing press. In fact the term *censor* comes from the Latin word, *censure*, which means "to give as one's opinion, to assess" (WGBH Educational Foundation, 1999, para. 1). The earliest censors were Roman magistrates who were concerned with the morals and ethical conduct of the day. Within fifty years of the invention of the printing press, Germany, England, and France all had governmental agencies charged with overseeing censorship of this new form of communication. The Catholic Church became involved in the censorship business when it published a list of banned books, *Index Librorum Prohibitorum* in 1559.[1] This list grew to ultimately contain over 5,000 titles and was in use until 1966!

Anthony Comstock led the way to modern book banning in the United States when he founded the New York Society for the Suppression of Vice in 1872. The following year, the United States Congress passed a law called "An Act for the Suppression of Trade in, and Circulation of, Obscene Literature and Articles for Immoral Use" (Kammeyer, 2008; Rierson, 2004). Ultimately known as the "Comstock Law," this act made it illegal to distribute what it termed "obscene, lewd, or lascivious" materials through the United States mail (Kendrick, 1987, p. 134). Materials designated as "obscene" included "accurate scientific information" about such topics as sexuality, homosexuality, abortion, and birth control (Gary, 2008, para. 12). Under the rallying cry of "Morals, not art or literature," the Comstock Law banned the works of many authors, including several whose works are now considered classics, such as: George Bernard Shaw, Honore de Balzac, Oscar Wilde, Ernest Hemingway, James Joyce, F. Scott Fitzgerald, Victor Hugo, D.H. Lawrence, John Steinbeck, and Eugene O'Neill, and censured several classical works, including *Lysistrata, The Decameron, The Canterbury Tales,* and *The Arabian Nights* (Heins, 1993; LaMay, 1997; Mullally, 2009).[2] The Comstock Law ultimately fell out of favor in 1933, when a federal court in *United States v. One Book Called "Ulysses"* unbanned *Ulysses,* coincidentally only months after a much publicized book burning of the work occurred in Nazi Germany (Mullally, 2009).

One of the most enduring forms of censorship targets children's and young adult resources. Parents and others will go to great lengths to restrict the right to read when they feel they are protecting young people. This essay will focus on this particular area of censorship and how people have attempted to restrict access to materials with LGBTIQ content.

Some Definitions

Despite centuries of censorship and defense of speech, there is no neat and tidy modern legal definition of the term. For purposes of this essay, we will use the American Library Association's (ALA) definition of censorship:

> Censorship is the suppression of ideas and information that certain persons — individuals, groups or government officials — find objectionable or dangerous ... Censors try to use the power of the state to impose their view of what is truthful and appropriate, or offensive and objectionable, on everyone else. Censors pressure public institutions, like libraries, to suppress and remove from public access information they judge inappropriate or dangerous, so that no one else has the chance to read or view the material and make up their own minds about it. The censor wants to prejudge materials for everyone [American Library Association, 2009f, para. 3].

Often censorship attempts take the form of challenges to library materials. ALA defines a challenge as:

> an attempt to remove or restrict materials, based upon the objections of a person or group ... Challenges do not simply involve a person expressing a point of view; rather, they are an attempt to remove material from the curriculum or library, thereby restricting the access of others" [ALA, 2009a, para. 1].

When challenges result in the removal of books from library shelves, these books are termed "banned books."

Using these definitions, this essay will explore several issues related to the censorship of children's and young adult books, including self-censorship by librarians, legal issues, and the importance and availability of professional guidelines and policies. Several examples of challenges are examined, ranging from challenges instigated by individuals and groups to legislative attempts to restrict or remove LGBTIQ resources. The essay concludes with strategies libraries can implement to mitigate or counteract censorship attempts and what individuals can do to combat challenges.

Self-censorship by librarians

Probably the most insidious form of censorship is that of self-censorship. Most librarians, if asked, would not consider themselves ardent censors of what their patrons read. In fact, only twenty-three percent of school librarians reported self-censorship on a survey conducted by *School Library Journal* (Whelan, 2009b). It is all too easy to rationalize collection development decisions which happen to disfavor LGBTIQ materials on ever-tightening budgets or the mistaken belief that "we don't have any of those students in our library" (Greenblatt, 2003).[3] Still others may attempt to preempt any challenges by taking the safer route and not ordering any materials which may be considered controversial. The key factor in distinguishing between careful collection development decision-making and self-censorship is the intent. A good teacher/librarian, children's librarian, or young adult (YA) librarian is expected to "choose a range of titles that best suits the curriculum or meets the reading needs of the students" or children (Whelan, 2009a, p. 28). Where those professional judgment calls turn into self-censorship is often hidden from view and difficult to identify.

In the previously mentioned *School Library Journal* survey, over six hundred teacher/librarians responded about reasons they rejected (or censored) certain materials with the following results: seventy percent of librarians say they would not buy certain controversial titles simply because they are terrified of how parents will respond. Other common reasons for avoiding adding particular items include potential backlash from the administration (twenty-nine percent), the community (twenty-nine percent), or students (twenty-five percent), followed by twenty-three percent of librarians who say they would not purchase a book due to personal objections. Additionally twenty-nine percent were concerned about the appropriateness of the materials to age groups and/or the curriculum (Whelan, 2009b).

The *School Library Journal* survey also ranked the types of content that lead librarians to censor material. Sexual content topped the list with eighty-seven percent of those surveyed citing it as the main reason they shy away from buying a book. Objectionable language (sixty-one percent) came in second, followed by violence (fifty-one percent), homosexual themes (forty-seven percent), racism (thirty-four percent), and religion (sixteen percent). Another ten percent cited additional topics, such as drug use, as well as inappropriate graphics (Whelan, 2009b).

"But if you reject a book just because of its subject matter or if you think that it would cause you some problems, then that's self-censorship. And that's going against professional ethics," says former school librarian Pat Scales, author of *Protecting Intellectual Freedom in Your School Library*. "Censorship takes place anytime a book is removed from its intended audience," Scales continues (Whelan, 2009a, p. 28). Moving books out of the children's section of the library, behind the desk, or otherwise restricting their use is still a form of censorship — as is the practice of applying content labels to rate books (much like movies or audio recordings) or expurgating certain portions of the text.

Although it is impossible to determine the level of self-censorship of books with LGBTIQ content, one study shows that less than one percent of school libraries and only twenty-one percent of public libraries in Arkansas contain books with gay themes or characters in their collections. A survey sent to 499 school media specialists received only 37 responses (Whelan, 2007). Commenting on this study, author Brent Hartinger, asks:

> If these appalling results are from only the librarians who felt comfortable enough to respond, how bad must the situation actually be? [Hartinger, 2007, para. 8].... I've argued for a long time that there is a strong and ongoing institutional bias against gay books, and that a sort of preemptive censorship is occurring in libraries all across the country. The results of this study suggest that that is almost certainly the case [para. 10].

Wendy Rickman, one of the co-authors of the University of Central Arkansas study, attributes the librarians' reticence to collect LGBTIQ-themed books to a variety of factors, including avoiding the possibility of challenges to the books, receiving negative feedback from school administrators or school board members, and fearing the possibility of job loss.

Linda W. Braun in a post to the *YALSA Blog* (2008) cautions young adult librarians not to let fear be the deciding factor in collection development decisions. Materials that answer the "tough questions" that teens have about life are essential to their successful development and growth. Making controversial materials available will not only improve the young adults' social abilities, but also give them a sense of empowerment. These materials can provoke discussions among adolescents, giving them insights beyond the opinions of their peers.

As Braun observes:

> Yes, it's important to know your community. But, knowing your community means focusing on the teens who might have the library as the only place where they can access the information they need in order to grow up successfully. Be a teen advocate by giving teens the resources they deserve [para. 9].

Legal Treatment

There is not much case law regarding censorship in school or public libraries. This is because most cases are decided outside of the traditional court system, usually by school boards or local governments. However, to trace any legal basis of censorship back to its roots, we should start with the language of the First Amendment which states: "Congress shall make no law respecting an establishment of religion, or prohibiting the free exercise thereof; or abridging the freedom of speech, or of the press" (U.S. Constitution, First Amendment). This First Amendment language is at the heart of all protection of the right to read. It gives a constitutional basis to any argument that without the right to read, there is no right to speak (or write).

One of the few actual legal cases involving censorship in a school library setting is *Board of Education v. Pico* (1982). This case established the right of library users in a school library to read ideas and information and connected this right to that of authors to "speak" or send ideas and information under the protection of the First Amendment. The Supreme Court in *Pico* allowed students standing to sue the school board for pulling books from the school library based on their right to receive this information. *Pico* has laid the foundation for lower courts' treatment of the right to send as well as receive information and ideas in a public or school library setting. So far, *Pico* is the only case in which the United States Supreme Court has dealt with this particular issue.

The issue of censorship in a public library setting was addressed in Federal District Court in the case of *Sund v. City of Wichita Falls, Texas* (2000). In this case, the District Court reversed a library board resolution which directed the transfer of several children's books to the adult section of the library, finding that public library users also have the right to receive ideas and information.[4]

Since the only nationally authoritative case law in this area is *Pico*, and most other decisions from school boards and lower courts regarding what constitutes censorship in school and public libraries are not binding (outside their jurisdictions) on the average school or public librarian defending their patrons' right to read, we, as librarians must look to other sources such as ALA guidelines, to guide us through the maze of censorship issues.

The ALA *Library Bill of Rights* and Its Interpretations

For most of our day-to-day guidance in drafting challenge policies and defending challenges, the best sources to turn to are the *Library Bill of Rights* and its numerous interpretations concerning censorship and the right to read. The *Library Bill of Rights* stresses inclusiveness, clearly stating that libraries should provide materials that present all viewpoints.

In case there is any question of whether the *Library Bill of Rights* pertains to materials containing LGBTIQ subject matter, there is an explicit interpretation of the *Library Bill of Rights* which states:

> The American Library Association stringently and unequivocally maintains that libraries and librarians have an obligation to resist efforts that systematically exclude materials dealing with any subject matter, including sex, gender identity, or sexual orientation [ALA, 1993/2004].

ALA has published several other interpretations of the *Library Bill of Rights* pertaining to diversity in collection development and the obligation of librarians to protect library collections from removal of materials based on prejudice, to the more active responsibility to select and support access to materials which reflect all viewpoints. There are even unequivocal limitations on librarians putting rating systems or labels on books when such a system effectively limits access to certain populations, including youth. Children's and young adults' First Amendment rights to read are explicitly addressed in "Free Access to Libraries for Minors."[5]

Armed with these very explicit edicts from ALA as far as the obligation of librarians to protect and enforce all library users' rights, including those of minors, let's look at several challenges to the right to read books containing LGBTIQ subject matter.

Examples of Censorship Attempts

The Heartland Has Annie on Its Mind

In 1993, a gay rights group donated two books, *Annie on My Mind* by Nancy Garden (1982) and *All American Boys* by Frank Mosca (1983), to the Olathe (Kansas) School District libraries. A committee of librarians from the school district reviewed both books and decided to "accept *Annie* but reject the other book for lack of literary merit" (Meyer, 1996, p. 22). Going against the librarians' decision, Superintendent Ron Wimmer turned down the donations and ordered librarians to remove three copies of *Annie* which had been on library shelves since the book first came out a decade earlier. There had been no formal request to reconsider the book, and in fact, it is easy to assume that the book would have remained on the shelves except for the donations which shed light on the book's existence. Students and parents sued the school district in 1995 and won reinstatement of the book in federal court. In *Stevana v. Unified School District No. 233* (1995), the Court found that the book, depicting two girls who fall in love, be returned to the libraries. Relying on *Pico,* the Court found that books could not be removed merely because of disagreement with the views expressed ("Annie goes back to school," 1996; Meyer, 1996).

Since that decision, *Annie* has been included in ALA's "Best of the Best Books for Young Adults" as well as *School Library Journal's* "One Hundred Books that Shaped the Century" (Jenkins, 2003). Most notably, *Annie* was the first lesbian-themed young adult book with a happy ending and the first to show two generations of lesbians — the girls and their teachers (Sutton, 2007). *Annie's* legacy lives on through the Johnson County (Kansas) First Amendment Foundation, established in 1999 by Shook Hardy & Bacon, the law firm that won the Olathe censorship case, with the $200,000 in fees paid by the school district.

The Foundation promotes awareness of First Amendment rights among Kansas students through the sponsorship of essay contests, the underwriting of college scholarships, and other programming (Lambe, 2009; Taylor, 2009).

Wichita Falls Rallies Against Picture Books

Probably two of the most well-known picture books containing LGBTIQ content are *Daddy's Roommate* by Michael Willhoite (1990) and *Heather Has Two Mommies* by Leslea Newman (1989). Although these books had been on library shelves for several years, they apparently did not come to the attention of the Rev. Robert Jeffress of the First Baptist Church in Wichita Falls, Texas, until 1998. The Reverend Jeffress effectively "stole" the public library copies of these books that a church member had checked out and brought to him. Refusing to return them to the library, he wrote a check for $54 to cover the costs of the books and fines[6] ("Daddy's roommate/Heather flap erupts in Texas," 1998; "Wichita Falls pastor's protest of gay books sparks donations of extra copies to library," 1998).

Following up on this action, the reverend took up a petition to have the books removed from all public library shelves in Wichita Falls. This campaign was so successful that a city ordinance was passed requiring the library to restrict access to ANY title that at least 300 people petitioned against. After receiving a petition against *Heather* and *Daddy* containing almost 600 signatures, the library removed the books from the shelves. The American Civil Liberties Union (ACLU) took the case to federal court which issued a temporary restraining order in August 1999, ordering the books to remain on the shelves of the children's nonfiction section of the library while the outcome of the case was pending ("Books to Stay on Wichita Falls Children's Shelves ... For Now," 1999). Ultimately, the federal court found the city ordinance to be an unconstitutional restriction of speech based on the viewpoint expressed in a petition ("Judge rules censorship by petition to be unconstitutional," 2000). The Wichita Falls City Council decided not to appeal the case.[7]

Ironically, as a result of the reverend's protest, the library received renewed interest and many requests for these two older picture books as evidenced by the number of holds on them. In fact, the library had to purchase additional copies (as per its own guidelines which dictated buying new copies based on exceeding six holds per title), and was the recipient of at least fifteen donated copies as well ("After protest by pastor, interest in gay books at library grows," 1998; "Wichita Falls pastor's protest of gay books sparks donations of extra copies to library," 1998).

Alabama Takes Censorship to the Legislature

During the 2005 Alabama legislative session, House Bill 30 was introduced attempting to prohibit the use of state funds "for the purchase of textbooks or library materials that sanction, recognize or promote homosexuality as an acceptable lifestyle" (Alabama, 2005, p. 3).[8] This far-reaching bill would also have forbidden classroom speakers to portray homosexuality in a positive light and banned theatrical productions, such as the Pulitzer Prize–winning *Cat on a Hot Tin Roof,* at state-funded institutions. Further it would hold any "public employee" (including librarians) criminally liable for violating the provisions contained in the bill (Alabama, 2005, p. 3).[9]

Sponsored by Alabama State Representative Gerald Allen, the bill would have prohibited the purchase of new books with gay themes and characters or those written by gay authors. And librarians would have had to remove classic works by Truman Capote, Tennessee Williams, Walt Whitman, Oscar Wilde, Herman Melville, Willa Cather, Carson McCullers, John Cheever, Alice Walker, James Baldwin, and Gore Vidal, among many others ("Alabama lawmaker wants to ban gay books," 2004). When asked what to do with all the materials purged from the library shelves, Rep. Allen replied, "I guess we dig a big hole and dump them in and bury them" (Sledge, 2004, p. D1). Rep. Allen did not see this bill as a form of censorship, stating:

> Homosexuals can freely practice their lifestyle choice. Books can be written, plays can be produced and spirited criticisms can be levied. At the end of the day, I feel strongly that we as a state should not spend tax dollars promoting such activities [2004, p. D2].

The bill raised many questions, such as: Who ultimately decides what constitutes inappropriate material? What standards should be used? (Liebler, 2005). In short, "Who does Allen think will read every word in every library in the state in search of a wayward thought that might corrupt?" (Norman, 2005, p. D1). All of which were moot as the bill ultimately failed due to lack of a quorum at the time of the scheduled vote (Holguin, 2005).

Oklahoma Wants Adult Only Sections in the Library

In 2006, the Oklahoma Legislature attempted to pass a similar bill which would have prohibited funding public libraries unless all children's and YA materials that contained homosexual or sexually explicit subject matter were placed in a special area restricted to adults only ("Oklahoma bill ties library funds to gay-free kids' collections," 2006). No distinction was made between books with gay themes which contain sexual references and the numerous age-appropriate picture books or YA novels containing no explicit sexual references but having gay characters or themes. The bill defined homosexual subject matter as "content that relates to the recruiting and advocating of same gender sexual relationships" (Oklahoma, HB2158, Section 1.B.1, 2006) and also mandated the establishment of a "State Library Material Content Advisory Board ... [to] annually develop a recommended [*sic*] list of child and YA materials that contain homosexual or sexually explicit subject matter ... [to] be distributed to every library ... in the state" (Oklahoma, HB2158, Section 3.A, 2006).[10]

The bill was introduced by State Representative Sally Kern who in 2005 requested the Oklahoma City Metropolitan Library Commission to place the picture book *King and King* in the adult section of the library, presenting the members with two petitions, one signed by over seventy legislators and another signed by approximately 600 local citizens ("Oklahoma lawmakers seek to dethrone *King and King*," 2005). The petition led to Kern's introduction of House Resolution 1039 which called for "Oklahoma libraries to confine homosexually themed books and other age-inappropriate material to areas exclusively for adult access and distribution" (Oklahoma, HR1039, 2005). The resolution passed in the Oklahoma House of Representatives by a vote of 81–3 (Walker, 2008; Hinton, 2005).

Following upon this victory, Kern introduced the aforementioned HB2158 which passed in the House of Representatives with vote of 60–33. However, the bill died in committee in the Senate (Walker, 2008; Hinton, 2005).[11]

"Safe Libraries" vs. "Free Speech" in West Bend

The West Bend Community Memorial Library (WBCML), located just outside Milwaukee, Wisconsin, was the focal point of one of the most highly publicized cases concerning book challenges.[12] The challenges were brought in February 2009 by residents Jim and Ginny Maziarka whose demands changed as the situation unfolded. Originally, they objected to a booklist featuring LGBTIQ young adult books on the library's website. Later, they asked that the library relocate, label, and/or remove these books which they referred to as "Youth-Targeted Pornographic Books" (Maziarka, 2009, March 26, para. 3) and also to balance the collection by adding "faith-based and ex-'gay' books that oppose a pro-homosexual ideology" (Maziarka, 2009, February 24, para. 8). A group calling itself "West Bend Citizens for Safe Libraries" quickly emerged, dedicating itself to "support[ing] a family-friendly, child-safe library environment, free of sexually-explicit materials for minors" (West Bend Citizens for Safe Libraries, 2009, para. 1).[13]

Other individuals and groups supporting the library's position also came forward and the situation quickly transformed from a local incident into a national media feeding frenzy.[14] Both sides circulated petitions, with West Bend Citizens for Safe Libraries collecting 700 signatures and an opposing group, West Bend Parents for Free Speech, collecting 1000 signatures on its petition to the library "to enforce (and if necessary, adopt) policies that protect the collection from attempts at censorship" (Hanrahan, 2009, para. 1; Goldberg, 2009).

For the next several months, the situation escalated. Turnout to the March library board meeting where the Maziarkas' complaint was to be discussed was so large that the over-capacity crowd had to be turned away by the fire department, and the meeting was postponed (Butler, 2009). Eventually, the library cancelled the meeting citing the Maziarkas' changes to the original complaint. In response, Ginny Maziarka called her own town meeting. Attendance was about half of those turned away from the original library board meeting, but representatives from both sides of the controversy were in attendance (Maziarka, 2009, March 27).

According to WBCML young adult librarian, Kristin Pekoll, although the West Bend Citizens for Safe Libraries "circulated the petition and blogged, nothing more was brought formally to the library, so the Board proceeded with business as usual" (Pekoll, 2009, p. 286). But toward the end of April, the West Bend Common Council, unhappy with how the process concerning the challenges had been handled, voted down the reappointment of four of the library board members. This sparked quite a bit of debate as the four members who were refused reappointment to the nine-member board consisted of a retired librarian, who had served on the library board for twenty-four years, an alderman who taught English at the local high school, an attorney, and a retired teacher (Rank, 2009, April 22).[15] Several individuals and organizations, including the American Library Association, sent letters condemning the Council's actions.

However, at its June meeting, the Library Board (including the four members who although not reappointed had not yet been replaced) voted unanimously to retain the books in the young adult section without any of the restrictions put forward by the group filing the complaint. In the aftermath of this controversy, the library staff has been recognized by two intellectual freedom awards, including the Robert B. Downs Award ("West Bend Community Memorial Library named Downs award recipient," 2009)[16] and the Wisconsin ProQuest Intellectual Freedom Award (Wisconsin Library Association, 2009), while Ginny Maziarska was recognized by an award from Phyllis Schlafly's Eagle Forum for her efforts in regards to the challenge attempt at the library (Rank, 2009, December 11).

The Case of Tango, or How a Couple of Penguins Raised a Ruckus

And Tango Makes Three by Justin Richardson and Peter Parnell, published in 2005, is a picture book based on a true story of two male penguins at the New York City Central Park Zoo who raised a chick together. *Tango* has been recognized by several diverse groups, garnering awards from organizations such as the American Society for the Prevention of Cruelty to Animals (ASPCA); Henry Bergh Children's Book Award (2005); and the Gustavus Myers Center for the Study of Bigotry and Human Rights Outstanding Book Award (2006), and appearing on best book lists including Notable Social Studies Trade Books for Young People (2006) and ALA's Notable Children's Books (2006). *Tango* also has the distinction of topping ALA's list of most challenged books from 2006 through 2008 (ALA, 2009d).

This seemingly innocuous story has touched off debates and challenges across the country. An AFP[17] article states that challenges to the book have taken place in at least fifteen states (Hussein, 2009). These challenges, issued by both individuals and organizations, have taken many different forms ranging from requests to move the book to a different location in the library to affixing a warning label indicating "mature content" to removal from the library altogether. For example, in Loudoun County, Virginia, School Superintendent Edgar B. Hatrick III pulled the book off the shelves in response to a parent who claimed the book promoted a "gay agenda." Despite the recommendations of two separate committees, composed of librarians, principals, teachers, and parents, who advised returning the book to the shelves, the superintendent ordered that it be placed in the professional collection, available only to teachers who wished to share the book with their students (Chandler, 2008a). Later, Hatrick reversed his decision due to "significant procedural errors that he believes void the process followed in this matter," most significantly that "the person who brought the request is not a parent" at the school in question, Sugarland Elementary School (Loudoun County Public Schools, 2008).

A parent in Lodi, California, asked the public library's board of directors to either remove the book from the library's toddler section or to label it for "mature content." Her request was denied by the board members, who cited the book's popularity and critical acclaim as the basis for their decision. Lodi Public Library Director Nancy Martinez also referenced the library's collection development policy which states that it is up to parents, not the library, to decide what types of materials are appropriate for their children (Reid, 2007).

One cannot help but compare *Tango* to other similar books featuring unusual animal relationships, such as a gorilla and her pet kitten (*Koko's Kitten*), a tortoise raising a hippo (*Owen & Mzee: The True Story of a Remarkable Friendship*), or a seeing eye dog for a cat (*Two Bobbies: A True Story of Hurricane Katrina, Friendship, and Survival*), all of which have been favorites in children's collections — and none of which have been challenged. The only difference is the gay element of the true story. One could venture to say that most librarians would find it bordering on absurdity if a parent were to claim that a relationship between a hippo and tortoise is unnatural and a book based on a true story about that relationship should not be on the shelves. Yet, despite the acknowledged high quality and appropriateness of the book, many librarians would not purchase *Tango* for their libraries based on the ongoing controversy.

As the above examples show, censorship attacks have not only taken the form of one or two angry parents attacking school or public libraries, but also well-organized citizenship attempts to pass censorship legislation from the city to the state level of government. This is not merely an argument over what Johnny or Janie will or will not read at the school or public library, but what will any of us have access to in our libraries, classrooms, or even publically funded theaters.

Most Frequently Challenged Books

Since 1990, ALA's Office for Intellectual Freedom (OIF) has tracked book challenges and published lists of those most frequently challenged each year. The OIF draws upon two sources for this data — news accounts and reports by individuals — and estimates that these account for only twenty to twenty-five percent of the actual amount, as many challenges go unreported (ALA, 2009d).

Although the list addresses challenges to books for children *and* adults, the three books in the 2008 top ten list challenged on the basis of "homosexual content" include two picture books and one young adult novel:

- No. 1: *And Tango Makes Three* by Justin Richardson and Peter Parnell (heading the top ten list for three years in a row). Reasons: Anti-Ethnic, Anti-Family, Homosexuality, Religious Viewpoint, Unsuited to Age Group
- No. 6: *The Perks of Being a Wallflower* by Stephen Chbosky. Reasons: Drugs, Homosexuality, Nudity, Offensive Language, Sexually Explicit, Suicide, Unsuited to Age Group; and
- No. 8: *Uncle Bobby's Wedding* by Sarah S. Brannen. Reasons: Homosexuality, Unsuited to Age Group (ALA, 2009, April 16; Whelan, 2009c).

In fact, between 2001 and 2008, 269 books out of over 3,700 challenges recorded by ALA's Office for Intellectual Freedom were challenged on the basis "homosexual" content (ALA, 2009e). And since the OIF began to tabulate results in 1990, 839 out of 10,415 books were challenged on the same basis (ALA, 2009g).

A New Strategy

Increasingly libraries are approached by outside groups and/or individuals with donations of books and media that express a particular viewpoint or agenda. This new tactic seeks to "enhance" library collections. For example, during Banned Books Week in 2008, a group of conservative Christian students attempted to donate books that present "a Christian viewpoint on homosexuality" which "show there's an alternative to living out a homosexual life" to a Fairfax County (Virginia) high school (Stand, 2008, para. 2 & 7). Conversely, that same year a gay activist donated copies of *Heather Has Two Mommies* and *Daddy's Roommate* to then Vice-Presidential candidate Sarah Palin's hometown library in Wasilla, Alaska (Petrelis, 2008). In both cases, these donations were rejected based on each of the libraries' respective collection development policies/standards.

Susan Thornily, the coordinator of information services for the Fairfax schools, explained that the books were rejected because they did not meet the district's collection development criteria which include receiving two positive reviews apiece from professionally recognized journals (Chandler, 2008b; Melloy, 2008; "Virginia high-schoolers rally for gay-cure books," 2008). Further, she stated that district librarians felt that the "nonfiction books were heavy on scripture but light on research" (Chandler, 2008b, para. 6) and that the books may make LGBTIQ students feel "inferior" (Melloy, 2008, para. 26) citing district precedents for rejecting books that "target minority groups" (Chandler, 2008b, para. 27).[18]

In an interview with Norman Oder of *Library Journal*, Wasilla Public Library Director K. J. Martin-Albright discussed her library's decision to reject the donated books:

> While the library agrees that *Heather* and *Daddy's Roommate* are important books because they were ground-breaking and because of the controversy and discussions that have occurred in the 15-plus years since they were published, there are better choices for a dynamic, current, and appealing children's collection [Oder, 2008, para. 9].

Martin-Albright also stated that while the library did own both books in the past, they are no longer on the shelves for several reasons, none of which are related to their subject matter. As a small library, retention needs to be justified and if books do not circulate, they cannot remain on the shelves. Additionally, the quality of the books is important — content, construction, and comparison to books on the same subject all need to be taken into consideration. Says Martin-Albright:

> All one has to do is look at the books in question next to *[And] Tango [Makes Three]*, or any other well-made picture book, to see that *Heather* and *Daddy's Roommate* are poorly constructed, lack engaging illustrations, and have too many words on the page to be useful to young readers [para. 8].

These two examples illustrate the importance of formulating selection policies/standards to adequately reflect the library's collection philosophy and support decision-making on accepting or rejecting donations, as well as supporting the library's position should challenges to particular titles occur.

Practical Tips on How to Deal with Challenges

The best way to deal with any kind of challenge to books on library shelves is to be prepared with solid policies and procedures. ALA offers many resources from drafting challenge policies to support from their Office for Intellectual Freedom, should a challenge occur. The "Essential Preparation" portion of the Challenge Section on ALA's webpage at http://www.ala.org/ala/issuesadvocacy/banned/challengeslibrarymaterials/essentialprepara tion/index.cfm provides lots of helpful tips and resources. Among these is "Kids and Libraries, What You Should Know," a resource directed to parents, at http://www.ala.org/ala/issuesadvocacy/banned/challengeslibrarymaterials/essentialpreparation/kidslibraries/inde x.cfm. It is an excellent explanation of the role of the library versus the role of parents and the fact that parents are the ultimate decision-makers in what their child, and their child alone, should read, not the library. It offers practical suggestions for parents in dealing with their children's use of the library, and explains the *Library Bill of Rights* and how it fits in with First Amendment rights.

ALA also offers a "Workbook for Selection Writing Policy" at http://www.ala.org/ala/issuesadvocacy/banned/challengeslibrarymaterials/essentialpreparation/workbookslctn/index.cfm which is aimed at school districts and library information centers. Crucial components of any selection policy include: setting objectives; defining responsibility for selection decisions; establishing the criteria upon which selection decisions will be based; and outlining and explaining the collection development process and procedures. Most importantly in relation to our purposes, the workbook contains sections on "Policies on Controversial Materials" and "Reconsideration," which feature sample reconsideration forms and list three essential parts of a challenge or reconsideration policy:

- asking the complainant to fill out a written complaint form
- assigning a reconsideration committee to examine the materials in question
- requesting that the committee report their findings to the school board (para. 39).

ALA also includes a sample selection policy on the website.

The National Coalition Against Censorship (NCAC) website also contains many resources related to dealing with challenges at http://ncac.org/resources, including a "Book Censorship Toolkit" at http://ncac.org/literature/bookcensorshiptoolkit.cfm directed to schools and parents, as well as authors, offering advice and sample letters on how to deal with book challenges.

The Cooperative Children's Book Center (CCBC) of the University of Wisconsin's School of Education is another organization providing several useful resources. One of these suggests steps to help individuals and institutions deal with a challenge to a book, such as reviewing your institution's collection development policy, particularly the selection criteria and reconsideration process; assessing where you are in the reconsideration process — i.e., what's been done so far and what still needs to be done; reviewing the complaint; conferring with your administration about the situation; identifying and understanding applicable ALA guidelines/policy statements; collecting information about the title in question, such as book reviews, awards, etc.; and reading (or re-reading) the book (CCBC, 2009a, para. 2). The CCBC website also features a searchable database of intellectual freedom questions it calls the "What IF?" forum, providing practical advice in response to such questions as:

- "How do you balance censorship and selection if you have an administrator who has implied that if there are complaints received about library materials, then the materials budget, or even your position, is in jeopardy?"
- "Is a selection policy that outlines 'acceptable' and 'unacceptable' topics for materials promoting censorship instead of selection?"
- "What should I do if my public library director orders me to move picture books about gay and lesbian families to the adult collection?"
- "I struggle with selecting materials for our school library which are not compatible with my personal beliefs" (CCBC, 2009b).

In addition to these websites, there is also a useful book on the topic: Pat Scales' *Protecting Intellectual Freedom in Your School Library: Scenarios from the Front Lines*. Based on the work of the ALA Office of Intellectual Freedom, Scales enhances these policies, procedures, and data with scenarios taken from real life situations and practical guidance gathered over a lengthy career as a library media specialist.

Consulting these resources and working with your colleagues in administration and your public library or school to create policies and procedures that are relevant to your institution's situation ensures that you will have a strong foundation to rely upon should challenges to your collection arise.

Banned Books Week — How to Celebrate Controversial Books

One positive way to combat challenges to all books, including those with LGBTIQ content, is to empower and educate children and young people as well as the general population by celebrating Banned Books Week. Begun in 1982 and sponsored in part by ALA, Banned Books Week is a way to educate all readers on the ways people attempt to restrict their right to read.

The general Banned Books Week <http://www.bannedbooksweek.org> and ALA Banned Books Week <http://www.ala.org/ala/issuesadvocacy/banned/bannedbooksweek/index.cfm> websites offer many ideas on how to promote the week in your library and provide resources such as videos and lists of frequently challenged books. Held during the last week in September every year, Banned Books Week conveniently coincides with Constitution Day which is observed on September 17, commemorating the signing of the constitution.

Banned Books Week can be celebrated with students as young as elementary school age. In fact, Laura has worked with sixth grade teachers, integrating Banned Books Week with Constitution Day as well as the sixth grade social studies curriculum involving the study of the Constitution. One very powerful lesson involved announcing that all books were being recalled by the school district. The classroom teacher instructed her students to bring all library books back to the library where a discussion was held about whether the district had the right to restrict what the students could read. Another lesson involved a display of frequently challenged books in the library. The students, who did not know all the books in the display had been challenged, were asked to work in groups to select which ones they thought had been. The books included titles from *Little Red Riding Hood* (challenged for depicting a bottle of wine in the picnic basket) to the ever popular R.L. Stine's *Goosebumps* series. Both of these lessons sparked significant discussion among the students, some of whom were confronted for the first time with the concept that someone would want to restrict their right to read.

There are many ways to defend challenges to the right to read books with LGBTIQ and other controversial content. Perhaps the best protection is an empowered and informed public, including children and young adults, who are aware of their protected constitutional right to read.

Conclusion

As we have discussed in this essay, censorship attempts have been around since before the printed word, and we expect them to continue into the future. Those who would like to restrict access to LGBTIQ materials have turned to different tactics such as donating anti-gay books or initiating local legislative attempts to circumvent First Amendment rights. When it comes to LGBTIQ-related materials in particular, parents and other concerned citizens will always be sensitive to the fact that school and public libraries make these materials available to children and young adults. But however much these parents and citizens would like libraries to stand *in loco parentis* as guardians of what children and young adults should read, this is clearly not the school or library's role. Rather the role of these institutions is that of vanguard of the right to read. It is the parents' responsibility to choose appropriate reading material for their children within the context of that particular family's values — not the librarian's. A well constructed collection development policy, clearly defined challenge responses, and an educated reading public will go a long way in protecting everyone's access to LGBTIQ materials.

APPENDIX: AMERICAN LIBRARY ASSOCIATION *LIBRARY BILL OF RIGHTS* AND SELECTED INTERPRETATIONS

The first date given here is the date of adoption; the second date pertains to the most recent revision.

- *Library Bill of Rights* (1939/1996)[1] http://www.ala.org/ala/issuesadvocacy/librarybill/index.cfm
- *Access for Children and Young Adults to Nonprint Materials* (1989/2004) http://www.ala.org/ala/issuesadvocacy/librarybill/interpretations/accesschildren.cfm
- *Access to Library Resources and Services Regardless of Sex, Gender Identity, Gender Expression, or Sexual Orientation* (1993/2008) http://www.ala.org/ala/issuesadvocacy/library bill/interpretations/accesslibrary.cfm
- *Access to Resources and Services in the School Library Media Program* (1986/2008) http://www.ala.org/ala/issuesadvocacy/librarybill/interpretations/accessresources.cfm
- *Challenged Materials* (1971/2009) http://www.ala.org/ala/issuesadvocacy/librarybill/interpretations/challengedmaterials.cfm
- *Diversity in Collection Development* (1982/2008) http://www.ala.org/ala/issuesadvocacy/librarybill/interpretations/diversitycollection.cfm
- *Evaluating Library Collections* (1973/2008) http://www.ala.org/ala/issuesadvocacy/librarybill/interpretations/evaluatinglibrary.cfm
- *Expurgation of Library Materials* (1973/2008) http://www.ala.org/ala/issuesadvocacy/librarybill/interpretations/expurgationlibrary.cfm
- *Free Access to Libraries for Minors* (1972/2008) http://www.ala.org/ala/issuesadvocacy/librarybill/interpretations/freeaccesslibraries.cfm
- *Importance of Education to Intellectual Freedom* (2009) http://www.ala.org/ala/issuesadvocacy/librarybill/interpretations/importanceofeducation.cfm
- *Labeling and Rating Systems* (1951/2009) http://www.ala.org/ala/issuesadvocacy/librarybill/interpretations/labelingrating.cfm
- *Privacy* (2002) http://www.ala.org/ala/issuesadvocacy/librarybill/interpretations/privacy.cfm
- *Restricted Access to Library Materials* (1973/2009) http://www.ala.org/ala/issuesadvocacy/librarybill/interpretations/restrictedaccess.cfm
- *The Universal Right to Free Expression* (1991) http://www.ala.org/ala/issuesadvocacy/librarybill/interpretations/universalright.cfm

NOTES

1. Some list 1557 as the original date of publication, see for example Halsall (1998).
2. Reirson (2004) states that Comstock "bragged that he had convicted enough people to fill sixty-one passenger cars on a train, approximately 4,000 individuals" (p. 168) although other sources state that while about 3500 people were prosecuted, only about ten percent were convicted (Mullally, 2009). Wright (1999) states that by the 1930s, 160 tons of information was destroyed as a result of the Comstock Law (p. 171).

3. See also the essay on "Barriers to Selecting Materials about Sexual and Gender Diversity" in Section Four.

4. For more on this topic, "Wichita Falls Rallies against Picture Books" in this chapter.

5. Please see Appendix for a listing of relevant ALA guidelines.

6. According to Kennedy (1998), the Reverend Jeffress raised the issue about these LGBTIQ-themed books at the same time that "he kicked off a $1.3 million capital pledge campaign" (p. 5).

7. Pruitt (2000) states that the Wichita Falls City Council made a deal with the ACLU "agreeing not to appeal in exchange for a 30 percent reduction in attorney fees" (p. 39A)—leaving a $26,558 legal bill for the city to pay.

8. The full text of the bill is available on the Internet at: http://www.alsde.edu/legislative_bills/2005Regular/HB0030_OR.pdf.

9. Daniel (2005) states that the Class A misdemeanor cited in the bill would include a maximum fine of up to $2000 along with a jail term of up to one year according to Alabama criminal code.

10. The text of this bill can be found by searching http://webserver1.lsb.state.ok.us/WebBillStatus/main.html by measure number and legislative session in the "Basic Search Form"—e.g., HB2158 and 2006 Regular Session.

11. Despite the failure of the bill, Rep. Kern has remained in the headlines. In 2008, the Gay & Lesbian Victory Fund uploaded a video to YouTube http://www.youtube.com/user/VictoryFund#p/search/0/tFxk7glmMbo capturing remarks she made to a Republican organization, including her characterization of homosexuality as "the biggest threat our nation has, even more so than terrorism or Islam." Later that year, Kern was stopped at the state Capitol building when she tried to bring her gun into the building—and not for the first time (Greiner, 2008).

12. For an overview of this incident from the vantage point of a librarian at the West Bend Community Memorial Library, see Pekoll (2009). A document outlining the situation was prepared by the library as a handout for a presentation on the topic at the 2009 American Library Association annual meeting and can be found at http://www.west-bendlibrary.org/alahandout.pdf. A collection of links to information chronicling the controversy can be found at http://www.west-bendlibrary.org/wbdnpublications.htm.

13. As the campaign ensued, another group, the Christian Civil Liberties Union (CCLU), joined the fray demanding that one of the books in question, *Baby Be-Bop*, be publically burned and that the four-member Milwaukee-based CCLU be awarded $120,000 in damages for their exposure to the book (Dorning, 2009; Goldberg, 2009).

14. For more information about this aspect of the controversy, see the essay on "The Internet and LGBTIQ Communities" in Section One.

15. Alderman Terry Vrana defended the Council's decision stating that the "ideology" of the board members ran counter to community interests and he was "concerned about the morality of this city." Pekoll (2009) added that one of the aldermen "compared the library to a 'porn shop'" (p. 286). Additionally, she observed that "Ironically, many alderman do not have library cards" (p. 286). Acting Director of ALA's Office for Intellectual Freedom, Deborah Caldwell-Stone, urged the Council to reconsider, citing their "obligation to distinguish between personal beliefs and the preservation of the public library's duty to represent the diversity of people, opinions, and ideas found in West Bend, Wisconsin" ("Politics heats up materials challenges," 2009, pp. 33–34).

16. The faculty of the Graduate School of Library and Information Science at the University of Illinois at Urbana-Champaign bestows this annual award to individuals and/or organizations that have advanced the cause of intellectual freedom particularly in the context of libraries.

17. Formerly Agence France-Presse.

18. Several conservative groups, including Americans for Truth about Homosexuality and Parents and Friends of Ex-Gays and Gays (PFOX), have or will be launching similar campaigns to get these types of books into libraries. Focus on the Family, which organized the Fairfax campaign, has created a website to help others with this process: True Tolerance http://www.truetolerance.org/.

REFERENCES

After protest by pastor, interest in gay books at library grows. (1998, May 24). *The New York Times.* Retrieved from http://www.nytimes.com/1998/05/24/us/after-protest-by-pastor-interest-in-gay-books-at-library-grows.html

Alabama bill would ban gay-interest items. (2004). *American Libraries News Archive.* Retrieved from http://www.ala.org/ala/alonline/currentnews/newsarchive/alnews2004/december2004ab/bamabill.cfm

Alabama lawmaker wants to ban gay books. (2004, December 3). *Advocate.* Retrieved from http://advocate.com/article.aspx?id=27075

Allen, G. (2004, December 26). It's not censorship — it's just protecting children from the "gay agenda." *Mobile Register,* D2.

American Library Association. (1993/2004). Access to library resources and services regardless of sex, gender identity, or sexual orientation: An interpretation of the Library Bill of Rights. Retrieved from http://www.ala.org/Template.cfm?Section=interpretations&Template=/ContentManagement/ContentDisplay.cfm&ContentID=31878

American Library Association. (2009, April 16). Attempts to remove children's book on male penguin couple parenting chick continue. Retrieved from http://www.ala.org/ala/newspresscenter/news/press releases2009/april2009/nlw08bbtopten.cfm

American Library Association. (2009a). Challenges to library materials. Retrieved from http://0-www.ala.org.sapl.sat.lib.tx.us/ala/issuesadvocacy/banned/challengeslibrarymaterials/index.cfm

American Library Association. (2009b). Coping with challenges: Kids and libraries. Retrieved from http://www.ala.org/ala/issuesadvocacy/banned/challengeslibrarymaterials/essentialpreparation/kidslibraries/index.cfm

American Library Association. (2009c). Essential preparation: How to deal with challenges to library materials. Retrieved from http://www.ala.org/ala/issuesadvocacy/banned/challengeslibrarymaterials/essentialpreparation/index.cfm

American Library Association. (2009d). Frequently challenged books. Retrieved from http://www.ala.org/ala/issuesadvocacy/banned/frequentlychallenged/index.cfm

American Library Association. (2009e). Frequently challenged books of the 21st century. Retrieved from http://www.ala.org/ala/issuesadvocacy/banned/frequentlychallenged/21stcenturychallenged/index.cfm

American Library Association. (2009f). Intellectual freedom and censorship Q&A. Retrieved from http://www.ala.org/ala/aboutala/offices/oif/basics/ifcensorshipqanda.cfm

American Library Association. (2009g). Number of challenges by year, reason, initiator, & institution (1990–2008). Retrieved from http://www.ala.org/ala/issuesadvocacy/banned/frequentlychallenged/challengesbytype/index.cfm

American Library Association. (2009h). Workbook for selection policy writing. Retrieved from http://www.ala.org/ala/issuesadvocacy/banned/challengeslibrarymaterials/essentialpreparation/workbookslctn/index.cfm

Annie goes back to school. (1996). *School Library Journal, 42*(1), 13.

Bill restricting gay material at Oklahoma libraries passes house. (2006, March 17). *Advocate.* Retrieved from http://advocate.com/article.aspx?id=35335

Board of Education v. Pico, 457 U.S. 853 (1982).

Books to Stay on Wichita Falls Children's Shelves ... For Now. (1999). *American Libraries News Archive.* Retrieved from http://www.ala.org/ala/alonline/currentnews/newsarchive/1999/august1999/booksstaywichita.cfm

Braun, L. W. (2008, July 19). What are we scared of? *YALSA Blog.* Retrieved from http://yalsa.ala.org/blog/2008/07/19/what-are-we-scared-of/

Butler, D. (2009, March 4). West Bend Library Board meeting postponed. *GM [Greater Milwaukee] Today.* Retrieved from http://www.gmtoday.com/news/local_stories/2009/March_09/03042009_02.asp

Chandler, M. A. (2008a, February 17). 2 guys and a chick set off Loudoun library dispute. *Washington Post.* Retrieved from http://www.washingtonpost.com/wp-dyn/content/article/2008/02/16/AR2008021600749.html

Chandler, M. A. (2008b, October 3). Banned books, chapter 2. *Washington Post.* Retrieved from http://www.washingtonpost.com/wp-dyn/content/article/2008/10/02/AR2008100203644.html

Cooperative Children's Book Center, University of Wisconsin-Madison. (2009a). Steps when materials are challenged. Retrieved from http://www.education.wisc.edu/ccbc/freedom/steps.asp

Cooperative Children's Book Center, University of Wisconsin-Madison. (2009b). What If? Questions and answers on intellectual freedom. Retrieved from http://www.education.wisc.edu/ccbc/freedom/whatif/default.asp

Crabtree, E. A. (2005, March 27). Don't let misguided state legislation wipe out our history. *Mobile Register,* D2.

Daddy's roommate/Heather flap erupts in Texas. (1998). *American Libraries News Archive.* Retrieved from http://www.ala.org/ala/alonline/currentnews/newsarchive/1998/may1998/daddysroommate.cfm

Daniel, J. (2005). Burying books in Alabama. Retrieved from http://www.campusprogress.org/features/205/burying-books-in-alabama/index.php

Delcour, J. (2009, June 7). Video: Oklahoma's roadside detraction. *Tulsa World*, G1.

Dorning, A. (2009, June 19). Library book riles small Wisconsin town: "Baby be-bop" and its gay teen angst too much for Christian Civil Liberties Union. *ABC News*. Retrieved from http://abcnews.go.com/US/story?id=7874866&page=1

Garden, N. (1982). *Annie on my mind*. New York: Farrar, Straus, Giroux.

Garden, N. (1996). Annie on trial: How it feels to be the author of a challenged book. *Voice of Youth Advocates, 19*, 79–82.

Gary, B. (2008). Morris Ernst's troubled legacy. *Reconstruction: Studies in Contemporary Culture, 8*(1). Retrieved from http://reconstruction.eserver.org/081/gary.shtml

Goldberg, B. (2009). Milwaukee group seeks fiery alternative to materials challenge. *American Libraries*. Retrieved from http://www.pla.org/ala/alonline/currentnews/newsarchive/2009/june2009/westbendbabybebop060309.cfm

Greenblatt, E. (2003). Lesbian, gay, bisexual, transgender library users: Overcoming the myths. *Colorado Libraries, 29*(4), 21–25.

Greiner, J. (2008, July 24). Kern says she didn't mean to take pistol into state Capitol. *The Oklahoman*, 1A.

Halsall, P. (1998). Modern history sourcebook: Index librorum prohibitorum, 1557–1966 (Index of prohibited books). Retrieved from http://www.fordham.edu/halsall/mod/indexlibrorum.html

Hanrahan, M. (2009). Petition. *West Bend Parents for Free Speech*. Retrieved from http://westbendparentsforfreespeech.webs.com/petition.htm

Hartinger, B. (2007, January 14). Just because I'm paranoid doesn't mean people aren't out to get me. *AS IF! Authors Support Intellectual Freedom*. Blog. Retrieved from http://asifnews.blogspot.com/2007_01_01_archive.html

Hatkoff, I., Hatkoff, C., & Kahumbu, P. (2006). *Owen & Mzee: The true story of a remarkable friendship*. New York: Scholastic.

Heins, M. (1993). *Sex, sin, and blasphemy: A guide to America's censorship wars*. New York: New.

Hinton, M. (2005, May 10). Limits urged on book access. *Tulsa World*, A9.

Hinton, M. (2006, April 9). Dead bills available as campaign fodder. *Tulsa World*, A17.

Holguin, J. (2005, April 27). Alabama bill targets gay authors: Proposed law could force many literary works off the shelves. *CBS Evening News*. Retrieved from http://www.cbsnews.com/stories/2005/04/26/eveningnews/main691106.shtml

Hussein, S. (2009, September 6). US libraries hit back over challenges to kids books. *AFP*. Retrieved from http://www.google.com/hostednews/afp/article/ALeqM5iMj2Fmuq6lqm4kdFfy5Vhp8-suQg

Jenkins, C. A. (2003). Annie on her mind. *School Library Journal, 49*(6), 48–50.

Judge rules censorship by petition to be unconstitutional. (2000). *American Libraries News Archive*. Retrieved from http://www.ala.org/ala/alonline/currentnews/newsarchive/2000/september2000/judgerulescensorship.cfm

Kammeyer, K. C. W. (2008). *A hypersexual society: Sexual discourse, erotica, and pornography in America today*. New York: Palgrave Macmillan.

Kendrick, W. M. (1987). *The secret museum: Pornography in modern culture*. New York: Viking.

Kennedy, B. (1998, May 23). Wichita Falls furor a tempest in a pulpit. *Fort Worth Star-Telegram*, 5.

Kenney, B. (2006). Do the right thing: It's easy to dismiss gay teens, but think about the consequences. *School Library Journal, 52*(1), 11.

LaMay, C. L. (1997). America's censor: Anthony Comstock and free speech. *Communications and the Law, 19*(3), 1–59.

Lambe, J. (2009, October 2). Lawyers toast program spawned by banned book. *Kansas City Star*. Retrieved from http://www.kansascity.com/news/neighborhood/leawood/story/1483755.html

Larson, K., & Nethery, M. (2008). *Two Bobbies: A true story of Hurricane Katrina, friendship, and survival*. New York: Walker.

Liebler, R. (2005, February 3). Bill to keep gay books out of libraries officially read by Alabama legislature February 1, 2005 — Text of HB30. *LibraryLaw Blog*. Retrieved from http://blog.librarylaw.com/librarylaw/2005/02/alabama_bill_to.html

Loudoun County Public Schools. (2008, March 3). *And Tango Makes Three* decision voided. Retrieved from http://cmsweb1.loudoun.k12.va.us/509759161361/cwp/view.asp?A=3&Q=474407&C=82592

Maziarka, G. (2009, February 24). West Bend Library thumbs nose at taxpayers. *WISSUP = Wisconsin Speaks Up*. Blog. Retrieved from http://wissup.blogspot.com/2009/02/west-bend-library-thumbs-nose-at.html

Maziarka, G. (2009, March 26). Petition for a child-safe, family-friendly library. *WISSUP = Wisconsin*

Speaks Up. Blog. Retrieved from http://wissup.blogspot.com/2009/03/petition-for-child-safe-family-friendly.html

Maziarka, G. (2009, March 27). West Bend library issue "town meeting." *WISSUP = Wisconsin Speaks Up*. Blog. Retrieved from http://wissup.blogspot.com/2009/03/i-said-id-blog-about-meeting-later.html

McNutt, M. (2008, March 11). Legislator's anti-gay words draw national focus. *The Oklahoman*, 1A.

Melloy, K. (2008, October 3). Christians use "Banned book week" to promote including anti-gay books in school libraries. *EDGE Boston*. Retrieved from http://www.edgeboston.com/index.php?ch=news&sc=&sc2=news&sc3=&id=81388

Melvin, L. (2008, February 13). Rep. Campfield wants gay references banned in schools. *Knoxville News Sentinel*. Retrieved from http://www.knoxnews.com/news/2008/feb/13/rep-campfield-wants-gay-references-banned-schools/

Meyer, R. (1996). Annie's day in court. *School Library Journal, 42*(4), 22–25.

Mosca, F. (1983). *All-American Boys*. Boston: Alyson.

Mullally, C. (2009, September 14). Libraries and First Amendment issues: Banned books. Retrieved from http://www.firstamendmentcenter.org/speech/libraries/topic.aspx?topic=banned_books

National Coalition Against Censorship. (2009, February 23). Book censorship toolkit. Retrieved from http://ncac.org/literature/bookcensorshiptoolkit.cfm

National Coalition Against Censorship. (2009). Resources. Retrieved from http://ncac.org/resources

Newman, L. (1989). *Heather has two mommies*. Boston, MA: Alyson Wonderland.

Norman, D. (2005, May 1). Lawmaker would bury books to save us all. *Gadsden Times*, D1. Retrieved from http://news.google.com/newspapers?id=j3cvAAAAIBAJ&sjid=d9wFAAAAIBAJ&pg=5790%2C107112

Oder, N. (2008). LJ talks to Wasilla Public Library Director KJ (Kathy) Martin-Albright. *Library Journal*. Retrieved from http://www.libraryjournal.com/article/CA6604854.html?desc=topstory

Oklahoma bill ties library funds to gay-free kids' collections. (2006). *American Libraries News Archive*. Retrieved from http://www.ala.org/ala/alonline/currentnews/newsarchive/2006abc/march2006ab/oklabill.cfm

Oklahoma lawmakers seek to dethrone *King and king*. (2005). *American Libraries News Archive*. Retrieved from http://www.ala.org/ala/alonline/currentnews/newsarchive/2005abc/april2005ab/oklaking.cfm

Patterson, F. (1985). *Koko's kitten*. New York: Scholastic.

Pekoll, K. (2009). Standup! Defending teens' right to read at West Bend Community Memorial Library. *Voice of Youth Advocates, 32*(4), 284–287.

Petrelis, M. (2008, October 15). Wasilla library rejects 2 gay children's books. *Petrelis Files*. Retrieved from http://mpetrelis.blogspot.com/2008/10/wasilla-library-rejects-2-gay-childrens.html

Politics heats up materials challenges. (2009). *American Libraries, 40*(6/7), 32–34.

Pruitt, B. (2000, November 11). Wichita Falls residents riled about books case: City stuck with legal bill in dispute started by church. *Dallas Morning News*, 39A.

Rank, D. (2009, April 22). Four tossed off Library Board: Council rejects reappointments on 5–3 vote. *The [West Bend] Daily News*, A1.

Rank, D. (2009, December 11). Young adult controversy has rewards for library. *The [West Bend] Daily News*, A1.

Reid, K. (2007, May 5). Tale's theme too adult for kids, patron says. *Recordnet.com*. Retrieved from http://www.recordnet.com/apps/pbcs.dll/article?AID=/20070505/A_NEWS/705050321

Richardson, J., & Parnell, P. (2005). *And Tango makes three*. New York: Simon & Schuster Books for Young Readers.

Rierson, S. (2004). Comstock Act (1873). In B. K. Landsberg (Ed.), *Major acts of Congress*, (Vol. 1). (pp. 166–169) New York: Macmillan Reference USA.

Scales, P. (2009). *Protecting intellectual freedom in your school library: Scenarios from the front lines*. Chicago: American Library Association.

Sledge, J. (2004, December 5). Proposed book ban deserves firm rebuttal. *Mobile Register*, D6.

Stevana v. Unified School District No. 233, Johnson County, Kansas, 895 F. Supp. 1463 (D. Kansas, 1995)

Strand, P. (2008, October 5). Christian students protest book ban. *CBN.com — Christian Broadcasting Network*. Retrieved from http://www.cbn.com/cbnnews/457606.aspx

Sund v. City of Wichita Falls, Texas, 121 F. Supp. 2nd 530 (N.D. Texas, 2000).

Sutton, R. (2007). Annie on my mind: A second look. *The Horn Book, 83*(5), 543–546.

Taylor, B. (2009, October 1). First amendment event targets free speech & privacy issues. Retrieved from http://www.shb.com/news_events_detail.aspx?id=713

Thomas Jefferson Center for the Protection of Free Expression. (2005). Muzzle archive 2005: Alabama State Representative Gerald Allen. Retrieved from http://www.tjcenter.org/muzzles/muzzle-archive-2005/#item10

U.S. Constitution, First Amendment.

Virginia high-schoolers rally for gay-cure books. (2008). *American Libraries News Archive.* Retrieved from http://www.ala.org/ala/alonline/currentnews/newsarchive/2008/october2008/fairfaxgaycure.cfm

Walker, D. (2008, March 12). Do comments create environment of hate? Oklahoma's legislature is homophobic, some say. *The Oklahoman,* 2A.

West Bend Citizens for Safe Libraries. (2009). Who we are. Retrieved from http://sites.google.com/site/wb citizens4safelibraries/Home/who-we-are

West Bend Community Memorial Library named Downs award recipient. (2009, December 8). Retrieved from http://www.lis.illinois.edu/articles/2009/12/west-bend-community-memorial-library-named-downs-award-recipient

WGBH Educational Foundation. (1999). Culture shock: Who decides? How and why? Definitions of censorship. PBS (Public Broadcasting Service). Retrieved from http://www.pbs.org/wgbh/cultureshock/whodecides/definitions.html

Whelan, D. L. (2007). Gay titles missing in most AR libraries. *School Library Journal, 53*(1), 18.

Whelan, D. L. (2009a). A dirty little secret: Self-censorship. *School Library Journal, 55*(2), 27–30.

Whelan, D. L. (2009b). SLJ self-censorship survey. *School Library Journal.* Retrieved from http://www.schoollibraryjournal.com/article/CA6633729.html

Whelan, D. L. (2009c). Gay penguins top ALA's most challenged books, again. *School Library Journal.* Retrieved from http://www.schoollibraryjournal.com/article/CA6653100.html?industryid=47055

Wichita Falls pastor's protest of gay books sparks donations of extra copies to library. (1998, May 22). *Dallas Morning News*, 39A.

Willhoite, M. (1990). *Daddy's roommate.* Boston, MA: Alyson Wonderland.

Wright, Les. (1999). San Francisco. In D. Higgs (Ed.), *Queer sites: Gay urban histories since 1600* (pp. 164–189). London: Routledge.

LGBTIQ Teens — Plugged In and Unfiltered: How Internet Filtering Impairs Construction of Online Communities, Identity Formation, and Access to Health Information

David Brian Holt

Introduction

The LGBTIQ community has a special relationship with the Internet. A number of studies have suggested that LGBTIQ people are more likely to use the Internet as an information resource than other patron groups. They are also more actively engaged in social media and online social networking (Harris Poll Interactive, 2008). They are more likely to be tech savvy and use the Internet to access information about health concerns, sexuality, and mental health. Consequently, the Internet has become a vital resource within the LGBTIQ community to access information crucial to community health and well-being. This is particularly true for LGBTIQ adolescents who must often contend with a hostile and homophobic environment and an insufficient social network. In response, the Internet has played a vital role in helping LGBTIQ adolescents reach out to other young people like themselves and to form online social networks that address their unique information and social needs. These social networks can act as a support system to help adolescents navigate the troubled waters of identity formation and the unique issues associated with adolescence among LGBTIQ youth.

The anonymity the Internet provides represents an invaluable resource where LGBTIQ youth can freely discuss their issues, concerns and problems without fear of reprisal from a frequently homophobic community. LGBTIQ youth may find the Internet, and its online communities and social networks, to be the only conduit through which they can express themselves, reach out to others, and access health information that addresses their particular issues and needs. LGBTIQ adolescents often deal with environments that lack sufficient social networks, such as empathetic adults or friends, and they may face daily discrimination due to their sexual orientation or gender expression.

The mandated use of Internet filtering in public libraries, however, threatens this special relationship. With the passage of CIPA (Children's Internet Protection Act), and its constitutionality subsequently affirmed by the Supreme Court, libraries are faced with the challenges presented by Internet filtering, and the obstacles to access it creates for disadvantaged patron groups. While library science literature has frequently discussed the problems of Internet filtering, LGBTIQ adolescents are often neglected by these studies despite filtering having a disproportionate impact on their communities. The need for anonymity, which the Internet can provide, is a more crucial need for LGBTIQ youth who often must construct their social networks in an environment hostile to their emotional, social and informational needs.

Internet Usage among LGBT Adolescents

In order to understand the implication of Internet filtering, it is important to recognize the significance of Internet use among all youth. In 2002, a study conducted by the Kaiser Family Foundation found that 74 percent of adolescents between the ages of 15 and 17 reported having Internet access at home, with 31 percent having access in their bedrooms (Rideout, 2002, p. 2). Along with an increasing reliance on the Internet in general, adolescents have increased their use of online resources to answer their health questions. In fact the Kaiser study found that some 70 percent report they have used the Internet as a health information resource (p. 4). Among these, 50 percent were found to use the Internet for information on general health topics such as cancer or diabetes, with 40 percent also using it for information about sexual health topics ranging from teen pregnancy and birth control to STD transmission. For issues such as depression and mental illness, 23 percent reported using the Internet as an information resource. The Internet ranked higher as a resource for health information above even friends (23 percent), or TV shows/movies (17 percent). When asked what made the Internet such an important resource, the most frequent response was its privacy and confidentiality. This element of confidentiality played a key role in the reason why adolescents felt comfortable using the Internet to access this information, with 82 percent reporting it as the most important reason in using the Internet as a health resource (p. 12). The results of the study suggest, therefore, that the Internet is increasingly vital for adolescents seeking out health and sexuality information they may be reluctant or unable to access via other means. The importance of privacy may also encourage adolescents to choose to use a library Internet connection rather than one available at home, as they may be under the impression that a public terminal will not keep a record of where they go online. According to the Kaiser report, 58 percent of adolescents reported not being concerned that their online activity would be documented on terminals available at their school or library (p. 13). Of course, public terminals at libraries are also outside the view of parents and that may be a major concern for LGBTIQ youth struggling with their identity formation.

Social Networking on the Internet

The anonymity provided by the Internet creates a unique resource for LGBTIQ teens looking to find peers with similar experiences. Gay teens may use the Internet to "try out" an identity before they ascribe to one themselves. The Internet, therefore, gives gay teens the unique opportunity to "prepare, discuss, and shape their gay identities before trying them out in real space" (Bernstein, 2004, p. 1026). Social networking sites, such as MySpace and Facebook, or virtual environments such as Second Life,[1] permit teens to construct an online identity without the same risk of community reprisal and enable these adolescents to connect with others who are constructing similar identities. Accordingly, the Internet is playing an increasingly important role in the "coming-out" process for these gay teens, enabling them to come out in an environment with little or no social consequences before they do so in "real space" (McKenna, Bargh, 1998, p. 686). Of course, the Internet is not free from social consequences as cases of "cyberbullying" and online harassment demonstrate.[2] However, for a teen who truly desires total anonymity and confidentiality for their identity construction, the Internet can provide this avenue in ways that "real-life" cannot.

This coming-out process, done online, may be conducive to the mental health of LGB-TIQ adolescents. Frequently, sexual minority or gender variant teens must deal with an environment where they feel marginalized and different from others. This may be particularly true in rural or conservative environments where there are few local resources for LGBTIQ adolescents. By finding other LGBTIQ youth on the Internet, a teen may experience a "demarginalization" of their sexual or gender identity and have reduced feelings of isolation (McKenna, Bargh, 1998, p. 691; Munt, Bassett, O'Riordan, 2002, p. 135). An online environment also allows teens to experiment in forming their identity as they navigate the stresses of adolescence. By creating an online identity before they come out to their "real-life" friends, gay teens are "motivated to come back to real life with their Internet life to verify their identity and make it 'real'" (McKenna, Bargh, 1998, p. 692).

The process of forming an identity online, rather than in "real-life," may also translate into lower rates of risk for these LGBTIQ teens as they are not forced into adult environments they are ill-equipped to handle (Bernstein, 2004, p. 1027). With the Internet, these adolescents are able to socialize with their peers and do so rather safely and without the same degree of risk that they will be forced into environments, or relationships, they are ill-equipped to handle. It is thus particularly ironic that the legislative intent of mandated Internet filtering is to protect teens when it pushes them into environments with greater risk of harm.

LGBTIQ Internet Revolution

That the Internet is playing an enormous role in the lives of LGBTIQ adolescents perhaps cannot be overstated. As the Internet moves from a Web 1.0 to a 2.0 environment with an increase in interactivity and social interaction, the ways in which LGBTIQ adolescents use online resources and communities have changed dramatically. LGBTIQ youth, particularly in conservative and rural communities, are able to connect with their peers and meet their unique socialization needs in ways that were impossible just a few years ago.

A recent Harris Interactive poll finds that LBGTIQ people use online social networking tools at a higher rate than their similarly situated heterosexual peers (Maul, 2009, p. 1). The survey found that 55 percent of LGBTIQ adults are on Facebook compared with 46 percent of adult heterosexuals. Further, 20 percent of LGBTIQ adults had a Twitter account, compared with only 12 percent of heterosexuals. This disparity between LGBTIQ Internet users, and their heterosexual peers, is perhaps even more pronounced among adolescents although quantitative studies of this group are hard to acquire given that many LGBTIQ adolescents are still in the process of identity formation.

This reliance on the Internet is also reducing the age at which LGBTIQ adolescents are navigating their identities. Journalist Benoit Denizet-Lewis, who formerly worked for the popular gay teen magazine *XY*, wrote an article for the *New York Times* that discusses how LGBTIQ adolescents are coming-out at younger ages (2009). There appears to be a generation gap emerging within the larger LGBTIQ community as the "coming-out" process is started at a much younger age. He attributes this shift to not only a decreasingly homophobic culture, but also from the identity-formation taking place in online communities. He writes that: "[G]ay teenagers ... still suffer harassment at school or rejection at home, but many [seem] less burdened with shame and self-loathing than their older gay peers. What had changed? Not only were there increasingly accurate and positive portrayals of gays and lesbians in popular culture, but most teenagers were by then regular Internet users. Going online broke through the isolation that had been a hallmark of being young and gay, and it allowed gay teenagers to find information to refute what their families and churches sometimes still told them — namely, that they would never find happiness and love" (Denizet-Lewis, 2009, p. 3).

The Unique Information Needs of Sexual Minority Youth

A study commissioned by the Gay, Lesbian Straight Education Network (GLSEN) on the online behavior of LGBTIQ adolescents found that 68 percent of respondents revealed that being online helped them to accept their sexual orientation, with 51 percent calling the Internet "crucial" to that acceptance (Garry et al., 1999, p. 20). The American Psychological Association (APA) recognizes that "coming-out" is conducive to mental health and is an important step towards the acceptance of one's sexuality and personal development. Additionally, the APA strongly recommends the inclusion of homosexuality and other LGBTIQ issues in sex education curriculum, and that access to important health and sexuality information is available to adolescents. In their statement on sexual orientation, the APA asserts that "the process of identity development for lesbians, gay men and bisexuals called 'coming out,' has been found to be strongly related to psychological adjustment — the more positive the gay, lesbian, or bisexual identity, the better one's mental health and the higher one's self-esteem" (APA, 2009, p. 1). This stronger sense of self also translates into making informed and wiser decisions about health, sexuality and gender expression.

Because the Internet plays this vital role in disseminating health and sexuality information, it is essential to understand the unique impact it has on the lives of sexual minority youth in particular. Interestingly, one study that attempted to measure the online information-seeking behavior of sexual minority youth indicated that 51 percent admit they revealed their sexual orientation to someone online before their friends or family (Garry et al., 1999). Other studies have found similar results indicating that LGBTIQ adolescents are heavy users of the Internet in comparison to their non–LGBTIQ peers (Koswic, Diaz, Greytak, 2007; Brooks, 2009). These statistics highlight the importance of Internet use among LGBTIQ youth, effectively demonstrating the importance of their ability to build communities in which they can discuss their particular concerns and issues. Building a social network of support and community is vital to mental health and social development, ultimately allowing adolescents to make informed choices about their health.

Indentity Formation in an Online Environment

Besides providing valuable health information and social networking, the Internet also plays a vital role in the formation of identity for LGBTIQ adolescents. Given that many of these young people live in environments which may not be conducive to the formation of their sexual orientation or gender expression, it is critically important that they find a safe, and affirming, place where they can explore and form their identity just like their non-minority peers. Unlike their peers, however, LGBTIQ adolescents must reveal their identity to receive appropriate support and may find hostility, or social stigmatization, by doing so (Friedman & Morgan, 2009, p. 921). The Internet, therefore, provides a safer environment where these adolescents can explore their identities without the same fear of social rejection.

Research indicates that sexual minority and gender variant adolescents who are able to find a supportive social network often have improved outcomes later in life including higher self-esteem, life satisfaction and lower rates of depression (p. 921). Social scientists have suggested that many adolescents negotiate two "master narratives" of sexual identity in the course of their development — "struggle" and "success" (Hammack, Thompson & Pilecki, 2009, p. 867). The first master narrative describes the period where sexual minority adolescents struggle with their external, and internal, challenges to their identity formation. The "success" element is usually typified by a "coming-out" experience where the adolescent identifies as LGBTIQ.

Recent social science studies indicate that many contemporary LGBTIQ adolescents are rejecting the identity "options" that were available to their predecessors. Termed "emancipation," this narrative of sexual identity and gender variance reflects the shifting discourse within the LGBTIQ community and the influence of Queer Theory, which frequently argued for a "critical perspective on society's need to create a sexual typology to regulate sexual desire" (p. 868). Some in the LGBTIQ community feel there is a need to reevaluate the sexual taxonomies which define them and replace them with more inclusive terms, reflecting the diversity of sexual desires and identities within the larger community (Hostetler & Herdt, 1998, p. 251).

The adolescent LGBTIQ community has readily adopted this "emancipation" from previous sexual taxonomies. Benoit Denizet-Lewis in his article, "Coming Out in Middle School," describes how adolescents are abandoning terms such as *gay* and *lesbian* and are creating their own vocabulary to describe their same-sex desires and gender expression. Denizet-Lewis describes a group of middle school students who use the term *woof* to describe their peers who have same-sex desires and how identifying as bisexual gives adolescents greater freedom to explore their gender and sexual identities (2009).

Legal History of Internet Filtering

The controversy regarding Internet filtering software in public libraries did not begin with the passage of CIPA. Although the library science literature tends to focus on CIPA, the fight against Internet filtering in public libraries actually started back in 1996. The Communications Decency Act of 1996 (CDA) was introduced in Congress as Title V of the Telecommunications Act of 1996, Pub.L. 104–104, 110 Stat. 133 (1996). The legislation intended to serve two functions: first, it aimed to restrict "indecency" available to minors, and secondly to restrict "obscenity." The legislation is also quite notable in that Section 230 releases Internet Service Providers (ISP) and hosting companies of liability for the content published on their sites by users (see 47 U.S.C. § 230).

First Amendment advocates quickly challenged the Communications Decency Act (CDA) in court on the rationale that it unconstitutionally infringed upon the free speech rights of adults. Just a year after its passage, the Supreme Court upheld a decision by the Eastern District Court of Pennsylvania that ruled the act unconstitutional as it was overly broad, extended into non-commercial speech and did not define the term "patently offensive," *ACLU v. Reno*, 929 F.Supp. 824 (E.D.Pa. 1996). The court left intact Section 230 of the act, which continues to indemnify web-hosting companies from liability for the content posted by their users.

The next attempt by Congress to restrict minors' access to materials they deemed "pornographic" was the Child Online Protection Act (COPA), Pub.L. 105–277, 112 Stat. 2681–736 (1998). This legislation is not to be confused with the Children's Online Privacy Protection Act, Pub.L. 105–277, 112 Stat. 2681–728 (1998), which requires websites to acquire parental consent when their sites are being used by those aged twelve and under. COPA attempted to prohibit access by minors to materials it calls "harmful" and was written to overcome the court's challenges to CDA. The definition used relied heavily upon community standards to define what is "harmful" using the test developed by *Miller v. California*, 413 U.S. 15 (1973). The courts quickly enjoined, and eventually overturned, the law for violating free speech guarantees and for applying the community standards test for online material. The court claimed that "COPA essentially requires that every Web publisher subject to the statute abide by the most restrictive and conservative state's community standards in order to avoid criminal liability ... [and] imposes an impermissible burden on constitutionally protected First Amendment speech," *ACLU v. Reno*, 217 F.3d 162, 166 (2000). Interestingly, the court claimed that filtering was a narrower means to achieve the goals of restricting minors from accessing pornography than the method COPA provided (Dobija, 2007, p. 52).

At issue with many of these cases is how speech can be regulated on government-owned property. Historically, the courts have organized government property into three types of "forums" when considering issues of free speech therein: traditional public, limited public and non-public forums (Bell, 2001, p. 200; Chemerinsky, 2006, p. 1126). This three-tier system of regulating speech on government-owned property was articulated in the case *Perry Education Association v. Perry Local Educators' Association*, 460 U.S. 37 (1983). Traditional public forums are public spaces that have been used for free speech activities either by tradition or government fiat. Some examples of traditional public forums include public streets and government-owned parks. In these traditional public forums, the government may not prohibit communicative activity and can only enforce restrictions if they serve a compelling government interest and are narrowly-tailored to further that interest (p. 45). This is similar to the "strict scrutiny" standard courts use to evaluate statutes which infringe upon a fundamental right, or affect a suspect class.

Limited public forums are those government-owned spaces reserved for a particular type of expression. The government may choose to close these limited public forums and they may designate them to be used by specific groups or to discuss particular topics (Bell, 2001, p. 202; Chemerinsky, 2006, p. 1137). Examples of limited public forums include public museums and public libraries. In these forums, "a state is not required to indefinitely retain the open character of the facility, as long as it does so it is bound by the same standards as apply in a traditional public forum. Reasonable time, place and manner regulations are permissible, and a content-based prohibition must be narrowly drawn to effectuate a compelling state interest" (Perry Education Association v. Perry Local Educators' Association, 1983). This standard is similar to the "rational basis" review used by the courts.

One of the most important cases regarding filtering, and what type of forums public libraries should be designated took place in 1997 with the *Mainstream Loudoun v. Loudon County* case in Virginia, 24 F. Supp. 2d 552 (E.D. Va. 1998). In this case, the court found that filtering infringed upon protected speech when it applied to both adolescent and adult library patrons. It also found that public libraries exist as a limited public forum. In response to this decision, the legislative push for Internet filtering directed its focus specifically on adolescents. In 1998, Senator John McCain introduced the Internet School Filtering Act, which ultimately languished in committee and never came to a vote on the floor (Garry et al., 1999). During the same time, challenges against the Child Online Protection Act (COPA) continued, with the ACLU winning a preliminary injunction against it in February 1999.

Congress responded to these constitutional challenges with the introduction of the Children's Internet Protection Act (CIPA) in 1999 (Pub.L. 106–554, 114 Stat. 2763, 2763A–335). Senators John McCain and Ernest Hollings introduced the bill, and it was signed into law by then President Clinton as part of a larger communications-spending bill. CIPA mandates that public libraries that receive funds through federal programs designed to offset their Internet costs must also install filters on their publically available terminals. It includes libraries receiving discounts through the E-rate program, schools that use Elementary and Secondary Education Act of 1985 funds to purchase computers, and libraries which receive federal grants from the Museum and Library Services Act. Ironically, these federal programs were designed with the intent to alleviate the "digital divide" between communities that enjoy high rates of Internet access and less-affluent communities that struggle in providing access.

CIPA was quickly challenged by the American Library Association, with the assistance of the American Civil Liberties Union. After an initial success in federal circuit court, the U.S. Supreme Court heard the case and found that CIPA does not impermissibly infringe upon First Amendment speech so long as adult library patrons can have their Internet access unfiltered at their request, *U.S. v. ALA*, 539 U.S. 194 2003. The court was unconvinced that filtering's history of overblocking was a concern due to the "ease with which patrons may have filtering software disabled" (p. 196). Furthermore, it found that CIPA did not compel librarians to infringe upon their patrons' First Amendment freedoms.

How Does Filtering Work?

Filtering software has undergone considerable change since the passage of CIPA back in 1999. Many of the criticisms directed towards filtering software, such as over-and under-blocking, have improved over the past decade. The problems still exist, however, as filtering software continues to trail behind web content and the various methods users engage in subverting it. The Brennan Center for Justice at New York University's School of Law has published a public policy report on Internet filtering software and its rates of over-and under-blocking. Published in 2006, the report indicates that filtering software continues to fail to meet its promised goals and prevents access to non-objectionable materials while also failing to block "obscene" materials (Heins, 2006, pp. 9–39). Additionally, the San Jose

Public Library recently published a report on the effectiveness of filtering software and evaluated the major commercial options including Barracuda, CyberPatrol, FilterGate and Web-Sense (Houghton-Jan, 2008, pp. 9–14).

The major technologies used by filtering programs can be divided into several major categories: network-based or stand-alone options, filtering by URL or keyword, blocking what the user sees, blocking by file type, and classification of URLs and keywords (Houghton-Jan, 2008, pp. 3–4). A network-based or stand-alone option is a filter that blocks the terminal used by a patron from requesting forbidden content over the network. If the program deems the content objectionable, then the system never makes a request for it over the Internet.

The second technology, filtering by URL or keyword, is particularly problematic and has a troubled history when it comes to LGBTIQ materials. These filters contain lists of terms that the filtering companies deem likely objectionable. "When the filtering program is in use on a computer, each Internet search result or direct entry of a web address is scanned against the list before results are displayed" (p. 3). Filtering software products have had terms on their keyword list that are particularly troubling. There have been cases of the word "breast" or "lesbian" appearing on these lists, which obviously significantly impair the ability for teens to access important health information or online LGBTIQ communities.

Responding to Mandated Filtering

When left with no other choice, libraries may be forced to use these commercial filtering products and struggle in constructing a practices policy which conforms with the principles of making "available the widest diversity of views and expressions, including those that are unorthodox, unpopular, or considered dangerous by the majority" (ALA Freedom to Read, 2009, p. 1). In effect, filtering products that restrict access to topics such as sexual and gender minority issues are doing so because they deem them controversial. This, of course, represents a value judgment on the part of these filtering companies and goes beyond what is required for CIPA compliance. Perhaps revealingly, there exists an established link between many of the popular filtering products (such as Symantec's I-Gear, N2H2's Bess, 836 Technologies' X-Stop, Solid Oak Software's Cybersitter, and WebSense) and largely Christian organizations, including prominent positions on the boards of several of the largest filtering companies (Ayre, 2004, p. 10). A University of Michigan study agrees with this sentiment concluding, "the main effect of the more restrictive settings [in these popular filtering products] is to block other categories of controversial material besides pornography" including LGBTIQ materials (Richardson et al., 2002, p. 2894).

Some recommendations are made in the *Library Technology Report* article "Filtering and Filtering Software" by Lori Bowen Ayre on how to deal with filtering mandates and work to lessen the damage done. She recommends disabling the monitoring feature available on many filtering products and to make this known to patrons so that they have a reasonable assurance that their privacy is maintained and that their online usage will not be documented (Ayre, 2004, p. 50). As mentioned earlier with the Kaiser survey, confidentiality ranked as the most important issue when adolescents look up health information online (Richardson et al., 2002, p. 10).

A second suggestion is to closely examine the category descriptions in the software product chosen. Many of the filtering products will hide exactly what URLs are blocked in a certain category so a librarian must be willing to investigate exactly what is contained in a category the filtering company self-defines as "sex" or "sexuality." For example, the two popular filtering products Smartfilter and N2H2 both have content categories called "Sex" yet Smartfilter's rate of overblocking health sites is much lower than N2H2's whose filter would block non-explicit sites dealing with adolescent sexuality (Ayre, 2004, p. 50). Essentially, a librarian should never trust the filtering company's category descriptions and should vigorously investigate the product's settings to attempt to lower the rate at which they block access to health and LGBTIQ information. Experimenting with the settings, and doing simulations, can prove beneficial.

Ayre continues with the recommendation that filters reinforce existing Internet use policy. For example, if the library's Internet use policy prohibits gambling, online gaming or chatting, the filtering software may have features that will block these services. Separate profiles can be made so that gambling, for example, could be blocked for everyone; whereas information about sexuality could be available via the teen profile in the teen library and blocked in the children's section (p. 51). Working closely with staff to create these profiles would be wise as they are often the best resources and will ultimately be the ones asked to turn off the filtering when it is blocking a requested site. Creating separate profiles enable libraries to comply with CIPA while demonstrating to their patrons that the library remains a safe place for young children to use the Internet (p. 52).

Ultimately, ensuring simple, and minimal, compliance with CIPA should be all that any librarian will need out of any prospective filtering product. As such, Ayre recommends that the librarian, or network administrator, who chooses the product and configures it keep in mind that compliance with CIPA is all that is necessary. Many popular filtering products used in libraries, such as CyberPatrol, contain broadly defined categories such as "adult/sexually explicit" which includes both materials that are objectionable, and sites that are not. Configuring the product to reasonably reduce the amount of overblocking will go a long way in reducing requests on staff (p. 53). Additionally, looking at usage studies, such as the one written by San Jose Public, may help a library system to choose an appropriate filtering product.

Another concern is the reliance on filtering once installed. Adult patrons with children may wrongly assume that because an Internet terminal is filtered this automatically results in a safer environment for children (Ayre, 2004, p. 54; Kranich, 2004, p. 14). Using specially designed search engines tailored towards sites appropriate for children may help, but a library should never put faith in filtering's ability to block all objectionable content from children. Accordingly, continuing to monitor the Internet viewing habits of very young patrons would be appropriate as long as adolescents have a reasonable degree of privacy and confidentiality.

After choosing and configuring the complying filtering product, staff should do testing before patron use. Training library staff on how to disable the filtering and how to monitor the accuracy of the configuration is needed. Included in this process is a method for patron feedback and a clear explanation of the filtering policy and what exactly is blocked to the public. Ayre recognizes that anonymity is essential in this effort when it comes to both patron feedback and requests to unblock permitted sites. She warns, "[p]atrons don't always want to ask for help or disclose what they are looking for. The embarrassed teenager looking for sex education information that has been erroneously categorized as sexually explicit and thus blocked is not likely to request the page be unblocked. If patrons could make override requests anonymously, they might" (Ayre, 2004, p. 59). Libraries would thus be wise to create a procedure where patrons could anonymously submit that a particular site be unblocked from the filtering.

When handling these unblocking requests a library should create an effective procedure to handle them as quickly and fairly as possible. Waiting until the end of the week to evaluate unblock requests, or at a specific time every day, may be a poor way to ensure equitable access. Instead, either immediately evaluate a blocked site or, if this is not possible, create a policy to automatically unblock sites and evaluate them after the fact may be more appropriate (p. 60). Because of the rapidly changing nature of online sources, expediency is critical in ensuring that processing requests for non-objectionable materials is done as quickly as possible.

A library should also create a policy on the use of online social networks. As the interactivity of the Internet rises, it is becoming increasingly important that adolescents are given freedom to connect with their peers through social networking sites of their choosing. A blanket policy that restricts access to Facebook or MySpace, for example, may have detrimental effects on the ability of these adolescents to connect with others and create an online social network.

Conclusion

While the current debate over Internet filtering remains unresolved, many libraries have little choice but to abide by the filtering restrictions mandated by the Children's Internet Protection Act. The ways in which filtering affects access to health information is clear, as is the disparate impact this mandate has on LGBTIQ youth. Internet filtering particularly affects LGBTIQ adolescents as it impairs their ability to create online communities and find healthy places to experiment during their crucial identity formation period. There is solid evidence that providing adolescents with the information they need to make informed choices about their sexuality and health, and environments conducive to their identity formation, leads to reductions in STD transmission, depression and teen suicide. It is a matter of public health that librarians remain proactive in combating Internet filtering and the issues of intellectual freedom it raises for sexual minority and gender variant patrons. Creating a clear and comprehensive Internet use policy and making a vigilant effort to reduce unnecessary overblocking will reflect the ideals of the profession and the values of intellectual freedom. Librarians have an important role in ensuring equitable access and providing critical health information to those in our communities who may be disadvantaged and unable to access this information elsewhere.

NOTES

1. See also the profile "It's Not Monopoly: Gender Role Explorations in Online Environments" in Section One.
2. For more information, see also "Queering Libraries and Classrooms: Strategies to Build Inclusive Library Collections and Services for Sexual Minority and Gender Variant Youth" in Section Two and also "The Internet and LGBTIQ Communities" in Section One.

REFERENCES

ACLU v. Reno, 929 F.Supp. 824 (E.D.Pa. 1996).
ACLU v. Reno, 217 F.3d 162 (3rd Cir. 2000).

ALA freedom to read statement. (n.d.). In *American Library Association.* Retrieved from http://www.ala.org/ala/aboutala/offices/oif/statementspols/ftrstatement/freedomreadstatement.cfm

American Psychological Association. (2008). *Answers to your questions: For a better understanding of sexual orientation and homosexuality.* Retrieved from http://www.apa.org/pubinfo/answers.html

Ayre, L.B. (2004). Filtering and filter software. *Library Technology Reports, 40*(2), 5–80.

Bell, B. (2001, March). Filth, filtering, and the First Amendment: Ruminations on public libraries' use of Internet filtering software. *Federal Communications Law Journal, 53*, 191–237.

Bernstein, G. (2004, April). Accommodating technological innovation: identity, genetic testing and the Internet. *Vanderbilt Law Review, 57*, 965–1039.

Bond, B., Hefner, V., & Drogos, K. (2009). Information-seeking practices during the sexual development of lesbian, gay, and bisexual individuals: the influence and effects of coming out in a mediated environment. *Sexuality & Culture, 32*(1), 32–50. doi: 10.1007/s12119-008-9041-y

Brooks, Caryn. (2009, June 2). How to come out on Facebook. *TIME Magazine.* Retrieved from http://www.time.com/time/nation/article/0,8599,1901909,00.html

Chermerinsky, E. (2006). *Constitutional law: principles and policies.* New York: Aspen.

Deibert, R., Palfrey, J., Rohonzinski, R., & Zittrain, J. (Eds.). (2008). *Access denied: the practice and policy of global Internet filtering.* Cambridge, MA: The MIT Press.

Denizet-Lewis, B. (2009, September 23). Coming out in middle school. *New York Times.* Retrieved from http://www.nytimes.com/2009/09/27/magazine/27out-t.html

Dobija, J. (2007). The first amendment needs new clothes. *American Libraries, 38*(8), 51–53.

Fedders, B. (2006, Spring). Coming out for kids: Recognizing, respecting, and representing LGBTQ youth. *Nevada Law Journal, 6*, 774–804.

Friedman, C., & Morgan, E. (2009). Comparing sexual minority and heterosexual young women's friends and parents as sources of support for sexual issues. *Journal of Youth and Adolescence, 38*, 920–936. doi: 10.1007/s10964-008-9361-0

Garry, J.M., Javier, L., Schneider, K., Spear, J., Walsh, J., Clayton, G., Smith, G.A., et al. (1999). Access denied version 2.0: The continuing threat against Internet access and privacy and its impact on the lesbian, gay, bisexual and transgender community. Retrieved from http://www.glaad.org/documents/media/AccessDenied2.pdf

Hamer, J. (2003). Coming-out: Gay males' information seeking. *School Libraries Worldwide, 9*(2), 73–89.

Hammack, P., Thompson, E., & Pilecki, A. (2009). Configuration of identity among sexual minority youth: Context, desire, and narrative. *Journal of Youth and Adolescence, 38*, 867–883. doi: 10.1007/s10964-008-9342-3

Harris Poll Interactive. (2008, April 21). *Gay and lesbian adults are reading and responding to more blogs than heterosexuals.* Retrieved from http://www.harrisinteractive.com/news/allnewsbydate.asp?NewsID=1300

Heins, M., Cho, C., & Feldman, A. (2006). Internet filters: A public policy report. In *Brennan Center for Justice, NYU School of Law.* Retrieved from http://www.fepproject.org/policyreports/filters2.pdf

Hostetler, A.J., & Herdt, G.H. (1998). Culture, sexual lifeways, and developmental subjectivities: Rethinking sexual taxonomies. *Social Research, 65*(2), 249–290.

Houghton-Jan, S. (2008, April). Internet filtering software tests: Barracuda, CyberPatrol, FilterGate & WebSense. In *San Jose Public Library.* Retrieved from http://www.sjlibrary.org/about/sjpl/commission/agen0208_report.pdf

Internet Filtering Software. (n.d.). A position paper from the Office for Public Policy of the Gay, Lesbian and Straight Education Network. In *GLSEN (Gay, Lesbian and Straight Education Network).* Retrieved from http://www.glsen.org/binary-data/GLSEN_ATTACHMENTS/file/282-1.PDF

Jaeger, P., & Yan, Z. (2009, March). One law with two outcomes: Comparing the implementation of CIPA in public libraries and schools. *Information Technology and Libraries, 28*(1), 6–14.

Kibble, M. (2008). Fear mongering, filters, the Internet and the First Amendment: Why Congress should not pass legislation similar to the Deleting Online Predators Act. *Roger Williams University Law Review, 13*, 497–528.

Kosciw, J.G., Diaz, E.M., & Greytak, E.A. (2007). The 2007 national school climate survey: The experiences of lesbian, gay, bisexual and transgender youth in our nation's schools. In *GLSEN (Gay, Lesbian and Straight Education Network).* Retrieved from http://www.glsen.org/binary-data/GLSEN_ATTACHMENTS/file/000/001/1290-1.pdf

Kranich, N. (2004). Why filters won't protect children or adults. *Library Administration and Management, 18*(1), 14–8.

Mainstream Loudoun v. Loudoun County. 24 F. Supp. 2d 552 (E.D. Va. 1998).

McKenna, Y.A., & Bargh, A. (1998). Coming out in the age of the Internet: Identity "demarginalization" through virtual group participation. *Journal of Personality and Social Psychology, 75*(3), 681–694. doi: 10.1037/0022-3514.75.3.681

Miller v. California, 413 U.S. 15 (1973).

Miltner, K. (2005, May). Discriminatory filtering: CIPA's effect on our nation's youth and why the Supreme Court erred in upholding the constitutionality of the Children's Internet Protection Act. *Federal Communications Law Journal, 57,* 555–578.

Munt, S., Bassett, E., & O'Riordan, K. (2002, July). Virtually belonging: Risk, connectivity, and coming out on-line. *International Journal of Sexuality and Gender Studies, 7*(2/3), 125–137. doi: 10.1023/A:1015893016167

Perry Education Association v. Perry Local Educators' Association, 460 U.S. 37 (1983).

Peters, R. (2007). It will take more than parental use of filtering software to protect children from Internet pornography. *New York University Review of Law and Social Change, 31*(4), 829–854.

Richardson, C.R., Resnick, P.J., Hansen, D.L., Derry, H.A., Rideout, V.J. (2002). Does pornography-blocking software block access to health information on the Internet? *Journal of the American Medical Association, 288*(22), 2887–2894.

Rideout, V. (2002, December). See no evil: How Internet filters affect the search for online health information. In *Henry J. Kaiser Family Foundation.* Retrieved from http://www.kff.org/entmedia/upload/See-No-Evil-How-Internet-Filters-Affect-the-Search-for-Online-Health-Information-Executive-Summary.pdf

Schmidt, C. (2008, March). Those interfering filters! How to deal with the reality of filters in your school library. *Library Media Connection, 26*(6), 54–55.

Spurlin, C., & Garry, P. (2009). Does filtering stop the flow of valuable information? A case study of the Children's Internet Protection Act (CIPA) in South Dakota. *South Dakota Law Review, 54*(1), 89–96.

Stein, E. (2003). Queers anonymous: Lesbians, gay men, free speech, and cyberspace. *Harvard Civil Rights-Civil Liberties Law Review, 38*(1), 159–213.

United States of America, et al., v. American Library Association, Inc., et al. 539 U.S. 194 (2003).

Van der Heide, J. C. (2008, Fall). Social networking and sexual predators: The case for self-regulation. *Hastings Communications and Entertainment Law Review, 31,* 173–191.

Wu, F. (2004). United States v. American Library Ass'n: The Children's Internet Protection Act, library filtering, and institutional roles. *Berkeley Technology Law Journal, 19,* 555–583.

Responding to a Challenge: A Letter from a Public Library Director — *Uncle Bobby's Wedding*

James LaRue

Recently, a library patron challenged (urged a reconsideration of the ownership or placement of) a book called Uncle Bobby's Wedding. *Honestly, I hadn't even heard of it until that complaint. But I did read the book, and responded to the patron, who challenged the item through email and requested that I respond online (not via snail-mail) about her concerns.*

I suspect the book will get a lot of challenges, so I offer my response, purging the patron's name, for other librarians.

June 27, 2008
Dear Ms. Patron:

Thank you for working with my assistant to allow me to fit your concerns about *Uncle Bobby's Wedding* by Sarah S. Brannen, into our "reconsideration" process. I have been assured that you have received and viewed our relevant policies: the *Library Bill of Rights*, the Freedom to Read, Free Access to Libraries for Minors, the Freedom to View, and our Reconsideration Policy.

The intent of providing all that isn't just to occupy your time. It's to demonstrate that our lay Board of Trustees — which has reviewed and adopted these policies on behalf of our library — has spent time thinking about the context in which the library operates, and thoughtfully considered the occasional discomfort (with our culture or constituents) that might result. There's a lot to consider.

Here's what I understand to be your concern, based on your writings. First, you believe that "the book is specifically designed to normalize gay marriage and is targeted toward the 2–7 year old age group." Your second key concern is that you "find it inappropriate that this type of literature is available to this age group." You cite your discussion with your daughter, and commented, "This was not the type of conversation I thought I would be having with my seven year old in the nightly bedtime routine."

Finally, you state your strong belief, first, "in America and the beliefs of our founding fathers," and second, that "marriage is a covenant between a man and a woman as stated in the Webster's dictionary and also in the Bible."

You directed me to the SarahBrannen.com site, which I also reviewed. I got a copy of

Uncle Bobby's Wedding today, and read it. I even hauled out my favorite Webster's (the college edition, copyright 1960).

First, I think you're right that the purpose of the book is to show a central event, the wedding of two male characters, as no big thing. The emotional center of the story, of course, is Chloe's fear that she's losing a favorite uncle to another relationship. That fear, I think, is real enough to be an issue for a lot of young children. But yes, Sarah Brannen clearly was trying to portray gay marriage as normal, but not nearly so important as the changing relationship between a young person and her favorite uncle.

Your second issue is a little trickier. You say that the book is inappropriate, and I infer that your reason is the topic itself: gay marriage. I think a lot of adults imagine that what defines a children's book is the subject. But that's not the case. Children's books deal with anything and everything. There are children's books about death (even suicide), adult alcoholism, family violence, and more. Even the most common fairy tales have their grim side: the father and stepmother of Hansel and Gretel, facing hunger and poverty, take the children into the woods, and abandon them to die! Little Red Riding Hood (in the original version, anyhow) was eaten by the wolf along with granny. There's a fascinating book about this, by the bye, called *The Uses of Enchantment: The Meaning and Importance of Fairy Tales* by psychologist Bruno Bettelheim. His thesis is that both the purpose and power of children's literature is to help young people begin to make sense of the world. There is a lot out there that is confusing, or faintly threatening, and even dangerous in the world. Stories help children name their fears, understand them, work out strategies for dealing with life. In "Hansel and Gretel," children learn that cleverness and mutual support might help you to escape bad situations. In "Little Red Riding Hood," they learn not to talk to big bad strangers. Of course, not all children's books deal with "difficult issues," maybe not even most of them. But it's not unusual.

So what defines a children's book is the treatment, not the topic. *Uncle Bobby's Wedding* is 27–28 pages long (if you count the dedication page). Generally, there are about 30 words per page, and each page is illustrated. The main character, and the key perspective, is that of a young girl. The book is published by G. P. Putnam's Sons, "a division of Penguin Young Readers Group." The Cataloging in Publication information (on the back side of the title page) shows that the catalogers of the Library of Congress identified it as an "E" book — easy or beginning reader. Bottom line: It's hard for me to see it as anything but a children's book.

You suggested that the book could be "placed in an area designating the subject matter," or "labeled for parental guidance" by stating that "some material may be inappropriate for young children." I have two responses. First, we tried the "parenting collection" approach a couple of times in my history here. And here's what we found: nobody uses them. They constitute a barrier to discovery and use. The books there — and some very fine ones — just got lost. In the second case, I believe that every book in the children's area, particularly in the area where usually the parent is reading the book aloud, involves parental guidance. The labeling issue is tricky, too: is the topic just homosexuality? Where babies come from? Authority figures that can't be trusted? Stepmothers who abandon their children to die?

Ultimately, such labels make up a governmental determination of the moral value of the story. It seems to me — as a father who has done a lot of reading to his kids over the years — that that kind of decision is up to the parents, not the library. Because here's the truth of the matter: not every parent has the same value system.

You feel that a book about gay marriage is inappropriate for young children. But another book in our collection, *Daddy's Roommate*, was requested by a mother whose husband left her, and their young son, for another man. She was looking for a way to begin talking about this with her son. Another book, *Alfie's Home*, was purchased at the request of another mother looking for a way to talk about the suspected homosexuality of her young son from a Christian perspective. There are gay parents in Douglas County, right now, who also pay taxes, and also look for materials to support their views. We don't have very many books on this topic, but we do have a handful.

In short, most of the books we have are designed not to interfere with parents' notions of how to raise their children, but to support them. But not every parent is looking for the same thing.

Your third point, about the founders' vision of America, is something that has been a matter of keen interest to me most of my adult life. In fact, I even wrote a book about it, where I went back and read the founders' early writings about the Constitution and the Bill of Rights. What a fascinating time to be alive! What astonishing minds! Here's what I learned: our whole system of government was based on the idea that the purpose of the state was to preserve individual liberties, not to dictate them. The founders uniformly despised many practices in England that compromised matters of individual conscience by restricting freedom of speech. Freedom of speech — the right to talk, write, publish, discuss — was so important to the founders that it was the first amendment to the Constitution — and without it, the Constitution never would have been ratified.

How then, can we claim that the founders would support the restriction of access to a book that really is just about an idea, to be accepted or rejected as you choose? What harm has this book done to anyone? Your seven year old told you, "Boys are not supposed to marry." In other words, you have taught her your values, and those values have taken hold. That's what parents are supposed to do, and clearly, exposure to this book, or several, doesn't just overthrow that parental influence. It does, of course, provide evidence that not everybody agrees with each other; but that's true, isn't it?

The second part of your third point was your belief that marriage was between a man and a woman. My Webster's actually gives several definitions of marriage: "1. the state of being married; relation between husband and wife...; 2. the act of marrying, wedding; 3. the rite or form used in marrying; 4. any close or intimate union." Definitions 2–4, even as far back as 1960, could be stretched to include a wedding between two men. Word definitions change; legal rights change. In some parts of America, at least today, gay marriage is legal. If it's legal, then how could writing a book about it be inappropriate?

Finally, then, I conclude that *Uncle Bobby's Wedding* is a children's book, appropriately categorized and shelved in our children's picture book area. I fully appreciate that you, and some of your friends, strongly disagree with its viewpoint. But if the library is doing its job, there are lots of books in our collection that people won't agree with; there are certainly many that I object to. Library collections don't imply endorsement; they imply access to the many different ideas of our culture, which is precisely our purpose in public life.

As noted in our policies, you do have the right to appeal my decision to the Board of Trustees. If you'd like to do that, let me know, and I can schedule a meeting. Meanwhile, I'm more than happy to discuss this further with you. I do appreciate many things: your obvious value of reading, your frank and loving relationship with your child, your willingness to raise issues of importance to you in the public square, and more. Thank you, very much, for taking the time to raise your concerns with me. Although I suspect you may not agree with my decision, I hope it's clear that I've given it a great deal of thought, and believe it is in accordance with both our guiding principles, and those, incidentally, of the founders of our nation.

Best wishes to you and your family,
James LaRue
Director, Douglas County (Colorado) Libraries

LGBTIQ Librarians and Workplace Issues

Rachel Wexelbaum

Introduction

Historically, LGBTIQ librarians have made notable contributions to the library profession. They have played significant roles in increasing access to resources and services for underserved populations, as well as to speak out against censorship. They have also served as role models for many library school students. Just like LGBTIQ individuals in the United States military, LGBTIQ librarians often serve on the front lines, fighting for intellectual freedom and free access to resources for all. In spite of the many contributions to the profession made by LGBTIQ librarians, many librarians remain unaware of LGBTIQ issues, let alone the history of LGBTIQ librarianship, because the LGBTIQ population has not always been included in the definition of diversity or in library school courses that may address diversity or social issues. Not only that, but acceptance of LGBTIQ librarians in the workplace is not always guaranteed, since (as of this writing) there is no existing federal employment non-discrimination policy addressing LGBTIQ individuals in any career field.

The Definition of Diversity

According to the *2007 State of Workplace Diversity Management Report*, only 30 percent of human resource professionals and diversity practitioners have an agreed upon definition of "diversity." Historically, the term "diversity" primarily addressed the recognition of people of color, immigrants, and people with disabilities. Not all institutions have included LGBTIQ individuals in their definition of diversity. The American Library Association defines workplace diversity in their "Diversity Vision" of their Staff Diversity and Inclusion Action Plan:

> in addition to race, creed, color, religion, gender, disability and national origin, there are a multitude of differences (language origin, regional and geographic background, economic class, education, learning and communication styles, sexual orientation and personal lifestyle) that individuals bring to the workplace. It is this diversity that contributes a deeper level of understanding and competence to our daily work [American Library Association, p. 1].

While this may be so, lesbian, gay, and bisexual librarians are still sometimes subject to discrimination in the workplace. As for transgender librarians, the ALA definition of diversity does not specifically include gender identity or gender expression as a distinct category from gender.

How Many LGBTIQ People Are in the Library Profession?

While the American Library Association collects statistics on the racial and gender breakdown of working librarians or library school students, it is difficult to gather accurate information on the percentage of working LGBTIQ librarians or library school students. Library school applications, as well as employment applications, do not ask candidates to identify their sexual orientation, gender identity, or marital status for affirmative action purposes. It is also illegal for employers to ask candidates about their sexual orientation, gender identity, or marital status during job interviews.

While older studies declared that one in ten people could be gay or lesbian, current studies from the United States and other countries reveal that one in twenty-five people may identify as gay or lesbian, while up to 13 percent may identify as bisexual (Savin-Williams, 2009). Calculating the percentage of transgender people in the population has been much more difficult; older studies only accounted for transsexuals who have undergone sex reassignment surgery, while more recent studies have included individuals who self-identified as an alternative category when asked to identify their gender identity. For this reason, the recorded percentage of transgender people in the human population has ranged from .25 to 8 percent (Human Rights Campaign, 2009).

Men, who compose the majority in most professions, remain the minority in librarianship. A demographic study of credentialed librarians revealed that roughly 18 percent identified as male (Davis & Hall, 2007). A 2009 report to the ALA Executive Board revealed that, from 1980 to 2005, four female credentialed librarians consistently existed for every male credentialed librarian in all age groups (Tordella & Godfrey, 2009). In library school programs, roughly 20 percent of library school students identify as male (Davis & Hall).

Although no accurate count of LGBTIQ librarians exist, some people believe that LGBTIQ librarians and LGBTIQ library school students may be overrepresented as compared to the general population. Historically, women who did not wish to marry entered the field of librarianship; there is no record of how many identified as lesbians. These unmarried female librarians may have remained closeted at work while serving as "the keepers of knowledge and the promoters of social morality" (Schell, 2001, p. 7). Due to the predominance of women in the library profession, men who became librarians were historically viewed as effeminate, and even in recent times are often stereotyped as homosexual (Carmichael, 1995).

How Library School Programs Address LGBTIQ Issues and Diversity

In addition to addressing diversity issues as they relate to resources and services, libraries must also address diversity issues in the workplace. Librarianship is still considered a predominantly "white" profession; as of 2007, only 11 percent of credentialed librarians identified as people of color (Davis & Hall). This lack of diversity begins in library school programs; in 2002 only 11.3 percent of library school students identified as people of color, as compared to 31.3 percent of the population (Kim & Sin, 2008).

Very few library school programs include the LGBTIQ population in their definition of "diversity." Some library schools and associations have programs to recruit a diverse pool of students, as well as offer scholarships to underrepresented groups in librarianship, but they do not specifically identify the LGBTIQ community in their definitions of diversity or minorities. The ALA Spectrum scholarship for minorities within the library profession, for example, does not apply to LGBTIQ students unless they are also students of color.

Over the past twenty years, library school programs have attempted to recruit more applicants from "underrepresented" populations. Many library schools have decided to address "diversity" by teaching future librarians about the information and service needs of "special populations." These populations often include Native Americans, African-Americans, Spanish-speaking populations living within the United States, immigrants, senior citizens, and people with disabilities.

A survey distributed to library school graduates asked whether or not social justice issues or LGBT issues had ever been addressed in their library school classes. While more than half of the graduates agreed that social justice issues were covered in their foundations and reference classes, the vast majority stated that LGBT issues and women's issues were not covered in any of their classes during library school, including classes that dealt with diversity, collection management, library administration, reference, and intellectual freedom (Carmichael, 1996). If students recalled a course where LGBT issues were addressed, it was often because the professor teaching the course was gay or lesbian.

In a review of online course descriptions of 57 ALA-accredited Masters of Library Science programs performed by the author of the current essay, one third address "diversity" in their curricula by offering at least one class that focuses on the information needs, user behavior, or resources and services for library patrons in underrepresented populations. Of those nineteen programs that offer at least one course about diversity, only three specifically address the needs of LGBTIQ patrons in course descriptions.[1] None of the library school programs directly address the specific career development needs of LGBTIQ library students. If a specific class on LGBTIQ librarianship is offered in the curriculum — even as an elective — it not only increases the comfort level of LGBTIQ students, but provides a safe forum for heterosexual library school students to learn about LGBTIQ issues in librarianship as well.

LGBTIQ Library School Student Preparation for Library Jobs

Every library school student is unique. While "traditional" library school students are "returning students" who are career changers or library paraprofessionals, a growing percentage may have started library school right after they received their bachelor's degree as full time undergraduate students. Library school students with minimal work experience often have a difficult time securing a full time library position after graduation, and struggle to adapt to the professional library workplace without mentoring and career guidance.

LGBTIQ library school students are especially at risk for failure or disillusionment within the library profession. Young students fresh out of a four year college may not have the self-awareness to determine what type of library environment would be right for them.

In an unfamiliar work environment, they may return to "the closet" if they feel isolated. They also may feel intimidated to speak out against homophobia or transphobia that they may observe or experience in the workplace. Not only that, but if LGBTIQ issues are not covered in library school programs, LGBTIQ library school graduates may apply for and accept library positions unaware of their rights (or lack of them) and how the lack of certain benefits may affect them.

LGBTIQ students may want to talk with self-identified LGBTIQ library school faculty about how to build a library career and navigate the professional library environment as an LGBTIQ person. Some library school programs do sponsor LGBTIQ library student organizations for professional mentoring and networking purposes. Those library school programs which require the completion of internship or practicum hours for graduation may inspire students to search for LGBTIQ librarians working in the types of libraries where the students aspire to work. Those library school programs which offer independent studies for students interested in library science-related subjects not addressed in the curriculum may also give LGBTIQ library school students the opportunity to network with LGBTIQ librarians through collaboration on research or working in special collections.

Being Out in the Stacks: Advantages to Being Out At Work

Most people entering the library profession do so with great humility. They do not always realize that, as librarians, they are also public figures who present a particular image of librarianship to the community that they serve. People who are new to the profession do not always realize that librarianship is more of a social gig than they had envisioned. In a big library, catalogers, sometimes stereotyped as misanthropes, must communicate with reference, circulation, systems, and collections staff in order to make the catalog as functional as possible. In a small library, the solo librarian will not only perform all library-related duties, but will also serve as tutor, babysitter, counselor, and fundraiser. No conscientious librarian these days can afford to hide in the stacks away from people.

Librarians go to a lot of conferences and network in many capacities. The stereotype of a shushing librarian soon falls flat when a flock of them congregate in a meeting or at the bar. They talk a lot about work, but they also talk about pets, hobbies, and significant others. If an LGBTIQ librarian is unsure of their social environment, they may not feel comfortable to "come out." Even worse, the LGBTIQ librarian may not feel comfortable addressing the needs of LGBTIQ patrons should they need assistance. The LGBTIQ librarian who is not out may subconsciously present a dishonest picture of themselves to the community that they serve, which may lead to a passivity that will do more harm than good.

Male librarians who identify as heterosexual have sometimes discriminated against gay male librarians in order to disassociate themselves from the perceived negative stereotype of an effeminate, ineffectual male librarian. According to a survey distributed to male librarians, straight male librarians are more likely to learn about this stereotype in library school, while gay male librarians become familiar with the stereotype from other librarians in the workplace (Carmichael, 1991). While male librarians identifying as straight are more likely to perceive discrimination predominantly from female coworkers, or a combination of male and female coworkers, gay male librarians are more likely to perceive discrimination predominantly from straight male librarians (Carmichael, 1995). Discrimination against straight and gay male librarians in the library profession will affect the number of male librarians who will self-identify as gay.

In the anthology *Liberating Minds: The Stories and Professional Lives of Gay, Lesbian, and Bisexual Librarians and Their Advocates* (Kester, 1997), thirty three lesbian, gay, and bisexual public and academic librarians shared their stories about different aspects of LGBTIQ librarianship. One of the librarians was inspired to come out as bisexual in the academic library where he worked because of the significant bisexual holdings he noted in the collection, and the fact that there was an ad hoc GLBT library task force in that state (Montgomery, pp. 56–59). Another librarian felt comfortable being out in the workplace because so many of his male coworkers were also openly gay (Garnes, p. 68). One librarian "came out" by writing book reviews for ALA's Gay and Lesbian Task Force, which led to invitations to write book reviews for scholarly journals, then to the physical presentation of her expertise to other librarians (Stone, pp. 82–83). Many of the librarians took proactive roles in selecting LGBTIQ materials for their collections; some were officially appointed to do so based on their "out" status. In general, being out at work empowered the librarians to take on leadership positions in the workplace and play a more active role in the communities which they served. Their presence as "out" librarians inspired colleagues or library patrons to open up to them and address information needs which previously had gone unexpressed. Not all librarians in the anthology came out with confidence to their employers; one librarian crossed out her LGBT affiliations on her curriculum vitae, thinking that those affiliations would affect her chances of being interviewed for an academic librarian position (Turner, pp. 143–144). One gay librarian of color noted many incidences where straight librarians of color were more likely to express homophobic thoughts or behavior in the workplace than white librarians, which sometimes made his work difficult when working with patrons of color (Kester, "Brother, Warrior," p. 64).

In school libraries, it is still difficult for many LGBTIQ librarians to be "out" in their environments, even in schools which may publish a non-discrimination policy in regard to enrolling, educating, and retaining students. Many school districts still lag far behind state legislation in regard to anti-discrimination policies to protect LGBTIQ teachers and librarians, particularly in rural areas, high poverty areas, and communities with lower adult educational attainment (Gay Lesbian and Straight Education Network, 2009). Sometimes school administrators want to be on good terms with parents, and will not always stand up for the rights of employees who may not fit the mold of teachers who promote "traditional" values. In school districts where books are banned due to LGBTIQ content, where students are allowed to call each other "faggot" and "queer" without reprimand, and where LGBTIQ students do not receive the support they need during their "coming out" process, LGBTIQ librarians may question their job security or acceptance among their colleagues should they come out. Even the American Association of School Librarians (AASL) seems to turn a blind eye to LGBTIQ school librarians when they describe themselves as "an open, friendly, welcoming organization that embraces cultural and ethnic diversity" making no reference to sexual orientation or gender identity (AASL Vision Statement, 2009). The Gay Lesbian and Straight Education Network (GLSEN) provides a wealth of supportive resources and training materials related to LGBTIQ acceptance for K–12 students and teachers interested in reducing homophobia in their schools, but it takes courage and support for a K–12 teacher or librarian in a homophobic community to initiate the process when few protections or forms of support are in place for those teachers or librarians themselves.

Workplace Challenges for Transgender Librarians

By fall 2009, only twelve states (California, Colorado, Illinois, Iowa, Maine, Minnesota, New Jersey, New Mexico, Oregon, Rhode Island, Vermont, and Washington) and the District of Columbia had banned discrimination against gender identity in all areas of employment. While some institutions have made the commitment to provide programs which educate employers about transgender issues and the transitioning process, it is still difficult for many transpeople to earn full acceptance in the workplace. In a study of Fortune-ranked corporations, more than 90 percent of the corporations prohibit discrimination against sexual orientation, while less than half offer the same protections for transgender employees (American Civil Liberties Union, 2007). In most cases, this discrimination stems from a lack of education regarding transgender issues. Even some gays, lesbians, and bisexuals do not support protections for transgender people in the workplace.

Public, school, and academic libraries are still behind the curve in regard to protections for transgender employees. One example of a library that has taken the lead in serving its transgender population is the Oak Park Public Library in Illinois.[2]

In states where there are no protections for LGBTIQ librarians, transgender librarians often suffer the brunt of discriminatory practices. In 2002, academic librarian Gypsey Teague was hired by Langston University, the only historically black university in Oklahoma, to serve as a branch librarian and an adjunct professor in the business department. In 2004, Teague decided to start the process of transitioning from male to female. While the administration was initially supportive of her decision, in 2005 a student circulated a petition calling for her removal from campus simply because she was transgender. When Teague spoke with the campus director about it, she was told that the student had a right to freedom of speech. The student continued to circulate hate-filled petitions and post flyers, leading the administration to implement a policy prohibiting use of classroom and library restrooms designated for students by faculty and staff that only Teague was directed to follow. Teague continued to file complaints and was told that she was "causing drama," resulting in a shift to an undesirable late night teaching schedule. This affected Teague's personal safety, as she was the last person to leave the building and had to walk through an empty unlit parking lot to go home. As many academic librarians serve as teaching faculty, and the percentage of their teaching hours can be as high as 50 percent, the failure of Langston University to stand up for Teague lowered her morale and affected the quality of her work in the library. With no recourse, Teague resigned from Langston University in 2005 to accept a library position at Clemson University in South Carolina (sadly, another institution which does not offer protection for transgender employees, in another state with no protection for transgender employees). As Teague herself sums it up:

> Had the administrators who were charged with my welfare stood up and supported me in the face of mean-spirited prejudice, I think I would have been able to stay and to prosper. When they failed to take decisive action, I was forced to choose between my safety, both emotional and physical, and my job [2009, para. 7].

Although the District of Columbia has banned discrimination in all areas of employment based on sexual orientation and gender identity, this legislation does not apply to federal employees. LGBTIQ federal employees can still be refused employment, denied promotion, or dismissed simply based on their sexual orientation or gender identity. Diane Schroer, a decorated military hero, had retired from military service and applied for the position of senior terrorism research analyst in the Congressional Research Service Division of the Library of Congress. Schroer applied for the position under her former name, David Schroer, and interviewed for the position in men's clothing. The Library of Congress offered Schroer the position when she was David, but rescinded the offer when she told her supervisor that she was transitioning and would start her new job as Diane dressed in traditional female attire. In spite of her flawless work record, her status as a veteran, and her loyalty to the United States government, the federal government intended to terminate Schroer simply because of her transgender identity. Diane took the Library of Congress to court and won. She also testified during the ENDA discussions in Congress, and her case, in addition to many others, is being used to fight for the rights of LGBTIQ federal employees.

Employment Policies and Benefits

In a 2000 survey by Hewitt Associates of nearly 600 companies in the United States, 22 percent of the companies offered domestic partner benefits for gay and lesbian employees. While two thirds of the companies provided those benefits primarily as a recruitment and retention tool, only 6 percent said that they offered the benefits "to be fair" (Braun Consulting News, 2005). Public, school, and academic libraries are often part of an administrative hierarchy, and their administrators cannot make decisions regarding domestic partner benefits or insurance plans without some form of state, local, or institutional support.

The Human Rights Campaign (HRC) conducts an annual survey of corporate responsibility in regard to LGBTIQ issues in the workplace. HRC tracks how many companies have policies, programs, and benefits that protect LGBTIQ employees and ensure their success in the workplace. Every year, the number of for-profit companies that include some form of protection and benefits to their LGBTIQ employees (as well as the number of for-profit companies that strive to improve their offerings to LGBTIQ employees) increases. This shows that many corporations have made a commitment to hire a diverse pool of employees, ensure that their employees are encouraged to be culturally sensitive, and provide assistance and support to them if they are in need.

Unfortunately, no organization at this time has developed a measurement tool or survey to collect data regarding policies, programs, and benefits that protect and support LGBTIQ library employees in public, school, or academic libraries. This does not mean that libraries are necessarily doing a better job than for-profit companies in regard to addressing the needs of LGBTIQ employees. In fact, libraries may have a worse social responsibility track record than private companies in regard to addressing LGBTIQ workplace issues, especially in states that have anti-discrimination legislation to protect LGBTIQ individuals in the workplace.

Minnesota is an example of a state which prohibits discrimination based on sexual orientation and gender identity in all areas of employment, but does not mandate that all employers must provide equal benefits to LGBTIQ employees. While Minnesota-based employers such as Target, 3M, and Cargill have received perfect scores on HRC's Corporate Equality Index for diversity training that includes gender transition guidelines, health insurance plans that include coverage for transition expenses, and full benefits for domestic partners, Minnesota libraries have not been held to the same standard. Most public school districts in Minnesota, for example, do not offer health benefits for domestic partners of librarians. Colleges and university systems in Minnesota vary widely in terms of diversity training and benefits that they may offer. The University of Minnesota system (U of M), for example, offers domestic partner benefits, but they are not equal to those benefits received by heterosexual U of M employees. The Minnesota State Colleges and Universities system (MnSCU) offers no domestic partner benefits at all, even though they have a significant LGBTIQ employee population, continue to hire LGBTIQ faculty and staff, and provide a great deal of support and resources for LGBTIQ students.

In 2009, as part of the LGBT Faculty/Staff Caucus at Saint Cloud State University, the author collected data on whether or not peer institutions of Saint Cloud State University offered domestic partner benefits if they were located in states that did not already recognize some form of same-sex partnership. Saint Cloud State University has twenty seven peer institutions; six peer institutions exist in states which recognize some form of same-sex partnership (California, New Jersey, and Iowa). Of the remaining twenty one peer institutions, only four offer equal domestic partnership benefits to their LGBTIQ employees.

Unless a state government has legalized some form of same-sex matrimony and included a clause to state that all institutions within the state must provide domestic partner benefits, public, school, and academic libraries may or may not provide domestic partner benefits. To add insult to injury, those domestic partner benefits provided, such as health insurance, are often taxable, unlike those given to heterosexual spouses. Sometimes the only domestic partner benefit offered is a library card, or use of the gym facilities — both of which are already offered in most cases to the general public.

Title VII of the Civil Rights Act of 1964 (42 U.S.C. §§ 2000e and following) prohibits employers from discriminating against applicants and employees on the basis of race or color, religion, sex, and national origin. It also prohibits employers from retaliating against an applicant or employee who asserts his or her rights under the law. Currently this federal law does not apply to sexual orientation or gender identity.

On June 17, 2009, President Barack Obama issued a Memorandum on Federal Benefits and Non Discrimination to the Director of the Office of Personnel Management and the Secretary of State to give a small number of federal benefits to same-sex partners of some federal employees (Obama, 2009). This memorandum, while a start, does not include full health insurance coverage. A proposed bill being discussed in the United States Congress called the Employment Non-Discrimination Act (ENDA) would ban discrimination against employees on the basis of sexual orientation and gender identity for civilian nonreligious employers. ENDA would provide protection against discrimination on a federal level to LGBTIQ librarians working for non-military, non-religious institutions, including federal institutions such as the Library of Congress.

Each state in the Union has chosen to address LGBTIQ discrimination in a different way. As of 2009, thirty states in the Union (and the District of Columbia) have state laws that address employment discrimination against LGBTIQ individuals. Unfortunately, not all of these states address employment discrimination equally:

- Twelve states (California, Colorado, Illinois, Iowa, Maine, Minnesota, New Jersey, New Mexico, Oregon, Rhode Island, Vermont, and Washington) and the District of Columbia have banned discrimination against sexual orientation and gender identity in all areas of employment.
- Nine states (Connecticut, Delaware, Hawaii, Maryland, Massachusetts, Nevada, New Hampshire, New York, and Wisconsin) only ban discrimination against sexual orientation in all areas of employment.

- Six states (Indiana, Kansas, Kentucky, Ohio, Michigan, and Pennsylvania) ban discrimination against sexual orientation and gender identity only in state employment.
- Four states (Alaska, Arizona, Montana, and Virginia) ban discrimination against sexual orientation only in state employment.

This leaves nineteen states in the Union without any form of protection against discrimination for LGBTIQ individuals in the workplace. If ENDA should come to pass, LGBTIQ librarians employed by non-religious institutions in all states will be protected from discrimination under federal law.

Unfortunately, anti-discrimination protections for LGBTIQ librarians in the workplace will not apply to domestic partner benefits, nor to health insurance coverage for the costs of transitioning. Even in states where domestic partnership, civil unions, or same-sex marriages are legal, there is no assurance that health insurance companies will provide benefits for same-sex partners.

Diversity Training for Librarians and Paraprofessional Staff

Education of library professionals on LGBTIQ issues not only strengthens the collection and services to patrons, but should also help library professionals gain a better understanding of their LGBTIQ coworkers. Diversity training which includes an LGBTIQ component will also help male librarians, who are insecure about their sexual identity due to the perpetuation of negative stereotypes, feel more comfortable on the job, and thus reduce the possibility that they will discriminate against their gay male coworkers.

Many academic librarians are required to attend some form of diversity training as part of a college/university initiative to "embrace diversity." As part of this initiative, many colleges and universities encourage faculty of color, and sometimes LGBTIQ faculty, to apply for residencies or full time positions. This sometimes serves as the impetus to provide diversity training for all employees. Unfortunately, not all colleges and universities include an LGBTIQ component in their mandatory diversity training program, even if the institution has an LGBT Resource Center and/or a faculty/staff LGBT organization to address workplace issues. The LGBT Resource Center may offer "Safe Space" training for interested faculty and staff who wish to be "point people" around campus for students and coworkers who may need resources or support, but this training is not mandatory. It is up to individual library administrators to determine whether or not to make more in-depth LGBTIQ sensitivity training a priority for their staff.

Public library systems provide diversity training to their employees if they are classified as state employees and if the training is mandatory for all state employees. If this is not the case, then it is up to the individual library administrator to initiate the process of selecting an established trainer or developing a unique program tailored to the needs of the library employees. The probability that the public library director will initiate some form of diversity training for its employees will increase if the public library serves a large LGBTIQ population or is located in a diverse urban community. Traditionally, diversity training in public libraries has not focused on employee relations; instead, it has focused on collection development issues, customer service, and implementation of new services.

School librarians receive the least support in regard to diversity training. While many organizations have developed programs to teach K–12 students about diversity, bullying, and homophobia, the enforcement of diversity training varies from state to state and district to district, and is rarely made mandatory for K–12 employees. It is possible that school administrators assume that new K–12 employees responsible for teaching receive diversity training through new teacher certification requirements that require specific coursework that may address underrepresented populations. As budget cuts force many public school districts to lay off certified librarians and replace them with paraprofessionals or volunteers who may or may not be responsible for classroom teaching, the probability that those school "librarians" have received even the minimum of formal cultural sensitivity training through coursework is very small. Some well-meaning school librarians will order books with LGBTIQ content for the students, but will not necessarily provide teacher resources including LGBTIQ content unless asked. School librarians who identify as lesbian, gay, bisexual, or transgender may or may not feel comfortable initiating conversations regarding diversity issues if the administration, the faculty, and the community are not supportive.

LGBTIQ Library Organizations and Resources for Support

In order for LGBTIQ librarians to be out in the workplace, they must have a support system outside as well as inside the library. LGBTIQ professional associations can serve as a source of support, especially for new librarians.

The premiere professional group for LGBTIQ librarians, the American Library Association Task Force on Gay Liberation (now known as the Gay, Lesbian, Bisexual, and Transgendered — GLBTRT — Roundtable) was founded in 1970. While the initial impetus for GLBTRT was to provide support for LGBTIQ librarians in the workplace, its main focus is now on improving access and resources for LGBTIQ library patrons and their allies rather than librarians themselves. Informally, however, the GLBTRT serves as a social networking venue for LGBTIQ librarians who are ALA members.[3]

Unfortunately, as of 2009, most state library associations do not have distinct groups for LGBTIQ librarians or issues in librarianship. The author of this current essay reviewed the committees, divisions, roundtables, and interest groups of all fifty state library associations and three regional library associations. As of fall 2009, only four state library associations and one regional library association include a specific LGBTIQ roundtable or interest group. Those groups are included in the resource list below. LGBTIQ librarians in most states may have to join a diversity, social responsibility, or intellectual freedom group to address their concerns.

LGBTIQ Professional Library Organizations

National Associations

American Library Association, Gay, Lesbian, Bisexual, and Transgendered Round Table (GLBTRT) <http://www.ala.org/ala/mgrps/rts/glbtrt/index.cfm>. According to their mission statement, "The Gay, Lesbian, Bisexual, and Transgendered Round Table of the American Library Association is committed to serving the information needs of the gay, lesbian, bisexual, and transgendered professional library community, and the gay, lesbian, bisexual, and transgendered information and access needs of individuals at large" (American

Library Association Gay, Lesbian, Bisexual, and Transgendered Round Table, 2009). Their main responsibility is to promote the improved quality, quantity, and accessibility of library materials of particular interest or usefulness to lesbian, bisexual, gay, and transgendered people of all ages. They also evaluate LGBTIQ fiction and non-fiction for the annual Stonewall Awards, organize panel discussions, and run a booth at the annual ALA Diversity Fair where they provide handouts and presentations on LGBTIQ resources and LGBTIQ issues in librarianship. ALA GLBTRT works together with ALA's Intellectual Freedom Round Table, ALA's Social Responsibilities Round Table, ALA's Ethnic and Multicultural Information Exchange Roundtable, and ALA's Offices for Diversity and Intellectual Freedom to ensure that there is easy access to appropriate, objective LGBTIQ materials in libraries, as well as fair treatment of LGBTIQ library patrons and librarians.[4]

American Association of Law Libraries (AALL), Standing Committee on Lesbian and Gay Issues <http://www.aallnet.org/sis/srsis/lgbt/index.html>. Founded in 1985 as a standing committee of the AALL Social Responsibility Special Interest Section, this committee "promotes non-discrimination policies and diversity in all aspects of the employment and professional life of law Librarians" (American Association of Law Libraries Standing Committee on Lesbian and Gay Issues, 2008). They have organized educational programs on lesbian and gay legal collection development, AIDS, and lesbians and gays in the military. They also have a gay and lesbian mentor program.

Medical Library Association (MLA), Relevant Issues Section, Lesbian, Gay, Bisexual and Transgendered Health Science Librarians Special Interest Group (SIG) <http://lgbt.mlanet.org/>. According to their position statement, the Lesbian, Gay, Bisexual and Transgendered Health Science Librarians SIG will "identify, collect, and disseminate gay/lesbian/bisexual health care information within this organization in order to enhance the quality and quantity of information available to our colleagues within MLA and within our institutions in order to support the physical and psychological health care concerns of our clients" (Medical Library Association Lesbian, Gay, Bisexual and Transgendered Health Science Librarians Special Interest Group, 2008). They also publish a newsletter, maintain an online discussion group, and resource bibliographies on LGBTIQ library issues, lesbian health, LGBTIQ mental health, and HIV and AIDS, among other general health resources.

Society of American Archivists, Lesbian and Gay Roundtable (LAGAR) <http://www.archivists.org/saagroups/lagar/>. According to their mission statement, "[LAGAR] is committed to bringing information about lesbian, gay, bisexual, and transgender archives to the public through projects such as *Lavender Legacies*, and to helping small community-based archives with information about archival practices" (Society of American Archivists Lesbian and Gay Roundtable, 2009). The group is concerned about lesbian and gay history, the role of lesbians and gays in the archival profession, and preservation and research use of LGBTIQ primary sources. LAGAR serves as a liaison between LGBTIQ archives and the Society of American Archivists.[5]

Special Libraries Association (SLA), Gay, Lesbian, Bisexual & Transgender Issues Caucus (GLBTIC) <http://units.sla.org/caucus/kglic/>. GLBTIC is a forum within SLA for resource sharing and discussion of issues of interest to the LGBTIQ members and allies of SLA. GLBTIC consists of LGBTIQ librarians who work in subject specific collections, health sciences libraries, law libraries, archives, museum collections, television and film studio collections, and other research institutions and resource centers which serve industry professionals or a targeted group of scholars or students.

Regional Associations

HQ76.3/New England: Lesbian, Gay, Bisexual, and Transgendered Librarians and Library Workers (GLBT Section of the New England Library Association) <http://www.dartmouth.edu/~jcd/hq763.html>. HQ76.3/New England is a social/professional organization of gays, lesbians, bisexuals, and transgendered people working in libraries in New England. According to their mission statement, "HQ76.3/New England seeks to make substantial contributions toward enhancing the visibility, recognition, and acceptance of all lesbian, gay, bisexual and transgendered library workers ... to support the work of regional lesbian, gay, bisexual and transgendered librarians and other library staff and to meet the broader needs of the library community, both staff and users" (HQ76.3/New England, 2008). Established in 1993, HQ76.3 has faithfully marched in Boston's Gay Pride Parade, hosted potlucks, sponsored readings, produced bibliographies, and served as a networking resource for other LGBT and library-related organizations.[6]

State Associations

Florida Library Association, GLBT Library Services Support, *not online*. The GLBT Library Services Support Group was founded to address the needs of all library patrons and library employees. Since its establishment, the group has presented annual programs on transgender etiquette, the importance of young adult GLBT titles in collections, and Leslea Newman's challenges during the writing and publishing process of *Heather Has Two Mommies*. According to founder Jerry Notaro, "to address the needs of any library patron is to address the needs of all." (J. Notaro, personal communication, November 16, 2009).

New Jersey Library Association, Lesbian, Gay, Bisexual, Transgendered and Intersexed (LGBTI) Roundtable <http://njla.pbworks.com/LGBTI>. According to their mission statement, the "Lesbian, Gay, Bisexual, Transgendered and Intersexed Roundtable has advocated and educated on behalf of librarian, support staff, and patron lesbian, gay, bisexual, transgender, and intersexed communities" (New Jersey Library Association Lesbian, Gay, Bisexual, Transgendered and Intersexed Roundtable, 2009). This Roundtable has taken a proactive role in collection development, reference and access support, and working together with other library organizations.

South Carolina Library Association, Gay, Lesbian, Bisexual, and Transgendered Round Table <http://www.scla.org/index.php?n=GayLesbianBisexualAndTransgender RoundTable.HomePage>. The Gay, Lesbian, Bisexual, and Transgendered Round Table provides "a forum for discussion and an environment for education and learning regarding the needs of the gay, lesbian, bisexual, and transgendered professional community and population at large" (South Carolina Library Association Gay, Lesbian, Bisexual, and Transgendered Round Table, 2009). They are not only committed to the information needs for LGBTIQ patrons, but also to advocacy for LGBTIQ librarians and library workers.

Texas Library Association, Gay, Lesbian, Bisexual, and Transgendered Interest Group <http://www.txla.org/groups/glbtig/glbt.html>. The purpose of the GLBT Interest group is "to address issues of concern to gay, lesbian, bisexual and transgendered library staff and patrons. Issues addressed may include fairness and discrimination in personnel decisions and in collections; censorship; collection development; networking; and sharing information" (Texas Library Association Gay, Lesbian, Bisexual, and Transgendered Interest Group, 2008).

Electronic Discussion Lists[7]

GAY-LIBN <http://www-lib.usc.edu/~trimmer/gay-libn.html>. A discussion list for LGBTIQ librarians and all others interested in relevant resources and issues.

GLBTRT Discussion List <http://lists.ala.org/wws/info/glbtrt-1>. The official discussion list of the American Library Association Gay, Lesbian, Bisexual, and Transgendered Round Table.

LAGAR (Lesbian and Gay Archives Roundtable, Society of American Archivists) <http://www.archivists.org/saagroups/lagar/listserv.html>. The LAGAR discussion list was created to stimulate discussion and the exchange of information related to collecting, preserving, and making accessible LGBTIQ historical documents.

LEZBRIAN <http://groups.yahoo.com/group/LEZBRIAN/>. Discussion list for lesbian and bisexual library workers and all others interested in relevant resources and issues.

Trans Library Workers Group <http://groups.google.com/group/tglibn>. Anyone with a Google account can become a member of the Trans Library Workers Group. Topics posted have included transitioning at work, relevant news articles, job postings, and calls for submissions to books and journals.

Conclusion

Many LGBTIQ librarians and library workers still face discrimination in the workplace due to a combination of factors. Discussion of LGBTIQ issues in library school, diversity and sensitivity training that addresses LGBTIQ issues for all library employees, legal protection against discrimination, and supportive social and professional networks will reduce discrimination against LGBTIQ library employees. Not only that, but increased LGBTIQ acceptance in the workplace also improves the work environment for other underrepresented groups in librarianship.

NOTES

1. San Jose State University (SJSU) offers an online section of LIBR 220: Resources and Information Services in Professions and Disciplines as a class on LGBTQ Library Resources and Issues at http://slisweb.sjsu.edu/classes/coursedesc.htm. Through the Web-based Information Science Education (WISE) program at http://www.wiseeducation.org, participating schools have access to online classes taught at the other member schools. And through this reciprocal program, students from the University of Illinois, Syracuse University, and the University of British Columbia have been enrolled in the SJSU class. At Clarion State University in Pennsylvania, the course description for LS 540: Multicultural Services and Sources for Education and Libraries states that "resources and services are examined particularly as they relate to ethnicity, race, gender preference, and disability" which implies that gay and lesbian issues are discussed in this class. See http://www.clarion.edu/1317/?directory-query=LS%20540

2. For more information, see "When Collection Development Leads to Staff Development: The Transgender Resource Collection," also in this section.

3. For more information about the GLBTRT, see the profile included in this section.

4. For more information about the GLBTRT, see the profile included in this section.

5. For more information about LAGAR, see the profile included in this section.

6. For more information about HQ76.3-New England, see the profile included in this section.

7. Many LGBTIQ professional library groups also have other means of communicating with members, including blogs, wikis, and social networking sites such as Facebook.

References

American Association of Law Libraries Standing Committee on Lesbian and Gay Issues. (2008, July). *Standing Committee on Lesbian and Gay Issues Home Page*. Retrieved from http://www.aallnet.org/sis/srsis/lgbt/index.html

American Library Association. (n.d.) *American Library Association staff diversity and inclusion action plan*. Retrieved from http://www.ala.org/ala/aboutala/offices/diversity/ALA_Diversity_Action_and_Inclusion_Plan.pdf

American Library Association Gay, Lesbian, Bisexual, and Transgendered Round Table. (2009). GLBT Round Table. Retrieved from http://www.ala.org/ala/mgrps/rts/glbtrt/index.cfm

Carmichael, J. V. (1995). The gay librarian: A comparative analysis of attitudes toward professional gender issues. *Journal of Homosexuality, 30*(2), 11–57.

Carmichael, J. V., & Shontz, M. (1996). The last socially acceptable prejudice: Gay and lesbian issues, social responsibilities, and coverage of these topics in M.L.I.S./M.L.S. programs. *The Library Quarterly, 66*(1), 21–58.

Cooke, J. C. (2005, Fall). Gay and lesbian librarians and the "need" for GLBT library organizations. *Journal of Information Ethics, 14*(2), 32–49.

Davis, D. M, & Hall, T. D. (2007). *Diversity counts*. Chicago: ALA Office for Research and Statistics/Office for Diversity. Retrieved from http://www.ala.org/ala/aboutala/offices/diversity/diversitycounts/diversitycounts_rev0.pdf

Egan, P. J., Edelman, M. S., & Sherrill, K. (2008). *Findings from the Hunter College poll of lesbians, gays, and bisexuals: New discoveries about identity, political attitudes, and civic engagement*. New York: The City University of New York. Retrieved from http://www.nyu.edu/public.affairs/pdf/hunter_college_poll_report_complete.pdf

Few organizations define diversity. (2008, March 4). *HRM Guide*. Retrieved from http://www.hrmguide.com/diversity/job-market.htm

Fikar, C. R. (2004). Information needs of gay, lesbian, bisexual, and transgendered health care professionals: Results of an Internet survey. *Journal of the Medical Library Association, 92*(1), 56–65.

Garnes, D. (1997). Rip Van Winkle in Connecticut. In N.G. Kester, (Ed.), *Liberating minds: The stories and professional lives of gay, lesbian, and bisexual librarians and their advocates* (pp. 68–72). Jefferson, NC: McFarland.

Goodson, P. (2008, October). Male librarians: Gender issues and stereotypes. *Library Student Journal*. Retrieved from http://www.librarystudentjournal.org/index.php/lsj/article/viewArticle/100/187

Griffiths, J.-M., King, D. W., & Choemprayong, S. (2009). *IMLS study: The future of librarians in the workplace: Overview and key findings* [PowerPoint slides]. School of Library and Information Science, University of North Carolina at Chapel Hill: Institute of Museum and Library Services. Retrieved from http://www.sla.org/PDFs/SLA2009/2009_SLAIMLS_update.pdf

HQ76.3/New England. (2008, October 23). *HQ76.3 New England: Lesbian, Gay, and Bisexual Librarians and Library Workers*. Retrieved from http://www.dartmouth.edu/~jcd/hq763.html

H.R. 3017: The Employment Non-Discrimination Act of 2009: Hearing before the House Committee on Education and Labor, 111th Congress, (2009).

Human Rights Campaign. (2009). Corporate equality index. Retrieved from http://www.hrc.org/issues/workplace/cei.htm

Kester, N.G. (1997). Brother, warrior: The black gay librarian-writer — some personal reflections. In N.G. Kester (Ed.), *Liberating minds: The stories and professional lives of gay, lesbian, and bisexual librarians and their advocates* (pp. 62–67). Jefferson, NC: McFarland.

Kester, N.G. (Ed.). (1997). *Liberating minds: The stories and professional lives of gay, lesbian, and bisexual librarians and their advocates*. Jefferson, NC: McFarland.

Kim, K.-S., & Sin, S.-C. J. (2008). Increasing ethnic diversity in LIS: Perspectives from librarians of color. *Library Quarterly, 78*(2), 153–177.

Lupton, B. (2006). Explaining men's entry into female-concentrated occupations: Issues of masculinity and social class. *Gender, Work, and Organization, 13*(2), 103–128.

Medical Library Association, Lesbian, Gay, Bisexual and Transgendered Health Science Librarians Special Interests Group. (2008, May 22). *Lesbian, Gay, Bisexual and Transgendered Health Science Librarians Special Interest Group (SIG) of the Medical Library Association*. Retrieved from http://lgbt.mlanet.org/

Montgomery, M. (1997). Of books and bisexuality. In N.G. Kester, (Ed.), *Liberating minds: The stories and professional lives of gay, lesbian, and bisexual librarians and their advocates* (pp. 55–59). Jefferson, NC: McFarland.

New Jersey Library Association Lesbian, Gay, Bisexual, Transgendered, and Intersexed Roundtable (2009, November 11). *LGBTI.* Retrieved from http://njla.pbworks.com/LGBTI

Obama, B. (2009, June 17). *Memorandum for the heads of executive departments and agencies.* Retrieved from http://www.whitehouse.gov/the_press_office/Memorandum-for-the-Heads-of-Executive-Depart ments-and-Agencies-on-Federal-Benefits-and-Non-Discrimination-6-17-09/

Savin-Williams, R. C. (2009). How many gays are there? It depends. In D. A. Hope (Ed.), *Contemporary perspectives on lesbian, gay, and bisexual identities* (pp. 5–41) New York: Springer Science + Business Media, LLC. doi: 10.1007/978-0-387-09956-1

Schell, L. E. (2001). *Workplace identity management issues of lesbian and bisexual librarians* (unpublished master's thesis). University of North Carolina at Chapel Hill. Retrieved from http://ils.unc.edu/MSpa pers/2690.pdf

Society of American Archivists Lesbian and Gay Archives Roundtable. (2009, November 12). *Society of American Archivists' Lesbian and Gay Archives Roundtable.* Retrieved from http://www.archivists.org/ saagroups/lagar/

South Carolina Library Association Gay, Lesbian, Bisexual, and Transgendered Round Table (2009, January 13). *Gay, Lesbian, Bisexual, and Transgendered Round Table.* Retrieved from http://www.scla.org/index. php?n=GayLesbianBisexualAndTransgenderRoundTable.HomePage

Stone, M.E. (1997). My destiny: Librarianship. In N.G. Kester, (Ed.), *Liberating minds: The stories and professional lives of gay, lesbian, and bisexual librarians and their advocates* (pp. 79–86). Jefferson, NC: McFarland.

Teague, G. (2009, October 18). Why ENDA matters: True stories of anti–LGBT employment discrimination from the ACLU. *The Bilerico Project.* Message posted to http://www.bilerico.com/2009/10/ why_enda_matters_true_stories_of_anti-lgbt_employm.php

Texas Library Association Gay, Lesbian, Bisexual, and Transgendered Interest Group. (2008, August 18). *TLA — Gay Lesbian Bisexual Transgendered Interest Group.* Retrieved from http://www.txla.org/groups/ glbtig/glbt.html

Tordella, S., & Godfrey, T. (2009, July 13). *Librarian retirements and ALA memberships* [Powerpoint slides]. Retrieved from http://www.ala.org/ala/aboutala/governance/officers/ebdocuments/2008_2009ebdoc uments/ebd12_58lib_retire.pdf

Turner, D. (1997). Where should the closets be in a library without walls? In N.G. Kester, (Ed.), *Liberating minds: The stories and professional lives of gay, lesbian, and bisexual librarians and their advocates* (pp. 143–148). Jefferson, NC: McFarland.

Winfield, L. (2005). *Straight talk about gays in the workplace: Creating an inclusive, productive environment for everyone in your organization.* New York: Harrington.

Workplace diversity: Does it work? (2004/2005, Winter) *Braun Consulting News: News on Personnel, Labor Relations and Benefits.* Retrieved from http://www.braunconsulting.com/bcg/newsletters/winter2004/ winter20042.html

Integrating LGBTIQ Representations Across the Library and Information Science Curriculum: A Strategic Framework for Student-Centered Interventions[1]

Bharat Mehra

Introduction

Contemporary American society has bestowed a popular mandate on library and information science (LIS) educators to train future librarians in critically applying their knowledge and expertise of information creation-organization-dissemination processes to effectively meet the unique social, cultural, and technological challenges of the twenty-first century (Bishop, Van House, & Buttenfield, 2003; Borgman, 2007). One such challenge especially relevant in today's intercultural and intertwined global networked information society is regarding the representation of diversity, recognition of multiple viewpoints, and integration of content of, for, and by disenfranchised populations (Abdullahi, 2007; Mehra, Allard, Qayyum, & Barclay-McLaughlin, 2008). Often "left out" in the representation of the "intercultural" (Sanlo, Rankin & Schoenberg, 2002) in LIS education are the needs and expectations of lesbian, gay, bisexual, transgender, intersex, and questioning (LGBTIQ) communities and experiences (Mehra & Srinivasan, 2007; Stringer-Stanback, 2009), considered "invisible" and the disenfranchised group in almost every corner of the world who are sometimes given the "token treatment" in a special population LIS course or marginally addressed in the LIS curriculum in an isolated and fragmented manner (Lovaas, Elia, & Yep, 2007; Mehra & Braquet, 2007a). Such limited efforts fail to adequately and systematically address the underlying heterosexual assumptions and biases that are almost ubiquitously taken for granted in any information-related teaching and learning environment (Ben-Ari, 2001; Szymanski & Carr, 2008).

This essay addresses these missing gaps and suggests a strategic framework for infusing LGBTIQ representations (e.g., experiences, informational content, point of views, behaviors, practices, etc.) in the LIS curriculum to address a perceived lack of fair, complete, and accurate information for and about people of diverse sexual orientations and gender identities in American communities and library settings (Mehra & Braquet, 2006; Mehra, Merkel, & Bishop, 2004). The strategic framework identifies goals and digital and non-digital actions/interventions that LIS educators can facilitate in their classroom in support of LGB-TIQ people. A focus on student involvement in digital and non-digital actions as part of their LIS course assignments is proposed to provide tangible and low-cost outcomes that are responsive to the current budget-cuts and appropriate for the digital age of the twenty-first century. Research methods in this study involved mapping information-related LGB-TIQ-relevant criteria with existing course syllabi in the curriculum of the University of Tennessee's (UT) School of Information Sciences (SIS) to propose student-centered interventions that further LGBTIQ representations, social justice activism, and promote community-wide socially progressive changes on behalf of LGBTIQ populations. These interventions in the LIS curriculum will help educate and train future librarians and others to become socially progressive curators of world knowledge (Shera & Egan, 1953; Rayward, 1975). It will transform them to become true leaders involved in the organization/management of information (Taylor, 2003; Stueart & Moran, 2007) who realize the worth of questioning heterosexist assumptions in LIS work and take appropriate actions that rectify these biases in a systematic and holistic manner that may bring about community-wide social, cultural, political, legal, and economic changes for LGBTIQ people.

Research Context

The goal of this research is to promote student-centered digital and non-digital actions/interventions in the LIS classroom that lead to fairness and equity in representation of LGBTIQ content in terms of its creation and inclusion in information-related work that is often found to be inaccurate, incomplete, and/or ignored owing to cultural inertia, administrative lethargy, prejudice and bias, and/or deliberate or unintentional ignorance, amongst other reasons (Mehra & Braquet, 2007b). In order to achieve this goal the essay proposes concrete examples of digital and non-digital actions/interventions for LIS student participation in course assignments and identifies the "how-tos" to address the specifics and particulars in information-related work to support LGBTIQ people. Such efforts will help develop more LGBTIQ-related content and opportunities for equitable digital and non-digital representation; it will lead to greater awareness of LGBTIQ issues in the LIS professions, academy, and surrounding communities. Implementing initiatives to further LGBTIQ representations in LIS education will also invigorate the profession and extend public relations via generating greater LIS visibility and involvement in the development of appropriate web and print content for marginalized groups (e.g., LGBTIQ people). This will help gain political support of local administrators and legislative power-brokers, community decision-makers, and the general public at large.

The findings reported in this paper are informed by qualitative studies and action research conducted by the author and others on behalf of LGBTIQ people at the UT since spring 2005. The essay extends and redefines (in a digitized and non-digitized context) select variables from a study entitled "A Website Analysis of the University of Tennessee's Peer Institutions to Assess their Support of Lesbian, Gay, Bisexual, and Transgender People" that the author led as Vice-Chair of the Research Committee of the UT's Commission for LGBT People during January–June 2007 (Mehra, Braquet, White, Weaver, & Hodge,

2007). Twelve peer institutions recognized by UT's Office of Institutional Research and Assessment were included in the study that assessed their web representation of LGBT issues based on select variables from the list of "gay friendly" criteria identified in *The Advocate College Guide for LGBT Students* (Windmeyer, 2006). The initial assessment of UT's support for LGBT people (based on the select variables) showed that the UT was ranked in the bottom two universities as compared to its peer institutions at the time.

Since the variables used in the UT's peer institution web assessment study were developed in an academic context they had to be partially redefined to apply to a broader community context. The process helped identify the role of LIS educators and students in taking digital and non-digital actions for progressive social change on behalf of LGBTIQ people. Re-definition of variable meanings were generated also in response to a contextual understanding of the UT's climate in support of LGBTIQ people and helped develop consistency between the different coders. The emerging digital and non-digital actions were mapped to existing syllabi of LIS courses in the UT's SIS to identify specific classroom interventions that can be taken in support of LGBTIQ people via student involvement in LIS course assignments. Grounded theory applications of open, axial, and selective coding practices were used to generate themes and patterns in digital and non-digital interventions. The findings were shared via the "LGBTANet," a local e-mail discussion list, and distributed to the members of UT's Commission for LGBT People for feedback that was integrated into the findings shared in this essay.

Findings: LGBTIQ Actions in the LIS Classroom

Table 1 summarizes the LIS classroom actions based on redefined LGBTIQ variables that helped generate meanings in a digital and non-digital community context.

Table 1: LIS classroom actions based on redefined LGBTIQ variables in a digital and non-digital community context.

No.	LGBTIQ Variable in an Academic Environment	Variable Redefined in a Digital/Non-Digital Community Context	LIS Classroom Actions
1.	LGBTIQ and ally student organizations	Creation of LGBTIQ print content and links from agency's main homepage to active/current LGBTIQ internal and external resources	Web and print resource development, LGBTIQ community analysis and needs assessment
2.	LGBTIQ resource center (office)	Physical and virtual space demarcated for use as a centralized LGBTIQ resource center for comprehensive access	Development of an information project management portfolio, policies, and bylaws for the LGBTIQ resource center
3.	Formal LGBTIQ representation (e.g., taskforce, commission, etc.)	Formal LGBTIQ representations in the agency's administrative and management structure	Proactive information analysis and use for social justice advocacy

No.	LGBTIQ Variable in an Academic Environment	Variable Redefined in a Digital/Non-Digital Community Context	LIS Classroom Actions
4.	Safe zone programs	Designated safe space programs especially for LGBTIQ people that have a trained support system to facilitate their operation and implementation	Development and print/electronic marketing of the library as an LGBTIQ "safe space"
5.	LGBTIQ social activities and educational events	Social activities and events for LGBTIQ people; Educational events on LGBTIQ topics and concerns	Event planning and development of the library as an LGBTIQ "safe space"; Information dissemination
6.	LGBTIQ studies (courses and curriculum)	Specialized courses on LGBTIQ issues and representation of LGBTIQ content throughout the curriculum of various disciplines	Digital and non-digital LGBTIQ information collection
7.	Nondiscrimination statement inclusive of sexual orientation and gender identity	Inclusion of the terms "sexual orientation" and "gender identity" in the Equal Employment Opportunity/Affirmative Action Statement (EEO/AA) to provide legal protection	Proactive information analysis and use for social justice advocacy; Creation of effective marketing and press coverage
8.	Domestic partner benefits for same-sex couples	Extending benefits for domestic partners of LGBTIQ members in the agency	Proactive information analysis and use for social justice advocacy
9.	LGBTIQ sensitivity training	Sensitivity training to create awareness, skills, and expertise in LGBTIQ concerns	Information creation and dissemination
10.	Procedures for reporting LGBTIQ bias, harassment, and hate crimes	Procedures and policies to address LGBTIQ discrimination and prejudice	Proactive information analysis and use for social justice advocacy
11.	LGBTIQ housing options	Adequate choices, options, and representation for LGBTIQ in housing	Information analysis and use
12.	LGBTIQ-inclusive health services	Visible health services (e.g., testing) to meet the needs of LGBTIQ people	Proactive information analysis and use for social justice advocacy
13.	LGBTIQ-inclusive counseling	Adequate counseling services (e.g., support groups) to meet the needs of LGBTIQ people	Proactive information analysis and use for social justice advocacy
14.	LGBTIQ student scholarships	Specific LGBTIQ scholarships and financial support provided by the agency	Proactive information analysis and use for social justice advocacy
15.	Services for trans-concerns	Representation of trans-concerns	Proactive information analysis and use for social justice advocacy
16.	LGBTIQ alumni group(s)	Visible groups for agency LGBTIQ stakeholders	Proactive information analysis and use for social justice advocacy

No.	LGBTIQ Variable in an Academic Environment	Variable Redefined in a Digital/Non-Digital Community Context	LIS Classroom Actions
17.	LGBTIQ faculty and staff group(s)	Visible groups for agency LGBTIQ stakeholders	Proactive information analysis and use for social justice advocacy
18.	"In-links" to main LGBTIQ service website	Connections within the agency to the LGBTIQ service website and resources	Web and print resource evaluation and use
19.	LGBTIQ print and online resources	Access to paper-based and electronic bibliographies, local resources, LGBTIQ listserv/mailing lists, and chatrooms, etc.	Print and digital collection development
20.	At least 4/10 top LGBTIQ-relevant hits using the University search engine and Google search engine	Functional assessment of the agency search engine and Google to effectively represent LGBTIQ concerns	Web resource development

As the select LGBTIQ variables were assessed in a broader community context that went beyond an academic setting, a few points of consideration emerged in the process. First, some aspects were similar in the LGBTIQ expectations within an academic environment and an expanded community context (e.g., a need for procedures for reporting on LGBTIQ bias, harassment, and hate crimes, as well the significance of LGBTIQ-inclusive health services and housing options). Other variables were somewhat different when superficially examined even though they had underlying aspects of similarity if one examined them closely. For example, the need for having more LGBTIQ courses and curricula seems applicable only for academic settings. Though if one looks at the broader goals of such courses to dispel ignorance and support expanded learning in areas of student limited knowledge, then this variable can be applicable in the larger community context as well where there may be a need for addressing homophobia and LGBTIQ prejudice in religious, educational, and social welfare agencies, amongst others, by offering workshops, seminars, and intergroup dialogue sessions on LGBTIQ concerns.

Further, the boundaries between digital and non-digital actions were not so distinct (Jones, 1998) and there was a need to see them as more inter-related and intersecting in terms of their socio-technical aspects and relationships in order to provide a more relevant and holistic approach (Ashraf & Anand, 2010). For example, the electronic creation of LGBTIQ web (and print) materials on existing resources available in the community (the "technical" or digital dimensions) is very much dependent on conducting a needs assessment and community analysis of the available LGBTIQ resources (quality and quantity), their impact and effectiveness, barriers to use, and suggested improvements, amongst other aspects, that are involved in the processes of collecting and analyzing informational datasets from actual people (the "socio" or non-digital dimensions).

Third, nearly all digital and non-digital actions that are proposed in a community context in this essay can have applicability irrespective of the nature of the specific environment under question. For example, having legal and political protection for LGBTIQ people via development of fair and equitably representative nondiscrimination statements and policies that are inclusive of sexual orientation and gender identity in their terminology is important in all kinds of environments (public, private, non-profit) such as government agencies, educational settings, business and corporations, community-based religious organizations, and others, in order for these agencies to attract the best and remain competitive and economically viable entities.

The proposed intertwining digital and non-digital actions listed in Table 1 extend the concept of an "information ecology" comprising of a system of people, practices, values, and technologies in a particular local setting (Nardi & Day, 2000) in that they integrate the important elements of taking progressive actions to further principles of social justice and social equity for LGBTIQ people (Mehra, Rioux, & Albright, 2009). In other words, at their heart the actions propose that the information reality and experience in a particular context (i.e., the information ecology in an organization/community) has to be extended to further the principles of social justice (e.g., fairness, justice, equality, and equity) via proposing change and improvements in the existing circumstances. In these progressive scenarios, the LIS educator and student and the library and information professional are no longer taking a passive role as neutral bystanders, but instead, the author proposes that these individuals become active participants and beacons of change to represent the marginalized and socially forward-looking ideologies in order to revitalize and expand the role of the professions (Mehra, 2008).

Discussion: Student Interventions in LIS Courses

The emerging digital and non-digital actions were easily translated into concrete interventions that LIS educators can help their students make in their local communities to further LGBTIQ content and representations while working on different assignments in their various LIS courses. Mapping the digital and non-digital actions on behalf of LGBTIQ people with existing syllabi of LIS courses in the UT's SIS proved an important step in this process. The syllabi of the courses listed in the following discussion can be found on the UT's SIS homepage (available at URL: http://www.sis.utk.edu/courses/listings). The proposed interventions in support of LGBTIQ people include:

• Web resource building, management, and maintenance
• Digital collections development and organization
• Analysis of digital use, users, and information seeking behaviors
• Research into LGBTIQ issues in different information environments
• Development of digitized social/communication technology
• Proactive information use for social justice and advocacy
• Digital information access/dissemination, marketing, and advertisement

LIS students' work in their course assignments related to web resource building, management, and maintenance can be tailored to provide them with opportunities to regularly assess and evaluate web representation in terms of fair and equitable support for LGBTIQ people in various kinds of information environments. The expectation may involve either developing primary web-based/print information (e.g., developing web pages for community-based agencies on LGBTIQ-related information resources) or managing and maintaining existing web information resources (e.g., broken links or incomplete information). For example, one member of the UT's Commission for LGBT People suggested having an LIS student work on developing new functionalities in the Commission's website (e.g., a

"Giving" link for donors to provide financial and other resources) to support LGBTIQ concerns. These assignments can be orchestrated in a course that focuses on a particular information environment (e.g., IS 552: Academic Libraries) or introduces the general topic of information and communication technologies (e.g., IS 585: Information Technologies). Developing and managing databases and content management systems for websites of community agencies unable to do so (e.g., UT's Office of Equity and Diversity) was another work category identified for potential LIS student involvement in courses like IS 584 (Database Management Systems) and IS 585 (Information Technologies).

Student interventions related to digital collections development and associated information organization activities include selecting authoritative and accurate LGBTIQ materials (print, electronic) in a course like IS 560 (Development and Management of Collections), developing LGBTIQ digital libraries in IS 565 (Digital Libraries), and technology implementation plans for delivering electronic LGBTIQ collections (IS 585: Information Technologies). For example, developing local/non-local community information directories/web portals of LGBTIQ people, activities, and events and appropriate centralized web resources were important community needs that can get met by student assignments in different LIS courses. Another area of information-related work that LIS students can undertake in their courses involves developing well-rounded and useful collection development policies for LGBTIQ materials (e.g., in IS 560: Development and Management of Collections) and multimedia collections (e.g., in IS 522: Organization and Representation of Multimedia Information Resources). Developing LGBTIQ keywords, authority control, subject headings, index terms, classifications, and metadata descriptions are other relevant activities in courses like IS 520 (Information Representation and Organization), IS 521 (Cataloging and Classification), IS 522 (Organization and Representation of Multimedia Information Resources), and IS 523 (Abstracting and Indexing).

Student intervention in analysis of LGBTIQ digital use, online users, and information seeking behaviors in electronic and face-to-face environments in their LIS courses can involve conducting community analysis and needs assessment while working with various LGBTIQ stakeholders in localized settings. An important area in this work is developing and evaluating sources, services, and access methods for LGBTIQ information in courses such as IS 530 (Information Access and Retrieval) and IS 531 (Sources and Services in the Social Sciences). User instruction and electronic reference services for LGBTIQ populations are other domains of work for potential student assignments in their LIS courses (e.g., IS 557: User Instruction). So are developing LGBTIQ fiction (various genres) and non-fiction collections for adults and young adults in courses like IS 572 (Resources and Services for Young Adults) and IS 574 (Resources and Services for Adults).

LIS course assignments for students can also be tailored to address specific LGBTIQ concerns in different information environments. For example, LIS students can conduct user-centered assessment and evaluation of select digital/non-digital public library services for LBGTIQ people for improved service design in a course like IS 554 (Public Library Management and Services) within the existing course goals and course activities. LIS students can potentially develop the entire academic library as an LGBTIQ "safe space" by working on a semester-long proposal to conceptualize and operationalize their efforts via developing appropriate library programming, hosting of events, activity planning, policy formulation, and marketing, amongst other activities, in a course like IS 552 (Academic Libraries).

LIS students can also be involved in their courses to design, develop, and use social and digital technologies to connect LGBTIQ people and resources (e.g., in IS 567: Information Network Applications). Another example of student work is developing, analyzing, and evaluating the use of Library 2.0 tools and applications for LGBTIQ users (e.g., in IS 574: Resources and Services for Adults). For example, as a master's student enrolled during spring 2009 in IS 574, Samuel "Jason" Ezell (2009) researched reader's advisory programs for LGBTIQ populations and completed his final project on "Using 2.0 Tools To Support a College Gay-Straight Alliance's Book Discussion Group."

Proactive information use for social justice and advocacy on behalf of LGBTIQ populations involves students to assess and evaluate legal LGBTIQ policies and procedures in various profit-based organizations, corporations, and companies around the world to highlight progressive trends and address unfair practices (e.g., in IS 553: Specialized Information Agencies and Services). LIS course assignments can be developed in courses like IS 552 (Academic Libraries) and IS 558 (Library Services in a Diverse Society) to have students document LGBTIQ-related information on non-discrimination policies, support services, and digital representation at local, regional, and national agencies to convince administrators, Board of Trustees, and political representatives to create an equitable and fair environment. For example, as master's students enrolled during fall 2005 in IS 558, Amy Elliott and Angela Woofter developed a hypothetical grant proposal entitled "Develop Safe Programs and Services for the Gay, Lesbian, Bisexual, Transgender, Questioning, and Allies at the University of Tennessee" following the funding guidelines for grant proposals identified by the Appalachian Community Fund.

LIS students can get involved in courses on digital information access/dissemination, marketing, and advertisement to identify and build partnerships with government and community agencies and others to participate in development of LGBTIQ-friendly print and electronic information in a course like IS 534 (Government Information Resources). Students can also participate in print/electronic information development and dissemination (e.g., developing workshop and diversity training materials) to help remove ignorance and support fair and equal constitutional rights for all individuals in a course like IS 560 (Development and Management of Collections). For example, as a master's student enrolled from 2005 to 2009 in various SIS courses (including IS 560), Roger Weaver worked with Donna Braquet, Vice-Chair of the UT's Commission for LGBT People, to establish the "Voices of Diversity" project that was created as an online multimedia archive of stories submitted by LGBTIQ students, faculty, staff and alumni of the UT (Braquet & Weaver, n.d.).

LIS students can also work in special topic courses that specifically focus on LGBTIQ concerns as and when they are offered. For example, as master's students in IS 590 (Problems in Information Science: Race, Gender, and Sexuality in the Information Professions) during spring 2007, Krishna Adams and Cason Jones were involved in a semester-long project entitled "Development of Community Information Services for the East Tennessee LGBTIQ Youth Project" that involved developing community bibliographic resources on library and information support services for LGBTIQ youth, assessing and evaluating community-based digital/non-digital resources and LIS agencies for LGBTIQ youth, surveying information support agencies for child welfare and juvenile justice programs in Knox and surrounding counties, and conducting qualitative research with LGBTIQ youth about their experiences in child welfare programs, juvenile justice programs, and/or secondary school systems.

In addition, LIS students can also enroll in practicum and independent studies to pursue an individualized and unique area of research that may include LGBTIQ topics and concerns. For example, on March 3, 2010, a call for a student practicum was made by Donna

Braquet, Vice-Chair of the UT's Commission for LGBT People, that was forwarded to the UTKSIS-L, the main UT SIS electronic list, that sought student practicum involvement in the UT LGBT and Ally Resource Center to conduct a literature review on LGBTIQ collections, analyze existing collection holdings, revise/implement a collection development policy, develop tailored web pages based on user needs, and revise a research guide for LGBT Studies using web editing tools and other Library 2.0 initiatives.

Conclusion

Elements of the strategic framework proposed in this essay were delivered and well received in a faculty retreat facilitated by the author on diversity infusion in the curriculum of the School of Information Studies at the University of Wisconsin-Milwaukee on January 29, 2010. The strategic framework presented in this essay to integrate LGBTIQ content across the LIS curriculum is "strategic" in terms of at least two levels of interpretation: 1) In its reliance on student-centered interventions that are orchestrated as part of LIS course assignments, the proposed strategic framework identifies a low-cost strategy that delivers concrete outcomes and tangibles, especially relevant in the context of the contemporary economic crunch and financial budget-cuts. Such efforts in service learning and community engagement (Mehra & Robinson, 2009) to further LGBTIQ concerns provide real problems for students to apply their information-related knowledge, skills, and experiences, and produce solutions that are significant in the process of growth of American society. 2) By training current LIS students to get involved in developing information-related work that has explicit social equity agendas for LGBTIQ populations the goal is to shape the direction of future LIS professions (including libraries) to become more visible and involved in social justice efforts. Currently, LIS tends to adopt a position of neutrality in justifying its limited advocacy role (Mehra, 2004; Phenix & McCook, 2007); the LIS professions have also traditionally gravitated towards a missionary service role in mainstream practice of "helping people" rather than "helping people help themselves" (Mehra, Albright, & Rioux, 2006) that views people as needy, impoverished, and asset-less that reflects unquestioned dynamics of power imbalances embedded in its conceptualization (Mehra, 2008). More equitable directions are important for future marketing, public relations, and continued survival of the LIS professions in the face of competing interests and sharing of LIS functionalities with community-based agencies and online stakeholders like bookstores, businesses, government agencies, and others (Mehra & Sandusky, 2009). Not only does it require a willingness of LIS students to engage in partnerships with community-based agencies to develop community relevant projects and further socially progressive ideologies; moreover, for successful adoption and implementation of the framework to integrate LGBTIQ content across the LIS curriculum, it is essential that LIS educators and researchers become more concerned with the impact of their endeavors that have traditionally taken place within the classroom, to critically reflect and evaluate how those can shape local communities to become more inclusive, fair, and welcoming places to live and grow for all people (Mehra, 2009). Providing LIS students with classroom opportunities to promote digital and non-digital interventions for LGBTIQ people will: generate greater LIS visibility/involvement in the development of appropriate web and print content for marginalized groups (and thereby extend public relations); gain political support and recognition for LIS professions by local managers/administrators, community decision-makers, and the general public as advocates for disenfranchised populations; make the community climate more conducive for LGBTIQ peoples' safety, learning, and participation in everyday life; distinguish such communities amongst others by attracting the best who want to live in welcoming and diverse environments; and give impetus to investing companies and multinational corporations searching for progressive regions for economic investments.

All identified actions and interventions presented in this research are equally important, inter-related, and need to be applied concertedly to present a holistic framework that integrates LGBTIQ experiences and content throughout the LIS curriculum to represent different community facets, in addition to developing specialized LIS courses on the topic. Future directions for LIS educators can be to promote student leadership in helping local LGBTIQ communities develop and implement a comprehensive diversity plan of action beyond piecemeal efforts to systematically concretize tangible outcomes in support of LGBTQ individuals. LIS professionals can play a significant role in wearing their dual hats as information providers and community action researchers to develop high prioritized community actions in support of LGBTIQ issues. Efforts call for LIS partnerships with outside community agencies and building of meaningful relationships between the academy and the broader community (e.g., public and school libraries) to help facilitate course assignments that further student involvement in LGBTIQ social justice activism via their information-related work. It may require creative strategizing to work around management and administration that is immersed in maintaining status quo and perpetuating cultural inertia via serving as mere communication conduits rather than taking leadership roles as proactive advocacy initiators.

NOTES

1. The author is grateful for feedback collected during the research process from the members of the University of Tennessee's Commission for LGBT People and others. A word of appreciation is offered to the audience for their feedback during a juried panel presentation of an earlier version of this paper at the Association for Library and Information Science Education 2009 Annual Conference.

REFERENCES

Abdullahi, I. (2007). Diversity and intercultural issues in library and information science (LIS) education, *New Library World, 108*(9/10), 453–459.

Ashraf, T., & Anand, P. (eds). (2010). *Developing sustainable digital libraries: Socio-technical perspectives.* Hershey, PA: Information Science.

Ben-Ari, A. (2001). Homosexuality and heterosexism: Views from academics in the helping professions, *British Journal of Social Work, 31,* 119–131.

Bishop, A. P., Van House, N., & Buttenfield, B. (eds.). (2003). *Digital library use: Social practice in design and evaluation.* Cambridge, MA: MIT Press.

Borgman, C. L. (2007). *Scholarship in the digital age: Information, infrastructure, and the Internet.* Cambridge, MA: MIT Press.

Braquet, D., & Weaver, R. (n.d.). Voices of diversity: An online LGBT story archive. Retrieved from http://lgbt.utk.edu/vod/

Ezell, S. (2009). *Using 2.0 tools to support a college gay-straight alliance's book discussion group.* University of Tennessee, School of Information Sciences. Retrieved from http://athena.cci.utk.edu/bmehra/IS574/IS574Sp09/IS574StudentList.htm#Samuel_Ezell

Jones, S. (ed.). (1998). *CyberSociety 2.0: Revisiting CMC and community.* Newbury Park, CA: Sage.

Lovaas, K. E., Elia, J. P., & Yep, G. A. (2007). *LGBT studies and queer theory: New conflicts, collaborations, and contested terrain.* Florence, KY: Routledge.

Mehra, B. (2004). Service learning in library and information science (LIS) education: Connecting research and practice to community. *InterActions: UCLA Journal of Information and Education Studies,* Volume 1, Issue 1, Article 3. Retrieved from http://repositories.cdlib.org/gseis/interactions/vol1/iss1/art3/

Mehra, B. (2008). *The cross-cultural learning process of international doctoral students: A case study in library and information science education.* Saarbrucken, Germany: Verlag Dr. Muller.

Mehra, B. (2009). A road map for integrating socially relevant research projects into a required library and information science course: From a service model to community engagement. In L. Roy, K. Jensen, and A. H. Meyers (Eds.), *Service learning: Linking library education and practice.* Chicago: American Library Association (ALA) Editions.

Mehra, B., Albright, K. S., & Rioux, K. (2006). A practical framework for social justice research in the information professions. *Proceedings of the 69th Annual Meeting of the American Society for Information Science & Technology 2006: Information Realities: Shaping the Digital Future For All.* Volume 43. [Short Paper], Austin, TX, November 3–8, 2006. [Available on CD-ROM].

Mehra, B., Allard, S., Qayyum, M. A., & Barclay-McLaughlin, G. (2008). Aquí y allá (here and there) information-based learning corridors between Tennessee and Puerto Rico: The five Golden Rules in intercultural education, *Education for Information, 26*(3), 151–168.

Mehra, B., & Braquet, D. (2006). A "queer" manifesto of interventions for libraries to "come out" of the closet! A study of "queer" youth experiences during the coming out process, *Library and Information Science Research Electronic Journal, 16*(1), (March 2006). Retrieved from http://libres.curtin.edu.au/libres16n1/

Mehra, B., & Braquet, D. (2007a). Process of information seeking during "queer" youth coming-out experiences. In M. K. Chelton and C. Cool (eds.), *Youth information seeking behaviors: Contexts, theories, models and issues* (pp. 93–131). Toronto, Canada: Scarecrow.

Mehra, B., & Braquet, D. (2007b). Library and information science professionals as community action researchers in an academic setting: Top ten directions to further institutional change for people of diverse sexual orientations and gender identities, *Library Trends, 56*(2), 542–565.

Mehra, B., Braquet, D., White, E., Weaver, R., & Hodge, C. (2007). *A website analysis of the University of Tennessee's peer institutions to assess their support of lesbian, gay, bisexual, and transgender people.* Unpublished report. Retrieved from https://web.utk.edu/~bmehra/final.pdf

Mehra, B., Merkel, C., & Bishop, A. P. (2004). Internet for empowerment of minority and marginalized communities, *New Media & Society, 6*(5), 781–802.

Mehra, B., Rioux, K., & Albright, K. S. (2009). Social justice in library and Information science. In M. J. Bates & M. N. Maack (eds.), *Encyclopedia of Library and Information Sciences.* New York: Taylor & Francis.

Mehra, B., & Robinson, W. C. (2009). The community engagement model in library and information science education: A case study of a collection development and management course. *Journal of Education for Library and Information Science, 50*(1), 15–38.

Mehra, B., & Sandusky, R. J. (2009). LIS students as community partners in elective courses: Applying community-based action research to meet the needs of underserved populations. In L. Roy, K. Jensen, and A. H. Meyers (Eds.), *Service learning: Linking library education and practice.* Chicago: American Library Association (ALA) Editions.

Mehra, B., & Srinivasan, R. (2007). The library-community convergence framework for community action: Libraries as catalysts of social change, *Libri: International Journal of Libraries and Information Services, 57*(3), 123–139.

Nardi, B. A., & O'Day, V. L. (2000). *Information ecologies: Using technology with heart.* Cambridge, MA: MIT Press.

Phenix, K., & McCook, K. de la P. (2007). A commitment to human rights: Let's honor the qualities required of a librarian dedicated to human rights. *Information for Social Change, 25* (Summer 2007). Retrieved from http://libr.org/isc/issues/ISC25/articles/A%20COMMITMENT%20TO%20 HUMAN%20RIGHTS.pdf

Rayward, W. B. (1975). The universe of information: The work of Paul Otlet for Documentation and International Organization, *FID, 20.* Moscow, Russia: VINITI.

Sanlo, R., Rankin, S., & Schoenberg, R. (eds.). (2002). *Our place on campus: Lesbian, gay, bisexual, transgender services and programs in higher education.* Santa Barbara, CA: Greenwood.

Shera, J. H., & Egan, M. E. (1953). A review of the present state of librarianship and documentation. In S. C. Bradford (ed.), *Documentation* (2nd ed., pp. 11–45). London: Crosby, Lockwood.

Stringer-Stanback, K. (2009). *Young adult lesbian, gay, bisexual, transgender and questioning non-fiction collections (LGBTQ) and countywide anti-discrimination policies.* An unpublished master's paper for the M.S. degree in Library Science, School of Information and Library Science, University of North Carolina at Chapel Hill.

Stueart, R. D., & Moran, B. B. (2007). *Library and information center management* (7th ed.). Englewood, CO: Libraries Unlimited.

Szymanski, D. M., & Carr, E. R. (2008). The roles of gender role conflict and internalized gay and bisexual men's psychological distress: Mediation models, *Psychology of Men and Masculinity, 9*(1), 40–54.

Taylor, A. G. (2003). *The organization of information* (2nd edition). Englewood, CO: Libraries Unlimited.

Windmeyer, S. L. (2006). *The Advocate college guide for LGBT students.* New York: Alyson.

When Collection Development Leads to Staff Development: The Transgender Resource Collection

Bleue J. Benton and *Sharon Grimm*

Oak Park, Illinois, located eight miles west of downtown Chicago, is well known as home to Frank Lloyd Wright and also to Ernest Hemingway, whose youngest son coincidentally was known as a cross-dresser and transsexual (Hemingway, 2007). Oak Park Public Library offers three locations and serves over 53,000 residents. In 2007 we unveiled the transgender resource collection, a groundbreaking project that combines materials selection with staff and building issues to offer a holistic model of collection development. In addition to putting materials on shelves, we conducted a self-study looking for barriers to service to transgender users, and launched an ambitious project of staff awareness workshops to help all library employees become more familiar with gender identity issues.

This process began in 2005 when Oak Park Public Library undertook an extensive general collection evaluation project. Using collection- and user-centered methods of evaluation and assessment, we produced a report that included quantitative statistical analysis combined with qualitative subjective narratives for 90 areas of the collection. For each category, we looked at size, circulation, turnover rate, age, physical condition, currency, scope and depth, and significance. We also conducted a materials availability survey, and analyzed interlibrary loan use. The 46-page report of this collection evaluation is available at http://www.oppl.org/about/depts/collection.htm.

As part of this collection evaluation, we additionally wanted to assess our overall collection from the point of view of specific population groups. Concerned that there are groups of people who may be ignored or neglected, we attempted to analyze our collections in terms of diversity. A work group was formed to look at this, and started with the premise that it's common for library collections to be influenced or determined by a selector's limited range of experiences and perceptions. It is very easy for librarians to avoid materials that seem different to them. Some materials are held to higher standards than other materials with which staff are more comfortable. While acknowledging the difficulty of discussing the needs of a population group without overly generalizing, we hoped to increase awareness and also to see that the library's collections represented genuine diversity and didn't simply offer token titles. We decided to take a first step, one emphasizing questions and concerns.

What populations make up Oak Park's diverse community? How do we judge a collection's effectiveness in reflecting, welcoming, or serving a particular group of people? What is being missed or forgotten? How can we incorporate these questions into an ongoing process?

The diversity evaluation process began by targeting nine groups of people for consideration: African-Americans, LGBT persons, Latinos, Asian-Americans, people with disabilities, senior citizens, poor people, and men. We chose key parts of the library collection to examine. For each location, we looked at adult, young adult, and children's print and audiovisual materials. For each category of materials, we asked the following questions:

- Is this collection welcoming to people within the population group? Does it reflect them? Are there materials by authors (or directors, actors, musicians, and so forth) who belong to this group? Are there titles, subjects, and content that represent the population group?
- Are there issues, concerns, and trends that are particularly important or relevant to people within this population group? Do we have materials on these subjects?
- Is the age of this collection an issue? Do we see outdated and offensive references, illustrations, use of language?
- Is there a canon of literature to use as a measuring stick for this collection? Are there any helpful checklists? How does this collection measure up?
- What are our goals? What should this collection look like?

This was an extremely valuable process. When the diversity work group report regarding our LGBT-related collection materials was presented, it was very clear that while the collection was reasonable for gay and lesbian library users, there were very few bisexual or transgender resources. In addition, we were strongly influenced by an excellent (and well-timed) program on serving transgender users at the 2005 American Library Association annual conference, with speakers Jami Taylor, K.R. Roberto, and Adam Davis. The point was well made that Oak Park Public Library was not alone in overlooking transgender users.

Shortly after this, mini-grants of $3,000 were announced by the Illinois State Library for the purpose of bridging the gap between communities and collections. The Illinois State Library's third goal in its *Long Range Plan for the Use of LSTA Funds* that year was to ensure that all Illinois residents had access to a full range of sources and formats of information. It seemed that a collection of transgender materials would provide pioneering service to a group of people with strong information needs who had largely been ignored. Our application stressed the fact that although there were some materials in large universities and archives, transgender people constituted an overlooked population who were not being served, welcomed, or reflected adequately in public libraries in Illinois. We believed that the open access environment of a public library offered the best venue for raising community awareness and understanding of gender identity issues, and for serving transgender people. This marginalized group facing widespread — often socially condoned — discrimination, harassment, and violence was drastically underserved. Our well-publicized project, with its commitment to diversity and inclusion, would help to promote libraries as welcoming and safe places for everyone.

Because *transgender* is an umbrella term that applies to people whose identity or behavior falls outside stereotypical gender expectations and refers to many types of people, there are a variety of information needs in the transgender community. The collection was planned to include areas of common concern such as body characteristics, gender roles, and the perceptions of others. We saw a particular need for medical and legal information.

Oak Park Public Library applied for and received the grant. We viewed this as a large success — a serious stamp of approval by three levels of government: federal money, awarded through a state agency, and administered by local government. We selected, purchased, classified, and processed $3,000 worth of circulating nonfiction books, audiobooks, and DVDs on transgender topics. We also purchased transgender fiction and feature films with funds from the regular materials budget. Our children's librarians compiled a reading list of nontraditional gender role books for kids. The library now owns about 190 items which are identified in the catalog with the local subject heading "Transgender Resource Collection." The outstanding collections of large urban public libraries were invaluable as we looked for appropriate titles to purchase, especially San Francisco and New York. We also used World-Cat and various lists of recommended books from the Internet.

Books selected included popular titles like *Hollywood Androgyny* (Bell-Metereau, 1985) and *Miss Vera's Cross-Dressing for Success* (Vera, 2002), as well as more technical titles like *Voice and Communication Therapy for the Transgender/Transsexual Client* (Adler, Hirsh, & Mordaunt, 2006). We now subscribe to the magazine *Transgender Tapestry*.

After much discussion, the decision was made not to create a separate physical space to shelve all the materials together. We were concerned about the stigma and ghettoization of a transgender aisle. Materials are classified on a title-by-title basis, ending up in their individual Dewey locations. This creates a natural grouping of numerous books in 306.768 and that serves as a good place to start with visitors who ask to see the collection. But because the materials are scattered throughout the library, various finding aids have been produced including our local subject heading and a brochure of selected titles.

Because *Transgender people* was not a Library of Congress subject heading at the time, our technical services manager created a very helpful worksheet for staff to use when searching the catalog. It outlined the available Library of Congress subject headings and also offered a list of keywords that might be helpful. We were delighted later in the year when the Library of Congress finally approved the subject headings of *Transgender people* and *Transgenderism*.

We knew that it was crucial to promote the transgender resource collection in a vigorous and creative way, and we still have a long way to go in this regard. We partnered with the Chicago Gender Society who distributed our eye-catching palm cards in very untraditional places, including bars, nightclubs, electrolysis offices, therapists offices, and makeover beauty shops. We sent a blitz of press releases to appropriate media and organizations. We created and launched a webpage, which includes our Library Toolkit that offers title lists, our self-study report, training materials, and the *$200 Transgender Bookshelf* for public libraries looking to add books to their collection. The Library Toolkit is available at http://www.oppl. org/media/trc_toolkit.htm.

Because we anticipated increased visits to the library by people who are transgender, we decided to conduct a self-study to look at our practices and policies, and to raise staff awareness. Our goals were to look for any barriers that transgender people face as patrons or employees, to work with staff so that the transgender resource collection would be available in a nonjudgmental environment, and to see that all staff were prepared to provide excellent customer service to people who are transgender.

We formed a service focus committee made up of six people from across departments, not all of whom were managers. The committee was charged to identify barriers and recommend changes to remove barriers to serving and employing people who are transgender. The committee began its work with the assumption that there were inadvertent barriers and quickly expanded this charge to look for ways to better welcome, reflect, serve, and employ people who are transgender. Thus the committee went beyond looking for barriers, which was deemed as negative, and expanded to looking for what could be added that would be positive.

Working definitions were established and agreed upon. *Barriers* were considered to be anything that gets in the way of providing great customer service at the library. *Welcome* meant that library users would feel comfortable in the library, and *reflect* meant that library users would see themselves in the library: in collections, in images and other materials used for public relations, and on the staff. *Serve* meant library users would find what they need. The committee laid out a four-step process that included education of the committee itself, evaluation of the library, recommendations to remove barriers along with ways to become a better library, and completion of a report.

For committee education, the first step involved reading about the populations. For that, of course, we turned to items in the collection, in particular the documentary *Trans-Generation*. We sought out information on the needs of transgender people as library users. The committee also attended awareness workshops, and not only did this further the education process, but also offered an excellent opportunity to observe staff reactions and thus inform the evaluation process. There was definitely a learning curve among the committee members, especially in understanding the breadth of populations under the transgender umbrella, and that some transgender people consider themselves outside the gender binary.

For the evaluation component, we looked at eight areas: collection, staff, facilities, communications to the public (including signs), Board-approved policies, procedures (like handling library card applications, interlibrary loan, booking meeting rooms), practices (what we say or don't say when checking out books, how we answer telephone calls, for example), and employment. The committee put forth 41 questions using the framework of reflecting, welcoming, serving, and identifying barriers. And we were not just looking for barriers (or negatives) but what we might do that would add positives.

To illustrate, here are some of our evaluation questions:

• Do library communications reflect transgender library users?
• Do procedures welcome transgender library users?
• Does the staff serve or know how to serve transgender library users?
• Are there any facility barriers to transgender library users?
• Are there any policies that are barriers to employing transgender people?
• What more could the library be doing to create a welcoming environment?

To answer these evaluation questions the committee was in discussion with other staff, walked through the three buildings, and continued to learn via print, video, and online sources. We looked at best practices at other libraries and in other fields. We did not meet with a focus group of people who are transgender and learn directly from them, but we hope to do so in the future. The service focus committee then developed recommendations based on this evaluation and our discovery of best practices. The final report included 35 recommendations to remove barriers and make the library more welcoming. These recommendations ranged from small to grand, from easily implemented to philosophical.

The committee recommended making transgender resource collection items easily findable by creating printed finding tools and by using a unifying subject heading to facilitate catalog searches. We recommended changing our restroom signs. We had four public single-use restrooms that could be used by anyone and we recommended keeping these unlocked to remove the barrier of having to ask for a key. We recommended staff be aware of stereotypes in communication and use images of multiple people to better represent diversity. We recommended staff consider diversity in displays — so when a women's history month book display focused on women, it might include books about a broad range of women, including transgender women. We recommended removing the salutation line from automated email notices to avoid using Mr. and Ms., and we removed the male/female check boxes from our library card applications and replaced them with a space for people to self-identify their gender. We added "gender identity or expression" to our diversity statement policy. We recommended that staff be welcoming in all interactions and that they use their best judgment when addressing others by name and/or pronoun. The committee also recommended that the library infuse staff training with sensitivity for working with gender and transgender issues. The final step was a 19-page report which is available as part of our Library Toolkit.

The committee was not charged with implementation of the recommendations, and the lack of continuity made for an uneven start. We were able to make some changes quickly and had a volunteer applying corrective stickers to our library card applications to save us from reprinting costs. Other changes were more difficult, such as changes to signage. In addition, the locking mechanisms on our restrooms proved challenging because we were switching from a swipe card lock to a mechanical lock.

An additional unique aspect of our approach to this collection is that it prompted staff development. We offered mandatory basic transgender awareness workshops that were two hours in length, and offered them three times, over a period of three months in 2007. They were conducted by an outside presenter, Shannon Sullivan of the Illinois Safe Schools Alliance. We had administration buy-in for attendance being mandatory at the basic workshop — which was critical, and in a large part due to our executive director's commitment. There were some voiced concerns from some of our management team that participation wasn't necessary for behind-the-scenes staff, but other managers were clear that all staff serve the public in some capacity. We were quite intentional about naming this an *awareness* workshop, rather than a *training* session. We wanted to reinforce the idea that staff should be aware of who all our patrons are. We didn't want to send the message that we were training people in how to think or what to believe about the transgender populations.

The basic awareness workshop covered gender roles and expectations for women and men, the pervasiveness of gender in our language, and the pressures to conform and difficulties of conforming to those expectations. Definitions were offered of biological sex, gender, and sexual orientation; the fact that these are often conflated was included. There was discussion of populations within the gender variant umbrella, for example, transsexuals and cross-dressers. Importantly, the workshop provided basic guidelines for creating a safe space for people who are transgender.

In terms of outcomes, we consider our basic transgender awareness workshops to have been a success. There was good attendance: 94 out of approximately 120 staff attended. This is a higher number than have participated in our staff in-service days over the years. Obviously, even by offering the workshop three times and making it mandatory, it would not be possible for all staff to attend, but some of our part-time librarians took time off from day jobs at other libraries to attend the workshop. We collected written evaluations after each session and the results indicated that staff learned a great deal of information about the topic of gender identity, gained sensitivity for working with others, and believed that the general conversation of the entire topic was important. We also received constructive feedback concerning the workshop's length and content. There were indications of interest in a smaller group setting; desire for role-playing, video, or a transgender person as a speaker;

need for specific library or real-world examples of how they would use the information; and concern that we should be respectful of everyone's feelings. We also realized that the workshops were helpful in communicating to staff what was happening with the collection — how much we had purchased, where it was in processing, and to answer questions about shelving. Additionally, offering the three workshops over the course of three months did exactly what we had hoped. It sustained the conversation over those three months. Each month the group that attended the workshop talked about it afterwards with their coworkers, which meant that it wasn't a single moment in our history. Rather than just the one month that we talk about this diversity topic, we had created a longer dialogue.

We then offered an optional advanced transgender awareness workshop. This two-hour workshop was offered once. We set a prerequisite of attendance at the basic workshop, and 12 staff attended. This workshop was offered as a chance for staff to ask remaining questions and engage further in the topic. We also took to heart the feedback we received on the basic workshop evaluations and used the advanced workshop as a chance to talk more about library specifics. We developed scenarios describing possible library work situations and discussed them in pairs and then as a whole group. The scenarios made the topic of gender identity more relevant to day-to-day work and helped us identify procedural gaps — how we handle complaints, for example.

It was crucial to us to continue to make this topic relevant to the day-to-day work of our staff. Following the advanced workshop, members of the service focus committee met with staff at their departmental meetings. We took a few of the scenarios that were relevant to each department. (Our branch staff talked about more of these since they are more generalists.) We divided staff into pairs or groups of three and gave each group a scenario to work on. We asked them to talk about the issues in their scenario and make recommendations for the staff that were portrayed. Then we asked them to share with the larger group. This was planned to take about 30 minutes of the department meeting, but some of the conversations went longer. This follow-up conversation with staff proved to be an excellent group-learning process. As the department problem-solved, this really became a time to share tips and develop customer service skills. We were also able to share recommendations from one department to the next, for example our maintenance workers had thoughts on handling restroom situations that we were able to share at other department meetings. Two of the scenarios are presented here. All 13 are available as part of the Library Toolkit.

First Scenario

Mark is working a busy afternoon shift at a public service desk. A patron approaches the desk looking for a book that is checked in but can't be found on the shelf. Mark asks for the title of the book.

PATRON: It's called *Ethics and Intersex.*

MARK: I'm sorry, *Ethics and?*

PATRON (leaning in): *Ethics and Intersex.*

MARK: I'm sorry, I'm still not hearing you, can you spell that for me?

Another patron is now waiting in line.

PATRON (nervously): I-n-t-e-r-s-e-x.

MARK: Oh, I see it in the catalog now. It was last checked out four years ago, so it shouldn't be still on a shelving cart. And you say it wasn't on the shelf?

PATRON: No.

MARK: Well, let's go have a look.

After a search Mark hasn't found the book on the shelf.

MARK: I'm sorry we weren't able to locate *Ethics and Intersex*. I'll have to put a trace on it.

What are the issues in this scenario?
What recommendations do you have for the staff member(s) involved?

Issues/Recommendations:
• Read the body language and clues from the patron to be aware of nervousness or discomfort.
• Search for "Ethics and" to bring up titles that might match the patron's request.
• Move to the public catalog to search together with the patron, or ask the patron to write down the title.
• Be aware that "last checked out four years ago" could be perceived as a value judgment.
• Let the patron know that we will find our copy or borrow it from another library. *Trace* is too much library jargon.

Second Scenario

Will, a staff member, is near the front entrance when three middle school girls enter. They are louder than usual so Will overhears their conversation about another person.

GIRL 1: I don't know and usually I can tell.

GIRL 2: I know, I mean really, people usually want you to know.

GIRL 3 (giggles loudly): Well it must just be an it!

GIRL 1: I don't know, it's not saying anything.

GIRL 2 (laughing): It's an it.

Will watches as the three girls continue their conversation, following the patron into another part of the building.

What are the issues in this scenario?
What recommendations do you have for the staff member(s) involved?

Issues/Recommendations:
• Wear your identification card or nametag visibly to be identified as staff.
• Be aware of developing situations that may become unsafe for library users.
• Understand that the targeted person could be in danger, or minimally be made to feel unwelcome in the library.
• As appropriate, notify security guards and other staff of the situation.
• Monitor the situation so that it does not escalate.
• Address the behavior of a group if necessary, according to the library's rules of behavior.
• Address the group to redirect or distract them. Use phrases like "May I help you?" or "Welcome to the library" to indicate they have been seen.
• Be visible to and near the targeted person to be available if they feel threatened.

- Approach the targeted person to communicate they are welcome. Use phrases like "May I help you?" or "Welcome to the library" to indicate they have been seen.
- Understand your responsibilities in maintaining a safe library environment for all library users.

It was extremely rewarding to see how staff applied skills and tactics that they already developed in their work — for example they already were printing nicknames or preferred names on library cards, and noting the preference on the account record that had the patron's official name. Our shelvers were already being asked sensitive questions from patrons in the stacks and tactfully referring them to librarians. After this week of department meetings, we posted all the scenarios and all the recommendations we gathered on the staff blog, so that it offered a larger group learning process. These meetings also furthered staff engagement on the topic and continued the conversations around this topic another month. We used this time with each department as an opportunity to share the procedures developed to fill the gaps identified earlier in the process. These department meetings also gave us the opportunity to share talking points that we developed to respond to questions from the public about the collection.

The staff awareness and self-evaluation process was a significant investment of library time, and it involved some money to bring in the workshop presenter. But it was successful in the high level of commitment our staff demonstrated to this process. The number of staff involved and the depth of conversation that occurred exponentially increased the level of staff awareness. The service focus committee benefited from staff insights and it truly seemed to give a library-wide focus on the topic. Ultimately our library is better prepared to welcome, serve, and employ people who are transgender.

As we have worked through all this, many nice things have happened with this collection. The project was designated an exemplary grant project by the Institute for Museum and Library Services. We have been contacted by a number of organizations, and have received numerous requests to link to our webpage. A transgender agency in the Canadian Maritimes contacted us for help in compiling a basic list of titles for their area libraries. Two publishers contacted us wishing to donate books to our collection. Members of the Chicago Gender Society shared a very emotional reflection on their joy that a public library is actively welcoming them. For many years their only information sources were found in adult bookstores, and their only gathering places were bars in dangerous locations.

Materials in the transgender resource collection are circulating. A traditional output measure for libraries is circulation, and ours is better than we had hoped. We had cautious expectations, realizing that there might be stigma attached to checking out books on this subject and also because of the issue that identification required for library cards might cause problems for some transgender people. One of our regular patrons indicated that she now leaves with her arms full of books each time she visits; we had not realized that she is transgender.

In summary, we believe that this pioneering project has implications that go far beyond library shelves. Our holistic approach, combining practical information for and about transgender people with a self-study and awareness workshops, is an excellent model for collection development in other libraries.

REFERENCES

Adler, R. K., Hirsch, S., & Mordaunt, M. (Eds.) (2006). *Voice and communication therapy for the transgender/transsexual client: A comprehensive clinical guide.* San Diego, CA: Plural.

Bell-Metereau, R. (1985). *Hollywood androgyny.* New York: Columbia University Press.

Hemingway, J. (2007). *Strange tribe: A family memoir.* Guilford, CT: Lyons.

Vera, V. (2002). *Miss Vera's cross-dress for success: A resource guide for boys who want to be girls.* New York: Villard.

The History of the GLBT Round Table

Anne L. Moore

Profile

Name	Gay, Lesbian, Bisexual and Transgender Round Table
Parent Organization	American Library Association (ALA)
Website	http://www.ala.org/ala/mgrps/rts/glbtrt/index.cfm
	See also:
	ALA Connect — http://connect.ala.org/glbtrt
	MySpace
	Facebook
Discussion list	glbtrt-l@ala.org
Membership	Open to all members of ALA
Meetings and programs	Meets semi-annually at ALA conferences. Roundtable meeting consists of two Steering Committee meetings and all-committee meeting. Membership meeting, programs and Stonewall Book Awards brunch held during Annual Conference.
Leadership	Rotating co-chairs, secretary and treasurer elected for two year terms.
Established	1970

The Gay, Lesbian, Bisexual and Transgendered Round Table (GLBTRT) of the American Library Association, founded in 1970 as the Task Force on Gay Liberation, is the oldest professional organization devoted to LGBTQ issues. With a current membership of approximately one thousand, the focus of the group is to promote accessibility to quality LGBTQ library materials, and to provide a forum for discussion of programs, events and challenges for LGBTQ librarians, library workers and other information specialists.

The group was founded during the 1970 ALA Annual Conference in Detroit, Michigan, within the Social Responsibilities Round Table (SRRT) which had itself been founded a mere two years before in response to a push for librarians and ALA to get involved in social issues in the larger community beyond libraries themselves. It was SRRT's intention for task forces to be "problem-oriented" and short-term, unless purposely continued by interested members. Israel Fishman, a librarian from New York City attending the conference to search for employment, filed the necessary papers to create the Task Force and became the first coordinator. Fishman recollected that he was inspired by thoughts of the first Gay

Pride Day in New York City in 1970 (K. Fattig, personal communication, June 29, 1995). A series of well-attended meetings were held in the SRRT hospitality suite throughout the conference. The original goals of the Task Force were developing greater understanding of homosexuality, ending its relegations to classification as "aberrant sexual behavior" and ensuring that homosexuals were not discriminated against in employment (Kniffel, 1970, p. 2622). Throughout the following year the group met several times in New York City. During this time, gay activist Barbara Gittings became involved with the Task Force, becoming coordinator in 1971, a position she held for the next fifteen years. She established many of the functions the group continues to this day, including producing and distributing bibliographies and other materials which discuss gay and lesbian (now LGBTQ) issues in a positive light, promoting books via a book award, and sponsoring programs during ALA conferences.

The annual ALA Conference, held in Dallas, Texas, in 1971, was a watershed event for the group. Isabel Miller was presented with the first book award for her novel, *Patience and Sarah*. The "Hug a Homosexual" booth, staged by the Task Force in the exhibit hall, drew enormous crowds and coverage by local TV stations and newspapers as well as the library media. And a sit-in of an Intellectual Freedom Committee meeting organized by four Task Force members pushed for action in supporting Michael McConnell, who was denied a job he had been offered at the University of Minnesota after he and his male partner applied for a marriage permit.[1]

After the 1971 conference, Gittings settled in as coordinator, handling all the various tasks associated with the position. Gittings, a gay activist involved on many fronts, used her skills and connections to publicize and promote the work of the Task Force. One of Gittings' most significant contributions was the creation and dissemination of *The Gay Bibliography*. In the fall of 1970, she produced a short bibliography of print materials with a positive perspective of gay life, consisting of thirty-seven items (books, articles and pamphlets). The sixth edition of the bibliography, produced in March 1980, grew to include more than 560 entries. These bibliographies were distributed widely. For example, Gittings estimated over 33,000 copies of the fifth edition were distributed. More topic specific and shorter bibliographies were also produced as the volume of gay and lesbian related material grew in the late 1970s and 1980s, and as the Task Force was recognized as an authoritative source for material. One of the most important of these was the "Gay Materials Core Collection List" designed as a buying guide for small and medium sized libraries.

From 1971 until 1986 Barbara Gittings was the face of and the force behind the Task Force. Ultimately the Task Force membership wanted broader involvement and participation. In June 1986, Gittings stepped down and was replaced with a new governance structure, consisting of a five-member steering committee, composed of two co-chairs, a secretary/treasurer, a programming committee chair and a book award committee chair. During the transition, Ellen Greenblatt acted as the sole chair until an election conducted by mail in November selected the first elected officers; among them, Ellen Greenblatt and Dee Michel as co-chairs and Roland Hansen as secretary/treasurer. The name of the Task Force was also changed to The Gay and Lesbian Task Force. One of the major efforts of the group was the work of the Clearinghouse, created in 1987, which was based on Gittings' work to distribute positively oriented material contributing to the educational awareness of gay and lesbian issues. Under the leadership of Cal Gough, the Clearinghouse grew rapidly, and by 1988, 116 items were available and 519 requests for those materials were filled. In 1993, the Task Force Steering Committee began discussing loading materials onto the Internet and making them available publicly. Currently over 22 bibliographies and lists are posted on the GLBTRT website.

One of the most visible activities of the GLBTRT is bestowal of awards for LGBTQ books. These book awards became official ALA awards in 1986, and, in 1998, became known collectively as the Stonewall Book Awards, with the literature award renamed to honor Barbara Gittings and the non-fiction award renamed to honor Israel Fishman. In 2002, an endowment was established to raise money for book awards, and, by June of 2008, a goal of $75,000 was reached. With this milestone attained, the existing book awards can be funded through this endowment and focus can be placed on developing a third award, specifically for Young Adult-Children's books.

In 2009, a related endeavor, the Rainbow Project, which presents an annual bibliography of quality books with significant and authentic LGBTQ content recommended for people from birth through eighteen years of age, officially became a joint project of the GLBTRT and SRRT.

Beyond producing bibliographies and recognizing outstanding LGBTQ books, a major focus of the group has been the programming offered at ALA Annual Conferences. Some of the more notable programs include "Let's not Homosexualize the Library Stacks" (1974), "The Children's Hour: Must Gay Be Grim for Jane and Jim?" (1975), "It's Safer to Be Gay on Another Planet: Gay Images in Science Fiction and Fantasy" (1981), "Gay Materials for Small-town, USA?" (1985), "AIDS Awareness: The Library's Role" (1986), "Positively Out: Gay and Lesbian Librarians in the Work Place" (1988), "Gay and Lesbian Library Service: Exploding the Myths, Dismantling the Barriers" (1991), "I Read You Loud and Queer: The Increasing Demand for Gay and Lesbian Literature" (1993).

Throughout its history, the organization has initiated several actions and resolutions. In 1971, a resolution was approved by ALA Council condemning discrimination against minorities (including non-heterosexual library users and employees). A stronger resolution was passed in 1977, in the wake of Anita Bryant's homophobic crusade. This resolution ultimately led to ALA personnel policy 54.7, which reads:

> Gay Rights — The American Library Association Council reaffirms its support for equal employment opportunity for gay librarians and library workers. The Council recommends that libraries reaffirm their obligation under the Library Bill of Rights to disseminate information representing all points of view on this topic.

The Steering Committee meetings, in January 1989, raised discussion of an ALA publication (1986) *Library Disaster Preparedness Handbook*, in which a section on "Problem Patrons" includes a section entitled "Homosexual Loiterers."

Perhaps the most public protest staged by the group occurred at the 1993 midwinter conference held in Denver. The Colorado electorate passed Amendment 2 to the state's Constitution in November 1992, which excluded sexual orientation from the list of groups protected from discrimination. While the ALA Executive Board issued a resolution opposing Amendment 2, Executive Director Peggy Sullivan conceded that the conference could not be moved (Memo, 11-10, 1992, Peggy Sullivan, Executive Director ALA to membership). During the conference, the Task Force organized a rally, which included remarks by the ALA President, Dr. Marilyn L. Miller, and a march to the State Capitol steps. Over 150 marchers participated and 2000 lapel pins, reading "It's a civil rights issue, it's a library issue" were handed out during the conference.

Since its inception, the Task Force has advocated for bibliographic accessibility to

LGBTQ materials. From the 1971 program on "Sex and the Single Cataloger" through contemporary battles over transgender terminology, the Task Force has worked diligently to ensure that the Library of Congress Subject Headings are non-biased and accurately reflect the realities of LGBTQ existence. Another project undertaken by the Task Force addressed the need for broader inclusion of lesbian and gay periodicals in indexing resources, primarily H.W. Wilson's *Readers' Guide*.

During ALA Annual Conference 1999, the Task Force gained status as a Round Table; moving the group out of the "temporary" nature of being a task force, giving it direct ALA staff liaisons and potentially direct representation on ALA Council. Throughout its four decades of existence, the name of the group has evolved from the Task Force on Gay Liberation to the Gay Task Force (1975) to the Gay and Lesbian Task Force (1986) to the Gay, Lesbian, and Bisexual Task Force (1995) to the Gay, Lesbian, Bisexual and Transgendered Round Table (1999). In 2007 the membership voted to change the bylaws removing "male" and "female" co-chairs and changing the wording to require co-chairs of differing gender identity. The debate around the wording and need for this bylaw has continued through 2009.

Over the course of almost forty years, the group has transitioned from a small group meeting monthly in members' apartments in New York City to a Round Table with its own representative on ALA Council (the association's governing body). The work of the group has evolved from filling requests for individual bibliographies by "snail mail" to offering resources on a web page. Book Award winners, originally acknowledged with hand-make tokens of appreciation, now receive a plaque accompanied by a check for $1000. And while being LGBTQ is no longer identified as "an aberrant sexual behavior" (as per the 1970 article in *Library Journal*), there is still, unfortunately, employment discrimination, particularly towards individuals who identify as transgendered. Intellectual freedom issues are also still a concern as some of the most frequently challenged books are children's and young adult books with LGBTQ characters or themes. Older issues, such as hate crimes and religious acceptance of same sex life styles, are still being discussed, though far more openly. New issues, such as those related to aging, same-sex marriage, and protection of legal rights, are topics warranting increased education in the profession and community. Forty years after humble beginnings in a hospitality suite in Detroit, the oldest LGBTQ professional group still has an important role to play in the library and information professions as well as the communities served by libraries.

NOTES

1. The Task Force continued to present motions urging ALA to act against the University of Minnesota through 1975. Ultimately no substantive action was ever taken as the issue was transferred from committee to committee (Shamin, 1988).

REFERENCES

Cain, P. D. (2002). *Leading the parade: Conversations with America's most influential lesbians and gay men.* Lanham, MD: Scarecrow.

Gay and Lesbian Task Force. (1978, December) Press release with header "For issue # 51" (December 1978) of SRRT NEWSLETTER (Social Responsibilities Round Table, American Library Association).

Gay and Lesbian Task Force. (1995) Highlights of Task Force activities: 1970–1995. *25th Anniversary 1970–1995 Program.* (pp. 36–51)

Gittings, Barbara (1990). Gays in library land: The Gay and Lesbian Task Force of the American Library Association: The first sixteen years. Unpublished manuscript.

Israel David Fishman papers. Manuscripts and Archives Division. The New York Public Library. Astor, Lenox and Tilden Foundations.

Kniffel, L. (1999). Gay liberation: From Task Force to Round Table. *American Libraries, 30*(11), 74–76.

Lerro, M. (1989, July 14). Gay/lesbian librarians keep up with gay history: Task force presents program on maintaining gay material. *Dallas Voice,* 7 & 23.

Samek, T. (2001). *Intellectual freedom and social responsibility in American librarianship, 1967–1974.* Jefferson, NC: McFarland.

Shamin, A. (1988). The Gay Liberation Task Force: Its origins, activities, and effectiveness. Unpublished manuscript.

Shamin, A. (1990). 20 years of the Gay and Lesbian Task Force: A personal reflection. *ALA SRRT Gay and Lesbian Task Force 20th Anniversary Program.*

LAGAR (Lesbian and Gay Archives Roundtable)

Mary Caldera

Profile

Name	Lesbian and Gay Archives Roundtable (LAGAR)
Parent Organization	Society of American Archivists (SAA)
Website	http://www.archivists.org/saagroups/lagar
Listserv	lagar@forums.archivists.org
Membership	Open to all
Meetings and programs	Meets annually at the meeting of the Society of American Archivists. Roundtable meeting consists of a business meeting and program of interest to members.
Leadership	Rotating co-chairs and steering committee by election.
Established	1989

Introduction

The Society of American Archivists' (SAA) Lesbian and Gay Archives Roundtable (LAGAR)[1] "promotes the preservation and research use of records documenting lesbian, gay, bisexual, and transgender history and serves as a liaison between lesbian, gay, bisexual, and transsexual archives and the Society of American Archivists" (Lesbian and Gay Archives Roundtable, 2007). Its mission, as outlined in its bylaws, is to:

A. Bring together people who are concerned about the collection, preservation, description and research use of archival materials documenting lesbians, gay men, and their institutions.

B. Keep lesbian and gay-male issues in archives and history more visible within SAA.

C. Educate archivists about the importance of identifying and preserving historical records documenting the lives, accomplishments, and culture of lesbians and gay men.

D. Act as a liaison between SAA and community-based lesbian and gay-male archives. Encourage and facilitate the participation of lesbian and gay-male archivists in SAA activities and the professional archival community.

E. Exchange information with other lesbian and gay-male professional groups [Lesbian and Gay Archives Roundtable, 2008].

The roundtable was established in 1989 by members of SAA "who were concerned about the preservation of the records documenting gay and lesbian history and the role of lesbians and gays in the archival profession" (Lesbian and Gay Archives Roundtable, 2007). Novak (2004) credits Elizabeth Knowlton's session, "Documenting the Gay Rights Movement," presented three years earlier at the 1986 annual meeting of SAA, as the catalyst for the establishment of the roundtable. Knowlton (1987) reported on her survey of gay and lesbian community-based and mainstream archives. She found a lack of interest and awareness of lesbian and gay documentation by traditional archives and the lack of training and resources of community-based lesbian and gay archives problematic and saw a need to open communication and collaboration between the two. In 1988 SAA members petitioned for a new roundtable that did just that, and more.

Throughout its twenty-year history, LAGAR has reached each of its objectives to varying degrees, but has been most focused and successful at bringing people, especially professional archivists, together, making lesbian, gay, bisexual, transgender, and queer (LGBTQ) archivists and archival issues more visible within the SAA, and educating archivists about the importance of preserving the LGBTQ historical record. Serving as a liaison between community-based archives and the archival profession is one of the roundtable's objectives, but its success at doing so is difficult to assess. As will be seen below, LAGAR has brought more awareness about LGBTQ community-based archives to the archival profession, however, the extent to which it has brought professional awareness and training to community archivists is not easily knowable. The roundtable does not track membership, email inquiries, or website usage in a way that would indicate how community-based archivists are using LAGAR's resources. Finally, making and sustaining connections with other professional LGBTQ organizations, the last objective listed in the by-laws, does not appear to have been a priority for LAGAR in the past few years.

Beyond its mission, LAGAR's value to those interested in LGBTQ archives, libraries, and documentation lies primarily in three non-mutually exclusive areas: Connections, Education and Resources. Each of these areas will be outlined separately.

Connections

One of LAGAR's most valuable contributions to the profession is the opportunity it affords for dialogue among LGBTQ archivists and between professional and non-professional caretakers of the LGBTQ archival record. Membership to LAGAR is open to all who share its objectives; however, SAA members get the fullest benefits of belonging to the organization.

The roundtable meets at the annual SAA conference. The event provides members an opportunity to meet, network and exchange ideas. The meeting program often includes an opportunity to connect with members of an LGBTQ archive, library, or collection in the host city. Its welcoming atmosphere, democratic leadership structure and small numbers encourage participation at every level, from suggestions for programming to self-nomination for office. Serving as a roundtable co-chair or steering committee member provides valuable experience which can lead to additional leadership roles within SAA.

The LAGAR listserv at lagar@forums.archivists.org is another way the roundtable facilitates dialogue, providing a forum for individuals to connect with each other and to seek and share information. Many of the foremost LGBTQ archives experts are subscribed to the LAGAR listserv allowing posters access to a wide variety of professional expertise. Common exchanges on the listserv include requests for information and resources, updates on archives projects and programs, and offers of archival materials.

Education

One of the roundtable's primary goals is to educate its members and the profession on the value of preserving LGBTQ records. One way it does this is in its annual meeting, which includes a program on LGBTQ issues and often highlights a local LGBTQ collection, archive, library or activist. The programs often offer unique learning opportunities. Recent programs included a political activist in Washington, DC, who spoke about his experiences in DC's LGBTQ community and a panel of heads of Chicago's LGBTQ community archives, libraries and museums, who discussed their work and challenges. The roundtable also develops and endorses SAA conference session proposals. Its leaders and members develop, shepherd, and endorse sessions on various topics relevant to LGBTQ archivists and documentation including diversity, collections and collection development, description, privacy, and confidentially. The number of SAA conference sessions at SAA with LGBTQ content has grown since LAGAR's inception (Novak, 2004). While LAGAR and its members may not be solely responsible for the increase, they have certainly played a role.

Roundtable leaders and members also serve as advocates within the SAA. They are consulted by and bring LGBTQ issues to the SAA Council, the organization's governing body, and the larger SAA membership. A recent example is their challenge of a recommendation made by the SAA Task Force on Sections/Roundtables, which recommended that roundtables be required to maintain a minimum of fifty members. LAGAR and other roundtable leaders successfully argued that the membership requirement runs counter to the organization's diversity initiative, as it threatened the existence of its minority roundtables (Cartwright, 2009).

Resources

LAGAR also makes an impact beyond its membership through the resources it makes available on its website at http://www.archivists.org/saagroups/lagar/. One of its most notable resources is *Lavender Legacies*, an online guide to repositories, both mainstream and community-based, with substantial LGBTQ collections. First compiled in 1998, the online guide now includes entries for approximately 90 repositories in the United States and Canada. Repositories can add and edit their information through a convenient online form. The guide was also published as an appendix in the *Encyclopedia of Lesbian, Gay, Bisexual, and Transgender History in America* (Stein, 2003).[2] Although entries are not updated regularly, the guide is a valuable resource for archivists, potential donors and researchers alike.

Another resource available on the website is the "GLBT Archives, Libraries, Collections and Related Subjects: A Select Bibliography," compiled by the author (Caldera, 2005). The bibliography is particularly valuable for students and other researchers interested in the history of LGBTQ documentation in archives and libraries. The *LAGAR Newsletter*, now titled *InQueeries,* is another professional resource. In addition to reports on the roundtable annual meetings, updates on LGBTQ documentation, library, and archival projects are common. Additionally, the editors often include briefs on broader LGBTQ issues, such as civil rights.

A more recent addition to the resources on the website is the "Information for Community Archives," a guide to archival management for non-archivists, edited by Paula Jabloner and Stephen Novak (2009). A work in progress, the guide aims to provide basic information on various archival activities including appraisal, arrangement and description, user services and preservation. Although intended for LGBTQ community-based repositories run by volunteers who are not trained archivists, the guide is a useful resource for other community archives as well.

Conclusion

Whether one is interested in making connections, learning about issues, or finding resources relevant to LGBTQ archivists and archives, LAGAR has much to offer. While the organization suffers from the same ills as any other volunteer organization, lack of time and resources, it has had significant successes. The group is currently focused on completing the "Information for Community Archives," and continuing to keep LGBTQ archives and archivists visible within SAA and the profession.

Notes

1. The members and leaders of the group are keenly aware that name suggests a lack of inclusiveness and have discussed changing it. As of this writing, that has not been done.
2. The royalties from the publication allowed LAGAR to offer two scholarships to attend the 2006 SAA Annual Meeting in Washington, D.C.

References

Caldera, M. (2005). *GLBT archives, libraries, collections and related subjects: A select bibliography*. Retrieved from Society of American Archivists' Lesbian and Gay Roundtable: http://www.archivists.org/saa-groups/lagar/bibliography/index.html

Cartwright, J. (2009, August 27). Review of annual meeting. *LAGAR Listserv*.

Jabloner, P., &. Novak, S. (Eds.) ([2009?]). *Information for community archives*. Retrieved from Society of American Archivists' Lesbian and Gay Archives Roundtable: http://www.archivists.org/saagroups/lagar/communityarchives/index.html

Knowlton, E. (1987, Spring). "Documenting the Gay Rights Movement," *Provenance, 5*(1), 17–30.

Lesbian and Gay Archives Roundtable. (2007, August 27). *Mission*. Retrieved from Society of American Archivist's Lesbian and Gay Archives Roundtable: http://www.archivists.org/saagroups/lagar/mission.html

Lesbian and Gay Archives Roundtable. (2008, October 28). *By-laws*. Retrieved from Society of American Archivists' Lesbian and Gay Archives Roundtable: http://www.archivists.org/saagroups/lagar/bylaws.html

Novak, S. E. (2004, August). Outreach and inreach: The SAA Lesbian and Gay Archives Roundtable, 1988–2004. *Paper presented at the Society of American Archivists Annual Meeting* . Boston, MA.

Stein, M. (. (2003). *Encyclopedia of lesbian, gay, bisexual, and transgender history in America*. New York: Thomson Learning.

HQ76.3/New England: Lesbian, Gay, Bisexual and Transgendered Librarians and Library Workers

John DeSantis

Profile

Name	HQ76.3/New England
Parent Organization	New England Library Association (NELA)
Website	http://www.nelib.org/hq76.3/index.htm
Listserv	HQ763-L@listserv.dartmouth.edu
Membership	Open to library workers in New England
Meetings and programs	Sponsors a program at the annual conference of the New England Library Association. Business meeting takes place during the program.
Leadership	Rotating convener by election.
Established	1993

On a weekday evening in the fall of 1993 a group of 40 or so queer librarians gathered in a seminar room in the Harvard Law School Library. Excitement was in the air, as we knew that we were about to embark on the groundbreaking activity of establishing a professional organization for gay and lesbian librarians in New England. The timing could not have been more perfect for this type of activism: it was the first year of Bill Clinton's presidency; the 1993 March on Washington had just taken place earlier that year; gays in the military was prominent in the public's consciousness; and a year earlier the American Library Association's Gay and Lesbian Task Force had caused a furor in the library community by appearing as a contingent in San Francisco's 1992 Gay Pride Parade on the cover of *American Libraries*. The proposed name of our group, HQ76.3/New England, came from Karen Whittlesey and David Ferris, two brave Harvard librarians who organized the meeting. Because so many library workers were still closeted at that time, it was felt that the name of the organization should not be branded with the words "gay" and "lesbian." Of course, this made many of the public librarians feel as if they were joining a secret society à la Mattachine or One. Those of us who worked in academic libraries, however, immediately recognized the name as the Library of Congress classification number for homosexuality (subdivided by geographic location). The name was therefore meaningful, yet discreet.

Printed newsletters could be sent out to members at their workplace without concerns about outing them.

Perhaps based on the model of ALA's Gay and Lesbian Task Force, the group decided that it should be led by two co-chairs (the organizers of our initial meeting becoming the first two). We also appointed a newsletter editor and treasurer. A regular meeting schedule, at first monthly, in the Boston area was set up. Eventually a mission statement was drafted:

> HQ76.3/New England seeks to make substantial contributions towards enhancing the visibility, recognition and acceptance of all lesbian, gay, bisexual and transgendered library workers.
>
> The mission of HQ76.3/New England is to support the work of regional lesbian, gay, bisexual and transgendered librarians and other library staff and to meet the broader needs of the library community, both staff and users

- by providing a support network for gay, lesbian, bisexual and transgendered staff in the libraries and library systems of New England
- by advocating and organizing around issues of concern and interest both within libraries and within the larger public area
- by offering the skills and expertise of lesbian, gay, bisexual and transgendered institutions, organizations, and agencies with particular interest in gay, lesbian, bisexual and transgendered issues, and
- by exchanging information with other gay, lesbian, bisexual and transgendered professional groups.

By the late fall of 1993 HQ76.3/New England had well over 100 dues-paying members. (A $10 annual dues was established to cover print mailings and to create a financial base for the organization.) The early *HQ76.3/New England Newsletter* was published every other month and contained notices of our upcoming meetings and events in New England, such as readings, plays and library programs, as well as the occasional calls for submissions, news about members' activities, and book recommendations (the "Purple Prose" column). The group enjoyed a flurry of activity during the years 1993 through 1996. Our regular meetings were combined with potlucks, usually held at a member's home. We regularly marched as a group in Boston's Gay Pride Parade during those years. We had our own banner and had printed brochures, and even HQ76.3 t-shirts for sale! Initially people seemed surprised to see a contingent of librarians in the parade, but still cheered us on warmly.

By 1995, our monthly meetings had become day-long annual meetings held at a member's home. While most of these meetings were social in nature, we continued to set aside time for the business portion. Almost all of these meetings were held in Boston, but at least one annual meeting was held in Western Massachusetts.

HQ76.3 was involved in some early fundraising events for our organization as well. We held yard sales at members' homes, often earning hundreds of dollars in one day. In May 1994, we held a very well-attended reading at Boston's Club Café, which featured gay author Stephen McCauley reading from his novel-in-progress, *Man of the House.*

One of our members and at one time a co-chair, the late Joanne Goodman, found herself on the planning committee for one of the early OutWrite gay and lesbian writers' conferences held annually in Boston throughout the 1990s. Joanne organized a caucus for HQ76.3 at the conference (as part of our mission to enhance the visibility of library workers), which was surprisingly well attended. We subsequently organized a caucus at every subsequent OutWrite conference right through what was to be the final conference in 1999. The caucus regularly attracted librarians, library staff, library school students and curious writers.

The 1996 caucus featured such luminaries as a curator at the Lesbian Herstory Archives, an editor at *Library Journal*, the director of the James C. Hormel Gay and Lesbian Center at San Francisco Public Library, and the editor of this book.

In June 1996 several HQ76.3 members collaborated with the Boston Area Lesbian and Gay History Project on a large exhibit mounted at the Boston Public Library. Entitled "Public Faces/Private Lives," the exhibit covered 350 years of gay and lesbian history and resulted in the publication of the book *Improper Bostonians: Lesbian and Gay History from the Puritans to Playland* (Beacon, 1998). Two HQ76.3 members also compiled an extensive GLBT bibliography with the same title as the exhibit, which included Boston-area periodicals and newspapers, works by local authors, and fictional works and memoirs with Boston as the setting.

HQ76.3 maintained liaisons with a number of other gay organizations, including ALA's Gay and Lesbian Task Force, GLSEN, and *Gay Community News*. We regularly sponsored display ads in the anniversary program books of ALA's Task Force (later Round Table). In addition, we provided financial support for the indexing project for Norman G. Kester's anthology, *Liberating Minds: The Stories and Professional Lives of Gay, Lesbian, and Bisexual Librarians and Their Advocates* (McFarland, 1997), to which several HQ76.3 members contributed essays.

For a number of reasons it became difficult to maintain the initial energy of the organization over a period of several years, and so by 1997 to 1998, activity in HQ76.3/New England had tapered off. Occasional dinners in the Boston area were still held, but the group was clearly flailing and needed new energy. Once again Joanne Goodman came to our rescue by suggesting that we align ourselves with the New England Library Association (NELA) as a subsidiary group. After years of no meetings, HQ76.3 reconvened at the 1998 NELA conference in Providence, Rhode Island, to discuss organizational issues and the possibility of becoming an official section of NELA. Members at the meeting expressed support for the idea, and Joanne performed the necessary research and made an application on our behalf to the Executive Board of NELA. Soon after, HQ76.3 was accepted as an official NELA special interest group. A year later at the NELA conference in Manchester, New Hampshire, we held a well-attended discussion group on coming out in libraries and also organized a program "New HIV/AIDS Resources for the New Millennium." Since then HQ76.3 has sponsored a program at almost every NELA conference. In 2001 HQ76.3/New England was upgraded from a special interest group to an official section of NELA.

The sense of community and friendship resulting from membership in HQ76.3 should not be overlooked. The support network which we formed exists to this day, and close friendships forged among the original members continue to thrive. In June 2006, several original members of HQ76.3 gathered at the home of Joanne Goodman and her wife on Cape Cod. As usual, it was a potluck, and we all enjoyed reminiscing over the past 13 years. Joanne died in the fall of 2007 after a long illness. Many members of HQ76.3/New England attended and spoke at her memorial service at the Boston Public Library. Aside from losing a cherished friend and true leader of our organization, it felt as if it were the end of an era.

In many ways it seems extraordinary that this organization has survived in so many incarnations for this number of years. Times have changed, and the grassroots activism so prevalent in the early 1990s seems, for better or worse, no longer as urgent today. The same can be said of the situation for GLBT library workers today. HQ76.3/New England may never have the vibrant enthusiasm it enjoyed in the 1990s, but it will always have relevance to those of us who live and work in New England.

About the Contributors

Melissa Adler attends the School of Library and Information Studies at the University of Wisconsin–Madison and is pursuing a Ph.D. minor in gender and women's studies. She also works as a cataloger for the SLIS Laboratory Library. Before starting the doctoral program she worked as a cataloger and archivist at a private college. Her research interests fall broadly under the heading of access, with an emphasis on access to LGBTQ collections, and queer theory and taxonomies as they relate to library and information studies.

Tami Albin is the undergraduate instruction and outreach librarian and liaison to women, gender and sexuality studies at the University of Kansas. She holds an M.L.I.S. from the University of Western Ontario and is the director of *Under the Rainbow: Oral Histories of Gay, Lesbian, Bisexual, Transgender, Intersex and Queer People in Kansas.* She can be reached at *albin@ku.edu.*

Bleue J. Benton is collection development manager at Oak Park Public Library in Illinois. She is middle-aged, English-speaking, female, white, straight, and able-bodied and believes that library collections shouldn't be. She earned her M.S.L.S. in 1981 from University of Illinois at Urbana-Champaign. She can be reached at *benton@oppl.org.*

Peter Bernier has several bachelor degrees (BSc, mathematics; B.B.A., marketing; B.A., psychology and history), an immigration practitioner's certificate with high honors, and a certificate of appliance repair. He operates his own Canadian immigration business, Immigration Link, specializing in immigration for same sex couples. He has served on the Pride Toronto Board and the Board of TAGL (Toronto Area Gay and Lesbian Phoneline and Crisis Counselling) and is an education and training director of the Canadian Association of Professional Immigration Consultants and is setting up Rainbow Link as a national charity to help bring LGBT culture to LGBT people across Canada and help them contribute to their LGBT community. He can be reached at *Peter@RainbowLink.ca.*

Aimee Brown received her M.L.I.S. from Simmons College and is the special collections and archives librarian at Mesa State College in Grand Junction, Colorado. She will always be especially grateful to the mainstream and community archives that preserve and make accessible material on lesbian culture and women's history and to everyone who helped her with this essay including her partner Mary, her sister librarian Margaret Brown-Sica, her co-workers and friends, and especially Ellen Greenblatt. Aimee may be contacted at *aimbrown@mesastate.edu.*

Mary Caldera received her B.A. and M.L.S. from Texas Woman's University. She is an archivist in manuscripts and archives at Yale University Library, where her duties include arrangement and description, reference, instruction and collection development. She is documenting the lesbian, gay, bisexual and transgender communities of southern Connecticut. She is the former co-chair and steering committee member of the Society of American Archivists Lesbian and Gay Archives Roundtable. She can be contacted at *mary.caldera@yale.edu.*

James V. Carmichael, Jr., is a professor of library and information science at the University of North Carolina in Greensboro, where he has taught since 1988. He has written extensively in the areas of southern library history, gender difference in the workplace, and aspects of GLBT history.

He edited the 1998 collection, *Daring to Find Our Names: The Search for Lesbigay Library History*, and chaired the 1995 joint program of the Gay, Lesbian, Bisexual and Transgendered Round Table with the Library History Round Table on the methodological challenges presented by GLBT library history. He may be contacted at *Jim_Carmichael@uncg.edu*.

Ben Christensen earned an M.L.I.S. at the University of Washington after earning a B.A. and M.A. in English from Brigham Young University. He has published an article on lesbian and gay representation in LCSH and LCC in *Knowledge Organization*. He works as a program manager for the Butler Hill Group and volunteers as a cataloger at the Orem Public Library in Orem, Utah, where he lives with his spouse and three children.

K.L. Clarke has been the librarian since 1999, for the Department of Gender, Women, and Sexuality Studies at the University of Minnesota, Twin Cities, in Minneapolis. Research interests include diversity, instruction, and public services.

Lisa A. Cohen is the founder/director of the Pacific Northwest Lesbian Archives. Lisa graduated from Evergreen State College in Olympia, Washington, and went on to receive training in archives and records management at Western Washington University in Bellingham. Lisa can be contacted at the Pacific Northwest Lesbian Archives, PO Box 27671, Seattle, WA 98165, (206) 654-447, *lisa@pnw lesbianarchives.org*.

tatiana de la tierra was born in Villavicencio, Colombia, in 1961 and landed in Miami, Florida, with her family in 1968. Her writings have been published in books and periodicals since 1987. She is author of the books *Xía y las mil sirenas* (2009) and *For the Hard Ones: A Lesbian Phenomenology/ Para las duras: Una fenomenología lesbiana* (2002). She was co-founder and editor of the latina lesbian publications published in the 1990s *esto no tiene nombre, conmoción*, and *la telaraña*. Over the years she has been a pagan, a pawnbroker, a massage therapist, a freelancer, and a librarian. She lives in Long Beach, California, and can be reached through her website at: *http://delatierra.net*.

John DeSantis is one of the original members of HQ76.3/New England. At various times he has served as its newsletter editor and webmaster. He also has a long involvement with ALA's Gay, Lesbian, Bisexual and Transgendered Round Table and has served that organization in various capacities. He received his library degree from the University of Toronto and has worked at academic libraries in New England for almost 20 years. He works as a catalog librarian and bibliographer at Dartmouth College.

K. (Ken or Kenna) Fisher (aka Rumifan Heron in Second Life) is transgendered, lives in Berkeley, California, works as an original manuscript cataloger for a major university library archive, is completing a master's degree in library and information science and constantly struggles with having to choose what name and pronouns to go by and wonders why it has to be this way. So much so that she/he has recently written and performed a solo performance piece called "What's in a name?" at the Marsh in San Francisco. She/he encourages persons interested in any aspect of the transgendered experience to contact her/him at *rumifan@hotmail.com* using any name or pronoun they wish.

Cal Gough (M.L.S., Emory University, 1979) has worked at the Atlanta-Fulton Public Library System since 1981. His current duties include managing the gay and lesbian collection at the system's Ponce de Leon Branch Library. With Ellen Greenblatt, he co-edited *Gay and Lesbian Library Service* (McFarland, 1990).

Ellen Greenblatt works at Auraria Library, University of Colorado at Denver. Previously she worked at the State University of New York at Buffalo and Princeton University libraries. Active in LGBTIQ librarianship for a quarter century, she co-edited (with Cal Gough) the book *Gay and Lesbian Library Service,* compiled several thesauri, and served on various boards including the EBSCO LGBT Life Database Advisory Board and the GLBTQ Online High School Advisory Board. She also teaches an online graduate course on LGBTIQ Resources and Issues at the San Jose State University School of Library and Information Science. Contact her at *ellengreenblatt@gmail.com*.

Sharon Grimm is communications coordinator at the Oak Park Public Library. She has an M.Ed. in college student personnel from the University of Maryland. Before working at the library, she led diversity training and coordinated diversity programming for college students.

Lauren J. Gutterman has been the project coordinator of OutHistory.org since 2008. She is also a doctoral candidate in the History Department at New York University, where she is studying the history of gender and sexuality in the twentieth-century United States. Her dissertation is about heterosexually-married women who engaged in sexual relationships with other women from the 1950s through the 1970s.

Karen P. Hogan lives in Minneapolis with her partner and daughter. She wears many library hats: she works in technical services at Augsburg College's Lindell Library, is an M.L.I.S. graduate student at St. Catherine's University, and a long time volunteer at the Quatrefoil Library.

David Brian Holt is the electronic resources reference librarian at Santa Clara University's School of Law. He lives in Santa Cruz County with his partner. He received his undergraduate degree from Southern Oregon University in Ashland, Oregon, and his M.L.I.S. is from San Jose State University. He is a law student at Santa Clara and intends on remaining in law librarianship. David can be reached by email at *dholt@scu.edu* or on Facebook at *http://www.facebook.com/david.holt*.

Jessica L. Howard is reference and web services librarian at Gettysburg College in Pennsylvania. She earned an M.S. in library and information science from the School of Information Studies at Syracuse University.

Arla A. Jones grew up in rural Kansas, getting her M.A. in librarianship and information management at the University of Denver. After working in public and school libraries in New York City for ten years, she and her partner Kimberley moved to Lawrence, Kansas, where Arla is the librarian and GSA faculty sponsor at Lawrence High School and has been working on launching an Lawrence Area GSA for all those junior high and high school students who don't have a GSA in their own school. Arla can be reached at her school: Lawrence High School, 1901 Louisiana Street, Lawrence, KS 66046-2999, or by email at *arlajones@gmail.com*.

James LaRue has been the director of the Douglas County Libraries since 1990. He is the author of *The New Inquisition: Understanding and Managing Intellectual Freedom Challenges*, and has written a weekly newspaper column for over 20 years. He was the Colorado Librarian of the Year in 1998, the Castle Rock Chamber of Commerce's 2003 Business Person of the Year, and in 2007 won the Julie J. Boucher Award for Intellectual Freedom.

Dale McNeill is grateful to the high school librarian in Ada, Oklahoma, who added *I'll Get There, It Better Be Worth the Trip* to the high school library — even though it probably was by mistake. Having worked as a children's librarian, branch manager, central administrator, and director of branches in public libraries, he's maintained a constant philosophy of inviting and encouraging library use by every individual the library is supposed to serve. He has worked in libraries in three states, and served on the Stonewall Book Award Committee. Dale works as the director of community libraries, Queens Library, New York City.

Bharat Mehra is assistant professor in the School of Information Sciences at the University of Tennessee. His research explores diversity and intercultural issues in library and information science to further social justice agendas to meet the needs of minority and underserved populations. His action research and community building efforts have involved working with international groups, LGBTIQ minorities, racial/ethnic groups, and most recently rural LIS professionals in Southern and Central Appalachia, amongst others, to promote progressive community-wide changes. Dr. Mehra applies a community engagement model in teaching courses on diversity services in libraries, public library management, collection development, resources/services for adults, grant writing for information professionals, and information representation and organization. He can be reached at *bmehra@utk.edu*.

Anne L. Moore is a special collections librarian at the W.E.B. Du Bois Library, University of Massachusetts Amherst. She has been active in the GLBT Round Table (formerly GLB Task Force) of ALA since 1997, serving on the book award committee (including chair) and as female co-chair of the group from 2002 to 2006. She is a member of the External Relations Committee and the 40th Anniversary Committee. In 2008 Anne began gathering records and correspondence and researching the history of the task force/round table. Her ultimate goal of this work is to publish her research and ensure records of the group are preserved at the ALA Archives. She may be contacted at *amoore@library.umass.edu.*

Analisa Ornelas feels at home in technical services as well as public services, and therefore has experience with both. She has worked in a variety of library environments — public, academic, law, and now for an integrated library system software company — and likes to incorporate her passion for LGBTIQ history, arts, and culture into her life and work.

Laura Reiman has worked as an elementary teacher/librarian for over ten years in New York and Colorado. Her interest in intellectual freedom and constitutional law issues began when she clerked at the ACLU in Cleveland, Ohio, as a law student. She was an attorney for the Legal Aide Bureau of Buffalo, working on cases involving constitutional rights for four years, before pursuing a much more enjoyable career working with children and books.

Catherine Ritchie is a selector of adult materials in the selection services/acquisitions department of the Dallas (Texas) Public Library. She also spent nine years as the theatre/film librarian in the Library's Fine Arts Division, and she is co-chairperson of the library's GLBT Adult Programming Committee. In addition to degrees in English and library science, she holds a certificate of advanced study in collection development from the Graduate School of Library & Information Science, University of Illinois, Urbana-Champaign. In 2001, her statistical study of gay/lesbian/bisexual/transgender non-fiction in mid-sized Illinois public libraries was published in *Illinois Libraries*. In addition, her book reviews and articles have appeared in *Library Journal, Public Libraries* and *Broadside*, the official quarterly of the Theatre Library Association. She has also given presentations on LGBT collection development at meetings of the Texas Library Association, Joint Conference of Librarians of Color, and the Public Library Association. She can be reached at *catherine.ritchie@dallaslibrary.org.*

Linda Rudell-Betts is a librarian and former information science consultant. Over the course of fifteen years, she designed, compiled and managed information retrieval vocabularies for periodical databases, Internet software applications, and records management systems. For the past several years, she has been a reference librarian at the Los Angeles Public Library Central Library, passing on her version of best practices in information retrieval to her patrons.

Alvin M. Schrader is currently director of research at the University of Alberta Libraries and professor emeritus at the University of Alberta. His research and teaching profile as a lifelong advocate of freedom of expression, including Internet access to LGBTQ information, is well known in the library community and beyond, and was recognized in 1997 with the Canadian Library Association's highest intellectual freedom award. He has served on the intellectual freedom committee (FAIFE) of the International Federation of Library Associations and Institutions, and was the only Canadian member of the American Library Association's Core Values Task Force I. In 1998 he was recognized by the Pride Awards Committee of Edmonton for his defense of free speech within library systems. In 2006 he was elected to the presidency of the Canadian Library Association and served on CLA Executive Council from 2006 to 2009. In 2009 he received the Distinguished Alumni Award from the Faculty of Information, University of Toronto, and the Honorary Alumni Award from the School of Library and Information Studies, University of Alberta.

Jennifer K. Snapp-Cook is an M.L.I.S. student at San Jose State University's School of Library and Information Science. She holds a B.A. in communications from the University of California, San Diego and an A.A. in museum studies from San Diego Mesa College.

Martha E. Stone received her library degree from Simmons College in 1990. She is the coordinator for reference services at Treadwell Library, Massachusetts General Hospital, Boston, and is a member of the Academy of Health Information Professionals. She is also the literary editor at the *Gay & Lesbian Review/Worldwide*. Her book reviews, essays, and articles appear in a wide variety of publications. She can be reached by email at *marthastone67@yahoo.com.*

David Cameron Strachan served as the first appointed intersex member to the San Francisco Human Rights Commission's Lesbian, Gay, Bisexual, Transgender Advisory Committee from 2003 to 2006 and was a member of their Intersex Task Force. Previously he served on the San Francisco Transgender Civil Rights Implementation Task Force 2000–2001, working to implement the Gender Identity law. David wrote Chapter 8 in *Intersex and the Age of Ethics*, served on the boards of the Intersex Society of North America and Advocates for Informed Choice. He also acted as the USA Human Rights Spokesperson for Organization Intersex International. David was a recipient of the 2008 KQED's Local hero award for his Intersex Community Volunteer Activism. He was Marriage Equality USA's Intersex Outreach Director until 2009.

Jim Van Buskirk was program manager of the James C. Hormel Gay and Lesbian Center at the San Francisco Public Library from 1992 to 2007 and appears in the documentary *Not in Our Town: Northern California*, representing "Reversing Vandalism," the project in which mutilated library books were transformed into artworks. Jim's reviews, articles and essays appear in a variety of books, magazines, newspapers, and websites. He co-authored *Gay by the Bay: A History of Queer Culture in the San Francisco Bay Area* (Chronicle, 1996) and co-edited the nonfiction anthologies *Identity Envy: Wanting to Be Who We're Not* (Harrington Park, 2007) and *Love, Castro Street: Reflections of San Francisco* (Alyson, 2007). Jim can be reached through his website at: *http://www.jimvanbuskirk.com*.

Jack van der Wel was one the founders of Homodok in 1978 and is head of collections and information services of IHLIA in the Netherlands. One of the projects he has done is the reconstruction of the historical Schorer gay library. He is working on a revised edition of the *Homosaurus/Queer Thesaurus* and on a project to provide major public libraries in the Netherlands with an LGBTIQ collection

Karen Vigneault is a member of the Iipay Nation of Santa Ysabel (also known as the Kumeyaay) which is located in the mountains of San Diego, California. She attended San Diego State University (B.S., television, film, and new media, 2001) and Drexel University (M.L.I.S., 2008). Karen has been a lesbian native activist for 32 years and the leader of the LGBT Nations of the 4 Directions since 1991. She was awarded the Soroptimists Women Making A Difference Award in 2007 and inducted into the San Diego Women's Hall of Fame in 2008. Karen can be reached at: kumeyaayindian@hotmail.com.

Michael Waldman is the head of collection management at Baruch College, City University of New York in New York City, overseeing electronic resources, acquisitions, serials and cataloging. He is interested in creating vibrant and diverse library collections, which are innovative both in their subject scope and in their forms of delivery. He was on the organizing committee for the GLBT Archives, Libraries, Museums, and Special Collections (ALMS) Conference in 2008 in New York City. He can be contacted at *Michael.Waldman@baruch.cuny.edu*.

Kristopher Wells is a Killam Fellow and Social Sciences and Humanities Research Council of Canada (SSHRC) graduate scholar with the Institute for Sexual Minority Studies and Services (http//www.ismss.ualberta.ca), Faculty of Education, University of Alberta. His award-winning research, teaching, and service work centers on creating safe, caring, and inclusive schools and communities for sexual minority and gender variant students and teachers. He is a founding board member of the Society for Safe and Caring Schools and Communities and the chair of the Alberta Teachers' Association's Sexual Orientation and Gender Identity Educational Subcommittee. Kristopher is also the co-founder and co-director of Camp fYrefly (http://www.fYrefly.ualberta.ca), which is Canada's largest leadership retreat for sexual minority and gender variant youth. In 2005, his community service work was recognized with an Alberta Centennial Medallion as bestowed by the Alberta Legislature. He can be reached at: *kwells@ualberta.ca*.

Rachel Wexelbaum is collection management librarian at Saint Cloud State University. She is also a film reviewer for the St. Cloud GLBTA Film Festival, facilitator for the group St. Cloud OUT, and chair of the Lambda Literary Award judging committee for children's and young adult literature. Rachel has written articles on many subjects, not limited to LGBTIQ studies, librarianship, culinary history, the challenges of research, and Jewish folklore.

Index